TRADE AND SOCIETY
IN THE STRAITS OF MELAKA

TRADE AND SOCIETY
IN THE STRAITS OF MELAKA

DUTCH MELAKA AND ENGLISH PENANG, 1780–1830

Nordin Hussin

NUS PRESS
SINGAPORE

NIAS Monographs, 100

First published in 2007 by NIAS Press
NIAS – Nordic Institute of Asian Studies
Leifsgade 33, DK–2300 Copenhagen S, Denmark
Tel: (+45) 3532 9501 • Fax: (+45) 3532 9549
E–mail: books@nias.ku.dk • Website: www.niaspress.dk

First published in 2007 by NUS Press
an imprint of NUS Publishing
National University of Singapore
AS3-01-02, 3 Arts Link, Singapore 117569
tel: (+65) 6776 1148 • fax: (+65) 6774 0652
e-mail: nusbooks@nus.edu.sg • website: www.nus.edu.sg/npu
for sale in the ASEAN countries, Japan, Korea, China,
Hong Kong, Taiwan, Australia and New Zealand

British Library Cataloguing in Publication Data
Hussin, Nordin
  Trade and society in the Straits of Melaka : Dutch Melaka and
  English Penang, 1780–1830. - (NIAS Monograph ; 100)
  1.Commerce - Malacca, Strait of, Region - History 2.Pinang
  (Malaysia) - History - 18th century 3.Melaka (Malaysia) - History
  - 18th century 4.Pinang (Malaysia) - History - 19th century
  5.Melaka (Malaysia) - History - 19th century
  I.Title
  959.5'03

ISBN 978-87-91114-47-2 (NIAS hardback)
ISBN 978-87-91114-88-5 (NIAS paperback)
ISBN 978-9971-69-354-1 (NUS paperback)

Typesetting by NIAS Press
Produced by SRM Production Berhad Sdn
Printed and bound in Malaysia

For Aishah, Imran and Azmi
in memory of our days in Holland and England

Contents

LIST OF ILLUSTRATIONS

LIST OF TABLES

ONLINE APPENDICES

The full set of appendices to Nordin Hussin's thesis ('Melaka and Penang 1780–1830: A study of two port towns in the Straits of Melaka', Ph.D. thesis, Amsterdam: Vrije Universiteit, 2002) can be accessed at http://www.niaspress.dk/extras/ as PDF files.

Acknowledgements

THIS BOOK HAS ITS BEGINNINGS as a doctoral thesis. Here, I would like to thank my supervisor at Vrije Universiteit Amsterdam, Professor Heather Sutherland, not only for her wise counsel, tolerance of my views and the generous amount of time she spent discussing both the intricacies of archival research and broader questions concerning the period under study but also for shaping some of the ideas that eventually found their way into the book. This book would not have been completed if not for the forbearance and insightful comments of Remco Raben, Gerrit Knaap and Barbara Andaya; my thanks for their kind advice and direction during the course of the research. I would also like to thank Leonard Blusse from IGEER Leiden, who had introduced me to the Dutch language course and Dutch archives.

This study would not have been possible without assistance and support of various organizations and the help and encouragement of faculty, colleagues, friends well-wishers and kin. I therefore welcome this opportunity to express my deep appreciation and thanks to them all. I am grateful to the Universiti Kebangsaan Malaysia for a generous scholarship and grant of leave of absence to pursue my study. To the Vrije Universiteit Amsterdam in particular, my heartfelt thanks for their generous financial support during the course of my study. I also owe a special debt to the officers at the Algemeen Rijksarchief (now Nationaal Archief) in The Hague, the KITLV Library, Leiden University Library, India Office Library London, SOAS Library London, UKM Library, Arkib Negara Malaysia, University Malaya Library, and the University of Amsterdam Library, for their cooperation, help and kind hospitality in the course of my research.

It is not possible here to thank each person individually, but a special note of thanks must be made to Khasnor Djohan from Canberra and Pamela Sodhy from Washington who helped me refine some of the ideas in this book. I am also particularly indebted to Professor Shamsul Amri from ATMA-UKM for suggesting that this work be published as well as for introducing me to Gerald Jackson and Janice Leon at NIAS Press. I also take this opportunity to thank Liesbeath Dolk and her husband, Hans, Jaap de Moor, Ibu Wurian, Jan van der Meulen, Professor Wahab, and all my Dutch and Indonesian colleagues in Leiden for having made my stay in the Netherlands a more stimulating intellectual experience. I would also like to thank Mohd. Shah for helping me with the photos as well as Norhizan and Syed Osman for their assistance in preparing the maps. In addition, I would like to extend my gratitude and thanks to the Centre for Southeast Asian Studies (CSEAS) at the University of Kyoto, Japan, for giving me a six-month fellowship at the Centre. I used this fellowship to revise and review the whole manuscript of this book. My short stay in Kyoto also broadened my intellectual experience.

Finally, I am indebted to my own family especially my wife Aishah, and my two sons Imran and Azmi, to whom I dedicate this work.

Bangi, July 2006

List of Abbreviations

ARA	Algemeen Rijksarchief, The Hague
BKI	Bijdragen tot de taal-, land- en volkenkunde van het Koninklijk Instituut voor Taal-, Land- en Volkenkunde
EIC	English East India Company
GM	Generale Missiven van Gouverneurs-generaal en Raden aan Heren XVII der Verenigde Oostindische Compagnie
JAS	The Journal of Asian Studies
JCBRAS	Journal of the Ceylon Branch of the Royal Asiatic Society
JIA	Journal of the Indian Archipelago and Eastern Asia
JMBRAS	Journal Malayan Branch of Royal Asiatic Society
JRAS	Journal of the Royal Asiatic Society
JRASSLB	Journal of the Royal Asiatic Society Sri Lanka Branch
JSEAS	Journal of Southeast Asian Studies
Rjk	Rijksdollars
SpD	Spanish Dollars
SSFR	Straits Settlements Factory Records
VOC	Verenigde Oost-Indische Compagnie (The United Dutch East India Company

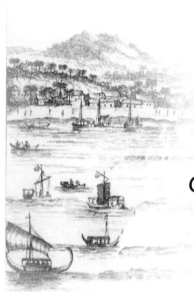

Currencies, Weights and Measurements

THE EXACT CONVERSION OF THESE UNITS is very hard to determine due to value fluctuations over time and because many places assigned different values to the same unit. For further reference, see Gerrit Knaap, *Shallow Waters, Rising Tide*, Leiden: KITLV, 1996, p.189–193.

CURRENCIES AND COINS

Exchange rates stated here are for 1824, taken from C.D. Cowan, 'Early Penang and the Rise of Singapore 1805–1832', *JMBRAS*, 23(2), 1950, p. 21.

100 Spanish Dollars	210.85 Sicca Rupees
100 Sicca Rupees	47.42 Spanish Dollars
100 Spanish Dollar	252.27 Dutch Guilders
1 Duit	1 Kupang (copang)
10 Pice	1 Kupang
10 Kupang (100 Pice)	1 Spanish Dollar
1 Rijksdaalder (rijksdollar)	48 stuiver

WEIGHTS AND MEASURES

1 tahil	1.3 oz
16 tahils	1.3 lbs
1 pikul	100 katis or 133.3 lbs
1 bahara	3 pikuls or 400 lbs
1 koyan	40 pikuls or 5,333.3 lbs
bos	0.5 pikul
bundle	a book
buyong	1 pot
corgie	1,000 lbs or 8 pikuls (if cloth, 20 pieces)
kranjang	Chinese tobacco: 0.5 pikul; Javanese tobacco: 0.2 pikuls; gambir: 1.2 pikuls; other products: 1 pikul
laksa	10,000 pieces
last	4,000 lbs or 32 pikuls
legger	360 kan

LAND MEASURE

1 jumba	12 square feet
20 jumbas	1 orlong or 1.3 acres

Introduction

IN RECENT YEARS THERE HAS BEEN A GROWING INTEREST in studies of colonial cities and towns in Asia; this interest has endeavoured to describe more of the life and society in port-towns. Some of the recent studies shedding new light on colonial cities and towns in Southeast Asia include the works of Heather Sutherland, Gerrit Knaap and Remco Raben.[1] The increasing recognition given by scholars that studies of society should not be confined to palace or state politics and the elite, but must extend to the common people, has made research on towns and ports a flourishing enterprise. This is because it is in cities, towns, and ports that the everyday life of the people and their activities can be examined in detail.[2]

This growth of interest in the development of urban centres in Asia has also led to works on the theoretical aspects of colonial cities and towns, such as those produced by Ronald J. Horvath, David Simon, M.E.P. Bellam, Anthony D. King and Luc Nagtegaal.[3] These have opened new dimensions of knowledge about colonial administration, everyday life and the socio-economic and political aspects of colonial towns and cities. Geographers such as Rhoads Murphy and Horvath paved the way to studies of colonial port-towns by historians who, in the 1970s, began to show increasing interest in the development of urban centres in Asia. Many historians writing on colonial port-towns have derived their initial inspiration from Rhoads Murphy, whose article 'Traditionalism and Colonialism: Changing Urban Roles in Asia' was published in 1969.[4] His work was carried on by S.J. Lewandowski who, in 1975, published her research on the colonial city of Madras.[5] Interest in the subject was further advanced by seminars and conferences, such as the gathering of historians in Santa Cruz to discuss the rise and growth of colonial port-cities in Asia and the multi-disciplinary conference in Perth in 1989, which reviewed the concept of port cities.[6]

Horvath's work on colonial cities was a response to G. Sjoberg's book, *The Preindustrial City* in which the idea was advanced that pre-industrial cities everywhere displayed similar social and ecological structures. It was this generalization that Horvath took issue with, observing that Sjoberg's theory did not match the pattern of urbanization in Third World countries. In focusing on colonial port-cities and identifying characteristics that were unique to them, Horvath, in fact, had taken the argument a step further. He had put forward the concept that European-ruled cities in Asia, which first came into existence in the sixteenth century, were different from other types or categories of cities. His idea found support among some scholars of Asia who subscribed to the view that, indeed, colonial port-cities had distinctive features that distinguished them from native or indigenous cities.

Writing in 1969, Horvath described a colonial city as a heterogeneous but distinct urban type distinguishable from other types of urban centres found in Asia. He identified its distinctive features in terms of the diversity of people who lived in the town, their different racial, cultural, social and religious backgrounds, all of which created a plural society. Further, the social structure of a colonial city was unique in that the ruling elites were usually European settlers and the role of natives or Asians elites, even if they were employed in the administration, was minimal and merely designed to pacify their own people.[7] In 1993, Luc Nagtegaal, in putting together the distinguishing elements of colonial port-towns that have been identified by other scholars, listed such features as European imposed urban concepts, a European fortress or castle as the focal point or centre of the town, most inhabitants were migrants, a large part of the population were slaves until the middle of the eighteenth century and the cities were poorly integrated into the hinterland.[8]

The view that colonial port-towns can and should stand as a separate urban type, however, has not gone unchallenged. Some scholars have rejected the colonial city typology as misleading, arguing that there was no funda-mental difference between a colonial port–town and any native port-city in Asia.[9] Others, while not rejecting the terminology, have expressed the view that it is flawed and that some of the dominant features have been exagger-ated or overstated. A third view comes from Kidwai who argues that just because some do not agree with the term 'colonial' being used, this does not mean that it should be thrown out.[10] In his opinion, many features of this type of city that were not found in a native setting, such as the role of the Europeans in the port-towns or cities, the role of the colonial port-city in the process of integration and interaction, the relationship between the colonial city and its hinterlands, the role of trade and commerce, the large and diverse populations comprising a substantial proportion of migrants who created a cosmopolitan world and the various ethnic groups who live in the town.[11] Further, one should not only look at the activities of the Europeans but also at their dominance in certain important sectors such as shipping, the control of political institutions, the control of market information from abroad and the control of funds to indigenous entrepreneurs.[12]

Nagtegaal, in the same article mentioned above, gave a critical review of the concepts that have been put forward by historians in relation to urban development in Southeast Asia in general and in Indonesia in particular. He sees the concept of 'colonial city' as flawed for two main reasons, namely, that it does not fit the available historical data and that it is a fixed concept that does not provide room for change. His work therefore reflects the continuing interest in the study of colonial port-towns and the ongoing debate regarding the theoretical aspects of such investigations. More importantly it highlights the existence of a knowledge gap between theory and historical reality in this field.

In getting to the crux of the problem of matching the theory with the historical data, Nagtegaal observes that scholars have failed to explain the differences between colonial cities and those not ruled by European powers. According to him most writings on colonial port cities have tended to be merely self-affirmative, with no attempt made to compare colonial cities with other types of cities in order to see if in fact those so-called defining features were really unique to the former. He points out that many European aspects of the colonial city which have been cited as unique have in fact been exaggerated. For example, the claim that European urban concepts had been imposed on the colonial city does not fit the facts as the evidence shows that only the European part looked Western and that the rest, which constituted the largest section of the city, looked more Asian then European. Morphologically, Nagtegaal argues that the colonial city in Southeast Asia was not much different from any other native town and port. Even the physical division of the colonial city into castle, town and kampong was not unique, as that also resembled the situation in other native Southeast Asian cities.[13] Nagtegaal further pointed out that even Batavia, which was built by the Dutch, began to resemble a traditional Javanese city as time went by.[14] The only significant difference was that the Europeans were the colonists and that although they were in the minority, they held all the power and control of the town. In this respect he sees the colonial city as an externally induced settlement and not one that had organically developed within the society itself.[15]

In light of the ongoing debate and the assertion, such as that seen in Nagtegaal's article, that there is a knowledge gap between theory and historical evidence, the need to conduct more empirical studies of colonial port-cities seems evident. The study undertaken here is one such attempt and it is hoped that an examination of Melaka and Penang between 1780 and 1830 will help to provide additional information and shed light on the nature of the societies in these two colonial port-towns. This would then help to ascertain to what extent the two port-towns fitted into the theoretical framework that has been presented by the scholars and to establish if such a framework is meaningful in explaining the situation in Melaka and Penang. The study will return to the idea of "colonial port-town" as a category at the end of the book. The term "colonial port-town" used in the course of the text is intended to be descriptive rather than endorsing the idea of a specific type.

This book will attempt a comparative study of Melaka and Penang in the context of overall trends: policy, geographical position, nature and direction of trade; also morphology and society and how these factors were influenced by trade and policies. An examination of this sort will require a look at all aspects of the development of Melaka and Penang. Thus trade, administration and policies, physical characteristics of the settlements and nature of the societies will be examined and the interplay of some or all of these factors will be shown. A comparative study of Melaka and Penang between 1780 and 1830 has to take into consideration as starting points, firstly, the fact that Melaka had a long history as an entrepot, has seen indigenous rule before it was colonized and been for a long time under the Dutch, while Penang was a newly opened English port; and, secondly, that both were run in the interests of rival trading companies. Conclusions will then be sought regarding the position of the ports in the region: nature and direction of the trade of both port-towns; the physical nature of the towns and type of societies that were fostered by the trade that was conducted and the policies pursued.

In the period under study, Melaka was under the Dutch until 1794, ruled by the English between 1794 and 1818 and returned to the Dutch in 1818. In 1824 the demarcation of spheres of influence agreed upon by the Dutch and the English finally saw Melaka transferred over to the latter, remaining under English rule until 1957, when Malaya (later Malaysia) attained its independence. Penang was opened by the English and remained English throughout the period under study. There was a difference in the attitude and approach to trade between the Dutch and the English. The Dutch East India Company had not only marginalized Melaka but also enforced the retention of the monopolistic trade policy that was first introduced by the

Portuguese in Melaka. On the other hand, the English had introduced free trade in Penang. How these contrasting policies impacted on the role and development of the ports will be pertinent. The study will also determine if the approach of the Dutch to administration differed to that of the English and show how such differences, if they existed, influenced the development of the physical and social environments of the port-towns. The main emphasis of the book will be on establishing the nature of trade, port and society in Melaka and Penang and to compare and contrast the development of these aspects of the two ports.

The above findings will then be used to relate the two port-towns to developments in Southeast Asia in attempting to provide a 'big picture' look at Melaka and Penang. At this level, conclusions will be drawn regarding two aspects. The first will try to see where and how Melaka and Penang fit in the urban traditions of Southeast Asia. The second will try to see the significance of the fact that the period under study coincided with the shift from the height of the 'Age of commerce'[16] in Southeast Asia towards the period of heightened imperialist activities which occurred in the second half of the nineteenth century,[17] as well as the 'Chinese century'.[18] During this transition period there was an expansion of English commercial networks in Southeast Asia and China. Furthermore, the expansion of the China trade, led by their forward thrust, had seen an increase in Chinese migrations to and activities in Southeast Asia. Both these developments were crucial to the eighteenth century economic development of Southeast Asia.

As trade was the raison d'être for the presence of the Dutch in Melaka and the English in Penang, it is assumed that it was central to the development of the two port-towns. The Straits of Melaka was situated along the important trade route between India and China and was also well placed to command the trade of the Malay-Indonesian archipelago and the regions of the Southeast Asian mainland facing the Bay of Bengal. Both these port-towns were therefore strategically positioned within the context of the trading activities of the period and control of these ports provided opportunities to exploit the lucrative trade that passed through the Straits. Moreover traders travelling between India and China had to take refuge in the Straits from the changing monsoon winds and to refit their ships. Yet one was geographically better situated than the other. Melaka, located closer to the southern entrance to the Straits of Melaka, was better placed to command the trade of the archipelago, a factor that ensured it an enduring role and good reputation as an entrepot for more than four centuries. Penang, geographically positioned at the northern end of the Straits and at the northeast corner of the archipelago, was not as strategically located as Melaka. It was also a newly opened port.[19] To what extent these factors affected the development and character of the trade and each of the port-towns, are questions that have to be answered. The interplay of these factors and the players and commodities involved also have to be examined to show the direction and nature of the trade of the two port-towns.

Under the theme of the development of trade, trading routes, networks and linkages of the two ports will be examined. The major and minor traders will be identified in terms of their ethnic origin, and the main commodities imported and exported will be shown. In this respect, shipping lists will show the number of out-going and in-coming ships, their port of embarkation and their destination, the frequency of their movements, the flags they sailed under, their size and the cargoes that they carried and, where possible, the size of the crew and the identity of the captain.

The development of trade over time and the shifts in the trading patterns of Melaka and Penang will be shown and some indication of the influence of external factors on trade, such as change in the political situation in Europe and within the region, will be made. The period under study saw the Napoleonic wars being fought in Europe, which, as already mentioned, saw Dutch Melaka taken over by the English in 1794. In the Straits the long and protracted rivalry between the Malay trading centre of Riau and Melaka, first under the Portuguese and later under the Dutch, led in the period under study to open conflict in the 1780s. Apart from wars that could affect trade, the attitude of the native states in the region towards the Dutch and the English and their ports will also be examined. The role of Aceh as a major player in the politics and trade of the region is a case in point.

Port-towns did not exist in isolation from one another but operated in their surroundings and were in many ways connected and tied together. By looking at the two port-towns, new light might be shed on the Straits. It is expected that there was fierce competition between Melaka and Penang and that, indeed, Penang was established to attract trade and wealth away from Melaka. This study will look at the ways in which Penang and Melaka were positioned and how each became rooted in its own networks and environs. Thus, the Straits will be seen not just as a gateway between the Indian Ocean and China Sea systems, but as a world of its own, and a differentiated one at that.

Internally, the nature of the administration, the urban tradition and the morphology of Melaka and Penang will also be discussed. The extent to which the administrative policies and urban traditions of the Dutch differed from those of the English will be discussed. How these policies and traditions affected the morphology of the town will be shown. It should be noted that in respect to urban development other factors such as trade and legacies of an earlier period will be considered.

The third theme will focus on society. The character of the society, the ethnic composition and the relationship between one group and another will be examined. As colonial port-towns have been said to foster plural societies, an attempt will be made to see to what extent the societies in Melaka and Penang exhibited such pluralistic tendencies and to what extent they differed from the expected norm. Further, the theory that the population was made up of mostly migrants (Europeans, Burghers,[20] Chinese, Keling,[21] Chulias[22] and Moors[23]) will be tested. As Melaka and Penang are well known for having fostered mixed groups, such as the Portuguese-Eurasians,[24] the *Jawi-Pekan*[25] and the Chinese *Peranakan*[26], the extent of ethnic amalgamation will be studied.

As mentioned above, the development of Melaka and Penang during this period places the study in an important transitional phase, which saw the beginnings of English ascendancy in the China trade as well as the influx of Chinese migrants and the spread of their economic influence in the region. This brings into focus the rise of European trading activities and the simultaneous decline in the role of native and Asian traders in long distance intra-Asian trade. The bigger players in the trade, European company traders as well as the country traders who, with the backing of shareholders in Europe, had greater resources and bigger ships, were able to a large degree to establish a stronger presence. This can be seen from their ability to establish more colonial ports during the whole of this transition period. Thus, if a late eighteenth century traveller made a voyage from Europe to East Asia, navigating round the African continent, across the Indian Ocean and into the Malay-Indonesian archipelago to China and Japan, he would encounter various strategically located port-towns, a fair number of which were already controlled by Europeans, namely, the Portuguese, Dutch, English, French and Spanish.

Using these port-towns as bases, European traders, especially the Dutch and English, who were the most aggressive during the period under study, made inroads into and gained considerable control of the intra-Asian trade networks. In Southeast Asia, the control of trade can be seen, for example, from the Dutch ability to impose a policy of trade monopolies that was implemented through a system of trade regulations and duties and the signing of trade treaties with native chiefs and rulers. Similarly, English traders who were establishing a strong presence in the Indian subcontinent and, from there, were launching attempts to gain entry into the lucrative China tea trade, were seeking a greater share of the products offered by Southeast Asia to reduce the drain on English bullion. The search for a strategic location in Southeast Asia which could enable the English to command the region's trade and control the trade route between India and China had in fact led to the acquisition of Penang in 1786. While trade and commerce expanded in Southeast Asia, this era saw the decline of the Asian traders, when fewer of them appear to have had the means and resources to participate in long distance trade. Foremost among those who survived as long distance traders were the Indians and Chinese, some operating from India and China respectively, and others from ports in Southeast Asia. In sharp contrast to the situation before the eighteenth century, native Southeast Asian traders increasingly were reduced to operating within the region mostly engaging in short distance trade, sailing in small boats along the coastlines of Southeast Asia and carrying with them small quantities of jungle products, food items and other produce for exchange.

Along with this development and as a result of the expanding commercial networks within Southeast Asia brought about by the expanding China trade, the region saw a corresponding expansion in the role of the Chinese in many aspects of its economic life. This phenomenon roughly coincided with the period between 1740 and 1840, inspiring Reid and Trocki to label it as the 'Chinese century'.[27] During this period, Southeast Asia saw an increased influx of Chinese migrants, an increase in Chinese settlements, trading networks and Chinese trade, a vigorous Chinese involvement in agricultural, mining industry, revenue farms and an increase in the Chinese population in many port-towns and their hinterlands. According to Reid, the influx of Chinese to Southeast Asia in 1754 was due to relaxation of hitherto strict rules imposed by the Chinese authorities on overseas travel. In that year the Chinese government declared that any Chinese living overseas with valid reasons would be entitled to return home and have his property protected. Due to the effect of this more lenient rule, an outflow was seen of traders, miners, planters, shipbuilders, mariners and others from China into Southeast Asia. In 1830 the total Chinese exodus to Southeast Asia was estimated at 'nearly a million' people, which represented about 3 per cent of the Chinese population.[28] These Chinese migrants were an essential resource for many port-towns and native kingdoms in Southeast Asia.

It is suggested here that the general trends, both in terms of the players in the trade and the position of the Chinese were largely reflected in the trading activities as well as the development of Melaka and Penang. The position and activities of the Chinese in Melaka and Penang and the attitudes of the Dutch and the English to them will be discussed. Finally, the acquisition of Singapore by the British in 1819 was a crucial factor in the long-term future of the two ports under study and the implications of the development of Singapore on the position and role of Melaka and Penang will therefore be discussed as well.

NOTES

1   Remco Raben, 'Batavia and Colombo: The Ethnic and Spatial order of Two Colonial Cities 1600–1800', Ph. D, thesis, Rijksuniversiteit te Leiden, 1996. See also Heather Sutherland, 'Ethnicity, Wealth and Power in Colonial Makassar: A historiographical Reconsideration'. In Peter J.M. Nas (ed.), *The Indonesian City: studies in urban development and planning*, Dordrecht: Foris Publications, 1986, pp. 37–55. See also Heather Sutherland, "Eastern Emporium and Company Town: Trade and Society in Eighteenth-Century Makassar", in Frank Broeze (ed.), *Brides of the Sea: Port cities of Asia from the 16th to the 20th Centuries*, NSW: University Press, 1989, pp. 97–128; and G.J. Knaap, *Kruidnagelen en Christenen: De Verenigde Oost-Indische Compagnie en de bevolking van Ambon 1656–1696*, Dordrecht: KITLV, 1987.

2   Heather Sutherland, 'Ethnicity, Wealth and Power in Colonial Makassar', p. 38.

3   Luc Nagtegaal, 'The Pre-modern City in Indonesia and Its Fall From Grace With The Gods'. In *Economic and Social History in The Netherlands*, Amsterdam: Het Nederlandsch Economisch-Historisch Archief, Vol. v, 1993, pp. 39–60; Ronald J. Horvath, 'In search of a Theory of Urbanization: Notes on the Colonial City', *East Lakes Geographer*, 5, 1969, pp. 69–82; David Simon, 'Third World Colonial Cities in Context: Conceptual and Theoretical Approaches with Particular Reference to Africa', *Progress in Human Geography*, Vol. 8, No. 4, 1984, pp. 493–514; M.E.P. Bellam, 'The Colonial City: Honiara, A Pacific Islands' Case Study', *Pacific Viewpoint*, Vol. II, No.1, May 1970, pp. 66–96. Anthony D. King, *Urbanism, Colonialism, and the World-economy: Cultural and Spatial Foundations of the world urban system*, London: Routledge, 1990.

4   Rhoads Murphy, 'Traditionalism and Colonialism: Changing Urban Roles in Asia'. In *Journal of Asian Studies*, 29, 1969, pp. 67–84.

5   S.J. Lewandowski, 'Urban Growth and Municipal Development in the Colonial City of Madras, 1860–1900'. In *Journal of Asian Studies*, no. 2, 1975, pp. 431–360.

6   Dilip K Basu (ed.), *The Rise and Growth of the Colonial Port Cities in Asia*, University of California, Berkeley, Centre for South and Southeast Asia Studies, Monograph Series no. 25, Lanham: University Press of America, 1985. See also Frank Broeze (ed.), *Brides of the Sea: Port Cities of Asia from 16th–20th Centuries*.

7   Ronald J. Horvath, 'In search of a Theory of Urbanization: Notes on the Colonial City', pp. 69–82.

8   Luc Nagtegaal, 'The Pre-modern City in Indonesia', pp. 39–60. See also, Heather Sutherland, 'Ethnicity, Wealth and Power in Colonial Makassar: A historiographical Reconsideration", pp. 37–55; Heather Sutherland, "Eastern Emporium and Company Town: Trade and Society in Eighteenth-Century Makassar', pp. 97–128.

9   Luc Nagtegaal, 'The Pre-modern City in Indonesia', pp. 39–60.

10 Atiya Habeeb Kidwai, 'Conceptual and Methodological Issues: Ports, Port Cities and Port-Hinterlands'. In Indu Banga (ed.), *Ports and Their Hinterlands in India (1700–1950)*, New Delhi: Manohar Publications, pp.32–33.

11 Ibid.

12 Ibid., p. 31.

13 Luc Nagtegaal, 'The Pre-Modern City in Indonesia', pp. 45–47.

14 Ibid., p. 56.

15 Ibid., p. 46–47.

16 Anthony Reid, *Southeast Asia in the Age of Commerce 1450–1680*, New Haven: Yale University Press, 1993, p.326.

17 D.K. Fieldhouse, *Economics and Empire 1830–1914*, Hong Kong: MacMillan, 1984.

18 Anthony Reid, *The Last Stand of Asian Autonomies: Responses to Modernity in the Diverse State of Southeast Asia and Korea 1750–1900*, London: Macmillan, 1997, pp. 1–25; see also Carl A. Trocki, 'Chinese Pioneering in Eighteenth-Century Southeast Asia'. In Anthony Reid (ed.), *The Last Stand of Asian Autonomies*, pp. 83–102.

19 See T. Braddell, *Statistics of the British Possessions in the Straits of Malacca With Explanatory Notes*, Penang: Pinang Gazette Printing Office, 1861. For further reference,

see also Wong Lin Ken, 'The Trade of Singapore 1819–69', *JMBRAS*, vol. 33, pt. 4, 1960, pp. 11–215.

20 Dutchmen and their descendents who had settled in most parts of the Dutch colonies. For further reference, see Jean Gelman Taylor, *The Social World of Batavia: European and Eurasian in Dutch Asia*, Madison: The University of Wisconsin Press, 1983.

21 The term used during the Dutch occupation of Melaka was Jentief or Kelings. It was used to distinguish between Indian-Hindus and Indian-Muslims. The Dutch classified the Indian-Hindus as Jentief or Keling and Indian-Muslims as Moors. In this book, the term Keling is used for the Indian-Hindus and the term Moors for the Indian-Muslims. During the English occupation of Melaka, they used the term 'Chulias' to refer to the Indian-Muslims, as the term was used in Penang, while the term Hindus was used for the Kelings.

22 'Chulia' is a term used by the British to describe Indian Muslims from the Coromandel Coast of India who traded and settled in Penang and Melaka. For further reference, see S. Arasaratnam, *Islamic Merchant Communities of the Indian Subcontinent in Southeast Asia*, Kuala Lumpur: University Malaya Press, 1989.

23 Moors was a term used by the Dutch to describe Muslim traders who came from the Indian subcontinent.

24 The Portuguese-Eurasians were the descendents of the Portuguese who intermarried with the local inhabitants or with Indians. Sometimes, the term was used to refer to the Christian Catholic community in Melaka. For further reference, see Colin Jack-Hinton, 'Malacca and Goa and the Question of Race Relations in the Portuguese Overseas Provinces', *JSEAH*, vol. 10, No. 3, 1969, pp. 513–559.

25 The term is used to describe the offspring from intermarriage between a Chulia Muslim male and a local woman. For further reference, see James Low, *A Dissertation on the Soil and Agricultural of the British Settlement of Penang or Prince of Wales Island*, Singapore: Singapore Free Press, 1836, p. 250.

26 The term Chinese *Peranakan* is used to describe the descendants of mixed-marriage unions between Chinese males and local women. Sometimes they are also known as Baba.

27 Anthony Reid (ed.), *The Last Stand of Asian Autonomies*, pp. 1–25; Carl A. Trocki, 'Chinese Pioneering in Eighteenth-Century Southeast Asia'. In Anthony Reid (ed.), *The Last Stand of Asian Autonomies*, pp. 83–102.

28 T.J. Newbold, *Political and statistical Account of the British Settlements in the Straits of Malacca, Pinang, Malacca and Singapore*, London: John Murray, 1839, vol. 1, p. 9. "The Chinese, it is well known, are emigrants from China…where there numbers is estimated at nearly a million". See also Anthony Reid, (ed.), *The Last Stand of Asian Autonomies*, p. 12.

Map 1: Port and polity in Sumatra and the Straits of Melaka in the eighteenth and early nineteenth centuries. Adapted from John Anderson, *Acheen and the Port of the North and East Coast of Sumatra*, London: W.H. Allen, 1840.

CHAPTER ONE

The Straits of Melaka and the Trading World

THE MALAY-INDONESIAN ARCHIPELAGO is situated on the trading route between India and China. This location, within which the Straits of Melaka is situated, is in the centre of one of the busiest trading routes in the East. Geographically fragmented, the Malay-Indonesian archipelago covers a very wide area that consists of the Malay peninsular and many islands. From the early part of the first millennium A.D., many settlements emerged as ports and service centres at strategic coastal and riverine locations.[1] Although not all of these settlements and ports became important trading centres, some of them emerged as important regional exchange ports or entrepots. Ports that were strategically located and had the power to command local trade later grew into regional and inter-regional trading markets and the foci of commercial wealth and exchange for the zones of economic activity that they serviced. For example, Aceh, Melaka, Jambi, Banten, Makassar, Ambon, Brunei, Semarang and Palembang grew from local ports into important regional and inter-regional centres for trade. The majority of these ports were located in strategic locations by the rivers that regulated and dictated the trading patterns and networks in the hinterlands and overseas.

In the period under study, the Straits maritime trade covered a network within the Malay-Indonesian archipelago and also formed part of the Indian Ocean trading world with vital linkages with South China.[2] The Straits served as a place of transit and fresh supplies of goods and provisions for long-distance voyages and a point of collection of all goods from the archipelago, which were later distributed to traders from India and China. In addition, it also acted as a place of distribution of goods from the two

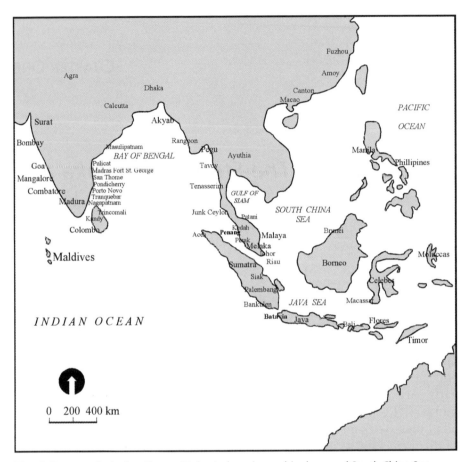

Map 2: Ports on the Indian Ocean, Malay-Indonesian archipelago and South China Sea

regions to the whole archipelago. The Straits also provided a convenient place for traders to stop while waiting for the changing winds to the east and the west.

Through the ages, many ports had risen and declined along the Straits on the west coast of the Malay peninsula and on the east coast of Sumatra. Some of the most important were Srivijaya, Melaka, Aceh, Kedah, Riau, Palembang and Siak. As early as the third century A.D., traders from India had been trading with various ports in the Straits to seek products such as gold, spices and medicinal herbs, which were brought to these ports from other areas of the archipelago. These Indian traders were later followed by the Arabs and Persians. Chinese traders from South China had also been trading with the ports in the Straits and beyond, although since the sixteenth century they rarely ventured west of the Straits. The importance of the Straits ports as hubs regulating the exchange of goods between the Indian Ocean and the South China Sea had, therefore, been long established, dating from at least the beginning of the first millennium AD.[3]

Trade between the West and East and also between the Straits and archipelago was dependent on seasonal winds.[4] These seasonal winds were

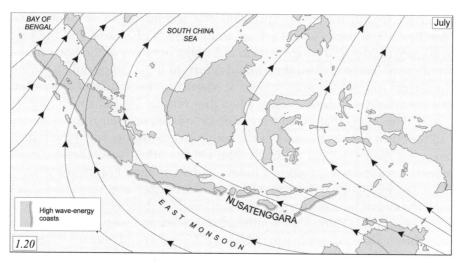

Map 3: Wind patterns in the Malay-Indonesian archipelago – east monsoon.

Map 4: Wind patterns in the Malay-Indonesian archipelago – west monsoon.

Both maps from Robert Cribb, *Historical Atlas of Indonesia*, Richmond, Surrey: Curzon Press, 2000. Reproduced by permission of the author.

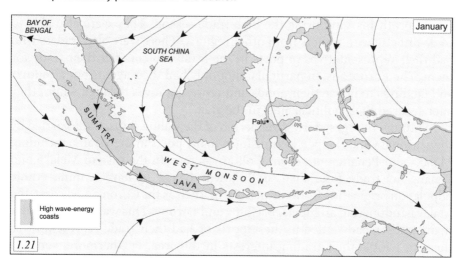

seen as a uniting element for the traders from the Indian Ocean, the Malay-Indonesian archipelago and China. In the Malay archipelago, the western monsoon brought traders to the spice islands while the eastern monsoon took them to Sumatra and to the ports on the Straits. Although Melaka was accessible during all monsoon seasons, its trading activities were determined by the seasonal winds. Two monsoons were used by the merchants to sail from India to the Straits of Melaka and to the East or China. The first monsoon season began in April and the second began in September. Merchants from India would set sail to the Straits of Melaka and the East beginning in May and would remain at Melaka or at any of the ports in the Straits until January, when they would return to India. Ships sailing during the second monsoon season arrived at Melaka in the middle of November and remained there until January, when they returned to India with cargoes from China. Ships that sailed from Melaka to India on their return journey had to return before the onset of the southwest monsoon, when the Indian coast was sealed off due to rough seas. On the other hand, the southeast monsoon was advantageous to Chinese traders on their homeward voyage. Chinese merchants arrived in Melaka in December and remained there until the end of June for their return journey. Merchants from Java and the archipelago came during the southeast monsoon and remained in Melaka until the northerly winds began to blow in December and January. Thus, the time of arrival at and departure from Melaka of the traders was dictated by the wind system so that, in effect, Melaka had a marked high as well as a low trade season.

The seasonal winds also had an impact on the profits earned by traders who travelled to the Straits. Those who arrived early and stayed longer were able to buy and stock up on precious goods at low prices and sell them for a higher profit margin during the high trade season. They were also able to trade directly with traders from other regions. There were also traders who had their representatives in ports in the Straits to conduct their trade for them. The Europeans, in particular, not only had their agents but also forts and factories to house their goods and representatives through whom they later secured their political aims in the area.

Through the ages, during the period of the sailing ships, trade carried by the seasonal winds helped to transform many ports in the Straits, including Melaka and Penang, into cosmopolitan centers. In the case of Melaka and Penang, as trade flourished, both towns began to have a multi-ethnic population originating from various places, such as the Coromandel coast, the Malaya-Indonesian archipelago, China and Europe. This was partly because many traders had settled in these ports or had their trade representatives there to handle their trading interests in the area. Furthermore, some of these traders had intermarried with the locals, thus creating new ethnic and cultural groups which added more intriguing features to an already complex trading society.

THE MARITIME TRADING WORLD OF SOUTHEAST ASIA

The maritime trading world of Southeast Asia covers a vast geographical area. Diverse in terms of its peoples, religious beliefs and languages, it was united by one main activity, namely, trade.[5] During the mid-seventeenth century the Indian Muslims (Chulias), the Indian Hindus, the English and Dutch East India Company (EIC and VOC) officials, and Danish, Portuguese, French and English country traders who had established their bases on the Coromandel Coast made up the majority of merchants from the Indian subcontinent. Many merchants kept bases on the Coromandel Coast because of the trading facilities, such as ship building and good ports and favourable trading policies adopted by local kingdoms who welcomed the presence of both the Europeans as well as the local traders. Joint ventures were also entered into by the local merchants (Chulia Muslims and Hindus) and the Europeans.[6]

There had been a lull in Chinese trading activities for several centuries following the period of increased official interest in the region, as seen in the fifteenth century during which Southeast Asia witnessed the expeditions of Admiral Cheng Ho (Zheng He). Only in the second half of the eighteenth century did the Chinese begin to make their presence felt once again. This period was marked by an increased number of Chinese migrants arriving in the region, which ushered in the so-called 'Chinese century' during which they began to make their presence felt in many sectors of the Southeast Asian economies.[7] The more relaxed policy on external trade adopted by the Chinese government in China had encouraged not only Chinese traders but also Chinese migrants to trade and settle in the western regions of Southeast Asia. The western part of the archipelago was preferred by many of these Chinese traders and migrants because the eastern regions of Southeast Asia were facing anarchy and turmoil.[8]

The activities of many Chinese traders and migrants in this part of Southeast Asia were different from the pattern seen in traders who arrived from the Indian subcontinent. As will be seen, many early Chinese migrants in Penang and Melaka did well by investing in revenue farms in Melaka and Penang and in the trade of the region. Some later turned into investors and financiers in the 1830s and expanded their businesses to include the tin mining industry in the Malay states. Some of the rich Chinese traders in Penang and Melaka had trading networks that covered a large part of the

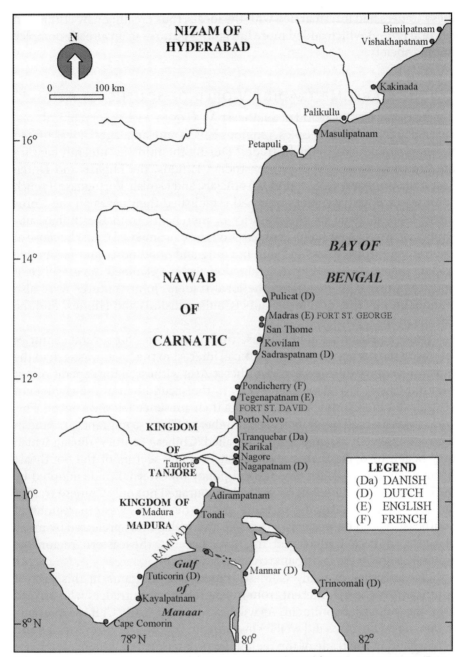

Map 5: Major ports on the Coromandel Coast, c. 1700. Adapted from S. Arasaratnam, 'European Ports Settlements in the Coromandel Commercial System 1650-1740'. In Frank Broeze (ed.), *Brides of the Sea: Port Cities of Asia from the 16th to 20th Centuries*, Kensington: New South Wales University Press, 1989.

north of the Straits of Melaka, northern Sumatra, Southern Siam and the Malay states. With these connections and having their proxies managing their business in many port-towns, many were able to exploit the agricultural and tin mining businesses in the region. These traders also brought in Chinese labourers to work in the enterprises in which they had invested, such as the mining industry and agricultural production. In both Melaka and Penang Chinese migrants undertook a variety of tasks. They not only traded in the town but also grew fruits and vegetables and pepper and gambir in the hinterland area. The opening up of lands in Penang's hinterland and the encouragement by the East India Company (EIC) to make Penang a pepper producer led to the influx of Chinese migrants who were mostly labourers to work in the agricultural sector. Even in Melaka, before the 1784 war with Riau, there were gambir plantations that had been opened by the Chinese merchants using Chinese labourers.

Since the abolition of slavery and the slave trade in the early nineteenth century, labour had become scarce in many parts of Southeast Asia. Penang and Melaka were also hit by a labour shortage. By the nineteenth century labour was always a scarce commodity in the Straits and the new wave of arrival of Chinese migrants had filled the gap. According to Trocki, many investors in the mining industry, including the Malay chiefs, preferred the Chinese to the indigenous people as labourers. This was partly due to the more systematic handling of Chinese labourers, the fact that they were easily controlled and that they also worked harder in order to pay back their passage before they were finally released from their contract. Therefore the coming of the Chinese migrant labourers to the Southeast Asian market provided the first alternative to slavery. The end result of the influx of Chinese migrants during the period under study was the dawn of a new era in most of Southeast Asia, in which the Chinese dominated the sphere of commerce and played important roles in many economic activities during the period of high imperialism.[9]

From the sixteenth to the nineteenth centuries, there were many port-towns that rose and fell along the shores of the Indian Ocean. A similar trend also occurred on the shores of the Malayan-Indonesian archipelago. A common characteristic shared by the majority of these port-towns was an exceedingly diverse population made up of representatives from all the major seafaring communities of Asia, including the Indian Ocean areas, archipelagos, China, and also representatives from various parts of Europe. These various ethnic or social groups tended to live under conditions later known as extra-territoriality. This implied a common residential area, a headman under various titles, use of their own law codes and considerable inter-group economic co-operation.[10]

During most of the seventeenth to nineteenth centuries, many of the port-towns along the Indian Ocean–Southeast Asia–South China Sea route came under European control. The Portuguese, who were the earliest of the Europeans to set foot in many of these port-towns, were challenged by the Spanish, Dutch, English and French. Control of port-towns such as Surat, Colombo and Melaka thus changed hands from one European power to another. In addition, new port-towns such as Madras, Calcutta, Penang and Batavia were created by the Europeans to tap the lucrative trade routes in this region. Therefore, many new port-towns emerged on the west coast of India and on the Coromandel coast. Almost all of the major European powers – Portuguese, Dutch, English, French and Danish – were active in building their own trading networks, establishing their forts and settlements on both sides of the Indian continent.[11] The Coromandel coast was especially important to the Europeans because geographically it was strategically located. Further, supply of Indian goods was readily available there, the infrastructure for refitting ships from Europe bound for the East was adequately provided and a good relationship existed between the Europeans and the local kingdoms, especially with regard to trade and the freedom to build settlements and forts in this area. The Coast also acted as the key passage to Southeast Asia and China.[12] The European powers were also very active in occupying and acquiring port-towns in the Malayan-Indonesian archipelago. Their main interest was to secure a constant supply of spices and other commodities that could be traded in the intra-Asian trade. Melaka was the earliest port-town that fell to the Europeans. Other port-towns which later came under European occupation were Batavia, Riau, Benkulen, Makassar, Ambon, Manila and Timor. Similarly, in the South China Sea region, several European powers established their own trading settlements on the Chinese mainland. In this way, by the end of eighteenth century many of the important trading centres on the Indian Ocean-Southeast Asia–South China Sea area came under European control.

Aceh, on the northern part of Sumatra, became an important port-town from the early seventeenth century. It came to power as a coastal kingdom of Sumatra under Sultan Iskandar Muda (1607–36). The extent of Aceh's dominance on the northern region of Sumatra stretched as far as Deli (Aru) in the east and Padang in the west. At some stage Aceh also held sway over a part of the Malay peninsula. Its capital, Bandar Aceh Dar-es-Salam, was an important centre of Asian trade.[13]

In addition to Aceh, other port-towns on the shore of the Southeast Asian mainland were also frequently visited by traders, both European and Indian, from the Indian subcontinent. Among the most important of these port-towns were Tenasserim, Mergui and Kedah. The island of Junk Ceylon, off the coast of southwest Thailand, was also a long-standing port. There-fore, there were very complex connections and networks between the ports of the western coast of India, the Coromandel coast, the Bay of Bengal and the port-towns on the northwest corner of the archipelago. Traders from all these places converged at specific port-towns during certain seasons as dictated by the monsoon winds. Likewise, traders from Aceh travelled as far as the Coromandel coast and frequented the northern region of the Malay peninsula. While the main trade between the major ports was carried by long distance traders, the connecting trade with various other small port-towns in the interior was served by local traders and merchants.

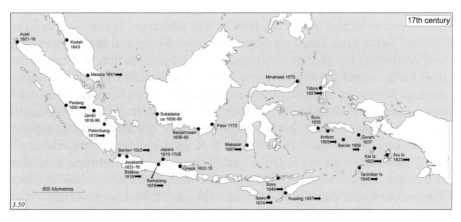

Map 6: Major VOC posts and forts in the archipelago, seventeenth century.

Map 7: British expansion in the archipelago, 1786-1797.

Both maps from Robert Cribb, *Historical Atlas of Indonesia*, Richmond, Surrey: Curzon Press, 2000. Reproduced by permission of the author.

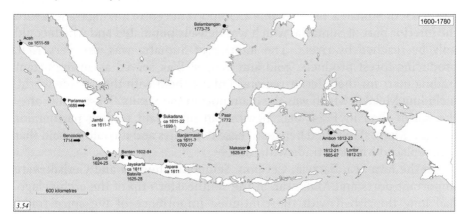

Further south in the Straits and beyond, within the archipelago, the important port-towns that served as important trading centres were Melaka, Johor-Riau, Siak, Batavia, Makassar and various port-towns on the north coast of Java such as Cheribon, Juwana and Semarang. These port-towns were connected to the wider network that extended to China and the Indian sub-continent while at the same time serving other small port-towns in the region.

Riau, at the southern end of the Straits of Melaka, became an important port-town in the middle of the seventeenth century, serving as an important centre of trade in the Straits. After the death of its last king in 1699, the kingdom was thrown into a turbulent period which witnessed a succession dispute between the followers of the Bendahara and the Laksamana.[14] Later, in the 1720s, the succession dispute became more complicated when Bugis princes, earlier driven out by the Dutch from Makassar, became involved in it.[15] The Johor-Riau kingdom was undermined by the Bugis princes and most of the decisions regarding trade and administration in Riau came under their control. Perhaps because Riau was indirectly ruled by the Bugis, who were renowned traders, trade continued to flourish there so that it once again became a leading centre of trade in the Straits in the mid-eighteenth century.[16] Traders from China, the archipelago, the Indian subcontinent and Europe came to Riau. However, as politics in the Straits became more volatile and uncertain towards the end of the eighteenth century, Riau was caught in a dispute with its closest rival, Dutch Melaka. A minor conflict between the Bugis leader, Raja Haji, and the Dutch-Melaka governor led to open war in 1784 and Riau's defeat.[17] The majority of Bugis traders and merchants fled to other ports along the Straits as well as on the east coast of the Malay peninsula. Thus in the aftermath of the war, far from being crushed or sidelined, Bugis traders continued to trade in the region from new bases such as Selangor, Johor, Trengganu and Siak.[18]

Another important port-town in the Straits was Siak, which lies on the east coast of Sumatra. Siak became an important centre linking traders with the interior part of Sumatra, which was densely populated and which could only be reached by rivers. The interior of Sumatra was also very rich, producing forest products, gold and pepper. Siak served as an important trading mart for the interior regions, linking them with the outside world, including Melaka, which was the main port in the Straits.[19] Especially after the fall of Riau in 1784, Siak became an important trading partner for Melaka. Many ships plied between these two ports and it could be said that Siak replaced Melaka's trade with Riau.[20]

In the Java Sea, Batavia, Ceribon, Semarang, Juwana and Gerisik were important ports and Makassar, at the southeastern tip of the archipelago, had long flourished with the continued importance of the spice trade.

Batavia, as mentioned earlier, was the centre of Dutch administration in the East and it became the centre of trade in the Java Sea, linking it with the port-towns in China. The Dutch administration made it a policy that the Chinese junk trade with the archipelago should be centred at Batavia.[21] Such a policy caused very few Chinese traders to arrive at Melaka and affected Melaka's direct trade with China. Therefore, port-towns on the mainland of China, such as Amoy, Canton and Macao, had important trading connections with the archipelago mainly through Batavia and, later, west Borneo.[22] The archipelago was also connected with the long-distance trade conducted by the Spanish galleons in Manila that traded between Southeast Asia and South America.[23]

Traders who arrived at many of the important port-towns of Southeast Asia could be divided into two major categories. The first group consisted of long distance traders who came from Europe, the Indian subcontinent or China. The second group consisted of the regional and short-distance merchants and traders who arrived from various ports on the archipelago. These traders and merchants could again be classified into four main groups. Firstly, there were the European merchants and traders from the major trading companies, the VOC and the EIC, and other European traders, such as the Portuguese, Danish, Spanish, French and the English country traders; secondly, the Indian traders who came from the Indian subcontinent, including the Chulia Muslims, Hindus, Moors and Gujarati; thirdly, the Chinese merchants from China; and, finally, there were the traders from the archipelago (the natives, Burghers, Chinese, Arabs, Chulias and Hindus).[24]

The VOC and EIC traders were long-distance and regional traders who travelled from ports in Europe and had close connections with many port-towns that came under their control in the East. They belonged to big companies funded by shareholders in Europe and also trade profits in Asia. These companies were very powerful and were supported by a large and strong bureaucracy, protected by strong armies and aided by large fleets of merchant and naval ships. Although the headquarters of these companies were located in Europe, they also had their centres of administration in the East. The Dutch VOC was centred at Batavia on the island of Java while the English East India Company chose Calcutta as its headquarters. Since these companies had shareholders with much capital, they were able to build up trading bases, networks and connections with various port-towns that were under their direct dominion in the Indian subcontinent, the archipelago and China. Matters regarding administration and regulations on trade in these port-towns were governed and dictated by the higher authority in the East.[25]

Apart from the VOC and EIC, there were other Europeans, such as the Portuguese and Spanish who owned port-towns in the Indian subcontinent,

China and the Philippines.[26] The Danish and French private companies owned factories and forts in many port-towns in the Indian subcontinent. Although the Danes and French were not as powerful and active as the others, they were able to capture some of the trade in the Indian Ocean, Southeast Asia and China.[27] There were also the English country traders who traded independently.[28] They were considered more robust and aggressive and their principal trading connections were with the native port-towns not directly under the control of the VOC or EIC. In addition to the European traders, Asian merchants from the Indian subcontinent and China were also long distance travellers. While the majority of the Chinese junk merchants were forced to trade at Batavia, the Indians traded freely at ports in the Straits and on the Java Sea although they were mostly seen in Aceh, Melaka, Riau and Junk Ceylon.

Most of the regional traders used port-towns in Southeast Asia as their bases. They were mainly natives, the most numerous being the Malays and Bugis, but a sizeable number of non-native traders such as the Chinese, Moors, Chulias, Arabs, Kelings (Hindus) and the Burghers also operated from within the region. In addition, there were also the VOC, EIC and the English country traders. Many non-natives had in fact settled permanently in Southeast Asia and become important merchants who traded within the archipelago. Some of them owned large ships capable of sailing longer distances to ports along the coast of the Indian subcontinent.

The types of goods that were traded by merchants from the Indian subcontinent-Southeast Asia-South China Sea can be divided into five main categories. They were manufactured goods, products for human consumption, mineral ore, forest products and human slaves.[29] The main commodities traded by the majority of merchants from the Indian subcontinent-Southeast Asia-South China Sea were the basic necessities of life, such as salt, sugar, grains and clothing.[30] The main manufactured products from these areas were silks, cotton textiles, porcelain and glass, jewellery and finely cut precious stones.[31] Raw materials for industries were exchanged in the maritime and overland trade of Asia. Although some of these materials were also produced locally, the demand for similar products in certain areas shows that imported goods were appreciated.[32]

Some of the commodities produced in Southeast Asia were not in great demand in the Indian subcontinent but were well sought after among the Chinese traders from China. For example, sea slugs or trepang which were harvested from the seas of the archipelago, were in high demand in China but not in the Indian subcontinent. However, some items were universally in demand, such as rice, the staple food of most Asians. Rice was also sought after by port-towns not as an exchange item but to feed their local population.

Other commodities, for example, gum resin and aromatic woods, items used in the preparation of incense in temples and religious gatherings, were sought after by the Chinese, Arabs and Indians.[33] Spices such as cloves, nutmegs and mace were in great demand among the Arabs, Persians and Indians but not by the Chinese, who preferred pepper. Pepper was also sought after by the majority of merchants from Asia and Europe.[34] Edible bird's nests, elephant's tusks and medicinal herbs were in higher demand in China than in India.

Most of the commodities traded remained largely unchanged throughout the seventeenth and eighteenth centuries except for a marked increase in the demand for Chinese tea from Europe, which was exchanged with opium from India and tin from Southeast Asia. Neither did the pattern of trade change. Throughout these centuries, the main commodities sought after were generally pepper, spices, gold, tin and forest products, such as rattan and aromatic woods, from the Southeast Asian regions. In return, there was the demand for cloth, opium and various manufactured products from India and China. Therefore, the trend of this exchange of goods shows that commodities exported from Southeast Asia were mostly food items and raw materials while the goods imported from India and China were mainly manufactured products. Goods like chinaware, porcelain, paper, sugar, salt and cloth originated mainly from India and China. Although Southeast Asia produced cloth, for example Java, Bugis and Aceh cloth, the demand for Indian cloth was greater and for different purposes, in part due to the superior quality of the Indian variety.[35] The majority of the Asian population also appreciated the various colours offered in Indian cloth.[36]

PORTS AND TRADING NETWORKS: MELAKA AND PENANG

The Straits of Melaka was an integral part of the international sea route linking the East with the West. Its importance as a waterway and passage through which most of the trade between China and India and beyond was conducted had long been recognized. The arrival of the Europeans took this recognition to a different level for they were inclined to put into action the belief that whoever controlled the Straits would ultimately take control of the lucrative trade that passed through it.

Since their occupation of Melaka in 1641, the Dutch aspired to establish it as a base that could tap the trade covering the India-Straits-China route.[37] However, their hope was challenged by Riau, capital of the Johor-Riau kingdom.[38] Aggravating the situation was Batavia, capital of the commercial empire of the VOC in the East, which also transcended her competitor, Dutch-Melaka. Whilst Batavia was a key rallying point for the VOC's trade and administration, it was also the most strategic focal point within the planned empire.[39] Ultimately, Dutch-Melaka was provided with a small garrison to control the trade,which formed a demarcation between the East and West. Melaka was therefore more of a guard post than an independent hub of its own. With the increasing focus and attention given to Batavia,

> Malacca thus lived in the shadow of Batavia, and it was possible for the governor-general and council to write to Amsterdam in 1698: 'It has been known for a long time that Malacca has been more a place of necessary residence and garrison than of trade'. Imhoff, in his report of 1741, compared Malacca with Malabar as a deficit post of the company: it produced little trade and was of no importance in relations with indigenous states. It could be reduced in size but not completely abandoned because of its strategic position.[40]

After the fall of Riau in 1784, the English feared that the Dutch would gain complete control of the commercial activities in the Straits and the Malay peninsula.[41] Meantime, beginning from the middle of the eighteenth century, there was a great expansion in the commercial activities of both the English East India Company (EIC) and English country traders with China.[42] But the English did not have a port that could supply fresh provisions and goods such as tin and pepper in the Straits for their trade to China. To resolve this problem, the director of the EIC suggested that a new English port prefer-ably on the east of the Bay of Bengal must be found in order to provide a constant supply of cargo for the trade to China as well as a base that could protect the safety of ships engaged in the China trade. However, this was not the sole motive of the EIC because the Company anticipated that it should also profit from the lucrative spice trade in the region.[43] The English believed that this was a right that should be conferred to them due to the fact that they had been driven from the archipelago by the Dutch.[44] In addition, the EIC needed a post to utilize as a naval base in the archipelago and to stem the growing power of the Dutch in the Malay peninsula.[45] After the 1784 war with Riau and following an active Dutch presence in Perak and Selangor, the English increasingly felt that the Dutch were a real threat to their activities in the Straits. Thus, a new English base in the Straits was seen to be a necessity and the case for its existence was strengthened by the need to prevent the emergence of French fleets in the area.[46]

As the movement of ships in the eastern seas was completely at the mercy of the monsoons or trade winds, this compelled the EIC to seek a suitable harbour situated on the eastern coast of the Bay of Bengal. The Company began to search for a suitable base, preferably in Aceh in north Sumatra or in the Andaman islands.[47] However, its attempts were in vain. Following the start of negotiation, which Francis Light conducted with the kingdom of

Kedah, attention was turned to a base near the Straits of Melaka leading to the opening of Penang on Prince of Wales Island by the English in 1786.[48]

Penang's location at the northern end of the Straits of Melaka and Melaka's position in its southern section meant that each port commanded a strategic site at the trading crossroads between India, China and the archipelago. Due to the fact that Penang is located at the northern end of the Straits, it had a closer link with the trading areas that cover that part of the Straits, including north Sumatra, the southern part of Thailand, the northern section of the Malayan peninsula, the southern region of Burma and the Coromandel Coast of India.[49] On the other hand, Melaka had more control over the southern part of the Straits, including the centre and southern part of Sumatra, the southern region of the Malayan peninsular and the Malay-Indonesian archipelago. It was also able to capture, to a small degree, the China trade.

The eighteenth century saw an increase in the activities of English and Danish country traders in the Straits.[50] This was due to an increase in trade between China and Europe. The most important commodity traded was Chinese tea to Europe, which was very lucrative. However, the tea trade intensified the problem of remittances to China. Thus, in order to reduce the flow of bullion from Europe to pay for Chinese tea, other goods such as pepper and tin from Melaka were instead used in exchange. Tin was therefore in great demand for the China trade. This increased the rivalry between the Dutch, English and Danish traders since they were competing to control the tin trade in the Straits. Subsequently, this development caused strained relations between Dutch-Melaka, the European traders and the Malay kingdoms, especially Riau.[51]

After the fourth Anglo-Dutch war (1780–84), the India-Straits-China trade was completely dominated by the English.[52] As we have seen, the importance of the China trade to the English also led them to look for a new post in the Straits for their ships on their way to China, resulting in the opening of Penang in 1786. In addition, the Dutch in Melaka also confronted the problem of competition with Bugis traders in Riau, leading to the 1784 war between Melaka and Riau.[53] Finally, the English increased their penetration into the Southeast Asian trade in those areas not under the control of the Dutch and even challenged the Dutch monopoly. The major challenge came from the activities of the English Country traders. As a consequence, after the 1770s, the English dominated the trade between the Coromandel Coast and Malaya.[54] Melaka's shipping lists clearly illustrate that in the 1780s and 1790s most of the trade between Melaka and the Coromandel Coast was conducted by the English, both Company and English country traders, and the Portuguese.[55] In the early days after the English established themselves in Penang, traders from the Coromandel Coast began to use its port. The most notable were the Chulia merchants whose ships called regularly there. Their networks linked various ports on the Coromandel Coast, such as Proto Novo, Nagore and Nagapatnam to Penang, as well as to Mergui, Junk Ceylon, Melaka, Aceh and Pedir. The most popular route used by their ships was from South India to Penang and back through Pedir and Aceh.[56] Some of the Chulia merchants settled down in Penang, making trading more convenient between the Indian subcontinent and Southeast Asia as the merchants based in India were able to rely on their partners in Penang to look after their business dealings. These partners not only bought goods required for the Indian trade but were also in a position to store valuable items bought during the low season at lower prices to be sold later at profitable prices in the high season. They could also make trading arrangements with native ports, such as Kedah, Aceh, Mergui and various other ports on the Sumatran coast. Thus, a multilateral trading pattern was organized by these traders. However, their main trading route was always between the Indian subcontinent and Penang.

Prior to the opening of Penang, traders from other ports in the Bay of Bengal area such as Pegu in Burma, Junk Ceylon, Mergui and Tenasserim had already established close trading connections with Melaka. At the same time merchants from Melaka also traded at these ports.[57] Merchants from the Coromandel Coast, on their trading journey to the Straits, also stopped at various places in these areas. Thus the Bay of Bengal region had had long connections with the ports in the Straits both directly through their own traders and indirectly through the visits made by ships coming from outside their region. Once Penang was established, trade from the Bay of Bengal region began to also flow to the island. This was in part due to the fact that Francis Light, who was based in Junk Ceylon before opening Penang, had had long trading connections with the region, in particular Kedah, Melaka and the Coromandel Coast. When Light ceased to trade after he became the first Superintendent of Penang, these contacts were maintained by his co-partner, James Scott. Penang also benefitted from the trade from the east. From the east, long-distance traders came mostly from the main ports of southern China, namely, Amoy, Canton and Macao, sailing through the South China Sea to other ports along this trade route such as those in Indo-China, Thailand and the Philippines before arriving in the Straits. Chinese ports were mostly served by English country traders, Portuguese and English East India Company ships.[58] Most of these long-distance traders who had their bases in the Indian subcontinent travelled from the Coromandel Coast and stopped at various Straits ports, including Melaka, Aceh and Penang, on their journey to and from Canton or Macao in Southern China.

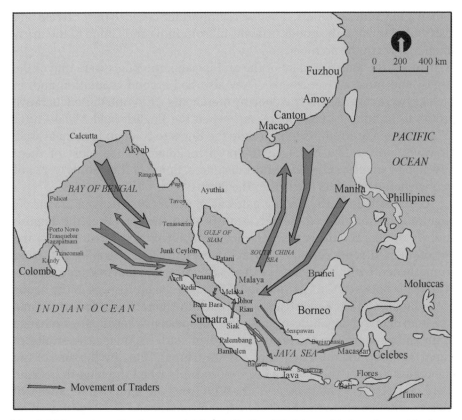

Map 8: Main ports on the Coromandel Coast, Straits of Melaka and Indonesian archipelago.

As a result of Dutch regulations that required all Chinese junks to trade at Batavia rather than at Melaka, fewer Chinese traders from China traded in the Straits.[59] The limited number of Chinese junks from Amoy usually did not go beyond Melaka where their presence was eagerly awaited. Most Chinese traders exchanged their goods with products from the archipelago and from India.[60] After the 1780s, only one or two Chinese junks from Amoy landed at Melaka per year.[61]

Foreign and local regional traders who had close trading networks with Melaka also included Penang on their route after 1786. These traders came from Batavia, Semarang, Juwana, Gerisik, Makassar and the Borneo areas, the major ports in the archipelago.[62] From these ports came food products such as rice, spices and sugar, which supplied Melaka and Penang with provisions. The presence of these traders at Melaka and Penang was important because they brought most of the goods that were needed at both places and provided the supply of spices, medicinal herbs and forest products for the

Indian and Chinese traders. They were important because they carried and distributed most of the goods brought in from India and China to the many smaller ports in the archipelago.

Among the native traders of the archipelago, the Bugis were one of the largest and most active groups. They also had a good reputation and, in Melaka, were regarded as trustworthy merchants who contributed lucrative profits to its trade.[63] For this reason, when the English held Melaka after 1794, they made attempts to persuade the Bugis to trade in Penang as well. However, only a few managed to travel to Penang since most of them travelled in smaller ships over short distances. Some of their ships were not strong enough to travel further up the Straits.[64]

As stated before, the trading patterns in the Straits changed drastically beginning in the mid eighteenth century with the arrival of the English country traders and the active presence of the EIC in Southeast Asia. By the end of the eighteenth century, the English presence in the Straits was further strengthened with the decline of the VOC. After the fourth Anglo Dutch-War, trade between the Coromandel Coast and the Straits was in the hands of the English.[65] The English also controlled the lucrative trade with China. The high demand for Chinese tea for the European market and the exchange of tin and pepper from the Straits for Indian cloth had made the Straits an important stop for the English traders to China. Thus, by the end of the eighteenth century there was a big shift in trade when the English became dominant players. The decline of the VOC and the temporary transfer of Melaka and Batavia to the English further strengthened the English trading network in the Straits.[66]

SHIPPING LIST, CURRENCIES, WEIGHTS AND MEASUREMENTS

One of the good things about the series of VOC records under the heading of *Overgekomen Brieven en Papieren* (OBP) is that they provide a detailed account of the events that happened in the port-town of Melaka and the surrounding areas.[67] The most important section on the political atmosphere of the port-town is found under the Secret Resolutions in the OBP series. This series of documents contains information not only on the Dutch administration of the town but also its trading activities. Detailed trade figures such as the type and quantity of commodities exchanged as well as prices and price fluctuations are given in the regular reports. The most important section in the OBP series is the Shipping List (incoming and outgoing ships at Melaka). This section, also referred to as *Boomsboeken*, was compiled and kept and then submitted each year, along with the general letter, to the Governor-General. All arrivals and departures of vessels were carefully listed and compiled. The data in the shipping list include information on the name of the owner of a vessel, the name of the captain, his origins, the port where he came from, the day the ship departed from the port and date of arrival in Melaka, the number of days on the journey, the size of the vessel, the weight of the vessel, the name of the vessel, the type of vessel, the total number of crew on board, the number of passengers on board, the type of weapons and cannons on board, the type of commodities loaded, the value of the commodities in weights and units and the number of days the ship anchored in the port.

Although accounts of trade in the OBP's Shipping List are very detailed, there remain some weaknesses. The value, volume and weight of goods were not standardized. For example, there was no standardization of the unit used to measure the volume of cloth. Sometimes the unit of measurement was the corgie, and at other times it was in bales, and certain documents did not even mention the volume involved. Similar problems are also encountered with other commodities where no standardized unit was used. Measuring units such as koyan and picul were not consistently applied but were used with many others, such as *buyong, kranjang, bundel, bottel, baal, bos, kati, legger, kist, laksa, kanaster, gantang* and *zak*.[68] This leads to difficulties in converting the various units, weights and measurements of commodities into currency value. Therefore it is very difficult to compare one commodity with another in currency value, as there was no standard method to assess value in currency terms. To overcome this problem, this study merely lists the more important commodities judged from the frequency of their appearance in the Shipping List. Commodities such as textiles, opium, grains, tin and forest products are considered important because they appear regularly in the list. Another problem encountered arises from the Dutch practice of omitting in their data the activities of VOC ships. At the same time, ships which were involved in the smuggling trade were also not recorded. However, despite the fact that the records are incomplete and problematic, they compare more favourably to those provided by the English on trade activities both in Melaka and Penang.

The English had their own method of compiling data on trade but it was not as detailed and painstaking as that of the Dutch. For instance, no mention was made of the identity of the captain of a ship arriving in Melaka, and other details about the goods brought in and other information usually found in the Dutch records are also not available. The reports on the whole were confined to providing information on the value of trade coming from and going to each area or port and lists of goods imported and re-exported. All the goods were valued in Sicca rupees. Thus it is difficult to determine the identity of the traders and their ethnic origins and their port of origin and destination. Although the data were standardized according to the value in money, the English documents did not provide an accurate and detailed picture of the trade at that time.

Therefore it is a challenging task to compare and contrast the two sets of documents on trade in Melaka and Penang. In addition, it is difficult to analyse in statistical form the decline of Melaka's trade during the English occupation from 1795 to 1818. This is because there is no complete shipping record listing incoming and outgoing ships for Melaka during this period. There are also no detailed reports on the trade itself. The only report on Melaka's trade, compiled by the English, was in 1817–18 before they handed Melaka back to the Dutch.[69] Even this report has limited usefulness as it only contains observations and opinions that emphasized the importance of keeping Melaka as an English port, since it was situated near the archipelago, and the only data given relate to Melaka's import of goods for 1810. It is also emphasized here that during this period of English administration, they made great effort to promote Penang as an important port of call for the India-Straits-China trade. The English considered their occupation of Melaka as a temporary commitment so that all their attention should be given to promoting the development of Penang rather than the former. As a result, during the English occupation of Melaka its trade declined with a considerable volume of it being diverted to Penang.[70]

In addition, there are too few documents available to give a complete picture of trade trends during the brief period from 1818 to 1824 when the Dutch reoccupied Melaka. Nevertheless, judging from long-term trends and new developments around the region, it can be safely concluded that Melaka's trade did not improve. The opening of Singapore in 1819 by the English might even have worsened the situation, as many rich Melaka-Chinese moved their business to Singapore.[71] As the trade in Singapore increased the effect on Melaka was clearly seen in later years.[72] Thus, the period from 1795 to 1824 could be considered as a period of uncertainty in the future of Melaka, not the least because it was transferred from one colonial master to another. During the English occupation, their policy appears to have been to maintain but not develop the port-town because they wanted to promote the success of Penang as a trading centre.

MELAKA'S TRADE IN THE EIGHTEENTH AND NINETEENTH CENTURIES

Melaka is situated on the west coast of the Malay peninsula by the Melaka river, which flows into the Straits of Melaka. The early history of Melaka's commercial monopolies and the imposition of the pass system on traders trading in the Straits can be traced to the Portuguese occupation of Melaka from 1511 to 1641. In order to tap its wealth and the lucrative trade between the Indian subcontinent and the Straits, the Portuguese issued passes to all merchants using the Straits.[73]

When Melaka was occupied by the Dutch in 1641, they retained the Portuguese system. According to Arasaratnam, there were two conflicting aims in relation to Melaka's trade during the early period of Dutch administration. One was to preserve and develop the emporium character of Melaka while the other was to ensure Melaka's commercial monopoly on trade and prices in the interests of Dutch trade in the Straits.[74] In 1641, for example, the Dutch administration imposed a duty of 10 percent on imported goods and 5 percent on exports and both were higher than those which had been introduced by the Portuguese.[75] The Dutch felt that the presence of many Asian traders in the Straits threatened their trade, and believed that by eliminating them they would finally increase their trading returns on commodities such as tin and Indian cloths.[76] In the long term, this policy led to the decline of Melaka's trade.

In order to secure full monopoly on the supply of tin from the Malay kingdoms in the peninsula, a constant supply of pepper from Sumatra and sole monopoly of the Indian cloth trade in the Straits, the Dutch embarked on a policy of making exclusive contracts with Malay rulers to gain full control of the trade in these products. Hence, treaties were signed with many Malay kingdoms: Kedah in 1642,[77] Junk Ceylon in 1643,[78] Bangery in 1645,[79] Perak in 1746[80] and Siak in 1754.[81] However, the trade monopoly policy had its drawbacks, as it encouraged smuggling in controlled goods such as opium, Indian cloth and tin. In addition, many traders tried to avoid going to Melaka.

After the Dutch occupation, laws and regulations were enforced in Melaka to regulate traders who purchased merchandise imported to, or exported from, Melaka.[82] Taxes were also applied to opium, betel leaf (*sirih*), pork, arak, gaming houses and fish markets. The Boom farm or customs house was given the power to collect duties on several commodities, such as 15 Spanish dollars per chest on opium, 1.25 Spanish dollars per picul on tin, and 1.25 Spanish dollars per picul on pepper. The customs house was also authorized to collect taxes for all piece goods (cloths) that entered Melaka, whether from the East or West. As for raw silk, it was taxed at 7 per cent of its value at the time of import.[83]

Goods, both imported and exported, that were not listed as taxable products paid a flat rate of 6 per cent levy. However, silk material that was to be re-exported was not taxed. Goods not displayed for sale but loaded on ships for export were required to have a certificate attached to them from the customs house, declaring that they were for re-export and not for sale in Melaka. If goods were offered for disposal, then the usual duties on imports were charged.

The customs house was entitled to receive one-third of the established import duties on all goods re-exported. In the case of goods sold and trans-shipped without landing, the customs house was allowed to collect half the established port duties. The value of all goods imported and exported was determined by the customs office and the merchants. This Dutch regulation of taxing various goods and commodities in Melaka's port was continued during the English occupation.[84]

After the Dutch occupation in 1641, Melaka continued to depend on trade as its major source of livelihood.[85] No agricultural activities were developed in the hinterland. As Melaka emerged into the eighteenth century under the Dutch it was not able to revive its former position as an important port.[86] But the intra-Asian trade, which had existed in Melaka since the Sultanate period, remained important to its well-being.[87] In the eighteenth century the main commodities in the intra-Asian trade were opium, tin, gold-dust, forest products and Indian cloth.[88] Many of these items were traded with the ports in the Straits and the archipelago. Possession of opium and tin was, in theory, restricted by law and exclusively monopolized by the VOC. Although the Dutch authorities had enforced exclusive rights to carry and sell opium and tin, smuggling activities among the European country traders were rampant in the Straits.[89] In the eighteenth century, most of the opium, which was jealously guarded by the Dutch, came from India. The income derived from the opium trade was profitable since the product was also in great demand at native ports. The Dutch administration in Melaka imposed regulations that gave sole rights to its vessels to carry the article. These regulations were strict and the penalties were severe. For example, one provision stated that if a ship was caught in possession of opium the cargo and ship would be confiscated and sold, with the proceeds going to the VOC. There were many records of such confiscations.[90] The opium trade was very profitable and it was reported that a chest of opium sold in the West Coast of Sumatra could fetch 300 Spanish dollars. It could then be sold again for twice the value of the purchase price.[91] But despite the strict regulations, the VOC only made a small profit out of the opium trade in the long term because it was unable to capture the largest share of the market; by the second half of the eighteenth century opium was traded in large quantities by the English country traders at Riau, where it was sold to Bugis traders in exchange for tin and pepper.[92]

Tin procured in the Malay states of the peninsula was mostly exported to Europe and China. Since the Dutch occupation of Melaka in 1641, the administration had made a great effort to monopolize the tin trade in the Straits, but it failed to capture the tin trade to Europe.[93] During the eighteenth century there were various efforts by the Melaka authorities to control the tin trade. The Dutch signed several treaties with the Malay kingdoms, such as with Perak in 1746, and made attempts to disrupt the tin trade of the Johor-Riau kingdom. However, all these efforts failed and the Dutch in Melaka could not compete in the tin trade with the English, Portuguese, Danish and Asian merchants.[94]

In the earlier period gold was a valuable item exported by Melaka, and it remained an important article for export in the eighteenth century. Gold formed a large proportion of the VOC's total imports at the Coromandel Coast of India.[95] Gold for export came from Sumatra and from the interior of the peninsula. Most of it came from the Minangkabau areas, the important gold producing states of Patapahan, Indragiri and Jambi. In 1749, the value of gold obtained from these areas reached a total of 53,640.7 guilders.[96] As the Siak river provided access to these areas, the Dutch tried to control them by frequently patrolling the Siak river and maintaining a small fortress on Pulau Gunting. However, their attempts failed to stop the smuggling activities that went on and by 1777, the Dutch monopoly of the gold trade had completely collapsed.[97]

In addition to gold, forest products were traded such as rattan, ivory, sago, wax, resin and sapanwood, and valuable medicines such as bezoar stones,[98] mainly from Sumatra and the interior of the peninsula. However, the trade in forest products was not considered important to the VOC in Dutch Melaka, so it was carried out mainly by the Dutch burghers there, with the administration profiting from this trade only through customs and anchorage tolls.[99]

Besides forest products, pepper was an important export from Melaka, and was obtained from Sumatra and surrounding areas. Melaka was in fact not regarded as a primary source for pepper, but rather as a watchdog, receiving occasional shipments from Palembang and Jambi. Again, the Dutch lost their control over the pepper trade in the Straits due to the activities of the country traders and because pepper was easily obtainable from Riau.[100]

Indian cloth was another important commodity which was re-exported by Melaka to various Malay ports in the archipelago. In the earlier period, Indian cloth came from the Coromandel Coast and was mostly carried by Indian and Moor traders from India. As the Dutch were determined to control the flow of cloth to the Straits, they denied passes to Indian traders carrying cloth there. Further, passes had to be purchased in Melaka, a policy aimed at forcing all traders carrying cloth to the Straits to land at Melaka. However, by the end of the seventeenth century, the policy of monopolizing the cloth trade in the Straits had to be abandoned because many Indian traders managed to avoid going to Melaka and, instead, traded directly with Malay ports such as Aceh, Ujong Salang, Kedah, Perak and Riau.[101]

By the end of seventeenth century the trading monopoly that was inherited by Dutch-Melaka from the Portuguese began to reveal its negative effect. Dutch-Melaka's trade in the Straits had declined and all policies regarding trading monopolies and the pass system began to fall apart. The situation was made worse with the coming of the EIC and the English Country traders to the Straits. With their greater capacity to mount an effective challenge to the Dutch position and power, the old monopoly and pass system became unworkable. The founding of Penang by the English and the new English policy of free trade signalled a bleak future for Dutch-Melaka, and its position as the great trading emporium never revived again to its old glory.

Two main factors contributed to the decline of trade in Melaka during this period. One was the stiff competition faced by the Dutch from the English country traders in the Straits and the other was the enforcement of the trade monopoly by the Dutch in Melaka together with the policy of the VOC at Batavia to maintain it only as a second class Dutch port-town.[102] Thus, Melaka was not a profitable settlement for the VOC during the greater part of the eighteenth century. But while the Directors came to see Melaka as a burden, since the cost of maintaining it was not covered by the income from the port, they were, however, not prepared to abandon it. This was due to its strategic importance both as a base from which the Dutch could attempt to control trade in the Straits and for the important role it could continue to play in the intra-Asian trade. In the meantime, Melaka's position as an entrepot was being challenged by the Bugis in Riau. Although the Dutch-Bugis war of 1784 that marked the climax in the acrimonious relationship between the two rivals ended in Dutch victory, the rivalry had also affected Melaka's trade in the long term. Thus, by the end of the eighteenth century some evidence showed that Melaka's trade was declining.[103] The opening of Penang in 1786 and Singapore in 1819 further reduced the status of Melaka as an important port in the east. Steps were taken to promote and improve Melaka's commercial status during the brief Dutch reoccupation (1818–24). However, this could not save the situation. Subsequently, the nineteenth century witnessed Melaka as a declining commercial port.

Melaka's trade and trading network also declined from decade to decade due to changes in the political atmosphere in Melaka and in the Straits. From November 1795 to September 1818 Melaka was ruled by the English and later returned to the Dutch administration, until March 1825. After the Anglo-Dutch treaty in 1824, Melaka was under the control of the English. When the English occupied Melaka from 1795 to 1818 and set up a caretaker government, they made no changes to the Dutch regulation regarding taxes on trade in Melaka. The Dutch system of administration and control was also continued. Meanwhile, in the early nineteenth century, Penang was beginning to transform into an important port and centre of trade in the northern part of the Straits. Many regular traders to Melaka, such as those from India, the European country traders and other Asian traders such as the Malays, Bugis and Acehnese, were attracted to shift their trade to Penang.

EARLY PENANG AND ITS TRADE

Towards the end of the eighteenth century, the English were active in Asia, replacing the old colonial masters such as the Portuguese and the Dutch in the Indian subcontinent. Their presence could be seen in the activities of English country traders and the English East India Company in the Bay of Bengal and in Southeast Asia.[104]

The strong English position on the Indian subcontinent was also clearly marked by their occupation of various ports and towns, such as Madras, Nagapatnam and Calcutta.[105] However, their presence in the archipelago was not on the strategic sea lanes. British Benkulen on the west coast of Sumatra was not a profitable post, being too far from the main trading route. As Furber describes, 'for this new fleet of "country" ships, as well as for the older ships, new bases not under Dutch control were needed. Bencoolen, the English East India Company's only outpost in the Malay archipelago, was not in the proper geographical position to be of most benefit to this trade. Hence, the founding of the British settlement at Penang, then known as Prince of Wales Island, was the natural consequence of the growth of Bengal "country" trade to China'.[106] The Napoleonic wars, which broke out in Europe (1789–1814) followed by the presence of the French fleet in the Indian Ocean and Southeast Asia, had a great impact on the English due to their fear of the French.[107] Thus the defence of English possessions on the East coast of India became paramount. The English authorities also needed a port that could provide a refitting station during the northeast monsoon on the eastern trade route to China. The northeast monsoon forced English ships from the Coromandel Coast to break their journey when sailing to the East and West. Therefore, the English administration in India was keen to secure a strategic place that could provide fresh provisions and a safe port during rough seas. Their concern with French danger to their Indian possessions due to the sudden increase in the French presence in the Indian Ocean strengthened their interest in a new base.

The occupation of Penang in 1786 allowed for the monitoring of French activities in the Indian Ocean and also served as an important port for the

English traders from the northeast monsoon.[108] The English also believed that Penang would later free English traders from the need to use Dutch ports in their trading journeys to the East. In addition by occupying Penang the English could also attempt to put an end to Dutch power in the Straits, as Penang would serve as a base from where they could counter Dutch efforts to control the sea routes to China.[109] Once Penang developed into an important port, it was expected that the income from the island's revenue would enable it to pay for its own administration without any help from the Company. In the long run, it was hoped that if Penang's revenue increased it could even contribute to the income of the Company.

The English first considered several other choices suitable for a new colony in the East Indian Ocean, such as the Andaman islands, Aceh and Junk Ceylon, before deciding to occupy Penang.[110] Located at the farther end of the archipelago, early Penang, unfortunately, was unable to control a large percentage of trade in the Straits, and Melaka still held the bulk of the important trade, both from the archipelago and from the Straits.[111] Traders from the archipelago and many English country traders from India still stopped at Melaka on their way to China.[112] Furthermore, the majority of Asian traders from the southern regions of the archipelago preferred Melaka to going further north to Penang.[113] During the English administration of Melaka between 1794 and 1818, they even resorted to the policy of persuading the Asian traders to go to Penang.

After the occupation of Penang, the English administration in India doubted whether Penang was the ideal location for controlling the lucrative trade between China and the West. The burden of proving that Penang was worthy to be a potential colony lay on Francis Light, the first Superintendent of the new colony. As pointed out by Skinner,

> the task of governing this mixed multitude fell entirely on the shoulders of Captain Light himself, for he received but little encouragement from the Indian Government, who long regarded the Establishment at Penang with doubts and even with jealousy. There had been a rival settlement formed at the Andamans in 1791, under the patronage of Admiral Cornwallis; but it never prospered, and in 1796, was abandoned.[114]

From its occupation until 1810, the English administration in India was uncertain whether Penang would become an important port or be able to raise sufficient revenue to meet its administrative expenditures.[115] Furthermore, from its foundation until 1810, the main theme in the government's master plan for the island was to make Penang a naval arsenal and centre of shipbuilding.[116] However, this idea was later abandoned due to lack of resources and manpower. Instead, the British decided to transfer the naval arsenal in Penang to her earlier base at Trincomalee, mainly because of the difficulty in obtaining a good supply of suitable timber at Penang as most timber had to be imported from Rangoon.[117] Thus, a ship built in Penang would cost more than one built in the Indian subcontinent. In addition, Penang had no skilled manpower to construct docks and large shipways, nor, above all, the capital to start the ambitious project. In any case, the idea of creating and promoting Penang as a centre for shipbuilding and a naval arsenal was not taken seriously by the administration in England. After the naval victory at Trafalgar, the English felt that there were no real threats to English possessions in the East and that any scheme to build a naval arsenal and dockyard was unnecessary.[118] The Company also faced financial difficulties and any grand scheme was seen to be likely to overburden the administration.[119]

Thus, from 1786 until 1810, not much change was seen in the attitude of the administration in India towards Penang. As Stevens argues, 'Light's difficulties on landing at Penang were very great. The Company had accorded only half-hearted support to his project. It was Light himself who persuaded the Directors to found the Settlement. But for many years, they remained unconvinced that Penang was the best place for their experiment. Indeed, during the whole of Light's administration, and for some years afterwards, it was a matter of constant discussion whether Penang should be abandoned in favour of some more suitable place, such as the Andaman Islands. In consequence of this the support accorded to Light was very niggardly.'[120] Therefore, in the early period, as Penang was still not regarded as an important colony, India did not provide the administration in Penang with enough support. This left considerable space for private initiative. Although trade flourished on the island, it was controlled and dictated by a few people, in particular the merchants at James Scott and Company. Scott and the small mercantile community controlled most trade and were united in their view on how trade should be carried out in the colony.[121] They wanted trade in Penang to be determined by them. They also demanded that some power be given to them to decide on taxes levied on goods imported and exported and also the right to fix the prices of goods sold and bought in the island. Thus, in the early period, Penang's trade was run by a few English merchants.[122] In the later period these merchants transformed Penang into an important port and trading centre in the Straits.[123]

Besides the English and other Europeans, there were also Chinese, Chulias and native merchants. Some of the wealthy Chinese in Penang had trading networks that covered the island, northern Sumatra, southern Thailand and the northern region of the Peninsula.[124] There were also Chinese merchants from the island who traded with Benkulen, Nias, Melaka and Selangor. Chulia merchants from Penang covered the Coromandel Coast, northern

Sumatra and part of the peninsula.[125] Native merchants mostly came from Kedah, and the Bugis came from Makassar and other native ports in the archipelago.[126] Native merchants from Kedah had a limited network, which only linked the island and the mainland. In the case of the Bugis, they mostly came from Makassar and stopped at many ports in the archipelago before landing on the island.[127] All these merchants can be considered as the pioneers who contributed to the development of Penang's trade.

CONCLUSION

For many centuries, the Straits of Melaka had been pivotal to the development of the trading world of Asia. It was an important waterway linking East and West Asia, its strategic location between the two regions and its sheltered position between the island of Sumatra and the Malay peninsula giving it an advantage not available to other areas fronting the China Sea on the east and the Indian Ocean on the west. At the same time, the integration of the Southeast Asian region, in particular the Malay-Indonesian archipelago, into this trading world, due to its huge variety of natural resources and the market demands of its people, increased its strategic importance. Thus ports within the Straits of Melaka had the potential to grow as important centres of trade, serving functions such as collecting and distributing centres and refitting stations and shelters from strong monsoon winds. It was within this context that Melaka and Penang rose and became vitally connected to the regional and wider trading patterns and networks that linked them with the Indian Ocean–Straits–South China Sea trading system. Further, their strong position was ensured by the fact that both were controlled by European powers, the Dutch in Melaka and the English in Penang, who dominated the region's trading activities.

As the nature of the Asian trade had not changed for many centuries, Melaka and Penang fitted into the pattern, reflecting similar trends. Both served as collecting and distributing centres, exporting goods for human consumption (agricultural produce) and forest products that were collected from many places, such as Aceh, Kedah, Perak, Selangor and the archipelago. These were then exchanged with manufactured goods imported from the Indian subcontinent and China, which were then re-distributed to other places where demand was high. Thus throughout the period under study, the character of Melaka's and Penang's trade remained virtually unchanged but the similarity of their function within the Asian trading world meant that their activities placed them in competition with one another. This was further aggravated by the fact that, in this period, Melaka was for some time under Dutch control while Penang belonged to the English.

NOTES

1 Leong Sau Heng, 'Collecting Centres, Feeder Points and Entrepots in the Malay Peninsula 100 B.C. – A.D. 1400', in, J. Kathirithamby-Wells and John Villiers, (ed.) *The Southeast Asian Port and Polity Rise and Demise*, Singapore: Singapore University Press, 1990, p.23.

2 See, for example, K.N. Chaudhuri, *Trade and Civilization in the Indian Ocean: An Economic History from the Rise of Islam to 1750*, Cambridge: Cambridge University Press, 1990; G.B. Souza, *The Survival of Empire: Portuguese Trade and Society in China and the South China Sea, 1630–1754*, Cambridge: Cambridge University Press, 1986; and Cheong Weng Eang, *The Hong Merchants of Canton: Chinese Merchants in Sino-Western Trade*, London: Curzon Press, 1996.

3 J. Kathirithamby-Wells, 'Introduction: An Overview', in, J. Kathirithamby-Wells and John Villiers, (ed.) *The Southeast Asian Port and Polity*, p. 1.

4 A good discussion on the function of the monsoon winds and how they determined the movements of traders in the Indian Ocean can be found in Alan Villiers, *Monsoon Seas: The Story of the Indian Ocean*, New York: McGraw-Hill, 1952.

5 K.N. Chaudhuri, *Trade and Civilization in the Indian Ocean: An Economic History from the Rise of Islam to 1750*, p. 21.

6 Ibid., pp. 23–32.

7 C.A. Trocki, 'Chinese Pioneering in Eighteenth-Century Southeast Asia', pp. 83–102.

8 Ibid.

9 Ibid.

10 M.N. Pearson, 'Introduction I: The State of the Subject'. In Ashin Das Gupta and M.N. Pearson (eds), *India and the Indian Ocean 1500–1800*, Calcutta: Oxford University Press, 1987, p. 13.

11 S. Arasaratnam, 'European Port Settlements in the Coromandel Commercial System 1650–1740'. In Frank Broeze (ed.), *Brides of the Sea, Port Cities of Asia from the 16th to 20th Centuries*, pp. 76–96.

12 S. Arasaratnam, 'Factors in the Rise, Growth and Decline of Coromandel Ports circa 1650–1720'. In *Maritime Trade, Society and European Influence in Southern Asia 1600–1800*, Aldershot, UK: Variorum, 1995, pp. 19–30; see also S. Arasaratnam, 'European Port Settlements in the Coromandel Commercial System 1650–1740', pp. 76–96.

13 Das Gupta, 'Aceh in the Seventeenth Century Asian Trade'. In *Bengal Past and Present*, January-June, 1962, p. 45. See also Ito Takeshi, 'The Elephant Trade of Aceh in the 1640s–60s', *Journal of East-West Maritime Relations*, vol. 3, 1994, pp. 1–11; and D.K. Bassett, 'The British in Southeast Asia during the 17th and 18th Centuries', *Occasional Paper No. 18*, University of Hull: Centre for Southeast Asian Studies, pp. 78–79.

14 For further detail, see L.Y. Andaya, *The History of Johore 1641–1728: Economic and Political Developments*, Kuala Lumpur: Oxford University Press, 1975.

15 For further detail, see Raja Ali Haji ibn Ahmad, *The Precious Gift: Thufat al-Nafis*, (trans.) Virgina Matheson and Barbara Watson Andaya, Kuala Lumpur: Oxford University Press, 1982; see also L.Y. Andaya, "The Bugis-Makassar Diasporas", *JMBRAS*, vol. 68, pt.1, 1995, pp. 119–138.

16 See, for example, Raja Ali Haji ibn Ahmad, *The Precious Gift*; and R. Vos, *Gentle Janus: Merchant Prince, The VOC and the Tightrope of Diplomacy in the Malay World 1740–1800*, Leiden: KITLV, 1993.

17 For a more detailed account, see R. Vos, *Gentle Janus*.

18 See also Appendix 11: Melaka Shipping Lists, 1780–82 and 1791–93, in Nordin Hussin, 'Melaka and Penang 1780–1830: A study of two port towns in the Straits of Melaka', Ph.D. thesis, Amsterdam: Vrije Universiteit, 2002, pp. 459–480.

19 See, R. Vos, *Gentle Janus*. See also D. Lewis, 'The East India Company and the Straits of Malacca 1700–1784: Trade and Politics in the Eighteenth Century', Ph.D. thesis, Australian National University, 1970; and Anthony Reid and Radin Fernando, 'Shipping on Melaka and Singapore as an Index of Growth 1760–1840', *South Asia*, vol. xix, 1996, pp. 59–84.

20 See also Appendix 11: Melaka Shipping Lists, 1780–82 and 1791–93, in Nordin Hussin, 'Melaka and Penang 1780–1830', pp. 459–480.

21 For further discussion on this subject, see L. Blusse, *Strange Company: Chinese Settlers, Mestizo Women and the Dutch in Batavia*, Dordrecht: KITLV, 1986. 'All junk trade was "once and for all" forbidden to Ambon, Banda, Ternate, Celebes, the east coast and south coast of Borneo (Sukadana included), Java, Sumatra and the Malay peninsula', p. 148.

22 See, for example, Cheong Weng Eang, *The Hong Merchants of Canton*; Che'en Kuo-tung, 'Shipping and Trade of Chinese Junks in Southeast Asia, 1730–1830: A Survey'. In S.P. Ville and D.M. Williams (eds), *Management, Finance and Industrial Relations in Maritime Industries: Essay in International Maritime and Business History*, St. John's: International Maritime Economic History Association, 1994, pp. 203–214; see also P.W. Klein, 'The China Seas and the World Economy Between the 16th and 19th Centuries: the Changing Structure of Trade'. In D. Fritschy (ed.), *Kapitaal ondermemerschap en beleid*, Amsterdam: NEHA, 1996, pp. 385–408; L. Blusse, *Strange Company.*

23 See, for example, J. F. Warren, *The Sulu Zone 1768–1898*, Singapore: Singapore University Press, 1981. See also Robert R. Reed, *Colonial Manila: The Context of Hispanic Urbanism and Process of Morphogenesis*, Berkeley: University of California Press, 1977.

24 Most of these ethnic groups had settled permanently in many port-towns in Southeast Asia. Many Indian and Chinese traders in the region maintained trading networks with their counterparts in India and China.

25 See, for example, F.S. Gaastra, *De Geschiedenis van de VOC*, Zutphen: Walburg Pers, 1991. See also C.H. Phillips, *The East India Company 1784–1834*, Manchester: Manchester University Press, 1961.

26 See, for example, G.B. Souza, *The Survival of Empire.*

27 See, for example, S. Arasaratnam, 'European Port Settlements in the Coromandel Commercial System 1650–1740', pp. 75–96.

28 See D.K. Bassett, 'The British Trader and Mariner in Southeast Asia c. 1660–1715'. In *The British in Southeast Asia during the 17th and 18th Centuries*, Occasional Papers, No.18, University of Hull: Centre for Southeast Asian Studies, 1990 p. 1. See also D.K. Bassett, 'The British Country Trader and Sea Captain in Southeast Asia in the 17th and 18th Centuries', *Journal of the Historical Society*, no.1, vol.2, 1961, pp. 9–14.

29 For further reference, see Anthony Reid, *Slavery, Bondage and Dependency in Southeast Asia*, St. Lucia: University of Queensland Press, 1983.

30 K.N. Chaudhuri, *Trade and Civilization in the Indian Ocean*, p. 19.

31 Ibid., p. 20.

32 Ibid., pp. 19–20.

33 See, for example, J. Villiers, 'The Vanishing Sandalwood of Portuguese Timor', *Itinerario*, 18/2, 1994, pp. 86–96. See also A.T. de Matos, 'Timor and the Portuguese Trade in the Orient During the 18th Century'. In A.T. de Matos, and L.F.F. Reis Thomaz (eds), *As Relacoes Entre a India Portuguese, a Asia do Sueste e o Extremo Oriente*, Macao-Lisbon, 1993, pp. 437–445.

34 See, for example, D. Bulbeck and Anthony Reid (eds), *Southeast Asian Exports Since the 14th Century: Cloves, Pepper, Coffee and Sugar*, Singapore: Institute of Southeast Asian Studies, 1998.

35 For further detail, see S. P. Sen, 'The Role of Indian Textiles in Southeast Asian Trade in the Seventeenth Century', pp. 92–110.

36 For a more detailed account on this subject, see Barbara Watson Andaya, 'The Cloth Trade in Jambi and Palembang'. See also R. Laarhoven, 'The Power of Cloth' and S. P. Sen, 'The Role of Indian Textiles in Southeast Asian Trade'.

37 See, for example, C.R. Boxer, *The Dutch Seaborne Empire 1600–1800*, London: Hutchinson, 1965.

38 Leonard Y. Andaya, *The History of Johor*. See also, Reinout Vos, *Gentle Janus*.

39 Sinnappah Arasaratnam, 'Dutch Commercial Policy and Interests in the Malay Peninsula, 1750–1795'. In, Blair B. Kling and M.N. Pearson (eds), *The Age of Partnership, Europeans in Asia, Before Dominion*, Hawaii: University of Hawaii Press, 1979, pp. 157–189.

40 Sinnappah Arasaratnam, 'Dutch Commercial Policy and Interests in the Malay Peninsula, 1750–1795', pp. 160–161.

41 In 1784, the Dutch occupied Riau, the capital and commercial centre of the Johor kingdom. In this period the Dutch were also engaged in the tin trade with Selangor and Perak, raising British fears that such activities would later extend Dutch control over the whole peninsula. For further reference, see, for example, C.D. Cowan, 'Early Penang and the Rise of Singapore', *JMBRAS*, vol. 23, Part 2, 1950, pp. 3–18. See also D.K. Bassett, 'British Commercial and Strategic Interest in the Malay Peninsula During the Late Eighteenth Century', pp. 50–70.

42 C.D. Cowan, 'Early Penang and the Rise of Singapore', pp. 3–18.

43 See, for example, N. Tarling, *Anglo-Dutch Rivalry in the Malay World 1780–1824*, London: Cambridge University Press, 1962.

44 See, for example, Holden Furber, *Rival Empires of Trade in the Orient, 1600–1800*, Minneapolis: University of Minnesota Press, 1976, pp. 31–78.

45 C.D. Cowan, 'Early Penang and the Rise of Singapore', p. 3.

46 Ibid., p.3. See also Anthony Reid, 'The French in Sumatra and the Malay World', 1760–1890, *BKI*, cxxix, 1973, pp. 195–238.

47 For further discussion, see, for example, D.K. Bassett, 'British Commercial and Strategic Interest in the Malay Peninsula During the Late Eighteenth Century'.

48 See, for example, R. Bonney, *Kedah 1771–1821:The Search for Security and Independence*, Kuala Lumpur: Oxford University Press, 1971; D.K. Bassett, 'British Trade and Policy in Indonesia and Malaysia in the Late 18th Century'; and D.K. Bassett, 'British Commercial and Strategic Interest in the Malay Peninsula During the Late Eighteenth Century'.

49 See, for example, the discussion on the activities and the trading pattern of the Chulia or Islamic merchants from the Coromandel Coast by S. Arasaratnam, in *Islamic Merchant Communities of the Indian Subcontinent in Southeast Asia*. He notes that: 'The ships came from Proto Novo, Nagore or Nagapatnam and from Penang they sailed to Mergui, Ujang Selang, Melaka, Acheh and Pedie. The most popular schedule was from South India to Penang and back through Pedie and Acheh', p. 20.

50 See Holden Furber, *John Company at Work*, Cambridge: Harvard University Press, 1948 and Holden Furber, *Rival Empires of Trade in the Orient 1600–1800*.

51 See Reinout Vos, *Gentle Janus*.

52 Sinnappah Arasaratnam, 'Dutch Commercial Policy and Interests in the Malay Peninsula, 1750–1795', p. 162.

53 See Reinout Vos, *Gentle Janus, Merchant Prince*. For the stiff competition and problems of controlling the supply of tin and important commodities for the China trade, see Sinnappah Arasaratnam, 'Dutch Commercial Policy and Interests in the Malay Peninsula, 1750–1795', pp.161–186. For the importance of the China trade and how the English were able to control the inter-Asian trade, see P.J. Marshall, 'Private British Trade in the Indian Ocean Before 1800'. In Ashin Das Gupta and M.N. Pearson (eds), *India and the Indian Ocean 1500–1800*, Calcutta: Oxford University Press, 1987, pp. 276–300.

54 Sinnappah Arasaratnam, 'Dutch Commercial Policy and Interests in the Malay Peninsular, 1750–1795', p. 162.

55 See Appendix 11: Melaka Shipping Lists, 1780–82 and 1791–93, in Nordin Hussin, 'Melaka and Penang 1780–1830', pp. 459–480.

56 S. Arasaratnam, *Islamic Merchant communities of the Indian Subcontinent in Southeast Asia*, pp. 19–21.

57 Such trading networks existed between Melaka and Mergui. For example, on 30 March 1780, a 100-*laasten* ship with 10 cannons and 28 people on board, which belonged to Tsoe Anko of Melaka, was captained by a Melaka Moor. The ship was travelling from Mergui to Melaka. The goods on board included 900 *pikuls amballo*, 90 pieces elephant tusk, 25 *pikuls* cardamom, 28 *koyan* rice and 4 *pikuls* wax, VOC 3582. Another trading network established by Melaka merchants with Pegu was carried out by a Melaka Dutch Burgher, named Joost Koek. On 16 March 1780, a 100-*laasten* ship belonging to him went to Pegu laden with 900 *laxa* arak, 10 *sijpen* arak, and 10,000 pieces of porcelain, VOC 3582.

58   See Appendix 11: Melaka Shipping Lists, 1780–82 and 1791–93, in Nordin Hussin, 'Melaka and Penang 1780–1830', pp. 459–480.

59   For further discussion see, for example, Leonard Blusse, *Strange Company*, pp. 95–155. See also D.K. Bassett, 'British Commercial and Strategic Interest in the Malay Peninsula During the Late Eighteenth Century', p. 60.

60   For example, on 2 February 1782, a 150-*laasten* Chinese wankang with 200 people on board arrived at Melaka from Amoy. The goods carried by this ship consisted of 7 *laxa kommen in sort*, 6 *laxa schotels en pierings*, 20 *pikuls cassombar*, 10 *pikuls zijde*, 50 *kisten* tea, 50 *kisten* gold thread, 70 *corgs* Chinese linen, 50 *karanjang* Chinese tobacco, 30 *karanjang* Chinese *gadong*, 200 bundles Chinese paper, 1,000 pieces of *sombriels* and 2,000 *vloer steenen*, VOC3625.

61   See Appendix 11: Melaka Shipping Lists, 1780–82 and 1791–93, in Nordin Hussin, 'Melaka and Penang 1780–1830', pp. 459–480.

62   Ibid.

63   See extract letter from Governor to the Chairman and Deputy Chairman dated 7 November 1808, and report by Raffles, 31 October 1808 in SSFR vol. 9. See also Memoranda on Melaka in SSFR vol.10.

64   Ibid.

65   Holden Furber, *John Company at Work*, pp. 103–176.

66   Ibid.

67   For further information on this see, for example: 'Archives and Fieldwork: The Dutch East India Company Documents as Source Material on Indian History in the Seventeenth and Eighteenth Centuries', *Itinerario*, no. 2, vol. vii, 1983, pp. 38–49. See also 'Historical Sources and the Writing of History', (unpublished paper presented at the Seminar on Asian History and Dutch sources, 17th and 18th centuries, University of Leiden).

68   For further explanation on these units of measurement and weights, see Gerrit J. Knaap, *Shallow Water, Rising Tide*, Leiden: KITLV, 1996, pp. 189–193.

69   Memoranda on Malacca 1817/1818 in SSFR Vol. 10.

70   Ibid.

71   See, for example, Lee Poh Ping, *Chinese Society in Nineteenth Century Singapore*, Kuala Lumpur: Oxford University Press, pp. 11–35.

72   T. Braddell, *Statistics of the British Possessions in the Straits of Malacca: with Explanatory Notes*, Pinang: Pinang Gazette printing office, 1861, pp. 17–18.

73   S. Arasaratnam, 'Some Notes on the Dutch in Malacca and the Indo-Malayan Trade 1641–1670', in *JSEAH*, Vol. 10, No.3, 1969, p. 480.

74   Ibid., p. 482.

75   Ibid.

76   Ibid.

77   Ibid. 'By this treaty a half of all the tin produced in Kedah or imported into the State from outside was to be sold to the Dutch at a fixed price', p. 483.

78   Ibid. 'According to its terms the ruler promised not to allow any traders from Kedah, Perak, Java, Coromandel, Bengal and other neighbouring places to trade there unless they have shown their passes to the Dutch, touched at Malacca and paid their tolls there', p. 483.

79   Ibid. 'Here the Governor promised to deliver all the tin found in his state to the Dutch as well as forbid his subjects and merchants there from buying cloth from any foreign vessels. All the tin brought by these merchants was to be sold to the Dutch and no tin was to be transported from there by any of his subjects', p. 483.

80   S. Arasaratnam, 'Dutch Commercial Policy and Interests in the Malay Peninsula': 'By this treaty the sultan agreed to sell all the tin found in his kingdom to the Dutch', p. 165; see also Dianne Lewis, 'The Tin trade in the Malay Peninsula during the Eighteenth Century'.

81   The treaty gave the Dutch authorities the right to build a fort on Pulau Gontong, an island at the entrance to the Siak River. Thus no cloth was to be imported except from Melaka and no vessels were to sail upriver except with a pass from Melaka. For further reference, see Dianne Lewis, 'The Dutch East India Company and the Straits of Malacca'.

82 Farquhar, Malacca, 10 December 1805 in SSFR Vol. 16.

83 Ibid.

84 Ibid.

85 See, for example, Dianne Lewis, *Jan Companie in the Straits of Malacca 1641–1795*, Athens: Ohio University Center for International Studies, 1995; and P.A. Leupe, 'The Siege and Capture of Malacca from the Portuguese in 1640–1641', pp. 1–178.

86 See, for example, Charles Lockyer, *An Account of the Trade in India*, London: Samuel Crouch, 1711, and S. Arasaratnam, 'Dutch Commercial Policy and Interests in the Malay Peninsula, 1750–1795', pp. 159–189.

87 Dianne Lewis, 'The Dutch East India Company and the Straits of Malacca', p. 38.

88 Ibid., pp. 37–71.

89 See 'Malacca in the Eighteenth Century: Two Dutch Governor's Reports', in *JMBRAS*, Vol. 27, Pt. 1 (1954) pp. 24–34; 'Trade in the Straits of Malacca in 1785: A Memorandum by P.G. de Bruijn, Governor of Malacca,' in *JMBRAS*, Vol. 26, Pt. 1 (1953), pp. 56–62; Dianne Lewis, 'The Tin Trade in the Malay Peninsula during the 18th Century', pp. 52–69.

90 See, for example, the case of the English ship *Betsey* in 1784, which carried opium on board, in Reinout Vos, *Gentle Janus*; this led to war between Raja Haji and Gabenor Bruijn. For the case of a vessel belonging to Alexander Hamilton, which was confiscated by the Dutch in Melaka, see Dianne Lewis, 'The Dutch East India Company and the Straits of Malacca', p. 57.

91 William Marsden, *The History of Sumatra, Containing an Account of the Government, Laws, Customs and Manners of the Native Inhabitants*, (Third Edition), London: Longman, 1811, p. 277. See also J. Kooeing, 'Journal of a Voyage from India to Siam and Malacca in 1779', *JSBRAS*, 26, 1894. During times of scarcity, the price of opium could equal the weight of gold, see p. 78.

92 Dianne Lewis, 'The Dutch East India Company and the Straits of Malacca', p. 58; See also T. Forrest, *A Voyage from Calcutta to the Mergui Archipelago*, London: J. Robson, 1792, p.32.

93 Graham W. Irwin, 'The Dutch and the Tin Trade of Malaya in the Seventeenth Century'. In N. Tarling (ed.) *Studies in the social history of China and South-east Asia*, London: Oxford University Press, 1970, pp. 72–105 and pp. 267–87; see also Dianne Lewis, 'The Growth of the Country Trade in the Straits of Malacca, 1760–1777', *JMBRAS*, 43. 2, 1970, pp. 114–30; Dianne Lewis, 'The Tin Trade in the Malay Peninsular During the 18th Century', pp. 52–69.

94 Dianne Lewis, 'The Tin Trade in the Malay Peninsular During the 18th Century', pp. 58–59.

95 Dianne Lewis, 'The Dutch East India Company and the Straits of Malacca', p. 39.

96 Brian Harrison, 'Malacca in the Eighteenth Century', *JMBRAS*, XXVII, I, 1954, p. 29.

97 Dianne Lewis, 'The Dutch East India Company and the Straits of Malacca, 1700–1784', p. 44.

98 This article was obtained from a type of animal called babirusa (hog-deer), For more information, see, Charles Lockyer, *An Account of the Trade in India*, pp. 46–49.

99 Dianne Lewis, 'The Dutch East India Company and the Straits of Malacca, 1700–1784', p. 48.

100 Ibid., pp. 47–48.

101 Ibid., pp. 51–55.

102 See, for example, Graham W. Irwin, 'The Dutch and the Tin Trade of Malaya in the Seventeenth Century'. In Jerome Chen and N. Tarling (eds), *Studies in the Social History of China and Southeast Asia*, London: Oxford University Press, 1970, pp. 267–87; Dianne Lewis, 'The Tin Trade in the Malay Peninsula during the Eighteenth Century', *The New Zealand Journal of History*, vol. 3, no. 1, April 1969, pp. 52–69; S. Arasaratnam, 'Dutch Commercial Policy and Interests in the Malay Peninsula, 1750–1795', pp. 159–189. See also G.W. van Imhoff, 'Consideratien over den Tegenwoordige Staat van de Neder-landsche Ooste-Indische Maatschappy', *BKI*, vol. 66, 1912 p. 513. He stresses that Melaka

was more of a frontier settlement and the Dutch did not want to abandon Melaka, but rather maintain it as a small port and colony.

103 See Reinout Vos, *Gentle Janus, Merchant Prince;* and Sinnappah Arasaratham, 'Dutch Commercial Policy and Interests in the Malay Peninsula', pp. 159–189.

104 Holden Furber, *John Company at Work*, pp. 103–176.

105 Ibid., p. 105.

106 Ibid., p. 176.

107 Ibid.

108 There are many reasons for the English occupation of Penang. C.D. Cowan, in 'Early Penang and the Rise of Singapore', emphasizes political motives when he notes that: 'The motives which prompted the Company to sanction this step were almost entirely political...', p. 1.

109 C.D. Cowan, 'Early Penang and the Rise of Singapore', p. 3.

110 Penang was not the only place that fulfilled these requirements. Aceh, Junk Ceylon (Ujong Salang), the Nicobars and the Andamans were all investigated and recommended as alternatives in the period following 1763, when the Court of Directors first gave orders to search for a suitable base to the East of the Bay of Bengal. For further reference on this matter, see D.K. Bassett, 'British Commercial and Strategic Interest in the Malay Peninsular during the late Eighteenth Century', pp. 50–70.

111 Extract letter from Governor Macalister to the Chairman and Deputy Chairman, dated 7 November 1808 in SSFR vol. 9; see also the report by Raffles, 31 October 1808 in SSFR vol.9.

112 See Appendix 11: Melaka Shipping Lists, 1780–82 and 1791–93, in Nordin Hussin, 'Melaka and Penang 1780–1830', pp. 459–480.

113 Extract letter from Governor Macalister to the Chairman and Deputy Chairman, dated 7 November 1808 in SSFR vol. 9; see also the report by Raffles, 31 October 1808 in SSFR vol. 9.

114 A.M. Skinner, 'Memoir of Captain Francis Light', *Straits Branch*, 28, August 1895, p.5.

115 C.D. Cowan, 'Early Penang and the Rise of Singapore', p. 5. See L.A. Mills, 'Penang 1786–1830', pp. 36–59.

116 C.D. Cowan, 'Early Penang and the Rise of Singapore', p. 5.

117 Ibid.

118 Ibid.

119 Ibid. See also the discussion on the project to extend and fortify the fort of Cornwallis which was later abandoned by the administration in SSFR G/34/7: Letter from Major Kyd to Governor General in Council, 2 August 1795.

120 F.G. Stevens, 'A Contribution to the Early History of Prince of Wales' Island', *JMBRAS*, Vol. VII, Part III, October 1929, p. 379.

121 F.G. Stevens, 'A Contribution to the Early History of Prince of Wales' Island', pp. 376–414. See also James Scott, 'The Settlement of Penang', *JMBRAS*, 28, Part 1, 1955, pp.37–41; 'Notices of Penang', *JIA*, Vol.5, 1851, pp. 93–119.

122 See 'Notices of Penang', *JIA*, vol 5, 1851, p.97.

123 'Notices of Penang', *JIA*, vol iv, 1850, p. 662.

124 For further reference see, for example, Lee Kam Heng, *The Sultanate of Aceh Relations with the British 1760–1824*, Kuala Lumpur: Oxford University Press, 1995; and Jennifer W. Cushman, *Family and State: The Formation of a Sino-Thai Tin-mining Dynasty 1797–1932* (edited by Craig J. Reynolds), Singapore: Oxford University Press, 1991.

125 See petition of Pulicat merchants Mohammed Syed and partners, 6 October 1814, in G/34/45. See also, for example, S. Arasaratnam, *Islamic Merchant communities of the Indian Sub-continent in Southeast Asia*.

126 Extract letter from Governor Macalister to the Chairman and Deputy Chairman, dated 7 November 1808 in SSFR vol. 9; see also the report by Raffles, 31 October 1808, in SSFR vol.9.

127 Ibid.

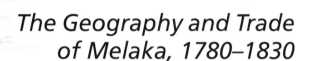

CHAPTER TWO

The Geography and Trade of Melaka, 1780–1830

PRIOR TO THE EMERGENCE OF PENANG and Singapore as important ports, Melaka was the grand emporium of the archipelago. However, by the end of the eighteenth century it had lost its status as an important port in the East.[1] This study tries to establish that the old trading pattern of the intra-Asian trade and the India-Melaka-China trading route remained the main focus of trade in Melaka. The extent of this trade at the end of the Dutch period and during the English period will also be examined. This chapter will also analyse the position of traders and merchants in Melaka and the commodities imported and re-exported by the port. It will also show that, in the period under study, Melaka was sustained by its advantageous geographical position in the Straits of Melaka and its long-standing trade relations with the central region of the Straits and the archipelago.

TRADING PATTERNS IN MELAKA

In the 1780s and the early 1790s, Melaka was still an important centre of trade in the Straits of Melaka. The Dutch war with Riau had decimated the port and eliminated it as a rival in the Straits, while Penang, founded in 1786, was not yet in a position to compete. In those days around 300 ships from various parts of Asia visited Melaka annually, bringing in traders from many different ethnic backgrounds and a huge variety of goods. This annual flow of traders into and out of Melaka followed a pattern determined by the winds and the monsoon. Thus trade at Melaka, as with many other ports, was seasonal with its high and low periods coinciding with the tropical monsoons.

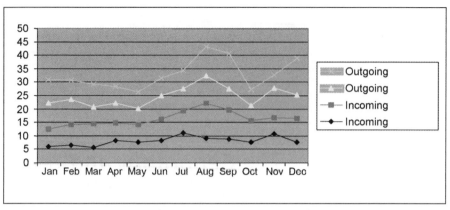

Figure 1: Monthly percentage of incoming and outgoing ships for Melaka, 1780–82 and 1791–93. *Sources:* VOC 3582, VOC 3599, VOC 3625, VOC 3650, VOC 3940, VOC 3961, OIC 107.

Figures 1 above and 2 below show the monthly movements of ships both in and out of Melaka. It can be seen that there were two peak periods during which traders converged on and then sailed away from Melaka. These were the periods between June and September, when the highest number of traders came to Melaka, and between November and December, and which trading activities peaked a second time in the year. Most of the ships that came from Amoy and Macao in China arrived in November to March. Ships from Bombay mostly arrived from July to September and from Bengal, from March to August.[2] Traders from Java mostly arrived in August to November, while most of the traders from Riau, Siak, Selangor, Kedah, Penang, Batubara, Rokan and Asahan came all year round, as they were not effected by the monsoon winds.

Traders came to Melaka in almost as many types and sizes of ships as the variety of goods they brought, for many kinds of ships that sailed in Southeast Asian waters during the late eighteenth century.[3] Ships from Europe were large and well equipped with cannons and weapons. These were mostly long-distance ships that travelled from Europe to the Indian Ocean, the archipelago and to China. Besides these, there were also ships that travelled within the archipelago, for example, from ports in northern Java to ports in the Straits of Melaka. Small ships normally travelled short distances between the ports in Sumatra and the Malay peninsula or within the Straits.[4]

The largest ships that anchored at Melaka port belonged to English traders such as those representing the English East India Company and the English country traders, which travelled between India and China. These ships were usually between 100 to 400 *lasten* in size.[5] Ships belonging to

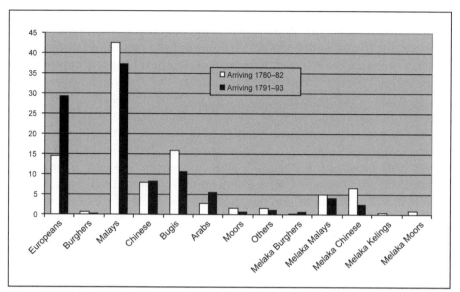

Figure 2: Traders arriving at Melaka in 1780–82 and 1791–93, in percentages and by ethnicity. *Sources:* VOC 3582, VOC 3599, VOC 3625, VOC 3650, VOC 3940, VOC 3961, OIC 107.

other Europeans tended to be smaller, ranging between 40 to 450 *lasten*, and Portuguese ships that sailed between India and Macao were even smaller still at around 20 to 40 *lasten* in size. The largest Asian ships belonged to the Chinese traders from China and Java. These Chinese traders, with large cargoes, came in brigantine ships.[6] However, the short distance Chinese traders mostly came in various smaller ships, such as the *balo, banting, bark, chialoup, wankang* and *pencalang*.[7] The Malays, mostly from Sumatra and the archipelago, also travelled in a variety of ships of which the most popular were the *balo*,[8] *banting*,[9] *kakap*,[10] *pencalang*[11] and *pencacap*.[12] The Bugis, mostly from Riau and Selangor, used the *paduwakang* and *pencalang*.[13] On the other hand, the majority of the Dutch burghers used the *bark* and the brigantine. The Moors, who travelled between India, Pegu and Melaka, sailed in fairly large ships, 80 to 200 *lasten* in size.

According to the records, the commonest vessels trading in Melaka were Malay and European ships followed by those brought in by the Bugis, Chinese, Melaka-Malays and Melaka-Chinese.[14] In the European category, the English fleet (EIC and English country traders) was the largest.[15] The English East India Company traders who visited Melaka were usually travelling the India-Melaka-China route. The records show that they were regular visitors, although for 1782 there is no record of English ships calling at Melaka.[16] This was probably due to the outbreak of the Anglo-Dutch war in Europe when it was felt unsafe for English ships to visit a port that was under the control of a hostile nation. No doubt, there would have been a constant flow of VOC ships coming in and out of Melaka's habour but the records do not provide information on this, as was mentioned earlier. The next biggest group of European merchants were the Portuguese, followed by the Danes and the French.[17]

The Malays represented more than 42 per cent of total arrivals in 1780–82 and 37 per cent in 1791–93.[18] The Bugis made up more than 15 per cent in 1780–82 and 10 per cent in 1791–93.[19] The majority of the Bugis skippers who arrived in the years 1780–82 came from Riau, but after the Dutch-Riau war in 1784 most of the Bugis skippers came from Selangor, Trengganu, Trantan and Tembelan.[20] Chinese ships made up more than 7 per cent of arrivals in 1780–82 and 8 per cent in 1791–93. Most of them came from Javanese ports such as Surabaya, Semarang and Cheribon and less than 1 per cent were recorded to have come from the Chinese mainland.[21] Local traders from Melaka made up more than 12 per cent of the total in 1780–82 and 7 per cent in 1791–93. Out of these, the largest group was the Melaka-Malays followed by the Melaka-Chinese, but later their numbers declined in the period 1791–93.[22]

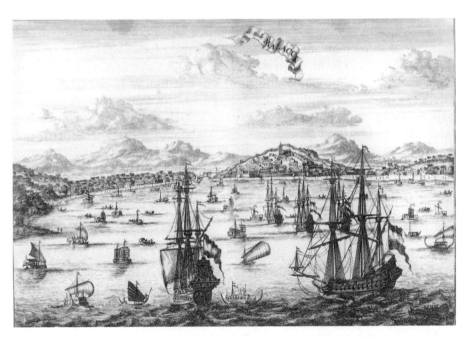

Plate 1: 'Malacca'. In J.W. Heydt, *Allerneuester geographisch und topographischer Schauplatz, von Africa und Ost-Indien*, Willermsdorff: Tetschner, 1744. Courtesy of the Royal Netherlands Institute of Southeast Asian and Caribbean Studies (KITLV), Leiden (Bibl. 3c 102).

As can be seen, not only did the Europeans come in large ships and engage in long-distance trade but they also came in large numbers, thus clearly showing their dominance in the Asian trade as a whole. But while they had the lion's share of that trade, the huge Malay and Bugis presence in the short-distance regional trade goes to show that, at this stage, native traders remained an integral part of the trading activities of Southeast Asia. It should also be noted that, while the number of Melaka-Malay traders remained steady throughout the periods 1780–82 and 1791–93, the Melaka-Keling and Melaka-Moors were not seen in the period 1791–93.[23] This could be because many of them had shifted to Penang. As Penang was closer to the Indian subcontinent and had attracted, from its opening, a large number of Chulia traders and merchants to settle there, it was probable that the majority of Melaka-Keling and Moors had also chosen to base themselves on the island.[24]

In order to have a clearer picture of merchants who traded at Melaka during the last decades of the eighteenth century, a short discussion on their arrival and the commodities they traded in at Melaka is worth discussing. A well-known English skipper who frequented Melaka, James Scott, moved from his base in Junk Ceylon to Penang sometime after its opening. In 1780, he was known to have travelled the Bombay-Melaka-China route with his ship, *The Prince*, a 250-*lasten* vessel, equipped with 6 cannons and 60 crew on board.[25] The main cargo he took from China to Melaka on the way to Bombay in that year was manufactured goods.[26] Scott's trading pattern is a good example of the sort of activities that the long-distance European traders engaged in. The records show that in January 1780, most of the English merchants who travelled from China to Melaka on their way to India carried with them saltpetre, porcelain, tea and silk, while those travelling from India to Melaka en route to China brought with them Indian cloth, opium and cotton.[27]

The arrival of the English merchants was much awaited by traders from the archipelago. English merchants brought goods that were usually in great demand by these traders, such as sugar, silk, Indian cloth and saltpetre, although the last item was not listed in the latter period. This was probably due to the fact that as saltpeter was a major component in the making of gunpowder, its trade had been restricted due to the Anglo-Dutch wars in 1780–84 and the volatile political situation in the Straits as a result of strained relations between Melaka and the Bugis in Riau and the surrounding Malay kingdoms.

The Portuguese merchants who travelled from China to Melaka on their way to Madras and the Malabar coast brought with them sugar, saltpetre, silk, porcelain, alum[28] and redwood. One of the Portuguese skippers, Simon

Plate 2: 'De stad Malacca'. In Francois Valentyn, *Oud en nieuw Oost-Indien*, Dordrecht: Joannes van Braam, 1724-1726.

Plate 3: Cyrille Laplace, 'Entrée de la riviere de Malacca'. In *Voyage autour du monde par Les mers de l'Inde et de la Favorite*, Paris: Imprimerie royale, 1835.

de Araujo Rosa, who travelled in January 1780 on the Macao-Melaka-Madras route in a 40-*lasten* ship, *St. Antonio Almas*, took with him mainly manufactured items.[29]

Traders from Java – Java-Chinese, Java-Malays and Java-Dutch Burghers – often came to Melaka bringing with them agricultural produce, food and forest products.[30] In September 1780, nine ships arrived in Melaka from various ports of Java; 4 from Gresik, 1 from Surabaya, 3 from Semarang and 1 from Cheribon.[31] Two of the skippers were Java-Dutch Burghers, 3 Java-Malays and 4 Java-Chinese. Goods that came from Java consisted mostly of rice, salt, beans, oil, Java cloth, Java tobacco and Java sugar, while goods taken from Melaka by the majority of traders from Java consisted of *gambir*, *amballo*, *dammar*[32] and *belacan/terasi*.[33] The pattern of travel appears to have been one in which many sailed from their port of origin directly to Melaka, stopping at other ports in the Straits or in Batavia only on their homeward journey.

Moor traders mostly came from Surat, Negapatnam and Porto Novo in India. A regular visitor to Melaka was the skipper, Syed Mohammad, from Porto Novo. He sailed between Nagapatnam and Melaka in a 200-*lasten* ship armed with 8 cannons and 59 crew on board. In February 1780, on his return journey from Melaka to Nagapatnam, he brought with him mostly food and agricultural products.[34] Syed Mohammad came again to Melaka in October 1780, bringing mostly goods from the Coromandel Coast, which consisted of Indian cloth and salt.[35] He stayed in Melaka for four months and, in February 1781, went back to Nagapatnam with goods that came mainly from China and the archipelago.[36] In general, Moor traders brought with them Indian cloth and salt to Melaka and took away with them gambir, arak, sugar and goods from China.

The majority of Malay traders came from Sumatra. The most common items brought by them were forest products (rattans) and food items, such as sago, rice and paddy. Most traders tended to bring only one particular product on their journey to Melaka but returned to Sumatra with a variety of Indian cloth and other sought after goods, such as salt and Java tobacco. Bugis traders mostly came from Riau and Selangor but later in the 1790s the majority came from Selangor, Trengganu and Trantan. A regular route covered Riau, Melaka and Selangor. The majority of the Bugis traders brought Bugis cloth or came without any goods but bought various types of Indian cloth in Melaka.

Among the European traders who came to Melaka in smaller numbers were the Danes, French and Spanish. In 1780–82, 10 Danish ships arrived in Melaka but in the period 1791–93 none came. The highest number recorded in one year was in 1780 when 6 Danish ships called at Melaka, frequently trading between Tranquebar in India to Melaka and China. The French traders were mostly from India and Pegu. In 1780–82, 11 French ships traded at Melaka.[37] The same number of ships was also seen in the period 1791–93. In 1780, two French ships arrived in Melaka from Rangoon and sailed on to Riau and Aceh before heading home to their base. The number of Spanish traders to Melaka was very small. In the period 1780–82 only one Spanish ship arrived and in the latter period none came.[38]

Chinese traders from mainland China, Siam and Indo-China were also relatively small in number. In the period 1780–82, there were five Chinese traders from Siam and in the period 1791–93 only two arrived in Melaka.[39] In each of these two periods, only one Chinese ship arrived from Amoy.[40] Similarly, only two Chinese traders came from Indo-China, both arriving in the period 1780–82. One Siamese-Chinese, named Koij Tioe, came from Siam to Melaka in March 1780 in a 80-*lasten wankang*.[41]

Local traders from Melaka could be divided into five groups: Dutch Burghers, Malays, Chinese, Moors and Keling. However, together, they were a small group compared to the total number who traded at Melaka. Of this group, those who owned larger ships went as far as India, Pegu/Rangoon and Mergui. Traders with medium sized ships operated within the archipelago, covering places like Batavia, Riau, Cheribon, Gresik, Surabaya and Semarang. Those with even smaller ships traded within the Straits, visiting ports along the eastern coast of Sumatra, such as Siak, Batubara, Asahan, Indragiri and Palembang and also other parts of the Malay peninsula. All these ships were captained by various ethnic groups such as Malays, Keling, Moors and Chinese.

One Melaka merchant who owned several ships was a Moor named Mirsa Mohammad Sia who was trading between Melaka, Riau, Mergui and Pegu. Besides Mirsa Mohammad Sia, a Melaka-Chinese named Tso Anko also owned more than one trading vessel and had a trading network between Melaka, Nagapatnam, Mergui, Batavia, Semarang and Riau. Another wealthy merchant from Melaka who also owned several ships was Malik Faizullah, a Melaka-Moor who appears to have been trading at Melaka and Nagapatnam.[42] A wealthy Melaka-Keling named Muthu Chitty, who held the position of captain of the Melaka-Moor and Keling communities, also owned ships travelling between Melaka and Riau. One of the wealthiest merchants in Melaka was a Dutch Burgher captain named Joost Koek. He owned a 100-*lasten* brigantine, named *De Concordia*, which traded between Melaka and Pegu. The majority of Melaka Malays and Chinese who owned smaller types of ships, such as the *kakap, pencalang, perahu mayang, balo, pencacap* and *banting,* traded between Melaka and Sumatra to ports such as Batubara, Asahan, Siak, Rokan, Indragiri, Selangor and Riau.[43] The cargoes that they

Table 1: Melakan ship owners in 1781–82

Name of merchant	Type of ship	Place made and purchased	Length (feet))	Breadth (feet)	Lasten	Age (years)	Trading network
Joost Koek	brigantine	Melaka	72	22	100	5	Pegu-Melaka
Joost Koek	brigantine	Melaka	80	24	120	11	Cochin-Melaka
Muthu Mara Chitty	brigantine	Melaka	75	24	80	31	Riau-Melaka
Malik Faizullah	brigantine	Melaka	86	22	150	21	Nagapatnam-Melaka
Tso Anko	brigantine	Melaka	80	20	100	7	Nagapatnam-Melaka
Tso Anko	brigantine	Melaka	60	18	60	9	Nagapatnam-Melaka
Mirsa Mahommad Sia	chaloup	Melaka	45	15	40	10	Pegu-Melaka
Malim Muda	chaloup	Java	48	14	40	2	Samarang-Melaka
Brahim	pencalang	Java	35	13	20	12	Asahan-Melaka

Sources: VOC 3599, VOC 3625.

brought out from Melaka were mostly salt, Indian cloth, Java tobacco, and the goods they brought to Melaka were mostly rice, sago, rattan, fish and forest products. In 1782, the bigger Melakan merchants and traders who owned ships were as follows (see Table 1).

From Table 1, it is evident that there were two Malays among the wealthier Melakan merchants and traders; that those who travelled beyond the archipelago went mostly to India and to ports in present-day Burma, while within the archipelago, trade was mostly conducted with Java and Sumatra. Interestingly, from the table we can see that there was a ship-building industry in Melaka capable of producing ships of 150 *lasten*; that the type of big ship mainly produced in Melaka was the brigantine; and that while it is not known if the industry catered only for a local clientele, it was long established, going back as far as the 1750s if not earlier. Thus, even though Melaka produced almost none of the products that it traded with, it nurtured a substantial group of local traders whose activities appear to have kept a shipping industry alive.

MELAKA'S TRADE AND TRADING NETWORK, 1780s–1830

Ships visiting Melaka in the 1780s to 1790s came from five major areas, namely, Sumatra and Riau, Peninsular Malaya, India and Europe, Java and East Asia (China, Indochina and Luzon).[44] Table 2 (opposite) illustrates Melaka's trading network in the 1780s and 1790s. From the table it can be concluded that much of Melaka's trade during this period was conducted within the Straits of Melaka. However, while the numbers of ships arriving from outside the region, especially from India and China, were comparatively fewer, they were larger ships with bigger cargo space. More importantly, they provided the link between Melaka and the trading world outside the Straits, thus maintaining its position as an international rather than just a regional or local port.

In the period 1780–82, a total of 1129 ships visited Melaka out of which 60 per cent or 677 ships came from Sumatra and Riau. Further, out of the 677 from the two areas, 208 ships came from Riau alone. There appears to have been a decline in the number of ships visiting Melaka in the period 1791–93, as only 946 ships, or 183 fewer, arrived at the port. Out of the total of ships arriving, 464 came from Sumatra and Riau. Thus, in absolute terms, there was a decline in the number of ships coming from Sumatra and Riau, with a decrease of 213. For ships arriving from Riau alone the total was 70 ships, representing a decrease of 138 from the earlier period. Thus there was not only a decline in the overall arrival of ships in the latter period but also a big decrease in the ships coming from Riau. Undoubtedly, the decline in

Table 2: Percentage of incoming ships at Melaka in 1780–82 and 1791–93

Regions	1780–82	1791–93
Sumatra and Riau	60.04	48.71
Peninsular Malaya	17.75	20.12
India and the West	10.46	14.52
China and the East	4.83	10.32
Java	5.82	4.73
Others	1.0	1.26

Sources: VOC 3582, Voc 3599, VOC 3625, VOC 3650, VOC 3940, VOC 3961, OIC 107.

the number of ships visiting Melaka in the early 1790s was closely associated with the decline in the number of ships coming from Riau. This, in turn, could be linked to the 1784 Dutch-Bugis war, which devastated Riau and caused the traders there, mostly Bugis, to disperse and find new bases in the region, such as in Johor, Selangor, Trengganu on the Malay peninsula and Siak, Rokan and Asahan in Sumatra, from where they continued to conduct their trade with Melaka.

The Bugis were undoubtedly one of the main players in the trade in the Straits and also of Melaka, as seen from the large number of ships arriving from Riau in the early 1780s. In fact, in that period, the total number of Bugis ships that arrived in Melaka was 178. Most of them would have come from Riau, and the rest would have arrived from Selangor, Johor and some ports in Sumatra. The lower number of arrivals from Riau, seen in the early 1790s, although indicative of the Bugis dispersal, also shows the revival of the Malay port to some degree.

In the early 1790s, there was a perceptible increase in the number of ships coming from India and China, which was clearly linked to the increase in the Chinese tea trade. Europeans, such as those representing the EIC, Portuguese, Danes, French and Spanish traders, as well as the English country traders, who were very active in this trade, stopped at Melaka and various other native ports in the Straits to collect tin and pepper that were then exchanged for Chinese tea. This increase marked the future trend of increasing dependence on tin, particularly on the part of the English traders, in order to pave their way into, and to gain a controlling share of, the lucrative tea trade. This had far reaching implications for the position of Melaka in the overall trading activities of the region, as we shall see.

When Melaka was occupied by the English from 1795 to 1818, the extent of its trading network gradually shrank. Traders who arrived in Melaka in the first decade of the nineteenth century can be divided into two main groups.[45] The majority came from the Straits, the northern region of Java and the eastern archipelago. Most of them were Bugis, Javanese and Malays (peninsular).[46] The second group of traders, those involved in long-distance trade from India and East Asia (China and Indo-China areas), still called at Melaka although their numbers had declined compared to earlier years.[47] This decline meant that Melaka was no longer a big player in the intra-Asian trade as it once was and its main function had shrunk to being a collecting and distributing centre for areas adjacent to it as well as the southern section of the archipelago. The rise of Penang and its ability to capture part of the network and markets that once belonged to Melaka were largely responsible for this state of affairs.

As the Dutch provided no clear value of trade in currency, it is difficult to compare the earlier period to developments in the nineteenth century. However, if the arrivals of ships are compared, it becomes obvious that there was a decline in Melaka's trade. In the 1780s and 1790s the annual arrival of ships stood at more than 300, whereas in the period 1813–14 there were only 208 arrivals annually at Melaka.[48] Thus, there was a decrease of more than 100 ships, representing a loss of about one-third of its trade. Out of the 208 ships that arrived in Melaka, 43 were from Penang and the rest, which amounted to 165 ships, came from other places. This meant that about 21 per cent of all ships arriving came from Penang, indicating that Melaka's trade with the other areas of the Straits and the archipelago had also shrunk.

In 1810, Melaka's imports were valued at SpD 973,000, while those of Penang's stood at close to SpD 2 million, reflecting the shrinking trade of Melaka and the fact that its main network covered ports in Sumatra and the archipelago. The existence of Penang also reduced the need for the long-distance traders to call at Melaka, so that the port's share of the China and Indian trade also decreased. In addition, many of the Asian traders such as the Bugis, Javanese and Malays had already left Melaka for Penang. In fact, when the English were in control of Melaka they had tried very hard to encourage the remaining Asian traders to trade in Penang rather than in Melaka.[49]

No detailed records are available on Melaka's trade in the early nineteenth century. Only in the late 1820s were more detailed reports kept and a clearer picture of Melaka's trade and trading network in that period began to emerge. Table 3 above illustrates the main trading network of Melaka and also shows the value of imports and exports in 1828–29. Although Melaka's trading network in the late 1820s remained quite extensive, the size of its trade had declined compared to the earlier period. This is because the number of European ships visiting had slowly declined. By 1826 only six

Table 3: Melaka's trading network and value of imports and exports, 1828–29

Place/ports	Imports (SpD)	%	Exports (SpD)	%
Native ports	124,987.73	24.5	224,846.67	67.7
Madras	115,302.2	22.6	25,404.316	7.6
Java	63,236.94	12.4	30,348.8	9.1
Calcutta	53,76.42	10.5	8,224.52	2.5
Siam	66,833.74	13.1	–	–
England	46,353.05	9.1	–	–
Deli	7,642.20	1.5	4,557.06	1.4
Kedah	3,295.69	0.6	–	–
Aceh	10,200.04	2.0	7,086.919	2.1
Ceylon	3,172.39	0.6	–	–
Bombay	639.95	0.1	1,217.27	0.4
China	15,285.83	3.0	30,608.66	9.2
Total	510,325.97	100.0	332,294.2	100.0

Source: SSFR, vol. 162.

English ships came to Melaka compared to 51 in 1780.[50] These ships brought long-distance traders from their bases in India and China. However, the arrival of short-distance traders was not reported, and since Melaka was not an important hub compared to Penang or Singapore, it could be assumed that the number of short-distance and regional traders had definitely declined. Furthermore, Singapore had by then become an important trading centre in the Straits and the archipelago and would have attracted many of those traders who once went to Melaka;[51] Melaka was no longer a vital port in the Straits.

Nevertheless, it should be noted that while the overall picture of Melaka's trade was one of decline from a position of some strength in the late eighteenth century, the reduction in its trade was not drastic. If one were to take, as a starting point, Melaka's position in 1791–99, it could be seen that in a period of 20 years up to 1813–14, the number of ships arriving had declined by one-third of the earlier figures. While that represented a fairly large reduction, it was by no means disastrous. Further, if the value of Melaka's imports in 1810, which stood at SpD 973,000, was compared with that of 1828–29 – almost 20 years later – when its imports were valued at

SpD 510,326, representing a reduction of almost one-half, the decline in Melaka's trade over a period of almost 40 years from 1791 to 1828 was gradual rather than sudden. That Melaka did not suffer a death blow due to competition from Penang and Singapore is significant. It points to the fact that its strategic position in the Straits and its long established standing as a trading centre sustained it throughout the period under study.

MELAKA'S TRADE AND TRADING NETWORK

Riau, Sumatra, Java and the Malay Peninsula

In the 1780s and 1790s, the largest number of traders arriving in Melaka were from Sumatra, Riau and the archipelago. These traders made up more than 60 per cent of all arrivals in that period and 48 per cent in the years 1791–93. The relative decline seen in the latter period was due to the increase in the number of traders from Peninsular Malaya, India and China. In addition, there was a big reduction in ships coming from Riau in the period 1791–93. The majority of Sumatran traders came from the eastern ports of Sumatra, in particular Siak.[52] Other important Sumatran ports with close connections to Melaka were Batubara, Asahan, Aceh, Kampar, Panji, Rokan and Appong. The majority of traders from these ports were Malays, with a very small number of Arabs and Chinese. Most of the Chinese traders from Sumatra came from Siak and the Arabs were mostly from Palembang and Siak.[53]

The single largest number of traders came from Riau, as we have seen. In the 1780–82 period, more than 18 per cent (208 ships) of all traders arrived from Riau, representing the largest number of traders from any one place.[54] However, their numbers declined in the 1791–93 period to only 8 per cent (70 ships). The majority of the Riau traders were ethnic Bugis with a small number of Malays and Chinese. By the early nineteenth century, Melaka's trade with Riau had declined. But many Bugis traders continued to arrive in Melaka, although in the first decades of the nineteenth century most of them came from Makassar, Pasir, Banjarmasin, Bali, Mandai and Sumbawa.[55] As stated before, the Dutch war with Riau in 1784 had led to an exodus of Bugis traders from Riau to other ports on the Malayan peninsula and East Sumatra. Thus, immediately after the 1784 war, many of the Bugis came from the Malayan and Sumatran ports, but in the nineteenth century the majority of them came from the Eastern Indonesian archipelago. This could be because many of the Bugis traders had resettled themselves in the latter region.

The pattern of trade of the Bugis traders from the Eastern Indonesian archipelago was one in which they set sail during the southwest monsoon and arrived in the Straits in July, their numbers increasing in August, September and October. Most of these traders stopped at various places, for example in Borneo and Java, on their journey to Melaka. Their main cargo consisted of Bugis cloth, mats, bird's nests, diamonds, gold dust, rice, tobacco, oil and specie (Spanish dollars). On their return journey from Melaka they carried with them opium and Indian cloths. Some of these traders went on to Penang in order to procure opium, which was sold cheaper there than in Melaka.[56] However, in the late 1820s, the Bugis traders were not listed among the important traders who arrived from the archipelago. The 1828–29 trade report on Melaka only mentioned traders from Java, who were the fourth most important group after traders from the Indian subcontinent and native ports and China and Siam.[57]

The role played by the Bugis in Melaka's trade is hard to determine for the whole period under study, but we know that up to 1808 they remained very active. However, if one were to look at the 1828–29 trade figures, the value of Melaka's imports from native ports was the highest compared to the rest. As the Bugis were among the most active traders of the natives of the archipelago, it could be concluded that most of the trade from the native ports was conducted by them. It should also be noted that Java, Deli, Kedah and Aceh were treated as separate categories from native ports. This further strengthens the case for believing that the Bugis came under the 'native ports' classification. Continuing Bugis trading activities during the period under study can be seen from the strong Bugis presence in Penang and later in Singapore. Ships from Makassar and Eastern Indonesia, which were mostly owned by Bugis traders, carried forest products and agricultural goods to Singapore in exchange for manufactured goods.[58]

Apart from the Bugis, other native traders, including those from Sumatra and the peninsula, brought mainly tin to Melaka. In the early nineteenth century, the annual supply of tin from Palembang and Lingga was 1,300 *pikuls*.[59] The interior Malay states of the peninsula also brought tin to Melaka but its supply was very irregular. In the last decade of the eighteenth century trade between Melaka and Siak in Sumarta was excellent. There was a large number of ships from Siak to Melaka. However, in the early nine-teenth century this lucrative trade declined to its lowest level due to the interruption caused by a civil war in Siak.[60] Melaka provided mainly raw silk, Indian cloth and opium, while in return the Siak traders brought gold, wax, sago, salted fish, fish roe, elephant's tusks, gambir, hogslard, camphor and rattan to Melaka. Other small ports in Sumatra, such as Batubara and Jambi, brought in rattan, wax, rice and Dragon's blood[61] to exchange for opium and Indian cloth. On average, Melaka re-exported between 100 and 130 chests of opium annually to native ports.[62]

Traders from Java who arrived at Melaka were mostly Chinese, Malay, and Dutch-Burghers.[63] They accounted for around 5 per cent of all arrivals in the 1780–82 and 1791–93 period. The major ports in Java with close trading connections with Melaka were Batavia, Semarang, Surabaya, Cheribon, Rembang and Juwana.[64] Traders from Java were considered important to Melaka's trade because they brought with them goods that were greatly in demand, such as rice, salt and tobacco.[65] Ships from Java were usually captained by Arabs, Malays and Chinese. Most brought in rice, sugar, arak, coffee, spices (cloves) and a small quantity of tin, which they collected at Banca on their way to Melaka. In return, these traders took with them Indian cloth, gambir, salted fish, fish roe and Surat cloth from Melaka.

Chinese traders comprised more than 3 per cent (38 ships) of all traders from Java in 1780–82, but 10 years later, in 1791–93, their numbers had decreased to 25 ships or 2 per cent.[66] In the period 1780–82, the majority of Java-Chinese traders came from Semarang, with a total of 18 followed by Cheribon (7) and Surabaya (6), Batavia (3), Juwana (2) and one ship each from Rembang and Gresik. In addition to them were Chinese traders who came from Siak. In 1780–82, 30 Chinese-owned ships came from Siak to Melaka, and in 1791–93 there were 22 ships.[67] Although few detailed accounts about traders from Java in the early nineteenth century are available, the evidence shows that they constituted only a small proportion of all traders who arrived in the period 1828–29. Their numbers had declined tremendously due to the fact that the majority of them had taken their trade to Singapore.

In the 1780s and 1790s, the second largest group of traders who came to Melaka were Malays from the Malay peninsula. They comprised more than 17 per cent of total arrivals in 1780–92 and 20 per cent in the period 1791–93, the majority coming from Selangor, Perak, Kedah and Trengganu.[68] After the fall of Riau in 1784, a large number of Riau Malay traders migrated to Trengganu,[69] while the Riau Bugis moved to Selangor, which was under Bugis rule.[70] In the first decades of the nineteenth century, Malay traders were not specifically mentioned as a group yet, given the fact that the main traders in Melaka were from Borneo, Trengganu and Pahang (all Malay centres), it seems plausible to conclude that, like the Bugis, the Malays continued to play a big role in Melaka's trade.[71] Traders from Borneo brought with them bird's nest, camphor, pepper and sago, while those from Trengganu and Pahang brought pepper and gold respectively.

By the late 1820s traders from the peninsula and Sumatra were the second most important group next to traders from Indian ports.[72] Such traders were classified as those who arrived from 'native ports'. The term 'native ports' refers to ports located in the Straits of Melaka on the west coast of the Malay peninsula and also small ports on the east coast of

Sumatra. More than 24 per cent of Melaka's imports and more then 67 per cent of its exports were conducted with these ports.[73] Melaka's imports from native ports consisted mostly of forest products, such as rattan and birds nest, food products, such as rice and spices (pepper), and minerals (gold and tin). In return, the native ports imported mostly Indian cloth and opium from Melaka.

The Indian Subcontinent

In the 1780s and 1790s traders who came from India and the western regions were mostly Europeans, namely the English, Portuguese and a very small number of Danes, French and Spanish.[74] There were also a small number of Moor and Keling traders from these areas. The English traders, the largest number engaged in the India-Melaka-China trade, had increased tremendously in the period 1791–93.[75] Some of them, such as Francis Light and James Scott from Penang, traded goods on the Penang-Melaka-Coromandel-Bengal route. On the whole, the India–Melaka–China trade was controlled by the English traders with a small percentage captured by the Portuguese who travelled the India–Melaka–Macao route.[76] However, it is strange that the Melaka records do not show visits by English ships in the first decade of the nineteenth century, although if one were to go by the Dutch practice of not recording VOC ships, it could well be that the English in Melaka also went by that norm in not recording the movements of their own ships.

In the first decade of the nineteenth century the majority of Indian traders from India came from Pulicat on the Coromandel Coast. Pulicat merchants from India brought with them 80 to 150 bales of Indian cloths annually to Melaka valued at 80–140,000 Spanish Dollars (SpD).[77] Some three to four ships from Pulicat were regularly engaged in the trade with Melaka. In addition to these, there were also two ships from Surat that came to Melaka annually on their way to Siam. Surat merchants mostly brought with them silks and chintzes, very colourful and expensive types of cloth.[78] However, according to Arasaratnam, by the early nineteenth century the majority of Indian merchants who arrived in the Straits were the Chulias. Most of them were textile traders trading between the Coromandel Coast and Penang. Since the Dutch still imposed trading restrictions on the carrying of Indian cloth, the majority of these traders had made Penang their bases rather then Melaka.[79]

In the late 1820s, trade between the Indian subcontinent and Melaka was still significant. More than 33 per cent of Melaka's imports came from this area.[80] The bulk of goods re-exported by Melaka came from Indian ports such as Madras, Calcutta and Bombay. However, Melaka's exports to

Table 4: Excess imports and exports in Melaka's trade, 1828–29

Countries/ports	Excess of imports (SpD)	%	Excess of exports (SpD)	%
Calcutta	45,151.90	15.36	–	–
Madras	89,897.88	30.59	–	–
Bombay	–	–	577.57	0.49
England	46,353.05	15.77	–	–
China	–	–	15,322.82	13.23
Java	32,888.14	11.19	–	–
Ceylon	3,172.39	1.07	–	–
Siam	66,833.74	22.74	–	–
Aceh	3,113.12	1.06	–	–
Deli	3,085.14	1.05	–	–
Kedah	3,295.69	1.12	–	–
Native ports	–	–	99,858.93	86.26
Total	293,791.08	100.00	115,759.33	100.00

Sources: SSFR, vol 162, G/34/123.

Indian ports were tiny compared to the goods it imported from India. Indian cloth and opium were the most important items imported by Melaka. Thus, in general, Melaka's well-being was dependent on its position as a collecting and distributing centre. More importantly, the imbalance seen in its trade with India indicates that it remained an important centre from which manufactured goods were distributed to the archipelago, as shown in Table 3. Table 4 above shows the excess in Melaka's trade with India for the period 1828–29.

What is clear from Table 4 is that Melaka had a trade deficit with Calcutta, Madras, England, Java and Siam from which it imported manufactured goods and food products. However, Melaka enjoyed a favourable balance of trade with native ports (86 per cent of excess export), which was accounted for by the re-export of manufactured goods it imported from outside the region. Its good position vis-à-vis China (13 per cent of excess export) could be explained by the fact that while long-distance traders took from Melaka products from the archipelago to China, Chinese products were mostly destined for Europe and were therefore not offloaded in Melaka. Table 4 also shows that Java, Aceh, Deli and Kedah continued to trade with Melaka, although, with the exception of Java, the volume traded was small and did not exceed SpD 4,000 in value. At the same time, Melaka did not export goods to these areas, indicating that it no longer was the distributing centre for them. The case of Kedah, Deli and Aceh could be explained by the fact that Penang had by then superseded Melaka's position as the distributing centre for goods, especially from India for these areas. Although Melaka's trade had declined in the 1820s, it was still a participant in the intra-Asian trade, albeit on a much smaller scale. The volume of trade was small compared to that in the early period and the number of incoming ships had also declined. [81]

China and East Asia

In the 1780s and 1790s, the majority of incoming traders from China were the English country traders and those from the English East India Company, followed by the Portuguese and other Europeans. Most of the English traders travelled from Canton while the Portuguese came from Macao. Only a small number of ethnic Chinese traders came from Chinese ports.[82] In 1780 and 1781, no Chinese trader arrived from China and in 1782 only two came to Melaka. Melaka was not an important destination for Chinese traders from China, who mostly traded at Bangkok and Batavia.[83] The majority were local residents (Melaka-Chinese), who comprised more than 45 per cent of all Chinese who traded in Melaka in 1780–82 and about 24 per cent in the period 1791–93.

The overall decrease in Chinese traders arriving in Melaka in the 1791–93 period is difficult to explain. A total of 163 ships captained by Chinese arrived in the 1780–82 period, but in the 1791–93 period the number was 101. The decline was seen across the board, except for ships from Batavia, which increased from 3 to 4, Rambang, from 1 to 2, Gresik, from 1 to 3, Kedah from 1 to 16. Significantly, even the number of ships captained by Melaka Chinese declined to 24 from 74 in the period 1780–82. This, coupled with a big rise in the number of arrivals of Chinese traders from Kedah, seems to suggest that many Melaka Chinese had moved north, to Penang and especially Kedah, by this time. However, in the 1791–93 period, only 2 Penang-Chinese traders arrived at Melaka bringing with them powdered sugar, nuts, Javanese tobacco and garlic, and taking back Chinese chairs to Penang. The small number of Chinese traders from Penang could perhaps be explained by the fact that Penang was still in its infancy as a port so that the Melaka Chinese were inclined to move to a more established trading base such as Kedah. Melaka suffered a decline in trade and the number of merchants arriving at its port had also declined, especially after the Anglo-Dutch wars so that this might have had an impact on the Melaka-Chinese traders, encouraging some to leave Melaka and others to avoid it.

In the first decades of the nineteenth century the number of ships visiting Melaka from the Indo-China regions, such as Siam,[84] also decreased with only three to four Siamese junks arriving at Melaka annually.[85] Siamese traders mostly brought with them rice, salt, saltfish, sappanwood[86] and sticlac.[87] They also brought goods produced in China, such as silk, chinaware, paper and Chinese tobacco. In return they took away tin, fish roe, *dammar*, rattan, bird's nest and champor.[88] Although in 1828–29 Melaka's imports from China and Siam stood at 15 per cent of its total imports and its exports to them stood at 9 per cent of the total, the number of ships arriving from these areas was not recorded.[89]

The low number of Chinese traders coming to Melaka was due to the VOC policy of forcing all Chinese junks to trade at Batavia rather than at Melaka. However, during this period many EIC, Portuguese and English country traders who made their journey between the Indian subcontinent to Macao and Canton in China stopped at Melaka to collect local commodities for the China trade. Many of these ships on their return journey also carried Chinese passengers to Melaka, besides goods from China. Some of these Chinese passengers disembarked there. Many of these new arrivals did not remain in Melaka due to limited job opportunities. Instead, they made their way into the interior of the peninsula, some working in agricultural plantations, such as gambir and pepper, and others in the tin mining areas. Some also went across the Straits to Lingga, Bangka, Siak and Palembang. By the end of the eighteenth century these migrants to the Straits had formed many Chinese ('coolie') settlements based on agricultural production and the mining industry.[90] Products from these settlements mostly catered for the China market and some were also sold to European traders. In addition to tin, agricultural produce such as pepper and gambir were in demand in China, which encouraged the opening of Chinese agricultural settlements that produced pepper and gambir in Kedah, Riau, Johor, Trengganu and elsewhere.[91] Thus during the 'Chinese century' in Southeast Asia, Melaka became an important port of disembarkation for Chinese migrants, from whence they travelled to Sumatra or into the interior of the Malay peninsula where the demand for labour was higher in the agricultural and tin mining industries.[92]

COMMODITIES OF TRADE, 1780–1830

As mentioned earlier, the main commodities brought to Melaka in the period before the 1780s were opium, tin, Indian cloth, gold and forest products, and in the 1780s and 1790s the main commodities were three types of cloth (Indian, Bugis and Java cloth), rice, salt, *belacan/terasi* (shrimp paste), gambir, sugar and rattan. Beside these, there were also small items such as chinaware, amballo, saltpetre, opium, tin, Japanese copper, sago, tobacco, arak/liquor and fish products. Although tin and opium were still important commodities in the 1780s and 1790s, facts and statistics on these two items are difficult to ascertain. Although opium was mentioned in the shipping list as an item brought in by English ships from India, its volume was not mentioned. Similarly when opium was brought in by Asian traders the amount was also not stated.

Indian cloth, opium, tin and grains still constituted the major import items for Melaka in the second decade of the nineteenth century. Thus, not much change had occurred in the types of goods imported by Melaka compared to the 1780s and 1790s.[93] Most of Melaka's imports were re-exported, except for grains, which were mostly consumed in Melaka. One change relates to the position of gold in the trade. In the 1780s and 1790s, gold was the third most important import item after opium and Indian cloth. The increase in the amount of gold imported during the 1780s was due to the increase in its production in the interior of Pahang, Sumatra and also Borneo. As the gold producing areas were under the control of local chiefs and not interrupted by external political disturbances, supply of the metal to Melaka did not decrease. However, in the early nineteenth century, gold was not listed as an important item probably due to its irregular supply from the major producing areas in Sumatra. By then tin, which was an important item for the China tea trade, had made a comeback on the import list. Nevertheless, opium and Indian cloth remained the most important imports that Melaka then re-exported to various places in the archipelago. Table 5 below illustrates a comparative analysis of the major commodities imported and exported by Melaka in the years 1810, 1824–25 and 1828–29. It can be clearly seen that the value of Melaka's imports declined between 1810, when it stood at SpD 973,000, and 1824–25, when it was SpD 532,615, and slid down further by 1828–29 to SpD 510,325. However, it should be noted that the figures for 1824–25 are estimates made by Newbold. The figures given for opium for 1824–25 show a big gap between imports and exports, at 7 per cent and 1 per cent respectively, which erroneously implies that most of it was consumed locally.

No changes were implemented to revive trade during the brief period of Dutch administration in Melaka from 1818 to 1824. The Dutch failed to change the trading pattern that had existed under the English, with the result that they could not arrest Melaka's decline. Before Melaka was finally transferred to the English, about 22 per cent of its total imports was cloth (Indian and native cloth such as Bugis and Java cloth). This was followed by rice which constituted more than 19 per cent.[94] Next came tin, which was

Table 5: Melaka's major commodities imported and exported, 1810, 1824–25 and 1828–29

Major types of commodities	1810 Imported %	1824–25 Imported %	1828–29 Exported %
Textiles	36.53	23.51	21.34
Opium	25.17	7.40	1.17
Tin	9.76	8.11	17.46
Pepper	1.84	1.02	0.52
Grains	4.62	19.03	2.00
Rattans	-	1.48	3.08
Salt	-	1.19	0.90
Tobacco	-	4.72	2.97
Others	22.08	33.47	50.5
Total Value (SpD)	973,000	532,615	328,421

Sources: SSFR, Vol. 10; SSFR, Vol. 162; G/34/123; T.J. Newbold, *Political and Statistical Account of the British Settlements in the Straits of Malacca*, Vol. 1, London: John Murray, 1839, p.149. The exchange rate in 1824 was 100 Sicca Rupees to 47.42 Spanish Dollars.

more than 9 per cent, followed by opium, which was 7 per cent. The bulk of Indian cloth was re-exported, which also made it the most important export item from Melaka followed by tin. In 1828–29, the main goods that Melaka imported were cloth valued at more than SpD 202,009.[95] Most of the cloth came from India, which constituted more than 22 per cent of all cloth brought into Melaka, followed by English cloth, which made up more than 5 per cent. The next important imported item was rice and paddy – more than 16 per cent of all goods imported to Melaka. This was followed by opium and tin. As seen earlier in the chapter, in the eighteenth century, Indian cloth, opium, rice and tin were important goods imported by Melaka. The same goods appeared in the 1828–29 list. Melaka's trade had declined between 1810 and 1829 as reflected in the value of its imports, as shown earlier, while its exports increased only slightly from SpD 328,421 in 1824 and to SpD 332,294 in 1828.

From the shipping lists of 1780–82 and 1791–93, it is hard to assess whether the Dutch in Melaka were able to maintain an exclusive monopoly of the Indian cloth trade, because the data only covers ships that called at Melaka. Many ships did not stop at Melaka so as to avoid purchasing a pass for carrying items into the Straits, as required by the Dutch regulations. In addition, there were also many European country traders coming to the

Straits who called at various native ports, notably at Riau and some at Kedah, Selangor and Perak, where most of them went for tin in exchange for Indian cloth and opium. Furthermore, the data on the import of Indian cloth to Melaka are incomplete since there were many ships that carried Indian cloth to Melaka but did not state its volume. In addition, the units used to measure the cloth were not uniform.

More than 20 per cent of all cloth imports came from India in the 1780–82 and 1791–93 periods. The figure on import of Indian cloth shows that there was an increase between the periods 1780–82 (1606 *corgie*)[96] and 1791–93 (2003 *corgie*). An interesting trend can be seen in the trade of cloths produced in the region. The import of Bugis cloth was high in the period 1780–82, at 3,568 corgie, but declined in the period 1791–93 to 2,416 corgie. This was because most Bugis cloth came from Riau, which was the centre of Bugis cloth in the Straits, and the Dutch war with Riau had disturbed this trade. In contrast, Melaka's import of Java cloth increased in the same period from 1,498 corgie in the period 1780–82 to 4,808 corgie in the period 1791–93, showing a co-relation between the two trends. The import of Bali cloth and other types of cloth, such as Chinese linen, was small compared to the three major cloths above.

Indian cloth constituted more than 90 per cent of the total volume of cloths exported by Melaka in 1780–82. This represented about 5,144 corgie of cloth. Ten years later, the volume of Indian cloth exported had increased to 6,388 corgie. Despite the Dutch war with Riau, export of Bugis cloth from Melaka rose from 310 corgie in the early 1780s to 982 corgie ten years later. However, it should be noted that the import figures were much larger than the export figures for the same period, which suggest that the huge discrepancy between the two lies in the fact that much of the Bugis cloth for the two periods was for Melaka's consumption. The same pattern was seen in the trade in Java cloth in the two periods. The bulk of Indian cloth came directly from India, while a very small percentage came from elsewhere in the region, such as Selangor and Riau. This was due to the fact that English country traders who visited native ports sold their Indian cloth there, from where it was carried to Melaka by the local traders. In the period 1780–82, more than 44 per cent (3322 corgie) of the supply of cloth in Melaka came from Riau but in the latter period its position was overtaken by Java.

The supply of cloth from the Malay ports in the peninsula, such as Kedah, Selangor, Perak and Trengganu, increased from 1,094 corgie in 1780–82 to 2,236 in 1791–93. Similarly, the supply of cloth from Sumatra increased from 211 corgie in 1780–82 to 1,005 corgie in 1791–93. Aceh, Siak, Batubara and Asahan in Sumatra had become sources of supply for Melaka due to their increasing trade with Indian and country traders who brought Indian cloth and opium to exchange for pepper and tin. Thus, two factors were responsible for this trend, namely, the fact that more country traders were trading directly with these ports where tin or pepper could be procured cheaply in exchange for Indian cloth and opium, and because some Bugis cloth was being traded from these ports by the relocated Bugis traders. [97]

Most of the cloth imported by Melaka was re-exported. The bulk of the Indian cloth was exported to Riau in the period 1780–82 although, as to be expected, only a small amount went there in the period 1791–93. Instead, Sumatra became the largest exporter of cloth from Melaka in the latter period, most of it going to Siak, Rokan, Indragiri, Panai, Asahan and Batubara. The rather small amount of cloth exported by Melaka to the ports on the peninsula could be explained by the fact that they were receiving it directly from the country traders. The bulk of Java cloth came from Semarang, which supplied more than 80 per cent of Java cloth to Melaka. However, only a small fraction of Java cloth was re-exported, as was the case with Bugis cloth. Thus, the majority of people in Melaka used Bugis and Java cloth probably because they were cheaper. As for Indian cloth, the figures show an inconsistency in that the volume of Indian cloth imported was lower than the amount exported. A possible explanation for this is that much of the cloth might have been smuggled into Melaka and therefore not officially recorded. As mentioned earlier, Indian cloth was the most important item imported and re-exported by Melaka. More than 39 per cent of the imported Indian cloth was re-exported. A large share went to native ports and only 19 per cent was exported to Java. Only a small amount went to Sumatran ports because of direct trade with India, as mentioned before, as well as the fact that Penang had become an important source especially for the northern section of Sumatra.[98]

The amount of opium imported and then re-exported by Melaka in the 1780s and 1790s is hard to ascertain because the volume of the import was not mentioned in the shipping lists. Most of the opium was carried by VOC ships and was, therefore, not recorded. Although from time to time Portuguese and English ships brought in opium, its value was not stated in the documents. As mentioned earlier, both opium and tin were considered restricted items by the VOC, as they were important and were traded under a strict monopoly and regulated by the Dutch authorities in Melaka. Until 1828–29, opium was still one of the most lucrative goods sought after by most native traders in Melaka. Much of the opium came from India. In 1828–29, only 20% of the opium imported was used in Melaka while the rest was exported to various native ports (SpD 28,836) and to Aceh (SpD 4,870).[99] Most of the opium exported, about 85%, went to native ports and the rest was exported to Aceh.

As the Dutch period in Melaka came to its end in the late eighteenth century, the VOC was losing control of the tin producing areas in the peninsula and the islands of Billiton Singkep and Bangka, in Sumatra.[100] As stated by van Braam Houckgeest in his 1790 memoir before the transfer of Melaka to the English, Melaka's tin trade was already declining. Although Melaka had signed treaties with several tin producing areas, such as Junk Ceylon, Kedah, Perak, Palembang and Selangor, they only received a limited supply of tin annually from these places.[101] According to Houckgeest's memoir, most of the tin trade at the end of the eighteenth century was in the hands of the English, as the tin from Junk Ceylon, Kedah, Perak, Selangor and also Banca was in the hands of the English traders.[102] Although the Dutch succeeded in their wars with the Bugis in Riau and Selangor, their main sources of tin supply, and managed to destroy their greatest rival in the tin trade, namely, the Bugis, this only led to the establishment of an English settlement in the Straits. As tin was vital in securing the lucrative tea trade with China, the English saw the urgency of setting up their own settlement in the Straits in order to capture the tin trade in the region. Thus Penang was opened and developed into an important settlement and port for trade. The Dutch monopoly on the tin trade could not be successfully enforced due to competition from the English, who offered higher prices. For example, the Dutch tin trade with Perak collapsed when the kingdom refused to renew the agreement to deliver tin to the VOC in Melaka.[103] Although after the fall of Riau, in 1784, the Melaka Governor attempted to persuade the higher authorities in Batavia to review the monopoly on tin, it fell on deaf ears and no other reforms were carried out up to 1795 when Melaka was transferred to the English, which led to its further decline in commercial importance.[104]

There are some puzzling aspects to the figures given for tin import and export in the 1828–29 period. The report on Melaka's trade for 1828–29 shows that Melaka imported SpD 34,794.42 worth of tin from native ports and re-exported tin to the value of SpD 37,046.87 also to native ports. This is almost inexplicable unless an error had been made in the records. The only plausible explanation is that, as neither Penang nor Singapore was listed in the records, they might have been included in the category of 'native ports'. By that period, Melaka had become the depot for collecting goods from the areas adjacent to it, which were then sent on to Singapore for export. It is therefore strange that the trade link between Melaka and Singapore was not highlighted in the data. Further, it makes sense to assume that most of Melaka's tin went to Singapore, from where a good proportion of it would have been exported to England. The tin export figures of almost 10 per cent which went to China and the 3.1 per cent which went to India show that there was still direct trade between Melaka and China and India in that commodity although the amounts were very small. Most of Melaka's gold dust came from Pahang and Sumatra. In 1828–29 most of it was exported to Madras (SpD 25,404) with only a small amount going to China (SpD 1,043). Gold dust had been one of the most important items of export from Melaka since the mid-eighteenth century and it remained an item for export in the 1828–29 period.

Since the Dutch in Melaka did not encourage the local population to cultivate paddy or produce agricultural products, most of its food had to be imported.[105] Rice came mainly from Java, which supplied more than 61 per cent (2080 *koyan*)[106] of total import of the food item in the period 1780–82 and more than 79 per cent (1,373 *koyan*) in the period 1791–93. Other areas that supplied rice to Melaka were Sumatra, Pegu/Rangoon and also the Malay peninsular. However, in 1828–29 most of Melaka's rice came from Siam, valued at SpD 37,656.22, with Java as the next largest exporter at SpD 30,979.48.[107] A large number of Siamese junks came to the Straits and the archipelago during this period so that Melaka's link with Siam increased.[108] Besides Siam and Java, Melaka also imported rice from Calcutta, Aceh and Kedah although, together, they supplied less than SpD 4,742 worth of rice.[109]

Besides rice, Melaka also imported a large quantity of other food items from Sumatra. Sago was considered an important product after rice and was imported mostly from Siak. During periods of rice scarcity, sago was used as a substitute.[110] Most of the traders from Melaka and Siak brought with them sago on their journey to Melaka. Since the value of sago was not in standard units such as *gantang*,[111] *pikuls* and *buyong*,[112] it is difficult to compile the data.

Fish and other food products were also important items mostly for local consumption. Dried fish and fish roe were imported from Siak, Rokan, Indragiri, Asahan and Batubara. Only a small amount was re-exported to China and various places. It is also difficult to assess the import of fish since it was not recorded in uniform units and there were various types of fish imported to Melaka. Other food products imported were coconut oil, coconuts, paddy, groundnuts, bird's nests, tamarind and various types of beans. Different types of arack/liquor were also imported from Java and Sumatra. In the 1780s and 1790s, the bulk of food products came from Sumatra and also Java. However, in the 1828–29 period, the main supplier of food products such as rice, oil, salt, sugar and tobacco was Siam, with Java coming in second followed by native ports.[113]

A major foodstuff imported and also re-exported was salt. Since it was very difficult to produce salt around the sea coast in the Straits due to its muddy sea shore, salt had to be imported from places such as Java and India.[114] However, the bulk of Melaka's import of salt in 1828–29 came from

Siam, which was valued at SpD 12,177.45 followed by Java at SpD 912.83.[115] Salt was used as a seasoning in the preparation of food and also formed an important ingredient in the preparation of *belacan/terasi* and dried fish. Nearly half the salt imported in the 1780–82 period was re-exported but only a quarter of the item was re-exported in the 1791–93 period.

More than 56 per cent of salt imported in the 1780–82 period came from Java and this figure increased to more than 79 per cent in the 1791–93 period. Salt was also brought in from Sumatra, China and India. However, in the 1791–93 period almost 80 per cent of the salt imported came from Java. It was later re-exported from Melaka to various places, such as Sumatra and the Malay peninsula, with the former taking the bulk of it, namely, about 87 per cent in 1780–82 and 75 per cent in the 1791–93 period. The ports of Sumatra that imported salt were Siak, Rokan, Indragiri, Asahan, Batubara and Pasai. This trend continued to the 1828–29 period, when most of the imported salt was re-exported to native ports.[116]

One of the most important commodities of export from Melaka was *belacan* or *terasi*. *Belacan*, a paste prepared from small prawns or shrimps and salt, is an important ingredient for the preparation of food among many Asians. Since Melaka has a long shoreline and a good supply of shrimps from the sea, manufacturing of *belacan* was an important industry in and around Melaka, for the fishermen and people who lived near the shore. In the 1780–82 period the export of *belacan* from Melaka was more than 1,500 *pikuls* and it increased to more than 2,400 *pikuls* in the period 1791–93. Most of the *belacan* from Melaka was exported to Java, at more than 64 per cent (1780–82), increasing to more than 82 per cent in the period 1791–93. However, in the period 1828–29 *belacan/terasi* did not appear in the commodities exported from Melaka. Perhaps the volume of *belacan/terasi* exported was too small to be included in the list of small items exported from Melaka.[117]

The most important item of human consumption after rice and salt was powdered sugar. Powdered sugar was produced from cane but there were other types, such as kandji, Java and jager sugar,[118] which had been produced for centuries. Most of the powdered sugar was produced from cane and as Melaka did not grow sugar cane most of the powdered sugar was imported. In the period 1780–82, more than 84 per cent (27,400 *pikuls*) of the supply came from China and only 15 per cent (4,934 *pikuls*) came from Java. The import of powdered sugar was very high in the period 1780–82 compared to 1791–93 mainly due to the influx of powdered sugar from China. In the period 1791–93 no powdered sugar was imported from China. Surprisingly, no powdered sugar was exported to the Malay peninsula in the 1780–82 period, but in the period 1791–93 77 per cent (792 *pikuls*) of all powdered sugar exported by Melaka went to this area. In the period 1828–29, the major supplier of sugar to Melaka was Siam – valued at SpD 5,978.54.[119] Although tobacco is not really a food item, it was a consumable and used by the peoples of Southeast Asia as a medicine, for smoking, chewing and snuff. Most tobacco came from the Javanese ports of Semarang, Cheribon, Surabaya and Juwana. Some of the Java tobacco was re-exported to various Sumatran ports.

Since the early period, rattan was one of the items on the list of Melaka's exports and it remained an important export item in the 1780s and 1790s. However, it is quite difficult to prepare an accurate table on the import and re-export of rattan from Melaka since the units used were in various forms, such as pieces, *pikuls*, *bossen*,[120] etc. Most of Melaka's rattan came from Sumatra and the Malay peninsula and the main importers were China and Java. However, in 1810 there was no mention in the record of rattan imported to Melaka; it appeared again only in the period 1824–25 when only a small amount seems to have been traded. A similar situation was seen in the period 1828–29 where the value of rattan imports and exports was small compared to the other commodities. Most of the imported rattan came from native ports and in the 1828–29 period SpD 15,447.06 worth of the product was brought in. More than 90 per cent of this item was exported to China to the value of SpD 10,242.72.[121] Java was not listed as an important market for Melaka's rattan, as it was in the earlier period.

There are many records and also reports to support the view that the Melaka government, on the whole, did not encourage the development of plantation agriculture and the cultivation of paddy. However, there was a period when there appears to have been some encouragement to plant gambir in the interior of Melaka beginning in the 1750s, when the plant was introduced into Melaka from Pontian.[122] Had the scheme taken off, by the 1780s Melaka would have been an important producer of gambir. However, due to the fact that many land proprietors in Melaka tended to leave much of their land uncultivated, or left the cultivation to others, the development and expansion of gambir production was not properly monitored.[123] The fact that the land proprietors were disinclined to open up their land for cultivation meant that much of it was also inaccessible. Further, when land proprietors such as Adrian Koek and Westerhout encouraged some Chinese to open up land for the purpose of planting gambir the enterprise did not last long because the price of gambir fell and the land was abandoned. In the nineteenth century, most gambir plantations were destroyed or left untended. Nevertheless, in the period 1780–82 Melaka produced more than 14,000 *pikuls* of gambir, and in the period 1791–93 its production increased to more than 16,000 *pikuls*. Most of the gambir was exported to Java (more than 95 per cent) and a small amount was sent to China. However, there was no mention of gambir export in the early nineteenth century or the late 1820s period, showing that the enterprise was short-lived.

CONCLUSION

Several patterns are discernible in Melaka's trade in the late eighteenth and early nineteenth centuries and the trade reflected the general trend of that period when the India–China trade continued to be hinged to the trade of the archipelago. This mutual dependence, as we have seen, was based on the nature of the goods produced by the three regions, namely, manufactured goods from India and China and natural products from the archipelago. This being the case, there was a convergence of interests between the long-distance India-China traders on the one hand, and short-distance traders of the archipelago on the other, which met at, and were served by, Melaka. This pattern remained intact for several centuries, giving to Melaka its pre-eminence as the trading centre in Southeast Asia.

Another pattern was related to the long-distance India–China trade being controlled mainly by Europeans, in particular the English, with a few Indian and Chinese traders covering the India–archipelago, and China–archipelago routes respectively; the archipelago's trade was largely handled by the short-distance native traders. This European concentration on long-distance trade meant that native trading activities were left well alone, thus giving the traders of the archipelago a significant but not dominant role in the intra-Asian trade as seen from their contribution to the trade of Melaka. Finally, the period under study saw the emergence of Penang and, later, Singapore to threaten Melaka's position. This, combined with the outdated Dutch trade policies, the aggressive English competition and political changes in Europe, weakened Melaka's trade so that its position as a commercial and trading centre in the Straits was seriously challenged and then lost. This challenge was reflected in the decline of its trade, the shrinking of its networks and the diminution of its status. While the products it handled remained the same, their amounts and value decreased. Similarly, Melaka maintained contact with more or less the same areas and regions, but the number of ships which visited became fewer. However, Melaka's fall was one from the great height of famous trade emporium and entrepot to that of insignificant regional port.

NOTES

1   Charles Lockyer, *An Account of the Trade in India*, London: Samuel Crouch, 1711: where the author described Melaka as a healthful place, but of no great trade, p. 66.

2   See Appendix 11: Melaka Shipping Lists, 1780–82 and 1791–93, in Nordin Hussin, 'Melaka and Penang 1780–1830', pp. 459–480.

3   For further discussion on the various types of ships and their sizes in Southeast Asian waters during this period, see Gerrit Knaap, *Shallow Waters, Rising Tide*, pp. 149–157. See also S. Arasaratnam, 'Coromandel Shipping and Seafaring in the Indian Ocean 1650–1800', *Journal of East-West Maritime Relations*, vol.3, 1994, pp. 19–41; P.Y. Manguin, 'The Southeast Asian Ship: An Historical Approach', *JSEAS*, 11, 1980, pp. 266–276; H. Warington Smyth, 'Boats and Boat-building in the Malay Peninsula', *The Indian Antiquary*, April, 1906, pp. 97–115; and A. Horridge, *The Prahu: Traditional Sailing Boat of Indonesia*, Singapore: Oxford University Press, 1985.

4   For a further account of the maritime traffic in Southeast Asian waters during this period, see Gerrit Knaap, *Shallow Waters, Rising Tide*, pp. 159–169

5   *Last* is a measurement of the volume of ships. One *last* is equivalent to 4,000 lbs, see Gerrit Knaap, *Shallow Waters, Rising Tide*, p. 192.

6   For a detailed description of the history and the size of these ships, see Gerrit Knaap, *Shallow Waters, Rising Tide*, pp. 30–43.

7   Ibid.

8   H. Warington Smyth, 'Boats and Boat-building in the Malay Peninsula', where the author describes *balo* or *balok* as 'A single-masted boat. The model suffers from a mast which is too short to hoist the lugsail. The boat has beam and fairly flat floors. There are washboards at the quarters and a peculiar slightly outrigged grating or staying over the stern post. The rudder is very small and short, and had a yoke and lines', p. 102.

9   Ibid. Where Smyth states that the banting was frequently used by traders from Aceh; and he further describes the boat as a two-masted trader type, built of *giam* wood. The boat's dimension was 90 feet by 27 feet by 7 feet with a 2-foot freeboard; it had a capacity of 12 *koy* and the number of on-board crew was 6. The length of the mainmast was 50 feet, it used cloth for its sail cloth but the size of the rig was uncertain, p. 102.

10   Ibid. Smyth notes that *kakap* or *kakap* Jeram is a typical Malay fishing boat from Selangor. The rig is practically the same as that of the *nadir* (a shallow-draft Malay fishing boat from Melaka and built from carvel wood with straight stem similar to those of the European type), pp. 103–105.

11   Ibid. Smyth mentions that the *pencalang* is a typical Bugis boat and a two-masted trader type built from hard *jati* wood. The dimension of the *pencalang* is 80 feet by 15 feet by 9 feet; 4 feet freeboard, a capacity of 15 *koy* and 30 crew, pp. 105.

12   Gerrit Knaap, *Shallow Waters, Rising Tide*, pp. 30–43.

13   A *padowakang* is a large merchant ship and the size could reach up to 300 tons. For further information see A. Horridge, *The Prahu*, p. 19; and H. Warington Smyth, 'Boats and Boat-building in the Malay Peninsula', pp. 97–115.

14   See Appendix 11: Melaka Shipping Lists, 1780–82 and 1791–93, in Nordin Hussin, 'Melaka and Penang 1780–1830', pp. 459–480.

15   Ibid.

16   Ibid.

17   Ibid.

18   Ibid. See also Figure 2 (traders arriving at Melaka).

19   Ibid.

20   The exact position of Trantan is not known. It could be Siantan, a group of islands that formed a part of the Johor-Riau kingdom and both places were part of the Johor-Riau kingdom.

21   See Figure 2 (traders arriving at Melaka); Appendix 11: Melaka Shipping Lists, 1780–82 and 1791–93, in Nordin Hussin, 'Melaka and Penang 1780–1830', pp. 459–480.

22   Ibid.

23   See Figure 2 (traders arriving at Melaka); Appendix 11: Melaka Shipping Lists, 1780–82 and 1791–93, in Nordin Hussin, 'Melaka and Penang 1780–1830', pp. 459–480.

24   See S. Arasaratnam, *Islamic Merchant Communities of the Indian Subcontinent*; S. Arasaratnam, 'The Chulia Muslim Merchants in Southeast Asia'; and S. Arasaratnam, 'Coromandel Shipping and Seafaring in the Indian Ocean'.

25 Copie lijsten van de aangekomen en vertrokken vreemde en particuliere schepen en mindere kielen in genoemde datum, VOC 3582: 19 January 1780.

26 The goods carried on board consisted of 4,000 *pikuls* of sugar, 3,000 *pikuls* of saltpetre and 150 *kisten* of silk.

27 It is not clear whether this item was a type of cloth or raw cotton.

28 A type of mineral.

29 Copie lijsten van de aangekomen en vertrokken vreemde en particuliere schepen en mindere kielen in genoemde datum: VOC 3582: 13 January 1780. The listed goods were 2,000 *pikuls* of sugar, 1,000 *pikuls* of saltpetre, 1,000 *pikuls* of alum, 80 *kisten* silk and 40 *kisten* of porcelain.

30 He brought with him 37 *koyan* rice, 16 *koyan* salt, 100 pieces paving-stones, 199 pieces of house planks and 10,000 pieces of Chinese planks.

31 Copie lijsten van de aangekomen en vertrokken vreemde en particuliere schepen en mindere kielen in genoemde datum: VOC 3582: 13 January 1780, VOC 3599: 1–30 September 1780.

32 See *branddamar*.

33 Shrimp paste.

34 The list of goods were 600 *pikuls* sugar, 200 *pikuls* onions, 50 *pikuls* arak, and 11 *pikuls* gambir. See Copie lijsten van de aangekomen en vertrokken vreemde en particuliere schepen en mindere kielen in genoemde datum, VOC: 3582: 22 February 1780.

35 Ibid. VOC 3599: 9 October 1780.

36 The goods were 600 *pikuls* of arak, 130 *pikuls* of sugar, 70 *pikul*s of alum, 70 *pikuls* of sago, 50 *pikuls* of gambir, and 22,000 pieces of *lanthesen* (from China and not sure what was this item).

37 See Appendix 11: Melaka Shipping Lists, 1780–82 and 1791–93, in Nordin Hussin, 'Melaka and Penang 1780–1830', pp. 459–480.

38 Ibid.

39 Ibid.

40 For reasons regarding the small number of Chinese ships coming to Melaka, see Leonard Blusse, *Strange Company*, pp. 95–155.

41 Copie lijsten van de aangekomen en vertrokken vreemde en particuliere schepen en mindere kielen in genoemde datum, VOC 3582: 10 March 1780.

42 Copie lijsten van de aangekomen en vertrokken vreemde en particuliere schepen en mindere kielen in genoemde datum, VOC: 3599: 29 September 1780.

43 For a detailed description of these ships, see Gerrit Knaap, *Shallow Waters, Rising Tide*, pp. 30–44.

44 The figures are taken from VOC 3582, 3625, 3599, 3625, 3961, 3940 and OIC 107. The data is compiled according to monthly incoming and outgoing ships in Melaka for the period 1780, 1781, 1782, 1791, 1792 and 1793.

45 Memoranda on Melaka 1817–1818 in SSFR Vol. 10. See also Extract letter from Governor MacAlister to the Chairman and Deputy Chairman, dated 7 November 1808, SSFR Vol 9.

46 Ibid.

47 Ibid.

48 Ibid.

49 Ibid.

50 Memorial of the inhabitants of Melaka 4 October 1826, in G/34/172; see also Appendix 11: Melaka Shipping Lists, 1780–82 and 1791–93, in Nordin Hussin, 'Melaka and Penang 1780–1830', pp. 459–480.

51 For further discussion, see Wong Lin Ken, 'Trade of Singapore, 1819–1869'.

52 See Appendix 11: Melaka Shipping Lists, 1780–82 and 1791–93, in Nordin Hussin, 'Melaka and Penang 1780–1830', pp. 459–480. See also, for example, Anthony Reid, 'A New Phase of Commercial Expansion in Southeast Asia, 1760–1850'. In Anthony Reid (ed.), *The Last Stand of Asian Autonomies: Responses to Modernity in the Diverse States of Southeast Asia and Korea 1750–1900*. London: Macmillan, 1977, pp. 57–81.

53   For further discussion, see, for example, Barbara Watson Andaya, 'Adapting to Political and Economic Change: Palembang in the Late Eighteenth and Early Nineteenth Centuries'. In Anthony Reid (ed.), *The Last Stand of Asian Autonomies*, pp. 187–215, and J. Kathirithamby-Wells, 'Siak and its changing strategies for survival, 1700–1870'. In Anthony Reid (ed.), *The Last Stand of Asian Autonomies.*

54   The figure for Sumatra is 42 per cent, which covers many places such as Batubara, Asahan, Aceh, Siak, Kampar, Indragiri etc.

55   Memoranda on Malacca 1817/1818, in SSFR Vol. 10.

56   Extract letter from Governor Macalister to the Chairman and Deputy Chairman, dated 7 November 1808, SSFR Vol 9.

57   See Table 4: Melaka's trade (excess of imports and exports) in 1828–29.

58   See Wong Lin Ken, 'The Trade of Singapore 1819–1869'.

59   Pikuls: Pikul: 122–125 lbs: Gerrit Knaap, *Shallow Waters, Rising Tide*, p. 192.

60   Ibid. See also Barbara Watson Andaya, 'Adapting to Political and Economic Change: Palembang in the Late Eighteenth and Early Nineteenth Centuries', pp. 202–209.

61   Dragon's blood: red gum or resin from some of the rattan palms, used as an astringent and for colouring varnishes, lacquers etc; see C.D. Cowan, 'Early Penang and the Rise of Singapore', p. 113.

62   Extract letter from Governor Macalister to the Chairman and Deputy Chairman, dated 7 November 1808, SSFR Vol 9.

63   See Appendix 11: Melaka Shipping Lists, 1780–82 and 1791–93, in Nordin Hussin, 'Melaka and Penang 1780–1830', pp. 459–480.

64   Ibid.

65   For a discussion on the activities of tobacco-smoking among people in Southeast Asia, see Anthony Reid, 'From Betel-chewing to Tobacco-smoking in Indonesia', *JAS*, vol. 44, No.3, 1985, pp. 529–47.

66   See Appendix 11: Melaka Shipping Lists, 1780–82 and 1791–93, in Nordin Hussin, 'Melaka and Penang 1780–1830', pp. 459–480.

67   Ibid.

68   Ibid.

69   There was a conflict between the Bugis and the Malays, supporters of the Bugis under a king and the Malay Sultan, respectively, in the Royal House of Johor-Riau. It is quite likely that on both sides there were some traders and merchants. For further discussion, see, for example, Barbara Watson Andaya, 'An examination of sources concerning the reign of Sultan Mansur Syah of Trengganu 1741–1793, with special reference to the Thufat al-Nafis', *JMBRAS*, 49, 1976, pp. 80–104; Leonard Andaya, 'The Bugis-Makassar Diasporas', *JMBRAS*, vol. 68, pt. 1, 1995, pp. 119–138; Raja Ali Haji ibn Ahmad, *The Precious Gift: Thufat al-Nafis*, (trans.) Virginia Matheson and Barbara Andaya, Kuala Lumpur: Oxford University Press, 1982.

70   See Anthony Reid, 'A New Phase of Commercial Expansion in Southeast Asia, 1760–1850'. He describes that 'the Bugis commercial centres of Riau and Selangor flourished up to the Bugis defeat of 1784', p. 65; for an earlier history of the Bugis in Selangor, see, for example, E. Netscher, 'Twee belegeringen van Malakka 1756–57 en 1784', *TBG*, vol. 13, 1864, pp. 285–361; see also Leonard Andaya, 'The Bugis-Makassar Diasporas', pp. 119–138.

71   Extract letter from Governor Macalister to the Chairman and Deputy Chairman, dated 7 November 1808, SSFR Vol 9.

72   See Table 3: Melaka's trading network and value of imports and exports, 1828–29.

73   Ibid.

74   See Appendix 11: Melaka Shipping Lists, 1780–82 and 1791–93, in Nordin Hussin, 'Melaka and Penang 1780–1830', pp. 459–480.

75   Ibid.

76   Ibid.

77   Extract letter from Governor Macalister to the Chairman and Deputy Chairman, dated 7 November 1808, SSFR Vol 9.

78 For further reference regarding this cloth, see Ruurdje Laarhoven, 'The Power of Cloth'.

79 See S. Arasaratnam, *Islamic Merchant Communities of the Indian Sub-continent in Southeast Asia;* and S. Arasaratnam, 'Chulia Muslim Merchants in Southeast Asia 1650–1800', *Maritime Trade Society and European Influence in Southeast Asia, 1600–1800,* pp. 126–143.

80 Report on the trade of the three settlements, Prince of Wales Island, Singapore and Malacca, Fort Cornwallis 29 April 1830, in SSFR vol. 162.

81 Report on the trade of the three settlements, Prince of Wales Island, Singapore and Malacca, Fort Cornwallis 29 April 1830, in SSFR vol. 162; see also T. Braddell, *Statistics of the British Possessions in the Straits of Malacca With Explanatory Notes.*

82 For further discussion on the rulings of the VOC in Batavia regarding Chinese trade to Southeast Asia, see Leonard Blusse, *Strange Company,* pp. 95–155.

83 See J. Cushman, *Fields from the Sea;* and Leonard Blusse, *Strange Company,* pp. 95–155.

84 For further discussion on the importance of Siamese (Bangkok) trade with China and Southeast Asian ports, see Anthony Reid, 'A New Phase of Commercial Expansion in Southeast Asia, 1760–1850', pp. 68–71.

85 Extract letter from Governor Macalister to the Chairman and Deputy Chairman, dated 7 November 1808, SSFR Vol 9.

86 Sappanwood, obtained from the jungle, was highly prized in all parts of the East for the fragrant scent it emits on burning.

87 Sticlac: secretion of insects obtained from the twigs and branches of trees; used either as dye or resin, C.D. Cowan, 'Early Penang and the Rise of Singapore', p. 113.

88 Camphor: champor oil: used in medicines.

89 See Table 3: Melaka's trading network and value of imports and exports, 1828–29.

90 See Carl A. Trocki, 'Chinese Pioneering', pp. 93–96.

91 Ibid. See also Carl A. Trocki, *Prince of Pirates: The Temenggongs and the Development of Johor and Singapore 1784–1885,* Singapore: Oxford University Press, 1979.

92 See, for example, Barbara Watson Andaya, *To Live As Brothers: Southeast Sumatra in the Seventeenth and Eighteenth Centuries,* Honolulu,1993, pp. 188–191; Carl A. Trocki, 'Chinese Pioneering'.

93 See Tables 2, 3, 4 and 5.

94 T.J. Newbold, *Political and Statistical account,* pp. 146–150.

95 Report on the trade of the three settlements, Prince of Wales Island, Singapore and Malacca, Fort Cornwallis 29 April 1830, in SSFR vol. 162; see also Report on the trade of the three settlements, Prince of Wales Island, Singapore and Malacca, in G/34/123.

96 A measurement for cloth which is equivalent to 20 pieces, see Garrit Knaap, *Shallow Waters, Rising Tide,* p.190.

97 P.J. Marshall, 'Private British Trade in the Indian Ocean Before 1800'. He describes how 'Indian commodities needed to be supplemented by items such as tin and pepper, collected en route to China in Sumatra or Malaya. Consequently more and more English ships called at Kedah and Selangor in western Malaya, at Trengganu on the eastern side of the Peninsular and Riau which became for a time the general mart for the junks and ships bound to China ...' pp. 297–298.

98 Report on the trade of the three settlements, Prince of Wales Island, Singapore and Malacca, Fort Cornwallis 29 April 1830, in SSFR vol. 162.

99 Ibid.

100 For a detailed discussion on the tin trade in the eighteenth century and the Dutch attempts to control the tin trade in the Straits, see Dianne Lewis, 'The Tin Trade in the Malay Peninsula During the Eighteenth Century'.

101 J. de Hullu, 'A.E. van Braam Houckgeest's memorie over Malakka en den Tin Handel Aldaar (1790)', *Bijdragen tot de Taal-Land en Volkenkunde,* 76, (1920), p. 299.

102 Ibid., pp. 299–300.

103 Dianne Lewis, 'The Tin Trade in the Malay Peninsula', pp. 67–68.

104 Ibid., p. 68.

105 See, for example, T.J. Newbold, *Political and Statistical Account of the British Settlements.* He states that, 'previous to the capture of Malacca, in 1795, no grain of any kind was permitted to be raised within the limits of the Malacca territory; thus rendering the whole of the population dependent on the island of Java for all their supplies', p. 119. See also, 'Balthasar Bort, Report of Governor Balthasar Bort on Malacca, 1678', *JMBRAS*, vol. 5 pt.1 (1927), pp. 1–232.

106 A local measurement for rice which is equivalent to 30 to 40 *pikuls* and it varies with areas and regions and one *pikul* is equivalent to 122–125 pounds. See Gerrit Knaap, *Shallow Waters, Rising Tide*, p.191–192.

107 Report on the trade of the three settlements, Prince of Wales Island, Singapore and Malacca, Fort Cornwallis 29 April 1830, in SSFR vol 162.

108 For further discussion on the increasing number of Siamese traders arriving in the Straits in the nineteenth century, see Anthony Reid and Radin Fernando (eds), 'Shipping on Melaka and Singapore as an Index of Growth 1760–1840', pp 59–84.

109 Report on the trade of the three settlements, Prince of Wales Island, Singapore and Malacca, Fort Cornwallis 29 April 1830, in SSFR vol 162.

110 Memoranda on Melaka 1817–1818 in SSFR, Vol. 10. See also Extract letter from Governor Macalister to the Chairman and Deputy Chairman, dated 7 November 1808, SSFR, Vol 9.

111 A local measurement for bulky materials such as sago and rice and one gantang is equivalent to 11.5 to 13.5 pounds. See Gerrit Knaap, *Shallow Waters, Rising Tide*, p.191–192.

112 A local measurement for bulky materials such as sugar or oil and is equivalent to 3–7 pounds. Ibid., p.191–192.

113 Report on the trade of the three settlements, Prince of Wales Island, Singapore and Malacca, Fort Cornwallis 29 April 1830, in SSFR vol 162.

114 For a good discussion of the salt trade between Java and the Straits, see Gerrit Knaap and Luc Nagtegaal, 'A forgotten Trade: Salt in Southeast Asia 1670–1813'. In Roderich Ptak and Dietmar Rothermund (eds), *Emporia, Commodities and Entrepreneure in Asian Maritime Trade, c.1400–1750*, Stuttgart: Franz Steiner Verlag, 1991, pp. 127–157.

115 Report on the trade of the three settlements, Prince of Wales Island, Singapore and Malacca, Fort Cornwallis 29th April 1830 in SSFR vol 162.

116 Ibid.

117 Ibid.

118 Kandji and Java are types of brown sugar. Jaggery is a coarse brown sugar, the product of the Jagera tree. See C.D. Cowan, 'Early Penang and the Rise of Singapore', p. 112.

119 Report on the trade of the three settlements, Prince of Wales Island, Singapore and Malacca, Fort Cornwallis 29 April 1830, in SSFR vol 162.

120 A local measurement for padi, rattan and dye-wood. For rattan is equivalent to 100 pieces. See Gerrit Knaap, *Shallow Waters, Rising Tide*, p.190.

121 Report on the trade of the three settlements, Prince of Wales Island, Singapore and Malacca, Fort Cornwallis 29 April 1830, in SSFR vol 162.

122 Beright, aangaande de Gamber derzelver planting en bewerking op Malacca door Abrahamus Couperus, onderkoopman aldaar, *Verhandelingen van het Bataviaasch Genootschap der kunsten en wetenschappen*, Tweede Deel, 1780, pp. 356–382.

123 For a good discussion on the ownership and administration of land in Melaka during the Dutch and the English period, see, K.T. Joseph, 'The Malacca Land Laws', *Federation Museums Journal*, Vol. 15 (1970), pp.129–179.

CHAPTER THREE

The Geography and Trade of Penang, 1786–1830

INTRODUCTION

PENANG, SITUATED OFF THE COAST OF KEDAH in the northern region of the Straits, was ceded to Francis Light, on behalf of the EIC, by the King of Kedah in 1786. One of the reasons why the English acquired Penang was trade.[1] The English believed that Penang was the best location to replace Benkulen, which was far from the main trading route. By the end of the eighteenth century the China tea trade was important to the English and the need for a port to break their journey between India and China became paramount to the Company. This chapter will highlight the question of how the new colony was able to tap the lucrative trade of the Malay-Indonesian archipelago although it was located on its periphery.

The discussion will begin with a short introduction on the trading network and links between the English East India Company, the English country traders and the Indian merchants from the Indian subcontinent and their connection with trade in the Straits, the archipelago and China. This will be followed by a brief discussion on the types of ships that arrived in Penang. The second part of the study will focus on the merchants and traders in Penang, their trading networks and the commodities traded.

TRADING NETWORKS AND LINKS IN THE INDIAN SUBCONTINENT

In the Indian subcontinent, Madras was the earliest English settlement to become a major Asian port, followed later by Bombay and Calcutta. From the mid-seventeenth century the three ports also served as the main centres for English country traders. Although there was strong opposition from the EIC to the activities of the English country traders, in the mid-seventeenth century there was an expansion of the latter in trade. This was partly because the majority of English country traders had established links and trading networks with many Indian merchant groups that had their own trading fleets. The relationship between the English country traders and the Indian merchants was complex. It involved questions of how trade was carried out, whether it was on land or sea, the people who provided the funds and capital, those who formed joint stocks, institutions and agencies to manage the import and export trade, the ownership of goods carried on board the ships, the types of goods imported and exported, the people involved in the trade, those who built the merchant ships and the ownership of the trading vessels. All these were part and parcel of the trading network between the English country traders and their Indian counterparts.[2]

The English merchants had their bases in either Madras or Calcutta.[3] In general, wealthy merchants, both English and Indian, had agents and proxies who roamed over a wide area transacting business on their behalf.[4] Partnership ventures among two or more individual merchants were common. For example, large partnerships were formed to invest in ships which could include not only the English at Madras but also those in Surat, Bombay and Calcutta. Therefore many rich private European and Indian merchants from the Coromandel and Bengal areas had huge fortunes, and they owned a stake in shipping either as part-owners or as financiers. John Palmer, Khwaja Wazid, the Seths and the Basaks were important financial houses that controlled and lent money to local Indians and private European merchants.[5]

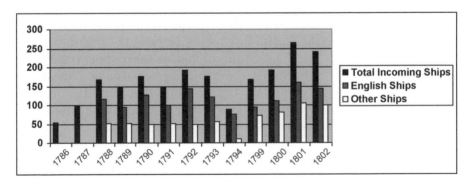

Figure 3: Incoming ships to Penang, 1788–94 and 1799–1802. *Sources*: G/34/2; G/34/3; G/34/4; G/34/5; G/34/6; George Leith, *A Short Account of the Settlement, Produce and Commerce of Prince of Wales' Island in the Straits of Malacca*, p. 89.

Many of the private English country traders who traded in the Bay of Bengal region (the Coromandel Coast, Bengal, Burma, southern Thailand, northern Sumatra and Malaya), the archipelago and China would have associated themselves with wealthy merchants from either Madras or Calcutta. These linkages, vital for their business, could be traced from the capital borrowed from various trading agencies. Some traders even travelled on vessels that belonged to trading agencies or carried commodities that belonged to these agencies, or they were partners in trade between the Indian subcontinent, the archipelago and China. In early Penang some private English traders who had resigned from the Company service to venture into trade were connected to these agency houses in Calcutta or Madras.

SHIPS ARRIVING IN PENANG AT THE END OF THE EIGHTEENTH CENTURY

Unlike Dutch-Melaka there is sketchy evidence and limited statistical data on the incoming and outgoing of ships for Penang. The earliest data on the shipping lists were collected by Francis Light in 1786 to 1794 when he was the Superintendent of the island.[6] These were followed by another document covering the years between 1799 and 1802, compiled by George Leith, the Lieutenant-Governor, during his term of office from 1800 to 1803.[7] In addition to these there is also complete data on arrivals of Malay traders or prahus to Penang, but only for the years 1786 to 1787 and 1799 to 1802.[8] However, the shipping lists compiled by Francis Light in 1786 to 1794 and the list on arrivals of Malay traders from 1786 to 1787 were by far the most detailed that the English produced in Penang. Although the shipping lists compiled by Francis Light are very detailed, they cannot match the Dutch shipping lists for Melaka. For example, the 1786 and 1787 data did not include information on the nationality of the commanders of ships. Furthermore, they did not mention the goods on board in detail. Nevertheless, the data on Penang trade are very useful as they provide a clear picture of the trends and trade networks that were developing in the early years before Penang was transformed into an important port at the northwest corner of the archipelago.

The early development of Penang's trade can be be traced from 1788, that is, two years after the port was opened. Figure 3 opposite traces initial growth over six years until 1794 and subsequent development until 1802. The shipping lists show that the number of ships coming to Penang increased over the years.[9] From the figure it can be seen that the number of incoming ships increased from 54 in 1786 to 265 in 1801. The decline in the number of incoming ships in 1794 is because the data for this year were only compiled from February to August. Similarly the number of incoming ships for the year 1786 was compiled from July to December, and for 1787 it was limited to January to July and October to December. The figure above only gives the number of incoming large vessels or ships to Penang but does not include incoming Malay prahus, so the numbers would be much higher if the latter were included. The English records did not combine both types of ships in one document. Furthermore, the data on Malay prahus were not regularly recorded and they only appeared in 1786–1787 and 1799–1802. The English records classified vessels according to size and weight. Vessels or ships more then 25 lasten (50 tons) were listed together, while prahus which had an average weight of more then 1.8 lasten or 60 *pikuls* (3.75 tons) but less than 50 tons were listed separately. Thus, Malay ships such as the banting (30 tons or 15 lasten) and the penchalang (37 tons or 18.5 lasten) were considered as prahus, while larger Malay ships such as the *jong* (125 tons or 62.5 lasten), and the *kichi* (150 tons or 75 lasten) and the *pinis* (75 tons or 37.5 lasten) were considered as large vessels.[10]

Thus the total number of incoming ships for the years 1786 to 1787 and 1799 to 1802 is very high. From 85 ships and prahus in 1786 the numbers rose to 3,569 in 1802. In just a decade Penang was able to attract more then 2,000 ships and prahus to its port. The number of incoming traders also shows a great achievement for Penang because, within a relatively short period, it was able to spread its trading network over a wide area.

Regular accounts of the number of incoming ships to Penang only show incoming vessels of 50 to 500 tons (25 to 250 lasten) which belonged to Europeans and Asian traders.[11] The largest ships to arrive at Penang were those of the English traders, with each ship averaging 275 lasten or 550 tons in weight. This was followed by the American, Danish and Portuguese traders whose ships were only slightly smaller at an average of 250 lasten (500 tons), while Asian traders mostly from the Coromandel Coast, China

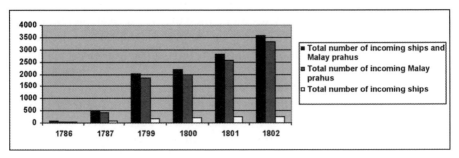

Figure 4: Total number of incoming ships and Malay prahus to Penang, 1786–87 and 1799–1802. *Sources*: G/34/2; G/34/3; G/34/4; G/34/5; G/34/6; George Leith, *A Short Account of the Settlement, Produce and Commerce of Prince of Wales' Island in the Straits of Malacca*, p. 89.

and the archipelago arrived in vessels weighing an average of 113 lasten (226 tons).[12]

In 1786 only 54 ships arrived in Penang but their numbers multiplied rapidly so that by 1782 more then 200 called in annually at the port.[13] Although some of the records did not give, in detail, the nationality of the commanders of the ships it is possible to conclude that the largest number of ships arriving at Penang brought in English traders followed by Asians and other Europeans. The most frequent arrivals were from ports in the Straits of Melaka (38 per cent) followed by ships arriving from the Indian subcontinent (35 per cent).[14] This trend continued throughout the years from 1786 to 1794 with one exception, the year 1788 when more ships arrived from the Indian subcontinental. Ports in the Straits of Melaka that had close trading relations with Penang were Pedir, Kedah, Melaka, Aceh and Selangor. Pedir, on the east coast of Sumatra and Aceh supplied Penang with pepper, betelnuts and forest products, while traders from Selangor, Kedah and Melaka brought tin and food products to Penang.

The majority of traders from ports on the Indian subcontinent came from Bengal, Bombay, Madras and Nagore. Most of them were English traders with a small number of Chulias, Moors and Portuguese. Other regional traders who arrived in Penang came from ports along the coastline facing the Bay of Bengal and ports in East Asia. From the Bay of Bengal the most important ports for Penang were Junk Ceylon, Rangoon and Pegu, and from the East Asian region traders came from China, Macao and Siam.[15]

From 1788 to 1794 there were 1,097 ships arriving at Penang and in 1799 to 1802 there were 867 ships. The highest number of traders were the English at 66 per cent (1,286 ships) followed by the Asiatic traders (Chulia, Malay,

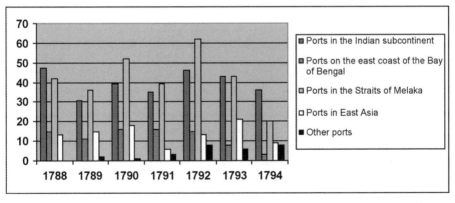

Figure 5: Incoming English ships to Penang according to ports of departure, 1788–94.
Sources: G/34/2; G/34/3; G/34/4; G/34/5; G/34/6.

Moor, Burmese and Chinese) at 19 per cent (381 ships) and the American, Portuguese, Dutch, French, Spainish and Danish traders at 15 per cent (297 ships). The volume of goods brought and carried by the English, American, Portuguese and Danish traders was larger than that of the Asiatic traders, because the Europeans had larger ships and most were long-distant traders travelling from India to China and the archipelago.

The sailing pattern of these traders was predictable. Those who came from the Indian subcontinent travelled from ports on the Coromandel Coast, such as Porto Novo, Nagore or Nagapatnam, Calcutta and Madras.[16] They arrived at Penang and later sailed to Mergui, Tenesserim, Pegu, Junk Ceylon, Melaka, Pedir, and Larut and Selangor. The long-distance traders would arrive at Penang from India and then sail on to Batavia, Siam, China and Macao.

The same period also witnessed a steady increase in the number of Malay and Bugis traders from the Straits arriving in Penang. Most of these traders travelled in prahus. In 1786, 31 prahus arrived in Penang but a year later the number had increased to 403. A decade later the number of prahus visiting Penang had increased by leaps and bounds. 1,836 prahus traded at Penang in 1799, and in 1802 the number stood at 3,328. These traders from the Straits normally brought a limited number and quantity of goods due to the size of a prahu, which could normally carry an average of 1.5 koyan (60 *pikuls*).[17] The prahus brought in forest products, for example, rattan and aromatic woods, and items such as rice, poultry, cattle, rice and paddy, and minerals such as gold dust and tin, and took away goods from India and China such as Indian cloth, salt, sugar and opium.

The majority of incoming Malay prahus were from Kedah, Perlis, Kuala Muda, Perak, Larut, Selangor, Kera and Batubara.[18] Malay traders from

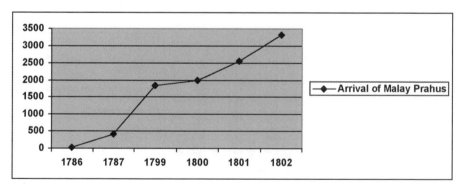

Figure 6: Arrival of Malay prahus in Penang, 1786–87 and 1799–1802. *Sources*: G/34/2; G/34/3; G/34/4; G/34/5; G/34/6; George Leith, *A Short Account of the Settlement, Produce and Commerce of Prince of Wales Island in the Straits of Malacca*, p. 91.

Larut, Perak and Selangor were important to Penang because they brought with them tin for the China tea trade.[19] Kedah, Batubara, Kera and Perlis were important suppliers of food products. One significant development to emerge from Penang's trade with the Straits region in the first decade or so of its opening was the close trading connection it forged with Pedir, on the east coast of Sumatra. Pedir and its hinterland were important producers of pepper and betelnuts and these two items were the major export earners for Penang in the earlier period.[20] However, in the late 1800s Pedir was replaced by Aceh as an important trading partner after the latter took control of northern Sumatra.[21]

MERCHANTS AND TRADERS IN PENANG

The success story of Penang's trade would be incomplete without mentioning the mercantile society which played a vital role in transforming it into an important port and trading centre. Very little is known about the backgrounds of the English merchants in early Penang. But among the pioneers largely responsible for the development and vitality of the new port and its trade were James Scott, McIntyre, Lindsay, Hutton, Roebuck, Brown, Sparran, Mackrell and Nason.[22] They were all merchants and traders who, before the founding of Penang, were based either in Bengal or the Coromandel Coast and had trading connections with places such as Junk Ceylon, Kedah, Aceh, Melaka, Pegu and Mergui. After Penang was established in 1786 they moved to the newly founded port-town.

After Penang was established, Francis Light, himself a merchant and trader who continued to engage in trade, gave his fellow merchants a free hand to determine and control trading activities on the island. They determined how trade should be conducted and this included the power to impose trade duties and taxes and decide the prices of goods imported and exported at Penang. Perhaps it was due to his own inexperience that Light decided to do this, or it could have been because of his friendship with some of them. Be that as it may, when Light died in 1796 his successor, Superintendent Major Forbes Ross Macdonald, was critical of the fact that Light had engaged in trading activities and was equally opposed to the idea that most of the trade on the island was controlled and dictated by its mercantile community. Thus very soon after he took over his new position, relations between him and the merchants deteriorated.

> Major Macdonald, on his arrival, seems to have fallen foul of the system practised by his predecessor, of being engaged in the trade of the place, whether incited thereto by the instructions of government, or by sense of duty, or by failure of the good will of the friends and

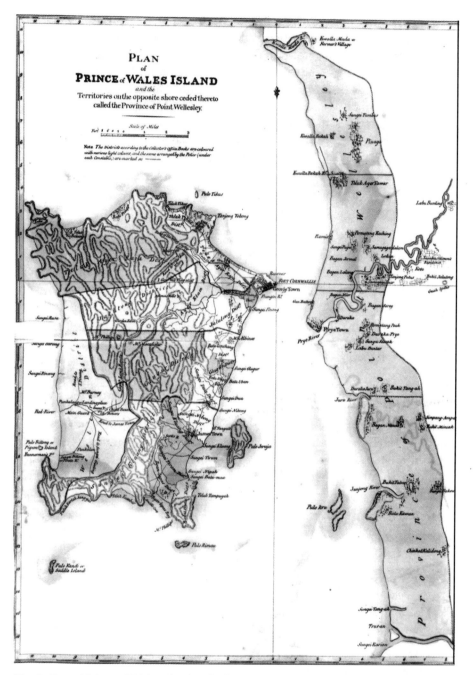

Map 9: Plan of Prince of Wales Island and adjacent coast, 1836. Courtesy of the Royal Netherlands Institute of Southeast Asian and Caribbean Studies (KITLV), Leiden (Bibl. a 58).

partners of his predecessor, it is impossible to say. No one could deny the evils of such a system, but in justice to Captain Light it must be remembered that he had some years before pointed out those evils to the government which he served, and earnestly entreated that a more liberal salary might be awarded him, to allow of his withdrawing himself from trade and devoting himself to his public duties, with a prospect of eventually securing a competence for himself. The request was not granted but no orders were ever issued to him to refrain from trade, and consequently Captain Light must be held wholly blameless, whatever the evils of the system as adduced by his successor. Major Macdonald and the mercantile community of the island very soon became hostile to each other, though the absence of any real ground of hostility, judging from the Major's own reports, raises a suspicion that the grapes must have been sour.[23]

Although these merchants were not on good terms with the administration of the island, their early contribution to its development helped Penang to get on its feet in the early years.[24]

Apart from the European merchants there were also Asian merchants and traders who helped make Penang a success. Of the Malays, two in particular, Tuanku Syed Hussain and Nakhuda Kechil, were very successful merchants. When Penang was established in 1786 the former shifted his trading base to the island and became a pioneer of the newly acquired colony. He was associated with several European merchants on the island and also in Calcutta. The Chinese towkey, Koh Lay Huan, alias Che Wan, was a prominent trader and Mahomed Syed was a Chulia merchant of great wealth.

Since Penang is in the northern part of the Straits, the majority of the early poineering traders, both European and Asian, had their trading networks linked to the coastal areas of the Bay of Bengal region. For example, most of the European merchants had their trading network with Bengal, Aceh, northern Sumatra and the Malayan peninsula. Similar patterns were followed by the Malays, Chinese and Chulia merchants. A good example of such trading connections can be seen from the trading activities of Tuanku Syed Hussain. Tuanku Syed Hussain was a wealthy merchant of Arab-Malay parentage who resided in Penang from the 1790s. He came from the Arab Aided clan and claimed to be the grandson of Sultan Jemal Syah of Aceh, who ruled Aceh between 1703 to 1726. In the 1770s Syed Hussain left Aceh for Riau where he settled down for a brief period. He then moved to Kuala Selangor before he finally settled in Penang. His wealth was based largely on his trade between Penang-Aceh-Calcutta. He was granted trading privileges in the Acehnese court including exemptions from trade duties. These privileges were given to him because of his royal descent and connections with the Aceh royal house. He was reputed to be the richest man in Penang and his connections with the Sultan of Aceh added to his prestige among the Arab and Malay population in Penang. He was so rich that even the government (EIC) asked his assistance for loans during difficult times. He had a close trading relationship with Aceh, Penang and also the Coromandel Coast and Calcutta. His association with John Palmer of Calcutta and merchants in Penang and his link with the royal family of Aceh made him a successful merchant and trader.[25] Due to his connection with the royal house of Aceh he was given trading preference there. His wealth strengthened his political and social influence in Penang. In July 1815, he offered a loan of SpD 50,000 to the Penang government when it was confronted with financial problems. On another occasion he gave a loan of SpD 30,000 to the government. It was also reported that he owned the official residence of the Governor. He became the native leader or Capitan of the Malay community, held official appointments in various government committees and was an influential personality in Penang to the extent that the government sometimes sought his assistance in matters concerning the defence of the island.[26]

European merchants and traders

Although many European merchants lived in Penang, references and documents pertaining to them are very limited. The available documents merely give information on their whereabouts and the value of their property but very few details on their trading activities. In 1793, there appear to have been four rich European trading houses in the town. They were James Scott and Company whose merchandise was valued at SpD 123,219, James Gardyne whose business was worth SpD 38,650, Thomas Pigou who owned a trading business worth SpD 5,000 and Abel Machell whose trading business was worth SpD 15,833.[27] In addition, James Scott had a total of seven trading vessels valued at SpD 131,073, James Gardyne had two valued at SpD 34,500 and Abel Machell owned one with a value of SpD 3,000.[28]

James Scott was among the most successful businessmen on the island. His trading network linked Penang and Junk Ceylon, his former base, the Coromandel Coast, Bengal, Aceh, Trengganu, Melaka and the archipelago.[29] He traded mainly in opium, tin, cloth and pepper. Tin was procured from Junk Ceylon or the Malaya Peninsula, opium from Bengal, cloth from the Coromandel Coast and pepper from Aceh and Trengganu. He also traded in Melaka for various merchandise. The main articles traded with these places were opium and Indian cloth.

However, not all European merchants were as successful as Scott. One failed merchant was James Douglas. He came to the island in 1803 as a superintendent of pilotage and harbour master of the port but later retired from the service to venture into business and trade, with disastrous results. Together with John Grant Wilson, an accountant from Calcutta, he formed a company with a paid-up capital of SpD 50,000 to carry out trading between Penang, North Sumatra and Bengal. John Grant Wilson later manipulated the business and cheated his partner, resulting in the insolvency of the company leaving the burden to Douglas to pay all debts.[30] Douglas's misfortune was made worse as a result of action taken by the notorious and corrupt police magistrate, Paul Kellner.[31] Kellner had detained his ships which were in transit to Aceh and demanded payment from the nakhoda of the ship. When the nakhoda refused to pay, Kellner forced the ship to anchor at the port and its goods were then illegally confiscated.[32]

Chulia merchants and traders

According to Arasaratnam, in the early eighteenth century, information regarding the activities of Chulia merchants was scarce and only in the later period of the eighteenth century did their activities appear in the European commercial records.[33] The earliest evidence regarding the activities of Chulia merchants in Penang indicates that most of them were from Kedah and not the Coromandel Coast, although their trading connections took them to the Indian subcontinent.[34]

> After Francis Light founded Penang, they realised that this was the port of the future and withdrew to Penang. This short transfer from Kuala Kedah to Penang gave the Chulias a head-start among all the communities settling in that port. They were able to secure some choice sites and establish themselves in a variety of commercial enterprises, ranging from the long-distance trade to Coromandel, the trade to Acheh and lower Burma, to the short haul between Penang and West Malayan ports to the very small peddling and retail on the island itself. The early ships lists of Penang show that Chulia vessels of about 200 tons and over were sailing in round trips from Cuddalore, Porto Novo or Nagore to Penang, Syriam, Ujong Salang and Acheh, trading in the commodities of textiles, tin, and pepper with sugar and betel nuts as the commodities appearing newly in this trade. Within ten years, the Chulias were one of the two largest communities settled in the area of the port.[35]

Of the Chulia merchants who came directly from India, Mohammed Syed and his partners, Mucktoon Saib, Boojoo Mohammed and Ismail Mohammed, all Pulicat merchants, were among those who became wealthy from their trading activities between the island and the Coast. Mohammed Syed and his partner came from the coast of Coromandel.[36] Their principal business was Indian cloth but they also traded in other goods from India. They arrived in Georgetown in 1787 and settled in the town as merchants and businessmen. From 1787 to 1814 their trading business was based on the island, trading between Penang and the Coromandel Coast. They owned brick shops at Chulia Street in Georgetown and most of the goods traded from the island to India and vice-versa were kept in the godowns and their premises. In 1814 their business revenue from Madras, Pulicat and the island was valued at SpD 112,000. This amount did not include the piece goods that were kept in their godowns, shops and bazaar, which were claimed to have a value of SpD 35,000. They also owned four brick shops with a value of SpD 77,000.[37] However, in 1814 all these properties were destroyed in a fire after which they applied for loans from the government to rebuild their business.[38] Yet, not much information can be obtained on them after the fire incident and some sources indicate that they migrated back to their homeland.[39]

The activities of these merchants and traders such as Mohammed Syed and his partners were among the few Indian merchant groups able to continue their activities in overseas trade in the late eighteenth and early nineteenth centuries.[40] Arasaratnam argues that these Chulia merchants sustained their trading activities until the late eighteenth century only because they were independent traders who did not receive or associate with any of the big financial houses in Bengal. The Chulias also 'continued to operate in specifically Asian commercial sectors, trading in commodities that were wholly dependent on supply and demand in the independent states of South and Southeast Asia. Thus, their relationships and ties were with these independent Asian states and tended to be continuous and long-lasting. Their operations were across a broad spectrum, from powerful merchant-magnates to itinerant peddlers and vendors'.[41]

Malay and Bugis merchants and traders

Few names of Malay traders appear in the documents and details of their business and trade are scarce. The number of Malay traders is hard to establish although there was a bazaar in Penang that belonged to, and was managed by, them. The name Nakhuda Kechil appears in the documents as a trader who had originally come from Kedah and later became the headman of the Malay bazaar for traders from Kedah. It was likely that his trading connections were between Penang and Kedah.[42] The commodities handled by him included rice, poultry, paddy and cattle.[43] Since Penang is situated off the coast of Kedah, there was a close trading network between the town and Kedah with most of the trade consisting of food products from Kedah in return for opium and cloth from India.[44]

Additionally, there was a significant trade between the island and Makassar and the Eastern archipelago, conducted by Bugis traders. They came in large numbers to the island, stopping in various Malay ports in the archipelago during their journey.[45] However, their names and their leaders are unknown. One name that came up in the documents is Haji Khussin, who owned property in the town but whose origin is not clearly known and whose name does not sound Bugis.[46] As the number of Bugis traders and merchants trading in Penang increased, many settled in a small town on the Penang River.[47] In 1800, the majority of the Bugis who came to trade and settle in Penang were from Borneo and the Celebes. They were commonly considered as Malays although their language was quite distinct. In a report, George Leith described the Bugis as 'bold, independent and enterprising, make good soldiers and if treated with kindness are attached and faithful'.[48] He also mentioned that the Bugis who had settled in Penang were mostly found in a small town on the Penang river and that their numbers fluctuated according to trading seasons.

The English had always admired the tradings skills of the Bugis. In fact, they had a preference for the Bugis traders who were encouraged to trade in Penang.[49] They even attempted to stop the Bugis from trading with Melaka.[50] According to the English, the Bugis were excellent and trustworthy traders compared to the Chinese and Chulias, who were considered shrewd and not to be trusted.[51]

While the main goods brought to Penang by Malays and Bugis traders consisted of food, forest products and minerals (gold and tin), they also traded in slaves. However, the exact numbers brought in by them are not known, although in 1792 they brought as many as 46 slaves to Penang to the value of SpD 1,840.[52] Nine slaves were brought into Penang in 1790 while in 1791 the number was seven. However, after 1792 no reports were made on the slave trade of the island.[53] Since the Eastern archipelago was known to be the main supplier of slaves to Melaka, they also could have been supplying slaves to Penang.[54]

Although traders from the Eastern archipelago were usually associated with trading slaves to the island, very little information is available about this trade. However, the records show that between 1786 and 1794 there was slave trading involved and that slaves were brought in from as far as the African coast of Mozambique. The shipping lists of Penang of these years reveal that of the three ships that arrived from Mozambique with full loads of slaves, one was owned by a Portuguese, another by a Moor and the third was owned by an English trader. The earlier two ships did not list down the number of slaves and other details but the third ship, *Ravenworth*, which arrived in June, 1787 brought 59 male slaves, 50 female slaves and 17 underaged children belonging to these slaves.

Chinese merchants and traders

Penang attracted Chinese merchants and traders right from the start and some of the early arrivals came from Kedah rather than directly from China. Although little is known about their trading activities, it could be assumed that those who came from Kedah would have already established contacts with ports in the Straits or in the Bay of Bengal region. At the same time, their presence in Penang would have opened the opportunity for some to trade between Penang and Kedah. One such trader by the name of Chewan, alias Koh Lay Huan, migrated from Kedah and still had family in that state so that it is probable that he traded between Penang and Kedah.[55] As he owned an opium farm on the island, he probably also exported opium to the Kingdom of Kedah. He was also known to have traded with Aceh, a connection which brought him some notoriety during the period after Jauhar al-Alam was forced to step down from his throne when the sultanate faced a succession struggle between the royal house of Aceh and Tuanku Syed Hussain.[56] The civil war that followed appears to have split the Penang mercantile community. Chewan, who had been given the trading preference by the disposed king of Aceh and who, in turn, gave assistance to the latter when he visited Penang, was seen as supporting the side opposed to Syed Hussain, who supported his son in the succession struggle.[57]

> The involvement of Koh on the side of Jauhar al-Alam indicated the beginning of a split in opinion within the Penang mercantile community over the civil war in Aceh. It was a division referred in Petrie's minute of 28 July 1814, in which he spoke of the lack of consensus among Penang merchants in response to the Sultan's introduction of commercial regulations. This split arose because some merchants who already enjoyed trading ties with the Sultan hoped to benefit further from the new regulations. They, therefore, did not raise objections to the regulations. Koh and several well-known Europeans did not sign the petition of 23 July 1814 against the Sultan's regulations. Koh could even have been part of a merchant group that was in competition with Syed Hussein and his associates.[58]

Another Chinese family whose head arrived in Penang in the 1820s was in later years to have extensive trading connections with Junk Ceylon, Kedah and southern Thailand. This was the Khaw family whose head, Khaw Soo Cheang, a migrant from Xiamen, China, started work as a labourer before he engaged in several kinds of business such as planting oranges and fruits and vegetable peddling.[59] Subsequently, after acquiring some wealth, he managed to purchase land and started his trading business within the island and the peninsula. Then he went to southern Thailand in order to start a trading base at Ranong. It was believed that he had business and family connections with the Captain of the Chinese in Penang, Chewan or Koh Lay Huan and also with the local Siamese chief, Na Nakhons, at Ranong. These connections helped his business relations with the Chinese in Penang and in Southern Thailand.

> [That] relationship would tie Soo Cheang back into the Penang Chinese and point to his inclusion in a network of other Hokkien Chinese. ... This connection would have given Khaw Soo Cheang an edge over others as he sought to establish himself as a political figure on the west coast. As it turned out, Soo Cheang's alliance with the Na Nakhons in the middle decades of the nineteenth century helped him consolidate his position and seize important commercial opportunities, mostly notably the regional tax monopoly, at the expense of competing interests.[60]

Since there was a profitable trade between southern Thailand and Penang, he decided to invest more money in procuring more trading vessels for trade between these two areas. One of his main trading items was tin as he had invested in the mining industry in Southern Thailand.[61] In general, it is hard to trace the activities of Chinese merchants in Penang in the period under study, but as Chinese traders were found in Melaka and other parts of Southeast Asia, it could be assumed that they would also have traded from Penang. Unfortunately, only when a problem occurred in which they were involved do they merit a mention in the documents. Thus, in view of the fact that there are few references to them, it could be assumed that they carried out their trading activities in a legitimate manner following the pattern of the other traders.

However, in 1828, the attention of the administration was drawn to an illegal trade in slaves conducted by some Chinese merchants who normally traded in cloth with some native ports in Sumatra.[62] In June of that year, a Chinese junk carrying 80 female minors was impounded on arrival in Penang from the West coast of Sumatra.[63] It turned out that the girls had been procured from Pulau Nias and were to be sold to various Chinese merchants in the town. The junk had been searched following an investigation which exposed that a racket in slave trading was still being carried out despite the trade being banned since 1807. The investigation had initially been conducted because of a complaint made by a Catholic clergyman, Mr Boucho. During the course of the inquiry, it was disclosed that young girls brought illegally into Penang in Chinese junks had become slaves as a result of coercion, and some were working in Chinese brothels as prostitutes. A check of all Chinese junks in the port revealed that three vessels had been trading slaves from the archipelago to Penang. When the slaves were interrogated, one of them, Nahao, who was regarded as the most intelligent of the Nias girls, revealed that the junk in which she travelled took more than 80 people on board to be sold as slaves. According to her, from Nias the junk had sailed to various Malayan ports on the West coast where most of the slaves were sold, and then on to Aceh before arriving at Penang with 16 girls. Of the 16 slaves left 13 had been sold while the remainder were still with the Chinese merchants.[64]

Obviously, the illegal trade had been going on for some time and as on earlier occasions, the Chinese merchants who brought the Nias slaves to Penang in 1828 had not reported or explained the reason for the arrival of the girls to the authorities, as was required by law. When confronted with their crime, they argued that the girls brought in were neither slaves nor servants but were to be their wives once they reached adulthood. However, the authorities found that most of the girls brought in were working in brothels and some had been sold as slaves in the town and concluded that the Chinese merchants involved were intentionally grooming minors from Nias to be slaves, who were later sold illegally.[65]

During the inquiry, one of the girls reported that three Chinese junks (*Khung Joo*, *Soan Sing* and *Khim Ee*) had landed at Pulau Nias where the girls were procured in exchange for blue cloth. One of the junks, *Khung Joo*, had traded 70 to 80 slaves at various ports. Eight of the slaves were sold in Penang and four were transferred onto the junk *Soan Sing*. The inquiry did not uncover the exact number of slaves carried by the *Soan Sing* from Pulau Nias, but it did find out that five slaves were brought to Penang and one girl died on board during the journey. The third junk, *Khim Ee*, had 15 slaves on board when it left Nias, of whom 10 had been disposed of at ports on the Malay coast before it arrived in Penang with the two remaining slaves.[66]

By the time the junks arrived in Penang after shedding most of their human cargo at ports along the route, only 19 slaves remained on board. Sixteen of them were traced by the authorities during their investigation to a house belonging to a merchant named Sim Tikloco, while three others were not found. The inquiry also discovered four other women and a little girl in the house. All the girls admitted that they were forced to work as prostitutes during their short stay in the house. It was also discovered that all the girls came from poor homes and did not appear to profess any religion. The three nakhodas of the Chinese junks and the owners of the vessels were than arrested and taken into custody at the police station and charged with slave trafficking.[67]

The investigation also discovered that most of the girls were content to live with their Chinese masters and refused to be sent home. One woman named Kafeeha, who lived with nakhoda Khung Too, was happy with him and had no intention of deserting him. Although the girls who had been in Penang for a while and the minors who arrived on the Chinese junks refused to leave their masters, the nakhodas of the three junks were still sentenced by the session court for illegal slave trading activities. The owner of the junks was also detained in connection with the slave trade and all the Nias girls and minors arrested in the Chinese junks were placed under the custody of Revd. Mr Boucho.[68]

From the few examples given of the legal activities of the Chinese traders, it could be concluded that they conducted their trade from Penang mostly with the west coast of the peninsula, north Sumatra and the southern Thailand region. They would have carried manufactured goods from Penang to the ports in the Straits and the southeastern section of the Bay of Bengal and brought back food, jungle products and tin.

The 'Chinese century' was clearly an important era in Penang because following the administration's encouragement to the Chinese to settle on the island, some among the community engaged in trade between Penang and other ports around it while others ventured into business such as revenue farming and retail trade. Some also opened up lands for agricultural plantations. In addition, many Chinese coolies worked in the pepper and betel nut plantations in Penang and skilled and semi-skilled men filled jobs in the servicing sector of the economy. In time, some rich Penang Chinese ventured into the tin mining industries in southern Thailand and the Malay states.

PENANG'S TRADE AND TRADING NETWORK 1786–1830

Penang, like Melaka, imported goods from abroad and then re-exported them to various places.[69] Little is known about the commodities that were imported to and exported from Penang in its early years. However, by the end of the eighteenth century the major goods imported by Penang came from the Indian subcontinent, China, northern Sumatra and the Malayan peninsula and were comprised of Indian piece goods such as Indian cloth, opium, pepper, betelnuts, rice, tobacco, oil and ghee, tin, silk, liquor, salt and various items, including products from Europe.[70] Exports from the island were mainly the imported goods, which comprised of Indian cloth, opium, tin, betelnuts and pepper.[71]

Six years after its foundation a detailed report was done on Penang's imports. The documents reveal that the island had close trading connections with Bugis and Malay traders who acted as the main carriers or conveyors of goods to Penang and out of it to ports in the northern half of the Straits of Melaka.[72] In 1792, the major goods brought to the island by these native traders were gold dust, bird's nests, tin, Bugis cloth, rice, pepper, sulphur, aromatic woods and rattan.[73] The main exports of Penang to the native ports of the Straits were opium,[74] Indian piece goods, Spanish currency, Bugis cloth, raw silk, sticlac[75] and cotton.[76] The trade pattern was therefore similar to that of Melaka except that while the old port-town captured the markets of the southern end of the Straits, Penang was gradually attracting traders from its northern sector. Unfortunately, there are few details on exports and imports with other major trading partners such as the Coromandel Coast, Bengal and China but, as the nature of the trade would not have differed from that seen in Melaka, it could be assumed that the major imports from the Coromandel Coast and Bengal were Indian cloth, opium, grains, salt, cotton, aromatic woods, oil and tobacco; and chinaware, torches and other manufactured items, in small quantities, from China.[77] The main attraction that China held for the European traders, especially the English, was its tea, which had a growing market in Europe but was not a major commodity for the archipelago.

Table 6 opposite illustrates the main goods imported to and re-exported from Penang by Malay traders from Aceh, the Malaya peninsula and the archipelago. From this table, it is evident that Malay traders mainly exported gold dust (17.11 per cent), bird's nest (14.60 per cent), tin (12.29 per cent), Bugis cloth (12.14 per cent), rice and paddy (9.33 per cent), and they mainly imported from Penang opium (54.78 per cent), piece goods/Indian cloth (21.39 per cent), currency in Spanish dollars (8.9 per cent) and Bugis cloth (2.15 per cent). As can be seen from the figures above, Penang had an import deficit of SpD 92,880.35. All of Penang's exports consisted of goods that were imported from abroad, such as opium, Indian cloth and specie (Spanish currency). Specie was in great demand by Malay traders from the Straits and the archipelago.

In its early years Penang relied heavily on the supply of food from abroad. Rice was therefore an important item of trade which was brought mainly by the native traders. In 1792 it constituted more than 7 per cent of the value of all goods brought in by these traders to Penang. Although paddy was grown on the island, this was not sufficient to meet the needs of a growing population. Penang's dependence on food from outside created a crisis in its early years when its major supplier, Kedah, threatened to stop sending rice due to unresolved political differences between the Kingdom and the administration in Penang.[78] But in later years and with the increase in the island's population, supplies were also obtained from Burma and Bengal.

In 1792, gold dust was the major item brought in by Malay traders, at 17.11 per cent of the total value of Penang's imports from these traders.

Table 6: Main imports and exports by Malay traders to Penang in 1792

Export items	Value (SpD)	%	Import items	Value (SpD)	%
Gold dust	38,422	17.11	Opium	173,880	54.78
Bird's nest	32,804	14.60	Piece goods	67,920	21.39
Tin	27,615	12.29	Specie (Sp. currency)	28,251	8.90
Bugis Cloth	27,280	12.14	Bugis Cloth	6,850	2.15
Rice and Paddy	17,775	9.33	Sticlac	4,350	1.37
Pepper	10,665	4.74	Chinese torches	3,480	1.09
Sulphur	10,533	4.69	Raw silk	4,540	1.43
Specie (Sp. currency)	9,250	4.11	Cotton	4,050	1.27
Rattan	8,825	3.93	Others	24,093	7.60
Algewood	8,825	3.93			
Piece goods	2,280	1.01			
Java tobacco	4,285	1.90			
Dammar	2,516	1.12			
White betelnut	2,487	1.10			
Others	17,770	7.90			
Total	224,534	100.00	Total	317,414	100.00

Source: *JIA*, 1850, vol. iv, p. 658.

Most of the gold dust came from the interior of Sumatra and the Malaya peninsula and Borneo. For as long as gold dust from the Malaya peninsula had been a commodity, its outlet was Melaka, to which it was brought from the interior. The gold dust from the peninsula which found its way to Penang was usually conveyed by Bugis traders who traded from all over the archipelago, including the principal gold producing areas or outlets, such as Borneo, Sumatra and Melaka.[79] A similar situation was seen in relation to Penang's import of bird's nests (14.60 per cent). The major bird's nest producing areas were Borneo and Junk Ceylon. Again, Malay and Bugis traders brought bird's nest to Penang from these places, which was then exported to China where it was a delicacy and therefore had a ready market.[80]

The next most important commodity brought in by the native traders was tin (12.29 per cent), which came mostly from the Malaya peninsula and the island of Bangka. Although the tin trade was monopolized by the Dutch at Melaka, Penang still managed to overcome the Dutch restrictions through smuggling activities and the Malay traders. Tin from Bangka was also brought by Bugis traders. The smuggling activities involved in the tin trade as well as the role of the native traders in conveying the tin to Penang is described by Cowan in the following terms:

> Trade with the Eastward was handicapped by Penang's position in the North of the Straits of Malacca, which made it necessary for the native prows to run the gauntlet of the pirates who swarmed in the Straits, and of the Dutch cruisers from Malacca, which endeavoured to force all passing native trade into that port unless in possession of a licence from the Dutch authorities. Nevertheless Dutch monopolies, especially the tin monopoly treaties with the native states, and the low prices they forced on the Banka and Selangor tin producers, led to a good deal of smuggling. By 1790 indeed, the Dutch at Malacca considered the English Company their masters in the tin trade of the Straits, but were prevented by the authorities at Batavia from raising their prices or lowering their port dues.[81]

Tin was a vital commodity for the English traders, whose desire to capture the lucrative tea trade in China meant that they had to find a commodity that could be exchanged or otherwise suffer a bullion drain. Thus, the role of the native traders was vital in the tin trade at least in the early years when the Dutch were still able to control the trade.

Although Indian cloth had for centuries found a ready market in the archipelago, Bugis cloth was also an important item in the cloth trade in the region. Bugis cloth was introduced to Penang by the Bugis traders from Makassar and the Eastern archipelago, though the volume of Bugis cloth exported was smaller compared to Indian cloth. It is difficult to assess the difference in price between the two types of cloth. Nevertheless, the value of Indian cloth was greater, as was its popularity, since it came in various forms and quality.[82] Some of the Indian cloth did not come directly to Penang from India but was brought in by Malay traders who had picked them up from ports in the Straits that had been visited by English country traders and Indian traders who came from the Indian subcontinent. However, the amount of Indian cloth brought in this manner was small (1.01 per cent) compared to Bugis cloth (12.14 per cent).

The native traders were also important in the pepper trade. The major suppliers of pepper to Penang were Aceh and Trengganu.[83] Due to the high demand for pepper in the markets in Europe, Penang in the early years after its opening made attempts to encourage the production of pepper. In the first two decades of Penang's existence, the enterprise was still in its infancy and the yields were too small for the purpose of export.[84] The jungle in the hinterland was still being cleared and the administration was trying its best to convince the new settlers, especially the Chinese and Europeans, to cultivate pepper, clove and nutmeg. The process was naturally slow as it took more than one year for the ground to be cleared. Furthermore, there was a short supply of labour in the newly acquired colony. Thus Penang had to rely on pepper brought in by traders. As can be seen, import from native traders brought SpD 10,665 worth of pepper to Penang in 1792.

One of the main contributions of the native traders to Penang's trade was their role in collecting a range of forest products such as bird's nest, rattan, gharuwoods, elephant's tusks, dammar, sapanwood and sulphur from ports in Sumatra and the Malayan peninsula and transporting them to the island for re-export to the Indian subcontinent and China. Some products such as sticlac and goods with medicinal properties, such as trepang, which they brought, in fact, went to ports within the Straits as these were found in some areas but not in others in the region. Thus native traders did not only bring in, from the archipelago, commodities whose ultimate destination was either India or China, but were also involved in a revolving trade chain within the Straits of Melaka.

In 1792, the main exports of Penang to Aceh, Kedah and the archipelago consisted of opium (54.78 per cent), Indian piece goods (21.39 per cent), specie or Spanish currency (8.9 per cent), Bugis cloth (2.15 per cent) and raw silk (1.43 per cent). Opium became the main item carried by Malay traders from Penang. Although between 1790 to 1793 these traders took away 105 to 483 chests of opium from Penang, the report did not specify where the opium was taken to except to say that it was exported to 'the surrounding areas'.[85] There is some indication that opium went to most ports in the Straits.

The second most important item bought by Malay traders at Penang was Indian piece goods/Indian cloth from the Coromandel Coast and Bengal, which, like opium, went to most ports in the Straits. In fact, cloth in general constituted a big item bought by native traders at Penang. Despite the popularity and availability of Indian cloth, Bugis cloth remained marketable in the region adjacent to Penang such as Aceh and the northern part of the peninsula, probably because it was cheaper yet distinctive.

A clearer picture is obtained of commodities imported by Penang in the early nineteenth century; however, the amount or value of each item was not given.[86] Nevertheless, an analysis can be made of the most important commodities traded between Penang and the archipelago. Opium, rice/grains, Indian piece goods, pepper, gold dust and tin remained the main imports of Penang. Most of these commodities were imported from the

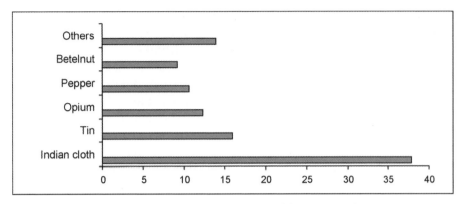

Figure 7: Percentage of goods imported to and exported from Penang in 1806. *Source*: T. Braddell, *Statistics of the British Possessions in the Straits of Malacca, Penang Gazette*, January 1861, p.5.

Coromandel Coast, Bengal, Bombay and the archipelago, while tea, sugar, paper, Chinaware and raw silk came mostly from China. Trade trends in the early nineteenth century had not changed to any significant degree from the situation in the early 1790s. However, the increasing demand for tin meant that more tin was being extracted from tin producing areas. In the earlier period the supply mostly came from the Malaya peninsula but Bangka and Junk Ceylon soon became important sources of the mineral.

By the early nineteenth century, Penang was acting as an entrepot for traders from Sumatra, the archipelago, China and India. In 1803–04, most of the Indian cloth was exported to Sumatra and the archipelago.[87] There was a high demand for opium in Sumatra, Trengganu, Java, Borneo, Celebes, Moluccas and China and, in addition to opium, commodities such as cotton, rattan, betelnut, pepper and tin were also imported by China. The commodities brought by traders to Bengal, Coromandel and Bombay consisted of pepper, tin, betelnut and gold dust.

By 1806, a clearer picture of the value of each individual item of import and export began to emerge. However, the documents do not give a detailed account of the sources of the commodities. They only give a summary of the value of imported and exported items. Since imports and exports were treated as one and the same thing and not as separate entities in determining value, it is difficult to determine the exact value of either imports or exports. But the fact that the English authorities presented the data in this manner indicates that Penang's imports were mostly re-exported and were very rarely aimed at the home market.

Figure 7 above shows that the major imports and exports of the island were Indian cloth, tin, opium, pepper, and betelnut. Again, the 1806 list of commodities imported and exported showed that little had changed since the 1790s. The major imported and exported goods did not change and Indian cloth, tin and opium remained the main items. Commodities appearing for the first time were betelnut and pepper, which by then were being produced locally but were also brought in from Aceh. Other minor changes were in commodities such as gold dust, bird's nests and Bugis cloth, which had earlier been Penang's major imports from the Malay and Bugis traders but which were now classified as small commodities and listed under 'others'. Thus from a situation in which many items were important to Penang's trade, by the middle of the first decade of the nineteenth century, a few items, namely, tin, Indian cloth and opium, dominated the trade. Of the three, most of the tin and a substantial quantity of opium were destined for China, while Indian cloth and opium remained important to the overall trade of the Straits and archipelago. Other small items, which appeared in the 1806 list of imported and exported commodities, were European goods, including iron, steel and textiles. Although in 1792 Penang sold iron and nails to Malay traders, there was no information on where these items came from so that it was hard to establish whether the nails and iron were brought by European traders from Europe or from the Indian subcontinent. However, European textile was a new commodity which first appeared, in small quantities, in the region in the early nineteenth century following the start of industrialization in England in the late eighteenth century.

From 1809 to 1818, while the main imports and exports of Penang – opium, tin, Indian cloth – remained unchanged, more European articles (textiles, iron and steel) and Chinese luxury goods (silk and chinaware) were finding their way to the region. At the same time, the increase in pepper and betelnut reflected the increase in the production of these agricultural items on the island. In 1812–13, there was an increase in the import and export of opium from Penang, with most of it going to Aceh.[88] This is probably because Penang's ties with Aceh were getting stronger and the latter had become an important distributor of opium for the northern region of Sumatra. By the second decade of the nineteenth century it became clear that Penang's fortunes were closely tied to the northern region of the Straits and the Indian subcontinent. Cowan observed that the healthiest branch of Penang's activities in 1815 was its trade, mainly with countries in its immediate vicinity, the states of the Malay peninsula and northern Sumatra, Burma and Siam, and that the island's main source of wealth was its entrepot trade.[89]

By Cowan's account, Penang was a flourishing port in 1815. Figure 8 overleaf shows Penang's position in terms of its imports and exports from 1806 to 1817. From 1809 to 1812 Penang's trade increased. However, for

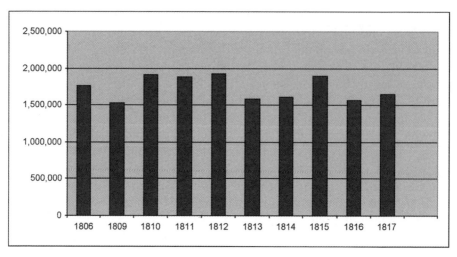

Figure 8: Penang's imports and exports, 1806–17 (in Spanish dollars). *Sources*: T. Braddell, *Statistics of the British Possessions in the Straits of Malacca*, *Penang Gazette*, January 1861, p.5, and Document no. 65, The Collector to the Secretary to Government, Prince of Wales Island, 28 December 1818, in C.D. Cowan, 'Early Penang and the Rise of Singapore', *JMBRAS*, Vol. 23, Part 2, 1950, p.86.

several years after that it registered some instability, going down in 1813, improving the following year and then slowing down again. But the movements in both directions were only slight, with the overall value of trade staying within the range of 1.5 to 2 million Spanish dollars. Thus it could be said that from 1806 to 1817, Penang's trade registered a steady growth, indicating that there had been no substantial change in the trend and pattern of intra-Asian commercial activities. Penang's import and export of opium increased throughout the 12 years but the import and export of Indian articles (Indian cloth) decreased. The English more and more dependent on opium to pay for tin and tea, also provided competition for Indian cloth by bringing in cloth from England. Tin, however, remained stable with only a small drop in 1812 and 1817–18, reflecting the steady demand for the commodity throughout the period.

Another clear pattern to emerge in this period was the close relations between Penang and Aceh. Indeed, Penang's chief trading partner was Aceh (see Figures 9 and 10). Most of Penang's export of Indian cloth and opium went to Aceh and her major import from Aceh consisted of pepper and betelnut. Although between 1806 and 1812 Penang's trade with Aceh increased steadily, from 1813 it began to decline. This was due to two reasons, namely, the political upheavel in Aceh because of the war of succession and because Java and the other Dutch Islands in the archipelago were under British rule.[90] As a result many traders from the Indian subcontinent and the

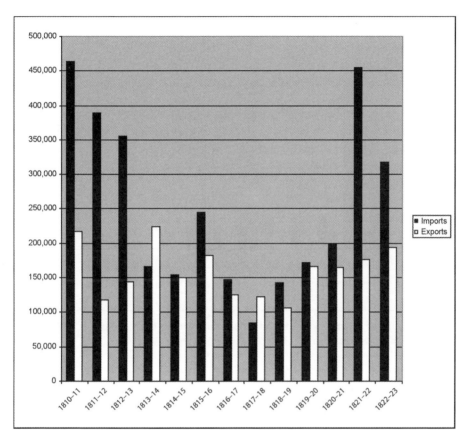

Figure 9: Penang's imports and exports with Aceh, 1810–23 (in Spanish dollars). *Sources:* Document no. 65, The Collector to the Secretary to Government, Prince of Wales Island, 28 December 1818 and Document no. 119, Minute by the Malay translator on the trade of Acheen, Fort Cornwallis, 15 March 1825, in C.D. Cowan, "Early Penang and the Rise of Singapore", *JMBRAS,* Vol. 23, Part 2, 1950, pp.86 and p. 153–158.

archipelago preferred to trade at Batavia rather than at Penang. Thus it is evident that the slight instability shown in Penang's trade between 1813 and 1817, as presented in Figure 8 opposite, was largely related to the situation in Aceh, its main trading partner.

As Aceh was very important to Penang's well-being, a closer look at the trade relations between the two ports will be attempted here. We have seen that political instability in Aceh in the second decade of the nineteenth century had repercussions on Penang's trade. The civil war in Aceh had resulted in the decline of trade and Penang was in short supply of pepper and betelnut for ships going to India and China.[91] In this period, Penang's

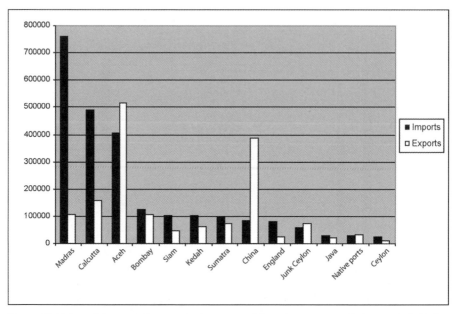

Figure 10: Value of Penang's imports and exports with various ports and places, 1828–29 (in Spanish dollars). *Source:* SSFR, Vol. 162.

export of pepper fluctuated also because of the state of the market in China, Europe, and India, but because Penang's main supplier of pepper was Aceh, the civil war there created an unexpected shortage.[92] The Aceh situation also affected the opium trade, as there was a decline in the volume imported into Penang between 1813 and 1818 following disruption to Aceh's trade. Figure 9 overleaf illustrates the trend and value of trade between Penang and Aceh. The value of Penang's export to Aceh remained in surplus except for 1813–14 and 1818–17 when it was in deficit of more than SpD 58,000 and SpD 37,000 respectively. Although the civil war raged on almost throughout the 1810s, and the Penang administration discouraged trade between the two ports, it was still carried out, albeit on a smaller scale by the Chinese merchants from Penang.

The internal conflict in Aceh had its origin in the struggle for the throne in that kingdom between the deposed king, Jauhar al-Alam, and Saif al-Alam. The latter was the son of Tuanku Syed Hussain, of the royal house of Aceh, who, as mentioned earlier, had settled in Penang and established himself as a wealthy merchant and leader of the Malay community there. Jauhar al-Alam's struggle against Saif al-Alam was boosted by the support of Chewan (Koh Lay Huan), a wealthy Chinese merchant and revenue farmer in Penang and other Chinese from Penang.[93] There were reports to indicate that Jauhar al-Alam had received a large sum of money from Chewan when he visited Penang, and it is likely that there was a continuation of such financial support.[94] This support appeared to have allowed these Chinese merchants to continue their trading activities in Aceh in areas that were sympathetic to the deposed king. Thus, the situation was mutually beneficial for both parties. Trade was vital to generate the revenue required by Jauhar al-Alam for his struggle while for the Chinese merchants it allowed them to continue their trading activities. The Penang administration's ban on trade with Aceh affected the European companies most as they abided by the ruling, whereas the Chinese and other local traders were more inclined to circumvent it.[95]

Penang's trade appeared to have steered a steady course in the 1820s despite the opening of Singapore, although with the latter's presence there was no question that it could, in the long term, become a more important international port. The fact that the British looked for another port in the Straits, which led to the founding of Singapore shows that they were aware of Penang's limitations. Nevertheless, as events were to prove, Penang succeeded in maintaining its position and role as the collecting and distributing centre in the northern region of the Straits of Melaka.

The figures for Penang's trade in 1828–29 show this role. These figures, which represent the most detailed account of the island's trade, show that Penang's trading partners were Calcutta, Madras, Bombay, England, China, Java, Ceylon, the Coast of Tenasserim, Aceh, Deli, Kedah and other native ports.[96] Furthermore Penang's report on trade in 1828–29 also shows that there was an increase in Penang's volume of trade as compared to the figures in 1806 to 1817. The value of import in Spanish dollars in 1828–29 was 2,394,006 and the value of export was SpD 1,625,830. Figure 10 illustrates the value of imports and exports in 1828–29 with Penang's major trading partners. It was only in this report that the commodities are clearly listed separately showing the goods that were imported and exported and the ports from which the goods came and the destination of goods exported from Penang.

As stated earlier, the major imports of Penang in the 1780s through to the early 1800s were cloth, opium and pepper. The same trend also appeared in the 1828–29 statistics. In 1828–29, 35.92 per cent of Penang's imports were piece goods from India, which was Indian cloth. This was followed by opium (14.78 per cent), pepper (7.98 per cent) and rice (7.02 per cent) respectively. The major exports of Penang in 1828–29 comprised Indian cloth (16.49 per cent), opium (15.70 per cent), pepper (10.67 per cent), betelnut (9.01 per cent) and tin (9.01 per cent).[97] This confirms that Penang had served as an important collecting and distributing centre for the north-western part of the archipelago. The commodities imported and exported had not changed much from the early period. Indian cloth was still on top of the list of commodities imported from India, followed by pepper, rice and betelnut.

Thus, at the end of the period under study, Penang had established itself as a player in the intra-Asian trade. However, due to the presence of Singapore, which had become the main centre for that trade in Southeast Asia, and its location at the northern end of the Straits, its role was confined to serving the northern section of the Straits of Melaka as well as the regions facing the Bay of Bengal.

TYPES OF COMMODITIES IMPORTED
AND EXPORTED BY PENANG

Cloth was a very important commodity in Penang's trade. As we have seen, Penang traded in Indian, Bugis, English and a small amount of Chinese cloth. Indian cloth came mostly from Gujarat (Surat), Coromandel and Bengal, while Bugis cloth, produced mostly in Makassar, was brought to Penang mostly by Bugis traders based in the Straits. English cloth was first introduced to the archipelago in the early nineteenth century with the purpose of penetrating the monopoly of the Indian cloth market.[98] However, it received a poor reception as the quality was inferior, so that when first introduced much was left unsold. On the other hand, Indian cloth was of a high quality, came in many colours and was of several varieties, such as cotton, silk and voile.

In 1828–28 the majority of Indian cloth that arrived in Penang came from Madras (80 per cent), and Calcutta (10 per cent). This item was distributed to the surrounding ports in the Straits of Melaka and the Bay of Bengal. Aceh was the major importer of Indian cloth from Penang, with more then 64 per cent, followed by Kedah (12 per cent), Southern Siam (12 per cent) and native ports and Java less than 10 per cent. The importance of cloth as an item of import and re-export for Penang merchants can be established by referring to the trade between the island and the Coromandel Coast, Bengal, and with the archipelago. The pattern of the cloth trade in the region clearly shows that Penang was the centre for the distribution of Indian cloth in the northern part of the Straits. The trade between Penang and Aceh verifies the importance of the cloth trade on the island. In 1828, Aceh took the largest share of Penang's trade in Indian cloth at 64 per cent and of British cloth at 73 per cent. Although Aceh imported a large amount of cloth from Penang, it is not certain whether Aceh re-exported the item to the other parts of the region. However, as Aceh was an important port on the northern part of Sumatra it can be assumed that it also catered to the demands of the other areas around the kingdom.

Opium was the second most important commodity imported to and re-exported from Penang. Most came from Calcutta and was an important item in the overall trading activities of the English. The profitability of opium can be seen from the practice of the Dutch and the English of opening opium revenue farms in Melaka and Penang, respectively. In Penang, opium was farmed out by the government and the revenue from these farms brought in the highest income to the government. Since being introduced in the 1790s, Chinese merchants had always gained control of the farms. In 1828–29, the consumption of opium on the island represented 27.87 per cent of the total value of opium imported while the rest was re-exported to various places in the archipelago and to China. In 1828–29, the major importers of opium from Penang were Aceh (69.48 per cent), China (10.32 per cent) and Sumatra (6.41 per cent).

Pepper was the third most important import and re-export commodity of the island. In 1828–29, more than half of the total amount of pepper came from Aceh (54.97 per cent), 43.82 per cent came from Sumatra and 1.19 per cent came from Siam. Most of the pepper was re-exported to Calcutta, China and England. The pepper trade with Aceh was so important to Penang's Chinese merchants that they sought to preserve it at all cost. As we have seen, during the civil war they continued their contacts, evading the ban by declaring that they were trading with Padang.[99] Furthermore, the Chinese merchants from Penang even went to the extent of stationing a ship in the territorial waters off Aceh, which acted as a floating collecting centre for pepper, betelnut and other commodities traded with Aceh.[100]

Due to the importance of pepper in the intra-Asian trade and a demand for it in Europe, Penang attempted to encourage the production of the condiment on the island. Thus pepper planting was first introduced as early as the 1780s.[101] In the meantime, the bulk of pepper exported originally came from Sumatra. The pepper plantations on the island represented the first export-oriented agricultural enterprise to be developed in a British settlement in the Malay Peninsula.[102] In its early development, pepper planting was a joint European-Chinese venture. It was first introduced by Francis Light, who had encouraged Chewan to plant pepper vines obtained from Aceh.[103] In the 1790s, the EIC established their experimental pepper gardens at Sungai Kluang and Ayer Itam on the island and some European planters, including Light, planted their newly acquired estates with pepper. By 1789, a total of 533,230 pepper vines had been planted on the island, covering some 900 acres of land. Between 1798 and 1801 a total of 1,700 to

2,200 acres of land were planted with pepper. In 1802, Penang produced between 16,000 to 20,000 *pikuls* of pepper, making it the most important export commodity produced on the island. By 1805 the production of pepper had increased to 27,000 *pikuls*, of which three-quarters went to Europe. By 1806, the annual production stood at 30,000 *pikuls*.[104]

However, in 1806–07, the British found themselves shut out from the markets in Europe. This was due to the Decrees of Berlin (1806) and Milan (1807), which closed the Company (EIC) from its Continental markets, as a result of which the stocks of pepper, spices and coffee in the Company's London warehouse could not be re-exported and were left unsold.[105] As demand on the London market declined, pepper prices fell drastically. This resulted in a major setback for the pepper planters on the island leading to a situation where many plantations had to be abandoned and eventually returned to jungle. Although the price of pepper revived in 1814, it was short-lived and prices fell further in 1817. In the 1820s, many of the farmers had to abandon their land again and some switched to the cultivation of nutmeg or cloves.[106]

Another local produce that gradually grew in importance was the betelnut, which became a major export product in 1828–29. In that period, 87 per cent of the betelnut exported from the island was locally cultivated and only 12.58 per cent came from Aceh. Thus, in 1828–29 the major product of the island was betelnut. In the early years, although Penang was already producing betelnut locally, the bulk of the product which was re-exported by Penang, came from Aceh. From 1810 to 1823, betelnut was an important item of trade between Aceh and Penang, reaching its height in 1814–15 when the former sold SpD 84,972 worth of the product to Penang.[107]

Tin was the fifth most important export of Penang in 1828–29 but the mineral represented only 1.73 per cent of total imports for the period. Tin amounted to 7.76 per cent of the island's total exports. The bulk of tin imported to the island came from the native ports, Kedah and Thailand. Tin that came from Thailand was mostly from Junk Ceylon, which already had close trade links with the Khaw clan and other Chinese merchants on the island. During this time the Khaw clan was already involved in the extraction of tin in the Ranong district of southern Thailand.[108] These connections meant that most of the tin from these Thai areas found its way to Penang.[109]

Although rice was grown in Penang it was never enough to feed its growing population and up to 1830 rice and other food products formed important import commodities. In 1828–29, 7.02 per cent of all imported goods to the island consisted of rice. Rice came from Kedah, which supplied 50.49 per cent, of the total rice import, followed by Calcutta at 24.20 per cent. The rice trade between Penang and Kedah was mostly carried out by Malay and Chinese traders. Most of the rice was sold in the market by petty-traders, mostly Malays and Chinese, who had close links with their trading partners in the Kedah mainland.[110] In addition, many small trading boats owned by the Malays and Chinese carried cattle and poultry between the mainland and the island. Penang also had to import wheat, grains and paddy from Calcutta, Bombay, Aceh and the Tenasserim Coast.

The Straits, as a whole, did not produce much salt but obtained its supply mainly from India and Java. The main suppliers of salt for Penang were Madras and Bombay. From 1806 to 1808, the government tried to introduce salt farms on the island but the attempt failed due to poor management and a lack of manpower to supervise the supply of salt.[111] Moreover, imported salt was cheap and supply in the market was more than sufficient to meet the demand. Salt was mainly exported to Sumatra, Kedah and other native ports.

CONCLUSION

At the time when Penang was founded, the main aim of the EIC and the English country traders was to capture the China market. Penang featured in this scheme of things as a half-way base, strategically located, to facilitate this ambition. For this reason, its early history revolved more on political and strategic factors than on economic decisions. From its foundation in 1786 until 1810, the main theme in the history of Penang was the attempt of the government of the island to implement the scheme to make Penang a naval arsenal and a centre of shipbuilding, both aimed at strengthening the EIC's ability to guard the sea route between India and China.[112] However, this idea was later abandoned due to lack of resources and manpower.

Nevertheless, Penang's trade flourished. This was because penetration into the China market could also be facilitated by making available goods that were in demand in China. It was in this context that Penang played an important role, as it was well placed to enter into the trade of the Malay archipelago, the longstanding provider of goods that interested the Chinese market. In the years after its opening, and despite Melaka's established position as the centre of trade in the Straits, Penang succeeded in wresting much of the trade that once went to Melaka and proved itself more than able to create a new trading network which took advantage of its position at the northern end of the Straits, facing the Bay of Bengal. The cumulative effect of these events was the steady decline of Melaka as an international entre-pot. In the circumstances, the British should have been pleased with the resulting boost to the position of Penang (so, too, the Dutch with regard to

Batavia). But for a few short years following Melaka's return to Dutch rule, the precarious nature of Penang's new-found dominance became apparent. As we have seen, the nucleus of Penang's trading network was located in the northwestern part of the archipelago, where its trade with the northern part of the Malaya peninsula and, particularly, Aceh was characterised by a system of exchange that saw Penang importing primarily food, minerals and jungle products from these areas and exporting to them manufactured goods and luxury items from India and China. This pattern of trade was established right from the start. While Penang was able to flourish, it was never able to achieve pre-eminence as the commercial centre in the Straits in the way that Melaka had done in the fifteenth century and for several centuries thereafter. This was because it was not as well situated as Melaka. As a result, although its trade developed, Penang did not develop in the way that Melaka once did, nor with the rapidity that Singapore achieved after its opening in 1819.

NOTES

1   For further discussion on this see, for example, Dianne Lewis, 'British Policy in the Straits of Malacca to 1819 and the Collapse of the Traditional Malay State Structure'. In Brook Barrington (ed.), *Empires, Imperialism and Southeast Asia*, Clayton: Monash Asia Institute, 1977, pp.17–33.

2   P.J. Marshall, 'Private British Trade in the Indian Ocean Before 1800'. In Ashin Das Gupta and M.N. Pearson (eds), *India and the Indian Ocean 1500–1800*, Calcutta: Oxford University Press, 1987, pp. 276–316. See also S. Arasaratnam, 'Indian Commercial Groups and European Traders 1600–1800: Changing Relationships in Southeastern India'. In S. Arasaratnam (ed.), *Maritime Trade, Society and European Influence in Southern Asia, 1600–1800*, Aldershot: Variorum, 1995, pp. 42–53.

3   Om Prakash, "Europeans, India and the Indian Ocean in the Early Modern Period", *South Asia*, vol. xix, Special Issue, 1996, p.21.

4   S. Arasaratnam, 'Indian Commercial Groups and European Traders 1600–1800: Changing Relationships in Southeastern India', p. 47.

5   See, for example, Lee Kam Heng, *The Sultanate of Aceh* and Sushil Chaudhury, 'Merchants, Companies and Rulers: Bengal in the Eighteenth Century', *Journal of the Economic and Social History of the Orient*, vol. xxxi, 1988, pp. 90–100. The author describes that European Companies freely borrowed money from the Jagat Seths' agencies in Calcutta, Kasimbazar, Dacca, Hughli and Patna. Robert Orme, the English Company's official historian who was in Bengal in the early 1750s, described the Jagat Seths as 'the greatest shroff and bankers in the known world'.

6   A List of arrivals and departures of shipping in Prince of Wales Island from 1786 to 1794, in G/34/2; G/34/3; G/34/4; G/34/5 and G/34/6. See also Appendix 12: Penang's Shipping Lists 1786–1794, in Nordin Hussin, 'Melaka and Penang 1780–1830', pp. 481–497.

7   George Leith, *A Short Account of the Settlement, Produce and Commerce of Prince of Wales' Island in the Strait of Malacca*, p. 89.

8   Account of Prahus arriving at Prince of Wales Island 1786 to 1787 in G/34/2. See also George Leith, *A Short Account of the Settlement, Produce and Commerce of Prince of Wales' Islands in the Strait of Malacca*, p. 89.

9   See extract letter from Light dated 20 June 1788: 'That the commerce of this port is annually increasing needs no proof. The Buggesse prows alone have brought gold and silver this year to the amount of two or three hundred thousand dollars to purchase

opium and piece goods, and if they meet with such favourable markets as to induce them to continue the trade, I entertain little doubt from the information I have received of the purchases they were accustomed to make formerly at Rhio, that they will in a few years import gold and silver annually to the extent of half a million of dollars, part of which will be carried in gold to the coast of Coromandel in payment of the coast piece goods and the other part will form a fund for the purchase of goods for the China market. Thus by encouraging this branch of commerce the coast of Coromandel will be benefited and the remittance to China be facilitated'. In *JIA*, Vol. iv, 1850, p. 647.

10 See H. Warington Smyth, 'Boats and Boat-building in the Malay Peninsula', pp. 97–115.

11 See A List of arrival and departures of shipping at Prince of Wales Island, 1 Feb to 25 August 1794, in G/34/6.

12 George Leith, *A Short Account of the Settlement, Produce and Commerce of Prince of Wales Islands in the Strait of Malacca*, p. 89. See also S. Arasaratnam, *Islamic Merchant communities*, p. 20.

13 List of arrivals and departures of vessels at Prince of Wales Island from July 1786 to Dec 1786, in G/34/2; George Leith, *A Short Account of the Settlement, Produce and Commerce of Prince of Wales Island in the Straits of Malacca*, p. 89

14 See Appendix 12: Penang's Shipping Lists 1786–1794, in Nordin Hussin, 'Melaka and Penang 1780–1830', pp. 481–497.

15 Ibid.

16 For further discussion on the trading pattern of the Chulia merchants, see S. Arasaratnam, *Islamic Merchant Communities of the Indian Subcontinent in Southeast Asia*, Kuala Lumpur: University Malaya Press, 1989, p. 18.

17 George Leith, *A Short Account of the Settlement, Produce and Commerce of Prince of Wales Island in the Straits of Malacca*, p. 89. See also S. Arasaratnam, *Islamic Merchant communities*, p. 20.

18 An account of goods imported by Malay prahus into Prince of Wales Island March 1789 in G/34/4.

19 An account of prahus arriving at Prince of Wales Island between 1 May and 9 July 1787 in G/34/2.

20 A list of arrivals and departures of Shipping at Prince of Wales Island in G/34/2; G/34/3; G/34/4; G/34/5 and G/34/6; see also An account of goods imported into Prince of Wales Island from 1 August to 31 December 1788, in G/34/3.

21 See Report on the trade of Prince of Wales Island 1828/29, in SSFR vol. 162; C.D. Cowan, 'Early Penang', p. 140. See also Lee Kam Heng, *The Sultanate of Aceh*, p. 249.

22 *JIA*, Vol.5, 1851, p. 98.

23 Ibid., p. 93.

24 See the conflict between the Superintendent Major Forbes Ross Macdonald with the mercantile society in 1796, in, "Notices of Penang", *JIA*, Vol.5, 1851, p. 93–119.

25 H.P. Clodd, *Malaya's First British Pioneer: The Life of Francis Light*, pp. 119–120. See also Lee Kam Heng, *The Sultanate of Aceh*, p. 219.

26 For a good and detailed discussion of Tuanku Syed Hussain's role in the civil wars in Aceh and his political activities during the war, see Lee Kam Heng, *The Sultanate of Aceh*, pp. 194–321.

27 *JIA*, 1848, Vol. II, p. 662.

28 Ibid.

29 For example, on 19 January 1780, James Scott travelling in his 250-laasten ship arrived at Melaka from China on his way to Bombay. On board the ship he carried 4,000 *pikuls* of sugar, 3,000 *pikuls* of saltpeter and 150 *pikuls* of silk; in Incoming and outgoing of ships at Melaka in January 1780, in VOC 3582; on 30 November 1780 James Scott arrived at Melaka from Kedah and sailed on to Selangor; in Incoming and outgoing of ships on November 1780, in VOC 3599.

30 See a letter by James Douglas, dated 28 September 1807, in G/34/18.

31 See the report of the investigation conducted by the Committee of Assessors which was formed in 1806, in F/4/262 5837. See also a protest letter from Douglas Wilson, 12 August 1806 in G/34/14.

32 A protest letter from Douglas Wilson, 12 August 1806, in G/34/14. See also the report of the investigation conducted by the Committee of Assessor, which was formed in 1806, in F/4/262 5837.

33 S. Arasaratnam, 'The Chulia Muslim Merchants in Southeast Asia 1650–1800'. In *Maritime Trade and Society and European Influence in Southern Asia, 1600–1800*, Aldershot: Variorum, 1995, p. 141. Arasaratnam suggests that the reason for little evidence regarding the activities of Chulia merchants was: '... that the companies had opted out of inter-Asian trade, by and large, in this period and their records do not contain observations on trade in the great Asian trading centres of Southeast Asia. There is a good deal of private European trade within Asia but, unfortunately, this has not generated records for the historian'.

34 Ibid., pp. 142–143.

35 Ibid.

36 Petition of Pulicat merchants Mohammed Syed, Mucktoon Saib, Boojoo Mohammed and Ismail Mohammed 6 October 1814, in G/34/45.

37 Ibid.

38 Ibid.

39 See, for example, Report on the 1814 fire, in G/34/45.

40 S. Arasaratnam, 'The Chulia Muslim Merchants', p. 143.

41 Ibid., p. 143.

42 *JIA*, 1850, Vol. iv, p. 630.

43 See Report of the fire by the enquiry 8 October 1814, in G/34/45, see also *JIA*, 1850, vol. iv, p. 630; *JIA*, vol. iv, p. 641.

44 *JIA*, 1850, Vol. iv, p. 630; see also, *JIA*, Vol. iv, p. 641.

45 Extract letter from Governor Maclister to the Chairman and Deputy Chairman dated 7 November 1808, in G/34/9 and also report by Raffles on 31 October 1808, in G/34/9.

46 See report of the fire by the enquiry 8 October 1814, in G/34/45

47 George Leith, *A Short Account of the Settlements, Produce and Commerce of Prince of Wales Island in the Straits of Malacca*, London: J. Booth, 1805, p.51.

48 Ibid.

49 Ibid.

50 Extract letter from Governor Maclister to the Chairman and Deputy Chairman dated 7 November 1808, in G/34/9, and also report by Raffles on 31 October 1808, in G/34/9.

51 Letter from Francis Light, 25 January 1794, to Governor General: 'The Bugesses the few inhabitants here at present yet as they come annually to trade and remain two or three months ashore to the number of one or two thousand they are during the time of their residence a part of our society, they are Mahomedans, proud warlike independent people easily irritated and prone to revenge .... they are the best merchants among the eastern islands .... their cargoes either in bullion or goods with the quantity of opium and piece goods they export make their arrival much wished for by all mercantile people', in G/34/6. See, also, Farquhar letters in Memoranda of Malacca: 'They are certainly far more honest in their dealings than either the Chinese or Choolias'. In SSFR Vol. 10.

52 *JIA*, vol. iv, 1850, p. 658.

53 *JIA*, vol. iv, 1850, pp. 600–647.

54 See Heather Sutherland, 'Slavery and the slave trade in South Sulawesi, 1600–1800s'. In Anthony Reid (ed.) *Slavery, Bondage and Dependency in Southeast Asia*, St. Lucia: University of Queensland Press 1983, pp. 263–285.

55 Wong Choon San, *A Gallery of Chinese Kapitans*, Singapore: Government Printing Office, 1964, pp. 9–26.

56 Lee Kam Heng, *The Sultanate of Aceh*, pp. 230–233.

57 Ibid., p. 231.

58 Ibid.

59 Jennifer W. Cushman, *Family and State: The Formation of a Sino-Thai Tin-mining Dynasty 1797–1932*, Singapore: Oxford University Press, 1991, pp. 10–11.

60 Ibid., pp. 10–11.

61 Ibid., pp. 56–87.

62 See *JIA*, Vol. iv, 1850, pp. 600 and 647.

63 See a report on an enquiry on the subject of slave trade 23 June 1828, in F/4/1130.

64 Ibid.

65 Ibid.

66 Ibid.

67 Ibid.

68 Ibid.

69 See an extract letter from Captain Light dated 20 June 1788, in *JIA*, Vol. iv, 1850: 'As the island produces nothing of a commercial nature in itself, but every article fit for the China market to be procured at it is brought from the surrounding countries by the Malays, whose chief inducement to visit it has been the great freedom of trade that inducement ceasing the imports would become too inconsiderable defray the expense of collecting duties on them', p. 647.

70 George Leith, *A Short Account of the Settlement, Produce and Commerce of Prince of Wales Island*, p. 83.

71 Ibid., p. 85.

72 See *JIA*, 1850 vol iv, p.658. See also Extract letter from governor Maclister to the chairman and deputy chairman dated 7 November 1808, in G/34/9; and also report by Raffles on 31 October 1808, in G/34/9.

73 *JIA*, 1850 vol iv, p. 658.

74 The quantity of opium imported by Malay traders from the surrounding area and the archipelago had increased annually at a rapid rate: from 105 chests in 1790 to 193 chests in 1791 and 483 chests in 1792, see, *JIA* Vol. iv, 1850, p.660.

75 Sticlac: Secretion of insects obtained from the twigs and branches of trees; used either as a dye or a resin, see, C.D. Cowan, 'Early Penang and the Rise of Singapore 1805–1832', p. 113.

76 *JIA*, 1850 vol iv, p.658.

77 George Leith, *A Short Account of the Settlement, Produce and Commerce of Prince of Wales Island*, p. 83.

78 Captain Light's letter dated 7 October 1787: 'The King of Kedah at other times he seems to have an intention of starving us. The inhabitants here like all other Indians make no provision against accidents. I am therefore obliged to advance money to the King's merchant at Kedah to provide a continual supply of rice and this is retailed to the troops and others at the same price I purchase it', in G/34/3. See also Light's letter dated 16 November 1787: 'The king of Kedah has stopped the exportation of rice since the month of September. On the 10 instant I sent Lieut. Blair with letters to him requesting to know if he would supply me or not. The Raja sent word he would send rice in three days but at the former price. It is not from any scarcity of grain the king prevents the rice from being brought here but from policy he thinks his case desperate and that he shall not obtain anything from the Company. He has therefore laid a duty of 23 Spanish Dollars per coyan on rice for exportation. This deprives those who would deal in rice of all emolument and is equal to prohibition. The country people find no purchasers for the surplus paddy (the king excepted) who buys it at a small price and sells it again at 50 Spanish Dollars per coyan to strangers. The consumption of this place is 25 coyan per month exclusive of foreign demands', in G/34/3.

79 Report by Raffles 31 October 1808, in SSFR Vol. 9.

80 Ibid.

81 C.D. Cowan, 'Governor Bannerman and the Penang Tin Scheme 1818–1819', *JMBRAS*, Vol 23, Part 1, 1950, p. 54.

82 See R. Laarhoven, 'The Power of Cloth: The Textile Trade of the Dutch East India Company 1600–1780'.

83 C.D. Cowan, 'Early Penang', p. 7.

84 C.D. Cowan, 'Governor Bannerman and the Penang Tin Scheme', p. 53.

85 *JIA*, vol. iv, 1850, p. 660.

86 George Leith, *A Short Account of the Settlement, Produce and Commerce of Prince of Wales Island*, p. 83.

87 For a discussion on the importance of Indian cloth trade in Sumatra, see Barbara Watson Andaya, 'The Cloth Trade in Jambi and Palembang Society During the Seventeenth and Eighteenth Centuries', pp. 27–46. See also R. Laarhoven, 'The Power of Cloth: The Textile Trade of Dutch East India Company 1600–1780'.

88 C.D. Cowan, 'Early Penang', p. 7.

89 C.D. Cowan, 'Governor Bannerman and the Penang Tin Scheme 1818–1819', p. 53.

90 Ibid., pp. 6–7. See also Lee Kam Hing *The Sultanate of Aceh*.

91 Lee Kam Heng, *The Sultanate of Aceh*, pp. 247–48.

92 See Document no. 108, Fort Cornwallis, at a Council meeting held on the 21st August 1823 in C.D. Cowan,'Early Penang', p. 140.

93 King Jauhar al-Alam was overthrown as the King of Aceh, Saif al-Alam, a contender, was the son of Syed Hussain and Panglima Sagis was a territorial chief. See Lee Kam Hing, *The Sultanate of Aceh*.

94 Lee Kam Hing, *The Sultanate of Aceh*, p. 244.

95 Ibid., p. 244.

96 Report on the trade of Prince of Wales Island 1828–29, in SSFR, Vol. 162.

97 Ibid.

98 Ibid.

99 Ibid., p. 244.

100 Ibid., 'One such boat was the Lam Hin belonging to Che Toah and Che Seong, two Penang Chinese. In 1816, the Lam Hin, under a Chinese known only as Attai, sailed for Padang, the declared destination, but it was to the Acehnese west coast that the ship headed. .... The Lam Hin, therefore, functioned as a floating trading factory, serving ships from Penang which for various reasons could stop only briefly in the west coast', p.244.

101 See Light's letter, 14 January 1790, in G/34/4.

102 James Jackson, *Planters and Speculators: Chinese and European Agricultural Enterprise in Malaya, 1786–1921*, Kuala Lumpur: University of Malaya Press, 1968, p. 32.

103 Ibid., p. 95.

104 Ibid.

105 C.D. Cowan, 'Early Penang', p. 5.

106 James Jackson, *Planters and Speculators*, pp. 93–100.

107 Lee Kam Hing, *The Sultanate of Aceh*, p. 251.

108 Jennifer W. Cushman, *Family and State,* p.11.

109 Ibid.

110 Proceedings of a special Committee of Assessors held on 18 August 1806, in F/4/262 5837; see also Report of the Committee appointed by the Governor in Council on 22 August 1806, in F/4/262 5837.

111 Tax farming a review from 1805–1825, in G/34/105.

112 See, for example, M. Stubbs Brown, 'The Failure of Penang as a Naval Base and Shipbuilding Centre', *JMBRAS*, vol. 32, part 1, 1959, pp. 1–32.

CHAPTER FOUR

Trade in the Straits: Melaka and Penang, 1780–1830

INTRODUCTION

ALTHOUGH MELAKA IN THE EIGHTEENTH CENTURY was not a great port for trade it still commanded a significant strategic location, attracting some traders from the Indian subcontinent, the archipelago and the South China Sea who passed through the Straits. As the eighteenth century drew to a close, political changes occurred rapidly in the Straits as a result of which drastic changes for the future of Melaka and its trade were set into motion. The Napoleonic wars that broke out in Europe had the political impact of Melaka being transferred from the Dutch to the English, engendering a big shift in its trade and trading network. As Dutch power weakened due to the events in Europe, for most of the early nineteenth century, English presence and success in Malay waters led to the replacement of Dutch power and influence in most parts of the Straits. For Melaka it meant the diminution of its stature as a player in the intra-Asian trade and a slow slide into obscurity.

On the other hand, Penang, which became an English colonial port-town in the last quarter of the eighteenth century, began to flourish into an important port on the northern region of the Straits. Penang, which faced the Bay of Bengal, was able to attract a large number of traders from the northern region of Sumatra and the Malay peninsula as well as the Indian subcontinent. In contrast to Melaka, which still maintained her old trading policy through imposing taxes on traders, Penang had embarked on a new course of action by having a free port, a new phenomenon in the Straits.

This was to have an adverse effect on Melaka's trade and in the long run the once famous trade emporium and entrepot never recaptured its glorious past.

The discussion in this chapter will focus on three main areas. Firstly, the trading network of Melaka and Penang, followed by an analysis of the changes that took place in both places. The discussion will also include a comparative analysis of the trading patterns of Melaka and Penang. Secondly, the volume, value and trends of trade in both Melaka and Penang will be examined. Finally, an analysis will be made of the main commodities and products traded.

TRADING NETWORK

Throughout the seventeenth century Melaka and Riau were rival port-towns in the Straits. This rivalry became more intense as Riau became a trading centre for many English country traders, and goods that were restricted by the VOC such as tin, opium and cloth could be easily found there. Nevertheless, Riau still maintained close trading connections with Melaka, as many Bugis and Malay traders from Riau continued to call there every year. This was because Melaka remained an important collecting and distributing centre for the region. After the 1784 Dutch-Bugis war and the defeat of the Bugis warrior-prince, Raja Haji, Riau's importance as a trading mart began to diminish, a situation that worked to Melaka's advantage. However, this good fortune was short-lived as two years later, in 1786, the English opened Penang as a free port to rival Dutch Melaka.

Melaka's trading activities could be divided into three major periods. The first covered the period before and after the war with Riau (1780–93), the next phase was when Melaka was temporarily occupied by the English, between 1794 and 1818, and finally the period between 1819 and 1830 which coincided with Melaka's return to the Dutch and the years under English rule following the permanent transfer of Melaka. A detailed analysis of the three periods is not possible because of difficulties arising from the different ways of compiling data adopted by the Dutch and English. As stated earlier, the Dutch shipping lists were very detailed but the English data on trade were very general and little information was given about the traders who arrived in Melaka, especially in the years 1794 to the 1820s.

In the period leading to and after the war with Riau until the English occupation, Melaka enjoyed a wide trading network. Many ships from the Indian subcontinent, China and the archipelago traded there. The shipping lists for incoming and outgoing ships for the port reveal that Melaka still commanded an important position in the Straits. From 1780–82 there were a total of 1,129 incoming ships to Melaka but in the 1791–93 period the number seems to have decreased by 183 ships to a total of only 946. Many reasons contributed to this slight but significant decline, although the most immediate were the consequences of the 1784 war and the establishment of Penang. The Anglo-Dutch war in Europe also impacted on the number of English ships visiting Melaka from the Indian subcontinent. Dutch defeat and the collapse of the VOC in 1794 led to the transfer of Malacca and other VOC possessions, including Batavia, to the English. Thus it could be said that the major events that led to the irreversible decline of Melaka's trade began in the last two decades of the eighteenth century.

However, Melaka's trade within the Straits was an enduring enterprise. This was because ports in the region had long been dependent on Melaka as the main collecting and distributing centre for goods. In particular, the eastern section of Sumatra was a rich area with ports all along the coastline, and while some were more important than others, they were, directly or indirectly, linked to one another and to the western part of the Malay peninsula. The linkage patterns changed from time to time depending on various factors, including the rise or fall of a port and changing alliances, both political and economic. An example of change in trading patterns can be seen after the Dutch-Bugis war in 1784. After the war, a significant change was seen in the pattern of trade with the Bugis. Before the war, the majority of Bugis traders came directly from Riau but following the Dutch raid on the Malay port, many Bugis traders who were based there left to make their homes elsewhere in the region. The effect of this shift was a reduction of Melaka's trade with Riau, but it did not significantly reduce Melaka's overall trade within the Straits, as the Bugis, who were among the most numerous traders to visit Melaka, now came from other ports such as those situated in Selangor, Perak and Trengganu on the peninsula and Siak, Jambi and Deli on the east coast of Sumatra. Further, with the fall of Riau, Siak emerged as Melaka's main regional trading partner. Siak was strategically located with a good connection through rivers and overland with many towns and villages in the interior of Sumatra, an important source of agricultural and forest products.

The importance of the Straits' trade to Melaka can be seen from the large number of traders involved. Coming from small native port-towns on the Malay peninsula, such as Selangor, Perak and Johor, and from other small ports in Sumatra, such as Batubara, Jambi, and Deli, in small ships with limited cargo, the value of these traders lay in their function as distributors and collectors of goods within the region. They did not travel long distances but within their travelling range they were able to make many stops, thus ensuring the widest possible coverage of the areas within the

Straits of Melaka. Their presence in Melaka in the 1780s and 1790s was constantly high and such a trend continued to prevail in the 1828–29 period.

Melaka's trade with other parts of the archipelago, mainly the northern coast of Java – Batavia, Cheribon, Semarang, Gerisik and Juwana – remained intact in the last quarter of the eighteenth century. Traders from these parts arrived regularly in Melaka throughout the 1780s and 1790s. Although there is no evidence to show trading activities between Java and Melaka for the first two decades of the nineteenth century, the fact that the English were in control of Melaka as well as the Dutch areas of Java during most of this period suggests that the old links could not have been severed. Indeed, in the late 1820s the records indicate that these trading connections remained intact and that they continued despite the existence of Singapore after 1819. Nevertheless, the figures for 1828–29 show that the number of traders from Java had declined, probably due to Singapore's increasing importance and Melaka's own exclusion from the Dutch trading network after 1824.

Beginning from the last decade of the eighteenth century, Melaka's position as a port of call for long-distance traders plying the route between India and China gradually weakened. As the most important long-distance traders to visit Melaka were the EIC and English country traders, the opening of Penang and the efforts of the English administration to lure traders away from Melaka reduced its importance in the overall trading activities connected to the India–archipelago–China trade network. The opening of Singapore hastened the process not only because the new port was more strategically located but also due to Melaka's proximity to it and the conscious decision of the English authorities not to develop further both Melaka and Penang as international trading centres. Thus, by the end of the 1820s, Melaka's trading network had shrunk considerably, covering mainly the Straits, and it received a smaller share of the trade from the archipelago and an even tinier share of the trade of China and the Indian subcontinent.[1]

The temporary transfer of Melaka to the English (1794–1818) had a big impact on Melaka's trade and her trading network. This could be seen from the shrinking trade experienced by Melaka and the simultaneous growth of Penang as a thriving port. As the English were promoting Penang, the majority of the traditional Melaka traders were encouraged and even forced to trade at Penang rather than at Melaka. As part and parcel of their programme to promote Penang as a vital port in the East, the English also made attempts to encourage Melaka's inhabitants to migrate to Penang by reducing taxes and transforming Penang into an entrepot.[2]

As Penang began to prosper with the implementation of a free-trade policy, Melaka's long-distance trading network was slowly absorbed and swallowed by Penang, leaving it with a very limited number of long distance ships arriving at its port. Although many of Melaka's long-distance and regional trading partners were diverted to Penang, native traders from many small ports on the coast of Sumatra and the Malay peninsula still maintained Melaka as a regional trading centre. For many traders in small ships which travelled short distances Penang was beyond their range.

When Melaka was returned to the Dutch in 1818 and the opportunity was opened to its administrators to stem the tide of decline, Batavia's attitude remained a stumbling block. Back in the late eighteenth century, in the face of Penang's growing importance as a trading centre, Melaka had proposed to Batavia that the monopoly system of trade, which was the core of the VOC trading policy, be abolished and replaced by a policy of free trade. The proposal appeared to have been influenced by the success of the English trading policies and the conviction that the old VOC trading style was outdated and had resulted in the decline of Melaka's trade.[3] But the intended change was far too radical to be accepted by the higher authorities in Batavia. More importantly, the freedom of trade requested by Melaka would definitely jeopardize Batavia's status and her trade with China, which had been exclusively preserved by the authorities at Batavia. The changes would have made Batavia impotent as a centre of Dutch trade in the archipelago and the East. Moreover, these changes would affect the main commodities such as opium and textiles which were the VOC's exclusive monopoly. The impact of free trade on these two commodities would greatly affect the VOC's trade in Java and the archipelago. Furthermore, Melaka as a free port would attract traders who would otherwise have traded in Batavia. Certainly, Batavia was unwilling to see such changes that could finally lead to the freedom of Chinese junks to visit Melaka.[4] Thus, the proposals made by the Dutch officials in Melaka were not implemented and as the Napoleonic wars had extended to the Netherlands, Melaka was transferred to the English from 1794 to 1818; during this period Melaka's importance as a trading centre was further reduced.[5]

Once again denied a free hand in managing its own future, Melaka's decline could not be arrested after 1818. It fared no better after its permanent transfer to the English following the Anglo-Dutch treaty of 1824. The English were more focused on Penang and, especially, Singapore, the two newly founded settlements and port-towns which were run on the principle of free trade. The free trade policy had proven successful in attracting many traders and had generated more income for the EIC. Thus, rather than rebuild Melaka as an important port, the view was taken that it was better to concentrate on developing Penang and Singapore.

The genesis of the English policy of building the Penang-Singapore trade axis in the Straits could be traced to the years before Singapore was founded and before the idea was even conceived that Melaka could be taken over permanently by the English. When the English occupied Melaka, they knew that they were there only temporarily. Thus they were fearful not only of the fact that Penang's trade could be jeopardized but that the Dutch would take retaliatory action by undermining English trade in the region. Therefore, to preempt this, they embarked on a policy of reducing Melaka's importance as a centre of trade in the region.[6] They had succeeded in doing this to a considerable degree since Melaka's regional and international trading networks were already being slowly usurped by Penang. However, the English wanted to go further than this and dislocate Melaka's trade with the Straits region. They wanted the native traders from the rich Sumatran ports, such as Langkat, Bulu China, Deli, Asahan, Rokan, Siak, Indragiri and Jambi, to trade in Penang rather than flourish in Melaka.[7]

The English were aware that the ports on the eastern coast of Sumatra were well served by the rich and populous interior of the island. The port of Langkat, for example, served the areas of Bubon and Batang Sarangan with their major produce of pepper, rattan, beeswax, gambir, gold, ivory, tobacco, belacan and paddy. Langkat imported a considerable amount of goods to be disposed of to the large population in the interior and also to the inland traders who arrived from the west coast of Sumatra. Their major imports were salt, opium, Indian, European and Bugis cloth and gunpowder.

Another important port on the east coast of Sumatra was Batubara whose inhabitants had a reputation for being good traders and who travelled to Melaka, Penang and other parts of the archipelago.[8] Some of its inhabitants had accumulated considerable wealth and were owners of several large vessels. In the report on Batubara's trade with Penang sent by the Shahbandar of Batubara to Penang, it was mentioned that 600 trading prahus made their base in the port of Batubara.[9] The traders from Batubara appear to have obtained their trading funds not only locally but also from merchants in Penang and, later, in Singapore as well.[10] Batubara's major exports included opium, silk cloth, rattan, slaves, horses and salt fish. Like most other ports on the east coast of Sumatra, it was well connected to the interior of the island by rivers and land.

All these Sumatran ports served as distributing centers for goods imported from Penang and Melaka. They also served as collecting centres for agricultural, forest and mineral products from the interior of Sumatra to be exported to either Penang or Melaka. Since Melaka still had close connections with these ports, the English sent several trade missions to major native ports on the eastern coast of Sumatra to forge closer ties with them. In 1806, John Scott was sent to Siak to persuade the kingdom to have a closer trading relationship with Penang. Since Siak was an important native port, a second mission was sent in 1807 under the command of F. Garling. In 1808, another mission under Lynch was sent by the English in Penang for similar reasons.[11] It would appear that Siak had not been won over and the English had to send Farquhar in 1818 to try and get the kingdom to sign a treaty that would allow the English to establish a settlement there.[12]

With the Dutch return imminent, the English became more worried about renewed rivalry in the Straits and Sumatra. They were also fearful that Penang's trade would be adversely affected should the Dutch authorities decide to lower Melaka's shipping dues. It was anticipated that this could result in an exodus back to Melaka of Asian traders who had only recently either made Penang their base or diverted their trade there. Basically, the majority of the Asian traders in Penang were formerly from Melaka, having been attracted there by Penang's free trade status and the promise of cheaper prices, especially of opium and Indian cloth. The crux of the matter was that, strategically, Melaka far outmatched Penang, for it commanded a better position by being situated in the centre of the trading network and closer to the archipelago than Penang. It had become obvious to the English that the majority of native traders from the southern half of Sumatra and the Malay peninsula still preferred to trade in Melaka because it was closer than Penang. In these circumstances the English began to look for another port, better located than Penang, which could overshadow Melaka completely and control trade in the Straits and the archipelago. This was to lead to the founding of Singapore in 1819.[13]

The English were not mistaken in their suspicion that the Dutch would attempt to regain their lost position and trade in Melaka and the Straits. The Dutch were in Riau and Melaka in the Straits and in Padang on the west coast of Sumatra, where an active Dutch presence there aimed to stop further English encroachment in the area. In fact the Dutch had instructed several native chiefs on the western as well as eastern coast of Sumatra not to enter into any agreement or trading treaty with the English. With an active Dutch presence in these areas, the English feared that their lucrative trade with the natives of Sumatra would be diverted to Melaka. They had made strides in their relationship with some ports in eastern Sumatra and the native chiefs of Deli, Serdang and Asahan had corresponded openly with Penang indicating their desire to have closer trading relations.[14] But there were others to win over and to this end further missions were sent in 1820 under the command of Ibbetson, who was instructed to visit the eastern coast of Sumatra from Timian to Jambi to gather more information on the people, administration and trade.[15] The main aim of the mission was also to prevent Melaka and Riau, which were under the Dutch, from diverting the flow of trade from eastern Sumatra to Penang. To reaffirm this aim, another mission was sent under the command of Anderson in 1823 to Deli, Bulu China, Langkat, Bubon, Batang Sarangan, Batubara, Asahan and Siak.[16]

The Dutch withdrawal from Melaka ended their quest to improve the port's position as an important centre of trade in the Straits. At the time of their withdrawal, Melaka's trade had shrunk to the extent that its contacts were limited to neighbours in the interior such as Sungai Ujong, Linggi, Rembau, Johol, Muar and to Siak, Jambi and the northeastern parts of Sumatra. The number of commodities traded also decreased and the principal goods were mainly agricultural and food products. Very few manufactured goods were found in Melaka because the number of long-distance traders had greatly declined. Although it still imported rice, the volume of such imports had greatly decreased due to the large supply from the interior regions.[17] Melaka had finally been reduced to a local port and the English authorities were happy to leave it that way.

As Melaka's fortunes dwindled, Penang was experiencing growth. Its location at the northern end of the Straits of Melaka, its free port status and the fact that it was the trading base of the nation that controlled the bulk of the Asian trade at that stage gave it a more than even chance to succeed as a trading centre. Penang's trading network soon covered the northern region of the Straits, northern Sumatra, notably Aceh, the northern Malay peninsula such as Kedah, southern Siam including Junk Ceylon, Tenessarim, Mergui, Pegu and southern Burma and the Indian subcontinent. It also developed a lesser trading network with the archipelago and the South China Sea. Penang's long-distance traders mostly came from the Indian subcontinent and China, its regional traders were mostly from the northern region of Sumatra, southern Burma and Thailand and also the archipelago, and its local traders were mostly from the Malay peninsula.

Penang's most important inter-regional connection was with the Indian subcontinent, the western terminal in the intra-Asian trade route. In the region, Aceh, an important trading partner, had been a political and economic power since the sixteenth century, and in the Straits of Melaka its position as an important native port was only rivaled by Riau. In the eighteenth century, although dynastic conflicts and civil wars caused its trade to be unstable from time to time, its port remained vital to the overall trading activities in the region. In the northern part of the Malay peninsula, Perak, Kedah, Ligor and Junk Ceylon became close trading partners. This was largely due to their close proximity to Penang and an already forged trading link with the English. Further, as the demand for tin grew to feed the tea trade with China, Penang's trade with Perak, Junk Ceylon and Ligor became more vital. Kedah, on the other hand, was important for its trade in foodstuffs, especially rice and poultry, to feed the growing population on the island.

Penang soon became the major focal point for traders who desired to exchange goods brought from the Indian subcontinent and also from China. Chulia traders from the Coromandel Coast were frequently seen in Penang travelling from there to Southern Burma and Thailand and Penang and later to Aceh before returning to their port of origin. In addition, EIC and English country traders based elsewhere frequently called at Penang on their journey to and from China and the Indian subcontinent.

One of the difficulties in analysing the trade network of early Penang is the scarcity of material. While there is some documentation on the movements of ships in and out of Penang for the early period, coverage of subsequent years is poor. No sustained effort appears to have been made to keep a complete record of the trading developments of Penang. Mostly, documents on Penang's trade provide very general information and are in fact summaries of trade figures without giving details such as movements of ships in and out of Penang, port of origin or destination. Most reports for the earlier period were presented in general terms such as stating that Penang had become an important port in the north of the Straits, and that traders from the Indian subcontinent, China, the northern region of Sumatra and the Malay peninsula were its main trading partners. However, a detailed account of Penang's import and export with Aceh is available. This is partly because Penang's trade with Aceh was very important, especially in view of the fact that it enjoyed a favourable balance of trade with the latter. A more detailed account of Penang's trade is also available for the 1828–29 period, when Calcutta, Madras, Bombay and China were Penang's four main long-distance trading partners. The major regional network encompassed Aceh, other ports in the northern region of Sumatra and the northern region of the Malay peninsula, namely Kedah, southern Thailand and Junk Ceylon. However Penang's trading network with ports in the archipelago, such as those in northern Java, the eastern archipelago and other native ports in the southern region of Sumatra and the Malay peninsula, was comparatively small. This was partly because Singapore had begun to dominate this network. In addition, Melaka still had some control of the trade with small native ports in the southern region of the Straits.

In the 1820s, Penang's inclusion in the expanding trading network of the English meant that it commanded a wider area compared to Melaka. Its position at the northern end of the Straits gave it the advantage lost by Melaka due to its proximity to Singapore. Although in the long term both Penang and Melaka suffered severely from Singapore's rise as an important entrepot, Penang was much less affected due to its proximity to the Bay of Bengal, an

Table 7: Comparative analysis of the number of ships arriving at and departing Melaka and Penang, 1780–1802

Years	Melaka		Penang	
	Arriving	*Departing*	*Arriving*	*Departing*
1780	380	367	–	–
1781	333	314	–	–
1782	416	352	–	–
1786	–	–	85	–
1787	–	–	504	–
1788	–	–	168*	–
1789	–	–	147*	–
1790	–	–	175*	–
1791	317	259	150*	–
1792	318	281	192*	–
1793	311	204	177*	–
1799	–	–	2,004	1,792
1800	–	–	2,173	1,710
1801	–	–	2,830	2,105
1802	–	–	3,569	2,986

*Note: Does not include the Malay prahus.

important trading region, and its continuing importance as a collecting and distributing centre for the northern Malay states and north Sumatra.

As mentioned before, charting Penang's rise as a trading centre is not an easy task. Nevertheless, in general terms it could be said that its transformation from a sparsely inhabited island into a thriving port was quite rapid. Table 7 below gives an idea of its increasing share of regional trade, while Melaka trade stagnated, as shown by the figures.

The table clearly shows that Melaka only received a small number of incoming ships compared to Penang. Even before Melaka was transferred to the English in 1794, the port only received fewer than 400 incoming ships. However, in 1799 Penang was able to pull in more then 2,000 vessels to its port and by the beginning of the nineteenth century more than 3,000 vessels arrived. Although no figures exist for ships coming to Melaka in the nineteenth century, the fact is that Melaka's position as an important port in the Straits was weakened with the opening of Penang.

Arasaratnam argues that the policy of free trade bore fruit quickly and that many traders from Aceh began to sail to Penang with their pepper, by-passing Melaka, while vessels from Rangoon, Mergui and other ports of the Kingdom of Ava, which used to trade with Melaka to fetch supplies of agricultural and forest products from the archipelago in exchange for the produce of their land, now went instead to Penang. Furthermore, there was also an increase in the smuggling of tin and pepper from the Dutch contracted states of Perak, Selangor and Palembang overland and by sea to Kedah and Penang. Penang's trade was boosted by the increasing importance of tin to the China trade. The Dutch, who had hitherto held the tin trade in their monopolistic grip through a system of trade treaties with the tin producing areas of the peninsula such as Perak and Selangor, gradually lost their grip on it due to the presence of the English traders, who offered better prices and encouraged the smuggling of the mineral to Penang.[18] Moreover, the English had prohibited ships flying their flag from calling at Melaka, which meant that the large number of English vessels that used to call there now visited Penang instead.[19] The aggressive trading policy adopted by the English was matched by the anti-Dutch propaganda they spread. Their country captains went around the area singing the praise of Penang and predicting the ruin of Melaka; a statement appeared in the Calcutta newspapers asserting that the establishment of Penang was to avenge the Amboyna 'massacre'.[20]

Penang was building a large trading network and despite the founding of Singapore in 1819, it continued to enjoy a close trading connection with the northern region of Sumatra, especially Aceh, the northern Malay peninsula, southern Thailand and Burma and also the Indian subcontinent. As a result of the trade missions sent to the east coast of Sumatra, over the years the import of pepper from that area rose from 1,800 *pikuls* in the period 1817–18 to 30,000 *pikuls* in 1822–23. Thus Penang had absorbed a large percentage of Melaka's former trading networks, thereby leaving Melaka with limited trading connections which covered short-distance traders from the west Malay peninsula and the east coast of Sumatra. Melaka's trade towards the 1820s began to decline and its trading network only covered a small area. The volume of its trade and earnings had declined tremendously compared to the 1780s. With Melaka's decline, the viability of Penang as a port was proven, Francis Light's faith in and aspirations for it were fulfilled and the massacre of Amboyna could be said to have been well and truly avenged.

VOLUME OF TRADE AND ITS TRENDS

As the method of compiling data between the English and Dutch documents was different, it is difficult to make a detailed comparative study of the trade

in Penang and Melaka. The VOC documents, although quite comprehensive, did not use standard units of measurement and weights. They also
did not mention the value of goods in currency. The English documents, on
the other hand, mentioned the value of imports and exports. Nevertheless,
if one looks at the number of ships that arrived and departed from Melaka
and their ports of origin, an analysis of Melaka's and Penang's trade trend
rather than the volume of trade is still possible. A detailed analysis of the
volume of trade in both places is only possible for the period 1828–29
because by this time they were ruled by the English and the data on imports
and exports were more standardized.

Although Melaka's trade was in decline towards the end of the eighteenth century, in the 1780s and 1790s it had a better trading record than
Penang because during this period Penang was still in its early stages of
development as a port. Penang, only established in 1786, took several decades
to emerge as an important centre for trade. Furthermore, Melaka had been
a convenient stop for traders travelling from the Indian subcontinent to
China, in addition to its reliability as a supplier of ample food and refitting
facilities for ships and traders while they waited for the changing monsoon
winds. Therefore, throughout the end of the eighteenth century, many ships
arrived at its harbour. Furthermore, Penang's early rise was plagued by
problems. There was uncertainty about its survival as a settlement because
of the negative attitude shown by the higher officials in Calcutta and their
unwillingness to provide financial assistance. Nevertheless, when Penang was
successfully established as an English settlement and the officials in India were
committed to making it an important naval and trading centre, it began to
shape the trading pattern and trends in the Straits.

Although it is difficult to determine the exact value and volume of
Melaka's trade in the 1780s and 90s, the value of the harbour taxes (customs
house/*boompagcht*) from 1780 to 1793 imposed on ships that arrived at
Melaka could be used as an index of Melaka's trade from 1780–93. In the last
two decades of the eighteenth century the harbour taxes in Melaka declined
from 68,350 rijksdollars in 1780 to 51,000 rijksdollars in 1784 and increased
to 77,555 rijksdollars in 1793.[21] This shows that during the Anglo-Dutch
war in the 1780s there was a decline in income and this trend reached its
lowest level during the war with Riau in 1784, picking up only after the war.
However, it was short-lived as Melaka was transferred to the English in 1794.

The earliest record giving the value of Penang's trade was confined to
Malay and other native traders in 1792. In that year these traders brought in
goods valued at SpD224,533.65 (566,431.03 Guilders[22]) and exported
products worth a total of SpD317,414 (800,740.29 Guilders).[23] Although
during this year Penang also received the arrival of long-distance traders

from the Indian subcontinent and China, there are no exact figures of their arrival or the value of their trade. That the value and volume of trade from these long-distance traders were not mentioned in the documents could be indicative of the fact that Penang was still struggling to become an important port of call for long-distance traders. But there is no doubt that the Penang authorities were keen to monitor the movements of the native traders, because the bulk of Penang's export to long-distance traders depended on the Malays who arrived with agricultural products and minerals, which had a ready market in the Indian subcontinent and China. Penang also depended heavily on Malay traders as distributors of goods brought in by the long-distance traders. At this stage, Melaka was still the main trading centre for Malay traders, and Penang had to convince them that it was worth their while to change course.

In the early nineteenth century, when Penang had succeeded in implementing the policy of free trade, its trade made great strides. From 1806 to 1818, trade increased and it became an important centre for opium, tin, Indian cloth and pepper.[24] During this period the administration appears to have kept better records of trading activities. However, a comparative analysis of the volume of the trade of Penang and Melaka during the early nineteenth century is not possible because there are no trade figures for Melaka for these years. Yet during this period when Melaka was ruled by the English, many Melaka traders were persuaded to trade at Penang, leading to the decline of the former in the long term. A comparative analysis of trade of the two port-towns is only available for the period 1828–29. Table 8 overleaf clearly shows that Melaka's trade was greatly affected by the existence of Penang.

In 1828–29, the total value of all imports for Penang stood at SpD 2,394,006 compared to Melaka's SpD 510,325.97, that is, about 82 per cent and 18 per cent respectively of their combined imports. Penang's exports were also higher in value at SpD 1,625,830 (more than 83 per cent) compared to Melaka at SpD 332,294 (less than 17 per cent). The main trade between the Straits with the Indian subcontinent was centred at Penang, with more then 90 per cent of imports and 90 per cent of exports conducted through Penang. The trade with the northern part of Sumatra and the northern region of the Malay peninsula was exclusively under the control of Penang. In fact there was no trade at all being conducted between these regions and Melaka. Even the trade with England and China was in Penang's favour, with 63 per cent import and 100 per cent export with England and 84% import and 92% export with China.

A similar pattern was seen in the movement of commodities in and out of Penang and Melaka. The major share of the export of Indian cloth (74 per

Table 8: Imports and exports of Penang and Melaka, 1828/29

Places/ports	Share of combined imports (%)		Share of combined exports (%)	
	Penang	Melaka	Penang	Melaka
Madras	90.20	9.79	80.87	19.12
Calcutta	90.20	9.79	95.07	4.92
Bombay	99.48	0.51	98.80	1.10
Ceylon	89.36	10.63	100.00	–
Aceh	97.55	2.44	100.00	–
Sumatra	100.00	–	100.00	–
Kedah	96.94	3.05	100.00	–
Junk Ceylon	100.00	–	100.00	–
Siam	61.09	38.9	100.00	–
China	84.56	15.43	92.69	7.30
England	63.17	36.82	100.00	–
Java	31.37	68.62	44.00	55.98
Native Ports	18.32	81.67	12.3	87.68
Deli	–	100.00	–	100.00
Total	82.40	17.50	83.00	16.90

Source: SSFR, Vol. 162

cent), opium (88 per cent), pepper (88 per cent), betelnut (100 per cent), tin (77 per cent), and British cloth (87 per cent) was in the hands of Penang. Similarly, import trends also show that Penang had the lion's share of all incoming commodities. Table 9 opposite shows the huge gap between Penang and Melaka in terms of control of trading activities passing through the Straits.

From the table above, Penang received the bulk of the main goods traded in the Straits, such as Indian cloths, opium, pepper, betelnut, rice and paddy, tin and British cloth. Penang also had the advantage over Melaka in terms of export activities in that its exports were on a much larger scale than Melaka's.

The decline in trade at Melaka in the 1820s was so serious that the Europeans (Dutch Burgers) and native traders residing there decided to send a

Table 9: Import and export of the seven main commodities for Penang and Melaka, 1828/29

Seven main commodities	Share of combined imports (%)		Share of combined exports (%)	
	Penang	Melaka	Penang	Melaka
Indian cloth	88.14	11.95	74.60	25.32
Opium	89.32	10.67	88.33	11.66
Pepper	96.16	3.80	88.70	11.29
Betelnut	100.00	–	100.00	–
Tin	54.00	45.90	77.5	22.49
British cloth	56.60	43.30	87.56	12.43
Rice and paddy	66.10	33.80	–	100.00
Others	75.70	24.29	81.37	18.62

Source: SSFR, Vol. 162

memorandum to the English to revive its trade. This memorandum revealed that only six English ships arrived in Melaka in 1826, compared to more than 40 ships in the 1790s.[25] The Melaka merchants also realized that Melaka's harbour was silting and that this caused difficulties for big ships to anchor at the port. Thus it was suggested that the English administration should build piers at the harbour. The British, however, did not respond positively to the request.[26]

COMMODITIES

The main goods and commodities traded in both ports were mostly imported goods from the Indian subcontinent, China and the archipelago. The only commodities produced locally in Melaka were gambir and belacan/terasi but they only appear in the records for the 1780s. Presumably, most of the gambir plantations were ruined due to the 1784 war with the Bugis, or were abandoned by the Chinese due to lower prices and unstable conditions in the interior part of the country, while the belacan produced might have been for home consumption. Likewise, Penang made some attempts to produce agricultural goods for export, such as pepper, cloves and betelnut but most of the plantations were not profitable for export purposes. Moreover, most of the spice plantations in the later period ended in failure due to low prices in the world market.

The main goods imported by Penang were Indian cloth, opium, tin, rice and pepper while its main exports consisted of Indian cloth, opium,

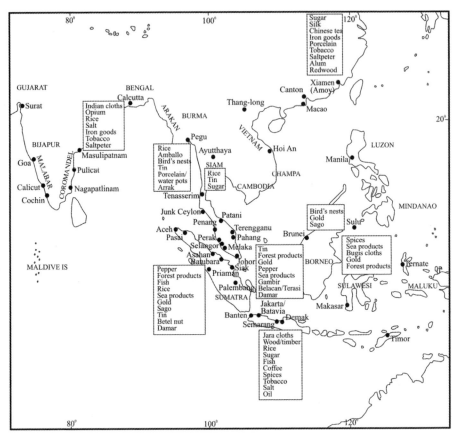

Map 10: Trading networks and connections. Type of commodities that arrived at Melaka and Penang from various ports and regions in the late eighteenth and early nineteenth centuries.

betelnut, pepper and tin. Melaka mostly imported various types of cloth (Indian, Bugis and Java cloth), opium, rice, salt, and various forest and food products and re-exported Indian cloth, opium, tin, belacan, gambir and salt. Thus both imported and exported more or less similar goods. Both also depended on food supply from abroad. Penang had to depend on her supply of rice from Kedah while Melaka procured it from Java and various native kingdoms. Thus, during times of difficulties, for example when Penang's relations with Kedah were strained, it had to depend on the import of rice from Rangoon or India. Thus, lacking in their own resources and even food supply, the colonial port-towns of Melaka and Penang were totally dependent on trade and on their function as collecting and distributing centres for commodities for their well-being.

CONCLUSION

In view of the similar function both Melaka and Penang performed in the intra-Asian trading world and the fact that they were in competition with one another, the success of one port had to be at the expense of the other. In this respect, Penang experienced growth at the expense of Melaka.

The circumstances that brought about this situation were many and varied. In 1780, Melaka's trade was already on the decline, hampered by a monopolistic policy which the Dutch could no longer successfully enforce, a VOC determined on maintaining Melaka only as a second-rate port, serious competition from the native port of Riau and the increasing encroachment of the English country traders and the EIC. While the Dutch in Melaka were able to eliminate the competition from Riau, they could neither convince the VOC to change its trade policies nor prevent the English advance into the trade of the region. In the long run, the two latter factors were largely responsible for Melaka's decline as the main centre of trade in the Straits.

Preoccupied by and defeated in the Anglo-Dutch war in Europe and forced to withdraw from their bases in the archipelago, the Dutch absence gave to the English more then two decades in which to establish themselves strongly in the trade of the region. It was an opportunity that the English used fully. Their role as caretakers of the administration of Melaka provided the excuse merely to maintain and not develop the port while Penang worked to undermine Melaka not only by the policy of free trade and giving favoured treatment to those willing to settle in the new port, but also by an active engagement with the trading regions in the Straits through trade missions. Penang's success was further assured by the fact that the English had already built the foundation for a thriving trade by their dominance in the long-distance trade between India and China. The manufactured goods they brought to Penang from India and China formed the magnet that drew the archipelago's traders to the port.

The Dutch reoccupation of Melaka between 1818 and 1824 was too short a time to arrest Melaka's trade decline and the unchanged VOC trade policy was too big an obstacle to overcome. Further, Melaka's problems were compounded by the opening of Singapore, whose rapid rise as an international port took away the strategic advantage that the former once had over Penang. After the Dutch withdrawal from Melaka to concentrate their resources on protecting the spice trade and to focus on the island of Java, and following the formation of the Straits Settlements, Melaka was sidelined by the English policy of developing Singapore and Penang rather than rebuilding the port that for centuries had been the most famous trade emporium in Southeast Asia.

NOTES

1   See Table 8: Imports and exports of Penang and Melaka, 1828/29, and also Table 9: Import and export of the seven main commodities for Penang and Melaka, 1828/29.
2   Memoranda on Melaka 1817–18 in SSFR, Vol. 10. See also extract letter from Governor Macalister to the Chairman and Deputy Chairman dated 7 November 1808, SSFR, Vol. 9.
3   Sinnappah Arasaratnam, 'Dutch Commercial Policy and Interests in the Malay Peninsula, 1750–1795', pp. 181–182.
4   Ibid., pp. 185–186.
5   See discussion in Chapter 2.
6   *An Exposition of the Political and Commercial Relations of the Government of Prince of Wales Island with the States on the East Coast of Sumatra, From Diamond Point to Siack*, Prince of Wales Island, 1824, pp.19–52.
7   For further information on these ports, see *An Exposition of the Political and Commercial Relations of the Government of Prince of Wales Island with the States on the East Coast of Sumatra*; John Anderson, *Political and Commercial Considerations Relative to the Malayan Peninsula and the British Settlements in the Straits of Malacca*, PWI: William Cox, 1824; John Anderson, *Acheen and the Ports on the North and East Coasts of Sumatra: with Incidental Notices of the Trade in the Eastern Seas and the Aggressions of the Dutch*, London: W.H. Allen, 1840; and John Anderson, *Mission to the East Coast of Sumatra in 1823*, London: T. Cadell, 1826.
8   An Exposition of the Political and Commercial Relations of the Government of Prince of Wales Island with the States on the East Coast of Sumatra.
9   Ibid.
10 Ibid.
11 *An Exposition of the Political and Commercial Relations of the Government of Prince of Wales Island with the States on the East Coast of Sumatra*, p.2.
12 Ibid.
13 See, for example, C.M. Turnbull, *A History of Singapore, 1819–1975*, Kuala Lumpur: Oxford University Press, 1977.
14 *An Exposition of the Political and Commercial Relations of the Government of Prince of Wales Island with the States on the East Coast of Sumatra*, p.3.
15 Ibid., p.4–10.
16 Ibid., p. 10–52.
17 T.J. Newbold, *Political and Statistical Account of the British Settlements in the Straits of Malacca, Pinang, Malacca, and Singapore*, Vol. 1, p. 150.
18 Ibid., p. 180.
19 Sinnappah Arasaratnam, 'Dutch Commercial Policy and Interests in the Malay Peninsula, 1750–1795', pp. 180–181.
20 Ibid., p. 181.
21 Rijksdollars or rijksdaalder is an imaginary standard coin of 48 stuiver used by the private sector for measuring for the different coins in circulation, see Gerrit Knaap, *Shallow Waters, Rising Tide*, p. 192.
22 Dutch currency.
23 The exchange rate is based on figures for 1824: 100 Spanish Dollars = 252.27 Dutch Guilders.
24 See C.D. Cowan, 'Early Penang and the Rise of Singapore', p. 86.
25 Inhabitants of Malacca to Robert Fullerton, Governor in Council of PWI, Singapore and Malacca, 4 October 1826, F/4/1044 28714; see also SSFR, Vol. 168.
26 For a detailed comparison of the three ports, see T. Braddell, *Statistics of the British Possessions in the Straits of Malacca*.

CHAPTER FIVE

Urban Traditions, Geography and Morphology

INTRODUCTION

THE AIM OF THIS CHAPTER is to look at the differences and similarities between an English and a Dutch colonial port-town. The scope of the discussion covers the definition of and the differences between a colonial port-town and a pre-industrial town. The chapter is arranged into two parts. The first section will highlight the characteristics of a colonial port-town and the differences and similarities between an English and a Dutch port-town. The second will deal with the morphology, foundation and geography of Dutch Melaka and English Penang. Finally this chapter will also highlight the problems of unplanned towns, which led to fires and their destruction. Initially, most colonial port-towns were unplanned and unorganized. As a result, there was no supervision of building materials so that many of these towns were exposed to the danger of fires. In fact, in the early seventeenth century, in the early stage of Dutch administration in Melaka, the town suffered from many fires, prompting the administration to introduce rules and regulations concerning building materials so that the port-town became relatively safe from destruction by fire in later years. In this chapter dis-cussion on the extreme vulnerability to fire hazards of an unplanned port-town will focus only on Penang in the early stages of its evolution.

Melaka was the first port-town in Southeast Asia occupied by a European power when in 1511 the Malay kingdom centred there was defeated by the Portuguese. In the ensuing decades and centuries, many more important port-towns of Southeast Asia were either seized or opened by other European powers, such as Manila by the Spanish, Batavia, Makassar and Melaka by the Dutch and Penang and Singapore by the English. This European intrusion into Southeast Asia resulted in the emergence of many colonial port-towns.[1] Although this development began in the early sixteenth century, the fundamental and radical changes in Southeast Asian society only took place in the mid-nineteenth century. From the sixteenth to the eighteenth centuries, colonial port-towns were confined to small areas and limited boundaries but by the mid-nineteenth century, the gap between the port-towns and their hinterlands had changed drastically. This was partly due to the expansion of the towns' population, which resulted in their boundaries expanding and merging with the hinterlands.

A definition of a colonial town is provided by Anthony D. King who notes the following characteristics:

> (i) dominance by a foreign minority, racially (or ethnically) different, of an indigenous population, and inferior from a material standpoint (ii) the linking of radically different civilisations in some form of relationship (this is perhaps the special task of the colonial city) (iii) the imposition of an industrialised society onto a non-industrialised one (this, of course, applies only from the late eighteenth or early nineteenth centuries) in (iv) an 'antagonistic relationship' where the colonial people were 'subjected as instruments of colonial power.[2]

A colonial town had unique features that distinguished it from pre-industrial towns.[3] As we shall see, these unique features can be seen in the administration, the society and the relationship between all the ethnic groups. Some colonial port-towns, of which Melaka is a good example, were formerly sites of native kingdoms later occupied and administered by colonial powers. Others, such as Penang, Singapore and Batavia, were newly created by the colonial masters who settled and built their administrative centres in strategic locations of Southeast Asia.

Most colonial towns were major ports which served as receiving and export centres for the colonial empires. As such, they became the focus of the colonial power's interest. Colonial port-towns served as a microcosm of colonial society and as 'a political, military, economic, religious, social, and intellectual entrepot between the colonizers and colonized.[4] Some colonial towns were set apart from the native societies in which they were placed. Nevertheless, over the centuries, the character of colonial towns changed. Most colonial towns had a low percentage of white inhabitants and a high percentage of natives and immigrants. Studies have suggested that colonial towns had a more pluralistic population composition than other towns and could accommodate separate ethnic communities with different lifestyles.

Most of these port-towns were established on sites which functioned as centres of trade, commerce, transport and administration. Since most of the population in the Southeast Asian region was concentrated in port-towns, the people there were cosmopolitan in nature and represented various ethnic groups.[5] This was also partly due to trade and the seasonal winds that dictated the movement of traders in the archipelago. According to Reid, the population in the urban areas of Southeast Asia was higher in 1600 than in 1850.[6] The commercial peak of the period, 1570–1630, brought a substantial increase in urbanization.[7] In the sixteenth and seventeenth centuries, about 5 per cent of the total Southeast Asian population inhabited large cities.[8] The most densely populated areas were, as Reid notes, in the area of the Straits of Melaka.[9]

The majority of the colonial port-towns in Southeast Asia grew and developed because they served as collection and distribution centres for goods from various places. For example, Melaka acted as a collection centre for goods from the archipelago and as a distribution centre to traders from India and China. Batavia, Penang and Singapore, likewise, served in the same manner as collection and distribution centres for trade.[10] While Melaka and Makassar were formerly the sites of native kingdoms, port-towns such as Ambon, Batavia, Manila, Penang, Madras and Colombo were created by the European powers. Since trade was the major force in determining the dynamism of these colonial port-towns, most were situated on strategic trading routes, for example Surat, Bombay, Goa, Colombo, Madras, Calcutta, Penang, Melaka, Batavia, Makassar and Manila. Many of these ports later grew into important towns administered by the Europeans and inhabited by people from various ethnic backgrounds.

TRADE AND PORT-TOWNS

The major trade routes used by the majority of traders to Southeast Asia were the Straits of Melaka, the Sunda Straits, the Java Sea and the South China Sea. Hence, many major port-towns emerged in these strategic parts of Southeast Asia, situated either by the sea or by a large navigable river.[11] On the eastern coast of Sumatra, the major port-towns in the Straits of Melaka, in a north to south direction, were Aceh, Pasai, Aru, Asahan, Batubara, Kampar, Indragiri, Siak, Jambi and Palembang. The main port-towns on the west coast of the Malay peninsula in the Straits of Malacca were Junk Ceylon, Kedah, Penang, Perak, Selangor, Melaka, Singapore and Riau. Most of the port-towns on the Sumatran coast were not under the direct control of Western powers, although they had a close trading relationship with ports under direct European control, like Melaka, Penang and Singapore.

In the eighteenth century, the main port-towns on the Java Sea were located in three geographical areas: the northern coast of Java, the southern coast of Borneo and the eastern part of the archipelago. On the northern part of the Java coast, the important port-towns were Batavia, Cheribon, Tegal, Semarang, Juwana, Rembang, Gerisik, Surabaya and Sumenep.[12] On the southern coast of Borneo, the important port-towns were Sukadana and Banjarmasin, and the main port-town on the eastern archipelago was Makassar. Although not all these port-towns were under direct Dutch control they had a very close trading connection with Batavia, the centre of Dutch administration in the East.[13] On the South China Sea, the main port-towns were Pahang, Trengganu, Patani, Ligor, Champa, Hue, Macao, Canton, Amoy, Manila and Brunei. Although most of these port-towns were not under foreign rule, they nevertheless enjoyed a close trading connection with ports under European control, such as Manila, Batavia and Melaka.

COLONIAL PORT-TOWNS

There have been many studies on the theoretical aspect of the urban morphology of colonial port-towns and various models have been used in this connection. For example, in early studies of urban development, Sjoberg modelled the colonial port-towns on pre-industrial cities. But his work has been heavily criticized because his model of a pre-industrial city did not fit the development of a colonial town.[14] Recent studies on colonial urban morphology have shown that the development of colonial towns differed from that of pre-industrial cities.[15] Although most of these studies have focused on the mid and late nineteenth century, during the peak of European imperialism and colonialism, they also shed light on the development of colonial port-towns in the late eighteenth and early nineteenth centuries and provide much information on colonial society.[16] A good description of a colonial society can be found in the work of Heather Sutherland. For instance, she describes seventeenth and eighteenth century Makassar as follows:

> The division of Makassar's society into three clusters, each with its own nucleus, would seem to suggest an obvious ranking. At the top the Castle, with its Europe-born male officials, backed by the power of the Company and the Netherlands. Below this, Vlaardingen, with its mestizos and Chinese, local merchants functioning within an Asian framework. At the bottom, the native kampung, the equivalent of the 'Black Towns' of British Indian settlements. But such an assumption must be modified by checking in which arenas of activity this relative ranking applied, and secondly, by asking to what extent differing groups would accept such an evaluation.[17]

As Sutherland's description of Makassar shows, various ethnic groups lived together in a colonial town. They included the colonialists (Europeans), immigrants (for example from China and India) and the natives. These ethnic groups were not a feature of pre-industrial towns in Europe.[18] On the other hand, people in a colonial town were from various ethnic groups and different backgrounds, with each ethnic group exhibiting its own ingrained cultural behaviour, traditions and institutionalized practices. The groups were then intertwined within a social matrix comprising newly constituted relations of domination and dependence between individuals and between collectivities of people.

Bellam describes the society and the economy in a colonial town as 'dominated by the European colonisers who occupy the apex of a "caste-like" hierarchy.' According to him, the Europeans, besides having virtually complete control of the power centres, monopolized the most important shares of administrative and economic activity. However, this was not always the case in many port-towns. Although political power was concentrated in the hands of a foreign white minority, they still had to rely on the Asian population in running the port-towns. In many cases, the economic structure of the city exhibited a broad dualism between a firm-centred European sector and a bazaar sector.[19] Thus, the heterogeneous nature of a colonial town clearly differentiated it from a pre-industrial city, which had a homogenous society.[20]

Another difference between a colonial port-town and a pre-industrial city was the stratification of society. According to Horvath, the stratification system of a colonial city consisted of three major components: the resident population from the colonial or imperial power; an intervening group; and the indigenous population from the surrounding countryside.[21] The highest stratum in the society, the elite, was made up of Europeans or the imperial masters, who possessed power and control and who determined the town's policy and administration. All policies regarding the administration of the ports, trade, law and order were vested in their hands. Although a minority group in the colonial town, they were powerful and could determine the daily life of the town dwellers.[22]

The issue of race was an important factor in determining social rank, occupation and relationships in a colonial town. Although there were Asian elites, the Europeans were at the top of the hierarchy, especially those born in the motherland and who held positions as officials in the administration, followed by the group active in trading and business.[23] The locally born white population held a lower status than those born and raised in the motherland. Even the religions, languages and economic activities of the elites and other ethnic groups differed from one another.[24] The only unifying factor was trade and commerce because it was the survival feature for the colonial towns.[25] In addition, trade and commerce formed the main reason for them to meet and interact with each other.

Horvath also argues that there were two types of intervening groups in colonial towns, those resulting from interracial mixing and those resulting from the migration of people from a third country. [26] Since most of the earlier migrants were men, this caused an unbalanced sex ratio among the new settlers in the town and led to intermarriage between them and the indigenous people. The offspring from these mixed marriages enjoyed a higher status than the indigenous inhabitants. The intermingling of Europeans and indigenous peoples produced a group called the Eurasians, while intermarriage between Asian immigrants and natives created new groups collectively called the mestizos (offspring of Chinese immigrants and natives) and Jawi Pekans (a mixture between Chulias with Malays). Besides the mixed groups of mestizos, Jawi Pekans, Eurasians and Anglo-Indians, there were the migrants from a third country. In most of the Southeast Asian colonial towns, these migrants were Indians and Chinese, some of whom were active in commerce and trade while others worked as semi-skilled and unskilled labourers in the towns.[27]

Besides the groups already mentioned, there were, of course, the indigenous peoples or natives and slaves who came from diverse places in the archipelago. The majority of the natives migrated from the immediate hinterland to settle in the town. In addition, migrants arrived from various parts of the archipelago. Melaka, for example, attracted the Javanese, the Bugis from the Celebes, and the Minangkabaus from Sumatra. In Penang there were also the Bugis, the Siamese and the Acehnese from Sumatra.

From the perspective of morphology, the early colonial town also had its own unique characteristics. First, the town was usually dominated by a fort, for example the towns and ports of Madras, Calcutta, Batavia, Galle, Penang and Melaka. Forts were normally built by the colonial administration as a place of defence against the enemy, from either land or sea. In some cases, another function of a large fort was to serve as the living quarters for the European administrative officers. In some towns the fort also accommodated the Europeans not employed by the colonial government. The fort was sometimes separated from the town by a ditch or canal and had a wall around it. Soldiers also patrolled the fort. If the fort was large, the administrative buildings of the town were situated within it.

The town, which was separated from the fort, was usually lined with streets and roads leading to the interior part of the country. It was in the town that the businesses and markets were located. The town also had various buildings of worship, for example churches, mosques and temples.

Moreover, the town provided the meeting point for residents to congregate. In some colonial towns, such as Madras, Calcutta and Batavia, the living quarters of the various ethnic groups were segregated. The colonial power controlled the administration and defence of the town and employed security guards to patrol at night. Nevertheless, these characteristics differed from one colonial town to another.

In addition to the above characteristics, a colonial town was connected to the hinterland. In most cases, the hinterland areas were not under direct colonial administration. The town's boundary was marked by a river or a canal that separated the town from the hinterland. However, some colonial towns were connected to the hinterland areas by roads, rivers or canals. In some colonial towns, the hinterland areas supplied agricultural and food resources produced by the native inhabitants. In some cases, the hinterland was under the direct administration of the town's colonial administration.

DUTCH COLONIAL URBAN TRADITIONS

Dutch imperial power was exercised through the occupation and administration of port-towns that stretched from the Indian Ocean through the Malay-Indonesian archipelago. These port-towns served as collection centres for trade and as distribution centres for goods to various places in the hinterland and other areas. Hence, a consequence of Dutch colonial activity in the East was the development of various colonial port-towns.[28] The first important port-town established by the Dutch in the Malay-Indonesian archipelago was Batavia, as early as 1619. It became the centre of Dutch imperial power in the East and was also the first city built by the Dutch on Asian soil.[29] The majority of port-towns under direct Dutch control were strategically located on the trading route between India and China, such as Colombo, Galle, Jaffna, Melaka, Batavia, Ambon, Makasar and Zeelandia. Some of these port-towns had formerly been built and occupied by natives as centres of trade for their kingdoms. A few, like Melaka, had been under Portuguese rule while others were newly founded. Batavia, founded by the Dutch, was an exceptional case, being planned and constructed according to a Dutch master plan for the town that was modelled on the work of Dutch architects and planners.[30]

The majority of Dutch ports and towns had certain distinguishing characteristics: a location at the mouth of a river or inlet or an island; the administrative, military, and economic centre in the form of a fort or citadel; the town separated by a stretch of open land; a main street or canal built running across the town; a special area for the civilian residents; and the sizes of housing lots often fairly irregular and narrow.[31]

Although most Dutch port-towns had some similarities, there was no strict type or blueprint planning for each town.[32] Dutch officers and administrators in each town played an important role in the planning and structuring of the town.[33] The town's fort was small and served as the main defence area. It was in the towns that most of the inhabitants resided and met. In the centre of the towns were the markets, bazaars, places of worship and residential areas. In places where the fort or castle covered a very large area, administrative buildings were located there and the majority of the Dutch administrators also lived there. The town, built and developed outside the fort, became the busiest area. Since most Dutch towns had various ethnic groups, some segregation policies were enforced in them. The layout and the morphology of a Dutch town are well illustrated in Makassar, which had a town where all the inhabitants met and a fort, a massive, typical seventeenth century defensive structure enclosing dwellings, storehouses, church and offices, and functioning as the living and working quarters for the Company officials. Makassar also had areas with houses of foreign merchants and native villages, or kampong, with local peoples.[34]

Most of the port-towns depended on commerce and trade in order to collect revenue for the local administration. There were also revenue farms, or *pachten*, which varied from one town to another.[35] For example, in Makassar one of the earliest documented farms was for alcohol.[36] The customs or *Boom* farms were very important in all Dutch port-towns. It was from the customs duties that the bulk of the revenue was collected because the Dutch administration was dependent on this revenue.

In most Dutch colonial towns, administrative power was shared by various officials. The most important post was that of the governor who was in charge of the town's political, military, criminal and civil affairs.[37] The *syahbandar* (harbour master) maintained patrols and watchouses on smuggling, supervised the weights and measures, inspected ships for contraband goods and kept a register of incoming and outgoing ships.[38] Other important administrative department posts were the *fiskaal* (prosecutor), who was head of the police, and the public prosecutor, who was in charge of suspected criminals and presenting cases before the Council of Justice.[39] The administration of the Christian community was undertaken by the *predikant* or Calvinist preacher.[40] There was also the *schutterij* or militia, the *wijkmeester* or town administrators, the *brandspuitmeester* or chief fireman and lamplighter.[41] In addition, there were charitable bodies, such as the *diakonij*, which supervised poor relief, and the *weeshuis*, or orphanages, in most Dutch colonial towns.[42] The orphanage funds served as a de facto bank providing financial resources for the inhabitants of the towns. The churches, mosques and temples of each ethnic group played an important role in society. Although the Dutch Reformed Church had full support from the administration, other churches, such as the Roman Catholic Church, were free to have their own services.

ENGLISH COLONIAL URBAN TRADITIONS

Like the Dutch, the English occupied various port-towns at many strategic locations on the Indian subcontinent and in Southeast Asia. Although in the beginning the English were not as successful as the Dutch, who started occupying various port-towns as early as the seventeenth century, they soon caught up by the mid-eighteenth century.[43] In fact, many port-towns earlier occupied by the Dutch and the Portuguese eventually fell into English hands.[44] Important port-towns situated on the trading route between India and China, such as Bombay, Madras, Calcutta, Penang, Melaka and Singapore, were occupied by the British. Distinctive English characteristics could be discerned in the colonial ports on Asian soil. The first Asian port-town to be built and occupied by the British was Madras in India.[45] Madras was a swampy and neglected part of the Coromandel Coast but the British transformed it by 1639 into an important port-town controlling the trading route from the interior part of the Coast to Southeast Asia, China and the Indian subcontinent.[46] Madras was largely the creation of the English East India Company's commercial interests on the subcontinent.[47]

Some features of English colonial towns were similar to those in Dutch colonial towns, for example the presence of various ethnic groups and, in some cases, ethnic segregation and race discrimination. However, a major difference was that English colonial towns did not have the careful proper planning found in the Dutch towns. They were less well planned, lacked infrastructure and their urban planning showed little influence from the metropolitan centre. However, they were similar to Dutch port-towns in the East in that the Asian inhabitants were allowed much freedom to manage their intra-caste affairs while the administration of the town was in the hands of the English, who were mostly merchants. This is well depicted in the case of Madras where the port-town was divided into three main areas: the inner fort or castle enclosing the factory house; the outer fort enclosing the inner fort housing the European quarter; and the unprotected native settlement of traders, merchants and artisans.[48] The English concentrated more on securing and protecting the fort – the centre of their administration – and less on establishing an urban colonial society subservient to their aims.

One of the main features of a colonial town that the English shared with the Dutch was the practice of ethnic segregation. In many parts of the Indian sub-continent ethnic group segregation by the English was common. Such a policy was tolerated and fostered, for example in Madras, because it was especially useful to British commercial interests and values.[49] Moreover, the local people had no say in the matter. Since segregation was already a working principle in Madras, when the English established their port-towns in Southeast Asia they commonly enforced the same pattern. A clear example of this was in Singapore,[50] a city planned by the British and inhabited by non-Europeans whose residential distribution continued to reflect the intentions of the European rulers.[51] The layout showed the clearly marked spatial segregation of the ethnic groups into separate areas. The Arabs and Bugis were located close to the Malay Sultan's areas and the mosque. The local Malays resided on the northern fringes of the Rochore River.[52] Other ethnic groups like the Chinese and Indian immigrants, seen as potential trouble-makers, were separated from the quiet and spacious European zones by the Singapore River.[53] The English and European areas were specially located on the high and well-drained site between the rivers Rachore and Singapore. It was here that the English colonial institutions – such as the cricket grounds, Anglican church, government buildings and the clubs – were found.

Since commerce was of such vital significance to the Dutch and the English, the posts of 'senior and junior Merchants' were of much importance in their colonial towns. Under VOC rule, the senior merchant also headed the administration while the junior merchant served as the secretary and bookkeeper. Both posts were important in the Dutch colonial towns because they could further one's career, up to the level of Governor. A similar practice was seen in the EIC, although in some cases the administration of an English colonial town was dominated not by EIC merchants but by English country traders. For example, in Penang the post of the Superintendent or Governor was held by a merchant, Francis Light, a former English country trader, who was assisted by a Committee of Assessors made up of mostly English country traders and wealthy merchants. Therefore, most of the officers in the administration were formerly merchants (country traders) or officers who had been given some freedom to venture into trade besides working as administrators. The conclusion can be drawn that an English colonial town was administered more by the merchant community than by officers appointed by the Company. These merchants were given some allowances to conduct their own trading activities in order to supplement their low incomes from the EIC.[54]

Both English and Dutch colonial towns showed similarities from a morphological perspective. For example, the main building of the town was the fort, and in colonial Madras the town was divided into three major areas, an Inner Fort or Castle enclosing the Factory House and defended by four corner bastions connected by curtained walls; an Outer Fort enclosing the

Inner Fort and the European quarter protected by four corner bastions and walls on three sides; and an unprotected native settlement of traders, merchants, weavers, and artisans serving English commercial trade and interests. The second area was called the 'white town' while the third area was called the 'black town'.[55] Beyond the town was the hinterland. The relationship between the hinterland and the town was very important in most English colonial towns. For example, in Madras the British administration later acquired several areas in the hinterland and incorporated them into the town. The town also came to depend on the hinterland areas for most of its trade and commerce.[56] Calcutta, for example, depended heavily on the internal trade in the Bengal area.[57] Singapore too depended on the hinterland areas (the archipelago and the Malay peninsula) for its trade.[58] Thus, although most hinterland areas were not under the direct control of the town, its survival and dynamics depended heavily on these areas.

The fort in Madras, named Fort St. George, was not large and consisted of a tower or house enclosed by a rectangular wall 400 yards long by 100 yards wide, with bastions at the four corners. This was the administrative heart and sanctuary for the Europeans or whites within which they could feel secure. Roche points out that 'all the lists of residents at Fort St. George over hundreds of years do not mention a single native living within the confines of the "White Town". The presence of numerous Dutch and Portuguese residents provides evidence of a planned process of assimilation – pulling together all who shared colour and race'.[59]

Nevertheless, not all English colonial towns had large forts or castles. Only towns vulnerable to invasion by powers from land and sea had them, for example Madras, Calcutta and Penang. But it was not just vulnerability that determined the existence of a fort or castle. It may be observed that many early port-towns were built around a fort, but those that were founded later did not follow this pattern. Singapore, for example, did not have any fort or castle, perhaps because by the time Singapore was founded methods of warfare had changed considerably and forts were no longer impenetrable, so that they did not provide the protection they once did. If a port-town had a fort, then the meeting places were situated on the outer side of the fort. Such meeting places allowed intermingling, mainly for business and trade which were the mainstays of a colonial port. In order to facilitate communications the towns were lined with streets and roads linking various sections with the hinterland.

For most colonial English towns, no master plan was used in the building of the fort; there was also no clear indication that plans for the structure of forts and castles in Europe had been used. The officer on the spot played an important role in deciding the structure and planning of the fort or castle, rather than a military architect brought in from Europe for that purpose.[60] Although no blueprints were found for most of the English colonial towns, there were definitely segregated areas in the town that separated the white population from the coloured inhabitants.

Most colonial English towns had a small white population. As marriages between this population and the natives were not encouraged the only way to increase the white population in some towns was through marriages within the various European groups. For example, in Madras, the presence of the Portuguese and the Dutch who lived in the same area as the English helped to ensure racial endogamy.[61] The Portuguese and Dutch had arrived in Madras long before the English arrived in Indian waters and a small community of their descendents, the result of mixed-marriages, remained when the English took over the port. Similarly, there was a small Portuguese-European community as well as a Portuguese-Eurasian group in Melaka when the Dutch took over the town. Although some mixing also occurred between the Dutch and the Portuguese-Eurasians in Melaka, this happened only on a small scale. In Penang, cases of mixed-marriages between the early English settlers and Portuguese-Eurasians from Siam were not uncommon.[62]

Social and religious facilities were not provided by the administration as a matter of course. As a consequence, more often than not places of worship such as the church were built by Christian communities themselves or by Christian organizations such as the missionary society. Little support came from the administration to raise money to construct churches. Unlike the Dutch, who had more government-sponsored plans, no charitable bodies, such as for the relief of the poor and orphanages or financial institutions such as the *weeshuis*, were established in most English colonial towns. In addition, most English colonial towns lacked sufficient funds and manpower to administer public utilities and social welfare activities.[63] Although taxes were imposed on the inhabitants, the social amenities provided were very poor.[64]

GEOGRAPHY, FOUNDATION AND MORPHOLOGY OF MELAKA

Melaka is located on the western side of the Malay peninsula, on the Straits of Melaka, the main gateway between East and West.[65] Although situated in the hot tropics, Melaka has fair and pleasant weather.[66] Its main assets were trade and location rather than its hinterland, which was left mostly uncultivated.[67] As a seventeenth century traveller pointed out, 'the harbour of Malacca is one of the finest in all the Indies, being navigable at all the seasons of the year, a conveniency belonging scarce to any other in the Indies.'[68]

During the Malay sultanate period, Melaka controlled a very wide empire that covered parts of eastern Sumatra and the western Malay peninsula. However, during the Portuguese occupation, they only controlled and occupied a small area, which included the fort of Melaka and the town and its suburb.[69] The exact area and its boundary cannot be clearly determined. It would appear that the Portuguese only had limited jurisdiction over the areas beyond the fort. The position of Naning, in the interior, was even less clear as there is no evidence of Portuguese occupation and jurisdiction in the hinterland of Melaka.[70] Although some scholars have claimed that the boundary of Melaka during the Dutch occupation was wide, studies have proven that the Dutch only had jurisdiction over a limited area.[71] For example, in 1660 'a VOC employer confidently claimed that the town's jurisdiction extended 64 leagues, from the island of Sembilan to the Cape of Singapore, but less than two decades later Governor Bort more modestly placed the northern boundary of the company's authority on the Pannagie (Penajis) River and the southern at Muar'.[72] According to Pieter van Dam, the famous Company lawyer, the government of Melaka never really controlled more than four miles south, five miles north and six miles inland from the town centre.[73] During the English occupation, they determined more clearly the boundary of Melaka, which extended along the coast from the Linggi River to the north of the town to the Kersang River on its south. The territory was 40 miles long at its greatest extent, and its breadth varied from 10 miles to 28 miles inland.[74]

Although Dutch Melaka had only a very limited area of jurisdiction, its hinterland came under the loose control of large land proprietors who lived in the town. The Dutch administration gave over the management of the hinterland areas to these land proprietors who in turn appointed the *penghulu* or local headmen, to supervise the collection of tax from the people who lived on the land. As long as these proprietors collected and paid the tax, the Dutch administration left them to their own devices. The proprietors who came from the Dutch Burgher, Chinese, Malay and Keling communities usually lived in town and were therefore absentee landlords.[75] One of the largest pieces of land alienated by the Dutch administration in this manner in the middle of the eighteenth century went to a Burgher named de Wind. This land covered an area of about 280 square miles.[76]

The Dutch approach to the question of land use contrasted sharply with the situation in Penang, where attempts were made to develop the hinterland into an important agricultural area and where land was granted in perpetuity during Francis Light's administration. For example, at Sungai Kluang there were 60 families, making up 250 people. A total of 600 *orlongs*[77] of land was distributed and cleared for planting. The area from

Sungai Pinang to Sungai Kluang which covered almost 6 miles, was occupied by Malays and Chinese settlers. Much of these pieces of land was planted with spices. In another region, which covered an area called Salisbury plain, 30 Malay families with their headman (*penghulu*), named Panglima Dato Hakim, had settled permanently. These lands were cultivated with food crops and spices. In addition to the above, the Company also gave the right to James Scott to own plantations, constituting 200 *orlongs* on newly cleared ground on the east side of the Penang River and another 200 *orlongs* on the southwest side of the Penang River.[78] Even the Company (EIC) owned large pieces of agricultural land in the hinterland of Penang; these were planted with spices such as pepper and nutmegs.[79]

Melaka under the Dutch had a large area of uncultivated hinterland covered, for the most part, with dense forest. Throughout the period from the Malay sultanate to the Dutch occupation little development seems to have taken place in this area.[80] For most of these centuries Melaka's position as an emporium of trade did not encourage agricultural activities. But with the Dutch, an additional factor was the deliberate policy of the higher authorities in Batavia to discourage Melaka's development so as not to undermine the commercial interest of Batavia. Therefore, only a few areas near the town were cultivated with fruit trees and paddy fields.[81] In some parts of Naning, paddy was cultivated and some of the agricultural produce from these areas was sent by river to Melaka. As noted by Sheehnan, 'it produces but little for the sustenance of life, except what is brought forth in gardens, and what grows among the mountains, where you meet with some rice and pease: the defect of which is supplied by vast numbers of small vessels, which come every day from Bengal and Sumatra, and bring thither rice and other eatables.'[82]

Studies of the early history and morphology of Melaka have so far been limited in their scope and have therefore shed little light on what the town was like in the early years of its existence. Although there have been many recent works on the town of Melaka, they tend to focus on the population and trade during the golden age of the Malay sultanate.[83] Many of these studies relied on the old Malay texts, which were mainly concerned with court history and genealogy, and on the writings of Western travellers and observers who mostly extolled the greatness of Melaka as a trading emporium.[84] This has meant that little is known about the streets, buildings, people or morphology of the town. Thus, knowledge about the town's layout in its early days is scant. Nevertheless, from the available material, it could be surmised that Melaka during the period of the Malay sultanate was not a walled town with a separate administrative area and a business district. It would also appear that after the introduction of Islam to Melaka, despite its

pervasive influence in many aspects of Malay life, it did not bring any fundamental change in the traditional structure and morphology of Melaka.[85]

Although for the Malay sultanate period clear information on the morphology of Melaka is not available, a close study of the Portuguese period can
help to give a picture of the layout and setup of the town. We know that the
site on which the Sultan's palace stood was taken over by the Portuguese and
used to build a castle and fort. Otherwise, in the early years of the
Portuguese administration, Melaka was left much the same as it was during
the Sultanate period. Over the years, however, some changes did take place
in the morphology and structure of the town.[86]

The former site of the palace became the centre of the Portuguese
administration. Dominated by St. Paul's Hill, this centre was enclosed by a
stone wall some 20 feet high and five feet thick. Inside the walls were many
buildings to house the administrative offices, the residences of the governor
and officers, the bishop, the town hall, a church and a hospital. The area
outside the wall – the town – was divided into various quarters to house the
different ethnic groups. There was Kampong Kling for the Indian community, Kampong China for the Chinese inhabitants and Kampong Java for
the Javanese settlers.[87]

More information is available on the morphology of Melaka as it entered
into the seventeenth century.[88] Important information is provided by a
traveller, John Nieuhoff, who entered the service of the Dutch West India
Company in 1640 after 13 years in Brazil. He made a voyage to the East
Indies and wrote about his visit to Melaka in 1660: 'This city is very large in
compass, being not many years before surrounded with a wall of square
stones and bastions, by the Dutch. It is very populous, the houses being built
very close, though it has some very broad and handsome streets, which are
planted on both sides with trees. In the midst of the city is a hill with a very
fair church dedicated to St. Paul, on the top of it, where divine service is
performed in Dutch: The steeple church and monasteries founded here by
the Portuguese are much decay'd. Most of the houses here are built of strong
bamboo-canes, which are very durable in dry weather, tho' there are also
some stone houses here; they are generally not very large, and low, provided
with small apartments and slenderly furnished.'[89]

Morphologically, the town of Melaka during the Dutch period could be
subdivided into three main sections; the Fort, in which only Company
servants and Dutch free burghers were allowed to reside; the town of
Melaka, which was lined with streets named by the Dutch as Herenstraat,
Jonkerstraat, Goudsmidstraat, Eerstbrugwalstraat, Secondebrugwalstraat,
Derdebrugwalstraat and Visherstraat; and its outer suburbs, Tengkera,
Bandarhilir, Bunga Raya and Bukit China. The busiest part was the town, in

the business area, the market place and the houses of worship where many of the inhabitants met. The town was located on the right bank of the Melaka River; the Fort was separated from the town on its left bank.[90] The Fort, or castle, covered a large area. Abdullah bin Abdul Kadir, a Jawi Pekan born in 1797 and bred in Melaka, and hailed as the father of modern Malay literature, in his writing, *The Hikayat Abdulah*, made the observation that 'the fort and the buildings within its walls were put up by the Portuguese after their occupation of Malacca in July 1511, as part of Alphonso d'Albuquerque's plan to have a chain of fortresses between Goa, the head-quarters of the Portuguese conquerors in India, and their possessions in the East where their ships could revictual'.[91] The original fortress, completed in January 1512, was a castle and four-walled keep facing the sea and commanding the entrance to the Malacca River on the south bank, on which it stood near the shore. It was the residence of successive Portuguese governors for nearly 130 years. During this period the fortifications were enlarged and the surrounding walls extended to enclose St. Paul's Hill. A map made in 1613 by Godinho de Eredia, Portuguese explorer and geo-grapher, shows the plan of the walls as an irregular pentagon with its apex towards the sea, and this is seen also in a map dated 1656 found by Leupe in the archives of the Dutch East India Company in Batavia. The distance round the perimeter was estimated in 1605 by de Eredia at about 1,100 yards, and in 1678, after the Dutch had strengthened the defences, by Governor Bort at about 1,400 yards. The fort was built to the same plan as that at Galle, shaped as a quadrilateral; there was a well in the middle so that in times of disturbance or war the people with their supplies could take refuge inside the circular of the protecting walls. The castle or tower was as high as the hill. It was not built on the top of the hill because it was preferable to place it at the foot, right on the sea, where it could easily be strengthened in times of war.[92]

As far as the VOC was concerned, the main focus of Melaka town was the fort or castle.[93] Many travellers to Melaka in the seventeenth and eighteenth centuries mentioned the fort. According to one description, it "was about a mile in compass. There are six small towers furnished with sufficient cannon, and a ditch towards the sea and channel. The two gates are one towards the river, and the other towards the south cape. The governor of the city commands in it, and has under him a garrison of one hundred and eighty soldiers".[94] Munshi Abdullah observed that there were four gates leading to the fort and three bridges connecting it to the town and to other parts of the suburbs.[95] The main bridge, located on the Melaka River, was a drawbridge and any ship entering the town through this bridge had to pay a levy tax. In fact, this was the tax on ships entering and leaving

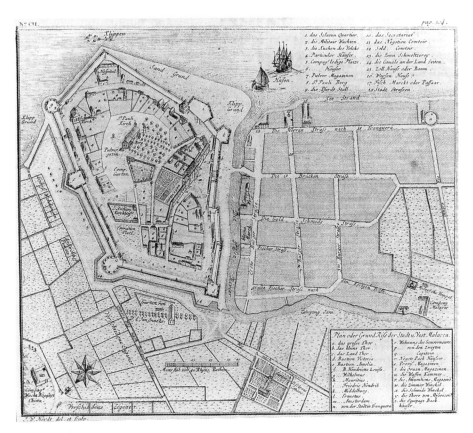

Map 11: Map of Melaka drawn in the early eighteenth century. From J.W. Heydt, *Geographisch und topographischer Schauplatz von Africa und Ost-Indien*, p. 304. Courtesy of the Royal Netherlands Institute of Southeast Asian and Caribbean Studies (KITLV), Leiden (Bibl. 3c 56).

the bridge. For security reasons, this bridge was raised and closed for pedestrian crossing at night and no one was allowed to walk near the fort without any lights.[96] Abdullah also described the morphology of the fort.[97] An old map of Melaka published in 1744 (see above) provides a very clear plan and layout of the buildings and the land used inside the fort.[98] It shows the buildings, the gardens, the churches and the bastions.

The fort of Melaka, so long the symbol of strength and power of the Europeans who had ruled Melaka, was destroyed in 1807 by the English with the aim of abandoning the town and closing the port to merchants and traders. This policy was implemented for the survival of Penang because the English believed that if the Dutch were to return to Melaka it would rival the British port at Penang, leading to stiff competition in trade.[99] The British believed that by destroying the fort, the Melakan population would be forced to evacuate and settle in Penang. It was also done to prevent Melaka from remaining a defendable place and threat to English interests in the Straits. However, this plan failed when the majority of the population refused to leave. In fact, the destruction of the fort was an ill-advised plan by Colonel Robert Farquhar, who became Lieutenant-Governor of Penang in 1804–05. Although there were some protests against the plan by William Farquhar, Resident of Melaka, the Board of Directors did not heed his protests and ordered the destruction. To Abdullah, who decried the fort's destruction, it was 'a pity that a building as fine as this should be brought low in an instant of time. For if they wished to repair it there is no knowing how many years it would take before it was finished. For the fort was the pride of Malacca and after its destruction the place lost its glory, like a woman bereaved of her husband, the lustre gone from her face'.[100]

Outside the fort and beyond the town lay the suburbs. The Tengkera area was located at the northern part of town and lay by the coast, and Bandarhilir was located south of the castle also by the coast. Bunga Raya and Bukit China were located further inland, on the outer fringe of the town. These areas were connected by roads and waterways to the town. However, as stated earlier, the area covered under the jurisdiction of the town for most of the VOC period until 1794 was no more than four to five miles in radius. The following is a description of Melaka made by William Dampier in 1729:

> Malacca is a pretty large town, of about 2 or 300 families of Dutch and Portuguese, many of which are a mixt breed between those nations. There are also many of the native Malayans inhabiting in small cottages on the skirts of the town. The Dutch houses are built with stones, and the streets are wide and straight, but not paved. At the north west of the town there is a wall and gate to pass in and out: and a small fort always guarded with soldiers. The town stands on a level low ground, close by the sea. The land on the back-side of the town seems to be morassy, and on the west-side, without the wall, there are gardens of fruits and herbs, and some fair Dutch houses: but that quarter is chiefly the habitation of the Malayans. On the east-side of the town, there is a small river which at a spring-tide will admit barks to enter. About 100 paces from the sea there is a draw-bridge, which leads from the midst of the town to a strong fort, built on the east-side of the river.[101]

During the Dutch administration the town area was populated by various ethnic communities, the major groups being the Dutch Burghers, Malays, Peranakan-Chinese, Kelings and Portuguese Eurasians. There were also large numbers of slaves. However, towards the end of the eighteenth and in the early nineteenth centuries, the Dutch Burgher population declined due to several reasons, including migration.

During the Portuguese period, each ethnic group lived in its own kampong or quarter, named after the particular group.[102] This practice survived during the Dutch period and was, in fact, expanded so that there was a Kampong Belanda (Herenstraat and Jonkerstraat), a Kampong Java (outside the town), a Kampong China (Goudsmidstraat and Eerstebrugwalstraat), a Kampong Serani (further north of the town), a Kampong Pali (between the Seconde and Derdebrugwalstraat) and a Kampong Kling (Colijstraat). Although during the Portuguese period and for a good part of the Dutch occupation there was ethnic segregation, by the end of the eighteenth century the divisions had been blurred and in the ensuing years there was evidence to show that the reasons which had in the first place brought about separation no longer applied. Areas formerly exclusively populated by the Dutch Burghers (Heren and Jonkerstraat) became the homes of the Chinese, reflecting a shift from an ethnic orientation to one in which wealth was the main criterion. Thus, the majority of the wealthy population of the town, irrespective of ethnic origin, resided on two important streets, Herenstraat and Jonkerstraat. The houses here were built from bricks and roofed with tiles. Due to the hazard of fire, which had burnt down many houses in the town area in the mid seventeenth century, the Dutch administration enforced regulations on the building of houses in the towns.[103] As a result, most houses were of brick and had roofs of tile.[104] All those who did not abide with these regulations were asked to move away from the town.

The map of Melaka in the mid-eighteenth century reproduced overleaf, which shows the layout of the town, the names of the streets, the markets, the orphanage home, the mosques, the bridges and the Malay kampongs, is testimony to the fact that during the Dutch period Melaka had seen important changes although it had not expanded to any significant degree. It also indicates that the Dutch not only preserved many old features of the town but also enhanced them. Although the fort was lost due to an English official's notion of expediency, some legacies of the past still remain.

GEOGRAPHY, FOUNDATION AND MORPHOLOGY OF PENANG

Penang, ceded to the English East India Company in 1786, is an island 15 miles long from north to south and 10 miles wide. The island, located on the northern part of the Straits of Melaka,[105] covers an area of 108 square miles and has ranges and hills reaching a height of 2,600 feet.[106] In its northeastern part lies a plain, shaped like a triangle, on which Francis Light established Georgetown, the first English colonial town in Southeast Asia.[107] This plain runs almost to the foot of the hills in a flat valley that became an important agricultural area. It consists of a strip of land three miles wide down the east coast, facing the Malay peninsula, from Penang to the south.

On the mainland opposite the island of Penang is an area called Prai, which belonged to the kingdom of Kedah. In 1800, the territory of Prai, which stretched from Kuala Muda to Sungai Kerian (about 45 miles long and eight miles deep), was annexed by the English from the Sultan of Kedah and renamed Province Wellesley. The English intended Province Wellesley to be an important agricultural hinterland which would produce paddy to provide rice to feed the people of Penang. It was also annexed from the kingdom because of its importance to Penang's defence. It could act as a buffer, protecting the island from invasion from Kedah as well as eliminating the possibility of a port growing there which could compete for Penang's trade. Before the invasion of Kedah there was a small port opposite the island which belonged to the kingdom. Due to its close proximity to Penang and because it was frequently used by many local and foreign traders, the English feared this port's rivalry. English control of Province Wellesley was also seen as necessary to halt smuggling and piracy in the narrow channel between Penang and the mainland.[108] Unlike Melaka, Penang had well-marked boundaries and the English administration held control over a wide area. This control covered the whole island and its territories, including Province Wellesley and a few small islands off Penang.

In the early period of the English occupation, there was much discussion as to whether Penang would make a suitable naval base. There was also discussion of the terms on which Penang was ceded. This led to bitter controversy as to whether the Company was bound to defend the Sultan of Kedah against Siam. A third concern was the rapid growth of population and trade, which led to 'extravagant hopes regarding its suitability as a means of gaining the control of a considerable part of the commerce of the East Indian islands'. Yet another problem was 'the difficulty of maintaining law and order amongst a turbulent native and European population when no legally constituted courts were in existence on the island'. This difficulty was only solved when the Recorder's Court was established in 1807. Other questions the administration had to deal with included the problem of piracy and the introduction of pepper, nutmeg and cloves in Penang so as to 'render Gt. Britain independent of the Dutch spice islands'.[109]

Although trade was the main focus at Penang, in the early period the English administration hoped that the island would become Britain's main naval base in the East.[110] Thus, various plans and monetary investments were put forward towards this goal. Unfortunately, the plan failed mainly due to insufficient artisans and building materials and a shortage of timber and trained personnel. The timber available on the island and from Province Wellesley was of poor quality, so that it had to be obtained from Pegu via Rangoon. This made it more expensive to build a ship in Penang. In addition, there were delays in obtaining from Europe essential items, such as ironwork, copper and nails.[111] As a result, Penang failed as a naval base and shipbuilding centre.

One of the motives of the Company (EIC) in promoting Penang was to take advantage of its strategic location to build a naval base there and to defend the east coast of India against rival European forces during the Napoleonic Wars. However, after the Battle of Trafalgar, which established Britain as the unchallenged naval power in Europe, there was a feeling among higher authorities in England that such an idea was unnecessary and the home government soon lost interest in the scheme. Furthermore, when the Admiralty withdrew its financial support, the Directors of the East India Company who were faced with heavy financial commitments in India also followed suit. Since Penang's revenues were not sufficient to pay for the project, the scheme for making Penang a naval base and shipbuilding centre was finally abandoned.[112]

Although Penang failed in this scheme, the administration never stopped attempting various economic activities that would help the new colony to develop into an important establishment. It encouraged people from the surrounding regions, especially the Chinese, Indians and Malays and the natives from the Indonesian archipelago, to migrate to the island and develop the hinterland so as to convert it into an important spice producer. Since occupying the island, the English introduced various crops.[113] Unlike Dutch-Melaka, lands in the hinterland were cleared for producing spices. Chinese, Indian and Malay immigrants from the surrounding areas were encouraged to clear and to own land for this purpose. As a result, numerous agricultural experiments were attempted on the soil of Penang. Under Light, rice was first grown followed by pepper. By 1805 the pepper produced by Penang came to 2,000 tons and for over ten years it was the staple product and economic mainstay of the island. The next valuable export was betelnut, followed by tin.[114]

The site on which the town of Penang was built was called Tanjong Penaigre.[115] Although there was no blueprint for the layout of the town, nor a master plan such as that produced for Batavia by the Dutch, Light, the first Lieutenant-Governor of the new colony, who was not devoid of ideas, did make an attempt to establish one.[116] According to his plan, the commercial areas would lie between Light Street, Beach Street, Malabar or Chulia Street and Pitt Street. These were the earliest streets in Penang, named by the founder of the island and town. The increase in population, largely due to

Table 10: Types of shop buildings/dwellings in Penang in 1818

Names of Streets	Attap	Plank with tile roofs	Brick	Total
Beach Street	21	39	277	337
Chulia Street	104	15	80	199
China Street	5	18	48	71
Penang Street	1	12	90	103
King Street	-	19	26	45
Church Street	1	2	7	10
Bishop Street	-	-	17	17
Market Street	-	8	37	45
Love Lane	1	-	-	1
Queen Street	-	-	24	24
Pitt Street	6	-	2	8
Leith Street	-	-	1	1
Praingin Road	38	8	12	58
Penang Road	89	3	10	102
Aceh Street	1	1	4	6
Chuckla[?] Street	26	-	-	26
Total	293	125	635	1053

Source: F/4/633 17169.

new arrivals from the surrounding regions, led to further expansion in the early nineteenth century. New roads were built, such as Farquhar Street, Love Lane, Penang Road and Battery Lane.[117] In 1800 Penang town was less than five miles in radius, with its boundary marked by a river on the southern part and a canal on the western part. This boundary separated the town from the hinterland.

The town of Penang had numerous shop buildings. Table 10 above shows that more than 32 per cent of the shops were situated on Beach Street, the busiest street in Penang. There were also godowns, the Customs House and warehouses on this street. Moreover, many government buildings were found in this part of the town, as were the majority of brick shops. It was also the first landmark for a traveller to Penang. Most European merchants and traders had their property, warehouses, godowns, shops or offices on the northern end of the street near the harbour and the Customs House.[118] At the southern end of the street stood shops that belonged to the Chinese, Indian and Malay traders. The street was connected to Light Street in the north and to Bishop Street, Church Street, China Street, Market Street, Chulia Street, Aceh Street, Malay Street and Praingin Road in the south.

At the southern end of the town was a marketplace privately owned by John Brown, a wealthy businessman who owned land and property. Brown was a government servant during the time of Lieutenant-Governor George Leith but later resigned to start his own business as a planter. In 1806 he built a marketplace on his own land at Beach Street near the Praingin River and rented out the premises to tenants. He was authorized by the Governor and the Council to sell paddy, rice, poultry and fish in the market and given the right to collect rent from the shops and the freedom to set the price of all goods sold in the market.[119]

Chulia Street was the second busiest street with more than 18 per cent of all shops in the town. The majority of the people who owned property or shops in the street were Chulias or merchants who came from the Coromandel Coast and Bengal. Only a few Malays owned property there, the most notable being Tuanku Syed Hussain, the richest Malay in Penang, but many lived in the street. The area surrounding the street was formerly the site of a Malay settlement, which had been incorporated into the town when Penang's population increased. Due to this it remained a predominantly Malay area with hardly any Chinese or European settlers. Many buildings in Chulia Street had attap roofs, which suggests that they were built as temporary homes; perhaps the majority of the people living in this street were seasonal occupants, such as sailors and traders, who lived in Penang for a few months in a year while they waited for the next wind season to trade. The attap houses were probably rented for a short period of stay.[120] Certainly, the Bugis and Malay traders made this area their base.

Although the length or span of China Street was shorter than either Beach Street or Chulia Street, there were more shops on it. This street could also be very busy at times, as it intersected with Beach Street. Moreover, it was situated in the middle of the town, between Chulia Street and Market Street on the south, Church Street and Bishop on the north, and was intersected by Pitt Street on the west. China Street had been earmarked by Francis Light as the centre of the commercial area and, reflecting its importance, there were more brick than attap houses here.

Penang Street and King Street, also situated in the commercial area, ran parallel to Beach Street on the east and Pitt Street on the west. They were also criss-crossed by Chulia Street, Market Street, China Street, Church Street, Bishop Street and Light Street. The shops in this area belonged to

Europeans, Chinese, Indians and Malays and most were built of bricks. This part of the town suffered from the fires that occurred in 1789, 1812 and 1814 so that by 1818 there was only one shop still roofed with attap on Penang Street while there were none on King Street. Similarly on Church, Bishop and Market Streets, which also suffered fires, most buildings were made of brick. Many of the properties situated on Bishop Street and Church Street belonged to European owners, though a smaller number were owned by Asians.

Love Lane, Queen Street and Pitt Street, also situated close to the commercial centre, were considered less important. Further away from the heart of town were Leith Street, in the western part, Praingin Road, at the southern end, and Penang Road, further southwest of the town. The majority of shops found in these areas were built from attap. A possible explanation for this was that this region was not affected by the fires. Most of the shops on these streets were not concentrated in one particular area that might easily catch fire.

Aceh Street, predominantly Malay, was also a former Malay town that had grown and expanded and later was incorporated into the main town area. The majority of the Malays had their property in this street, but there were few shops since the majority of the Malays living here were not merchants or shop owners. Many Malays owned houses here so that this street was in a Malay residential area and not a business area. Tuanku Syed Hussain also owned some property on Aceh Street.

Although there is mention of a Chuckla[?] Street, it is hard to trace its location. Most of the old maps do not show this street; there is the possibility that this was in fact Armenian Street. On the other hand, it could have been situated outside the town centre since all of the shops were built from attap.

Most of the government buildings were located on the northern and eastern part of the town. In the earlier period, the government had to rent most of its offices from James Scott and Tuanku Syed Hussain. This occurred because much of public land in Penang had been sold to private individuals, especially during the administration of George Leith, for the purpose of raising money to finance the construction of roads and streets and to carry out drainage and restructuring. As a result, there was little public land left for the building of government offices and houses.[121] At one point, the government tried to purchase land from the estate of the late Francis Light, though it had in the meantime been sold to James Scott.[122] Much of the northern beach area of the town, considered to be prime land, had belonged to Light. When he died, his property was inherited by his widow, Martina, who, for some years, lived on the northern beach on Leith Street Ghout.

Table 11: List of government buildings/houses and lands in 1827

District	Streets	Types of Property
Penang	Beach Street	(1) The master attendant's house and office. (2) The government warehouse. (3) The Customs House. Treasury. (4) The land belonging to the Committee of Assessors. (5) Government buildings and rice godowns. (6) The civil store keeper's office and godowns and a piece of land.
Penang	Light Street	(1) Two pieces of land. (2).Post office. (3). Library.
Penang	Bishop Street	(1) A ghee godown.
Penang	Penang Street	(1) Church. (2) School. (3) The Court House. (4) The Recorder's Chambers. (5) Prison.
Penang	King Street	(1) The engineer's yard. (2) A piece of land (unused?).

Source: G/34/119.

This street was later renamed Martina Lane. Later, Martina married a man named John Timmer, and in April 1802 the Timmers sold the northern beach property to James Scott. Two months later, Scott, as one of Light's executors, sold an adjoining site to Carnegy, who then passed it on to Messrs. Scott and Company. Thus, the greater part of the valuable land once owned by Light was transferred to James Scott during the Leith administration.[123]

As the government did not own much property, it had to rent premises and in time it was faced with rental problems. One such problem was related to a property owned by James Scott when he raised the rent to an exorbitant price. Without much land at its disposal, the government also found it difficult to have a public park. Nevertheless, the government managed to purchase lands from revenue farmers. This it did when there was a fall in the value of the property market and land could be purchased at a very low price. In 1827 the government owned the following property detailed in Table 11.

Most government buildings and the homes of a majority of the European community were found in the northwestern part of town.[124] The residences of the majority of merchants and businessmen, such as the Chinese and Chulia, were in the business areas, while most Malays and Jawi Pekan built their homes in the southern part of the town.[125]

Penang also had a fort that was built in 1786, named Fort Cornwallis which was less grand than the Portuguese-Dutch-Melakan fort.[126] Situated on the northeastern part of town, it covered only a small area. The town, on the northeastern part of the island, was built close to the fort. Certain parts of the town were close to the wall of the fort but there was no clear boundary which separated them. No ditch had been built for the purpose and nor was

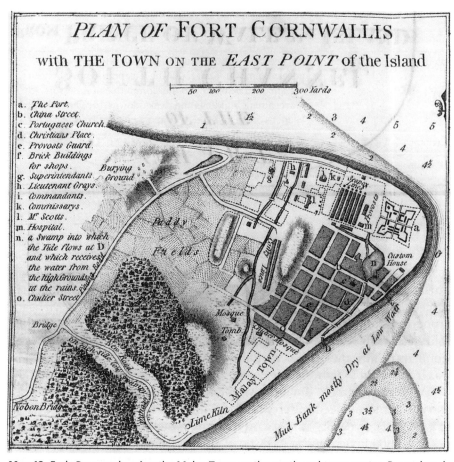

PLAN OF FORT CORNWALLIS

with THE TOWN ON THE *EAST POINT* of the Island

50   100   200   300 Yards

a. *The Fort.*
b. *China Street.*
c. *Portuguese Church.*
d. *Christians Place.*
e. *Provosts Guard.*
f. *Brick Buildings*
    for shops.
g. *Superintendants*
h. *Lieutenant Grays.*
i. *Commandants.*
k. *Commissarys.*
l. *M.r Scotts.*
m. *Hospital.*
n. *a Swamp into which*
    the Tide flows at D
    and which receives
    the water from
    the High Grounds
    in the rains.
o. *Chulier Street*

Map 12: Early Penang showing the Malay Town on the south and town centre. Reproduced by permission of the British Library (G7370 opp Appendix 0675617).

there a river to form a natural boundary. The fort itself was small and did not house the government buildings or facilities for the Company's servants and the Governor as was the case in Melaka. It was of square masonry with exterior sides measuring 500 feet, built by a local Chinese contractor. Not only was it badly built but it was incomplete in some parts. By the 1790s, the fort was in a deplorable condition and many parts of the walls had fallen down.[127] Although there was a suggestion to rebuild the fort and make it bigger and stronger, the administration was unable to do so partly because the cost of buying the adjacent lands from the rich European merchants was prohibitive. Moreover, a strong fort was not an urgent need for Penang, there being no serious threat from any external power.

FIRES AND LOSS OF PROPERTY

Most colonial towns had, at some time or other, suffered from fires that caused much destruction of property and loss of lives. For example, Melaka suffered many fires in its early history as a result of which the VOC enforced strict regulations regarding building materials and the layout of buildings. Only brick buildings were allowed and those unable to afford them were forced to move out of the town. Firefighting facilities and firefighters were always on alert. Thus, by the end of the eighteenth century, Melaka was better prepared to cope with fire hazards. However, Penang, then in its early stage of development, was without any fire regulations or firemen. It was also an ill-planned town without any strict regulations on building materials. Most of its houses were built from materials prone to catch fire.

Since the town's establishment, there were three major fires, namely, in 1789,[128] 1812,[129] and 1814.[130] These fires burnt down almost the whole town. The first outbreak, on 23 April 1789, burnt down Malabar or Chulia Street, including 56 six houses belonging to the Chulias. Most of the shops situated in this part of town were owned by Chulia merchants, as noted before. As retailers of Indian cloth, many of these merchants had their warehouses and godowns on this street. In the confusion caused by the fire, petty thieves took advantage of it to steal goods from the shops and warehouses so that many bales of Indian cloth were stolen and hidden away. The authorities appear to have succeeded in recovering the goods and apprehending the thieves. Some of the stolen goods were found on ships anchored in the port and in houses and shops in Aceh Street, and the petty thieves who were caught were whipped and exiled from the island. The cause of the fire could not be ascertained but the loss was said to amount to SpD 20,000. Those who suffered losses were given assistance by the authorities.

The authorities later encouraged the town dwellers to build brick premises and helped them by reducing the price of bricks to SpD 3.00 per mill.[131] Other expenses required for the rebuilding of houses made from brick were also reduced.[132] Since fire had destroyed many valuables and property belonging to the merchants and traders in the town, they became more conscious about the question of safety in their neighbourhood. Many responded by rebuilding their shops and other premises with bricks, although petty traders and small business merchants, perhaps due to the high expenses involved, still rebuilt their shops with materials that could catch fire easily.

However, a more cautious attitude or some degree of civic-mindedness developed and the administration began to receive petitions regarding acts of negligence or disregard for the safety of others. Thus, if a neighbour's mode of business and premises were thought to have the potential to endanger property and life, a complaint was lodged with the authorities. When

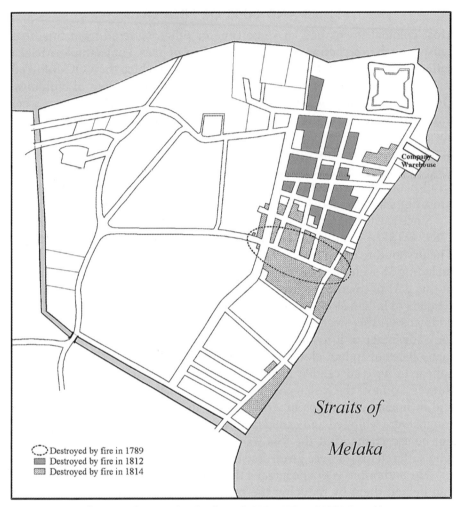

Map 13: Areas of Penang destroyed in the fires of 1789, 1812 and 1814. Based in part on map R.1.17x/3345 (British Museum).

complaints were filed, the authorities had to investigate the premises. For premises prone to fire, the owners were ordered to dig more wells and to have more fire fighting facilities, like buckets, firefighters and wells filled with water.[133] Premises such as those used by arak distillers were considered as unfriendly.[134]

Although the first fire caused much property loss and made the authorities aware of its adverse effects, many town dwellers remained negligent and continued to take risks. Thus, another fire broke out in 1812, which burnt down nearly half of the town area. The only place saved was the Beach Street

Table 12: Number of houses destroyed in the 1814 Penang fire

Ethnic Group	Brick shops/ houses	%	Attap shops/ houses	%	Total	%
Malays	34	25.00	131	17.28	165	18.45
Chulias	67	49.26	573	75.59	640	71.58
Armenians	1	0.73	nil	0.00	1	0.11
Arabs	29	21.32	nil	0.00	29	3.24
Chinese	5	3.67	54	7.12	59	6.59
Total	136	15.21	758	84.78	894	100.00

Source: G/34/10.

area, which housed most of the government warehouses, godowns and marine store houses. This fire appears to have destroyed a lot of the property belonging to the wealthy Chinese in. Records show that the majority of fire victims were Chinese, followed by a small percentage of Malay and Chulia merchants and traders who had their premises in the centre of the town's commercial area.[135]

The real extent of the damage and the actual number of people who lost their property during this fire cannot be ascertained from the records, as the list of fire victims only covered the town's major landholders and merchants.[136] The majority listed was Chinese merchants and landholders but some revenue farmers were also included. Only a small number of individuals from the other ethnic groups were recorded in the list. The 1812 fire burnt down nearly all of the property belonging to the wealthiest Chinese, for example, Tequa, Che Em, Low Amee, Khoo Hooan alias Chewan, Baba Yair, and By That Poye. The property losses of the European and other Asian ethnic groups appear to have been less extensive than those of the Chinese. The only Malay who seem to have suffered losses in the fire was Syed Harron, who claimed losses of SpD 10,000. However, many shopkeepers and house owners suffered losses in the fire, but their names were not entered in the list. This can be surmised from the official report: a total of 500 shop owners and house owners were affected by the 1812 fire, and out of all premises destroyed, 227 were owned by traders and merchants.[137]

The third fire, in 1814, also destroyed almost half the town. The worst affected areas included the whole of Chulia Street, Armenian Street, Market Street, the southern part of Beach Street, Penang Street, King Street, Queen Street and Pitt Street. The 1814 fire was believed to have started from Chulia Street in a house belonging to a Chulia named Cauther.[138] His house was attached to a shop selling prepared food. Many of the people interviewed about the fire confirmed that the fire started from the Cauther residence. At the time of the fire, Cauther's child was ill from small pox and it was believed that while preparing medicine for his sick child, he accidentally started the fire which spread immediately to the whole house and the neighbourhood. Cauther, however, denied the allegations.

In any case, the 1814 fire destroyed many of the town's residences, shop-houses, warehouses and godowns owned mainly by wealthy Chinese, Malay and Chulia merchants and traders.[139] Table 12 above shows that many of the properties destroyed were built from attap although a substantial number of brick buildings were also destroyed. The Chulias suffered the most, as 640 buildings belonging to them were destroyed. The Malays and the Chinese also suffered big losses, but far less than the Chulia community. This was because the fire destroyed the whole of Chulia Street before spreading to parts of Beach Street, Penang Street and King Street.

Table 13 below shows the number of people affected by the 1814 fire. As can be seen, the Chulias accounted for more than 68 per cent, the Malays 21 per cent and the Chinese 9 per cent. Although as many as 2,283 Chulias were adversely affected by the fire, the principal victims among this group were fewer, as can be seen from the number of buildings destroyed and the small number of brick buildings affected. This was because most Chulias affected were workers who were temporary migrants, merchants or traders who had come to Penang during the trading period and therefore did not own real estate property. With the Malays, few were listed as fire victims because not all appear to have reported their losses to the government, un-like the Chinese victims, who usually reported their losses. Moreover, as with the Chulias, the majority of the Malays affected in the 1814 fire were traders and merchants from the archipelago who came to Penang during the trading season. On the other hand, while the number of Chinese affected by the fire was smaller compared to the Chulias and Malays, principal sufferers among them were higher compared to the other two ethnic groups.[140]

Table 13: Number of inhabitants of houses/shops destroyed in the 1814 Penang fire

Ethnic Group	Number of People	Percentage
Malays/Arabs/Armenians Merchants	716	21.53
Chulias/Pulicats/Surat Merchants	2,283	68.66
Chinese	326	9.80
Total	3325	100.00

Source: G/34/10.

The report from the committee of inquiry after the 1814 fire stated that all attap buildings in the town would be demolished and replaced with bricks and tiles, distributed free to the poor. The government also requested that Melaka bricks and tiles be used in rebuilding the town.[141] The committee also discovered that actual losses in the fire had been exaggerated and that the actual loss sustained did not exceed the sum of SpD 500,000. They also identified a number of poor people who had been victims but whose names were not included in the list. The committee also concluded that the actual loss suffered by the merchants from the Coromandel Coast and native merchants and traders was SpD 150,000, while the sum of SpD 350,000 represented losses sustained by individuals and residents on the island. Out of the total amount evaluated, one-third was determined as loss in buildings and the remainder in merchandise and sundries. The government also distributed aid to the poor by giving rice and charity, and they were also given the opportunity to borrow money to rebuild their houses and shops provided the loan was repaid within five years.[142]

In the aftermath of the fire, the government ordered that only brick buildings were to be built east of Pitt Street, which was to be widened to 120 feet and extended in a direct line as far as the Praingin River. All houses in the street were required to be constructed with bricks and roofed with tiles within five years. The committee also discovered that the many attap buildings in Beach Street and in the lower end of Bishop Street, belonging to carpenters and blacksmiths, were vulnerable to fire and would affect the neighbouring warehouses. It was therefore suggested that buildings in the lower end of Bishop Street and on either side of Beach Street, as far as Armenian Street, be demolished and replaced by brick buildings, with similar aid for rebuilding. The government also passed a regulation that all houses situated in Pitt Street should be rebuilt using brick.[143]

After the fire incident, the government prohibited the building of huts or houses with attap roofs and those who could not afford or who refused to use bricks and tiles were ordered to move out of the town area. Attap houses had to be built away from the commercial areas. Orders were issued for the immediate removal of all huts or sheds within the fort or near the commercial area and new regulations required that a space of not less than five to six feet should be left between each building. Further, wells for fire prevention had to be frequently checked and maintained. Military officials were used to conduct and submit a full report on all types of houses belonging to the Company (EIC) or rented by the government for public purposes. The failure of the fire engine during the fire also led the government to take immediate action to create a fire department with more manpower and equipment.

The fire pressured the government into forcing the town dwellers to change their attitude when rebuilding their premises. Although the government was very firm about its policy of rebuilding the town with bricks and tiles imported from Melaka, the majority of town people were still unable to afford the high cost of rebuilding. Even officers in the committee owned attap houses in the commercial area of the town and they too refused to rebuild their houses with bricks.[144] Rebuilding was still costly even though the government had reduced the prices of bricks and tiles. Moreover, the money loaned by the government and payable in five years created financial problems for certain merchants, traders and house owners whose businesses were ruined. Most were unable to repay their debts and ended up insolvent.

Discussion of the physical development of Penang and the experiences the town went through during and after the fires shows that the new colonial port-town evolved and grew despite the ad hoc approach to its planning and the teething problems it faced. As can be seen, from a small beginning when it was inhabited by only a few hundred Malays, Penang was turned by the English into an important European colonial town with a multi-ethnic population and a port capable of rivalling Melaka in importance as a trading centre in the Straits of Melaka. With the arrival of the Chinese and Chulias as well as other ethnic groups, the new town was transformed into a cosmopolitan centre inhabited by more than 90 per cent immigrants who, along with the English administrators, helped to shape Penang into a viable colonial port-town.

CONCLUSION

A common feature of a colonial town was that despite its small European population, the Europeans were at the top of the social scale. A colonial town may not have been a city heavily populated by Europeans but it was a town administered by a European power. The European residents, clearly demarcated by the colour of their skin, their superior position in the social hierarchy and their responsibility as colonial rulers, lived in isolated communities segregated from the major part of the town's population.[145] The forts, churches and stone buildings were common features of the Western elements in a colonial environment. A fort existed in Penang and a castle and fort existed in Melaka. Penang was undoubtedly influenced by developments in British-India, where the population was segregated and clustered into separate areas, while in Melaka such a policy appeared to have been less important to the Dutch in the eighteenth century. All in all, both Melaka and Penang reflected these features and grew within the same scheme of things. There were of course some differences but, as we shall see, these differences were not fundamental and did not negate all the other characteristics that help to identify them as colonial port-towns.

NOTES

1   Some of the good studies on the theoretical aspects of colonial towns and ports include: L. Nagtegaal, 'The pre-modern city in Indonesia and its fall from grace with the Gods', pp. 39–60; Ronald J. Horvath, 'In search of a Theory of Urbanization: Notes on the Colonial City', pp. 69–82; David Simon, 'Third World Colonial Cities in Context: Conceptual and Theoretical Approaches with Particular Reference to Africa', pp.493–514.

2   Anthony D. King, 'Colonial Cities', p. 9.

3   'Preindustrial cities', a concept based on the development of cities in Europe, was put forward by G. Sjoberg, in *The Preindustrial City*, New York: Free Press, 1960.

4   Ronald J. Horvath, 'In Search of a Theory of Urbanization: Notes on the Colonial City', p. 76.

5   There were also inland towns and cities that were not necessarily dependent on trade but agriculture. However, the majority of towns in the Southeast Asian region depended on trade. For further discussion, see T.G. McGee *The Southeast Asian City*, p. 33.

6   Anthony Reid, *Southeast Asia in the Age of Commerce 1450–1680*, p. 68.

7   Ibid., p. 70.

8   Ibid., p. 75.

9   Ibid., pp. 75–77.

10   M.E.P. Bellam, 'The Colonial City', pp. 67–68.

11   Anthony Reid, *Southeast Asia in the Age of Commerce 1450–1680*, p. 85.

12   See the discussion on the various ports on the northern coast of Java, in Gerrit J. Knaap, *Shallow Waters, Rising Tide*, pp. 45–60.

13   Ibid.

14   See, for example, David Simon, 'Third World Colonial Cities in Context', pp. 493–514; and Ronald J. Horvath, 'n Search of a Theory of Urbanization: Notes on the Colonial City', pp. 69–82.

15   See the discussion on the development of the pre-industrial city in G. Sjoberg, *The Preindustrial City*; see also the discussion on the critique of Sjoberg's works by David Simon, in 'Third World Colonial Cities in Context', p. 498. Sjoberg's model of a pre-industrial city has also been criticized in Ronald J. Horvath 'In Search of a Theory of Urbanization: Notes on the Colonial City', pp. 71–72.

16   Luc Nagtegaal, 'The pre-modern city in Indonesia and its fall from grace with the Gods', pp.39–60.

17   Heather Sutherland, 'Ethnicity, Wealth and Power in Colonial Makassar', pp. 45–46.

18   See Ronald J. Horvath, 'In Search of a Theory of Urbanization'. To Horvath, 'The colonial city is viewed as a subsystem of a colonial society and, therefore, we may inquire briefly into the nature of the colonial society. The basic characteristic of a colonial society is that it is *heterogeneous*, unlike the models of industrial or preindustrial socities, which are basically or relatively more homogeneous'. p. 74.

19   Bellam interprets the 'firm-centred' as one 'where trade and industry occur through a set of impersonally defined social institutions which organise a variety of specialised occupations with respect to some particular productive or distributive ends'. The bazaar sector, on the other hand, is founded on 'the independent activities of a set of highly competitive commodity traders who relate to one another mainly by means of an incredible volume of *ad hoc* acts of exchange'. 'The bazaar sector is labour – rather than capital – intensive and the bazaar business generally is run on a personal, often kinship, basis'; see M.E.P. Bellam, 'The Colonial City: Honiara, A Pacific Islands' Case Study', p. 68.

20   Ibid., p. 68.

21   Ronald J. Horvath, 'In Search of a Theory of Urbanization', pp. 76–77.

22   Ibid., p. 77.

23 See T.G. McGee, *The Southeast Asian City*, pp. 59–60.

24 Ronald J. Horvath, 'In Search of a Theory of Urbanization: Notes on the Colonial City', p. 77.

25 See, for example, the case of Madras which at the end of the eighteenth century became an important port on the Coromandel Coast. For further discussion, see Susan J. Lewandowski, 'Changing Form and Function in the Ceremonial and the Colonial Port City in India: An Historical Analysis of Madurai and Madras', in *Modern Asian Studies*, II, 2, 1977, pp. 196–209.

26 Ibid. p. 77

27 T.G. McGee, *The Southeast Asian City*, pp. 58–59; see also Ronald J. Horvath, 'In Search of a Theory of Urbanization: Notes on the Colonial City', p. 78.

28 Ron van Oers, *Dutch Town Planning Overseas during VOC and WIC Rule (1600–1800)*, Zutphen: Walburg Pers, 2000.

29 Ibid., see also Remco Raben, 'Batavia and Colombo', p. 11.

30 Remco Raben, 'Batavia and Colombo', p. 11.

31 Ibid., pp. 33–34.

32 Ibid., p. 34.

33 Ibid., pp. 9–39.

34 Heather Sutherland, 'Ethnicity, Wealth and Power', p. 41.

35 For further discussion on the history of revenue farms in Southeast Asia, see Anthony Reid, 'The Origins of Revenue Farming in Southeast Asia'. In John Butcher and Howard Dick (eds), *The Rise and Fall of Revenue Farming: Business Elites and the Emergence of the Modern State in Southeast Asia*, London: Macmillan Press, 1993, pp. 60–79.

36 Heather Sutherland, 'Ethnicity, Wealth and Power', p. 113.

37 Barbara Watson Andaya, 'Melaka under the Dutch, 1641–1795'. In Kernial Singh Sandhu and Paul Wheatley, *Melaka: The Transformation of A Malay Capital c. 1400–1980*, p. 203.

38 Heather Sutherland, 'Eastern Emporium and Company Town', p. 114.

39 Ibid.

40 Ibid.

41 Ibid.

42 H.C. Gall, 'De Weeskamer in Nederlands-Indie Als Negetiende-Eeuws Instituut', in C.J.H. Jansen, E. Poortinga and T.J. Veen (eds), *Twaalf Bijdragen Tot De Studie van de Rechtsgeschiedenis van de Negentiende Eeuw*, Faculteit der Rechts-geleerdheid, Universiteit van Amsterdam, 1996, pp. 29–43; see also H.E. Niemeijer, 'Calvinisme en Koloniale Stadscultuur Batavia 1619–1725', Ph.D. thesis, Vrije Universiteit Amsterdam, 1996; Jean Gelman Taylor, *The Social World of Batavia*. For the laws regarding orphanages, see some discussion on this matter in Peter Burns, 'The Netherlands East Indies: Colonial Legal Policy and The Definitions of Law'. In M.B. Hooker (ed.), *The Laws of Southeast Asia*, Vol. II, Butterworths, 1988, pp.147–214.

43 See, for example, D.K. Bassett, *British Trade and Policy in Indonesia and Malaysia in the late 18th Century*.

44 See, for example, Holden Furber, *Rival Empires of Trade in the Orient, 1600–1800*; Holden Furber, *John Company At Work*.

45 S. Arasaratnam, 'European Port Settlements in the Coromandel Commercial System 1650–1740', p. 79; see also Susan M. Neild, 'Colonial Urbanism: The Development of Madras City in the Eighteenth and Nineteenth Centuries', pp. 217–246.

46 Ibid., See also Ashin Das Gupta and M.N. Pearson, *India and the Indian Ocean 1500–1800*, Calcutta: Oxford University Press, 1987.

47 Patrick A. Roche, 'Caste and the British Merchant Government in Madras', p. 381.

48 Ibid., pp. 384–385.

49 Ibid., p. 381.

50 T.G. McGee, *The Southeast Asian City*, pp. 69–72.

51 Ibid., pp. 69–72.

52 Ibid., p. 70.

53   Ibid., pp. 69–72.
54   Patrick A. Roche, 'Caste and the British Merchant Government in Madras', p. 387.
55   Ibid., p.385. See also Susan J. Lewandowski, 'Changing Form and Function in the Ceremonial and the Colonial Port City in India', p. 199.
56   Susan M. Neild, 'Colonial Urbanism: The Development of Madras City in the Eighteenth and Nineteenth Centuries', p. 218. See also Susan J. Lewandowski, 'Urban Growth and Municipal Development in the Colonial City of Madras', p. 347.
57   Rhoads Murphey, 'The City in the Swamp', pp. 241–243. See also P.J. Marshall, 'Eighteenth-Century Calcutta', p. 91.
58   Wong Lin Ken, 'The Trade of Singapore, 1819–69', *JMBRAS*, Vol. 33, Part 4, 1960. pp.11–105.
59   Patrick A. Roche, 'Caste and British Merchant Government in Madras', p. 386.
60   Susan J. Lewandowski, 'Changing Form and Function in the Ceremonial and the Colonial Port City in India', p. 205.
61   Ibid., pp. 388–389. See also George D. Winius, 'A Tale of Two Coromandel Towns: Madraspatam (Fort St. George) and Sao Thome de Meliapur', in *Itinerario*, Vol. XVIII, 1994, Number 1, p. 62.
62   Ibid.
63   See P.J. Marshall, 'Eighteenth-Century Calcutta', p. 92.
64   Rhoads Murphey, 'The City in the Swamp', pp. 251–253.
65   J.J. Sheehan, 'Seventeenth Century Visitors to the Malay Peninsula', *JMBRAS*, vol. 12, Pt. 2, 1934, p.100. See also Walter Caulfield Lennon, 'Journal of a Voyage through the Straits of Malacca on an Expedition to the Molucca Islands Under the Command of Admiral Rainier', *JSBRAS*, Vol.7, June 1881, p. 64.
66   See J.J. Sheehan, 'Seventeenth Century Visitors to the Malay Peninsula', p. 91. See also T.J. Newbold, *Political and Statistical Account of the British Settlements in the Straits of Malacca, Pinang, Malacca, and Singapore*, Vol. I, London: John Murray, 1839, p. 116.
67   The many writings on the uncultivated hinterlands of Melaka include: James N. Anderson and Walter T. Vorster, 'In Search of Melaka's Hinterlands: Beyond the entrepot'. In Dilip K. Basu (ed.), *The Rise and Growth of the Colonial Port Cities in Asia*, Monograph Series No. 25, University of California: Centre for Southeast Asian Studies, 1985, pp. 1–5; F.L. Baumgarten, 'Agriculture in Malacca', in *JIA*, Series 1, Vol. 3, 1849, pp. 707- 723; and E.A. Blundell, 'Notices of the History and Present Condition of Malacca', in *JIA*, Series I, Vol. 2, 1848, pp. 726–754.
68   J.J. Sheehan, 'Seventeenth Century Visitors to the Malay Peninsula', p. 76.
69   T.G. McGee, *The Southeast Asian City*, p. 50.
70   T. Braddell, 'Notes on Naning with a brief notice of the Naning War', *JIA*, Series II, Vol. 1, 1856, pp. 194–232. For further reference to Naning, see Jonathan Cave, 'Naning in Melaka', *MBRAS*, 1989, Kuala Lumpur.
71   See 'Valentyn's description of Malacca', *JSBRAS*, No. 13, 1884, p. 50, where it is stated that the territory belonging to Melaka extends over a length of 30 miles and over a breadth of about 10 miles.
72   See Barbara Watson Andaya, 'Melaka under the Dutch', p. 198.
73   Ibid., See also J.J. Sheehnan, 'Seventeenth Century Visitors to the Malay Peninsula', p.103, where Sheehnan mentions that the region that falls under Dutch-Melaka control only covered an area of not more than three miles round the city.
74   T. Braddell, 'Notes on Malacca', *JIA*, Series II, Vol 1, 1856 p. 43. For the problems of boundary and the question on Naning, see Jonathan Cave, "Naning in Melaka", and T. Braddell, 'Notes on Naning with a Brief notice of the Naning War'.
75   For a discussion on the problems of land ownership and the conflict between English and Dutch laws regarding land ownership, see, for example, K.T. Joseph, 'The Malacca Land Laws', *Federation Museums Journal*, vol. XV, 1970, and Paul H. Kratoska, 'Land Law and Land Tenure in British Melaka'. In Kernial Singh Sandhu and Paul Wheatley (eds), *Melaka*, pp. 497–534.
76   Brian Harrison, *Holding The Fort*, p. 110.

77   Orlongs or relong is a local measurement for the size of a piece of land. One orlong or relong is equivalent to 0.7 acres.

78   For a further detailed account, see Letter from Captain Light 14 January 1790, in G/34/4. See also an account of lands cleared and cultivated from Teehouse point to Penang as compiled in 1791, in G/34/5. See also Report of the Lieutanant Governor upon Prince of Wales Island in 1805 in G/34/9 and look at appendix 14 in G/34/9. See also statement of expenses incurred on accounts of roads and bridges at Prince of Wales Island from January 1804 to September 1805, in G/34/9; and Extract of Bengal Consultations 17 April 1802: an account of the spice plantations on this island belonging to the Company and to the inhabitants, in G/34/9.

79   Extract of Bengal Consultations 17 April 1802: an account of the spice plantations on this island belonging to the Company and to the inhabitants, in G/34/9.

80   T.G. McGee, *The Southeast Asian City*, p. 40. As McGee correctly points out, 'the economic base of Malacca was first and foremost trade. Malacca did not rely upon its hinterland for its wealth. The life blood of Malacca was commerce'.

81   Walter Caulfield Lennon, 'Journal of a Voyage through the Straits of Malacca on an Expedition to the Moluccan Islands Under the Command of Admiral Rainier', *JSBRAS*, Vol. 7, June 1881, p. 62. He notes that, '"Though situated in the most favourable way for uniting all the resources of a rich country with an easy communication by sea to foreign markets, Malacca now labours under every inconvenience that an island does, without its advantages, and though it has adjoining a soil capable of yielding the richest productions of every kind, and though under the dominion of an European power for about 250 years, it remains, even to the foot of the lines of the town, as wild and uncultivated as if there had never been a settlement formed here'.

82   J.J. Sheehnan, 'Seventeenth Century Visitors to the Malay Peninsula', p. 76.

83   See, for example, Anthony Reid, "The Structure of Cities in Southeast Asia", pp. 235–250.

84   See, for example, Tome Pires, *The Suma Oriental*, London: Hakluyt Society, 1944. See also M.A.P. Meilink-Roelofsz, *Asian Trade and European Influence in the Indonesian Archipelago Between 1500 and about 1630*, 's Gravenhage: Martinus Nijhoff, 1962.

85   J. Kathirithamby-Wells, 'The Islamic City: Melaka to Jogjakarta, c. 1500–1800', in *Modern Asian Studies*, 20, 2, 1986, p. 336.

86   T.G. McGee, *The Southeast Asian City*, p. 50. He states that the morphology of the city did not change dramatically apart from the addition of the stone buildings and walls of Fort A' Famosa.

87   Ibid., p. 49. See also Kernial Singh Sandhu and Paul Wheatley, 'From Capital to Municipality', in *Melaka*, pp. 495–597.

88   See, for example, 'Report of Governor Balthasar Bort on Malacca in 1678', in *JMBRAS*. Vol. 5, Part 1, 1927, pp. 1–232, and P.A. Leupe, 'The siege and capture of Malacca from the Portuguese in 1640–1641', pp. 1–175.

89   J.J. Sheehnan, 'Seventeenth Century Visitors to the Malay Peninsula', pp. 72–73.

90   See '"Valentyn's Description of Malacca', pp. 50–51. The author states that the town of Melaka was built in the form of a crescent. There was a respectable fortress of great strength, with solid walls and fortified, with bastions, well-provided with guns, able to withstand, with its garrison, a hard blow.

91   Abdullah Abdul Kadir, *The Hikayat Abdullah* (annotated translation by A.H. Hill), Kuala Lumpur: Oxford University Press, 1970. A.H. Hill says that Abdullah was the first writer in Malay to bring realism to his writing. Abdullah sees events of everyday life from the standpoint of a common experience of mankind and not through the tinted glasses of legend and romance. It was said that he began writing *The Hikayat Abdullah* after his wife's death. At that time he had settled permanently in Singapore. In the postscript it was mentioned that the first draft was completed in May 1843, pp. 1–28.

92   A.H. Hill, 'Munshi Abdullah's Account of the Malacca Fort', *JMBRAS*, Vol.23, Pt.1, 1950, pp. 88–89.

93   A good description of the Fort of Melaka can be found in, 'Report of Governor Balthasar Bort on Malacca 1678', pp. 14–27.

94   J.J. Sheehnan, 'Seventeenth Century Visitors to the Malay Peninsula', p. 101.

95 A.H. Hill, 'Munshi Abdullah's Account of the Malacca Fort', p. 85. According to him, one of the gates was connected by a large bridge and had in it a small door through which men went out after 8 o'clock at night. See also *The Hikayat Abdullah*, pp. 56–64.

96 See A.H. Hill, 'Munshi Abdullah's Account of the Malacca Fort', p. 87 It is stated that after six o'clock in the evening the authorities would not allow anyone to enter the fort and one could only walk round the outside. At eight o'clock the authorities fired a gun, followed by the raising of the drawbridges. After this anyone walking about without a torch was arrested, and anyone not answering a challenge was fired on from the fort above.

97 A good description of the layout of the inside of the fort can be gathered from, 'Munshi Abdullah's Account of the Malacca Fort', pp. 87–88.

98 See Map 11, 'Map on the layout of the fort and town of Melaka', in J.W. Heydt, *Geographisch und Topographischer Schauplatz von Africa und Ost-Indien*, p. 304.

99 See report by Raffles, 31 October 1808, in SSFR vol. 22.

100 Abdullah Abdul Kadir, *The Hikayat Abdullah*, p. 63. See also abstract of the statement about the fortification and public building demolished at Melaka, 10 August 1807 to 30 November 1808, in SSFR vol. 21.

101 William Dampier, *Voyages and Discoveries*, London: The Argonaut Press, 1931 (reprint), p. 110.

102 Kernial Singh Sandhu and Paul Wheatley, 'From Capital to Municipality', pp. 532.

103 Toine Ketellars, 'Van Inheemse stapelmarkt', pp. 10–30.

104 See 'Valentyn's Description of Malacca', p. 50.

105 The original name of Pulau Pinang was derived from the betelnut palms, or areca, found on the island. The palm tree was a prominent feature of the scenery on the island. It had straight stems, graceful leaves and bunches of fruits and became one of the major exports of the island. However, the original name, Penang, was seldom used in official documents since it was re-named the Prince of Wales Island when Francis Light took possession of it in 1786 from the Kingdom of Kedah. The town, which was created on the island, was named Georgetown after the Prince of Wales. Here, Penang will be used to denote the town (since Penang is more often used to refer to the town rather than to Georgetown) unless otherwise stated.

106 K. G. Tregonning, 'The Early Land Administration and Agricultural Development of Penang', *JMBRAS*, Part 2, Vol. 39, 1966, p. 34.

107 Although Benkulen was established earlier, in 1685, it remained only as an English factory and did not grow into an important port-town like Penang. For further reference on this matter, see William Marsden, *The History of Sumatra*, Singapore: Oxford University Press (reprint), 1986, pp. 44, 351, 363 and 451. See also John Bastin, *The British in West Sumatra (1685–1825) A selection of documents, mainly from the East India Company records preserved im the India Office Library*, Kuala Lumpur: University Malaya Press, 1965; and Kathirithamby-Wells, *The British West Sumatran Presidency 1760–1785: Problems of Early Colonial Enterprise*, Kuala Lumpur: Universiti Malaya Press, 1977.

108 L.A. Mills, 'British Malaya 1824–67: Penang 1786–1830', *JMBRAS*, Vol. XXXIII, Part 3, 1960, pp. 36–59.

109 Ibid., pp. 38–39.

110 Ibid.

111 M. Stubbs Brown, 'The Failure of Penang as a Naval Base and Shipbuilding Centre', *JMBRAS*, Vol. 32, part 1, 1959, pp. 30–31.

112 Ibid., pp. 28–29.

113 See James Jackson, *Planters and Speculators: Chinese and European Agricultural Enterprise in Malaya*, pp. 93–110.

114 K. G. Tregonning, 'The Early Land Development and Agricultural Development of Penang', p. 42.

115 'Notices of Pinang', *JIA*, vol.5, 1851, pp. 107–108.

116 F.G. Stevens, 'A Contribution to the Early History of Prince of Wales' Island', p. 390. He notes that 'within this area the network of roads laid out by Light survives almost without change to the present day, the original names of the streets, with the exception of Malabar Street, being still in use'.

117 Ibid., p. 390. F.G. Stevens states that 'Light Street came to a dead end, approximate at the point where the main gate of the Convent now stands. The only road from the town into the interior of the island was given the name of the Penang road. This road started where Farquhar Street now starts, between the Supreme Court and the Church, and followed the course of Farquhar Street, whence it pursued its course behind the back of the town, to meet the inner end of Malabar Street. Love Lane (so-called apparently from the earliest times) followed its present course. A narrow road called "Battery Lane" led from the Penang Road, past the old burying ground, along what is now the beginning of Northam Road, to the site of a battery guarding the north-west entrance of the town.'

118 See Report to ascertain the value of houses and lands in Penang in 1808, in G/34/19.

119 Report by the police magistrate regarding John Brown's application, in G/34/13. See also Letter from judge and magistrate, dated 29 July 1806, in G/34/14.

120 George Leith, *A Short Account of the Settlement*, p.49.

121 See letter to Secretary to Government, George Leith, 10 May 1800, in 'Notices of Pinang', *JIA*, Vol 5, 1851, p.162. This letter notes that, 'I find that the land belonging to the Company in the town and vicinity to be extremely limited and much dispersed. The only spot of any tolerable size is a square where it will be advisable to build the chapel. There is not a foot of ground on the sea beach from the Fort to the entrance of the harbour reserved for government. The whole has been given away to individuals who taking advantage of the situation are most exorbitant in their demands. I have been induced to make a purchase of a very excellent piece of ground on the beach, for the purpose of building the new hospital.... this being the sum offered by a merchant here.'

122 See F.G. Stevens, 'Early History of Prince of Wales Island', p. 381. See Account on sale of the Company spice plantation at public auction by order of the Lieutenant Governor in Penang 20 June 1805, where plantations containing clove and nutmeg were purchased by Mr. Smith and Scott, in G/34/9. See also Account on sale of Company spice plantation sold at public auction on 22 July 1807, where a total of 17 lots of plantations were sold at a price of SpD 9,656.00. All were bought by Mr. Smith and Scott, in G/34/9. See also report by Mr. Oliphant in 1805 on government premises and offices that were rented from James Scott's property, in G/34/11. For details of the real estate owned by James Scott see an account on the sale of his property on 11 September 1811, where his lands were sold for a total of SpD 35,721.00 to various people (Europeans, Malays, Chinese, Chulias), in, G/34/33. See also an account of Francis Light's estate and the estate of James Scott (n.d.), in G/34/37.

123 F.G. Stevens, 'A Contribution to the Early History of Prince of Wales' Island', p. 397.

124 Ibid., p. 390.

125 See Map 12, an old map of Penang (ref. British Library Museum, G 7370 opp Appendix 0675617), where on the southern part of the town is referred to as Malay Town. Further, as F.G. Stevens notes in 'A Contribution to the Early History of Prince of Wales' Island', 'The area south of Malabar street was reserved for a Malay Kampong, and here a large site was allotted to a Malay Mosque near the junction of Pitt street and Malabar street', p. 390.

126 Walter Caulfield Lennon, 'Journal of a Voyage Through the Straits of Malacca', p.57. He remarked that 'the fort is situated in the North-East point of the island, which I think the best, but it is in itself so childish a plan and scale, so near the sea, so ill-executed, and so crowded on by the town and houses adjoining, that I fancy, to afford a real security to their possessions, it will be found necessary to build another in a different place'.

127 See Extract of letter from R.T. Farquhar to the Governor General of India in 'Notices of Pinang', *JIA*, Vol. 5, 1851, p. 401.

128 See Captain Light's letter, dated 18 July 1789, in G/34/3.

129 Minute by Governor Seton, 2 July 1812, in G/34/35.

130 See the report of the fire in G/34/10.

131 A unit used to determine the price of bricks according to a process of producing bricks.

132 After the 1789 fire, Francis Light and Captain Glass built ten brick houses, shops and warehouses and encouraged the town dwellers to follow their example by reducing the prices of bricks and *chunam* (one of the ingredients for making bricks such as lime). He

also requested 20 bricklayers and 30 coolies from Bengal to be sent to Penang to help in rebuilding the houses. See Captain Light's letter dated, 18th July 1789 in G/34/3.

133 Fort Cornwallis, 29th September 1814, in G/34/10; See also Collector of Customs and Land Revenue, 30th April 1806 in G/34/13.

134 See the complaint by Mr. Douglas to the Collector of Customs and land revenues regarding an arrak farmer who had his distillery near his warehouse which could endanger his property, 30th April 1806, in G/34/13.

135 See Appendix 5.I, Fires in Penang: List of persons who were the principal victims of the fire in Penang on 29 June 1812 together with an estimate of their losses, in Nordin Hussin, 'Melaka and Penang 1780–1830: A study of two port towns in the Straits of Melaka', Ph.D. thesis, Amsterdam: Vrije Universiteit, 2002.

136 Ibid.

137 List of persons who were the principal victims of the fire of 29 June 1812, in G/34/37.

138 Superintendent of Police to the Secretary to the Governor, in G/34/45; see also minute by W.E. Phillips, in G/34/45.

139 See for example, the petition made by Pulicat merchants Mahomed Syed, Mucktoon Saib, Boojoo Mahomed, and Ismail Mahomed, dated 6 October 1814 in G/34/45.

140 See Appendix 5.II, Fires in Penang: List of the principal sufferers from the fire which broke out in George Town on 27 September 1814, in Nordin Hussin, 'Melaka and Penang 1780–1830', pp. 429–431.

141 Fort Cornwallis 10 October 1814, in G/34/10.

142 Fort Cornwallis 8 October 1814, in G/34/10.

143 Ibid.

144 Superintendent of Police, 18 January 1816, to Secretary to Governor, in G/34/54.

145 Patrick A Roche, 'Caste and the British Merchant Government', p. 390.

CHAPTER SIX

Population Growth in Melaka and Penang, 1780–1830

INTRODUCTION

THIS CHAPTER WILL EXAMINE POPULATION GROWTH in Melaka and Penang with the aim of showing the pattern of growth both in terms of spatial and numerical expansion. Factors and explanations behind the growth pattern will be discussed and linked to the question of how both colonial towns grew and who were the people that made their permanent and temporary homes there. The discussion will begin with the general population growth, followed by an analysis of the population dynamics that led to the population growth obtained. This includes an examination of the extent of natural growth that occurred as opposed to the increase caused by migration in Melaka and Penang. Finally, as slaves were an important component of the population, particularly in Melaka, where at some stage they were made up more than half of the inhabitants, some emphasis will be given to their growth.

THE POPULATION OF MELAKA TOWN

Problems arise in finding a good census or report on population in early Melaka. Although some estimates have been made for the periods of the Malay sultanate and the Portuguese occupation, the Dutch records provide the earliest accurate account of Melaka's population.[1] Even so, these records are by no means complete, as it does not appear that the Dutch were consistently conscientious in gathering information about the population.

Indeed, while during the early years of their administration of Melaka the Dutch took and kept some censuses, the practice appeared to have been abandoned later so that up-dates of population figures are not available. As a result it is hard to give an accurate picture of population growth in Melaka throughout the period under study.

The town of Melaka in this discussion refers to an area that covers the town centre (the fort of Melaka and the town) and the suburbs, which include Tengkera, Bandarhilir, Bungaraya and Bukit China. The total area of Melaka town and its suburbs was estimated to be about five square miles. The people who settled in this area were mainly Dutch civil servants (Europeans), Dutch Burghers (Europeans), Portuguese-Eurasians (a Portuguese-local mix, sometimes referred to as Christian Catholics, Inland Christians or Native Christians), Malays, Chinese, Kelings, Moors and slaves. The Dutch were mostly civil servants working with the company and the Dutch Burghers were Dutchmen who resided in the town but were not employed by the Company. The natives were composed of Malays and those who came from the Indonesian archipelago, such as the Bugis and Javanese.

The population of Melaka can be analysed from the census records. The earliest census appears to have been taken between 1675 and 1678 when Balthasar Bort was the Dutch Governor of Melaka.[2] After 1678, three more censuses were taken, in 1680, 1687 and 1688.[3] In these censuses, the population of Dutch Melaka was divided into various ethnic groups: VOC servants and their families, Dutch Burghers, Portuguese-Eurasians, Malays (Javanese and Bugis), Chinese, Kelings and Moors and slaves (Company slaves, slaves owned by Company officials and private slaves owned by Malays, Chinese, Kelings and Moors).

From the figures shown, we can conclude that the population of Melaka was very small in the seventeenth century. It is not known what the situation was when the Dutch first occupied Melaka but it would seem that the town expanded little during Dutch rule. Between 1675 and 1678 there was an increase of about 5.7 per cent with the population increasing from 5,324 to 5,970, but within two years the numbers had dwindled to 3,689 although in the 1680s they rose again, reaching 4,320 in 1688. Based on the seventeenth-century census the largest single group was made up Portuguese-Eurasians followed by the slaves (excluding those owned by the VOC), who between 1675 and 1788 increased from 1406 to 1987, showing an inexplicable downward trend only in 1680 when their numbers stood at 1260. Bearing in mind that Melaka was, since the fifteenth century, already settled by Malays, the figures suggest that Malays from the surrounding areas and from elsewhere had not been attracted to settle there in larger numbers. It is also worth noting that the Malay, Chinese and Keling populations increased perceptibly

Table 14: Total population of the town of Melaka in the seventeenth century

Ethnic groups	1675 No.	1675 %	1678 No.	1678 %	1680 No.	1680 %	1687 No.	1687 %	1688 No.	1688 %
VOC servants and family	674	12.6	666	11.1	NA	NA	NA	NA	NA	NA
Slaves of VOC servants	504	9.5	355	5.9	NA	NA	NA	NA	NA	NA
VOC slaves	57	1.0	65	1.1	NA	NA	NA	NA	NA	NA
Burghers	104	1.9	145	2.4	NA	NA	NA	NA	NA	NA
Portuguese-Eurasian	1463	27.5	1489	24.9	1420	38.49	1542	36.07	1445	33.58
Malays	597	11.2	690	11.5	523	14.17	521	12.18	443	10.29
Chinese	160	3.0	426	7.1	351	9.51	270	6.31	292	6.78
Kelings/Moors	356	6.7	547	9.2	135	3.65	120	2.80	135	3.13
Slaves	1409	26.5	1607	26.9	1260	34.15	1821	42.60	1987	46.18
Total	5324	100.0	5970	100.0	3689	100.00	4274	100.00	4302	100.00

NA: Not available (the census records do not contain figures for these years).

Sources: VOC 1361, folio 72–73 (for year 1680); VOC 1332, folio 561–563 (for year 1678); VOC 1452, folio 1013–1014 (for year 1687) and VOC 1453 folio 419–420 (for year 1688). See also Balthasar Bort, 'Report of Governor Balthasar Bort on Melaka, 1678'.

between 1675 and 1678 which coincided with Bort's governorship; this suggests that his policies might have been responsible for the situation.

The character and composition of Melaka's population changed over time. In the seventeenth century, as we have seen, there was a large slave population though the free individuals, the Portuguese-Eurasians, the VOC servants and their families and the Malays, were the largest groups. However, by the nineteenth century the demographic pattern had changed. The VOC servants were fewer, but there was an increase in the number of Dutch Burghers and Chinese in the town. The slave population had also dwindled, while the Portuguese Eurasians – once the most numerous of the free population – were no longer dominant due to the influx of Chinese, Kelings, Moors and also Malays from the surrounding areas. The Portuguese Eurasians, despite their long history in Melaka, were a closed community of devout Catholics who were disinclined to enter into mixed marriages with most other communities, except Europeans. But such unions were also rare due to differences in social and religious backgrounds.

As stated earlier, one of the problems with studying Melaka's population is the difficulty in locating the census records. The earliest censuses on Melaka, as we have seen, were very clear and provided a break-down of the population by ethnic groups thus offering the only detailed set of population statistics. Even information such as the number of households, the number of adults, children and slaves in each household and gender details were provided. No census appears to have been taken after this period until the English attempted a survey in the early nineteenth century and again at the end of the second decade of that century. In addition, a report written in 1824 by the Dutch before the transfer of Melaka to the English described the demographic patterns at Melaka and Naning.[4] This was followed by three censuses recorded in 1826, 1828 and 1829, the latter two providing more details than the first. T. Braddell, writing in 1861, provided statistics for the years 1750, 1766 and 1817, but his sources remain obscure.[5]

Braddell's statistics do not include the slave population and Europeans and Portuguese Eurasians are pooled together. The total population given for 1750 was close to 10,000, almost double the population in the second half of the seventeenth century, and although by 1766 the numbers had fallen to 7,216, they were still much higher than when the Dutch took the early censuses.[6] Braddell's figures also do not show the extent of coverage, but mention of Melaka's dependencies suggests that this population count covered the town of Melaka and its suburbs as well as the areas beyond, including the hinterland areas and perhaps also Naning. Perhaps this was why the population figures he gave are much higher than those in the seventeenth century. In any case, Braddell's population census should be

Table 15: Total population of the town of Melaka and its dependencies in 1750, 1766 and 1817

Ethnic groups	1750		1766		1817	
	No.	%	No.	%	No.	%
Malays	3,615	37.51	3,135	43.44	13,988	71.19
Chinese	2,161	22.42	1,390	19.26	1,006	5.12
Indians	1,520	15.77	1,023	14.17	2,986	15.19
Europeans/Portuguese-Eurasians	2,339	24.27	1,668	23.11	1,667	8.48
Total	9,635	100.00	7,216	100.00	19,647	100.00

Source: T. Braddell, *Statistics of the British Possessions in the Straits of Melaka with Explanatory Notes*.

treated with caution as it seems probable that his statistics were merely estimates of population; they lack in many details that a contemporary survey would have been able to provide. There was no elaboration on the settlement or residential areas of each ethnic group, the concentration of population, age or ownership of property.

Nevertheless, if we look at the figures provided by Braddell, some issues can be raised such as the reason for the decline in Melaka's population in 1766. It is possible that the war between the Dutch and the Bugis in Selangor, which erupted as a consequence of long rivalry between the two powers, had disrupted trade and caused many people to flee the port. [7] The reduction was seen in all the communities, for the total population of Malays was reduced by more then 19 per cent, the Chinese by 31 per cent, the Indians by 20 per cent and the European and Portuguese-Eurasian group by 27 per cent. In 1803–04, a partial census was compiled, as shown in Table 16 below.

Table 16: Partial *wijkmeester* census of Melaka in 1803

Ethnic groups	Adult males	Adult females	Male children	Female children	Male slaves	Female slaves	Adopted children
Christians	18	25	28	38	39	52	20
Chinese	138	70	96	93	54	73	89
Malays	1	1	[?]	[?]	[?]	[?]	[?]
Indians	10	9	3	[?]	17[?]	6[?]	1[?]
Total	167	105	127	131	110	131	110

Source: R/9/34/1.

This census might well have been the first taken after those conducted in the seventeenth century. It appears to have been derived from a regular exercise conducted by the Superintendents of the wards to record population changes within their wards.[8] This survey had been required by the Dutch administration but the practice had evidently been continued after the English took over Melaka as a practice under the English administration. As can be seen, this census covers only one ward, probably the Heren/Jonkerstraat ward. Many pages of this record are either damaged or missing so that the information that can be gathered is incomplete.[9] However, the retrievable material provides interesting information, for it can be seen that ethnic segregation had broken down in a ward that was once dominated by the Europeans. Further, the Chinese community was in a clear majority.

The reason for concluding that the ward involved was Heren or Jonker is because of the high number of Burgher and Chinese population, as compared to other ethnic groups. The Malay population in this quarter was very low compared to the Chinese, at 45.06 per cent, Christians at 12.37 per cent and Indians at 2.49 per cent of the total population. While in the eighteenth century Heren and Jonker were notably exclusive areas for the Dutch Burghers, by the nineteenth century many of them had left Melaka following the English takeover and their properties had been transferred or purchased by wealthy Chinese. Another development worth noting is that only a couple of Malays resided in the ward in 1803 whereas in the 1780s and the 1790s there were more.[10] The reason for the very small number of Malays is unclear, but their near absence along with the low numbers of Europeans and Indians had, drastically, changed the character of the ward, for it had virtually become a Chinese enclave.[11]

Not only were many slaves and adopted children recorded in the census, but the number of slaves per household, particularly in the Christian community, was quite high. Evidence shows that a person by the name of de Wind had 20 slaves and one adopted child.[12] The slaves owned by the Chinese represented 52.69 per cent of the total slave numbers while those owned by the Christians stood at 37.75 per cent. The high number of adopted children in Chinese families could be due to many of these children being illegitimate, produced by slaves or concubines.

The next set of statistics available relating to Melaka's population was that produced by Braddell for 1817, as seen in Table 15. The figures appear to confirm that this survey covered a wider area than the town because it recorded an unusually high number of Malays, completely out of proportion with the rest of the population. For the first time since 1680, the Indians had overtaken the Chinese in numbers. The reason for this is not immediately obvious and in subsequent years it was seen that there were more Chinese than Indians in the population, thus reflecting the long established trend.

Table 17: Population of the town of Melaka and its suburbs in late 1824

Ethnic groups	Total population	Percent of population
Europeans	405	3.62
Inland Christians	1,839	16.44
Malays	2,570	22.98
Chinese	2,741	24.51
Moors	1,105	9.88
Kelings	583	5.21
Slaves	1,314	11.75
Others	623	5.57
Total	11,180	100.00

Source: Collectie 57 Schneither ARA.

Due to the dearth of statistical material on Melaka for the first two decades of the nineteenth century, a more complete analysis of population trends and their implications cannot be made. In the 1820s, several population counts appear to have been conducted, the first by the Dutch in 1824, shortly before they handed Melaka over to the English, and the rest by the English.

The population count of 1824 (see Table 17 above) was compiled by the Dutch at the beginning and the end of the year. The records divided the population of Melaka into ethnic groups and place of residence. The survey covered the town and its suburbs, the hinterland areas and Naning and classified the population into eight groups, namely, Europeans, Portuguese-Eurasians (Inland Christians), Malays, Chinese, Moors, Kelings, slaves and others.

This population count was the first accurate and comprehensive one in a century and a half. Out of a population of 11,180, the Chinese made up more than 24 per cent of the total, followed by the Malays at 23 per cent and the Portuguese-Eurasians at 16 per cent. The number of Europeans/Burghers had decreased substantially to less then 4 per cent of the total population. Several reasons could be suggested for the decrease in the European/ Burgher numbers. The imminent transfer of Melaka to the English might have encouraged many to leave and relocate elsewhere. The obvious choice would have been Batavia, which was under Dutch rule although some might even have moved to Penang or Singapore where business opportunities were increasing rather than contracting, as was the case with Melaka.

The Dutch Burgher community, although always small in number, was an important group in Melaka chiefly due to their wealth, high status and position as the elite of society outside the official community. They would have constituted the largest group within the European community. Compared to other ethnic communities, their history is well documented, again because of their dominant position in Melaka society. In 1824 there were 95 adult Dutch Burgers listed among the people who attended the Reformed Church service (church members).[13] The total Burgher population was probably much bigger, as there were altogether 405 Europeans in that year. A genealogical list of Melaka's European and Dutch Burgher families in Melaka from 1818 to 1825 reveals 155 families.[14] Of the 155, seven had long association with Melaka, with some going back to the seventeenth century. They were the Dieterich, Koek, Kraal, Neubronner, Rappa, Velge, Westerhout and Wiederhold families.[15]

In the nineteenth century the town of Melaka was transformed into a predominantly Chinese town surrounded with a large Malay population in the suburbs and outer areas. Surprisingly, despite the English ban on slave trading, which was first introduced in the first decade of the nineteenth century, the number of slaves remained high in Melaka. The slave population was higher then that of the European, Moor and Keling. In 1675 they exceeded 37 per cent of the population and while in 1824 they had been reduced to less then 12 per cent, slaves remained an important group in society.

Few records are available to enable us to look closely at the Malay population of Melaka. However, in 1825 a census report produced by the English administration covered a fairly detailed study of the 14 Malay kampongs in the suburbs of Melaka.[16] Among the details sought by this survey were the names of heads of families, the total number in each household and whether they were free, slaves or debtors.[17] The statistics show that the total population of Malays in the suburbs was just over 1000, that the kampongs were small, the largest number of inhabitants in a kampong being 250 and the smallest 18, that there were more married males and females than single men and women, that the ratio between males and females was balanced, that the average number of occupants per household was 5–6 people and that there were with no slaves or slave-debtors. The population also appeared to have been relatively young, many of child bearing age, as there were 477 children in all. These kampong Malays supplied their excess agricultural produce such as fruits, vegetables and also paddy to the town dwellers.[18]

The more stable sex ratio in the Malay population compared to the other communities was understandable in view of the fact that they were not migrants. Although there were more boys than girls, this is considered normal because the mortality rate among girls was higher in the early age. As they came of age, the sex ratio became more stable because there was a higher mortality rate among the males.

Table 18: Census of Malay kampong in suburbs of Melaka town in 1825

| Name of kampong | No. of houses | Males | | Females | | Children | | Av. size of households | Total |
		Unmarr.	Married	Unmarr.	Married	Male	Female		
Ching	10	4	9	4	9	12	8	4.6	46
Kandang Hujong	5	3	3	6	3	5	6	5.2	26
Paia Nato	12	12	21	12	21	31	24	17.6	121
Malim	3	1	2	0	2	10	3	6	18
Pangkalan Arang	4	1	3	0	3	7	5	5.2	21
Ayer Petaling	6	0	6	3	6	9	6	5	30
Ayer Marbo	5	2	5	2	3	13	6	11.2	56
Pengkalan Jambu	4	4	4	1	4	6	6	6.2	25
Balai Panjang	70	23	61	20	64	44	38	3.5	250
Paya Rumput	24	20	24	15	19	19	29	5.2	126
Sungai Bandar	16	5	16	9	16	22	20	5.5	88
Rumbia	25	7	19	7	19	24	25	4	101
Ayer Poete	5	1	4	1	4	9	6	5	25
Ayer Gajah Mati	20	14	22	11	20	22	17	5.3	106
Total	209	97	198	91	193	260	217	5	1,056

Source: R/9/34/7.

One year after the transfer of Melaka to the English, a census was prepared by the British administration. The 1826 census was considered an important document for the English administration, which believed it would give information to indicate general issues pertaining to social conditions, wealth and property of the new colony.[19] It was hoped that the census would reveal facts on the distribution of the people, ownership of land and economic activities that would assist in determining policies for the future development of Melaka.[20] Such findings would also assist in determining the types of taxes that should be levied on the people.[21] The English administration was also unclear about how to approach the administration of land in Melaka, as the Dutch had left many related matters unresolved when they departed.[22] The new administration was also unsure where Melaka's boundary stood and which land belonged to the government.[23]

Table 19: Population of Melaka town and its dependencies in 1826

Ethnic groups	Free Citizens	Slaves	Slave-Debtors	Total
Christians	2236	353	31	2,620
Malays	16,121	120	77	16,318
Chinese	4,125	353	–	4,478
Chulias	1,475	147	–	1,622
Hindus	862	124	–	986
Naning	3,628	24	34	3,680
Total	28,447	1,121	142	29,770

Source: SSFR, vol. 165.

Unfortunately, the census made in 1826 was not done in a proper and detailed manner. It drew much criticism from Garling who expressed his opinion in a letter to Lewis dated 13 March 1827.[24] He questioned the method of collecting the information, which he thought should have been more meticulous and precise in order to achieve the objective of collecting data not only on the population, but also on the property of the inhabitants, houses, slaves, land area and ownership of land. In his opinion, the census did not gather enough information on the number of houses in various wards of the town and the outlying areas. Further, it failed to include details on wealth and property of all households.

One significant fact emerged from the census: the number of slaves was 1,121, lower than the figure for 1824 (1,314). Although the slave population was slowly dying out due to the ban on the slave trade, this decrease, which

Table 20: Birth and mortality rates in the town of Melaka and its suburbs in 1826

Ethnicity	Born in 1826		Died in 1826		Mortality rate %	Birth rate %
	Males	*Females*	*Males*	*Females*		
Europeans	8	4	3	4	0.55	0.94
Malays	77	89	64	59	9.69	13.08
Chulias/Moors	45	41	24	23	3.70	6.77
Hindus/Kelings	21	21	16	13	2.28	3.30
Chinese	87	81	75	74	11.74	13.23
Portuguese	68	66	50	38	6.93	10.55
Total	306	302	232	211	34.90	47.71

Note: The percentage of mortality and birth rates is calculated according to the total of births or deaths divided by the total number of the population for the year 1826 and multiplied by 1,000.

Source: F/4/1272 51026.

happened in a short period of two years, points to other than natural causes. It may well have been the case that the Dutch Burghers had emancipated their slaves before they left Melaka. Further, the change of administration might have provided opportunities to many, including slaves, to take a new course of action. There were some cases of slaves running away from their masters because of ill-treatment. At the same time, the teachings of the Christian missionaries were also liberating and could have influenced slaves to find their freedom.[25]

    Table 20 above shows the birth and mortality rates for 1826 in the town of Melaka. The highest birth rate occurred among the Chinese and Malays followed by the Portuguese-Eurasians, while the Europeans showed a very low birth rate. In the early period the Chinese population was tiny but in the 1820s their numbers increased rapidly so that they were able to surpass the Malay population. In fact, between 1824 and 1826 their numbers increased two-fold, which suggests an increase in the number of new arrivals rather than from natural causes. The 1820s was a period of increased economic activities in the western Malay states relating to the opening of tin mines, and Melaka was one of several entry points for new arrivals, mainly labourers, but also a financial base from which the Chinese launched their businesses in the interior. It should also be noted that in the 1820s, gender imbalance was no longer prominent in the Chinese population. There were still more single males compared to single females, but the disparity was not as great as it was

Table 21: Population of the town of Melaka and its suburbs in 1826

Ethnicity	Adult males Marr.	Single	Adult females Marr.	Single	Child ren Male	Female	Total	%
Europeans	32	23	42	29	55	52	233	1.6
Malays	676	556	758	545	701	657	3,893	27
Chulias/Moors	277	204	295	220	242	240	1,478	10
Hindus/Kelings	150	139	164	104	138	113	808	6
Chinese	588	960	702	636	616	487	3,989	28
Portuguese-Eurasians	413	346	465	346	397	322	2,289	16
Slaves/slave debtors	1,493	–	–	– –	–	–	1,493	10
Per cent	15.06	15.70	17.1	13.25	15.15	13.19		100
Grand Total	2,136	2,228	2,426	1,880	2,149	1,871	14,183	

Source: F/4/1272 51026. The total population was 14,180 (1,493 were slaves or slave-debtors).

before this period. In fact, many Chinese in this period had Chinese wives and the presence of a substantial number of single Chinese females suggests enough women were arriving from China to make the difference. At the same time natural growth also helped to increase the numbers.

Unlike the Chinese, the Moor/Chulia and Hindu/Keling communities did not expand. As most of them were engaged in one way or another with

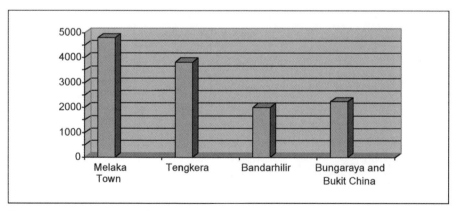

Figure 11: Population of the four major quarters of Melaka town and its suburbs, 30 April 1828. *Source*: SSFR, Vol. 168.

the trading sector of Melaka, the port's decline meant that few new arrivals were seen in the community.

Table 21 opposite also shows that for all ethnic groups adult married females out-numbered adult married males. This could be either due to a substantial number of them being widowed or that a big proportion of married males were away from Melaka engaged in some kind of business and thus absent when the census was taken.

Figure 11 opposite and Figure 12 below show the population of Melaka town and its suburbs. As can be learned from the 1828–29 census, the English administration had clustered the population into four main quarters, the town as one quarter, and the suburbs, three major quarters, Tengkera, Bandarhilir, and Bungaraya-Bukit China.[26] Formerly, during the Dutch administration, Bungaraya and Bukit China were two separate wards but the English classified them as a single quarter. By the end of the 1820s, the Malays and the Chinese constituted the largest groups in Melaka. While the Chinese were most numerous in the centre of town, the Malays showed a reverse pattern, predominating in the outer areas. But both communities lived in all four quarters, as was the case with the other groups. However, in the town quarter the Chinese made up more than 49 per cent of the total town population, with the Malays and the Chulias constituting less than 18 per cent each. The largest concentration of Malays was seen in the Bungaraya-Bukit China and Bandarhilir quarters, where 61 per cent of all Melaka Malays resided. In the Bandarhilir quarter, the Malays made up more than 44 per cent of all inhabitants. The Chulias, mostly merchants and traders, were found mostly in the town and Tengkera quarters. The majority

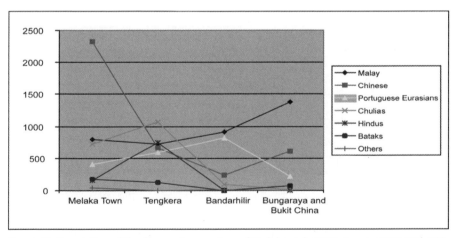

Figure 12: Population of the four major quarters of Melaka, July 1829. *Source:* SSFR, Vol. 169.

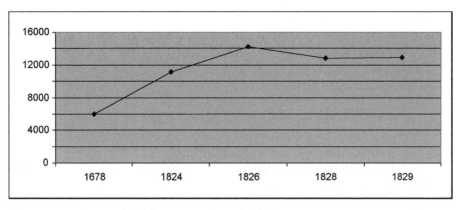

Figure 13: Population of Melaka town and its suburbs in 1678, 1824, 1826, 1828 and 1829. *Source:* Balthasar Bort, 'Report of Governor Balthasar Bort on Melaka,1678'; Collectie 57 Schneither ARA; F/4/1272 51026; SSFR vol.165; SSFR vol. 168; SSFR vol. 169.

of the Native Christians, or the Portuguese-Eurasians, were found in the Bandarhilir and Tengkera quarters.

Although the population reports in 1828 and 1829 mention 229 and 265 Europeans residing in Melaka respectively, no detailed accounts are given of their distribution. Traditionally the wards with a high number of European settlements were the town, Tengkera and Bandarhilir. These three quarters were the most popular places of residence among the Dutch Burghers/ European ethnic groups. But the number of Europeans had always been small compared to other major ethnic groups.

The figures also show that the concentration of population was in the town and the Tengkera area, while Bandarhilir had the smallest population of the four major quarters. But while the town was predominantly Chinese, the Tengkera area showed a more even distribution of ethnic groups, although the Chulia population was slightly higher than the rest. The Bandarhilir area, on the other hand, was dominated by the Malays and the Portuguese-Eurasians, with a small number of inhabitants from other ethnic groups. In Bungaraya and Bukit China, the Malays were in a clear majority, with the Chinese as the second largest group. However, it is highly probable that the former were concentrated in Bungaraya while the latter were mostly in Bukit China. Clearly, the population of Melaka was not segregated along ethnic lines and the dominance of one ethnic group over the rest in a particular area had less to do with ethnicity than with function and tradition.

The population of Melaka town and its suburbs was never large and probably never exceeded 10,000 before the nineteenth century. In the period under study, the long-term pattern was one of very slow increase, reaching its highest numbers in the 1820s. Thus the population trends did not coincide with trade trends, for, as we have seen, trade was on a downward roll throughout the period. Even the establishment of Penang in 1786 and Singapore in 1819 did not appear to have affected the overall pattern in Melaka's population. The majority still preferred to stay in Melaka although the port's importance in trade had greatly declined in the nineteenth century. Furthermore, the plan to force the majority of Melaka's population to settle in Penang ended in failure. Although the English authorities in Penang had tried to lure them by giving the Melaka-Chinese special offers, such as free land and lower taxes, these factors seem to have had little effect in influencing the majority of Melaka's population to leave Melaka for Penang.[27]

Thus the explanations for this population pattern have to be sought elsewhere. It is probable that those who had lived long in Melaka had property and family attachments, which kept them there. In any case, especially for the wealthy, the nature of their businesses would not have required them to physically move from one place to another. Moreover, the 1820s saw the beginning of new opportunities for business and investments with the opening up of the western Malay states to new economic ventures. Melaka was well placed to benefit from developments in the neighbouring states of Negeri Sembilan and Selangor. Not only did Melaka serve as the financial centre for these developments, but it also became the collecting centre for

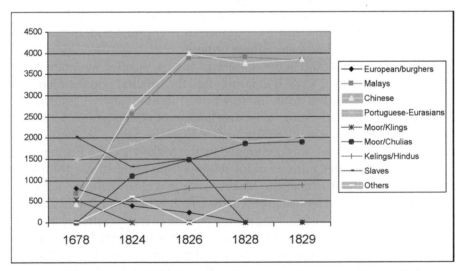

Figure 14: Population of Melaka town and its suburbs 1678–1829, according to ethnic groups. *Source:* Balthasar Bort, 'Report of Governor Balthasar Bort on Melaka,1678'; Collectie 57 Schneither ARA; F/4/1272 51026; SSFR vol.165; SSFR vol. 168; SSFR vol. 169.

goods from these areas which were destined for export through the international port of Singapore.

THE SLAVE POPULATION IN MELAKA

Since the early history of Melaka, slaves were vital to the society; slaves provided the work force. Those owned by wealthy masters were forced to work in the households, in the manufacturing sector, such as brick making, as entertainers and as crew in trading vessels.[28] In addition, slaves also provided pleasure and comfort to many lonely migrant males, and such liaisons were quite common among the Chinese, as observed by a writer, 'the slave women contributed so much to the happiness of the male population, and the general prosperity of the settlement [and]... became wives of respectable Chinese'.[29] The availability of slaves as sexual partners is also borne by the fact that prostitution was not endemic in the region. Reid points out that prostitution was uncommon in port-towns, as the needs of single migrant men were met by the buying or hiring of a bonded woman, who served frequently as cook, commercial assistant and local informant as well as sexual partner. But it was not only the Chinese who found their partners among the slave population. Living alone in a faraway land had also made European men follow this example. As time passed and the hopes of the Chinese and European settlers of returning to the fatherland receded, they were more likely than not to marry their concubines. By the early nineteenth century the trade in women came to resemble a large-scale 'marriage market' and the slave trade appears also to have provided a large proportion of the female population of the British Straits Settlements at their foundation.[30]

Ownership of slaves was a measure of one's wealth and the more slaves one owned the greater one's status and prestige.[31] Therefore the majority of the population that owned slaves belonged to the higher classes. The value of slaves also varied according to age and sex, adult male and female slaves normally commanding higher prices than minors.[32] Slaves in Melaka could be classified into two categories, namely, those owned by the Company (VOC) and those owned by private individuals.

Table 22 illustrates that in 1775, one hundred and six slaves were owned by the VOC, out of which more then 22 per cent were old. By 1806 the number of slaves owned by the VOC had dropped to only 34 people, of whom, 18 were men and 16 women.[33] Due to the ban on the slave trade, the number of slaves belonging to the Company had declined but those owned by private individuals was still high.

The practice of owning slaves had existed during the Sultanate period in Melaka. In the early period slaves were an integral part of Melaka, the

Table 22: Slaves working with the VOC in 1775

Age/ description	Total numbers	%
Very old	24	22.64
20–55 years	70	66.03
3–4 years	3	2.83
Sick	2	1.88
Blind	3	2.83
Insane	3	2.83
Paralysed/crippled	1	0.94
Total	106	100.00

Source: VOC 3467.

descendents of those who had lived within the socio-cultural context of the old Malay world. Both the Portuguese and the Dutch took advantage of this old practice and kept the slave trade alive as a cheap means of obtaining labour.[34] Prior to the transfer of Melaka to the English, the Dutch administration had kept a list of slave masters and the number of slaves owned by them.[35] However, the list was never complete, as the majority of masters did not register their slaves in the official registry for fear that they would be liberated by the authorities or taxed. Thus there is no way of knowing the actual number of slaves in Melaka.

When Melaka was occupied, the English administration made a compulsory order for all slave masters to register their slaves with the police. Regulation was passed and those who refused to register would see the slaves liberated. Although there was a lot of dissatisfaction among slave masters, the majority complied by registering them. This allowed a clearer picture to

Table 23: Slave owners in Melaka town and its suburbs based on ethnicity in 1824

Ethnicity/owners	Male slaves	%	Female slaves	%	Total	%
Europeans	277	41.59	238	40.33	515	41.00
Malays	193	28.97	84	14.23	277	22.05
Chinese	150	22.52	239	40.50	389	30.97
Kelings	46	6.90	29	4.91	75	5.97
Total	666	100.00	590	100.0	1,256	100.00

Source: SSFR, vol. 169.

emerge on the number of slaves owned. In 1824 the number in the town of Melaka was 666 males and 590 females, with 86 under-aged males and 75 under-aged females, making a total of 1,417 slaves, including 161 children born into slavery. This register of slaves provides detailed information regarding ownership, origin, age and gender.

The majority of slave masters in Melaka, in absolute as well as relative numbers, were the Europeans (Dutch Burghers) followed by the Chinese and Malays. Some owned large numbers of slaves in 1803, but by 1824 many were left with only one slave or none. One such person was J.B. de Wind, who owned 20 slaves in 1803, but the slave register of 1824 had him down as owning only one Malay slave.[36] It is not known what happened to the other 19, but the situation seems unusual especially when seen in the light of his great wealth and the fact that other Burghers, including Adrain Koek, still owned many slaves until 1824 despite the English having discouraged slave trading at the beginning of the nineteenth century.[37] Other masters known to own slaves before 1824 were de Rozaerio, a Portuguese-Eurasian, who had ten slaves; a Dutch Burgher, Isabella Velge, who owned nine slaves and had two adopted children; and a widow, de Grasia, a Portuguese-Eurasian, who owned six slaves and had five adopted children.[38] However, in the 1824 slave register they were not listed. The biggest slave owner in 1824 was Adrian Koek, who owned 63 slaves. Another, by the name of J.J. Timmerman Thyssen, owned 37 slaves, Hendrik Kraal had 30 slaves, Hubertus van Bragt kept 23 slaves and A.A. Velge owned 19 slaves.

The register shows that only one Malay came close to matching the slave numbers owned by the Dutch Burgers. He was Encik Mohamed Ariffin, who owned 19 slaves. Surprisingly, the number owned by the richest Chinese was smaller compared to the Dutch Burghers, although in 1803 the Chinese were the largest group of slave owners in Melaka (see Table 24). The 1824

Table 24: Slave owners in Melaka town and its suburbs in 1824 owning slaves under 8 years of age

Ethnicity/owners	Male slaves	%	Female slaves	%	Total	%
Europeans	41	47.67	42	56.00	83	51.55
Malays	15	17.44	7	9.33	22	13.66
Chinese	17	19.76	18	24.00	35	21.73
Kelings	8	9.30	6	8.00	14	8.69
Unknown	5	5.81	2	2.66	7	4.34
Total	86	100.00	75	100.00	161	100.00

Source: SSFR, vol. 169.

Table 25: The highest number of slaves owned by individuals in Melaka town and its suburbs in 1824*

Names	Ethnic groups	No. of slaves	Names	Ethnic groups	No. of slaves
A. Koek	Burgher	63	Siwa Sidambrong Chitty	Keling/Hindu	7
J.J. Timmerman Thyssen	Burgher	37	Catharina Koek	Burgher	7
Hendrik Kraal	Burgher	36	Widow Pavonarius	European	7
Hubertus van Bragt	Burgher	23	Lebe Pelae	Malay	7
A.A. Velge	Burgher	21	Tja Tong Kie	Chinese	6
Jan Henderick Stecher	Burgher	19	Valberg	Burgher	6
Mohamed Ariffen	Malay	19	S. de Souza	Portuguese-Eurasian	6
Widow of Greys	European	17	A. Kraal	Burgher	6
Widow Westerhout	Burgher	14	Tan Koseing	Chinese	6
Saibo Ahmad Sab	Malay	14	Hussain Yusoff	Malay	6
Sagrae Chetty	Keling/Hindu	14	Abdul Halim Tahir	Malay	6
Tan Toen Jet	Chinese	13	Seido Mira alias Tambi Besar	Keling/Hindu	6
Johannes Lodewykson	European	12	Abdul Oeatrap	Malay	6
Thomas Williamson	European	12	George de Souza	Portuguese-Eurasian	5
G.L. Baumgarten	Burgher	10	Jacob Dries	European	5

Table 25: The highest number of slaves owned by individuals in Melaka town and its suburbs in 1824 (continued)*

Names	Ethnic groups	No. of slaves	Names	Ethnic groups	No. of slaves
Tan Sang	Chinese	10	G. Derteriah	Burgher	5
China Jambi	Chinese	10	A. Minjoot	Burgher	5
Anthonij Stecher	Burgher	10	Tan Boenian	Chinese	5
Choa Chong Kiat	Chinese	10	Tan Bon Tjoen	Chinese	5
J.H. Overre	Burgher	9	Toe Ing Nio	Chinese	5
J.W. Baumgarten	Burgher	9	Ko Ing Ko	Chinese	5
Demar Mohamed Badaruddin	Malay	8	Tjan Oey Liem	Chinese	5
Danial Koek	Burgher	8	Tan Tun Kok	Chinese	5
Joseph Minass	Burgher	8	Salleh Mahomed Lebe	Malay	5
Widow Tan Tldg	Chinese	8	Shaikh Abdul Rahman Alowie	Malay	5
Ko Ing Siong	Chinese	8	Che Madar	Malay	5
Ahmad Badaruddin	Malay	8	Pelang Pillay	Keling/Hindu	5

*Note: Excluding minors or infants. Those who owned fewer than 5 slaves are not listed in the table.

Source: SSFR 169.

register shows that Chinese ownership of slaves was high but the numbers owned by individual Chinese were low, perhaps due to the fact that slaves were often assimilated into the family through marriage. In addition, the Chinese community sometimes regarded their slaves as a part of their family and thus did not register them. The 1824 slave register indicates that among wealthy Chinese, Tan Toen Jet owned the most slaves at 13, while among the Indians, Sagrae Chetty kept the most at 14. Table 25 above shows the number of slaves owned by rich individuals in Melaka in 1824.

Melaka's slaves came from areas far and wide although the Southeast Asian region was the main source of supply. In the archipelago, apart from Melaka as a source of supply, slaves were brought in from Kedah, Rembau, Borneo, Bali, the Batak areas, Makassar, Inas, Riau, Sumbawa, Batavia, Linga, Timor and several other areas. Outside the region traders obtained their supply from as far away as Mozambique in Africa, and Bengal, the Malabar Coast, Mandar and Mangary.

In 1826 the total number of slaves in the town of Melaka was 1,097 and in Naning it was 24. The highest number of slave masters came from the Christians (Dutch Burghers/Europeans) and Chinese ethnic groups. Both ethnic groups owned more then 31 per cent of all slaves. The Kelings and Malays owned slightly more then 10 per cent of all slaves. The data did not specify whether the Christians who owned slaves were Dutch Burghers or Portuguese-Eurasians, but as many Portuguese-Eurasians were poor and earned their living as fishermen it is unlikely that they owned slaves. Hence, it can be concluded that most of the slaves owned by the Christians belonged to the Dutch Burghers. Although the number of Dutch burghers was very small compared to the other ethnic groups, they owned the largest number

Table 26: The slave population in Melaka town and its suburbs in 1826

Owners/ethnicity	Men	Women	Male minors	Female minors	Total	%
Christians	135	143	35	40	353	31.48
Malays	61	59	–	–	120	10.70
Chinese	135	176	28	14	353	31.49
Chulias/Moors	56	61	23	7	147	13.11
Hindus/Kelings	49	43	18	14	24	2.14
Total for Melaka	436	482	104	75	1,097	97.85
Naning	5	14	3	2	24	2.14
Total	441	496	107	77	1,121	100

Source: SSFR, vol. 165.

Table 27: Slave-debtors in Melaka town and its suburbs in 1826

Ethnic groups	Men	Women	Male minors	Female minors	Total
Christians	14	8	4	5	31
Malays	71	6	–	–	77
Chinese	–	–	–	–	–
Moors	–	–	–	–	–
Hindus	–	–	–	–	–
Total	85	14	4	5	108
Nanings	12	18	2	2	34

Source: SSFR, vol. 165.

of slaves in their houses. Table 26 opposite shows the slave population of Melaka in 1826.

Besides slaves, there were also slave-debtors in Melaka, persons who had bound themselves with their families, often for trifling sums, to serve their creditors until the liquidation of their debt.[39] Table 27 above shows the numbers of slave-debtors in Melaka in 1826. The highest number came from the Malays at 77 per cent, followed by the Christians at 31 per cent. Most Christian slave-debtors came from the Portuguese-Eurasian category, or those who had become Christians and were serving their masters as slave-debtors.

Table 28 overleaf shows the number of Melaka's slaves and slave-debtors: a total of 1,493. This figure is higher than the number of slaves in 1826 because slave-debtors were included in the count. The table also shows 141 household slaves owned by the Dutch Burghers in Melaka. The most masters of slaves and slave-debtors came from the Chinese (34.89 per cent), the Malays (23.64 per cent), the Europeans (Dutch Burghers) (18.15 per cent), the Moors (15.02 per cent) and the Kelings (8.23 per cent). There were no slaves or slave-debtors owned by the Portuguese-Eurasian ethnic group.

Although the number of slaves had decreased since the seventeenth century, slaves were still considered an important of daily life. Slavery was vital for household services and in the manufacturing and trading sector in Melaka. The majority of the owners were Chinese, Malays and Europeans/ Dutch Burghers. In 1827 the number of slaves owned by the Dutch Burghers/ Europeans, Chinese and Malays were still relatively higher compared to the other ethnic groups. In 1827 the slave population in the town of Melaka was 10.52 per cent of total inhabitants, compared to more than 30 per cent in the mid-seventeenth century. Although the government tried to persuade slave

Table 28: Slaves and slave-debtors in the town of Melaka and its suburbs in 1827

Slave-owners and slave-debtors by ethnicity	Slaves and slave-debtors		Slaves and slave-debtors		Total % of ownership
	Male	Female	% of male	% of female	
Europeans*	130	141#	15.79	21.04	18.15
Malays	207	146	25.15	21.79	23.64
Hindu Moslems	126	99	15.30	14.77	15.07
Hindu Kelings	67	56	8.14	8.35	8.23
Chinese	293	228	35.60	34.02	34.89
Portuguese	–	–	–	–	–
Total	823	670	100.00	100.00	100.00

Notes: (*) Europeans and their descendents
        (#) These are household slaves belonging to the Dutch; the rest were mostly slaves or slave-debtors.
Source: F/4/1272 51026.

owners to emancipate their slaves, the old tradition of having slaves in the household was not easy to abolish.[40]

THE POPULATION OF PENANG, 1786–1830

When Penang was occupied by the EIC in 1786, there were 158 Malay settlers living on the island. Later another 154 new Malay settlers arrived between 1787–88. By August 1788 the population was 121 Chinese immigrants, 216 Chulias and 180 Christian settlers, bringing the total to 829. However, the census did not include European settlers and the number of Europeans working with the company. Between August and December 1788 immigration was so rapid that the population of Penang doubled in that short period.

From the early days after its opening, Penang attracted a mixed group of people. Among them were Europeans, Jawi-Pekans, Malays, Roman Catholics, Chinese and Chulias. Most Europeans who settled in Penang came from Britain and belonged to the Anglican Church. In addition to them, a number of people from Siam and Kedah professed the Roman Catholic faith. These individuals were classified as Eurasians, as they were the descendants of the Portuguese who had intermarried with Asians. But a number of Asians, such as Siamese and Burmese, were Christian converts and classified as Roman Catholics.

Most of Penang's population lived in the town, situated on the north eastern side of the island. Compared to the area controlled by the Dutch in

Melaka, the area over which the English held jurisdiction was very small, covering less than three square miles. In the 1780s, the population was made up of immigrants – mostly semi-skilled workers in the agricultural and manu-facturing sectors (artisans and craftsmen), although a large number were traders. The majority of the semi-skilled workers in the trades, such as car-pentry and blacksmithing, were Chinese. The Europeans were concentrated in the administration and related jobs and also in agricultural-planting and trade-related occupations. The Chinese and the Jawi-Pekans were mostly in the small trade-related activities selling merchandize such as cloth and household products, while the Malays were mostly involved in trade and in clearing the jungle.

The majority of Malays, Jawi-Pekans, Chulias and some of the early Chinese settlers came from Kedah and Siam. There were also Chulias who came directly from the Coromandel Coast. Other migrants from India were the Bengalis, but their numbers were small. Of the Chinese settlers, many came from the peninsula and not directly from mainland China. It is pos-sible that these migrants had settled earlier in the peninsula but, not having found a reasonable living there, then decided to move to Penang Island.

From the table below it can be deduced that almost 99 per cent of the population of Penang were immigrants. The highest numbers came from Siam, Kedah and mainland China. In the Jawi Pekan and Chulia com-munities more then 45 per cent came from Kedah, while of the Chinese 50 per cent came from Kedah and less than 20 per cent from mainland China and less than 7 per cent (35 people) came from Melaka. The majority of the European settlers came from Britain.

As most of the Jawi Pekan and Chulia settlers on the island in 1788 were from Kedah, the Company placed them and Malays under one ethnic cate-gory, namely, Chulias-Malays. Helped by the fact that they were Muslims, many Chulias from Kedah had intermarried with local Malays and were well

Table 29: Population of the town of Penang in 1788

Ethnic groups	Number of people	Percentage
Europeans (not including Company servants)	19	1.48
Portuguese-Eurasians	197	15.35
Jawi-Pekans/Malays	530	41.30
Chinese	537	41.85
Total	1,283	100.00

Source: G/34/3.

integrated into the local society. Their descendants were collectively known as the Jawi-Pekans. In Penang, these were shopkeepers, and by August 1788 they had built and settled in 71 shop-houses in Penang.[41] Although the 1788 population report had pooled the Malays, Jawi Pekans and Chulias under one category, in later years the Chulias were treated separately, and the Malays and Jawi-Pekans remained grouped together. The rationale for the earlier classification was that they were all Muslims. The Chulias, also small in number, were mostly from Kedah. But with the arrival of more Chulias directly from India, the community began to outnumber the Malays. Furthermore, the Chulias from the Coromandel Coast possessed distinctive cultural and social traits quite different from those who had come from Kedah.

In the period 1792–93, a new population count, which included information on the number of births, deaths, baptisms and marriages that took place from 1787 to 1793, showed some important features in the population pattern, including changes in the demographic character of Penang. It showed that in the Chinese community there were twice as many men as women and that most migrants had no intention of staying permanently, staying only long enough to build up savings. However, those who had married local women and had families were considered permanent settlers. The count also showed that most Chinese children born between 1787 and 1793 were the offspring of mixed marriages between Chinese and natives. As in Melaka, the early male settlers were usually unaccompanied by women. However, in 1792 it was reported that 14 Chinese families from Kedah, Ligor, and Melaka arrived at Penang.

The statistics also show that the birth rate among Christian Catholics was high in the 1787 to 1793 period. In particular, among new immigrants from Kedah and Siam, Christian Catholics traditionally had large families, a fact that contrasted sharply with Chinese-local mixed unions. Both males and females were well represented among Christian Catholics who migrated to Penang. In addition, families appeared to favour their children marrying only other Christian Catholics, which protected the religious identity of the group and made them a close-knit community. Since most Indian Moslem men from the Coromandel and Bengal did not bring their wives or family with them, they had little choice but to wed local Malays. Thus the Jawi-Pekan group became an important community in Penang and in later years became a defining feature of Penang society.

The 1792–93 count was limited in scope and confined to four communities, namely, the Christians, Malays, Chulias and Chinese who represented the most prominent groups in Penang. In 1810 a more accurate but still partial study was conducted. While all other communities that lived in Penang were also included, slaves were not counted although many other documents

Table 30: Total population of the town of Penang in 1810 not including persons in the Company's service

Ethnic groups	Number of people	Percentage
Europeans (not in the Company's service)	95	0.6
Portuguese-Eurasians	790	5.6
Chulias and Bengalis	5,604	40
Chinese	5,088	36.6
Malays, Jawi-Pekans, Arabs	2,069	15
Armenians	70	0.5
Persians	21	0.1
Half-casts	36	0.2
Total	13,885	100

Source: G/34/29.

mentioned the existence of slavery in the town. Table 30 above shows the breakdown.

In 1810 the largest ethnic groups of settlers in Penang were the Chulias and Chinese. The Malay group, which included the Arabs and Jawi-Pekans, accounted for slightly more than 15 per cent and Europeans were less than 1 per cent. For the first time ethnicity rather than religious affiliation was the main criterion for determining classification. The exclusion of slaves in the count was probably because officially they were not supposed to exist. As the slave ban was a company policy, admission of the presence of slaves would not have gone down well with the higher authorities.

Slavery in Penang can be categorised into two groups, namely, slaves controlled by the Company and slaves owned by the native peoples (Malays, Jawi-Pekans and Arabs). In the early days when the island had just been opened up to economic development, fuelling the demand for labour and work force, slavery would have been seen as an immediate means of fulfilling this demand and the Company probably kept slaves for this reason. But most of the slaves owned by the Arabs and native Malays were in domestic service. Domestic slaves were defined as those offering service to their master and working on lands, fields and households. They shared the homes of their overlords to whom they pledged their obedience.

Slaves owned by the native peoples were known to have existed in Penang at least by 1792, when Tuanku Syed Hussain and Syed Jaafer resided in Penang. These two Arab-Malay merchants from the royal house of Aceh had moved to Penang with their large families, including many slaves. It would appear that Francis Light had been inclined not to interfere in matters concerning the ownership of slaves. At some stage in the early period, *hakims* or native notaries were appointed to keep a register of slaves belonging to the Arab merchants on the island and Light left all matters to do with these slaves to these notaries and community, a policy implemented until the promulgation of the emancipation of slavery in 1808. However, there was no register for slaves belonging to the Company.

In 1801, there were 723 slave owners of whom the majority were Malays although a substantial number were Europeans and Chinese.[42] The total number of slaves in Penang in 1801 was estimated to be 1,200.[43] By 1805, estimates had risen to 1,400 with most slaves in domestic service.[44] A register of the sale and transfer from one master to another was kept but no tax or duty was levied upon importation. In 1807, records estimated that there were 3,000 slave-debtors in George Town, mostly owned by wealthy familes such as Tuanku Syed Hussain, the Pengeran families, Maha Raja Setia and Naquda Byan. Together, these men owned one third of all bondage slaves[45] in the colony.[46]

Despite the ban on the slave trade and the keeping of slaves, introduced in 1808, slaves continued to be kept by the people. This is evident from the fact that as late as 1820 a petition was sent by a group of Malays asserting that they should be given the liberty to practice their personal laws, which included ownership and administration of slaves.[47] However, that a petition was forwarded to the administration points to the fact that slavery was no longer a practice to be taken for granted in Penang although the authorities appeared to have been turning a blind eye to it, not only because slaves were useful in the labour force but also because the leaders would have met with strong resistance had they tried to implement the ban strictly.

After the 1810 census, the next count was conducted in 1818 (see Tables 31 and 32). This survey of the Prince of Wales Island and its territories showed that the total population of the island had increased to 30,200, out of which 12,135 people, or 40 per cent of the total, lived in the town. The population of Penang appears to have decreased by 2,150 but this could be because European settlers had been excluded in the count. In addition, there was also a decrease in the Chinese population. However, by 1822 the numbers had increased to 13,781, an increase due to incoming refugees from Kedah seeking to escape from the Siamese invasion. More than 94 per cent of the temporary migrants from Kedah were Malays, causing the Malay population to rise to 3,367, overtaking the Chinese for the first time since the earliest days.

The main cause for the drop in the population in 1818 emanates from the Chinese community, which accounted for 5,088 people in 1810 and had decreased to 3,128 persons in 1818. The decline might have been related to

Table 31: Population of the town of Penang by ethnicity in 1818

Ethnic groups	Number of people	Percentage
Europeans (including Company servants)	400	3.29
Malays	2,193	18.07
Chinese	3,128	25.77
Chulias and Bengalis	5,498	45.3
Portuguese-Eurasians	831	6.8
Arabs	84	0.69
Siamese/Burmese	1	0.0
Total	12,135	100

Source: F/4/633 17169.

economic problems faced by the island, especially the failure of the colony's spice plantations. Since 1806, pepper cultivators –mostly Chinese and Europeans – had faced the problem of declining pepper prices in the world market. This had caused many pepper plantations to be abandoned, a trend that continued into the 1820s. There was a small increase in prices in 1814 but they soon fell further and never recovered.[48] An indication of the hard times faced by pepper farmers can be seen in the many advertisements in the *Prince of Wales Island Gazette* seeking to sell property such as land, houses and premises in Penang.[49] Many owners had to sell in order to settle their debts before leaving the island. As a result of this economic problem the island witnessed the departure of many Chinese.

Table 32: Population of the town of Penang in 1818 by age and ethnicity*

Ethnic groups	Below 14 years			15–39 years			More than 40 years			Grand total
	M	F	Total	M	F	Total	M	F	Total	
Malays	293	287	580	639	816	1,455	63	95	158	2,773
Chinese	253	173	426	1,993	245	2,238	425	39	464	3,128
Eurasians	50	31	81	250	430	680	40	30	70	831
Chulias	1,043	162	1,205	3,098	379	3,477	116	46	162	4,844
Others	84	81	165	320	221	541	15	18	33	739

Note: Not including European settlers and Company servants.

Source: F/4/633 17169.

Table 32 above shows that the population of Malay females was higher then males in the categories of adults 40 years and above and adults from 15 to 39 years. This unusually high number had to do with the influx of women from Kedah due to the war situation there. The men had stayed behind to fight the Siamese army. The figures showing the state of the Chinese population confirm the traditional pattern in Chinese immigration in the region: more males than females. Fluctuations in the number of Chulias can be accounted for in the same way. Chulia males represented 26 per cent of the overall population while the females were just 3 per cent. Most Chulias tended to intermarry with the locals if unable to find a suitable woman from their own ethnic background. The Native Christians remained stable as a social group but had a higher number of females in the 15 to 39 years category. This could also be due to additional numbers coming in because of the Siamese invasion of Kedah.

Table 33 below shows that the biggest ethnic group residing in Penang was the Chulia community, who accounted for 36 per cent of the population, followed by the Malays at 26 per cent and the Chinese at 24 per cent. The

Table 33: Population of the town of Penang in 1822

Ethnic groups	Number of people	Percentage
Europeans (incl. settlers and Company servants)	400	2.9
Malays	3,367	24.43
Chinese	3,313	24.04
Chulias	4,996	36.25
Native Christians	763	5.53
Achinese	60	0.43
Bataks	294	2.13
Bengalis	411	2.98
Arabs	145	1.05
Armenians	16	0.11
Persians	11	0.07
Cafferes (or Kafirs)*	4	0.02
Total	13,781	100.00

*Note: A term used to denote a group of people who did not incline to any set of religious belief. Usually, it referred to those coming from the lowest class of society.

Source: G/34/89.

Eurasians only amounted to 5 per cent. While the Chulias remained the biggest community from 1818 to 1822, the Chinese – the second largest community in 1818 – were overtaken by the Malays by 1822.

The population of the island decreased by 2,300 between 1822 and 1823 chiefly owing to emigration of settlers to Province Wellesley because of the outbreak of diseases such as fever, small-pox and cholera on Penang Island.[50]

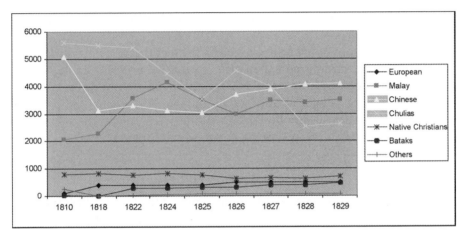

Figure 15: Population of the town of Penang according to ethnic groups, 1810–29. Source: F/4/633 17169,G/34/89,G/34/99, G/34/102, G/34/115, G/34/122, G/34/123, G/34/129.

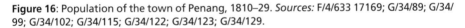

Figure 16: Population of the town of Penang, 1810–29. *Sources:* F/4/633 17169; G/34/89; G/34/99; G/34/102; G/34/115; G/34/122; G/34/123; G/34/129.

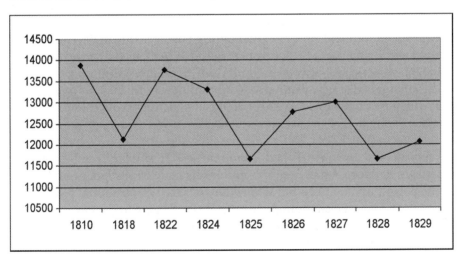

In general, Penang's population fluctuated from year to year. In 1810 the population of the town was 13,885, in 1818 it was 12,135, in 1822 it stood at 13,781, in 1824 it was 13,303, in 1825 it was 11,645, in 1826 it was 12,762, in 1827 it was 12,992, in 1828 it was 11,647 and in 1829 it was 12,060. The highest number was reached in 1810 and the lowest in 1825. But the fluctuations were not sharp. In the two decades after 1810, Penang's population was within the range of 11,600 to 13,900, which compares favourably to the situation in Melaka, especially bearing in mind that Penang was relatively new as a port-town.

Such fluctuations could be explained by the fact that as a new settlement dependent largely on migrants, Penang's population was less stable. Moreover, many in the population were traders, there only temporarily, creating a constant flow of people in and out of Penang. Also many had to leave because the agricultural slumped due to falling prices, but at the same time others arrived to try to make a living in a new environment.

CONCLUSION

As two colonial ports located in the same region of the Straits of Melaka and serving similar economic functions, it stands to reason that both Melaka and Penang would share similar demographic patterns. In fact it could be said that as the newer settlement, Penang replicated many of the features seen in Melaka. Thus it could be said that the concentration on trading activities and the nature of the trading networks that had developed in the region determined the demographic composition of the two port-towns. Both were cosmopolitan, multi-ethnic, multi-cultural and multi-religious in character, with a similar combination of ethnic groups. But the fact that they were both European trading colonies meant that there was also a small European component in the population. Further, the male dominated trading world and the fact that distant outposts were usually male domains made intermarriages between migrants and locals more common, resulting in the emergence of new distinctive communities. In Melaka, its experience of Portuguese control had already produced a distinct group of Portuguese Eurasians long before the arrival of the Dutch in 1641, while its long history as an international port had made possible the evolution of the Chinese Peranakan and the Jawi-Pekan communities. A similar trend of mixed marriages between Asian migrants and locals had already begun in Penang in the period under study, but it was the arrival of a substantial number of Eurasian and Jawi-Pekan immigrants that instantly gave to the newly opened, English-ruled island the European-Asian and Indian-local admixtures that had to evolve slowly in Melaka.

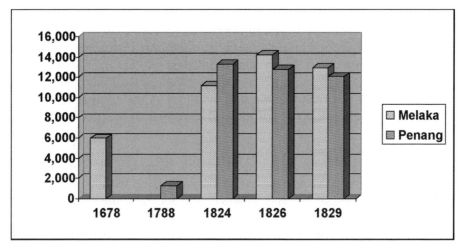

Figure 17: Population of the town of Melaka and Penang, 1678–1829. *Sources:* Balthasar Bort, 'Report of Governor Balthasar Bort on Melaka,1678'; Collectie 57 Schneither ARA; F/4/ 1272 51026; SSFR vol.165; SSFR vol. 168; SSFR vol. 169; F/4/633 17169; G/34/89; G/34/99; G/34/ 115; G/34/122; G/34/123; G/34/129.

Both Melaka and Penang had small populations reflecting their positions as essentially collecting and distributing centres of goods in the intra-Asian trade. At the same time both had a comparatively small home-grown entrepreneurial class depending, instead, on the support and activities of merchants and traders from outside. Further, the one-dimensional economic activity meant that the scope for population increase was limited. As we have seen, the Dutch did not encourage the development of agriculture in Melaka's hinterland, while in the case of Penang its efforts to diversify by developing an agricultural sector were thwarted by the fickle demands of the European market. The dependence on trade also meant the presence of a substantial floating population with no intention of settling permanently.

Historically Melaka was the seat of a Malay kingdom while Penang was on the fringe of another. Thus the Malay component of the population was never absent although when Penang was first opened, its Malay population was very small. In both ports most Malays were settled in the outer fringes of the town area, indicating their mainly marginal economic role. The policies of the colonial authorities were also responsible for the Malays being side-lined, for there was active encouragement of immigrants to settle in Melaka and Penang. There were, of course, some wealthy Malay traders but their numbers appear to have been small. In Melaka, it was firstly the Dutch Burgher community and later the Chinese who lived in the choicest areas in, while in Penang the commercial centre was dominated by the Chulias and Chinese.

As the European community represented a small part of the population, being limited to the official community and a small group of merchants and traders, the majority of whom did not regard the port-towns as home, their numbers did not expand to any significant degree. Further, the arrival of Asian migrants in larger numbers and the presence of the Malay population meant that they were completely outnumbered. Thus, by the end of the 1820s, both Melaka and Penang had been transformed into predominantly Asian towns.

In the period between 1780 and 1830, the long-term trend in the populations of Melaka and Penang was one of growth, rising to their highest levels in the 1820s when both port-towns had a population within the range of 11,500 to 14,500 people. Yet Melaka was on the decline while Penang was on the rise. Several explanations could be given for this situation. The opening of Singapore as the new centre of international trade was, in the long term, to relegate both ports to the position of regional rather than international trade centres. However, the peninsula's western Malay states were on the cusp of new economic developments especially in the tin mining industry, and with their trading infrastructures still intact, Melaka and Penang became the depots where tin and other goods from the interior were taken before being shipped to Singapore. Especially for Melaka, the 1820s provided a new lease of life to its trade. At the same time, both port-towns became the bases for launching and expanding business in the Malay states. Penang was also fortunate in that its distance from Singapore and its position at the southeastern tip of the Bay of Bengal allowed it, to some extent, to continue trading with the regions facing the bay as well as with other parts of India. Nevertheless, it could be said that beginning from the 1820s the fortunes of both Melaka and Penang were more tied up with the Malay peninsula than with the world beyond their shores.

NOTES

1   Balthasar Bort, 'Report of Governor Balthasar Bort on Melaka, 1678', pp. 1–232; see also Anthony Reid, 'The Structure of Cities in Southeast Asia, Fifteenth to Seventeenth Centuries', pp. 235–250.

2   Balthasar Bort, 'Report of Governor Balthasar Bort on Melaka, 1678', pp. 1–232.

3   VOC 1361, folio 72–73 (for year 1680); VOC 1332, folio 561–563 (for year 1678); VOC 1452, folio 1013–1014 (for year 1687) and VOC 1453 folio 419–420 (for year 1688).

4   See Collectie 57 Schneither ARA.

5   T. Braddell, *Statistics of the British Possessions in the Straits of Melaka with Explanatory Notes*. See also M.V. Del Tufo, *A Report on the 1947 Census of Population*, London: Crown Agents, p. 584. R. Montgomery Martin, *History of the British Possessions in the Indian and Atlantic Oceans*, London: Whittaker, 1837, p. 140.

6   Ibid.

7   See 'Miscellaneous Notes: Malacca in the Eighteenth Century', *JSBRAS*, 1883, No. 12, pp. 261–267.

8   Instructions to the *wijkmeesteren* (ward superintendents) to maintain a regular census of houses and inhabitants in Melaka, 3 Jan 1803–20 Nov 1804, in R/9/34/1.

9   Ibid.

10   Cassa Boeken (Cash Books of the Melaka Orphan Chamber 1780–1827, in R/9/3; Principaal Weeskamer's Journaal 1780–1830, in R/9/4; Grote Boeken 1780–1830, in R/9/9, Notitie Boeken van Debiteuren 1787–1799, in R/9/5; Melaka Wills 1780–1823, in R/9/11; Obligatie Boeken 1780–1821, in R/9/8; and Vendutie Boeken 1780–1822, in R/9/13.

11   Instructions to the *wijkmeesteren* to maintain a regular census of houses and inhabitants in Malacca, 3 Jan 1803–20 Nov 1804, in R/9/34/1.

12   Part of the document is missing, so that de Wind's first name or initials cannot be ascertained. However, it is probable that the person referred to was J.B. de Wind.

13   Kerk Boek: Miscellaneous: Naamen de Ledemaaten van Gereformeende Kerk welke in het jaare 1824 .

14   P.A. Christiaans, 'De Europese bevolking van Malakka onder het laaste Nederlandse bestuur, 1818–1825', *Jaarboek Centraal Bureau Voor Genealogie*, Deel 40, 1986, 's-Gravenhage: Centraal Bureau Voor Genealogie, pp. 257–287.

15   Ibid.

16   Census of Population in Melaka giving the names of heads of families, numbers in each household and whether free, slaves or debtors, for the year 1825, in R/9/34/7.

17   Ibid.

18   W.T. Lewis, 30 June 1827, in G/34/172.

19   S. Garling to Lewis, 13 March 1827, in SSFR, vol. 165.

20   Ibid., see, for example, Minute by R. Fullerton 5 July 1827, in G/34/172; see also Malacca 6 January 1827, in SSFR, vol. 165.

21   Ibid.

22   For further reference on this matter, see K.T. Joseph, 'The Malacca Land Laws', pp. 129–179.

23   See Brian Harrison, *Holding the Fort*, pp. 114–125.

24   S. Garling to Lewis, 13 March 1827, in SSFR, vol. 165.

25   See Petition of inhabitants of Melaka to Governor R. Fullerton, in SSFR, vol. 169. See also minute by Garling in enclosures C, E,H, I, K, M, N, in SSFR, vol. 169.

26   See population census for the town of Melaka for the year 1828, in SSFR 168.

27   Extract Letter from Governor Macalister to the chairman and deputy chairman, dated 7 November 1808, in SSFR, vol. 9; see also memorandum on Melaka 1817/1818, in SSFR, vol. 10.

28   For further discussion on slaves and their occupations, see Anthony Reid, 'Introduction: Slavery and bondage in Southeast Asian History', pp. 22–27.

29   Ibid., p. 27.

30   Ibid., p. 26.

31   Ibid., See also Heather Sutherland, 'Slavery and the slave trade in South Sulawesi, 1660s–1800s'. In Anthony Reid (ed.), *Slavery, Bondage and Dependency*, pp. 263–285; V. Matherson and M.B. Hooker, 'Slavery in the Malay texts: categories of dependency and compensation'. In Anthony Reid (ed.), *Slavery, Bondage and Dependency*, pp. 182–207.

32   See, for example, auction records of a Burgher, Benjamin Moll, on 17 November 1770: one man slave was sold for 106 rijksdollars; another male slave, probably an old man, was sold for 37.24 rijksdollars; and one slave girl, a minor, was sold for 19 rijksdollars, in R/9/13/1. For further discussion regarding the prices of slaves according to areas of origin, see S. Arasaratnam, 'Slave trade in the Indian Ocean in the seventeenth century'. In K.S. Mathew (ed.), *Mariners, Merchants and Oceans Studies in Maritime History*, New Delhi: Manohar, 1995, pp. 195–208.

33   Letter from Farquhar to Secretary, dated 27 March 1806, in SSFR, vol. 13.

34   V. Matheson and M.B. Hooker, 'Slavery in the Malay texts: categories of dependency and compensation', pp. 182–207. See, also, Anthony Reid, 'Introduction: slavery and bondage in Southeast Asian History', in, Anthony Reid (ed.), *Slavery, Bondage and Dependency*, pp. 1–43.

35 See minutes by the President, 9 November 1829, in SSFR, vol. 169.

36 Instructions to the *wijkmeesters* to maintain a regular census of houses in R/9/34/1; see See Appendix 9: List of Registered Slaves in Melaka 1819–1824 and Appendix 10: List of Registered Slave Children in Melaka 1819–1824, in Nordin Hussin, 'Melaka and Penang 1780–1830: A study of two port towns in the Straits of Melaka', Ph.D. thesis, Amsterdam: Vrije Universiteit, 2002. See also minutes by the President, 9 November 1829, in SSFR, vol. 169.

37 See Anthony Reid, 'Introduction: Slavery and Bondage', p. 30.

38 Instructions to the *wijkmeesters* to maintain a regular census of houses, in R/9/34/1.

39 For further reference regarding the definition of slave-debtors and how slaves turned into slave-debtors, see V. Matheson and M.B. Hooker, 'Slavery in the Malay texts: categories of dependency and compensation', pp. 182–207. See also Anthony Reid, 'Introduction: Slavery and Bondage in Southeast Asian History', in, Anthony Reid, (ed.) *Slavery, Bondage and Dependency in Southeast Asia*, St. Lucia: University of Queensland Press, 1983, pp. 1–43.

40 For further discussion on the emancipation of slaves, see W.R van Hoevell, *De Emancipatie der slaven in Neerlands-Indie*, Groningen: van Bolhuis Hoitsema, 1848.

41 See Appendix to consultation 25 August 1788, in G/34/3.

42 Letter dated 18 April 1805, in F4/266 5872. See also extract general letter from PWI dated 12 November 1805, in F/4/266 5872; see also Letter dated 4 February 1809 and 31 July 1787 and letter dated 18 April 1805, in F/4/279 6417.

43 Letter dated 18 April 1805, in F/4/279 6417.

44 Extract general letter from PWI dated 12 November 1805, in F/4/266 5872.

45 For further discussion on the meaning of bondage slaves, see Anthony Reid, 'Introduction: Slavery and Bondage in Southeast Asian History', pp. 1–43.

46 Extract general letter from PWI dated 12 November 1805, in F/4/266 5872.

47 Petition from certain Malays (signed by 12 people), 1 April 1820, in F/4/663 18439.

48 James C Jackson, *Planters and Speculators: Chinese and European Agricultural Enterprise in Malaya 1786–1921*, pp. 93–100.

49 See *Prince of Wales Island Gazette,* 1810–1825.

50 Minute by the President, dated 25 January 1825, in G/34/99.

CHAPTER SEVEN

Dutch Urban
Administration in Melaka

INTRODUCTION

THE DUTCH ADMINISTRATIVE SYSTEM in most of its colonial towns was more or less similar, although a more elaborate administrative structure was usually seen in the more important centres. As explained by Gaastra, the importance and the status of the establishments were expressed in the forms of address and the salaries of the chief officials. The large establishments, like Melaka and Ambon, were administered by governors, while other areas had directors, commanders or residents. In all cases, however, these officials were aided in the day-to-day running of the administration by various councils, such as the Political Council, the Council of Justice, the board of guardians of orphans, the heads of city wards, the board of commissioners for matrimonial and minor judicial matters and the Church Council. However, this was only in theory for in practice decisions were sometimes made without consulting the councils.[1]

A Governor, usually chosen through merit, patronage or family connections,[2] had the power to make decisions on various matters regarding the town, although all his decisions first had to be sent to VOC headquarters in Batavia for approval.[3] As head of the administration he was entitled to many privileges. His official residence was in the fort, the administrative centre. He also enjoyed the right to trade, including the illicit type, like smuggling.[4] Further, he was allowed to own property, such as slaves, land, farms and houses in and outside the town.[5]

During the Dutch period from 1641 until 1824, Melaka had 32 Dutch governors.[6] A Governor was assisted by several subordinate officers, such as the Senior Merchant (the most senior official after the Governor), the Merchant (who held the position as Treasurer), and several Junior Merchants of whom one was also the Bookkeeper and the Commandant of the *militie* (militia). The posts of Senior and Junior Merchants were important in the hierarchy because the Junior Merchant could be promoted to the post of Senior Merchant and from there to Governor.[7] For example, Abraham Couperus, a Junior Merchant, was later appointed to Senior Merchant and then promoted to the post of Governor. Nevertheless, there were other reasons for such promotions. Factors such as family ties and relationships also played important roles in determining one's career. A marriage between an ordinary VOC officer and a daughter of the highest ranking officer could also make one's career brighter.[8] The post of Governor carried much power, including the defence of the town under the direct jurisdiction of his office.[9] In all other matters, the Governor was assisted by the councils of which the most important was the Political Council *(Raad van Politie)*. But even within this body, the Governor as head of the council could overrule decisions made by it.[10] Table 34 shows the officials who were elected to posts in the Political Council (*Raad van Politie*) in Melaka in 1780 and 1793.

While the Political Council dealt with administrative and political matters, the Council of Justice was in charge of legal matters. Before 1734, the Governor was also the President of this council although his power in it was limited.[11] After 1734 he no longer sat on the Council of Justice but received monthly reports on its proceedings.[12] The Council consisted of nine permanent members who were mostly VOC servants. After 1737 the Senior Merchant acted as the President.

Table 34: The Political Council (*Raad van Politie*) of Melaka in 1780 and 1793

Name of Office	1780	1793
Governor	Pieter Gerardus Bruijn	Abraham Couperus
Senior merchant and Chief administrator	Anthonij Abraham Werndlij	Francois Thierens
Merchant and Fiscaal (exchequer)	Arnoldus Franciscus Lemker	David Ruhde
Junior merchant and secretary of the Political Council	Francois Thierens	Gerrit Pungel
Junior merchant and bookkeeper	Abrahamus Couperus	Walterus Adriaanus van Heusden
Captain Commandant of the militia	Johan Andreas Hensel	Johan Andreas Hensel

Source: VOC 3599, COIH 107.

Serious disputes among the population of the town were solved in the court of the Council of Justice. When such disputes involved the Asian communities, the Council usually sought the assistance of community leaders as well as interpreters. The Council's judgement, however, was not always unquestioned and there were cases of decisions being criticised biased and unjust.[13] When the British took over the administration in 1794, they retained the Dutch judicial system and the Council of Justice continued to be run by Dutch officials.[14] English law was only implemented after the Anglo-Dutch treaty and the transfer of Melaka to the English in 1825.[15]

As mentioned before, there were many councils set up to assist the administration and they came directly or indirectly under the administration of the governor's office.[16] As there were only a small number of Dutch officials, each had to hold several posts and each was a member of various councils at any one time. For example, in 1780, Anthonij Abraham, Senior Merchant (*Opperkoopman*) and Chief Administrator in the Political Council, also served as President of the Council of Justice and held a position in the Church Council.

The majority of the officers in the VOC administration in Melaka were Dutch or Europeans who had formerly worked in other Dutch colonial towns and ports in the East.[17] All official posts with executive power were held by Europeans. The Political Council and the Council of Justice were exclusively run by VOC officials, but the less important councils were run by the Dutch Burghers. The only councils whose membership was open to Asians were the council of *wijkmeesteren* (ward superintendents) and the *weeshuis* or Orphan Chamber. The office of the *Syahbandar* could also be held by an Asian.[18]

The Asian officials who represented their communities were usually wealthy individuals, well known in the society. These officials were known as captains. The practice of appointing a captain was a carry-over from the Portuguese period when each ethnic group had to have a leader who represented them in matters concerning the community. During the Dutch period, the Burgher, Malay, Chinese and Keling communities had a captain each. These captains were also elected as Superintendents of the Wards and members of the Orphan Chamber. Thus few duties were entrusted to non-Europeans. Some Asians were employed in the *militie* (militia) for the defence of the town. As for the Portuguese-Eurasians, they appear to have been left very much to their own devices without a captain to represent them. Portuguese-Eurasians were mostly poor fishermen who resided in their own quarter of the town.[19] Some were employed to do the night watch (*Burgerijwacht* or native patrol) for the town.[20] It is strange that there was no captain for the Portuguese-Eurasians but this was probably because their numbers were small and they were not regarded as an important group in terms of their contribution to the well-being of the port-town. There was, however, a Portuguese-Eurasian Superintendent of the wards. A similar situation appears to have developed in the Moor community, when, after its numbers declined, Moors were pooled together with the Keling as one group and a Keling was appointed as captain.

SUPERINTENDENT OF THE WARD

The ward system covered the areas of Melaka that fell under direct Dutch administration. This covered the 'urban' centre (the fort of Melaka and the town) and the suburbs or the outer fringes of the town. The majority of the population was concentrated in the town area, on the north side of the fort, which was well-lined with streets. The most important streets were Herenstraat and Jonkerstraat while others were Eerstebruggewalstraat, Secondebruggewalstraat, Derdebruggewalstraat, Goudsmidstraat, Coetijstraat, Moorsestraat and Visstraat.[21] The suburbs were divided into four main wards, namely, Tengkera to the north, Bandarhilir to the south and Bungaraya and Bukit China on the eastern part of the fort. The fort of Melaka did not come under the ward system. It was situated on the south of the town, covering an area slightly smaller than the town area. Only VOC officials and their families had the right to reside within the fort although from time to time some wealthy Burghers were given the privilege to live there.

The Superintendent of a Ward (*Wijkmeester*) came under the jurisdiction of the Governor's office. Superintendents played a big role in the day-to-day affairs of a port-town, as they were the eyes and ears of the administration at the ward level. Superintendents were required to provide regular reports to the Governor's office regarding the social, economic and political situation in their own ward.[22] The ward was the most important unit in the VOC urban colonial administration, and reports submitted by the Superintendents were considered important intelligence material for the Governor. Decisions on defence, economic, political and welfare strategies were based on the information received.

Therefore, the contents in the Superintendents' reports included detailed accounts of demographic patterns in the wards, among other things. Each Superintendent had to conduct a regular census of the population in his area to record information such as ethnic composition, age, sex and number of slaves in each household. The report also had to contain details about the wealth or types of property owned by each household, for example, size of land and number of houses, including the type of house, that is, whether brick or wooden. Other details sought include food items consumed in each household and the amount of food stored. Items such as rice and paddy were considered important and had to be recorded in the report. Each individual had to declare the amount of rice he or she consumed and the volume of rice and paddy stored in each household. The Superintendents of the wards also had to report on any new immigrants who arrived in their area as all new arrivals needed to be reported to the Governor's office.

All information collected was vital to the Dutch administration in order to determine population size and adequacy of food supply and to check on new suspicious immigrants who could threaten the town and the administration.[23] The supply of rice and paddy had to be carefully monitored as Melaka depended on imports to feed its population. In times of war and uncertainty supply and prices could be affected, and to maintain peace and order the administration had to be alert to any change or development. Information on property was also used to determine taxes on the wealthy. Therefore, the report of each Superintendent constituted an important social document about each ward. Unfortunately, very few have survived and those that have are in a very bad condition.[24]

A ward could have more than one superintendent. Appointment to the post of head of a ward was based on various factors, such as wealth, status and standing in his own community, although the VOC could chose an outsider to be superintendent of a ward. The position could also be held through an election. This appears to apply usually to wards where the inhabitants were mostly Dutch Burghers, thus indicating that the European community was more privileged in that it was allowed to select its own leader. An incumbent could be reappointed so that a superintendent could hold his position for many years or even for life. Although in theory the superintendent came from the largest ethnic group within a ward, in practice this was not followed particularly if there were Burghers residing in the ward. In such cases, a Burgher was invariably made Superintendent. No doubt the idea was that leadership must always be in the hands of the Europeans.

In 1744, for the purpose of administering the *wijkmeesteren*, Melaka was divided into three major wards, the Town, Tengkera and Bandarhilir. The small number of wards in the 1740s was probably due to the fact that the population was small then, and Bukit China and Bungaraya were included within the town ward. In 1744, the town ward, situated on the north side of the fort, had three superintendents or *wijkmeesteren*, namely, Jan Krijkman, Huijbertus Overre and Che Laoedin (Captain of the Moors). The town ward had a mixed population, with the Dutch Burghers, Malays, Portuguese-Eurasians, Chinese, Moors and Kelings. Although there were many ethnic groups, the Superintendents came from the two major groups, the Dutch

Table 35: Superintendents of wards (*wijkmeesteren*) in Melaka in 1744

Name	Ethnic group	Ward	Method of appointment
Jan Krijkman	Burgher	Town	by appointment
Huijbertus Overre	Burgher	Town	by appointment
Che Laoedin	Captain of the Moors	Town	by continuation
David Swerusz	Burgher	Tengkera	by election
David Perrinet	Burgher	Tengkera	by election
Ulrich Altheer	Captain of the Burghers	Bandarhilir	by continuation
Encik Soereen	Captain of the Malays	Bandarhilir	by continuation
Tsan Hionqua	Captain of the Chinese	Bandarhilir	by continuation

Source: VOC 2630.

Burghers and the Moors. During this period there was probably a large number of Dutch Burghers and Moors in the town of Melaka and fewer Chinese. Nonetheless, the Dutch Burghers in the early period would have been fewer in number compared to the Malays and Portuguese-Eurasians, as they never outnumbered the Portuguese-Eurasians and Malays throughout the Dutch period. In the early period, the Dutch also distrusted the Portuguese-Eurasians, who were mostly Catholic. However, such distrust proved unfounded and later the relationship with the Portuguese-Eurasians improved.[25]

The Tengkera ward had two Superintendents, both Europeans. It is hard to believe that in 1744 it had more European residents, as Tengkera was traditionally an area in which the Portuguese-Eurasians and Malays resided.[26] The Bandarhilir ward towards the southern part of the fort had three Superintendents, namely, Ulrich Altheer, a Burgher captain who had been the *Wijkmeester* for 25 years, Tsan Hionqua, captain of the ethnic Chinese community, and Encik Soereen, who was the captain of the Malays.[27] From the three names one can conclude that this ward had a mixed population of Dutch Burghers, Malays and Chinese. This area was also a predominantly Portuguese-Eurasian and Malay area.[28] However, a Portuguese-Eurasian was not elected as Superintendent until 1780, when Francisco Cardoza held that position.[29] Dutch Burghers owned land and property in Bandarhilir but many did not live there, choosing instead to live in town in Heren and Jonkerstraat.[30]

By the 1770s, the number of wards had increased to seven: the first, Herenstraat, the second, Jonkerstraat, the third, the Malay and Moor ward, the fourth, Tengkera, the fifth, Bandarhilir, the sixth, Bungaraya, and the seventh, Bukit China. In 1775 the Dutch administration instituted changes and increased the wards from four to seven, probably due to the fact that the population in the centre of town had increased and was too big to be administered as one ward, while the suburbs had also expanded and could justify the addition of two other wards, namely, Bungaraya and Bukit China. Thus there were three wards in the town and four in the suburbs. This division of Melaka into seven wards remained until 1794 when the English took over. There is no indication that the ward system was continued during the English administration, although the fact that they retained the judicial system and continued to use Dutch officials suggests that the wards remained intact, although more in their form than in their substance. Table 36 overleaf shows the Superintendents of Wards in 1775, 1782 and 1793.

Several questions can be raised regarding the geographical division of the wards. For example, why were Herenstraat and Jonkerstraat classified as separate wards? Heren and Jonker Straats were both close to the beach, parallel to each other, and only a few hundred meters long. Compared to the other divisional wards, the Heren and Jonkerstraat wards each covered a small geographical area. The main reason why this area was so important to the Dutch administration lay in its population being mainly Dutch burghers and Europeans.[31] They were also the wealthiest groups and therefore the most influential people in town. By dividing the European communities into two separate wards the Dutch administration probably anticipated that they would be able to monitor the living conditions and the security of these wards more closely than the other larger wards.

In 1775, three people were elected as the *wijkmeesteren* of the Herenstraat: Joost Koek, a Dutch Burgher captain, Quintiliano de Grace, a Portuguese-European, and Tan Tiko, the Captain of the Chinese.[32] That a Chinese became a Superintendent in an exclusive area of Melaka suggests that by then the demographic pattern had changed and that more Chinese lived there. This indicates that some Chinese there were very wealthy. Up to 1775, no Chinese had been a Superintendent in this area; Herenstraat was noted as the most famous street in Melaka and those who lived and had property there were considered as belonging to the top rung of society. Evidently, the Moors, once able to live on this street, had been replaced by the Chinese. However, the exact population of this area is not known. Neither is it certain that the Dutch Burghers remained the majority group. The names found in the list of estate papers, Melaka wills and bond books of the Orphan Chamber records reveal that most who lived or had property in this area were Burghers. They did appear to be in the majority the minority being made up of Chinese, Malays, Moors and Keling.[33] There were two

Table 36: Superintendents of wards in Melaka in 1775, 1782 and 1793

	1775		1782		1793
Superintendent	Ward	Superintendent	Ward	Superintendent	Ward
Joost Koek	Herenstraat	Joost Koek	Herenstraat	Adrian Koek	Herenstraat
Quintiliano de Grace	Herenstraat	Tan Tjapko	Herenstraat	Tan Tjapko	Herenstraat
Tan Tiko	Herenstraat	Abraham de Wind	Jonkerstraat	Carel Ferdenand Grejis	Jonkerstraat
Abraham de Wind	Jonkerstraat	Joh. Adr. van Moesbergen	Jonkerstraat	Gerrit Leendert Velge	Jonkerstraat
Anthonij Brouwer	Jonkerstraat	Tan Tinko	Jonkerstraat	–	–
Encik Zainuddin	Malay and Moor	Encik Astor	Malay and Moor	Encik Astor	Malay and Moor
Sewa Soeria Chittij	Malay and Moor	Sewa Soeria Chittij	Malay and Moor	Sewa Soeria Chittij	Malay and Moor
Johannes Barth. de Wind	Tengkera	Claas de Wind	Tengkera	Michiel Kilian	Tengkera
Jan Henderik van Robbig	Tengkera	Michiel Kilian	Tengkera	Adrianus van Moesbergen	Tengkera
Fransub. van Moesbergen	Bandarhilir	Gerrit Pungel	Bandarhilir	Pieter Puit	Bandarhilir
Berhard Janszen	Bandarhilir	Cornelis Adamsz	Bandarhilir	Cornelis Aćamsz	Bandarhilir
–	–	Franciso Cardozo	Bandarhilir	Francisco Cardoza	Bandarhilir
Johannes Speijkerman	Bukit China	Johannes Spijkerman	Bukit China	Jacob Rappa	Bukit China
Encik Draman	Bukit China	Encik Draman	Bukit China	Encik Roa	Bukit China
Encik Amal	Bungaraya	Baba Som	Bungaraya	Baba Som	Bungaraya
Tan Somko	Bungaraya	Encik Brahim	Bungaraya	Encik Abdul Aziz	Bungaraya

Source: VOC 3467, VOC 3625 and COIH 107.

Superintendents in Jonkerstraat in 1775, both Dutch Burghers, namely, Abraham de Wind and Anthonij Brouwer. Again, it is not clear whether this ward had a Burgher majority.

There is evidence to show that Jonker and Heren Straats had a substantial Burgher population even if they were not in the majority because records of the Orphan Chamber, Melaka wills, Estate papers and auction papers show that many Dutch Burghers whose names were mentioned in these documents resided in the two streets. At least from the 1770s to the 1790s, this appears to be the case. However, in the nineteenth century more Chinese names were associated with the two streets so that a change probably occurred in the meantime.[34]

The third ward, the Malay and Moor ward, was situated within the town but further up from the Heren and Jonkerstraat wards.[35] It was slightly larger than the Heren and Jonker wards combined. The Malay and Moor ward covered a few streets, such as Eerstebruggewalstraat, Secondebrugge-walstraat, Derdebruggewalstraat, Goudsmidstraat, Coetijstraat, Moorsestraat and Visstraat. There were three major ethnic groups in this area, the Malays, Moors and Kelings. The two *wijkmeesteren* elected in 1775 were Encik Zainuddin, Superintendent of the Malays and Sewa Soeria Chittij, Superintendent for the Moors and Kelings.[36] It seems that the Moors had declined perceptibly because, while in 1744 a leader was appointed them, in 1775 a Keling became Superintendent for both the Keling and Moor communities.

The wards in the suburbs of Melaka had large numbers of Malay and Portuguese-Eurasian inhabitants but fewer Chinese and Dutch burgher settlers. However, the majority of the people who lived in the Heren and Jonkerstraat wards owned land and property in these areas. The majority of the Malays could be found in the wards of Bukit China, Bungaraya, Tengkera and Bandarhilir, with a small percentage of Chinese in Bungaraya. However, Dutch Burghers were appointed as *wijkmeesteren* in Tengkera, Bandarhilir and Bukit China.

By 1782, the population of the Chinese in Melaka had increased tremendously. This could be seen from the appointments in 1782 of three Chinese as Superintendents of wards: in Herenstraat, Jonkerstraat and Bungaraya. In Herenstraat the Chinese Superintendent was Tan Tjapko; in Jonkerstraat, Tan Tinko; and in Bungaraya, Babba Som.[37] This could be explained not only in terms of an increase in the Chinese population but also by the fact that many rich Chinese had settled in these areas. It is indisputable that the Dutch administration had the tendency to elect only the wealthy to the post of Superintendent. The Chinese population in Melaka had been increasing since the first census was conducted in the mid-seventeenth century. However, in 1793, only two Chinese *wijkmeesteren* were appointed, in Herenstraat and Bungaraya, while the appointment of the Chinese Superintendent in the Jonkerstraat was terminated and he was not replaced by another Chinese.[38] This was not because the Chinese numbers had declined but due to a change in policy that saw the number of superintendents in each ward reduced from three to two.[39]

Although the main features of the ward system were maintained during the Dutch period, as we have seen, inconsistencies appeared and some details changed over time. Factors such as ethnicity and wealth remained vital. The Dutch preference for appointing their own ethnic representative over an Asian one remained unchanged because apart from everything else, they probably felt more secure with their own men and could deal better with their own kind. But while they would not impose a Dutch burgher as Superintendent over a ward with a clear Malay majority, they did not hesitate to appoint one in areas where the majority was Portuguese-Eurasian. However, as the distribution of population in the seven wards during the Dutch administration, and before the censuses in 1826 and 1828, is still unclear, it is hard to see, in its entirety, how the ward system worked.

After 1824, when Melaka was transferred to the English, the new administration did not maintain the ward system. The town was still divided into various quarters, but the practice of having superintendents was discontinued.[40] Under the new administration the town was regarded as one quarter, where formerly there were three, while the suburbs were divided into three major quarters: Tengkera, Bandarhilir and Bungaraya-Bukit China. Whereas during Dutch rule Bungaraya and Bukit China were separate wards, they were now merged into one quarter. Under the English a municipal council was established to take charge of the welfare of the town and its suburbs so that superintendents were no longer required.

THE ORPHAN CHAMBER (*WEESKAMER*) OF DUTCH MELAKA

A distinguishing characteristic of VOC administration was the attention it gave to promoting charitable works and the protection of orphans and the various activities that arose from this. As in other Dutch port-towns, the burgher elite in Melaka was actively involved in charitable bodies, such as the *diakonij*, giving supervision and relief to the poor, and the *Weeskamer*, or the orphanage.[41] The function of the Reformed *diaconij* (diaconate) was the most important charitable social welfare institution in Melaka. Financially the diaconate relied heavily on church offertories, collection boxes and money received from church activities.[42] But it was the Orphan Chamber that was the more important, as its role was multiple and its outreach much wider than suggested by its institutional name.

Since its inception, the Orphan Chamber of Melaka was formed with various socio-economic objectives.[43] It was first and foremost an institution for the management of orphans, which meant supervising the housing and education of orphans. But its role went further than that, as it had the authority to administer the intestate estates of deceased persons and to act as guardian of the families of such estates. As a guardian of estates its power was subject to the letters of the will. The Orphan Chamber was also authorized to receive accounts of estates when administered by executors and to register them for general reference. In line with the powers given to it to handle all matters related to estates of deceased persons, it also managed all inheritances that were deposited with it. These inheritances were usually invested for the purpose of generating dowries for the girls and to create business capital for the boys to be used by them when they came of age. The mode of operation was one in which the orphanage funds were used to set up a de facto bank that provided financial capital for the community.

Members of the Orphan Chamber were residents and local householders. Its managing committee was made up of a president, a vice president, a secretary, a treasurer and six additional members, three from the European community and three ethnic captains from the Asian population.[44] The Portuguese-Eurasians were not represented because their affairs were taken care of by the burger and European officials. In 1793, the directors of the Dutch-Melaka orphanage comprised the following officials: David Ruhde as President; Michiel Kilian as Vice President; Gerrit Leendert Velge as Secretary; and Jan Arnold Wiederhold as Treasurer. The three ordinary members from the European community were Adrian Koek, Jacob Frans Overre and Johan Wilhelm Davonarius, while the Malays, Chinese and Kelings were probably represented by Encik Astor, Tan Tjapko and Sewa Soeria Chittij respectively. The Asian representatives were not actually named in the document referred to but reports on the proceedings of the Orphan Chamber mention the presence of Asian representatives.[45] Asian participation is also evidenced by the fact that the regulations of the Chamber were written in Dutch, Portuguese, Malay, Chulia and Chinese.

Besides holding money derived from inheritances deposited on behalf of orphans, the chamber also offered various social and economic services, such as facilities to deposit money as savings, investments for interest, mortgages, loans, sale of bonds and preserving property such as houses.[46] Profits from the business were distributed to the owners of the funds and depository for the purpose of protecting orphans. The interest earned on the orphans' deposits and other individual and private deposits was at a rate of 6 per cent.

Estates and depositors' money and estates managed by the Chamber were therefore the main assets kept by the Chamber. The main source of investment and profit from this capital was interest charged on the assets. A person who wanted to borrow money was required to produce collateral in the form of land or a house, together with two guarantors. The interest charged was 9 per cent per annum and a borrower repaid his loan by installments paid once every six months. Such a practice was carried out during the Dutch period and also during the English administration. For example, in 1770, Encik Noeria borrowed a sum of 50 rijksdollars from the Chamber and was charged an interest of 9 per cent while the half-yearly payment was 2.12 rijksdollars.[47] Thus, she had to pay her installments within 12 years, a lengthy period of repayment because the chamber allowed a long grace period to pay one's debt. However, some people who borrowed large sums of money preferred to settle their debts within a shorter period, such as two or three months. In such cases, the interest was calculated on a monthly basis.

The Orphan Chamber was the only institution in Melaka that served as a bank for the public. It had the power to give loans not only to individuals but also to companies. In this connection, during the English occupation, the English East India Company borrowed SpD 60,000.00 from the Chamber to finance its administrative expenses.[48] The Chamber also approved loans applied jointly by several people. For example, in 1787, Ahmad Budiman, a Malay, and Ong Tinnio, a Chinese, together borrowed SpD 1,000.00, in one loan.[49]

The Orphan Chamber was also empowered to extend existing loans. If the borrower was unable to settle his debt, the Chamber would request more collateral to support the loan. Due to the long period given for settling loans, sometimes the market value of collateral could go down in the intervening years. When this happened and a debt was found to exceed two thirds of the value of the mortgage, the borrower was required to either pay off the debt or to take an additional mortgage. Another alternative for a debtor caught in this predicament was to sell the collateral at a public auction to settle the difference in the debt. If a borrower passed away before settling his debt, then the Chamber would issue a summons on the estate of his heirs. In 1825, the assets of the Chamber were valued at SpD 116,635.20.8. From this amount, a sum of SpD 27,664.20.8 was in cash and the rest was in the form of loans valued at SpD 88,971.00.[50]

As the Chamber was the trustee for the orphans until they attained adulthood, it also acted as the depository for title deeds and kept a list of all titles deeds it held. When a dispute arose between family members in regard to a will or estate of a deceased, the Chamber acted as a mediator, usually resolving the problem by mutual consent.[51]

In managing the education of orphans, the Chamber supervised the expenses incurred by each orphan and paid those costs. An example can be seen in the Chamber's handling of the affairs of two orphan sisters, Elisabeth and Anthonetta Stecher, who were under its care.[52] The records show that, for one particular quarter, each of the girls received a maintenance allowance of SpD 19.20, a school allowance amounting to SpD 9.00, washing and ironing allowance of SpD 3.60 and a personal allowance amounting to SpD 3.60. They also received a pair of long cloths each at SpD 14.00, six pairs of Melaka shoes costing SpD 4.64, five yards of silk amounting to SpD 5.00, two bonnet flowers at SpD 3.00, a pair of gloves at SpD 2.50, 6.5 yards of lace at SpD 3.00, one pair of Bengal shoes at SpD 2.00 each, one pair of silk stockings each at SpD 2.00 and six yards of cloth at SpD 8.00. Altogether, the expenses for both girls stood at SpD 79.54 per month for the three months involved. The Chamber did not merely look after Burgher orphans but took care of all orphans in the town.[53]

The Melaka Orphan Chamber was given privileged status by the administration by allowing it to use a common seal for all deeds and proceedings. Further, in the event that the Chamber's committee encountered difficulties pertaining to legal issues, it was able to seek free consultation from the Council of Justice.

After the transfer of Melaka to the English in 1825, the new administration ordered a review of the operations of the Orphan Chamber, which made many recommendations concerning its functions and regulations. While the practice was continued of administrating the estates controlled by the Chamber in accordance with the laws and customs of inheritance of the various ethnic groups, the English sought to overcome some of the weaknesses they found.[54] For instance, it was discovered that there were some irregularities in the Chamber's accounts. Personal loans were given to prominent individuals but with not enough collateral to support them. Furthermore, many individual borrowers failed to pay their installments on time and some could not afford to pay back their loans. Although there was collateral such as houses and land, sometimes, due to the fall in the value of property in the market, these did not raise sufficient money at auctions to pay off the loans. In addition there was also some money deposited in the Chamber that had not been claimed because the administrators could not locate the heirs.

Due to the Chamber's poor management, the English administration tried to carry out reform. Since the Chamber had a large amount of money deposited under its control and since most of the town's wealthy inhabitants relied on the Chamber for their credit and for the administration of their inheritance, a more prudent system of paying interest and providing credit was needed. Moreover, the last Dutch governor of Melaka, Jan Samuel Timmerman-Thyssen (1818–23) was found to have used certain sums from the Chamber for his own benefit.[55] As a result of these abuses, the British administration attempted to enforce new regulations on the Chamber.

After a few years and much effort, some changes did take place in 1828. Accordingly, the managing committee was made up of a president, one vice president, a secretary and a treasurer and three ordinary members who were all elected, while three native captains sat on it as ex-officio members.[56] The president was elected annually and by rotation. The secretary and treasurer and the three ordinary members were elected at the annual meeting of the Chamber, to be attended by the majority of the residents of Melaka who possessed property in land or houses to the amount of SpD 5,000. Those who sought election to the managing committee had to own property worth more than SpD 500.00. In order to discharge their duty, the secretary and treasurer had to post a bond worth SpD 480.00 at the Court of Judicature. Since the function of the Melakan Orphan Chamber was to help and benefit the public, no member of the managing committee could get private benefit from the Chamber.

The new regulation also gave the Resident of Melaka the power to appoint the President of the Chamber from the ranks of government officials or the inhabitants of Melaka who were good and trustworthy.[57] The elected members came from the Dutch burgher or European population and had to be inhabitants of Melaka. The secretary and treasurer were allowed remuneration for their services out of the profits of the chamber. Under the revised regulations, all Melaka residents were given preference in obtaining loans, provided they owned sufficient collateral for the sum borrowed. The rate of interest for personal loans was not changed but was maintained at 9 per cent per annum. The Chamber was also entitled to charge 2.5 per cent interest on profits from estates it administered. These profits were to be equally distributed to the secretary, the treasurer and the general fund.[58] The secretary and treasurer also received a salary, and remuneration for stationery expenses incurred by them in the performance of their duties. A committee was also appointed at each annual general meeting of the Chamber to inspect the accounts.

The Orphan Chamber showed a humane and practical approach to solving the social problem of orphans in a distant outpost. No doubt the motivating force was the protection of European children but orphans belonging to other communities also benefited. While the orphans were looked after, their inheritance was put to good use not only for them but also for society at large. Undoubtedly, the business ventures the Chamber engaged in benefited only those who had money to invest in the first place, or those with property to use as collateral in order to raise a loan, but one could not dismiss the fact that it also served to stimulate business in Melaka.

DEFENCE AND INTERNAL SECURITY OF THE TOWN
THE *BURGERIJE WACHT* AND *MILITIE*

For the defense and internal security of the town and its suburbs, the Dutch administration relied on its *Burgerije wacht* (Burgher watch) and the *militie*. The *Burgerije wacht,* or civil patrol, policed the town areas and suburbs. It was formed from a group of civilian residents with the majority of its non-ranking members coming from the Portuguese-Eurasian community. The administration of the Burgher watch did not come under the direct control of the Governor's office but was administered by the burghers. The financing of this organization came from the *Burgerije Cassa,* or Burgher Fund, which was derived from taxes collected from the Malays, Chinese, Kelings and Portuguese-Eurasians. As the civil patrol received no financial help from the administration, officers of the Burgher watch, who were mostly Burghers, received remuneration from the government in the form of tax relief. This benefited wealthy burghers who were officers of the Burgher watch because they were exempted from paying taxes on their property and wealth.

The internal security of the town was wholly under the Burgher watch, which conducted night patrols. In 1780, the officers were Joost Koek (Captain), Abraham de Wind (lieutenant), Johannes Adrianus van Moesbergen (*vaandrig/*second lieutenant), Jan George Abelven (sergeant), Jan van Kersbergen (sergeant), Francis La Fevre (sergeant), Godlieb Hampel (sergeant) and Jan George Frank (sergeant). Members of the watch had the power to apprehend suspicious or riotous persons and to confine them until morning, when they would be reported to the officer of the burghers. The watch could detain all persons who walked in the public streets without a lantern or a lighted torch after 9 o'clock at night and keep them in custody until morning. The Burgher watch also functioned as firefighters and crowd controllers. In the event of a fire or serious disturbance, a team was formed to help the affected community. The number of patrolmen on duty at any time was decided by the captain, who had the responsibility of submitting a report on the security of his designated area.

On the other hand, the *militie,* or militia, came directly under the VOC administration. It served as the army for the defence of Melaka and its members received their salary from the Dutch administration. Members came from almost all the ethnic communities: Europeans, Portuguese-Eurasians, Malays (Bugis and Javanese), Chinese and Kelings. The militia was divided into various units with each unit representing an ethnic group headed by its own ethnic captain.[59] If there was any external threat to the town, these units assembled at various points assigned to them. For example, the Malays were assigned at the *landpoort*, the Chinese to the plain close to

Table 37: The *militie* of Melaka in 1782

Ethnic Groups	QM Seamen	Capts Militie	Lieuts	Sub-Lieuts	Sergts	Corpls	Soldiers
Europeans	76	1	2	4	15	25	149
Malays		5	5	5	20	30	180
Chinese	40	1	1	1	4	6	90
Kelings		1	1	1	4	6	50
Port-Euras	61						74
Javanese	1						
Sepoys	-		1		2	4	56

Note: Port-Euras = Portuguese-Eurasians; Sepoys = Indian Sepoys; QM seamen = Quartermaster seamen; Capts = Captains; Lieuts = Lieutenants; Sergts = Sergeants; Corpls = Corporals.

Source: VOC 3625.

Victoria point and the Moors and Kelings to the Vischerstraat.[60] During the Dutch-Melaka war with the Bugis in Selangor in 1756 and the war with Johor-Riau in 1784, the militia played an important role in defending the town. Below is a table showing the *militie* in Melaka in 1782.

When Melaka was under English occupation, the Dutch defence force, *militie,* was abolished and replaced with an army made up of sepoys mostly recruited from India.[61] The English had been used to the services of Indian soldiers, whom they regarded as fearless and who could be trusted to be loyal. As for the enforcement of law and order in and around Melaka, formerly carried out by the Burgher watch under the Dutch, a modified system of policing was introduced under the name of native patrol.[62] As the new name suggests, the native patrol was aimed at involving all the communities with the policing of their own town, although most of the men who joined were Portuguese-Eurasians. This was probably because in 1825 a new regulation stipulated that all persons registered under the Burgher watch would automatically be registered in the native patrol. The native patrol was divided into divisions and each residential quarter was allocated a number of divisions. When the system was first introduced the situation was as follows: five divisions were assigned to the town area, ten to Tengkera, eight to Bandarlier (Bandahilir) and five to Bongaraya (Bungaraya).[63] It is not clear why the numbers differed from one quarter to the next, but presumably the decision was made based on considerations of security and community numbers in each division.

Table 38: List of native patrols in Melaka in 1825–26

Areas	Headman	Number of patrolmen
Town of Melaka	Albert Jonathan	51
Tengkera	Pedro Gomez	148
Bandarhilir	Domangio Merchona	119
Bungaraya	Felipe Dasker	48
Total		366

Source: R/9/32/1; R/9/32/10.

Each division of the native patrol would elect its own leader or headman. After approval from the English Resident, the top administrator, the headman would be officially appointed and would receive a salary of SpD 7.00 per month. The main duty of the headman was to submit a report every morning to the Superintendent of police regarding the welfare and security of his division. A watch house was built for each division as an assembly place for the native patrol. The native patrols were empowered to apprehend suspicious persons and detain them until morning in the watch house. The offender would then be sent to the police department and brought before the magistrate. Those who had served in the native patrol and wanted to terminate their services had to apply to the Resident's office for permission and they also had to pay the sum of SpD 0.75 monthly to the police department. However, those who continued their services were given exemption from paying taxes on godowns, shops and other taxes for which all other individuals were liable. In the event of a fire or other emergency, the four divisions of the native patrol had to assemble at their respective watch house and wait for an order from the Resident or the Superintendent of Police. The British administration continued to use the Dutch regulations, and members of Burghers watch were exempted from paying taxes.

In effect, the native patrol was the precursor of the police force. In 1825 a police department was created to take charge of the town's internal security.[64] In 1826, this department had a Superintendent of police who also served as the clerk to the magistrate. The native Captains were also incorporated into the police department.[65]

ADMINISTRATION OF ROADS, BRIDGES AND THE MUNICIPALITY

During the Dutch administration, the Company did not have an office for administrating the municipality, so this task was left to the burgher community. Thus, the burghers formed a *Burgerije Cassa*, or Burgher Fund,

Table 39: Statement on the *Burgerije Cassa* (Burgher Fund) in December 1780

Debit in rijksdollars		Credit in rijksdollars	
Money carried forward	908.17	Repairing expenses on the watch house at Bandarhilir	18.00
Tax imposed on Chinese	365.00	Repairing expenses on roads at Tengkera	48.00
Tax imposed on Malays, Kelings, Moors	260.00	Repairing expenses on roads at Bukit China	22.24
Tax imposed on Portuguese-Eurasians	88.00	Cleaning and repairing the fire brigade equipment	25.36
Tax on Bullcarts	6.00	Cleaning and repairing various equipment	75.24
Tax on Horses	18.00	Payment to various services	21.12
		Payment for buying equipment	25.00
		Building and repairing the walls on the river	97.36
		12 months salary for corporals and writer	420.00
Total	1,645.17		752.32

Source: VOC 3599.

which financed the municipal administration of road, bridges and sanitation services. Those forced to contribute to the Burgher Fund were the Malays, Kelings, Moors and Portuguese-Eurasians, whose taxes paid for financing the administration of the municipality.[66]

The burgher funds were also used for paying the salary of the night watchers/native patrolmen and to keep up the administrative offices. Therefore, under Dutch rule, the burden of providing the public and municipal facilities was borne by the Asian and Portuguese-Eurasian communities. In a different time and under a different regime, Abdullah the writer observed, 'they inflicted great hardship on the poor for every day people were obliged to pay money. Taxes were increased.....' Abdullah added that 'according to the accounts I have heard all these deeds of the Dutch were prompted by a desire for general cleanliness'.[67]

However, after 1825, with the transfer of Melaka to the English, the Burgher Fund was terminated and all municipal affairs were handled by a municipal council and funds were derived from the council tax on property and business premises.[68] Nevertheless, the British still retained, and further enforced, Dutch regulations on the cleanliness of the town.[69] In 1826, the English Resident Councillor, S. Garling, issued a regulation outlining the requirements for keeping the town clean. According to the regulation, every householder had to keep the space opposite his house swept and cleared of rubbish every morning at sunrise and again at 5 o'clock in the afternoon.[70] The rubbish had to be gathered into heaps and placed by the roadside. Later, convicts, led by an overseer, collected it in their carts and dumped it into an old ditch instead of into the river. It was the duty of an overseer to see that the public streets were swept clean and cleared of rubbish and to prevent the river from being used as a dumping ground. The river was to be kept clean and used for transportation. Thus, enforcement officers were sent to make sure that householders cleaned the streets of rubbish, not only in the urban areas but also in the suburbs. Persons who refused to execute this order after a second warning were made to pay the expenses of labourers hired by the superintendent of police to clean the area.[71]

The strict regulation also covered the bazaar, the grass along the sea coast and public wells.[72] In the suburbs, the superintendent of police enforced the regulations on cleanliness in the quarters of Bungaraya, Tengkera and Bandarhilir, where rubbish carts also visited. In terms of town cleanliness, one major focus was the Bazaar area, where the wet market (market selling fish, poultry, meat and vegetables) was situated. The bazaar also served as a meeting point for most town dwellers.[73] However, it was considered the filthiest part of town as it had a great deal of rubbish. The drains in the Bazaar were often obstructed, stopping the flow of water through the channel and so creating noxious smells. The owners of premises in the Bazaar area had the duty of keeping them clean and those who failed to do so were penalized. In the fish market area, three duits[74] were levied for every mat of fish exposed for sale. The person in charge of the administration of the fish market came under the control of the superintendent of police and he had to keep that market clean.

The scope of the regulations not only covered aspects of physical cleanliness but also included the physical siting of the buildings, especially those built near the river.[75] No building or construction could be built on the banks of the river below the water mark without special written permission by the chief local authority. Those who did not abide by this regulation were given a warning. After a second warning, the buildings were torn down and the owner had to bear the cost of hiring labourers for clearing the buildings. As the Melaka river was an important waterway, the regulation stipulated that there should be no enclosure for bathing or stakes driven into the bed of the river, which would form a barricade obstructing the free passage of boats.

The regulation also limited the extensions of shops and houses in the town, as they tended to impede pedestrians and affect the beauty of the town. So no extensions were allowed from houses bounding the road, irrespective of the use of durable or perishable materials, without special written permission.[76] Trees and hedges also had to be trimmed. Furthermore, no hedges were permitted beyond certain proper limits. Those negligent in obeying these rules were warned and punished. The English administration in Melaka did not incur problems in its enforcement of public cleanliness in the town areas, partly because they did not implement many changes to the existing Dutch regulations and practices. But enforcement of the rules was carried out by government officers and not by an association such as the Burgher watch, as was the case under the VOC administration.

Melaka already had a reputation for cleanliness during the time of the Dutch and was regarded as the healthiest town and port in the East.[77] A health report by Loftie (1802–1808) suggested that Melaka was a healthier place than Penang, Amboyna, Batavia or Calcutta.[78] That was no small praise and it is no wonder that when the English took over Melaka permanently in the mid-1820s they took steps to uphold this good reputation. In later years the sleepy port-town came to be considered as a worthy retreat for many colonial officers serving in the East and also for Asians.[79]

THE CHURCH COUNCIL

The Dutch VOC administration was a secular instrument of power which co-existed comfortably with the Dutch Reform Church in all Dutch colonies in the East. This was because most VOC officers, their families and the burghers belonged to the Dutch Reformed Church as well as the fact that there was, among the highest officials, a strong spirit for spreading the faith.[80] The church was also probably seen as necessary both to bind the small European community together and also to maintain high morals. This was a particularly desirable objective for a minority group of Europeans living as the rulers among the ruled Asian majority. Further, the church performed some of the most important of life's rituals, namely, baptisms, marriages and funerals and fulfilled the social and emotional needs of its congregation. Thus it is understandable that the Dutch administration supported the building of reformed churches and favoured the Church as the main religion in Melaka.

The Dutch administration's interest in and close relations with the Dutch Reform Church were maintained through the Church Council, headed by a senior VOC official who was one of at least two members, the second coming from the non-official community. However, records show that more than two people usually attended council meetings. The major function of the Church Council was to care for the welfare of the believers of the Reformed Church in general and to oversee marriages, baptisms, schooling, deaths and burials.[81]

The Church Council financed its numerous social activities from a church fund. The Dutch administration gave the Church Council the power to administer all marriages that took place in Melaka. These marriages were registered at the Church Council irrespective of religious belief. Christians not from the Dutch Reformed Church as well as non-Christians were required to pay a certain amount for the registration of their marriage. The Muslims, Hindus and Buddhists were required to pay two rijksdollars and the Catholics were charged six rijksdollars. The Dutch Reformed Church believers were given the liberty to pay any amount they wished.[82] The Church Council also obtained funding from facilities it provided, such as burial equipment which could be hired and burial plots which could be bought.[83] In addition, the church gathered funds through its collection of money during church services and from renting out of houses and property it owned.[84] The money thus collected was then spent on various activities, such as repairing the church, paying the expenses of the teachers at the school, buying books for the schoolchildren and giving allowances to poor native children.[85]

While the Dutch administration encouraged the activities of the Dutch Reformed Church, it did not discourage the practice of other religions. In fact, religious tolerance was practised in Melaka although the administration and financial affairs of the non-Dutch Reformed Christian believers were left to their own communities to handle.[86]

FINANCIAL ADMINISTRATION: REVENUE FARMS AS A MAIN SOURCE OF FINANCE FOR PORT-TOWN URBAN ADMINISTRATION

Besides trade, which brought income to the administration, revenue farms were also important financial sources for the Company's administration in Melaka.[87] Since the Dutch occupation of Melaka in 1641, many revenue farms were introduced. For instance, in 1700 there were 15 types of tax farming imposed by the Company in Melaka. There were taxes on the harbour or customs (*Boom* farm), *de stads Herberg* (the gentlemen's tavern), *de kleijne winkeliers* (small shops), *het boshout* (products from the forest i.e timber), *de arak* (liquor), *het Chinese bazaar* (Chinese market), *de waag* (weight-house), *de Vis bazaar* (fish market), *de top baan* (gambling), *Haanemat* (cockfighting), *het lijst van maaten* (weights and measures), *de rijs bazaar* (rice market), *het slagten van het beestal* (slaughter of animals, such as cows and pigs), *de beestal* (livestock), *de ophaal brugge* (drawbridges), and *de rivier vaartuijgen* (riverboats).[88] By 1780, the list included additional farms, such as a head tax on the Chinese and taxes on sea and river fish, betel leaf, bridges, the rice bazaar, opium and riverboats/prows.[89]

In 1700 income from tax farming amounted to rijksdollars 3,890, rising in the following year to 3,957 rijksdollars. The tax imposed on small shops had also increased to 840 rijksdollars from 804 rijksdollars in 1700. However, in 1702, the total income from tax farming was 3,948 rijksdollars, showing a slight fall.[90] In 1700–01 the major income from tax farming came from the fish market, followed by the small shops. These two farms contributed an income amounting to more than 800 rijksdollars. This was followed by income derived from public weights and customs houses, which amounted to 570 and 608 rijksdollars respectively. The income from the slaughterhouse and livestock was quite lucrative. Both tax farms produced an income of 300 and 400 rijksdollars respectively. The lowest income came from the taverns, this fluctuating between 18 and 40 rijksdollars.

Towards the middle of the eighteenth century, the income from the tax farms showed a large increase. The total tax farming income in 1742 was 5,991 rijksdollars and in 1743 it was 5,834 rijksdollars.[91] In 1742 and 1743, the major contribution to the tax farm income came from the head tax on Chinese and the fishing sector. In both years the head tax income amounted to more than 1,100 rijksdollars per year. This was due to the migration of Chinese to Melaka which took place during these years. The Company then decided to enforce this head tax, mostly traders, merchants, carpenters and labourers/workers who had just arrived and settled in Melaka. In 1742 and 1743, the total income from the sea and river fish trade was more than 1,400 rijksdollars per year. Meanwhile, income from livestock had doubled from the early eighteenth century to 700 rijksdollars. This was primarily due to the increase in Chinese settlers, which was followed by an increase in pig farms set up by them.

Through the years, there was an escalation in total income from tax farming as seen from the 1742 amount of 5,991 rijksdollars to 87,152 rijksdollars in 1792.[92] For the years 1792 to 1806, the highest total was reached in 1793 when the administration netted 89,065 rijksdollars (SpD 61,5172.66).[93] Between 1792 and 1798 the *Boom* farm contributed the most income. The *Boom* farm, a harbour tax imposed by customs on all ships coming to or leaving Melaka, was the oldest tax introduced by the Dutch in Melaka and covered the types of ships and the cargoes they carried. In 1793, the *Boom* farm alone produced 77,555 rijksdollars. The next major contributor came from gambling, *arak*, opium, fish and pork. From the year 1799, the *Boom*, opium, gambling, *arak*, pork and sirih farms were sold annually by sealed proposal, probably because they earned high incomes.

Plate 4: Cyrille Laplace, 'Debarcadere a Malacca'. In *Voyage autour du monde par Les mers de l'Inde et de la Favorite*, Paris: Imprimerie royale, 1835.

When the British occupied Melaka from 1795 to 1818, they continued the Dutch regulations imposed on persons who purchased incoming as well as outgoing merchandise.[94] There was also no change to duties on revenue farms such as opium, betel leaf, pork, *arak*, gaming houses and the fish market. Regulations on opium farms stated that no person, except the farmer, was allowed to sell opium, by retail in small quantities or in cake form. This restriction, however, did not extend to the sale of opium in chests. In the case of betel leaf farms, the tenant of the farm had the right to deduct 10 per cent of the income for his personal benefit. The tenant of the pork farm was the only person who could sell pork in the public market, but this restriction did not extend to the sale of live hogs. The farmer was also not allowed to increase the weight of pork by adding water into the meat and, if found guilty of this, was severely punished.

The farmer (owner) of the gaming farm was allowed to keep a total of four gaming houses in the city, namely, in the Tengkera, Bandarhilir and Bungaraya areas. He was prohibited from bringing any goods to the gaming houses, except money. He was authorized to prevent any European or native troops, the company's officials or slaves from entering the gaming houses. If they breached the regulation, they would be prosecuted 'in the most exemplary manner'. No person except the *arak* farmer was allowed to retail or sell *arak* in small quantities. The *arak* farmer was not allowed to own more than four retail shops and was prohibited from selling any *arak* except Batavia *arak* to the troops in the garrison or to the seamen of the squadron. Furthermore, the *arak* could not be adulterated, nor was any person allowed to drink alcohol in his house. The farmer of the fish farm had the right to take 10 per cent of all the fresh fish brought to the market, a custom implemented under the Dutch government. The selling of fish in any place other than in the public market was strictly forbidden. Punishment for those who breached this regulation was very severe.

Under the tax farming regulations, farmers were required to make monthly payments of rent imposed by the Company. The company would not accept excuses if a person defaulted on the monthly payment; if it occurred, the farm would be resold and any losses would be borne by the original purchaser. An application to purchase a farm contract could be made by a sealed proposal. This was done by disclosing the price agreed for the whole farm together with the names of two reliable sureties. In the early nineteenth century, most farms were sold by sealed proposal. Mainly these were bought by wealthy Chinese with joint-stock capital who thus acquired control and monopolies on the farms.[95]

During the British occupation from 1794 to 1818, nearly all farms were sold by sealed proposal. During this period, there was a significant decrease in the income of the revenue farmers because of the decline in trade and the growing numbers of Melakans migrating to Penang and also to Singapore after the 1820s.[96] The number of farms decreased to less than 12 as compared to 18 during the Dutch period. The most important ones during the English administration were the customs, gaming (gambling), opium, pork, sirih (betel leaf), *arak*, weights and fish trading. The timber farm was abolished due to a decline in demand for timber from traders coming to Melaka.[97] As trade declined from the end of the eighteenth century, its effect was seen in the gradual reduction of revenue earned from some farms. The first to suffer was the *Boom*, or customs farm, which had, hitherto, been a big revenue earner.

Farms directly dependent on trading activities were the most adversely affected. Among these were the timber farms, largely dependent on timber brought in by Chinese junks, the weights and measures farm which charged a fee for weighing and stamping incoming and outgoing articles, the head tax on new Chinese arrivals who travelled from Macau mainly in Portuguese ships, the bridge tax which was paid by traders who sailed up and down the Melaka River, and the tax on small boats/prows imposed on native traders using the river between Naning and Melaka. As revenue from these farms fell, they were abolished.

Since Melaka's lifeblood was trade, any changes in the trade pattern in the region had a great impact on the town's livelihood. With the opening of Penang and later Singapore, major trade from Melaka was taken away. Melaka had in fact few internal problems such as smuggling, poor regulation or enforcement of law but the decline in trade ensured that the revenue farms remained limited and produced a smaller revenue compared to Singapore and Penang.[98] In the 1820s, the main revenue farms in Melaka were the following: opium; *arak*/spirit; gaming/gambling; toddy and bang, a spirit prepared by the natives and Keling from the young shoot/flower of coconut plants and also from fermented rice; shops and carts; betel leaf/sirih; pork; the market; and rice.[99] As can be seen, many of these farms were not totally dependent on Melaka's trade.

ADMINISTRATION OF THE HINTERLAND

Soon after the Dutch occupation of Melaka in 1641, a report was prepared for the development of its hinterland.[100] However, little was done to transform it into an important agricultural area. For most of the Dutch period, Melaka depended on external supplies for its food and its main exports. Although the Melaka territory under Dutch administration included the hinterland, most of this area was covered by thick forest and jungle. There were a few settlements in the interior but they were administered loosely and left to the care of their proprietors.[101] So the Dutch administration did not have direct jurisdiction over these areas, their only connection being the lease of titles given to the proprietors to manage and administer the land.[102] The Dutch administration only collected taxes. As has been pointed out:

> According to Malay customary law (*adat*) all land belonged to the ruler, but the peasant cultivator had a right to security of tenure as long as he continued to farm the land and pay rent of one-tenth of the produce. Adopting this custom to Melaka territory, the Dutch had claimed the land-ownership rights of a ruler; but rather than attempt to collect the customary rents from the cultivators themselves, they had leased the right to do so to a number of landholders, or 'proprietors' as they were called, who were mainly Dutch or Dutch-Eurasian but also included some Malays and Chinese. In return, these proprietors undertook to open up and develop their lands to maximum cultivation, and to maintain all paths, bridges and waterways in good order.[103]

Thus, in the town of Melaka, in addition to those who owned property in the form of houses, or ships or business through trade, there were also a few individuals who were considered wealthy land proprietors. Some of these were de Wind, Adrian Koek, Westerhout and Manuel de Souza, who owned huge estates.[104] Some of these estates had been owned by private individuals since the seventeenth century and had been passed down within the family for several generations. Since the Dutch in Melaka did not develop the interior, it was left to the land proprietors to develop it. However, little effort was put in by them either and most of the land remained densely forested, and with no good roads connecting the town and the interior, it was also almost inaccessible. The only means of access was by rivers and through small jungle footpaths. Some of the proprietors could not even recognise their land areas and the only testimony was the grant map showing the areas, given to them by the Dutch administration in Melaka.[105] There were also cases of disputed land boundaries between land proprietors who shared a common boundary.[106]

Management of the land was usually given to a native *Penghulu,* or a village headman, who was given the task of collecting taxes in kind.[107] These taxes were paid by the people who lived on the land. However, the headman was exempted from paying tax because he collected taxes on behalf of the land proprietors, who in turn paid taxes to the administration. Under this arrangement, in which the administration was not directly involved and the proprietors were disinterested, cases of abuse of power were not unknown because the headman could easily demand more payment than was required from his people. The system of indirect governance is explained by Braddell in the following terms:

> ... in carrying on the government of the country districts the Dutch availed themselves of the Malay village system. Every community of 44 families constitutes a village, which is entitled to have a mosque and the regular officers, Imam, Khatib, Bilal and Penghulu. All these held their lands free, and formed a tribunal before which minor matters in dispute were adjudicated. The two first named are Mahomedan priests, the third is the 'Muezzin' while the last is the chief secular officer. Under a Christian government the chief, and in temporal matters sole, authority was lodged in the Penghulu, and in course of time, by the neglect of supervision from Melaka, these officers became invested with full power to hear and decide petty cases, and to collect the revenue of the district.[108]

Where there were inhabitants on the land, there was some land usage for agricultural purposes such as for paddy planting, fruit orchards and pepper and gambir plantations.[109] But more often than not, land was left uncultivated. Prior to the 1780s there was a gambir plantation cultivated by a Chinese from Melaka.[110] However, due to wars with Selangor and the neighbouring kingdom, production from the plantation was interrupted and later the land was abandoned. As the interior was densely forested, some of the land proprietors exploited the timber and wood from the jungle. Wood and timber were felled and carried by the rivers to Melaka and later converted into planks for houses and ships. But the industry was not fully developed partly because of lack of supervision from the land proprietors and due to the problem of transporting logs to the town.[111] The Dutch administration had begun to impose a tax on timber and wood brought out from the interior but as the enterprise was short-lived, the tax was soon scrapped.[112]

During the time of the English administration some parts of the estates were being cultivated and farmed by Chinese merchants from the town. De Wind's estate for example produced pepper, the Westerhout estate produced pepper and spices, and pepper was grown on land belonging to Daniel Koek. But the earnings for the Chinese merchants were small,[113] partly due to poor cultivation methods but also due to the lack of good road networks and communication with the town.

Altogether, the management of land in the interior was very poor. This led in some cases to socio-economic problems, such as a minimum amount of revenue, poor relationships between the land owners, the *penghulus* and the local people, and limited progress in land development. As a result the British administration had, in some cases, to take over the land and compensate the land proprietors.[114] For example, in one incident in 1828, the government declared its right to a 'tenth of the produce of all cultivated lands, as well as its right to resume possession of any waste land. The Land Department would henceforth collect all tithes, either directly or through the district penghulu. The former proprietors would be compensated by the grant of annuities equivalent to the amount hitherto collected in tithes from their cultivators'.[115]

A look at the extent of the land alienated by the Dutch to private individuals and not utilized well serves to show the degree of neglect of the interior over a long period of time. The estate of J.B de Wind covered an area of 280 square miles from the southern part of the Kersang River to the boundary of Melaka and Muar. In 1752, Claas de Wind purchased land in Pungor, named Old Melaka, for 915 rijksdollars, and it extended from the Duyong River to Tanjong Palas, about two miles along the coast.[116] However, the title deeds did not state how far inland the land extended, but merely mentioned that the area was located in the northeast and that deep jungle had obstructed efforts to measure the whole area. Later, in January 1753, he bought another piece of land that extended from Tanjong Palas to the Serkam River, the length of which was about six and a half miles along the shore.[117] The second title of deeds also failed to ascertain the boundaries

Table 40: Major land proprietors in Melaka

Proprietor	Land area*	Proprietor	Land area*
J.B. de Wind	280	J.B. Westerhout and J.C. Neubronner	2.5
Adrian Koek	66	Encik Ahmina	0.25
A.A. Velge	1	Encik Etam and Malay Capt. Abu Bakar	1.5
J.B. Westerhout	36.25	Encik Soerin	2.5
De Coasta	5	Encik Haroon	2
Daniel Koek	2	Encik Sainah and Ahmedah	1
Appo Katcjil	3	Encik Samsuddin	0.25
Mahomet Tahir	2.5	Encik Saedah	0.25
Manuel de Souza	10	Encik Ahmeedah	1
Total			417

Note: Land area in square miles.

Source: SSFR, vol. 168, G/34/172

inland. In March 1759, de Wind purchased more land in an area called Jadong, extending to Merlimau and Kersang from Serkam to the Kersang River for another 500 rijksdollars.[118] This area was about 7.5 miles long along the shore, but the exact area was not specified due to the thick forest and jungle. Thus, for the sum of 2,415 rijksdollars, Claas de Wind became one of the largest land proprietors in Melaka, with an area of about 280 square miles under his control. In the 1820s, revenue from the land consisted of duties levied on pepper, paddy and fruits cultivated on it, and on dammar, rattan and wood oil collected from the jungle. In addition, hardwood from the forest was felled and turned into planks and marketed in Melaka for building houses and bridges. The whole area did not yield more than 1,700 rijksdollars per annum to de Wind.[119]

The second largest and most talked about estate was owned by Adrian Koek. It extended in a southeasterly direction along the shore from the northwest area of Melaka at the mouth of the Linggi River to Kelebang Kecil. The area also reached inland towards Melaka to Bertam and from Panchor to the Linggi River, an area five miles inland as far as Ramuan China.[120] The total area of this estate was 66 square miles, exclusive of Ramuan China, which was seven square miles. In 1816 Koek extended this piece of property by purchasing Kelebang Kechil, a small area of about one square mile already planted with paddy, for 300 rijksdollars. The rest of the estate owned by Adrian Koek consisted of land granted by government on 13 Janurary 1794 to a Mr Ballemout but which was later bought by Adrian Koek in February 1804 for SpD 500. This area covered the beach southeast of Sungai Bano as far as the Linggi River. On the western side, the estate ran from the mouth of the Linggi River inland, passing Bukko Rendah, Bukit Beruang and Ramuan China to the hill called Bukit Pambaggean, which was the boundary with Naning. The chief produce from the Adrian Koek estate was pepper, gambir, dammar, wood oil, timber, firewood and paddy. After Adrian Koek's death in 1824, his land was annually farmed by Chinese merchants.[121]

The third largest land proprietor was the widow Westerhout. The area covered by the Westerhout estate, named Ago de Souphie, was originally purchased by her husband in March 1790 from a Chinese named Chan Samko for 1,100 rijksdollars.[122] The title deed owned by Westerhout can only be traced to 1764 since no documents have survived prior to that date. The estate covered about 13 square miles and was situated on the western side of the Melaka River. This land was low and swampy and produced paddy. The higher ground and forest area contained good timber and were fully guarded from illegal felling in order to maximize revenue from timber production. In addition, the Westerhout estate also included Little Ching, an area on the southwest of Melaka purchased in March 1778 for 525 rijksdollars.[123] Former holders of the land could be traced by documents to the year 1744.[124] The area occupied about 21 square miles, a good deal of which was planted with pepper. Together, the two areas covered under the Westerhout estate, Ago de Sophie and Little Ching, covered 36 square miles and produced paddy, pepper, fruits, *dammar*, firewood and timber.[125] Besides the three major land proprietors, each who owned more than 30 square miles, the following seven land proprietors had areas of 10 square miles or less each. The estate of Manuel de Souza, situated close to Naning, lay on the left side of the Melaka River in Pengkalan Benar and Tanah Merah. It was purchased by him in 1817 from a Chinese for 600 rijksdollars.[126] The original grant from the government could not be located but this land covered 10 square miles. It had few inhabitants and produced paddy and firewood.[127] Another piece, five square miles in size and covering an area of Durian Tung-gal, which had been purchased earlier, was in the possession of Gregory de Souza. Most of this land was covered by forest, though the area on the right side of the Melaka River produced paddy and timber.[128]

The second owner was Appa Katchee, an Indian, who owned a piece of land called Batu Berendam. This land was brought at an auction by his father for 3,070 rijksdollars. Situated upstream on the right bank of the Melaka, it was mostly lowland, producing pepper, timber and firewood.[129] The third owner was Daniel Koek, who owned an area covering two square miles in Penkalan Batu that formerly included Bukit Bruang. Originally granted to

Mohammed Budiman in September 1702, this land was in the hands of Governor Couperous when it was purchased in 1800 by Daniel Koek for 2,900 rijksdollars. The land produced wood and pepper.[130] Other small estates included a piece owned by a Malay captain, Abu Bakar, and his family, covering 1.5 square miles in Batu Ampa. This area covered the banks of the Melaka River up to the Roman Catholic Church and included land in Peringit and Pengkalan Rama, which was well cultivated with paddy and densely populated.[131]

The other small estates were owned by Mohammad Tahir, Syed Hussin and Seva Sangra. The estate owned by Mohammad Tahir extended from Adrian Koek's estate to that of de Wind's in Duyong, covering an area of 2.5 square miles. This estate land was passed from father to son in the same family for many years and can be traced back to 1738; its main produce was paddy, although a big part of it was not cultivated. Syed Hussin's estate, a piece land situated in Semabok, was originally owned by a descendent of his named Syed Hussin, an Arab who received it as a dowry from his bride. In 1796, it was sold for 500 rijksdollars. Most of the ground on its southwest side was covered with paddy fields, from Duyong to Ujong Pasir, but a large part of the area was uncultivated. It is estimated that this land was part of a larger piece covering at least 450 square miles, of which only 1/20 was cultivated. The other small estate, situated on the left bank of the Melaka River was owned by Seva Sangra, a Keling captain.[132]

Due to the fact that the large land owners were absentee landlords who lived in town and who probably never inspected their land due to the difficulty of access, disputes over boundaries cropped up from time to time, particularly when the original owners were no longer alive. One such dispute happened in 1788. In that year, Adrian Koek appeared in court claiming that a piece of land in Batang Tiga belonged to him. This land, which covered Kelebang Besar and extended to Tanjong Bruas, had been placed in 1770 under the administration of Encik Aroe, the Malay chief and Superintendent of the area. But upon Koek's application, the court, without recording any documents produced before, made a decision that he should be given full title to this area. After the court decision the government had to pay a sum of 900 rijksdollars to Encik Aroe as compensation for the area that was transferred to Adrian Koek.[133] In the 1820s Adrian Koek was yet again embroiled in a land dispute, this time with the de Wind family but also involving the Malay rulers of the Johor Kingdom, the native rulers in the disputed areas and the government in Melaka.[134] Adrian Koek was then an influential person in Melaka due to his close relationship with the English Governor and the Sultan of Johor, for whom he acted as an agent, and to his important position in the Court of Justice in Melaka.[135] This dispute also involved the boundary problem between Melaka and Johor.[136] Another piece of land belonging to Koek in the Ramuan China area was disputed by the *Penghulu* of Naning.

Although the Dutch administration had a comprehensive model of governing a colonial town, the hinterland was not regulated but left to the land proprietors, reflecting its policy of not encouraging the development of Melaka's hinterland for agricultural production. This caused a greater reliance on supplies from Batavia or from imports. These problems, later inherited by the English administration, demanded many years to solve before Melaka's hinterland was opened up for development.[137]

CONCLUSION

Melaka, as one of several subordinate seats of administration set up under the Supreme Government at Batavia, never had a large administration. The officials allocated to the port-town were few so that each had to hold several posts. But like other small Dutch port-towns, Melaka provided a good example of how limited resources were put to maximum use. The Dutch authorities achieved this through a system of civil administration whereby much of the work of running the port-town was carried out by the town folks themselves. Thus, while the more important aspects of governance, such as political, economic and security matters, were fully under the control of the Governor and his officials, the rest was left to a number of councils and organizations manned mostly by members of the community.

The ward system achieved the need on the part of the administration for keeping in close touch with developments in the community through the receipt of regular census reports. Yet it gave to the ward community representation through their superintendent or captain. The Burgher watch, essentially a citizens' policing unit, freed the administration of the expenses of setting up a police force, while at the same time giving the community a stake in the defense of their own town. As for the Orphan Chamber, it showed the humane as well as the pragmatic in the Dutch administration's approach to social problems for at the same time that the orphans were protected, their inheritance provided the capital for encouraging, in a limited way, economic activities in the community. The frugal but practical approach to financial administration saw the delegation of revenue collection to the community through the system of revenue farms. In essence, the role played by the land proprietors in collecting taxes from the hinterland for the Dutch administration was a form of delegated responsibility similar to that achieved through the revenue farms.

The proof of the effectiveness of the Dutch administrative system could be seen from the fact that when the English occupied Melaka in 1824 they did not introduce many changes to the existing system because it worked well. In fact, the English implemented some aspects of the Dutch system in Penang, such as appointing captains from the various ethnic groups and having revenue farms.[138] Unlike Penang, there were no serious internal problems in Melaka, and its beauty and lifestyle even drew praise from English travellers. For example, one traveller wrote that 'the houses in the town make a good appearance [and] are built with stone and ranged in street much like our small sea-ports in England'.[139]

NOTES

1　See F.S. Gaastra, 'The Organization of the VOC', p. 26.

2　See, for example, 'Some Old Private Letters from the Cape, Batavia, and Malacca, 1778–1788', *JMBRAS*, vol. 2, pt. 1, 1924, pp. 9–24; Barbara Watson Andaya, 'Melaka under the Dutch', p. 202.

3　Barbara Watson Andaya, 'Melaka under the Dutch', p. 200.

4　Ibid., p. 205.

5　See, for example, Abrahamus Couperus, Governor of Melaka (1788–95) who owned a piece of land planted with fruit trees situated at Bandarhilir. He also owned three houses built from bricks and land at Eerstebruggedwarstraat and Jonkerstraat, Notitie Boek van de Debiteuren 29 Feb 1792, in R/9/9/6; see also the last Governor of Melaka, Jan Samuel Timmerman-Thyssen (1818–23) who owned several properties such as houses and lands in the fort of Melaka, near the bazaar, at Eerstebruggewalstraat, and at Tengkera, in Obligatie Boek 15 Mar 1811–15 Dec 1821 in R/9/8/9. See also the Estate papers of the late Jan Samuel Timmerman-Thyssen, Governor of Melaka, who died on 15 Jan 1823, in R/9/12/39; and the Claims against the bankrupt estate of the late Jan Samuel Timmerman-Thyssen, Governor of Melaka, 26 Mar 1821–17 Feb 1825 in R/9/20/31.

6　W. Wijnaendts van Resandt, *De Gezaghebbers der Oost-Indische Compagnie op hare Buiten Comptoiren in Azie*, Amsterdam: Liebaert, 1944, pp. 200–230; see also Barbara Watson Andaya, 'Melaka under the Dutch', pp. 238–239. When the British occupied Melaka from 1795–1818 the post of Dutch Governor was replaced with that of a Commandant and later with that of a Resident, see Brian Harrison, 'Holding the Fort', pp. 45–125.

7　See A.P.M. Ketelaars, 'Van Inheemse Stapelmarkt tot Tweederangs Koloniale Stad een geschiedenis van Malakka van 1403 tot omstreeks 1690', Doctoraalscriptie geschiedenis, Rijksuniversiteit Utrecht, June 1985, pp. 83–84.

8　Barbara Watson Andaya, 'Melaka under the Dutch', p. 202.

9　See, for example, D.K. Bassett, 'The Surrender of Dutch Malacca, 1795', *BKI*, vol.117, 1969, pp. 344–358, and Graham Irwin, 'Governor Couperus and the surrender of Malacca, 1795', *JMBRAS*, vol. 29, Pt.3, 1956, pp. 86–113.

10　Barbara Watson Andaya, 'Melaka under the Dutch', p. 201.

11　In the earlier period, the Council of Justice was presided over by the Governor. See Schouten's report of his visit to Melaka, in P.A. Leupe, 'The Seige and Capture of Malacca', p. 134.

12　Barbara Watson Andaya, 'Melaka Under the Dutch', p. 201.

13　See, for example, the case of one Mr Alms criticizing the decision of the Court of Justice, which he thought was unfair, in a letter from Farquhar dated 20 September 1806 to Governor and Council in PWI, in SSFR, vol.14; see also the dispute regarding inheritance and wills, in extract from civil records of the court of justice, dated 8 December 1812, between Mr W. Chalmers and G.L. Baumgarten as heirs to the estate of the late J.H. Pungel against J.H. Stecker the will writers where the latter was given a large share of the inheritance by the court although he had no family connection with the heirs, in SSFR, vol. 40. See also the decision made by the court in the case of a Chinese woman, Oeij Kitnio vs. Maria Catharina Westerhout, in R/9/20/2.

14   Farquhar, 25 December 1795, in SSFR, vol. 16. See also the list of Dutch civil servants and others with their employment and monthly salaries, in Appendix no. 7, SSFR, vol. 16. See also The proceeding of the Dutch College of Justice, Farquhar 15 November 1808, in SSFR, vol. 20.

15   Papers regarding the administration of justice in Melaka in 1825/6, in F/4/1230 40216. See also papers regarding the administration of justice in Melaka in 1825/6, in F/4/1230 40215.

16   See Appendix 1: Dutch Administration of Melaka in 1780 and Appendix 2: Dutch administration of Melaka in 1793, in Nordin Hussin, 'Melaka and Penang 1780–1830: A study of two port towns in the Straits of Melaka', Ph.D. thesis, Amsterdam: Vrije Universiteit, 2002. See also Barbara Watson Andaya, 'Melaka under the Dutch', p. 203.

17   See W. Wijnaendts van Resandt, *De gezaghebbers der Oost-Indische Compagnie op hare buiten comptoiren in Azie*, pp. 200–231.

18   The office of *Syahbandar* was a continuation from the Sultanate period, having been adopted by both the Portuguese and the Dutch. For further reference, see Kernial Singh Sandhu, 'Indian Settlement in Melaka'. In Kernial Singh Sandhu (ed.), *Melaka*, p. 183. See also H.M. Elmore, *The British Mariner's Directory and Guide to the Trade and Navigation of the Indian and China Seas*, London: T. Bensley, 1802, p. 304.

19   P.J. Begbie, *The Malayan Peninsula*, Madras: Vepery Mission Press, 1834, p. 367. In 1827 there were 2,289 Portuguese-Eurasians, the majority of whom resided in Bandarhilir. Portuguese-Eurasians had their own church which was located at Bungaraya near the Melaka River, see W.T. Lewis, 30 June 1827, enclosure 5, in G/34/172.

20   See List of native militia in Melaka and environs, 8 June 1781, in R/9/41/1. See also List of Portuguese who served as daily watchmen in Melaka, Tengkera, Bungaraya and Bandarhilir, in R/9/32/1; List of Portuguese town guards at Melaka, R/9/32/4; List of Portuguese watchmen in the Bungaraya wards 31 Dec 1826, in R/9/32/12; and List of Portuguese watchmen in the Tengkera wards 31 Dec 1826, in R/9/32/13.

21   See J.W. Heydt, *Allerneuester Geographisch-und Topographischer Schauplatz van Africa und Ost-Indien*, p.304. Although the street names were written in old German, most of them can be constructed again by refering to the following sources: Obligatie Boeken (Bond Books) 1743–1821, in R/9/8/1 to R/9/8/9; Notitie Boeken van de Debiteuren 1787–1799, in R/9/9/1-R/9/9/11; and Estate papers, accounts and inventories (1743–1827), in R/9/12/1-R/9/12/42.

22   See Instructions to the *Wijkmeesters* (Ward Superintendents) to maintain a regular census of houses and inhabitants in Melaka, 3 Jan 1803–20 Nov 1804, in R/9/34/1; Census of population in Melaka, giving the names of heads of families, the numbers in each household and whether free, slaves or debtors, in R/9/34/7; and List of burgher property belonging to the wards of Bungaraya, Melaka and Tengkera, 31 Dec 1826, in R/9/34/10.

23   The Dutch feared the migration of Malays from the inland areas, especially the Minangkabaus (Naning) and Bugis (Selangor), who would pose a threat to the town. See, for example, D.F.A. Hervery, 'Malacca in the Eighteenth Century', *JSBRAS*, No.12, 1883, pp. 261–267.

24   Instructions to the *Wijkmeesters* (Ward Superintendents), in R/9/34/1.

25   Barbara Watson Andaya, 'Melaka Under the Dutch'. She notes that: 'A Catholic uprising in the Dutch-controlled area of Brazil in 1645 inevitably aroused doubt concerning the loyalty of the Catholics in Melaka. The activities of priests, "more harmful than the plague", was now especially suspect, and for many years after the Brazilian rebellion stringent measures were enforced to control priestly influence. In time, this distrust lessened and, though to some pious Catholics the Church's children in Melaka were ringed by "bloody wolves", a blind eye was usually turned to the presence of fugitive priests who secretly conducted services and gave instruction in the faith. ... Tolerance of Catholicism was no doubt facilitated by the fact that many Dutchmen had taken Eurasian wives', p. 211.

26 See, for example, 'Report of Governor Balthasar Bort on Malacca 1678', pp. 42–43. For further reference regarding this area in 1756 see, for example, D.F.A. Hervery, 'Malacca in the Eighteenth Century', *JSBRAS*, No. 12, 1883, pp. 261–267.

27 Ibid.

28 See W.T. Lewis, 30 June 1827, enclosure 5, in G/34/172.

29 See Table 43.

30 See Appendix 6: Property and Ownership in Melaka 1787/88 and 1805/11 in Nordin Hussin, 'Melaka and Penang 1780–1830', pp. 432–433.

31 Until 1827 there were 233 burghers residing in these areas and they continued to be the majority ethnic group, but the Chinese were fewer in numbers. See W.T. Lewis, 30 June 1827, enclosure 5, in G/34/172.

32 See Table 43.

33 See Malacca Wills, in R/9/11/1-R/9/11/21; Estate Papers, accounts and inventories (1743–1827), in R/9/12/1-R/9/12/42.

34 See Cassa Boeken (Cash Books of the Melaka Orphan Chamber 1780–1827, in R/9/3; Principaal Weeskamer's Journaal 1780–1830, in R/9/4; Grote Boeken 1780–1830, in R/9/5; Notitie Boeken van Debiteuren 1787–1799, in R/9/9; Melaka Wills 1780–1823, in R/9/11; Obligatie Boeken 1780–1821, in R/9/8; and Vendutie Boeken 1780–1822, in R/9/13.

35 List of Dutch Administration officers, in VOC 3467.

36 Ibid.

37 List of Dutch Administration officers, in VOC 3625.

38 Comite Oost-Indische Handel 107.

39 In 1793 there were seven *wijk* (wards): 1. In the Herenstraat ward: Adrian Koek and Tan Tjapko; 2. In Jonkerstraat ward: Carel Ferdenand Grejis and Gerrit Leendert Velge; 3. In Malay and Moor ward: Encik Astor and Sewa Soeria Chittij; 4. In Tengkera ward: Michiel Kilian and Adrianus van Moesbergen; 5. In Bandarhilir ward: Pieter Puit, Cornelis Adasz., and Francisco Cardozo; 6. In Bungaraya ward: Baba Som and Abdul Aziz; 7. In Bukit China ward: Jacob Rappa and Encik Roa, see Comite Oost-Indische Handel 107.

40 See population census in 1828, in SSFR 168.

41 For further discussion on the function and activities of the diaconij, see H.E. Niemeijer, 'Calvinisme en Kolonial Stadscultuur Batavia 1619–1725', pp. 275–304. See also, for example, in Makassar and Batavia. For further reference see Heather Sutherland, 'Ethnicity, Wealth and Power in colonial Makassar'; Margreet van Till, 'Social care in Eighteenth-century Batavia: The Poor House'; and H.C. Gall, 'De Weeskamer in Neder-lands-Indie'. See also Jean Gelman Taylor, *The Social World of Batavia: European and Eurasian in Dutch Asia*.

42 See Kerk Boek 1820–1822; Kerk Boek 1809–1819; Kerk Boek 1799–1808; Kerk Boek 1782–1799.Ibid.

43 Ibid.

44 Ibid.

45 Resolutie boeken van de Malaxe weeskamer (Orphan Chamber proceedings) 26 Jan 1797–20 Nov 1799, in R/9/1/6; Resolutie boeken van de Malaxe weeskamer 15 Jan 1800–13 Jun 1805, in R/9/1/7; Resolutie boeken van de Malaxe weeskamer 22 Jul 1805–9 Feb 1807, in R/9/1/8; Resolutie boeken van de Malaxe weeskamer 1 Apr 1807–28 Dec 1920 in R/9/1/9; Resolutie boeken van de Malaxe weeskamer 9 Jan 1821–18 Jun 1822, in R/9/1/10; and Resolutie boeken van de Malaxe weeskamer 16 June 1825–25 Apr 1831, in R/9/1/11.

46 See letter signed by A. Koek, A.A. Velge, J.H. Overree, J.W. Baumgarten, A. Manjoot, J. Williamson, G.L. Baumgarten, D. Koek, H. Krall, A.J. Wiederholds, P. Overree, J.B. Wester-hout, J. Lodewickson, J.Jonkman, A. Vander Beek, J.C. Neubronner, J.B. de Wind, Tan Olim (Captain of the Chinese), Abu Bakar bin Asman (Captain of the Malays) and Saugra Chitty (Captain of the Kelings), in letter to the Resident of Melaka, dated, 30 April 1825, in F/4/1230 40215.

47 Obligatie boek 15 Mar 1811–15 Dec 1821, in R/9/8/9.

48 Orphan Chamber proceedings 16 June 1825–25 Apr 1831, in R/9/1/11.

49 Notitie boek der debiteuren 28 Feb. 1787, R/9/9/1.

50   Orphan Chamber proceedings 16 June 1825–25 Apr. 1831, in R/9/1/11.
51   See discussion regarding the estate of J. Rappa, valued at 45,635, in R/9/1/11. See also the decision taken on the estate of, Oei Kong Hee, in R/9/1/11.
52   Maintenance of Orphan Chamber pupils, in R/9/6/20 and R/9/6/21. See also other list of children in R/9/10/1 and R/9/10/2.
53   Among the orphans who received money when they attained their age of majority were Ali bin Maukan, Abdul Kadir and Chio Longo. See Orphan Chamber Proceedings, 16 June 1825–25 Apr 1831, in R/9/1/11.
54   Acting Resident of Melaka, 4 June 1825, in F/4/1230 40215.
55   See Estate papers of the late Jan Samuel Timmerman-Thyssen, in R/9/12/39 and R/9/20/31; during his period of office, Jan Samuel Timmerman-Thyssen borrowed a sum of 16,800 rijksdollars and only 0.75 per cent interest was imposed on him, R/9/8/9; He then borrowed another 23,800 rijksdollars with only 0.75 per cent interest charged. See also Obligatie Boek 15 Mar 1811 to 15 December 1821, in R/9/8/9. He borrowed a further 1,500 rijksdollars at the rate of only 0.75 per cent interest, in R/9/8/9. All of his collateral was in the form of property. For further reference, on his family and career background, see D. Meyer Timmerman Thyssen, *Twee Governeurs en een Equipagemeester: in en om Malakka 1778–1823*, Buren: Knuf, 1991.
56   Extract Malacca Diary, 27 November 1827: Petition by the President of the Chamber W.J. Lewis, in F/4/ 1129 30176.
57   See letter Acting Resident of Malacca, 3 June 1825, in F/4/1230 40215; see abstraction of funds from the Orphan Chamber at Malacca by the outgoing Dutch government, proposals of the president of the Orphan Chamber for its future administration, February–November 1827, in F/4/1044 28713. See also Extract Malacca Consultation, 2 July 1827, in F/4/1044 28713; Extract Malacca Consultations, 5 July 1827, in F/4/1044 28713; Extract Malacca Diary, 3 February 1827: Report on the Funds of the orphan chamber, in F/4/1044 28713; see also Petition of the Malacca Orphan Chamber to be incorporated as a body politic with perpetual succession in November 1827–January 1828, in F/4/ 1129 30176; See also Extract Malacca Diary, 27 November 1827: Petition by the President of the Chamber W.J. Lewis, in F/4/ 1129 30176.
58   See Letter Acting Resident of Melaka, 4 June 1825, in F/4/1230 40215.
59   See, for example, E. Netscher, 'Twee belegeringen van Malakka: 1756/57 en 1784', *TBG*, vol. 13 (1864), pp. 285–361.
60   See a detailed account of the regulations to cover any attempted violation of the fort of Melaka, in VOC 3599.
61   Patrick Morrah, 'The History of the Malayan Police', pp. 30–31.
62   A regulation for the introduction of certain alterations into the present system of the Bughery watch, Melaka 28 April 1825, in enclosure 9, F/4/123 40215.
63   Ibid.
64   See Letters from the Superintendent of Police, Malacca, to the Acting Resident and others, in R/9/32/5; Records of the receipt of fees and fines by the Malacca Treasury from the Police Department, in R/9/32/6; Police regulation regarding gambling and cockfighting and the trade in opium, spirits, toddy, swine's flesh and sirih leaf, 1826, in R/9/32/9; List of the establishment of the Police Department, Melaka, with statement of salaries, August 1826, in R/9/32/10; See also Patrick Morrah, 'The History of the Malayan Police', *JMBRAS*, vol. xxxvi, Part 3, No. 202, pp. 29–33.
65   List of the establishment of the police department Malacca with statement of salaries, in Aug 1826 in R/9/32/10.
66   See, for example, the burgher fund report, December 1780, in VOC 3599.
67   Abdullah bin Abdul Kadir (an annotated translation by A.H. Hill), *The Hikayat Abdullah*, pp. 148–149. Abdullah was born in Melaka in 1797 when Melaka was ruled by the English for a period. He grew up during this temporary English rule (1794–1818) and during the Dutch return (1818–1824). Later he went to Singapore when it was opened by the English in 1819. In his autobiography, Abdullah wrote on everyday life in Melaka, comparing life under the English and the Dutch.

68 A good description of the Dutch administration's strict regard for cleanliness can be found in Abdullah Abdul Kadir, *The Hikayat Abdullah*. The incident mentioned happened during the administration of the last Dutch governor, Timmerman-Thyssen (1818–23). Abdullah wrote that: 'When Bamgoor [a Frenchman] and a senior official of the Dutch civil government who was next in importance to the Fiscal and the Shahbandar and had a seat on the Council came out of the Fort riding his horse there was everywhere a general rush for home to get brooms and to start sweeping in front of the houses, until the noise of sweeping rent the air. Because people were afraid of being fined, whenever Bamgoor went there was the sound of people sweeping. Yet when he had gone home three or four people would be fined. This happened every day until Bamgoor himself came to be known as Mr. Sweep', pp. 148–149.

69 S. Garling, Resident Councillor, August 1826, SSFR, vol. 165.

70 Ibid.

71 Ibid., see also Abdullah Abdul Kadir, *The Hikayat Abdullah*, pp. 148–149.

72 Ibid.

73 Ibid.

74 A local monetary unit: one duit is equivalent to one Kupang, 10 Kupang is equivalent to 1 Spanish dollar.

75 S. Garling, Resident Councillor, August 1826, SSFR, vol. 165.

76 Ibid.

77 Barbara Watson Andaya, 'Melaka under the Dutch'. She notes that: 'Melaka would be clean in body and spirit, a town in which VOC servants washed twice daily, refrained from excessive drinking, and avoided both the sun and local women', p. 197. See also Charles R. Lockyer, *An account of the trade in India*, London, 1711, p. 74; and J.J. Sheehnan, 'Seventeenth Century visitors to the Malay Peninsula', p. 91.

78 See Rhoads Murphey, 'The City in the Swamp: Aspects of the site and Early Growth of Calcutta'. See also Report of the number of European and natives discharged and who died in the hospital in Melaka for the period 1802–1808, by B. Loftie acting head surgeon, 14 July 1810, in G/34/9. See another letter by B. Loftie, acting surgeon Fort Cornwallis, 14 Feburary 1810, in SSFR, vol. 26. See also Walter Caulfield Lennon, 'Journal of a voyage through the Straits of Malacca', where he writes: 'Notwithstanding that this town is surrounded on the land side with impenetrable jungles and swamps, from the small proportion of sick in Hospital, it may be reckoned healthy for Europeans', pp. 61–62. T.G. McGee, *The Southeast Asian City*, p.51. McGee notes that in Batavia: 'The unhealthy physical environment of the stuffy Dutch houses and the malaria canals soon forced the Dutch citizens to move to a favourable location on the fringes of the city in the suburb of Weltevreden'. See also Ramco Raben, "Batavia and Colombo".

79 C.M. Turnbull, 'Melaka under British Rule', in Kernial Singh Sandhu and Paul Wheatley, (ed.), *Melaka*, pp. 242–296.

80 There are about 171 names listed in the Church book record. See Rolle der gemeene Christenen van Malacca, in Miscellaneous Book.

81 Officially, there were two members in the Church Council. The council was headed by an officer from the VOC usually the Senior merchant, and the other was a Dutch burgher not employed in the Company, see Appendix 1: Dutch Administration of Melaka in 1780 and Appendix 2: Dutch administration of Melaka in 1793, in Nordin Hussin, 'Melaka and Penang 1780–1830', pp. 418–421. However, minutes of Church council meetings give other names as well, mostly burghers, probably appointed to represent the Protestant Church community by the Church council. For further information regarding this matter see Kerk Boek 1820–1822, Kerk Boek 1809–1819, Kerk Boek 1799–1808 and Kerk Boek 1782–1799. A detailed account of the activities of the Dutch Reformed Church regarding the administration of marriages, baptism, schooling, death and burial can be found in: Baptisms 1742–1790; Resolutie Boek 1773–1825; Kerk Boek 1820–1822, Kerk Boek 1809–1819, Kerk Boek 1799–1808; and Kerk Boek 1782–1799.

82 See Trouwboek December 1798, in Kerk Boek 1782–1799, folio 11; Trouwboek 1787 in Kerk Boek 1782–1799, folio 29; Trouwboek 1796 in Kerk Boek 1782–1799; Huwelijk 1795 in Kerk Boek 1782–1799, folio 60; Notitie der trouwboekens van onchristenen 1795

in Kerk Boek 1782–1799, folio 61; Notitie der trouwboekens van christen 1795, in Koek Boek 1782–1799, folio 62; Huwelijkse 1794 in Kerk Boek 1782–1799, folio 118; trouwboetens van onchristen 1794 in Kerk Boek 1782–1799, folio 120; Trouwboek 1793 in Kerk Boek 1782–1799 folio 143; Trouwboek van de roomsch 1793 in Kerk Boek 1782–1799, folio 144; Trouwboek van onchristenen 1793 in Kerk Boek 1782–1799, folio 145; Extract uit het trouwboek van het commissarissen van huwelijks en kleijne gerigtbaaken 1792 in Kerk Boek 1782–1799, folio 157; Notitie der trouwboetens van de roomsch-gezinnen 1792 in Kerk Boek 1782–1799, folio 158; Notitie van trouweboeten van onchristen het jaar 1792,in Kerk Boek 1782–1799, folio 158; Extract uit het trouwboek 1791 in Kerk Boek 1782–1799, folio 171; Notitie trouwbotens van inlandsche christians 1791 in Kerk Boek 1782–1799, folio 172; Notie trouwbotens van onchristen 1791, 1790, 1789 in Kerk Boek 1782–1799, folio 173, 192, 216; Extract het trouwboek 1790, 1788, 1789, 1789 in Kerk Boek 1782–1799, folio 193, 205, 217, and 218.

83 Memorie van de ingekoommene collecte penningen in de onderstaande laaste het maanden die gecollecteerd Julie tot December 1798, Kerk Boek 1782–1799, Folio 13.

84 The details of such collection could be found from: Kerk Boek 1782–1799, Kerk Boek 1809–1819, and Kerk Boek 1820–1822.

85 The expenditure of the Reformed Church on school books in 1780 includes: 50 A,B,C books; 36 *catechesmusen klijne*, 20 letter *konsten*, 16 *trapen det jeugd*, 30 psalm books, 12 writing books, 6 *cijfferleijn*, 24 *cijffergriften* and 20 bibles, VOC 3599. For detailed expenditure on such activities, see Kerk Boek 1782–1799; Kerk Boek 1809–1819, and Kerk Boek 1820–1822; see also letter from C.M. de Groot and the first church warden A. Koek to Faquhar, dated 7 Feburary 1806, in SSFR, vol. 13.

86 See Barbara Andaya, 'The Dutch in Melaka', where she points out that: 'But the VOC was unwilling to be embroiled in religious disputes, and, although the Bible was translated into Malay, efforts to propagate Protestantism were half-hearted at best. Obvious failure forced even a zealous Churchman like Governor Bort to abandon the practice of preaching in Portuguese "to attract our Romish community". The general atmosphere of toleration is indicated by the fact that in 1669 there were about 2,000 Catholics in Melaka, and by the early eighteenth century they still outnumbered members of the Reformed Church by six to one', p. 211.

87 For further reference on the discussion regarding the early history of revenue farms see Anthony Reid, 'The origin of revenue farming in Southeast', in J. Butcher and Howard Dick (ed.), *The Rise and Fall of Revenue Farming Business Elites and the Emergence of the Modern State in Southeast Asia*, London: Macmillan Press, 1993, pp. 60–71.

88 Vier reackeningen van de eendemnatien gevallen in de jaren 1698, 1699, 1700 en 1701, in VOC 1661; See also Appendix 3: Melaka Revenue Farms 1742–1830, in Nordin Hussin, 'Melaka and Penang 1780–1830', pp. 422–425.

89 See Appendix 3: Melaka Revenue Farms 1742–1830, in Nordin Hussin, 'Melaka and Penang 1780–1830', pp. 422–425.

90 Vier reackeningen van de eendemnatien gevallen in de jaren 1698, 1699, 1700 en 1701, in VOC 1661.

91 See Appendix 3: Melaka Revenue Farms 1742–1830, in Nordin Hussin, 'Melaka and Penang 1780–1830', pp. 422–425.

92 Farquhar, dated 9 Feb. 1806, in SSFR, vol. 13. See also Report on Melaka farms, 31 December 1795, in SSFR, vol.16 and report by Farquhar, dated 10 December 1805, in SSFR, vol. 16.

93 Ibid.

94 Farquhar, dated 9 Feb. 1806, in SSFR, vol. 13, and see also Report on Melaka farms, 31 December 1795, in SSFR, vol.16. Also report by Farquhar, dated 10 December 1805, in SSFR, vol. 16.

95 Farquhar, 9 Feburary 1806, in SSFR, vol. 13.

96 C.M. Turnbull, 'Melaka under British Colonial Rule', p. 247. Turnbull states that: 'Governor Thyssen protested at the foundation of the British settlement, prohibited Melakans migrating to Singapore on pain of fines, imprisonment, and confiscation of property, and posted patrol boats at the river's mouth to enforce the regulation. Attracted by high

prices and good wages, many Melakans, both Malay and Chinese, defied the Dutch ban and dangers of piracy to seek their fortune in Singapore'.

97　Most of the timber from Melaka was brought by Chinese traders. In the early nineteenth century only a limited number of Chinese Junks stayed in Melaka and the timber farmers had problems in fulfilling their obligation to the government, see Letter, A. Koek 12 December 1805, in G/34/13.

98　For further reference on the differences between revenue farms in Melaka and those of Penang and Singapore, see T. Braddell, *Statistics of the British Possessions in the Straits of Malacca.*

99　See Appendix 3: Melaka Revenue Farms 1742–1830, in Nordin Hussin, 'Melaka and Penang 1780–1830', pp. 422–425.

100　See Schouten's report of his visit to Malacca, in P.A. Leupe, 'The Siege and Capture of Malacca', pp. 133–134.

101　See, for example, Brian Harrison, 'Holding the Fort', *JMBRAS*, Monograph No. 14,1985, pp.106–114.

102　See, for example, E.A. Blundell, 'Notices of the History and Present Condition of Malacca', in *JIA*, Series I, vol. 2, 1848, pp. 726–754. See also T. Braddell, 'Notes on Malacca', *JIA*, Series II, vol. 1, 1856, pp. 43–65. See also, K.T. Joseph, 'The Malacca Land Laws', in *Federation Museums Journal*, vol. VX, 1970, pp. 135–145.

103　T. Braddell, 'Notes on Malacca', p. 106.

104　Superintendent of Lands W.J. Lewis, 28 January 1828, in SSFR, vol. 168.

105　Ibid.

106　See, for example, the disputed land belonging to Adrian Koek and de Wind in G/34/168.

107　See Enclosure 4 and 5 in G/34/172. A *Penghulu* served as a headman of a village, see T. Braddell, 'Notes on Malacca', *JIA*, vol. 1, 1856.

108　T. Braddell, 'Notes on Malacca', p. 52

109　J.B. de Wind's estate produced pepper and timber; Westerhout's estate produced pepper and spices; Daniel Koek's estate produced pepper, report made by the land proprietors, in G/34/168.

110　Abrahamus Couperus, 'Berigt aangaande de Gamber, derzelver planting en bewerking op Malacca', *Verhandelingen van het Bataviaasch Genootschap der kunsten en weten-schappen,* Tweede Deel, 1780, pp. 356–382.

111　Minute by the President 5July 1827, in G/34/172.

112　Memo by Garling, in G/34/127.

113　For example, the largest estate could raise an income of SpD 4,000 per annum. For the details on each estate, see 'Statement of land transfer to the British administration', in SSFR, vol. 168.

114　For further discussion on the socio-economic problems of land in Melaka, see K.T. Joseph, 'The Malacca Land Laws', pp. 135–173.

115　Brian Harrison, 'Holding the Fort', p. 113.

116　Superintendent of Lands W.J. Lewis 28 January 1828, in SSFR, vol. 168.

117　Ibid.

118　Ibid.

119　Statement of land transfer to the British administration in 1828, in SSFR, vol. 168.

120　Superintendent of Lands, W.J. Lewis 28 January 1828, in SSFR, vol. 168.

121　Statement of land transferred to the British administration, in 1828, in SSFR, vol. 168. Part of this estate was farmed by Then Pong, Garling 20 March 1828, in G/34/168.

122　Superintendent of Lands W.J. Lewis, 28 January 1828, in SSFR, vol. 168.

123　Ibid.

124　Ibid.

125　Statement of land transferred to the British administration in 1828, in SSFR, vol. 168. See also The Chinese woman Oeij Kitnio, widow of Tjan Somko, versus Mrs. Maria Catherina Westerhout, nee de Wind, widow of Jan Jacobszoon Westerhout: Dispute regarding the ownership of a piece of land used for timber-cutting, 6 July 1803, in R/9/20/2.

126 Superintendent of Lands, W.J. Lewis 28 January 1828, in SSFR, vol. 168.

127 Statement of land transferred to the British administration in 1828, in SSFR, vol. 168.

128 Ibid. See also Superintendent of Lands W.J. Lewis, 28 January 1828, in SSFR, vol. 168.

129 Ibid.

130 Ibid.

131 Ibid.

132 Ibid.

133 Ibid. It was also said that the judgement was tampered with by Adrian Koek who was the president of the Council of Justice at the time.

134 See R. Fullerton 23 June 1828, in SSFR, vol. 168.

135 Minute by S. Garling 28 January 1828, in SSFR, vol. 168.

136 See translation of a document given by the Temenggong of Muar to Mr de Wind 7 Rabil Akhir 1243, in SSFR, vol. 168.

137 See K.T. Joseph, 'The Malacca Land Laws' and Paul H. Kratoska, 'Land law and land tenure in British Melaka'. In Kernial Singh Sandhu and Paul Wheatley, (eds), *Melaka*, pp. 497–534.

138 See, for example, Anthony Reid, 'The Origin of Revenue Farming in Southeast Asia' and Wong Lin Ken, 'The Revenue Farms', p. 60.

139 Charles Lockyer, *An Account of the Trade in India*, p. 74.

Plate 5: James Wathen, 'View overlooking Georgetown, 1811'. Reproduced with permission from *Early Views of Penang & Malacca 1660–1880*, Penang: Lembaga Muzium Negeri Pulau Pinang, 2002.

Plate 6: C. Sutton, 'Georgetown in Pulo Penang or Prince of Wales' Island, c. 1814'. Reproduced with permission from *Early Views of Penang & Malacca 1660–1880*, Penang: Lembaga Muzium Negeri Pulau Pinang, 2002.

CHAPTER EIGHT

British Urban Administration in Penang

THIS CHAPTER WILL LOOK AT how the English governed the colonial port-town of Penang. The scope covers the years from 1786 to 1830 and the chapter is arranged into two parts. The first section will discuss the administrative structure of English rule and the second will focus on the financial administration of Penang.

HISTORICAL BACKGROUND

Under the administration of the English East India Company (EIC), the highest body was the Board of Control in London, which consisted of 24 EIC directors.[1] The centre of the EIC administration, headed by a Governor-General, was, however, located at Fort William, Calcutta, in the Bay of Bengal.[2] Family ties and connections were important factors in determining the appointments of various Company officers serving in the colonies.[3]

Penang, one of many EIC colonies in the East, was first headed by a Superintendent (Francis Light, from 1786–94), then by a Lieutenant-Governor (the first being George Leith 1800–1803)[4] and finally by a Governor in 1805.[5] In the early period, the EIC establishment in Penang was very small, consisting of Francis Light as Superintendent, J. Gardyne as storekeeper, Mr Bacon as monthly writer, Adam Ramage as Beachmaster, Long, a Malay writer and Nakhuda Kecil, the security guard.[6] All official correspondence was sent from Penang to Calcutta and then from there to London for the final decision.[7] Although the British gained possession of the settlement in 1786, it was not until August 1794 that the Superintendent, Francis Light, was issued with instructions on legal matters by the Governor-General in Council in Calcutta. These instructions constituted the first regulations for the settlement and were called 'Lord Teignmouth's Regulations'.[8] They authorized Francis Light to be the Superintendent of the island and granted him power and authority.[9]

From 1786 until 1867 many changes took place in the administration. Between 1786 and 1805, Penang was administered from Calcutta in India but in 1805 it enjoyed the same status as the three other Presidencies of Bombay, Madras and Calcutta.[10] Another important change was effected in 1826 when Singapore, Melaka and Penang became known collectively as the Straits Settlements, with Singapore as the administrative centre or head-quarters. Although these possessions were initially administered separately as Presidencies, this was found to be too costly so their status was reduced to that of Residencies in 1830. As such, they came under the control of the Governor of Bengal in Calcutta. In effect, this meant that the Straits Settlements were administered as if they were part of the Bengal Presidency. Then, in 1851, the Straits Settlements were placed under the direct control of the Governor-General of India to reduce the financial expenditure of the administration. Due to much agitation from local merchants and British officials, the Straits Settlements, along with Labuan (ceded to the British in 1846) were separated from India in 1867. They were then administered directly by the Colonial Office in London.[11]

EARLY BRITISH ADMINISTRATION OF PENANG

When Penang was ceded to Francis Light in 1786, his first municipal act was to dig a well at the beginning of Light Street for the supply of water for the settlers. No other amenities were provided for the early settlers and all houses were built from *attap*.[12] This material, however, was easily inflammable so, not surprisingly, a fire broke out in 1789. The town was also swampy and without good drainage, thus contributing to the spread of fever and illness. The poor drainage system took its toll when Light himself became a victim of malaria, which eventually led to his death in 1794.

Light was replaced by Philip Manington in 1795. During Manington's term of office John McIntyre was appointed as Clerk of the Market and as Scavenger, besides having to cope with the municipal administration.[13] Since there was an increase in the municipal expenditure, Manington proposed a tax on the houses and shops owned by natives in the bazaar. It was left to McIntyre to collect the ground tax or rent property in the town as well as taxes on houses and shops.[14] These taxes were implemented for the first time in 1795. The taxes were used for clearing and draining the swampy areas, constructing a proper system of sewage and drainage and maintaining the streets.

However, disputes soon arose among the town's inhabitants over the taxes imposed. As a result, there was no income and hence no major improvements to the bad and unhealthy conditions. In addition, heavy rainfall caused floods and adversely affected the roads. The drains too were clogged with dirt, filth and stagnant water, giving rise to unbearable smells.

Tropical diseases could spread easily in such unhealthy living conditions, exposing the residents to the risk of contracting serious illnesses. Even the Superintendent who succeeded Francis Light, Philip Manington, suffered an illness that forced him to resign from his position in 1796. He was succeeded by Macdonald who held the post of Superintendent from 1796 to 1799.[15] The new Superintendent realized the unhealthy living conditions and made plans to move the administration centre to another vicinity south of the island, in a small town called Jamestown.[16] However, the idea was abandoned because of lack of financial support from the higher authorities in Calcutta who were even then entertaining the idea of abandoning Prince of Wales Island in favour of the Andamans.[17]

Macdonald was not on good terms with most people in Penang, especially the merchants, but his term in office saw many changes which helped to transform the town. [18] During his tenure the government decided to construct the Customs House, Hospital and Prison, streets were widened and a new road was constructed from the town into the interior of the island. Under him the streets and roads were clearly marked and extended to 65 feet wide. They were also reconstructed in straight lines with intersecting streets meeting at right angles. Macdonald introduced many ideas to improve the standard of living, town but his plans were interrupted by the Napoleonic wars in Europe (1789–1814), when the colony suffered financial problems and required financial assistance to strengthen its defence against French attacks in the East.

One potential source of revenue was taxes, in particular municipal taxes. At the point when Macdonald left little action had been taken to implement municipal taxes on property in the town, probably because of his antagonistic relationship with the business community. However, his successor, Lieutenant-Governor George Leith, was able to introduce taxes. In 1800 a proper planning and advisory body, the Committee of Assessors, was set up by the government to study the implementation of these taxes. The committee appointed by Leith consisted of three officials, namely, John Brown (Company officer), who held the posts of provost, sheriff, gaoler, coroner, bailiff, constable and police officer, James Scott (merchant) and David Brown (merchant).

Although its main purpose was to determine individual tax assessments the Committee of Assessors had wider functions, which included the supervision of road construction and drainage systems. At its first meeting it decided that convicts would be used for constructing Bishop and Church Street and that major improvements would be focussed on the commercial area, as planned by Francis Light. This area included Light Street, Beach Street, Chulia Street, Church Street, Pitt Street, King Street, Bishop Street and Market Street.

A dilemma faced by the Committee of Assessors was to set a tax rate that would give the administration the revenue it needed for development but not invite opposition from the citizens. Leith had begun the practice of using more convicts as labourers and had requested the government in Calcutta to supply even more from India for constructing and maintaining the streets. The number of convicts employed in 1800 was 130, increasing to 772 by 1805. This cheap form of labour saved the budget and improved living conditions.[19] The convicts received a minimum wage of 40 *pice* monthly. With the low cost labour force, there was no good reason for the Committee of Assessors to impose a high tax on the town's inhabitants. Furthermore, the committee realized that if it were to impose a high municipal tax, this would scare off prospective new settlers and the whole plan of transforming the colony into a new important settlement would fail.

Although many changes took place during the Macdonald and Leith administrations, the problem of keeping the town healthy remained a deep concern. In 1805, the administration discovered that within the Penang municipality, particularly within the boundary ditch northward and southward of Leith Street, the swamps and jungle extending to the south and the ditch itself was injurious to general health. Since the town was expanding, the European cemetery, an isolated area in earlier days, was soon surrounded by houses. The town was still unhealthy due to the practice of planting paddy nearby. This resulted in stagnant water, encouraging mosquitoes to breed and attracting rodents, especially during harvesting, thus further aggravating the poor health conditions.[20]

During investigation, the authorities discovered that the tract of land south of the town, extending from the sea three or four miles inland, was unhealthy because it was covered with jungle and swamp. It was also bounded on the seafront by a mud bank. The authorities were convinced that the acute infections of the liver, bunions, fevers, influenza and dysentery which occurred during the southwest monsoon, which lasted five months annually, arose from the wet conditions. At the same time newly cleared jungle areas for cultivation close to the town and poor drainage created a breeding ground for malaria. But while authorities were fully aware of the situation they were helpless due to lack of funds for the construction of a proper drainage system. Illness was common in Penang. In 1805, 302 Europeans were admitted to the hospital although 292 were discharged and found fit for duty and only nine, or 2.9 per cent, died. Among the natives 211 were admitted, with 202 discharged and six losing their lives.[21]

Penang, however, had one saving grace, the highland in its hinterland which had a temperature similar to a European spring. Its cool temperature which seldom deviated from 62 to 68 degrees Fahrenheit, was 12 degrees lower than that in the low lying areas – an ideal retreat for the European community to escape from the heat or to recover from sickness.[22] However, at that stage, the highland was a two-hour journey away.

Penang's early municipal history is poorly documented and there are few records available to make a closer study possible. The only early evidence of town administration was the appointment of John McIntyre as Clerk of the market and scavenger, in 1795. A Mayor appears to have been appointed but the date of his appointment is not available and his function and power were not clearly defined in the documents. The sole clear trace of the town Mayor was a case of his abuse of power through violence against a Chinese in 1807.[23] In addition to the civil servants who administered the colony, two important bodies regulated daily life in town, the Committee of Assessors and the Capitans of the various communities.

THE COMMITTEES OF ASSESSORS

From 1800, it seemed that the town was ruled and governed by several Committees of Assessors elected by the Governor in Council for the improvement of the town. The aim of forming various Committees of Assessors was to discuss, study and solve social and economic problems that affected the lives of the town's population. In effect, they were advisory bodies which could not pass or enforce regulations on their own. These were not permanent institutions, as they only existed for a specific purpose and term. Although the appointment of a Committee of Assessors was done on an ad hoc basis, it was nevertheless an important body because it assisted the government in making policy decisions. Each committee was chaired by a government official and its other members consisted of distinguished native chiefs and eminent Europeans not in the service of the government. In practice, the Europeans and natives nominated by the government to sit in the Committees of Assessors were wealthy.

A Committee of Assessors might exist for a few weeks or months depending on the task it was appointed to perform. For example, if it was felt necessary to build a road into the interior or to widen existing roads or build

Table 41: Committees of Assessors formed in Penang 1796–1814

Name of Committee of Assessors	Date/year formed
Committee of Assessors on obtaining a revenue from trade	1796
Committee of Assessors for the valuation of property for assessment	1800
Committee of Assessors on Kellner the police magistrate	18 August 1806
Committee of Assessors on Kellner the police magistrate	22 August 1806
Committee of Assessors on the regulation in the market	8 Sept. 1806
Committee of British Inhabitants of Prince of Wales Island	1806
Committee of Assessors on constructing water works and supply	1806
Comm. of Assessors on maintenance and building of roads and bridges	1807
Committee of Assessors on Land Holder of Penang	1807
Committee of Assessors to formulate regulations on road users	1807
Committee of Assessors to abolish slavery	1808
Committee of Assessors on the fire of 1814	1814
Committee of Assessors to guard against the possibility of future fire	1814

Source: 'Notices of Pinang', JIA, Vol.5, 1851, p. 97; G/34/14; G/34/13; G/34/18; G/34/20; G/34/10; G/34/45.

new bridges, the government would form a Committee of Assessors to discuss matters. This committee would then discuss and decide on the funding, cost, planning and building of the infrastructure.

From 1796 to 1814, as noted in Table 41 above, 13 Committees of Assessors were formed by the Governor in Council. Among these committees, the most important were the committee on obtaining revenue from trade,[24] the body for looking into the actions of the police magistrate, which brought about fundamental changes to the administration of the market,[25] and the one on the building and maintaining of roads.[26]

A difficult task for any committee was to raise funds or revenue. The Committee of Assessors on obtaining revenue from trade had as its term of reference the seeking of more income for the administrative expenditure of the town and for the colony as a whole. No tax, however, was levied on the port of Penang, as its founder, Francis Light, wanted it to be a free port in order to attract more merchants and traders. But with Light's death the new Superintendent of the colony decided to abolish the island's free port status. Macdonald hoped that the imposition of a tax would generate more income, which could then be utilized for the town's administration and thus further benefit the community.[27] But he was opposed by a strong group of English traders and merchants on the island and according to an observer:

> Major Macdonald however appears to have been a man of more firmness if not severity of disposition than Mr. Light and he went heartily to war with the difficulties that surrounded him. Under a friendly administration of the first Superintendent [Francis Light], and the three years interregnum which appears to have followed, the merchants had grown into as the major terms it 'a most contumacious body' and he directed his attention first to the reduction of these traders to a proper understanding of their position.[28]

As a result of his confrontational stance, the merchants united under their leader James Scott to oppose the taxes. These merchants had earlier worked with the government but had resigned to venture into trade and business so that their interests were not necessarily in tune with those of the administration. They took Macdonald's actions to be a personal attack on them and believed the administrator was envious of their wealth and success. The ill feeling engendered led to serious disputes and a strained relationship developed between the Superintendent and the merchants in the town. James Scott, leader of the merchant community and a powerful person in Penang, in particular, did not get on well with Macdonald, a factor partly responsible in forcing the latter to resign as Superintendent of the island in 1799. The idea of imposing a customs' tax was only successfully implemented during George Leith's period.

Two Committees of Assessors were set up to investigate the police magistrate Kellner.[29] In colonial Penang, the police magistrate administered law and order in the town and territories. His jurisdiction ranged from the administration of justice to the administration of the markets, the bazaar, the streets of the town and the island. With such extensive powers, possibilities of abuse and corruption existed. Even as early as 1800, there was evidence of anger and resentment among the inhabitants of Penang, with reports sent to the Governor and Council alleging abuse in the market by the police magistrate. However, a committee was only set up in 1806 to investigate the allegations and, even then, due to the power and influence of the police magistrate, it ended in failure. A new committee was set up under an official of higher ranking than the police magistrate. Strong evidence was obtained that the police magistrate was indeed corrupt and had abused his power by manipulating the prices and weights of goods in the market. Following the inquiry, he was replaced.

After the departure of the magistrate, a new Committee of Assessors was appointed to regulate market administration.[30] New regulations were introduced and changes in the management of the market which followed were effective in reducing manipulation of prices, and regulating the import of food products from Kedah. Under the new rules the police had to ascertain that goods were sold and purchased according to the proper regulations and not sold in huge quantities. However, these regulations had no effect on suppliers from Kedah, who sold most of their goods to traders in large quantities. In order to preserve stability in the markets and good negotiations between buyers and sellers, an official was appointed as superintendent of the markets.

This Superintendent was given an assistant to help him carry out his duties. He was required to maintain a register of all imported goods and daily internal suppliers, to enable the Committee to determine prices at a specific period. The committee suggested that the Superintendent should be vested with discretionary powers but in cases beyond his capacity, reference should be made to the police magistrate. The Superintendent was to be well equipped with adequate scales, weights and measures for his job in the market. He and his assistant were prohibited from buying and selling, either directly or indirectly, any of the restricted goods such as rice and meat. Nobody except the bazaar guard was allowed to wear any form of identification, such as a badge.

The new regulation was effective in curbing violence and aggression against the retailers. In addition, trading hours were specified, starting at seven o'clock in the morning and ending at six in the evening. These hours however, did not apply to the sale of fish and vegetables, which could be sold at most times. During regular market hours, the superintendent or his assistant was to be constantly present. Since the committee felt that no native was competent to be the superintendent, that post was entrusted to a European who understood Asia languages. An Englishman who professed a good command of Chinese and Malay, named McIntyre, was appointed as the first Superintendent of the market.

The committee also set up regulations for the bazaar and market of Penang, specifying that all persons were prohibited from selling fowl or other kinds of poultry in Penang except within the bazaar. If they broke the law, the punishment was in the form of fines, as follows: one fowl, one *kupang* and for every duck or goose, two *kupang*.[31] Part of the proceeds of the fine would be given to the informer and the rest used for expenditure for the maintenance of the streets.

With the enforcement of the new rules and regulations for the market, new problems emerged, especially in relation to the implementation of the new law on the sale of poultry. McIntyre declared that those who boarded prows/boats and fixed the value of the poultry based on their own self interest had caused problems and had deterred the natives from supplying goods to the market. The clerk of the market had to then appoint a *Panglima Pagar*, a security guard, to reside in the market for a specific period of time, from eight until 12 in the morning and from two to six in the evening.[32] This person was also to act as an intermediary between the buyer and the seller when necessary and should, as far as possible, seek justice for both parties. One of the main tasks of the *Panglima Pagar* was to act as an arbitrator in cases of disputes. A respectable Malay was chosen for this office and was paid SpD 25 per month.

THE OFFICE OF THE CAPITAN

Apart from the Committees of Assessors, the English administration in Penang instituted the practice of appointing a Capitan or Headman for each ethnic Asian group. The power and function of this office was similar to that of the Capitans in Dutch-Melaka.[33] When first introduced, the Capitan was empowered to administer justice and exercise social control in his own community. However, the capitan's judicial functions were abolished after 1808, when the Court of Judicature was set up and no more capitans appointed by the government. Despite this, the Chinese, Malays and Chulias continued to take their disputes to their elders rather than to the Recorder's Court.[34]

During the period when the capitan had judicial powers, the proceedings of the Capitan's court were held every Monday and Thursday at the Capitan's premises during which he was assisted by two persons called assessors. All judgments in cases of debts under SpD 10 were considered final. But in cases where the debt exceeded SpD 10 and a litigant was dissatisfied with the Capitan's verdict, he could lodge an appeal at the Magistrate's Court.[35] The power given to the Capitans covered small disputes that happened in their own communities.[36] They also had to assist the police department by rendering their help in fighting crime. Each Capitan was provided with five peons who also acted as police constables performing beat duties in the town during the day and night. In addition, the Capitans had to keep a register of the births and marriages of their own ethnic group, report new migrants, keep a regular count of the numbers of their ethnic community, regulate assessments of the standard of living and manage social and religious activities.[37]

The earliest known Capitan of the Chinese was Cheki alias Chu Khee alias Patcan alias Koh Lay Huan alias Chewan, who was appointed in 1794.[38] Sometime in the early nineteenth century, he was succeeded by Teaquah. The first Capitan of the Malays was Tuanku Syed Hussain[39] and for the Chulias it was Kadir Maiden alias Cauder Maydeen.[40] As the functions of the police department began to grow in maintaining law and order, the power of the native Capitans diminished and subsequently they merely held a ceremonial status in their ethnic group. However, the informal power of these Capitans was still very strong within their own ethnic group. For example, the majority of the Chinese still went to their Capitan to solve socio-economic problems, like settling land or family disputes.[41] Some of the Capitans were also very influential and the government usually sought their assistance in dealing with specific social problems. For example, during an outbreak of cholera in the Chulia community in 1819, the government requested the Capitan's assistance to explain the disease to the community in order to help curb its spread.[42]

POLICING THE TOWN

Prior to the establishment of the Court of Judicature in 1808, the Police Department in Penang was empowered with criminal and civil jurisdiction for the island.[43] It faced many challenges because, from its inception in 1786 until the early nineteenth century, it was confronted with difficulties.[44] The main problem was lack of sufficient manpower to administer law and order in the town and territory.[45] Secondly, it was plagued by inefficient administration as a result of unorganized laws and regulations. Thirdly, there was no separation of powers between the executive and the judiciary. As a consequence of these problems, on 22 November 1805 the Governor in Council passed a regulation to improve the policing of the island by dividing Penang town and the Prince of Wales Island into various divisions and districts.

For the purpose of administering law and order by the Police Department, the island was divided into six areas: Penang (the town or Georgetown), Jamestown, Kampong Pinang, Tanjong Tikus, Prai and Pulau Jerjak. The new Regulations created several posts, most importantly the position of Police Magistrate, and other executive posts for the island and Penang (Georgetown). All the new officials were Europeans. A General Police Office at Penang (the town or Georgetown) was also created, headed by the Police Magistrate who was assisted by a European Chief Clerk, four native clerks and a gong man.[46] The office or department was also equipped with a row boat.[47] The police establishment at Penang (the town or Georgetown) consisted of a Head Constable and Provost, two Deputy Constables, an Overseer of the market, four Police Constables (Jemedars), 16 peons and 24 night watchmen. If a European held the position of Deputy Constable, he received a salary of SpD 40, while a native was given only SpD 20.

The town (Penang or Georgetown) itself was divided into four wards or districts,[48] each under a Jemedar or Police Constable and ten peons and a watchman. They served under a Head Constable who was on duty every night, as were the constables and watchmen, who were usually Malays and Chinese. The Head Constable was assisted by two constables on alternate nights. He had to ensure that the police constables and peons were on duty. The police constables and peons were furnished with alarms to call for help from the Head Constable, his assistants and patrols from other wards when confronted by problems or fire.

The duty of these constables was to keep the peace and to arrest offenders who would then be sent to the General Police Office in Penang with a report on their behaviour. Other duties included keeping a register of the number of houses, inhabitants and immigrants and a list of marriages, births and deaths in the districts. The Police Magistrate had the authority to order all houses in every street within Penang to be numbered. This number had to be painted in English and Malay characters on a board to be hung over the main entrance of each household.[49] Such numbering of houses was carried out at police expense but if the number plate was destroyed, the owner had to replace it. The number plate of each house had to contain the names of the police constables (Jemedar) of the wards and the ethnic origin of the inhabitants in the house. Any false information given by the owner of the house resulted in a fine.

ADMINISTRATION OF ROADS, BRIDGES AND WATER WORKS

Penang, situated on the northeastern part of the island, was separated from its hinterland by ditches on its western side and by the Praingin River on its southern border. Straight streets criss-crossed each other at right angles. The longest street in town, Beach Street, was situated to the east and ran from the fort to the Praingin River in the south. Other busy streets in the town centre were Penang, King and Pitt Streets, which were parallel with Beach Street. The cross streets were Light Street on the north and Bishop, Church, China, Market, Chulia, Aceh and Malay Streets and Praingin Road on the southern end of the town. Other streets to the west were Farquhar and Leith Streets and Penang Road. These three were less busy than the streets mentioned earlier.

In 1804, the boundary or demarcation of the town was clearly drawn. This occurred when the authorities discovered that the population of Penang had increased since its occupation in 1786. Thus, the new town boundary was extended from the fort to the Praingin River in the south, where a drawbridge was constructed on the river. On the west, a canal or ditch had been constructed to join the Praingin River, which served as the boundary. Some canals had also been constructed in order to reclaim the swampy areas to the south.[50]

The improvement of the interior of the island had also been achieved by the construction of roads and bridges, through different districts, to the extent of 12 miles from Penang. From 1786 to the1790s, most roads were impassable during the rainy season, greatly affecting the agricultural production and movement of people within the town and from the interior to the ports.[51] The construction of regular streets and roads in the town area was undertaken and completed during the term of Lieutenant-Governor George Leith, leading to health improvement and prosperity in the settlement.[52]

In the early years, the financing of such major projects was done mainly by selling government land and property, although at times the administration was forced to borrow money from wealthy merchants. Not until the 1820s was a tax system regularized so that the administration could depend on a regular income to finance its projects. This was done in 1826, when proper regulations for assessment and taxes on all property, such as land and houses, were drafted to provide expenditure for cleaning, supervision, lighting and maintenance of streets and bridges in the town and hinterland.[53]

When Francis Light opened Penang much land was alienated to private individuals and Light himself acquired some prime property. Thus by the time the administration was ready to develop the island it found itself in the position of not having enough public land for its projects. It was therefore forced to purchase land or to rent premises from private individuals. Over the years, the administration took the opportunity to acquire land particularly when owners were in debt and had to dispose of their land. One way of acquiring prime land was to take over revenue farms from proprietors who could not settle their yearly payment. Most revenue farms were located in strategic areas so that they were valuable pieces of land. The total area of government land was small and some of it had been used for the construction of government buildings, such as administrative offices, customs office and police department.

In the early period, Leith sold land to the value of SpD 32,825.00 and used the money to improve and maintain the streets and roads and the drainage system in Penang.[54] During his tenure the government spent SpD 52,050 in drainage construction and the maintenance of streets and paying off government debts and loans obtained from the Committee of Assessors during the initial period of restructuring the town.[55] Roads were extended three to four miles from Penang town, spreading from the most fertile and cultivated area of the island, a vital project consistent with administration policy to transform the colony into a spice producing area.[56] In 1805, the government had to sell land and property amounting to SpD 18,406.13 in order to finance roads linking the interior to the town.[57] In 1804–05, the annual production of pepper from the island was 30,000 *pikuls*.[58] There were also many newly cultivated areas for pepper, clove and nutmeg. The government realized that the investment in communications was vital to the

Table 42: Government property sold in 1804–05

Sale of Government Property / cash received from other means	Amount in SpD
Government property sold at the corn market	230.00
Land on the east side of Beach Street sold by government	29,402.00
Land on the west side of Beach Street sold by government	1,793.00
Land in Market Street sold by the government	764.00
Land in Praingin sold by government	585.00
Land at Hujung Pasir sold by government	5,509.00
Land at Aceh Street sold by government	1,190.00
Green Bazaar sold by government	1,590.00
Land in Beach Street sold by government	1,200.00
Sale of government land at Sungai Kluang	4,113.04
Sale of government land at Sungai Kluang	785.02
Sale of government land at Ayer Itam	2,892.75
Sale of government land at Kampung Pulau Pinang	1,507.32
Sale of government land in Penang	9,048.00
Total	60,609.13

Sources: G/34/9; G/34/12.

economy of the island and town. Some of the roads had to be built across lands belonging to wealthy English merchants and traders.[59] However, since the majority of the English merchants had invested in agricultural business, such as planting pepper and nutmeg, the roads were allowed to be built. Therefore a symbiotic relationship developed between the English merchants and the government.

The problem in the early years was not merely confined to building new or more roads but also keeping them in good order as the surface was not sealed. Thus, after three years, all major roads constructed under George Leith were in bad condition as a result of the weather – heavy rainfalls made the roads impassable. During a meeting, the Committee of Assessors on roads suggested that more convicts be obtained to assist in the road and street maintenance work. Thus, in 1807, they requested 50 more convicts. There were suggestions that drainage ditches be constructed on each side of the roads and streets, especially in the low-lying and swampy areas. But it was realized that this might lead to fire since residents might dispose of their garbage into the ditches. They also feared that land owners would cover the ditches and convert them into cultivation areas. But the superintendent engineer felt this was the only means to drain the water from the swamp.

The Committee suggested that in order to derive more income for maintaining roads and streets, the government should order all carts to be registered.[60] Licensed carts had to use certain roads and streets only, and parking areas in the town were confined to the vicinity of the Customs House and on Chulia Street. Even the loads of the carts were monitored, the maximum allowed being two and a half *baharas* (six and a half *pikuls*).[61] The cart users had to pay for road usage, for example, four *kupang* for a full day and two *kupang* for half a day. All carts using the roads within the boundary of the town were charged one *kupang* per trip. If the master of any cart refused to abide by the rules, his license was terminated. A cart owner without a license was also punished. All coolies who worked for their masters involving the use of carts were ordered to wear badges with their names and registered number. The regulation also stipulated the working hours of these coolies: from seven in the morning to 12 in the afternoon and from two in the afternoon to six in the evening. Their salary was fixed at two *kupang* per day. These regulations were aimed at curbing the bad behaviour of road users, as excessive loads and frequent use affected the condition and durability of the roads.[62]

It was also proposed that all road users be taxed based on the nature of their carriages. Pleasure vehicles were to pay SpD 0.25. The tax on all carts was SpD 0.35 per cent, with SpD 0.25 tax on all horses. The owners of land in the hinterland were also required to pay road taxes, based on the size of the land fronting the road. All these sources of income were then utilized to maintain the roads, streets and bridges.[63]

Another concern of the administration was the supply of safe and clean water for daily consumption. In the early period, clean water was scarce, especially during the dry season, while water from wells was not sufficient to accommodate the increasing population. In the early years water was

Table 43: Income from the tax on carts and road users in Penang in 1807

Type of carriage	Income derived in SpD
120 pleasure carriages	360.00
100 carts	300.00
400 horses	1,200.00
Total	1,860.00

Source: G/34/18.

Table 44: Revenue from rents, duties and sale of government property, 1825 to 1828

Heads of revenue	1825/26	1826/27	1827/28	Grand total	Arrears 1825–1828
Quit rent	13,392.13	14,678.14	4,335.7	32,407.3	4,690.8
House rent	442.9	723.2	720.0	1,885.11	-
Duties on sales of houses and lands	2,703.1	1,696.15	1,986.9	6,386.10	-
Fees on bill of sale	1,025.1	683.3	509.0	2,217.4	-
Shop tax	497.12	153.1	157.4	808.2	-
Ground rent			147.5	147.5	-
Duties on timber		3,160.13	2,359.7	5,520.4	-
Ground sold		378.14	842	1,220.14	-
Total	18,060.35	21,472.16	11,058.2	50,592.15	4,690.8

Source: F/4/1140 30268.

carried by carriers from wells and rivers to public buildings and areas. Since Penang was a port for naval and commercial traders, there was a need for a good water supply system for the ships that called at the port. Many complaints were raised by port users that the port was supplying brackish water not fit for human consumption. Most water supplied to the vessels was taken from the Penang River at the junction where the river water met salt water, and its quality tended to deteriorate during the dry season. In 1805, Farquhar, the new Governor, devised a new system by taking fresh water from the interior.[64]

Under this new system, pipes were connected to the waterfalls and rivers in the hinterland, six miles from the town, to supply the whole community and the ports with fresh water. This system generated income. The price of water consumed by a household was determined by the number of people in the house. Homes with more than six inhabitants were charged SpD 2.00 per month while those with fewer paid half a dollar per month. During this period, there were 175 households with more than six persons and 2,545 houses contained fewer than six. The annual income from water supply to the town was estimated as SpD 19,470, while that to ships and vessels was SpD 5,000.00.[65] Fresh water was also supplied to the hospitals and the garrison. With a regular and efficient water supply system installed, the administration was able to dispense with paying water carriers.[66]

THE ADMINISTRATION OF BUILDINGS, SHOPS AND MARKETS

From the early days of the English administration a main problem was to create a town less exposed to the hazards of fire. As most of the buildings in the town were privately owned, and as the fastest and cheapest way of constructing a building was to use *attap* and planks, early Penang was mostly a town of timber and *attap* buildings. Most buildings then were elevated to a certain level in order to avoid floods, which occurred during heavy rains, their style imitating traditional native houses. A contemporary traveller's note provides some information on these buildings: 'the houses of the Europeans are all elevated from the ground eight or ten feet, on arches or pillars. They seldom consist of more than one floor and are built of wood and thatched with leaves of trees. The streets were regular but the houses were detached and were built according to the native custom'.[67]

However, after the 1789 fire the administration began to encourage owners to build houses from bricks. Since bricks manufactured on the island were of poor quality the authorities imported good quality bricks from Melaka, which were more expensive due to their better quality and additional cost of transportation.[68] Although the government had encouraged brick makers to produce better bricks, the quality of bricks on the island remained poor.[69] Thus, in the short term, due to the lack of technological skills and manpower and the great demand for bricks, they had to be imported.

By 1800, a few brick buildings had been erected, mostly owned by wealthy merchants and traders.[70] Most town dwellers, however, still lived in wooden and attap houses that were prone to fire. A few more fires had to occur before a majority of town dwellers changed course and built brick buildings, so that by 1818 more brick buildings existed than any other type, as shown in Table 45 below. The town had expanded very fast and by 1818 it had 1,053 shops, out of which *attap* buildings represented only 27 per cent, while the number of brick structures had increased to more than 60 per cent. Following the 1814 fire, the government had encouraged citizens to rebuild with brick by subsidising the price of bricks. However, some residents were reluctant to do so due to the high cost of rebuilding their property.

From a traveller's description, life in the town centre in the early nineteenth century was very busy.[71] Most of the small *attap* shops sold various goods, from cloth to rice to prepared food. But along Beach Street, there were many well-built shops, one belonging to a Mr Perkins who owned an auction house. Other shops were owned by various ethnic groups.[72] Further away from the main commercial centre the buildings were different, as was the lifestyle. According to the same traveller, the other areas were surrounded by trees and the houses were with gardens.[73] These were the residential areas, more green and tranquil, away from the hustle and bustle of the business centre.

Table 45: Types and total number of buildings in Penang in 1818

Types of buildings	Nos.	Percentage
Attap	293	27.82
Plank with tile roof	125	11.87
Brick	635	60.30
Total	1,053	100

Source: F/4/633 17169.

REVENUE FARMS AS A MAIN SOURCE OF FINANCE FOR PORT-TOWN URBAN ADMINISTRATION

In an attempt to save the new colony from being converted into a customs port, revenue farms were introduced by the founders of Penang.[74] The majority of the merchants in the colony opposed taxes on trade because they believed these would discourage the flow of immigrants to the new colony and therefore hamper the policy of enlarging the population. It was also argued that taxes would also hinder the progress of commerce in the port-town. Another means suggested for increasing immigration was to promote a liberal land policy by granting land in perpetuity for a nominal quit rent. Unfortunately this resulted in greedy settlers trying to own more land than they could manage.[75] The authorities also felt that if they decided to get revenue from taxes on cultivation, it would be impossible to encourage cultivators to venture into growing crops such as spices. Thus, the only choice for the government was to sell revenue farms, such as opium, *arak* (liquor made from rice and liquor extracted from coconut palm) and gambling, which would produce an income to maintain administrative costs.[76]

The five main revenue farms were the opium, *arak*, toddy (liquor made from rice) and *baang* (liquor made from rice and liquor extracted from coconut palm), *sirih* and pork farms.[77] They were sold through public auction and those who succeeded in their bidding had to give security in the form of land, property and a guarantor. The earliest revenue farm, introduced in 1788, was the *arak* farm, which yielded, in that year, a revenue of SpD 780.00. Three years later, it gave a revenue of SpD 4,835.00, six times the first year. The opium farm was introduced in 1791 and it immediately reaped a revenue of SpD 3,499.00. In 1793 the gaming (gambling) farm was introduced, yielding its first revenue of SpD 9,500.00. In 1799, the total revenue collected from the three farms was SpD 29,520.00. In 1800, two more farms were allowed, namely the *attap* (roofing made from leaves) and tobacco farms. However, the income from both these new farms was not as high as that from the earlier three farms. Later, in 1804, the *sirih*/betel leaf farm was also introduced. Then in 1805 five additional new farms were added: the pork, oil, ghee, hogslard (prepared pig's fat) and firewood farms. However, the oil, ghee and hogslard farms only lasted for three years, being abolished in 1807 because not much profit was obtained from them. Similarly, the tobacco farm was abolished in 1806. The government introduced two new farms, the salt farm in 1805 and the toddy and *baang* farm in 1808. The salt farm lasted for only two years again because of no profit. By the end of the 1820s, only five farms had survived: the opium, *arak*, *sirih*, toddy and *baung*, and pork.[78]

The gaming farms, which produced the highest revenue for the government, were abolished in 1811.[79] These were closed because most Europeans opposed them on the grounds that they encouraged immoral behaviour and brought social ills and vices to the town.[80] The opium, pork and *arak* farms were managed by the Chinese, as the majority of the people who consumed these items were Chinese, the other ethnic groups consuming only a small amount of the products from these farms. On the other hand, the *sirih* and toddy and *baang* farms were mostly frequented by the Chulias and Malays. These farms were almost always owned by the Chulias.

Although revenue farms provided the major income for the administration, the money received was irregular and sometimes the farmers did not fulfill their obligations as stated in the contract. Basically, the problems in irregularities of payment can be viewed from two main perspectives: firstly, the problems faced by the farmers, and secondly, by the government. The problems faced by most of the farmers were rivalry amongst the various Chinese groups to control the lucrative farms; natural disasters, such as fire;[81] epidemics, such as cholera;[82] and overestimation of the value of the farms.[83] On the other hand, the government's problem concerned its inability to police the smuggling activities by Chinese secret societies.[84] Despite regulations regarding the selling and buying of items listed under the revenue farms, enforcement was limited, so that smuggling was rampant.[85] Besides the weakness of the police department, abuses such as corruption amongst the higher officials aggravated the farmers' problems.[86]

In 1806–7, bad debts incurred by revenue farmers cost the government up to SpD 17,057. The highest bad debt, which amounted to SpD 8,250.00, came from the Georgetown *arak* farms.[87] This was followed by the oil, ghee and hogslard farms, with a total debt of SpD 1,900.00, while the pork farm had a debt of SpD 1,500.00. Although the government had foreclosed the mortgages of the Georgetown *arak* farms, it only retrieved a sum of SpD 1,185.00, because when the farmers offered their security in 1806, the value of land was very high, but when sold at an auction in 1815, the value had declined due to a depressed property market following a fall in trade and pepper prices.

Table 46: Unpaid arrears (bad debts) of revenue farms in Penang from 1806–13

Years	Arrears (bad debts) in SpD
1806–07	17,057
1807–08	8,374
1808–09	9,228
1809–10	1,575
1810–11	1,143
1811–12	17,461.30
1812–13	1,540
1813–14	7,890
1815–16	4,280
Total	68,548.30

Source: G/34/50.

Between 1810 and 1815, the largest number of bad debts from revenue farms was in the year 1811–12, when the government was owed SpD 17,461.30 as a result of the great fire in 1812, which nearly burnt the whole business district. Most of the large revenue farmers, for example those in the opium, *arak* and *sirih* (betel leaf) business, suffered greatly after the fire. However, the largest amount of bad debt came from the Georgetown and Jamestown *arak* farms, which owed SpD 9,235.00, a debt settled only on 11 January 1815. The Georgetown and Jamestown opium farms' debt in 1811–12 was SpD 6,500.00. The government only received part of the payment when the debtors sold rice and grains to the government storekeeper. However, due to the heavy losses incurred by the farmers after the fire, the government decided to write off the debt. The same thing also happened to the *sirih* farms, which were likewise affected by the 1812 fire and which owed the government SpD 1,726.30. The biggest debtors to the government were Che Wan, who owed SpD 5,070; Low Amee whose debt stood at SpD 7,465; Chee Seong and Che Toa with a debt of SpD 6,938.00; while Che Dee and Chee Sue owed SpD 3,000.00.[88]

Prior to 1806, there were no serious complaints by the revenue farmers. The first known problem only surfaced after 1806. Che Owe, owner of a betel leaf farm and indebted to the government to an amount of SpD 2,020.00, pleaded his inability to pay and proposed that his mortgage bond be sold.[89] However, after his securities were sold he still owed the government a balance of SpD 1,747.00. The Committee of Assessors on tax farmers was later informed that Chee Owe had been killed at sea in September 1806. His widow, Choo, and his father, Loksoon, pleaded their inability to pay the balance. Unfortunately, Che Owe's land that was mortgaged for the payment of his debt had depreciated in value. The government nevertheless insisted that the deceased's debt had to be settled by monthly payments of SpD 200.00. By the end of 1808, Che Owe's debt balance was SpD 400.00. His family was unable to settle that amount and insisted that their security be sold so that the proceeds would pay off the debt.

Several other cases of indebtedness had to be faced by the administration in1806. Teequa, owner of the Georgetown *arak* farm who owed the government SpD 8,250, absconded from the island after paying SpD 5,000. His father-in-law, Affong, the owner of the collateral property, then mortgaged his property to pay off the debt. Che Hap, a pork farmer, owed the government SpD 2,300 but paid off his debt by arranging to spread out the repayment in monthly installments of SpD 800.[90]

Most of the large debtors paid their debts to the administration by selling off their security or mortgages. Those who died left families or their executor to settle their debts.[91] For example, in 1818, when Che Im died, he owed the government SpD 11,938 in arrears from various revenue farms.[92] On 1 January 1818, the executor of Che Im's estate paid half of the amount owed and then paid off the other half through installments with surety and mortgages of property.

The question arises as to why many farmers in Penang were unable to pay their monthly installments and why some were heavily in debt to the government. The Collector of Customs and Inland Revenue thought there was no truth that the farmers were incurring losses. In 1825 they conducted an investigation of all farms in Penang. The results revealed that the farmers were making profits and yet they were always complaining of making losses. The government's conclusion was that farmers did not tell the truth, as they wanted to avoid paying higher taxes. Since the population of the colony was increasing every year, there was no reason why the farmers should end up with losses. For example, the *arak* farms catered to 5,000 to 6,000 people in the town who consumed *arak*. Almost all the communities drank *arak*, including the Europeans. Thus, the revenue from the sale of liquor could not be less than SpD 4,000.00 a month. The government believed that more than SpD 50,000.00 was collected yearly by the *arak* farmers. Therefore there was no reasonable explanation for the farmer ending up in debt.[93] Table 47 opposite shows the monthly expenditure of an *arak* farm in Penang. From the table it shows that a farmer's monthly expenditure was small and there was little justification for an arak farmer to claim that he had suffered losses.

Table 47: Monthly management expenditure of the *arak* farmers in 1825

Items	Costs per month in SpD
1 Chinese headman	30.00
1 Chinese writer	15.00
2 Chinese shopmen at 8 *pice**	16.00
2 Chinese distillers at 8 *pice*	16.00
2 Chinese assistant distillers at 7 *pice*	14.00
2 Chinese under-shopmen at 6 *pice*	12.00
4 Chinese woodcutters and servants	24.00
1 Chinese peon in charge of liquor godown	8.00
1 Chinese cook	7.00
8 peons at 6 *pice*	48.00
2 Chulia peons at 5 *pice*	10.00
Total expenditure of an *arak* farm	200.00

Note: See 'Currencies, Weights and Measurements' in preliminary pages.

Source: G/34/105.

Similar problems were unearthed by the government among the toddy and *baang* farmers. The average number of people who consumed toddy and *baang* was 1,000 and the majority came from the Chulia and Bengali communities, with a small percentage from the other Asians. About 800 to 900 bottles of toddy were sold per day in Penang and about 400 to 450 bottles were consumed in the interior. Toddy was sold at 5 *pice* per bottle and *baang* at 12 to 18 *pice* per bottle. Occasionally the price of *toddy* and *baang* would increase to 20 *pice* per bottle based on demand from consumers. The average earnings of the toddy and *baang* farms was 75 dollars a day. Thus, in a month, a toddy and *baang* farmer could earn SpD 2,250.00, and in a year up to SpD 27,000.00. Only during the rainy season was the supply of *bang* interrupted because heavy rainfall could spoil the liquor, which was collected from the palm trees. Hence, the government could not understand why toddy and *baang* farmers always complained that they were having problems. S*irih* or betel leaf farmers also made similar claims. Yet their monthly return was estimated at SpD 730.00, so the government found no truth in their claims to facing a predicament.[94]

In the 1820s, it was reported that about 10,000 persons consumed opium in Penang and its territory. About 5,000 people consumed opium daily and the volume of opium sold was 31.5 chests a year. In 1825 the consumption of a chest of opium was valued at 8,400 dollars and the total consumed over a year was set at SpD 100,800.[95] Table 48 below clearly shows that the farmers made profits and not losses. However, the figures do not take into account the smuggling and illegal trading that went on in the opium business. But even if losses due to smuggling activities were taken into account, the farmers could still make a profit, and not losses as stated in their complaints, because, as shown in the table below, most farmers enjoyed profits of 70 per cent or more from their business.

Table 48: Average annual expenses and net profit of revenue farmers on Prince of Wales Island in 1825

Farms	Receipts	Expenses	Net profit	Farmers' profit (%)
Opium	100,800	30,000	70,800	70.23
Arak	50,000	12,100	37,900	75.80
Toddy and baang	27,000	4,500	22,500	83.30
Sirih or betel leaf	8,760	1,500	7,260	82.80
Total	185,760	48,700	137,060	73.78

Source: G/34/105.

Although complaints were carefully investigated by the Collector of Customs and Inland Revenue, and occasionally the government appointed a Committee of Assessors to study them, in general complaints were responded to immediately only if they were related to the rules and regulations of farms. In these cases, the committee would analyse the problems carefully and then decide if amendments to the laws and regulations were necessary.

Although the administration was rather tardy in responding to the farmers' plight with regard to law enforcement, curbing smuggling activities and clan rivalry among the Chinese, from time to time it gave serious consideration to complaints and acted on them. In 1818, as a result of various complaints, the government passed a regulation affecting the sirih farmers.[96] They had complained of an inability to make profits due to smuggling. The government later introduced a new regulation effective from 22 June 1818, which stipulated that all hired carriages on hire by natives and buffalo carts would be subjected to examination by the sirih farmer in areas assigned to the farmer. The farmer and his assistant were authorized to search all premises or places and, if they discovered any sirih in hired carriages or in any buffalo carts, that sirih could be seized. The owner of the said carriage or buffalo cart would be convicted and fined SpD 5.00 for each and every offence committed and the *sirih* and vehicle, forfeited. Further regulations prohibited any person to land imported *sirih* at any place other than that for which a permit had been obtained from the farmer. Any person caught violating the regulation would be convicted, forced to forfeit their *sirih* and pay a sum of SpD 5.00 for each offence.

However, in 1824, the *sirih* farmers were not satisfied with the additional regulations. They demanded that stringent steps be taken to prevent smuggling.[97] For example, Jalabidin, a *sirih* farmer, proposed to the government in 1824 that the four shelter-houses for selling *sirih*, allowed by the regulations, should be reduced to only one. This was because, during his term as tenant in 1822–23, he had built four shelter-houses but only the shelter-house in Beach Street was being commonly used by the importers. He also suggested that the 20 bundles of *sirih* allowed to all persons importing *sirih* for their own consumption, which was not taxed, should be reduced to only five leaves of *sirih* individually. Moreover, if they were found to possess more than that amount, then the person should be punished. Jalabidin made these proposals because he had suffered losses of more than 1,500 dollars ever since he owned the farm, due to drought that affected the production of *sirih*. However, his ideas were rejected by the government on the grounds that they would create inconvenience to the public.

In 1825, three opium farmers, Che Ee, Che Toa and Beng, suggested to the government that the fines and punishments meted out to opium smugglers[98] be enforced to the fullest extent by the police and each fine imposed be shared equally by the farmer, the government and the informer. The practice had been to bring the offender to the police station, where he was usually made to pay a fine of only SpD 20.00. This was found to be inadequate and if the farmer preferred a heavier penalty, he had to appeal to the Court of Judicature. Many offenders were released by the court because they could not be charged twice for the same offence. The farmers therefore suggested that the police be given greater powers to impose heavier fines and not merely a maximum of SpD 20.00.

In 1814, the Governor in Council passed a regulation stating that any person not a tavern keeper or not authorized by the holder of a farm, who secretly obtained spirituous liquors, would be fined 100 dollars for the first offence. All persons found guilty smuggling liquor would be punished with the same penalty. The fines were to be shared equally by the three parties concerned, namely, the government, the informer and the farmer.[99]

Pork farmers also had their own reason for being discontented. In 1828 a pork farmer complained that hogs were being killed at a premise owned by a person by the name of Low Amee. An investigation was carried out and, when the farmer insisted on entering the premise, a fight broke out. The accused, however, denied having slaughtered the hogs on his premises even though there were traces of the deed having been done there. Despite the farmer becoming very upset and the presence of police at the scene, Low Amee was released and not prosecuted.[100] The pork farmer also made a complaint with regard to the clause in the 1814 regulations on illegal trading and killing of hogs which specified a fine of 50 dollars as fees for the court's proceedings. The farmer ended up having to hire a lawyer who charged a fee of 25 dollars, and the accused was fined only 5 dollars. If the accused had been convicted, he would have been fined 55 dollars. The farmer rightly complained that this was unfair because a settlement through court proceedings would have made him poorer by 20 dollars.[101]

A significant problem faced by revenue farmers was the attitude of the government in relation to the enforcement of law and the curbing of smuggling activities. Although the farmers were given the authority to bring smugglers before the court, the authorities did not take this matter seriously. Farmers were seldom assisted by the police and they themselves did not have sufficient men to look after their interests. The government was not sympathetic to their plight. The *arak* and the toddy farmers had made several complaints about smuggling activities but to no avail. In the end they had to handle their own problems in the best way they could to fight illicit trading. The office of the Collector of Inland Revenues had no resources to aid the farmers, and the excuse it gave was its powerless because local regulations were vested in the Governor's office. Furthermore, the government felt that it had already provided the channel for solving the problem through the provision of the courts, before which offenders could be brought. Beyond that nothing else could be done for the farmers. The government did admit that there was a serious problem with smuggling but claimed they did not have the manpower to control it. However, it assured the farmers that if sufficient proof of smuggling was given, then the police would act on it and even issue a warrant to enter houses and seize smuggled items.[102]

The activities of the Chinese secret societies had in fact created difficulties for both the farmer and the police in relation to the problems of smuggling. Many of the smuggling cases reported by the farmers were associated with such activities.[103] These secret societies were violent in character, and due to the lack of power and enforcement by the police, they were able to get away with illegal activities. The secret societies also interfered with pricing by intimidation in order to destroy a farmer's income and business. Thus, the farmers felt that major and drastic actions had to be taken in cases involving the activities of secret societies with large numbers of followers.[104]

The government regulations regarding farms were also unsatisfactory.[105] In 1829–30, the opium and *arak* farmers believed that by purchasing their farms they would be considered, through the regulations, as owners of the farms, possessing exclusive privileges recognised by the Court of Judicature. However, this was not so because when four cases involving smuggling were put on trial in the Magistrate's Court in Penang in 1829, it was discovered that the laws regarding tax farms were not binding. Of the four cases, judgements were made on two but the other two cases were put on hold until a reference was received from the judge of the Supreme Court in Calcutta.[106] Calcutta brought down the judgement that the regulations on the farms in the colony were illegal, which led to the offenders being acquitted and discharged from jail. The Supreme Court in Calcutta reached this verdict because the regulations regarding tax farms in Penang were not gazetted and made into law. As a result, the farmers suffered heavy losses.

As a result of this, there was a sharp increase in two offences: the smuggling of *arak* and opium and the selling of illegal goods in large quantities.[107] After the Bengal ruling all the regulations in the colony were reviewed in order to make them legal and binding on the community. The *arak* and opium farmers were required to pay their rent until the month of June 1829 and all farm activities were halted until the new laws and regulations could be enforced legally. The farmers sought compensation because they had to pay both legal fees and the expenses for maintaining the smugglers during their confinement in jail.[108] Some farmers were also required to show their account books to the authorities in order to prove that they had suffered losses. They included pork farmers who claimed that smugglers from Trang (southern Thailand) and Junk Ceylon (southern Thailand) had brought in cheap pork to Georgetown, which had affected their farms.[109]

SOCIAL AND WELFARE SERVICES IN PENANG

Unlike the Dutch, the British did not contribute much to social services for the benefit of the community in Penang. The government was reluctant even to build an Anglican church for the English Anglican community, while the Catholics built their own church as soon as the island was occupied in 1786.[110] Despite there being a Catholic church that served mostly the Portuguese-Eurasians and Asian converts, mainly from Siam, the English Anglican was without a place of worship for a long time.[111] In fact this drew a comment from Governor George Leith, who observed, 'there never has been either a clergyman or church at Prince of Wales Island. It is not necessary to dwell upon the many serious evils which must naturally result from this cause'.[112] But a church was not built during his term of office, probably because there were other more pressing needs to be met. Only in 1818 was an Anglican Church, called St. George Church, built after much persuasion and pressure from the Anglican community, made up mostly of Europeans.[113] The Church was built by Christian missionaries with a little financial help from the government.

In general, the religious affairs of the town were left to the various ethnic groups to organize. There were mosques, churches and temples in Penang as a result of the resourcefulness of the population. The Capitan mosque at Pitt Street was built in the early nineteenth century by the Capitan of the Chulia, Kadir Maiden, who was a *Jawi Pekan*. Most of the *Jawi Pekan* and the Chulia Moslems used the Capitan mosque as their major religious meet-ing place. The Malays, under their Capitan, Tuanku Syed Hussain, had the use of another mosque named the Aceh mosque, on Aceh Street, a pre-dominantly Malay area. The mosque was probably built in the 1790s by Tuanku Syed Hussain who was noted for his wealth.[114] The Chinese had their own temple on a piece of land given by the government. The funds to build the temple came from the Chinese community in the town and the island. Other communities also had their own places of worship. As noted by James Low:

> [T]he Hindus have a small temple in the town and there is another of moderate size but a chaste order of Indian architecture situated in the country near Suffolk House. ... The Siamese have a rather pretty temple at Pulau Tikus and on the opposite side of the road is a Bur-man. There is another and smaller Siamese pagoda at Batu Lanchang to the southward of the town.[115]

The government also did not provide any social services, such as an orphanage or credit facilities for the inhabitants. Unlike Dutch-Melaka, the only credit facility offered was established by the wealthy merchant, James Scott.[116] Furthermore, the Chinese Poor House, an institute established for humanitarian purposes, such as helping the poor and sick Chinese and also natives, was established by the Chinese community; revenue from the pork farm was used to maintain this institution. [117]

CONCLUSION

Penang, as the first English colony in Southeast Asia and the furthest of the EIC outposts in Asia, was a frontier settlement. For many years after its opening in 1786, it was not considered a vital settlement by Calcutta, so that its early history was one of struggle to prove that it could provide trade benefits and that its strategic location would enable the Company to control the Eastern trade route. No doubt this situation was an impediment to its development and shaped the way it was administered, at least in the early years. The burden of opening a new settlement was further exacerbated by the lack of financial support from EIC headquarters in Calcutta.

As we have seen, it was not until 1794, the year Francis Light died, that he was formally appointed as the Superintendent of Penang and received instructions from Calcutta on legal matters in the running of the new colony. In the circumstances, much was left to the ingenuity and resourcefulness of the pioneers who governed Penang. But it was founded by a country trader who, only later, became an EIC official and its early development was controlled by a few mercantile personalities whose main focus was on trade. This meant that less attention was given to the town's administration until the pioneers were replaced by better trained administrators. Thus, only after Light's death did the semblance of an ordered administration begin to emerge.

On the whole, Penang's administration was characterized by a makeshift and ad hoc approach to development. Not until 1795 was a tax of some sort introduced to raise revenues, while social and public amenities remained poor for a long time. It is not clear whether the ad hoc nature of the administration was due to a minimalist approach to governance or a lack of financial means, but the practice of selling public land in the early years to raise money for development and then of buying back land to develop further, could be said to be symptomatic of haphazard management.

It could also be seen that the administration did not utilize the talents of Penang's population to the fullest. Although the official community was small, instead of integrating it into the administration, as was the case with the Dutch in Melaka, the authorities in Penang chose a system of occasionally appointing influential private individuals to help run the town. This was done through the system of appointing ad hoc committees instead of permanent bodies. Again it is not clear why this was the case. It could well have been due to the bad experience Macdonald went through with the mercantile community, so that there was fear of giving their members more influence than they already had. But whatever the reason, the temporary nature of the Committee of Assessors discouraged continuity and experience and would have worked, to some degree, against effective administration.

On the whole, Penang progressed, albeit slowly and stumblingly, and proof of its success was the ability to attract new arrivals, not only traders but settlers who were prepared to engage in longer-term activities, such as in agriculture, and remain permanently. At the same time, as we shall see, the population of Penang created for themselves a social environment that had all the features of a viable and permanent society.

NOTES

1   C.H. Phillips, *The East India Company 1784–1834*, Manchester: Manchester University Press, 1961, p. 24.

2   For further discussion on the history of EIC and its administration, see K.N. Chaudhuri, *The English East India Company: The Study of an Early joint stock company 1600–1640*, London: Frank Cass, 1965; Brain Gardner, *The East India Company*, London: Rupert Hart-Davis, 1971; Philip Lawson, *The East India Company: A History*, London: Longman, 1993; and John Keay, *The Honourable Company: A History of the English East India Company*, London: Harper Collins, 1991.

3   See C.H. Phillips, *The East India Company 1784–1834*, p.16. To him: 'the method of appointing the Company servants by nomination had its merits; the nominees usually sprang from families with India, they carried out with them family traditions of service, and they were welcomed in India by family friends Indian and European'.

4   See, for example, 'Notices of Pinang', *JIA*, vol 5, 1851, pp. 400–429.

5   In September 1805, a new administration was formed for Penang, headed by a Governor and Council. Phillip Dundas was appointed as Governor and Treasurer. Governor Dundas had previously served in the Bombay marine and had been Master Attendant there. A nephew of Lord Melville, he was selected for the post of Governor of Penang because of his knowledge and experience of nautical affairs, qualifications suited to the aim of turning Penang into a naval depot and ship building port. Governor Dundas was assisted by his Council. At that time, the first and leading officer was John Hope Oliphant, the Warehouse Keeper and Paymaster. He was allowed a commission of 3 per cent on sales of Company goods and his income, including his commission, was to be revised annually. The second was Alexander Gray, Superintendent and Paymaster of marine, and a naval and military storekeeper. He was also allowed the same commission in addition to his salary. The third was Colonel Norman Macalister. The other officers included Henry Shephard Pearson, Council secretary; Thomas Raffles, assistant secretary; James Phillip Hobson, Accountant and auditor; William Robinson, Assistant accountant; Quintin Dick Thomson, Sub-warehouse-keeper and paymaster; W.E. Phillip, Collector of customs and land revenue; John Erskrine, Assistant to the Superintendent and storekeeper of marine and marine paymaster; William Dick, Surgeon; and 2 Assistant Surgeons and 10 writers. For further reference, see 'Notices of Pinang', *JIA*, Vol. iv, 1852, pp.18–22.

6   See 'Notices of Pinang', *JIA*, Vol. iv, 1850, p. 661. See also A.M. Skinner, 'Memoir of Captain Francis Light', pp. 1–17.

7   C.H. Phillips, *The East India Company 1784–1834*, p. 8. Phillips points out that '...each week the court of Directors met at least once, on Wednesday, and often 3 times. All letters from India and appeals from their servants were taken to court, final decisions were taken on reports of sub-committees and dispatches for India were read and signed by at least 13 Directors'.

8   For further reference, see, for example: M.B. Hooker (ed.), *The Laws of Southeast Asia, Vol. II: European Laws in Southeast Asia*, pp. 299–446; see also Tan Soo Chye, 'A Note on Early Legislation in Penang', *JMBRAS*, 23(1), 1950, pp. 100–107; and A.M. Skinner, 'Memoir of Captain Francis Light', pp. 1–17.

9   See also the development of law and order in Penang and the problems faced by Mr Dickens, judge and magistrate of Prince of Wales Island, regarding separation of power and authority between the Superintendent and the police magistrate and the court, in Appendix 1 in G/34/11.

10 For further discussion, see, for example, C.D. Cowan, 'Early Penang and the rise of Singapore', p. 4.

11 For further reference on the history of Straits Settlements, see M.C. Turnbull, *The Straits Settlements, 1826–67: Indian Presidency to Crown Colony*, Singapore: Oxford University Press, 1972.

12 Attap or Artab refers to the palm leaves used in thatching and house-building.

13 Letter from Phllip Mannington, dated 13 May 1795, in G/34/7.

14 This tax was to be collected on all houses and shops belonging to the Chinese, Malays, Bugis, Chulias, Moors, Malabars either merchants, shopkeepers or tradesmen of different occupations according to the extent of the grounds around the house or the size or rental price of the houses, see, G/34/7.

15 Under his administration, Major Macdonald drew up a list of officials to govern the colony. This list consisted of: First Assistant (a confidential counsellor and magistrate); Second Assistant (a collector of revenue and guardian of farms); Secretary (a confidential assistant to Superintendent); Three European clerks (for Superintendent and Assistants); two or four boys (from orphan school); Clerk of the Marshal (as superintendent of the department and of that part of Police which respects cleanliness); two European clerks (as assistants to clerk of the marshal); Head Constable and Jailor; three interpreters; three Malay writers; 12 Peons; three Native Capitans and three writers for the three native capitans. See 'Notices of Pinang', *JIA*, Vol. 5, 1851, p. 111.

16 The problems of the town were not only limited to the physical aspects, such as the hygenic level of the living quarters and the amenities but also the defence of the town. For further explanation on this, refer to a report prepared by Major Kyd in G/34/7.

17 See, for example, L.A. Mills, 'Penang 1786–1830', pp. 36–59; C.D. Cowan, 'Early Penang and the Rise of Singapore', pp. 3–7.

18 John Cameron, *Our Tropical Possessions in Malayan India*, London: Smith, 1865, p. 312. For further discussion on the disputes between Macdonald with James Scott and the English merchants and traders in Penang, see 'Notices of Pinang', *JIA*, Vol 5, 1851, pp. 93–119.

19 See, for example, Kernial Singh Sandhu, 'Tamil and other Indian Convicts in the Straits Settlements AD 1790–1873', *Proceedings of the 1st International Conference of Tamil Studies*, Vol.1, Kuala Lumpur, 1968, pp. 197–208.

20 Report by B. Loftie, acting head surgeon, 14 February, 1810' in G/34/9.

21 Ibid.

22 Ibid.

23 Complaint made by a Chinese shopkeeper named Gee against Captain Drummond, Town Mayor, 9th February 1807, in G/34/17.

24 This committee was formed by the new Superintendent of the colony after the death of Francis Light. It comprised Major Macdonald (Superintendent and President) Messrs Mc Intyre, James Scott, Lindsay, Hutton, Roebuck, Young, David Brown, Sparran, Mackrell, Nason. Young served as Secretary. This committee consisted of the mercantile community of Georgetown. See 'Notices of Pinang', *JIA*, vol.5, 1851, p. 97.

25 On 18 August 1806, a special Committee of Assessors was formed in order to investigate the allegation that the Police Magistrate had misused his power through corruption. This Committee comprised W.E. Phillips as Chairman, and its members included James Scott, George Seton, Thomas Jones, John Dunbar. N.B. Bone and N. Bacon. This group was appointed to represent the European community. In addition, Tegua, Chewan, Chee Im, Nakhuda Tamby Sahib, Jelanbebese, Cauder Maydeen alias Kadir Maidin, Che Amaat and Che Amat Gee, and Gee Pootee were elected on behalf of the native members. However, the Committee of Assessors was not able to make further investigations on the activities of the police magistrate. This led to the appointment of new members to sit on the Committee on 22 August 1806. The new Committee consisted of John Dickens, Chairman, J.P. Hobson, and James Carnegy. It was chaired by the magistrate who later charged and prosecuted the police magistrate for corruption. The police magistrate was found guilty of all the charges. The Kellner case created a great impact on the administration, leading to the formation of a special Committee of Assessors. The Committee was set up to legislate market regulation and its first meeting was held on 8th September, 1806, chaired by W.E. Phillips, with George Seton, John Dunbar and N. Bacon as the European members. The native community was represented by Che Wan, Chee Im, Gee, Gigee Pootee and Nakhuda Tombee Saib. The Committee passed a resolution that, in compliance with the direction of the Governor and Council, the Committee was required to submit suggestions for the administration of the markets of Penang. See proceedings of a special Committee of Assessors on 25 August, 1806, in F/4/262 5837.

26 See the discussion during the meeting of the Commitee on 17 Feburary, 1806, in G/34/13. See also 'Notices of Pinang', *JIA*, Vol.5, 1851, pp. 400–429.

27 See 'Notices of Pinang', *JIA*, Vol. 5, 1851, pp. 93–119.

28 John Cameron, *Our Tropical Possessions in Malayan India*, p. 312. For further discussion on the disputes between Macdonald with James Scott and the English merchant and traders in Penang, see 'Notices of Pinang', *JIA*, Vol. 5, 1851, pp. 93–119.

29 See letter dated 12 August 1806 in G/34/14 from Douglas Wilson, a merchant in Penang, to the secretary to Governor regarding a protest related to an act committed by Kellner in G/34/14.

30 See the discussion during the meeting held on 8 September 1806, of the committee of assessors to formulate market regulation in Penang in G/34/14. The committee was presided over by W.E Phillips while the European members were George Seton, John Dunbar and Nath. Bacon. The native members consisted of Chee Wan Chee, Eam Gee, Gigee Pootee and Nahkoda Tombee.

31 See 'Currencies, Weights and Measurements' in preliminary pages.

32 The term *Panglima* means 'warrior' and the word *Pagar* literally means 'fence'. Hence *Panglima Pagar* is a person who secures a property.

33 See 'Notices of Pinang', *JIA*, Vol.5, 1851, p. 106.

34 For further discussion on the function of this court and the early problems of the administration of justice in the town, see 'Notices of Pinang', *JIA*, Vol 5, 1851, pp. 292–305.

35 Wong Choon San, *A Gallery of Chinese Kapitans*, Singapore: Government Printing Office, 1964, p. 9.

36 See, for example, an application by Syed Hussain, who asked for a written declaration to allow the Muslims to practice Islamic law, in the letter from Captain Light, dated 30 July 1792, to the Governor-General in Council at Fort William, in G/34/5.

37 Wong Choon San, *A Gallery of Chinese Kapitans*, p. 10.

38 This name appeared in the list of mortgages granted at Prince of Wales Island on 24 February 1795. On 5 August 1794, Cheki, the Chinese Capitan, mortgaged his pepper plantation at Sungai Kluang to James Scott for SpD 1,300 with an interest of 12 per cent per annum, see G/34/7. Regarding Chu Khee, see the list of Chinese inhabitants residing in Georgetown, Prince of Wales Island, in December 1788. Chu Khee came from Kedah together with 18 members of his family. He was mainly a merchant. See G/34/3. A detailed account of Capitan Koh Lay Huan can be found in Wong Choon San, *A Gallery of Chinese Kapitans*, pp. 12–15.

39 See Report of Committee, 26 October 1819, in F/4/634 17218. See also H.P. Clodd, *Malaya's First British Pioneer*, p.119.

40 Information regarding Cauder Maydeen is limited and scattered. Nevertheless, his name appeared in some of the meetings of the Committees of Assessors, including one meeting regarding the curbing of cholera affecting most of the Chulia community. See report of Committee 26 October 1819, in F/4/634 17218.

41 According to Wong Choon San in his *A Gallery of Chinese Kapitans*: '...there is negative evidence to suggest that most of the disputes amongst the Chinese were dealt with by their elders without recourse to the English way of administration of justice', see p. 10.

42 'Police regulations', in F/4/262 5837.

43 For the problems of policing the town and the problems facing the judicial system in the town, see 'Notices of Pinang', *JIA*, Vol. 5, 1851, pp. 292–305.

44 For frequent complaints on robberies committed by the Europeans and Sepoys in the town and especially at the bazaar, see letter from Philip Mannington to Captain Robert Hamilton, Fort Cornwallis, 20 November 1794, in G/34/7.

45 See, for example, James Low, *A dissertation on the soil and agriculture of the British settlement of Penang or Prince of Wales Island*, Singapore: Singapore Free Press, 1836, p. 244, where he notes: 'The police of Prince of Wales Island is chiefly and unavoidably drawn from amongst the emigrants from Bengal or Madras, a few Chinese, Malays, and *Jawi Pekans*. The Bengals or Madras were people of problems: mind degrading morally low and bad character'.

46 A gong man literally means a person who holds a gong. In Penang at that time the gong was sounded along the streets in the town to signal to the inhabitants to assemble at a place where an announcement was to be made to them.

47 See the police establishment in the Prince of Wales Island, in G/34/8. As Penang and its territories consisted of the island and a strip of the mainland opposite it, the police needed boats to perform their duty. Further, some parts of the territory were not connected by roads so that the only means of access was by rivers.

48 See new regulation passed by the Governor and Council, 22 November 1805, in G/34/12.

49 Ibid.

50 See Report of the Lieutenant-Governor in 1805, in G/34/9.

51 George Leith, *A Short Account of the Settlement* p.24. He writes: 'Georgetown is extensive, bounded to the north and east by the sea on the south by an inlet of the sea, improperly called the Praingin river and on the west by the high road. The streets which cross each other at right angles are spacious and airy; but having been at first merely lined out, without being either raised or drained, they were frequently impassable after hard rain, and at all times were dirty and filled with stagnant water.'

52 See George Leith, *A Short Account of the Settlement.* p. 24. He notes: 'This serious inconvenience is now removed as the principal streets are properly raised and drained and the remainder are now finishing. The town has in consequence improved much in appearance and cleanliness and it is reasonable to suppose will also be more healthy.'

53 Ibid., see also report from the Chairman of Assessors 22 December 1826, in G/34/115. See also memorandum respecting additional sources of revenue at Penang for example taxes on exchanging money in the bazaar, taxes on Chulias quitting the country, in Appendix 16A in G/34/9.

54 Report of the Lieutenant-Governor, in G/34/9.

55 Ibid.

56 See minute and resolution of the Boards of Trade on Captain Light's letter, Fort William 14 January 1790, in G/34/4.

57 Report by the Lieutenant-Governor, in G/34/9.

58 Report by the Lieutenant-Governor in 1805, in G/34/12; see also an account of the spice plantations on the island belonging to the Company and on private land, in extract Bengal Public Consultations, 17 April 1802, in G/34/9. For further reference on the production of spices and agricultural produce in the hinterland, see, for example, James Jackson, *Planters and Speculators.*

59 See statement of expenses incurred for building roads and bridges, for example, Mr Smith building roads to Batu Lanchang; Penghulu Laung for building road across the hill to Ayer Hitam; Mr Smith for building road to Sungai Kluang; James Scott for building the Burmah Road; and Mr Smith for building and maintaining several roads in the town and in the hinterland, in G/34/9.

60 See the discussion at the meeting of the Committee of Land Holders presided over by James Scott and attended by other members, James P. Hobson, John Dunbar, Thomas McQuid, David Brown, Che Wan, Che Im and Amy on 6 August 1807, in G/34/18; see also the meeting of the committee on 17 August 1807, in G/34/18; and see the meeting on 3 September 1807, in G/34/18.

61 The term *bahara* is a measurement; one *bahara* amounting to 3 *pikuls* or 400lbs. See C.W. Cowan, 'Early Penang', p. 21.

62 See discussion at the meeting of the committee of land holders presided over by James Scott, and attended by other members, James P. Hobson, John Dunbar, Thomas McQuid, David Brown, Che Wan, Che Im and Amy on 6 August 1807, in G/34/18. See also the meeting of the committee on 17 August 1807, in G/34/18 and on 3 September 1807, in G/34/18.

63 Ibid., For further reference on the expenditure of the government on building and maintaining roads and bridges, see minute of the President, 18 August 1820, in G/34/76.

64 See report by the Lieutenant-Governor, in G/34/9.

65 See Appendix 6 in the Lieutenant-Governor's reports, in G/34/9.

66 Report of the special meeting of the Committee of Assessors, 17 February 1806, in G/34/13; see also the comment on the report, 20 February 1806, in G/34/13.

67 James Wathen, *Journal of a Voyage in 1811 and 1812 to Madras and China; Returning by the Cape of Good Hope and St. Helena,* London: J. Nichols and son, 1814, p. 130.

68   Superintendent of Engineers to Raffles, 28 Feb 1807, in SSFR, vol. 17.

69   In 1787, Francis Light had encouraged the Chinese to manufacture bricks for the buildings. Since the price of bricks sold by Chinese manufacturers was very high, Francis Light employed people from Bombay and Kafirs to keep the price down. However, the bricks produced by the Bombay and Kafir workers were of very poor quality. Thus, the production of cheaper bricks of good quality continued to be a major problem for the British administration. See letter by Captain Light, 7 October 1787, in G/34/3.

70   George Leith, *A Short Account of the Settlement*, p.26. Most of the brick buildings were owned by merchants and traders. For example, Francis Light owned two brick houses and offices valued at $16,000; James Scott had a brick house valued at $8,000; Thomas Pigou, a brick house valued at $4,500; James Hutton, a brick house valued at $2,500; James Gardyne, a brick house valued at $3,200; Geo Halsan, a brick house valued at $3,500; James Harrison, a brick house valued at $2,000; Mr Perkins, a brick house valued at $2,000; and Tuanku Syed Hussain, a brick house valued at $6,000. For further reference, see *Penang Past and Present 1786–1963*, City Council of Georgetown, 1966, p. 106.

71   Ibid. p. 133.

72   Ibid, p. 134.

73   Ibid. pp. 136–146.

74   A good discussion on the revenue farms of Penang can be found in Wong Lin Ken, 'The Revenue Farms of Prince of Wales Island, 1805–1830', in *Journal of the South Seas Society*, Vol. 19, 1964, pp. 56–127. See also T. Braddell, *Statistics of the British Possessions in the Straits of Malacca*. For further discussion on the history of revenue farms in Malaya, see John Butcher and Howard Dick (eds), *The Rise and Fall of Revenue Farming Business Elites and the Emergence of the Modern State in Southeast Asia*.

75   See dispatches from the Court of Directors, 20 September 1805, in 'Notices of Pinang', *JIA*, Vol. vi, 1852, p. 27.

76   See Appendix 4: Penang Revenue Farms 1788–1830, in Nordin Hussin, 'Melaka and Penang 1780–1830', pp. 426–428. See also minute by the President, dated 15 December 1825, on the review of tax farming, in G/34/105.

77   See minute by the President, dated 15 December 1825, on the review of tax farming, in G/34/105.

78   See Appendix 4: Penang Revenue Farms 1788–1830, in Nordin Hussin, 'Melaka and Penang 1780–1830', pp. 426–428.

79   The government had to abolish the gaming farm due to pressure from the town's European community. They believed that gambling was a great vice which adversely affected the way of life of the natives and the other inhabitants in the town. See minute by the President, 26 February 1818, in G/34/65. See also minute of the President, 26th February 1818, in F/4/633 17170 and minute by Mr. Phillip, 27th February 1818.

80   Minute by the President, 26 February 1818, in G/34/65. See also R. Counter, Superintendent of Police, 10 March 1818, in G/34/65; Minute of the President 26 February 1818, in F/4/633 17170; T. Braddell, 'Gambling and Opium Smoking in the Straits of Malacca', *JIA*, 1856, vol. 1, pp. 66–83; and, Wong Lin Ken, 'The Revenue Farms', pp. 84–92.

81   See the petition by Lowe Ammee, Teequa (*arak* farmer), and Che Im (opium farmer), in G/34/35.

82   See Petition of opium farmers, Cha Eu, Ben San and Che Sah, 22 November 1819, in G/34/72; see also petition from *arak* farmers Ahoo and Achee, in G/34/72; Petition of pork farmers Che Ee, Koke Tye and Che Toah, 25 November 1819, in G/34/72; Petition from *sirih* farmer, Boochuan 7 December 1819, in G/34/72; and a letter from Collector of Customs and Land Revenue to Secretary to Governor, dated 6 December 1819, in G/34/72.

83   See Petition of pork farmers, Amboon and Ah Keow, 31 May 1830, in G/34/33.

84   In 1829 the rivalry between the Chinchew and Cantonese was brought to the attention of the Collector of Customs and Land Revenue, based on the complaint made by the opium farmers. See the petition of Che Leong, Bengsan, Layho, Che Tong, Ko Kochye, Watsoye and Chew Ong, in G/34/129. See also the trial of the offenders, in G/34/130;

and see also Wong Lin Ken, 'The Revenue Farms', pp.122–127. See also the report on the Chinese secret societies in Penang by R. Caunter, dated, 21 May 1825, in G/34/101.

85 There were many petitions by the revenue farms regarding this matter. For example, see the petition by Chee Wan dated 13 October 1806, in G/34/15. See also petition from pork farmer Cha Sye, in G/34/38; and Petition of opium farmers Che Leong, Bengsan, Layho, Che Tong, Ko Kochye, Watsoye and Chew Ong, not dated, in G/34/129.

86 See, for example, testimony of Inchun and Chee Wan, gaming/gambling farmers on the Police Magistrate Kellner asking for favours, in Appendix to the report of the Committee appointed by the Governor and Council on 22 August 1806, in F/4/262 5837.

87 The Georgetown *arak* farm refers to the farm in Penang town. The Jamestown *arak* farm was located in Jamestown, a small town on the far south of the island. Jamestown was built by James Scott. Although there were suggestions that the town (Penang) would be relocated to Jamestown, the plan remained only on paper. Not much is known about the development of Jamestown. Later it vanished from the map of the island. According to W.H. Medhurst, 'Jamestown is a small village inhabited principally by Chinese and its distance about 10 miles from Penang (Georgetown) the seat of government. The country about Jamestown is well cultivated and inhabited by 4 to 5,000 Chinese and Malays....' See Medhurst's letter, dated 22 November 1820, in Council of world missionary archives of the London Missionary Society, Ultra Ganga Jacket C, folder 2, box 1.

88 See the petition from Che Wan dated 4 March 1814, in G/34/43. Abstract account of outstanding debts due to the Company from individuals on 30 April 1817, in G/34/61; see also petitioner of Oosoy opium farm, 28 April 1817, in G/34/61.

89 See report by Custom and Inland Revenue Office, in G/34/23.

90 Ibid.

91 Ibid.

92 See letter from Collector of Customs and Land Revenue, dated 25 January 1813, in G/34/38. See also letter from Che Im dated 18 January 1813, in G/34/38 and letter from R. Caunter, Superintendant of Police, 10 March 1818, in G/34/65.

93 See letter from Collector of Customs and Land Revenue, dated 25 January 1813, in G/34/38. See also letter from Che Im, dated 18 January 1813, in G/34/38, and letter from R. Caunter, Superintendant of Police, 10 March 1818, in G/34/65.

94 See Report by R. Caunter, dated 15 December 1825, in G/34/105.

95 Ibid.

96 *Sirih* farm regulations, 22 June 1818, in G/34/66.

97 See Drafts of regulation for the better security of these revenues and the protection of the privileges and monopolies vested in their renter with suggestions from the present renter of the *sirih* farm, 4 March 1824, in G/34/94.

98 Petitions of Che Ee, Che Toa and Beng renters of the opium farm, July 1825, in G/34/102.

99 Petition of Che Ee, Che Chiang and Guan So, in G/34/123.

100 Petition from the pork farmers, in G/34/123.

101 Petition from the Pork farm, 6 October 1828, in G/34/124. See also problems regarding illegal killing of hogs and the regulations on offenders in a complaint by a petitioner, dated 11 June 1806, in G/34/13.

102 Collector of Revenue 30 May 1829, in G/34/129. See also petition of the opium farmers, 18 May 1829, in G/34/129.

103 See petition of pork farmers, Amboon and Ah Keow, 31 May 1830, in G/34/33; petition of Che Leong, Bengsan, Layho, Che Tong, Ko Kcye, Watsoye and Chew Ong, in G/34/129; petition of opium and *arak* farmers 1829/30, in G/34/129; petition from *arak* farmers, 30 September 1829 and petition of *arak*, opium and pork farmers 30 November 1829, in G/34/129. See also Wong Lin Ken, 'The Revenue Farms', pp.122–127.

104 For further discussion on the activities of secret societies in Penang, see L.F. Comber, *Chinese Secret Societies in Malaya: A survey of the Triad society from 1800–1900*, New York: Monograph of the Association for Asian studies, VI, 1959.

105 See, R. Caunter, 17 August 1829, in G/34/130. See also petition of opium and *arak* farmers 1829/30, in G/34/129; petition from *arak* farmers, 30 September 1829 and petition of *arak*, opium and pork farmers 30 November 1829, in G/34/129.

106 See Petition of opium and *arak* farmers, 1828/29, in G/34/130.

107 Ibid.

108 Ibid., See also Petition from *arak* farmers, 30 September 1829 Achee Ahing and Achong, in G/34/130.

109 See Petition of *arak*, opium and pork farmers, 30 November 1829, in G/34/130.

110 For a good reference on the history and activities of the Catholic Church in Malaya, see F.G. Lee, *The Catholic Church in Malaya*, Singapore: Eastern University Press, 1963. Lee notes that: 'Persecution broke out in Siam in 1779 and missionaries were eventually driven out of the country. Among the expelled missionaries were Fr. Coude and Gernault who, after having gone to Pondicherry, came to Kedah in 1781 and found there about eighty Christians who had previously settled in Port Queda from Siam and Malacca... In 1782, Fr. Coude was nominated Vicar Apostolic of Siam and he left for that country on the invitation of the new king who was well disposed towards the missionaries. Fr. Garnault migrated with his parishioners to Penang when Captain Francis Light succeeded in annexing the island to the British Crown in 1786 and the Governor of Penang placed a house at the disposal of the French padre', pp. 45–46. See also Robert Hunt (ed.), *Christianity in Malaysia*, Kuala Lumpur: Pelanduk, 1992.

111 Most of the Portuguese-Eurasians came from Madras, Siam and Kedah. For a detailed account, see list of Roman Catholic inhabitants, men and women and children, in Penang in December 1788, in G/34/3. See also James Low, *A dissertation on the soil and agriculture of the British settlement of Penang*, where he states: 'Roman Catholic religion: a late statement in the Prince of Wales Island Gazette makes the number of conversions in Penang amongst the Chinese alone during the past 10 years to have been 759 but the actual present number of proselytes is not given. In the same statement the number of converts in Province Wellesley is rated at about 80 Chinese. The chief pastor was the Reverend Mr. Boucho. Some converts from the Samsams or mixed descendants of Siamese and Malays. There are two Roman catholic chapels on the island also a female seminary and several schools', p. 293.

112 George Leith, *A short account of the settlement, produce and commerce of Prince of Wales Island*, p. 69.

113 See Affairs of the united Companies of merchants of England trading to the East in G/34/10. A good reference on the activities of the Anglican Church can be found in a series of letters under the title 'Council of World Missionary Archives of the London Missionary Society Ultra Ganges', kept at the SOAS Library, London.

114 The exact date is not known. However, Syed Hussain and his family came to the island in the late 1780s. Probably after many years of residence and after making a fortune on the island, he built the mosque. For further reference, see H.P. Clodd, *Malaya's First British Pioneer: The Life of Francis Light*, p. 119.

115 James Low, *A dissertation on the soil and agriculture of the British settlement of Penang*, pp. 296–297.

116 See List of Mortgages granted at Prince of Wales Island, 24 February 1795, in G/34/7.

117 See report of the late Lieutanant-Governor, 1805, in Appendix 4 in G/34/12.

CHAPTER NINE

Melaka Society, 1780–1830

INTRODUCTION

MOST ASIAN COLONIAL TOWNS ARE IDENTIFIABLE by certain features, namely a society segregated along ethnic lines, a pluralistic population of emigrants and natives and an Asian majority ruled by a European minority. Since colonial towns were created and administered by European powers within an Asian environment, the manner in which various people with different social and cultural backgrounds interacted and intermingled was intriguing. A colonial town could provide the circumstances for the meeting of East and West or several Eastern cultures, thus shaping new communities with unique cultural and social backgrounds.

Melaka, between 1780 and 1830, had all the features of a society in a colonial town. The Dutch who were the rulers were a small minority ruling over a population made up of a small group of Europeans, essentially Dutch Burghers, and a larger group of Asians. The Asians consisted of Malays, Chinese, Kelings, Moors and slaves. There was, however, another fairly large and distinctive group that had emerged in Melaka due to its long history of European domination: the Portuguese-Eurasian community, which was large enough to exist as a separate entity and resist absorption into the larger native population. This was in contrast to the products of intermarriage between migrant Asians with local women, which in the case of the migrant Chinese created the Chinese Peranakan or Baba community, and in the case of the Indian Muslims, the Jawi Pekan. The Baba Chinese were more likely to identify with the ethnic identity of the male original, while the Jawi Pekan, being Muslims, were more easily integrated with the Malay community. That being the case, and due to the fact that each was a very small minority, the administration tended to classify the Baba and Jawi Pekan with the ethnic group with which they identified. Thus the official classification of the ethnic communities did not necessarily reflect the complete ethnic divisions in the population of Melaka.

Seen from an ethnic perspective, the Dutch officials in the service of the VOC and the Dutch Burgher community belonged to the same group. The Asians, on the other hand, were diverse, not only distinguishable by colour and looks but also by cultural and religious practices. Each ethnic community tended to segregate itself from the rest, living in clusters, which facilitated social interaction and the pursuance of customs and traditions and religious practices each in its own unique way. In Melaka, the segregation was not enforced by the Dutch but came about due to earlier practices observed by communities since the days of the Melaka sultanate, when each ethnic group lived in a separate quarter. It was during that early period that a residential entity was often named after the group residing in it, thus giving rise to names such as Kampung Melayu, Kampung Keling, Kampung Jawa and Bukit Cina.

During the Dutch period, certain areas could be easily identified as belonging to, or dominated by, a particular ethnic community. The divisions however, were fluid, allowing movement into, or out of, a quarter, but the tendency for each community was to live in a group rather than in isolation. The fact that Melaka society was made up largely of migrants who came in small numbers over time would have encouraged the situation in which new migrants sought, and lived among, their own kind. Thus, the official community made up of Dutchmen lived in the reserved area in the fort of Melaka, the Burghers and other Europeans were found mostly in Herenstraat and Jonkerstraat, the prime areas, and the Portuguese-Eurasians were identified with the suburbs of Tengkera and Bandarhilir. The Chinese and the Indians, both Kelings and Moors, many of whom were engaged in business, generally lived in the town, while most Malays lived in the outskirts, tending their vegetable garden and fruit orchard.

However, as a whole, the town was a cosmopolitan centre with a cross-section of all the ethnic groups. Thus Malays, Chinese, Kelings and Moors resided in most of the streets. Newbold, who was in Melaka for three years from 1832, observed of a particular street, rather longer than the rest, in which were 'many substantial well-built houses occupied by the Dutch gentry; by Portuguese, Chinese, Chulias, Kelings and Malay inhabitants'.[1] He also mentioned that the Malays who lived in the town were 'principally those engaged in native commerce, sailors, boatmen, wealthy Hajis, and their connections'.[2] Only the fort of Melaka was reserved for the whites, its inhabitants made up mostly of Dutch officials with a few Burgher families who had been given the privilege to live there.

While the tendency was for each ethnic community to congregate together, the motivation was not always to exclude others on ethnic grounds, but to facilitate the search or pursuance of common or complementary interests or goals. Thus, where those common interests cut across ethnic lines, there was a coming together. This can be seen from the fact that the wealthy, irrespective of ethnic origin lived side by side in substantial houses, as was observed by Newbold in the early 1830s, and while Herenstraat and Jonkerstraat were the two main streets identified with wealthy Dutch Burgers, rich Asian merchants and traders resided there as well. The cosmopolitan character of the town also presented another example where commercial activities, which were centred in the town and the port, drew people from differing backgrounds to live together. Nevertheless, social and cultural differences and distance remained, a reality witnessed by Newbold when he observed that in that long street where a mixed community lived stood 'the Anglo-Chinese College, the Mission Chapel, the principal Chinese temple and the two large mosques'.[3]

In view of this social separateness, it is possible and more meaningful to study each group in isolation from the rest. This chapter will therefore look at, firstly, the European community and then study the Asian groups. As most works on Melaka have been written by European authors, their observations have tended to concentrate on the Europeans, as a result of which there is more material on this group than the others.

THE EUROPEAN COMMUNITY IN MELAKA

Melaka's position as a Dutch colonial port-town meant that at all times there was a group of Dutch officials serving in the colony. But the commercial activities of the port had also attracted a small group of Europeans, mainly Dutch Burghers, who were engaged in trading and business activities available there. As Melaka had been an important port for a long time, and under the Dutch since 1641, it also became a permanent home to a sizeable number of Europeans, Company servants or Company relatives or Dutch Burghers, who had decided to settle in Asia rather than return to Europe. Most had made their fortunes and found they could also live comfortably in the colony. Many owned property in land and houses, and as the wealthy landed gentry, they held a higher status in Melaka society than they normally would in their own homeland. Others intermarried with Eurasians or the locals and, having created strong ties locally, saw little reason to return home.[4]

The presence of the Dutch in the East over a long period of time and their possession of several colonial-ports meant that there developed an overseas Dutch community, both official and unofficial, with mutual and complementary interests and the opportunity to enter into friendships or familial relationships. This situation was assisted by the tendency of the VOC to appoint men on merit and also on family ties, and the policy of moving officials from one colony to another. Over the decades, as the officials and other Dutch men spent long periods in the East, and as the colonies flourished and living conditions improved, more men set up homes in the colonies with their families and more women came out. This greatly eased the problems of gender imbalance although there were usually more European men than women in the colonies. In early Melaka and Penang there was a pattern of widows who remarried due to this gender imbalance. Nevertheless, the ingredients for the formation of a permanent overseas Dutch community already existed, a situation that was assisted, in later years, by the fact that there were Burgher communities in Batavia, Colombo and other Dutch towns in the East that allowed some Burgher males to meet or seek their brides in these places rather than in Europe. For example, some of the Melakan Burghers had chosen their brides from other Dutch settlements in the East, such as Makassar, Batavia and Colombo.[5]

Since the Dutch ruled Melaka for more than a century, the white population that lived there could also become close-knit. This was also helped by the fact that some families had been there for several generations and had married among themselves. For example, the Baumgarten, Dieterich, Koek, Kraal, Neubronner, Overree, Rappa, Velge, Westerhout, de Wind and Williamson families had been in Melaka for several generations.[6] Adriaan Koek, who later became a prominent member of society, was born in 1759 in Melaka to the family of van Joost and Catharina de Roth, and Gerrit Leendert Baumgarten was born in Melaka in 1789 to the family of van Christiaan Godfried and Maria Catharina Velge. Note that Baumgarten's mother was a Velge, one of the leading families in Melaka. Adrian Koek later married a Maria Dionicia Wilhelmina Dieterich from Melaka, while Jansz Sjouke Westerhout married Anna Maria Magdalena, a Burgher girl also from Melaka.

In any colony, whether or not there was a close relationship between the Dutch official and unofficial community depended on particular circumstances. In Melaka, at least, it would appear that the European community as a whole was a united group, as the officials, being few in number, were much dependent on the cooperation and goodwill of the Burgher community to run the day-to-day affairs of the town. As we have seen, Burghers were involved in many governmental and non-governmental activities, such as helping the administration with social and welfare issues like the administration of orphans and children. They were also involved in maintaining security and in managing roads and bridges.[7] In 1824, Gerrit Leendert Baumgarten worked as *pakhuismeester* (warehouse master), in the *weeskamer* (orphan chamber), the *diaconie* (Church administration) and as a *predikant* (Calvinist preacher). One of his brothers, Johan Willem Baumgarten, became a member of the Council of Justice in 1820–24. Adriaan Koek became the captain-lieutenant of the Burghers, Deputy Governor of Melaka, President of the Council of Justice and a Church minister. Thus, the presence of the Burgher community was an asset to the colonial town. Their role was more institutionalized than was the case with the unofficial European community in Penang.

In Melaka, the Europeans lived close together in one particular area in substantial brick houses. Many led a comfortable or even lavish lifestyle, served by a bevy of slaves. The records show that the Dutch in Melaka owned the most number of slaves compared to the other communities.[8] So good was life in the town and so attached were they to Melaka that many did not even leave when the Dutch administration withdrew in 1824. As noted by Newbold:

> The Dutch formed a highly respectable and wealthy class of the community. They are mostly the descendants of the officers of the old Dutch governments; who preferred, on the place being given up to the English, to remain without employment, rather than quit Malacca for Batavia, (the capital of the possessions of Holland, in India) and are much attached to the soil. Some of them find employment in the government offices, others are engaged commerce and agriculture, while a few live on the annual sum paid by government for the transfer of their landed rights.[9]

Relatively little is known about the business activities of the Dutch community, but that many owned property in land is obvious from the records. So much land was alienated to the citizens of Melaka, especially the Dutch, that Newbold stated: 'After the British had taken possession of Malacca, in 1825, it was found that scarcely a foot of land with the exception of a few spots near the town, belonged to Government; that the propriety rights in the soil of the whole territory of Malacca had been given away to various individuals, by the Dutch, reserving the right of imposing a land-tax on the whole.'[10]

Despite difficulties in accessing official statistics on the ownership of land and property in Melaka, the records from the Orphan Chamber reveal some patterns of property ownership. For example, from the list of mortgage documents in the Orphan Chamber records, not only can one conclude that the majority of borrowers were the Burghers, followed by the Chinese, Malays, Kelings and Portuguese-Eurasians but that many of these Burgers owned property such as houses and land.[11]

However, by the nineteenth century most property in elite areas had fallen under the control of the Chinese. The number of Burghers had decreased because most had migrated to Batavia due to the English occupation of Melaka. Thus, their property in the Heren and Jonkerstraats was bought by the rich Chinese. The displacement of the Burghers by the ethnic Chinese shows that Melaka in the nineteenth century underwent a drastic change from an Asian town with a strong European minority to becoming a town dominated by Asian migrants.[12]

An important component in building a community life for the European colonizers was the church. The situation in Melaka was no different and the close-knit nature of the community, the presence of family life and the occurrence of marriages and births and deaths would have ensured that the church had a strong influence in the life of the European community. In Dutch Melaka, the Reformed Church played an important role in the religious life of the Dutch community and was a focal point for their educational, social and welfare activities. The strong position of the Church was guaranteed

Plate 7: Auguste Nicholas Vaillant, 'Ancienne Église a Malacca'. In *Voyage autour du monde execute pendant les annees 1836 et 1837 par la corvette La Bonite*, Paris, 1845–52. Reproduced by permission of the British Library (P336 9660365).

by the support and encouragement it received from the VOC right from the start. In fact, the VOC appears to have been as much concerned about trade as it was about spreading Christianity. Thus the first Governor, Pieter Both, was entrusted with the supervision and power over the ministers and school teachers, who had not only to take care of the Europeans, but also to work for the conversion of the heathen, 'so that the name of Christ may be spread, and the advantage of the Company furthered'.[13]

Following the Dutch occupation, a strong anti-Catholic stand was taken which saw some of the Portuguese churches destroyed, while others were transformed into Dutch Reformed churches. The encouragement of religious activities by the administration can be seen in the fact that over 800 ministers and several thousand lay-readers were sent out to the colonies before 1799.[14] So close was the relationship between the Administration and the church that, when Melaka celebrated the centenary of Dutch occupation in 1741, a new church, named Christ Church, was built at the foot of St Paul's Hill to commemorate the occasion. The strong proselytizing spirit of the Dutch is captured in the comments made by a seventeenth century Catholic priest: 'The Dutch gave good alms even to the Catholick poor, but almost oblig'd them to be present at their service. A poor lame man said to me, Father, I cheat them very handsomely, for being lame, as I go up that hill I feign myself lamer, and sit down to rest every step, so that I never get to the top, nor never will'.[15] He had further observed in the context of the state of the Catholic faith under Dutch rule that 'in spirituals it was once a great colony and the church has many children there still, but they are among bloody wolves'.[16]

On the whole, Dutch society in Melaka had most of the appurtenances to enable them to lead a civilized existence. Many had their families with them, comfortable houses to live in, slaves to serve them, schools to educate their children, the church to fulfill their religious and ceremonial needs and an administration run by their own kind. Melaka was, indeed, a pleasant place to live in, as observed by the Catholic priest, albeit disapprovingly, when he described the town as 'a mere garden, and paradise for worldly pleasure' in which 'those who have some wealth are pleased and satisfied'.[17] The author was no doubt biased and saw Melaka as having been corrupted by the presence of the Dutch, but he confirmed the fact that the town was a pleasing place for people with wealth such as the Dutch.[18]

As in many colonial towns, most of the European settlements were usually situated in the best parts and were provided with good public utilities. Likewise, in Melaka, Heren and Jonker Straats, where most Europeans lived, were located in the best area with a good view of the sea.[19] Newbold described the view from the streets as 'extremely picturesque' and that it had 'the appearance of being situated in the bend of a crescent or bay; the southern horn of which is formed by a chain of beautiful islets, called the Aquadas, or Water Isles, stretching out seawards from the coast. On the north side, the shore trends to the west, terminating in an elevated and well wooded point called Tanjong Keling'.[20]

In the early days of Dutch rule, life for many Dutch men would have been lonely and even brutish. The near absence of Dutch women led some to seek companionship with local women. This situation was confirmed in the description given by Navarette, a Portuguese who visited Melaka in 1669 and stayed there for a few months.

> As I was going home with some friends, we found a jolly Dutch man with his table and bottles in the cool air; he invited us, and I accidentally ask'd, Are you married, Sir, in this country? He answer'd me very pleasantly, Yes, father, I married a black; since I cannot eat white bread I take up with brown.[21]

It seemed that this particular Dutchman had a sense of humour as well as the capacity to adjust to life in the tropics. But Navarette also saw the ugly side of life away from home when he observed: 'Some of us from a Catholick's house, saw a Dutchman lash two blackmoor women most cruelly, they seem'd to be catholicks; he had ty'd them to coco-trees, and beat them unmercifully; one of them call'd upon Jesus and Mary, and we saw him for that reason lash her again in a most outrageous manner'.[22]

However, with the passing of time, the Dutch population increased and the presence of more Dutch women in Melaka allowed the European community to create a social life that was in some ways akin to that which they or their ancestors had been accustomed to in Europe and to evolve as a separate social group. By the end of the eighteenth century certain patterns in their lifestyle were already in place and a permanent feature of their society.

The Dutch community also assimilated certain local customs and cuisine, perhaps due to the influence of slavery on the domestic life of most Dutch Burghers but also because it made life much easier to make those adjustments. Their houses and the food they ate reflected the impact of local influences. Even the habit of chewing *sirih* with betelnut, mainly practiced by the locals, might have been adopted by some Burgher women. There is evidence to show that the usually ornate silver and brass boxes in which the sirih was held and presented to those who found enjoyment chewing it and the equipment needed to prepare it, had been in the possession of some Burgher families although many could merely have kept them as ornamental objects or antiques.[23]

A long-standing local custom practiced by the Burghers was the owning of slaves, of whom they possessed the highest number. The majority were Indonesians from the archipelago and they worked in the homes of the Burghers and helped in their enterprises. Many slaves were also good merchants and traders and knew how to manufacture bricks and cultivate the land. A well-documented account of the relationship between the Burghers and their slaves is given by Captain Walter Caulfield Lennon, who served as principal engineer and secretary to an expedition from the Straits of Melaka to the Moluccas Islands under the command of Admiral Rainier in 1796. In his Journal, Lennon described the talents and duties of slaves at a dinner party in the home of the Dutch Governor of Melaka, Couperus (1788–95). In relation to the entertainment provided by the hostess, Lennon stated:

> In the evening she played on the harp, a plain instrument without pedals and only capable of a natural key, made at Batavia; she was accompanied by some of her slaves on violins; and altogether made a very good music for a Dutchman to sleep to; We were attended at dinner and during the evening by Malay slaves, male and female, some of the latter rather pretty, considering the general cast of Malay features. Couperus, I am told has above 130 slaves which must be a vast expense to him and he never sells one.[24]

Even though Couperus was the Governor of Melaka, it seems excessive for him to own 130 slaves. It does appear that the Dutch did not own slaves for economic reasons alone but, like the locals, they were also concerned with questions of status and prestige that ownership of slaves conferred on them. As they belonged to the ruling group and were wealthy, having more slaves than the other communities might have become a defining feature for them. Perhaps that was the reason why, as a whole, the Burgher community owned the most slaves and why Couperus never sold his, as owning slaves might not have been merely a matter of profit.

The Dutch Burghers appear to have devised certain ways of spending their leisure. The priest who was in Melaka observed of the Dutch that, 'Upon Sunday-nights the hereticks make their feasts in the streets' while Lennon's account of Couperus' dinner party shows that there was a degree of lavishness in the social events that the Dutch organized.[25] Lennon described the dinner as attended by 'a large company and not a bad dinner, allowing for Dutch cooking, of which I have not the most delicate idea' and while the ladies played, 'the Dutchmen smoked their long pipes and drank Klein beer, which is some of the best malt liquor I ever tasted.'[26]

The dinner party, as can be noticed, was attended by Dutchmen and their wives, showing that they partied and interacted among themselves.

However, an interesting point to note is the fact that the Governor's wife was probably a Portuguese-Eurasian, judging from her attire and the fact that Lennon took particular notice that she seemed ,very affable and well bred for a person never out of Melaka'.[27] Lennon's remark that the Governor had not once been offered the Government House 'though the only one proper for his residence' seems to hint at the fact that Couperus was deliberately kept out of the Governor's official residence and this could well be because of his wife. [28] If true, then it could be said that there was some resistance to any act that did not conform to the normal way of doing things in the community. However, in the case of the Governor's wife, the objection might well have been more because she was a Catholic than that she was ethnically different. Nevertheless, the prejudice existed and was shown by the fact that only marriages within the white community appear to have been recorded.

THE MALAY COMMUNITY

The Malays were the majority group in Melaka. Due to the fact that they were the native population, observers tended to compare them either favourably or unfavourably with the migrant Asian groups in terms of their behaviour and their input towards the economic development of Melaka. Thus Lennon observes the mild and inoffensive behavior of the Malays in the following terms:

> The disposition of the Malays about Malacca is quite inoffensive, nor has there been any act of treachery, that I could learn committed by them for a considerable time past. In their domestic habits they are free from the prejudices of the Hindoos, and are reckoned Mahomedans, though I fancy their chief tenet is abstaining from swine's flesh. Though very muscular in their make, and better formed for strength and activity than any of the natives of india, they are passionately addicted to gaming and cock-fighting, which are their chief amusements.[29]

Newbold also paints a similar picture: 'a Malay may be easily led, where force and compulsion would produce nothing but stubbornness and rebellion. The Malay, in his commercial dealings, is much more honest than the natives of China and of India, by whom, however, he is far surpassed in industry and perseverance'.[30] Such descriptions of the Malays were intended to show that they were pleasant but lazy, but it also gives a clear indication of the different character, way of life and habits of the Asian ethnic communities.

When Lockyer said that, 'the native Malayans live mean enough in the suburbs of the town' he was referring to the lot of the majority of the Malays who were farmers and fishermen, most of whom lived on the outskirts of

Melaka in more open spaces surrounded by greenery, as described by Thomson, above. [31] This observation coincided with the description given by Newbold, who stated: 'The agricultural classes reside in the country, in their native villages, under their respective penghulus or headmen; of whom, according to Malayan usage, there ought to be one to every forty-four families'.[32] Melaka's reputation as a producer of a variety of fruit had much to do with the Malays who had grown fruit since the days of the Melaka sultanate. Those who were fishermen appear to have been involved in fishing on a small scale, as noted by Thomson: 'we passed through hundreds of fishing boats manned by Malays and Indo-Portuguese. The fishermen held in their hands a bow strung with shells which they rattled in the water at a great rate. The object of this of course was not to frighten away the fish but to attract them'.[33] As mentioned earlier, the Malays were not regarded as hard working as the Chinese, but were nevertheless useful as farmers and fishermen who provided the town with some of its food.

A few Malays, mostly those living in town, were prosperous business-men, land owners and traders. Although there were wealthy Malays mentioned in the documents of the Orphan Chamber records, the details of their lives are vague. For example, there are names such as Encik Astor (Malay Captain), Encik Roa (Malay superintendent of ward), Ahmad Budiman (trader and land owner) and Encik Samsuddin (property owner), Mahomet Tahir (land owner) and Encik Noriea (property owner) but the details of their activities are hard to reconstruct.

That there were educated Malays is obvious from the fact that Munshi Abdullah, the father of modern Malay literature, was born and bred in Melaka. Abdullah, albeit a Jawi Pekan, identified with the Malay community, and his success as a writer attests that there was a form of Malay education and that the exposure brought about by Melaka's status as a port-town nurtured inquiring minds.

From the accounts of observers, it could be surmised that the Malays in Melaka continued to live in the way they were accustomed to, with their own headmen, following their own customs and traditions. As in the days of the Melaka sultanate, they farmed, fished and traded. Lennon noted their love of gambling and also asserted of the Malays that 'they are extremely indolent, and if not tempted by the hope of gain, would never exert them-selves'.[34] However, there was another perspective or picture of the leisure activities of the Malays, described by Ibrahim, the son of Munshi Abdullah. He described leisurely boating trips cruising down the Melaka River with singing and music on board and stopping to enjoy picnics along the river bank, which appear to have been a favourite pastime of wealthy Malays.[35] This type of leisure was open to them because they were wealthy and had slaves who worked in their households and also as traders and merchants on their behalf.

THE ASIAN COMMUNITIES

Since an Asian colonial town was founded, administered and controlled by a minority of European settlers, on Asian soil, the European administrators had to rely on the Asian ethnic communities to help make the town a success. As the focus of most colonial port-towns was trade, the European administrators sought profit for survival. Company servants viewed the presence of the Asians as a contributing factor for the encouragement of trade, which would benefit them.[36] Thus the Asians were encouraged to settle in the colonial port-towns although some groups were given more encouragement than others depending on their degree of usefulness in the estimation of the colonial masters. Such judgements were formed or made and were later perpetuated over time until they became the accepted notion of how a particular ethnic group behaved. Yet in most instances, the European perception of each Asian community was shaped more by their own goals and how a particular group could contribute towards achieving that goal. Their perspectives were therefore biased.[37] Asian ethnic groups that could bring wealth and help the Company in creating prosperity were encouraged to settle in the town. As a colonial town required much skilled and unskilled labour, those communities that could not provide such a work force were unwanted. In addition, those who created social and economic problems were considered a nuisance by the Company administrators.[38]

On these grounds, the European administrators felt that the presence of the Chinese was essential for the future development of Melaka.[39] The Dutch, like the Portuguese before and the English after them, also believed that they could rely on the ethnic Chinese to help them develop commerce and agriculture. The Dutch showed less enthusiasm for the Indian community but probably saw their usefulness in the intra-Asian trade in which they had long been involved, particularly in linking India and the archipelago. The other large group of natives under which were subsumed the Bugis, Javanese, Minangkabau, Batak and most others from the archipelago, formed the other big component in the native population. The Bugis made good trading partners but most of the native Malays were probably seen as useful farmers who provided the town with the vegetables and fruits for which Melaka was renown. Of the mixed or half-caste groups of Portuguese-Eurasians, the Babas or Peranakans and the Jawi Pekans, only the first was large enough to be classified and judged as a community in terms of their usefulness to the authorities. The Dutch had a strange relationship with the Portuguese-

Eurasians. They began by having doubts about the loyalty of the latter because they were descendants of the Portuguese from whom they had wrested Melaka, and due to the fact that they were staunch Catholics; they despised them for what they perceived as their state of degeneration, but ultimately found them useful as members of the town's security patrol.

Although their participation in the administration of the town was very limited and all decisions regarding the town were made by the minority group, the Europeans, the Asian community did play an important role in the economy and defence of the town and contributed to the overall flavour and character of Melaka.

THE CHINESE COMMUNITY

The history of the Chinese in Melaka can be traced to the Malay kingdom.[40] Beginning from the reign of the first ruler of Melaka, diplomatic and trade relations were forged with China. According to the *Sejarah Melayu* or *Malay Annals*, a Chinese princess was given in marriage to a sultan of Melaka and she lived on Bukit Cina. Although the truth of this claim cannot be proven, the fact that China went through a phase of open engagement with the outside world, as seen from the naval expeditions of Admiral Zheng He, and that Melaka developed into an important port meant that Chinese traders would have been attracted to settle in the port-town right from the start.

Three distinct periods marked the flow of Chinese immigrants to the Malay peninsula. The first stage covered the period of the Melaka sultanate and also includes the period of the Portuguese occupation and Dutch rule, until the end of the eighteenth century, the second stage was from 1800 to 1920 and the third stage was during the twentieth century (1920–42) when the British encouraged Chinese migrants to the Straits Settlements and later into the Malay states.[41] Right from the start, the Dutch and also the British made it clear that Chinese emigrants were needed to develop Melaka and Penang, and later Singapore, into important commercial and agricultural areas.[42] Most of the trade of the Straits Settlements was conducted by the Chinese and they monopolized the running of different types of government revenue farms, as in other places in the East.

Although it is not possible to be precise about the many economic activities conducted by the Chinese in Melaka, the fact that the Chinese population increased throughout the period under study indicates that Melaka offered them opportunities for work or earning a living. We have seen that some Chinese owned ships and traded between Melaka and the region, that they ran most of the tax farms in Melaka and that some were involved in the agricultural sector. They were predominantly town dwellers, suggesting that they were also involved in other businesses and prominent in the retail trade, as observed by Lennon, who said, 'They are very industrious, almost all of them keep little shops and sell groceries of all sorts. They all hitherto sold arrack and the consequent drunkenness of the place was abominable'.[43] Even in the early eighteenth century, Lockyer had observed that, 'The Chinese keep the best shops in the place which are well filled with the manufactures and produce of their own country and what else they can muck up to get a penny'.[44] The Chinese were also active in the labour force as skilled, semi-skilled and unskilled labourers although their influx as unskilled labourers came only after the formation of the Straits Settlements and with the subsequent exploitation of the tin mines in the Malay states.

Little has been written as well about the social activities of the Chinese in Melaka for the period under study. Activities centred on secret societies that engendered rivalry and conflict within the Chinese community did not happen during the Dutch administration of Melaka but only appeared in the 1830s when large numbers of Chinese immigrants entered the port-town during the British period. Apart from the fact that their numbers were small before the 1830s, and Chinese immigration was a very slow and gradual process, the absence of intra-ethnic conflict might also have been because the early Chinese migrants came from the Macao region, while those after 1825, who came in large numbers, were mainly from Fukien. Moreover, their arrival in large numbers gave scope for the rise of protection rackets as well as exploitation of newcomers.

In Melaka, the Chinese dominated the centre of the town, as is evident from the description given by John Turnbull Thomson, who visited Melaka in the late 1830s. Travelling from the centre of Melaka to its outskirts, he describes his journey thus:

> The first part of the drive was through the musty close and odorous china-town: but that passed, we entered into avenues of tall areca and coconut trees; thence we skirted the open plain, covered with rice plots. Now we entered orange, duku langsat and durian groves. Then we passed through rice fields at length we rise and wind round a grassy knoll, on whose top was set the capacious cool and snug bungalow of my friend.[45]

Thomson's description confirms both the tendency of ethnic communities to live among their own groups and the fact that the Chinese tended to live where they worked so that a Chinese area was crowded and full of smells, probably of food, joss-sticks and other odours.

Lennon had noted that the Chinese were addicted to gaming and liquor.[46] The existence of opium farms would also have encouraged opium smoking.

Thus such preoccupations would have filled the leisure hours of the Chinese. They were also fond of theatre performances, which Lennon observed as being remarkably good, saying that, 'They are also fond of theatrical exhibitions in which their merit is considerable, their chief performers are carpenters and other artificers.'[47] Although some of the pastimes of the Chinese as observed by the Europeans suggested over-indulgence, yet it was also obvious to them that the Chinese were hard working and an asset to the town.

That Melaka was both a place to seek work and settle. That it became a real home for many Chinese is evident from the fact that the English met with little success when they tried to persuade them to move to Penang, despite offering free passage and monetary grants to start a new life in the new settlement.[48] Moreover, the Chinese had also provided education for their children although the history of this Chinese education is not clear. However, Newbold's mention of the existence of an Anglo-Chinese school means that by the time he arrived in Melaka in the early 1830s, some Chinese were already educating their children in English. Thus Melaka was seen as a suitable and pleasant place to live in and its attractions were strong enough to bring other Chinese to it, as observed by Thomson: 'Malacca is the Brighton of the Singapore Chinese. To this place they come to spend their holidays, to eat the luscious fruit so abundant in the place, to indulge in recreation and repose from the merchantile anxieties of the great emporium.'[49]

THE INDIAN COMMUNITY

The Indians were sometimes referred as Kelings and those who were Hindus were mostly descendents of people from the Coromandel Coast who had come at different times to Melaka with their trade and cloth. They multiplied in Melaka through intermarriage with native women. During the Dutch administration, those who were Indian Muslims were termed as 'Moors'. Most Indians were traders and had shops and premises in the town and some also possessed lands. The rich Moor and Keling merchants of Melaka included Malik Farizullah and Muthu Manga,[50] the former a very wealthy merchant from Surat. His estate papers, accounts and inventories reveal his wealth to be in ships and other property. He owned vessels trading from Coromandel, Pegu, Melaka and Macao, had many houses, slaves, land and had his own 'de facto bank', which was involved in money lending. However, little is known about the social life of the Kelings and Moors but the richer sections of them were employed in trade and owned shops, and some of the shops were worth as much as SpD 20,000. Some of the rich also owned land and cultivated paddy fields but the majority were poor and employed in the shipping industry in the port of Melaka.[51]

THE PORTUGUESE-EURASIAN COMMUNITY

The Portuguese-Eurasians in Melaka formed the lower strata of society, partly because most of them were poor and lacked assets or skills needed by the European administration. In general, the Portuguese-Eurasians were regarded as degenerate, improvident and impoverished, 'subsisting principally by fishing, and upon the produce of the little gardens and enclosures attached to their houses. Many of them are employed as servants to gentlemen, and as writers in offices. They retain most of the pride, without the industry and energy of their ancestors; but under all these disadvantages, appear to be a light-hearted happy race'.[52] The Dutch administration's attitude was that the presence of the Portuguese-Eurasians did not confer any interest to them. Nonetheless, some were employed for the neighbourhood watch in Melaka.

The Portuguese-Eurasians were the remains of the once large population of Melaka, which in the 1820s had dwindled down to not more than 3,000 people. Although their ancestors originally intermarried with the native women, their descendants tended to set themselves apart from their native ancestors and were a distinct group with their own customs and habits. The attire of the women and the way they wore their hair reflected the blend between East and West. This is best seen in a description provided by Lennon of the Portuguese-Eurasian wife of the Dutch governor, Couperus:

> Madam Couperus was dressed in the most unbecoming manner possible, a mixture between Malay and Portuguese, her outward garment being made exactly like a shift, she looked as if she reversed the order of her dress altogether. Her hair was drawn so tight to the crown of her head, and the skin of her forehead so stretched, that she could scarce wink her eyelids.[53]

A habit that the Portuguese-Eurasian women adopted from their Malay mothers was betel chewing, as noted also by Sheehan, who said about Madam Couperus that, 'she chewed betel incessantly, as did the other ladies in company, and every chair in the room was furnished with a cuspidor to spit in...'.[54] While some Portuguese-Eurasian women were able to rise up the social ladder through marriage with the Dutch Burghers, as seen in the case of Madam Couperus, the men remained mostly poor, many living with their families in poor houses erected in Bandarhilir. It would appear that in their poverty they were sustained by a strong adherence to their Catholic faith. That the Portuguese-Eurasians retained this strong faith throughout the Dutch period despite attempts by the Dutch Reformed Church to woo them away is evident from the following account:

> That afternoon the stewards of the brotherhood of the Rosary invited me to go up the river at eight of the clock at night, where most of the

Christians live, there to sing the salve and litany of our Lady. I could not avoid it, but went; their church was adorn'd: after the rosary, the slave and litany were sung very well, I being in a cope, brought out the image of our blessed Lady, which was a very beautiful one. Then I heard some confessions, and having taken my leave of the people, went away to rest at the house of an honest Portuguese, who was married to a Malaye woman. I was twelve days ashore; the evening and morning was spent in hearing confessions. I said mass every day but one, and administer'd the blessed sacrament: the rest of the day I visited the sick, and that they might all be pleased, said mass one day in one house, and the next in another … .[55]

The writer asserted that the women were extraordinarily good Christians who wished they could get away from Melaka but could not because they were too poor. He further stated that: 'Among the rest there was a woman an extraordinary good Christian, she furnished bread and wine for the masses. She had a daughter whom she had educated with all possible care; yet when grown up, she married a heretick, who soon perverted her, and she prov'd a mortal enemy to catholicks'.[56] More than a century later, Newbold was to observe that a Roman Catholic Church erected near the river side of Bungaraya was a meeting place for the Portuguese–Eurasians and that priests regularly visited from Goa and Macao from where they were sent to help and preserve the religious and cultural beliefs of the community.[57] It would appear that the Portuguese-Eurasian identity was much determined by the tenacity with which they stuck to their religious affiliation and observances.

INTEGRATION AND THE FORMATION OF NEW ETHNIC AND CULTURAL IDENTITIES

While a prominent feature of a colonial port-town was the pluralistic nature of its society, Melaka's long history had created situations and circumstances that engendered some degree of social integration and even the formation of new ethnic and cultural identities. But at the same time that the process of bringing together the ethnics groups was occurring, resistance to this was still evident among almost all the communities. Thus, as we have seen, the Company servants and Dutch Burghers in Melaka were regarded and saw themselves as Europeans, and the children born of mixed parentage between the Dutch Burghers and the locals or the Portuguese-Eurasians were classified as Europeans. Further, the Dutch recognized mixed children as European if their Burgher fathers acknowledged them legally, and classified them as native if they were not acknowledged. Many Burghers were in fact of mixed descent but were legally accepted as Europeans. The Portuguese-Eurasians, on the other hand, were treated as a separate category by the Dutch and were not regarded as Europeans. In fact, the term 'Eurasian' was an English category and had no basis in any Dutch colonial port-town. On their part, the Portuguese-Eurasians saw themselves as a separate group, resisting integration with the local society. Among the Asian communities, sexual liaisons and mixed marriages between Chinese males and local women had produced the Baba community, which was distinct, speaking a kind of Malay dialect, the women wearing a distinctive Malay costume and possessing a distinctive cuisine; while in the Indian community such intermarriages gave rise to the Jawi Pekans with their own peculiar brand of cultural mix and traditions. Thus the official categories did not accurately reflect the true nature of the society and the more complex character of the population of Melaka.

The evolution of the complex cultural and racial mix began even in the days of the Melaka sultanate and was a continuing process throughout the period under study. An example from the early nineteenth century of which there is clear evidence is the case of the English Commandant and Resident of Melaka, Colonel William Farquhar (1803–18), of whom Brian Harrison wrote, 'Farquhar had already developed a sense of personal attachment to Melaka and its people. Melaka suited him well; he had learned to write Malay and could speak the language fluently. From his early days in the settlement, he had kept a Malay mistress by whom he had four children, three daughters and a son'.[58]

A more friendly environment existed in Melaka because the town had a small population and a lengthy period during which its inhabitants had co-existed side by side. This situation can be deduced from the *Obligatie Boeken* or Bond Books records of loans of money made by the Orphan Chamber on the security of houses and lands and the bonds of two individual sureties.[59] These records indicate that many individual guarantors were not from the same ethnic group. For example, a Dutch Burgher, Carel Ferdinand Greys from Heren Weg in Bandarhilir, borrowed 1,000 rijksdollars and one of the sureties was a Chinese named Tan Tun Tet. A Dutch Burgher widow, Dorothea Minjoot, the widow of van Hendrik from Tweede Brugge Dwarsstraat, borrowed 200 rijksdollars and one of her sureties was a Malay named Samsoedin Astor.[60] A widow by the name of Johanna Alwis, a Portuguese-Eurasian from Heren Weg, borrowed 200 rijksdollars and her two sureties were an Indian Moslem and a non-Muslim Indian, Seijdoe Mira and Majoom Tirwengedom, respectively. A Malay woman, Nonja Aij, who lived in Heeren Straat, borrowed 150 rijksdollars from the Chamber and her two sureties were Chinese, namely, Tan Tiongko and Kouw Tja Kong. A Chinese, by the name of The Tian Keeng from Jonker Straat, borrowed 200 rijksdollars from the Chambers and his two sureties were Indians, Baleatje

Plee and Annamale Chittij. A Malay by the name of Jachia Abdul Wayit from Kampong Melayu borrowed 300 rijksdollars and his two sureties were the Chinese, Ho Liem and Ko Hogoean. A Dutch Burgher, Jan Willem Baumgarten from Jonker Straat, borrowed 3,000 rijksdollars and one of his sureties was a Chinese, Tan Sang. A Dutch Burgher, Hubert van Bragt from Jonker Straat, borrowed 3,000 rijksdollars and one of his sureties was a Chinese, Ho Kong To. A Malay woman, Encik Mina from Bukit China, borrowed 200 rijksdollars and one of her sureties was a Chinese, Tjee Tiauw. A Chinese woman, Tjieuw Ingnio a widow from Goudsmith Straat, borrowed 1,930 rijksdollars and one of her sureties was a Malay, Achmat Saab. A Chinese, Tja Kong Tjouw from Bandarhilir, borrowed 200 rijksdollars and one of his sureties was a Dutch Burgher, Johan Hendrik.

In practice, it was difficult for a debtor to get a surety for his loan. Some factors that determined a surety were: relationship between debtor and guarantor; the capacity to guarantee the loan; and the ability to pay the loan by installments. The relationship between the debtor and the creditor was based on trust. From the record of Bond Books it can be established that there was cooperation and trust among the ethnic groups. Many were adequately comfortable in their cross-cultural relationships to be guarantors of individuals outside their own ethnic community.

Not only in the sphere of business did the Melaka population exhibit a willingness to have cross-cultural contacts. The presence of native slaves and their role as companions and concubines helped to break down ethnic barriers, particularly when such relationships resulted in the birth of children who were usually adopted into the family. Cross-ethnic adoptions were also practiced, as in the case of a wealthy Moor widow named Saida, alias Polobaaij, who had children of her own but also an adopted Chinese son. Problems arose after Saida's death regarding the inheritance for her children and her adopted child. Saida did leave wills but some of her children disputed the share given to her adopted child.[61]

Although, on the whole, cultural separateness was maintained, opportunities to interact were not only confined to the marketplace or during business transactions. In Melaka, during the Dutch period, the auction house provided an important and useful venue for inter-communal gatherings as it was the focal point where the population met to view and buy goods. It seems that the auction house attracted people from all communities and was always regarded as a big event.

More importantly, cultural barriers were being continually challenged especially by intermarriages, but also by friendships that were being forged by individuals of different ethnic backgrounds, as can be seen from Ibrahim Munsyi's account of his friendship with a Baba Chinese.[62]

Human relationships alone did not determine or shape the integrative forces at work in Melaka. A strong influence existed in the realm of ideas and practices that cut across ethnic lines. In this respect, aspects of the European way of life were cherished and adopted by the local society. The practice of writing wills, inheritance law, guardians of the orphanage and auctions were all European legacies that emerged in Melaka from the Dutch administration. The Asian ethnic groups had been introduced to these Dutch practices and seem to have been happy to follow them. For example, the writing of wills was done by a Dutch Burgher whose role as testator was to assist a bedridden and sick person to write his will before death.[63] After the person's death, the will was read to his beneficiary. Although the Malays had their own system of inheritance based on *adat* and Islamic law, some preferred to have a will written according to Dutch law. A similar pattern was also seen in the guardianship question where some Asian ethnic groups preferred the orphan guardianship system to be practised and administered by the Dutch administration. Social security in Dutch-Melaka was very well administered and the majority of Asians favoured this system.

CONCLUSION

Although Melaka society in some ways exhibited certain pluralistic tendencies, its long history had blurred the lines of divisions. There remained some form of segregation in terms of the social relationships among the different ethnic groups. Social gatherings of more than one group seldom occurred and many only met and gathered in order to deal with their business and daily life in general. However, as we have seen, the cross-ethnic relationship was not based purely on mutual business interest. The supportive and trusting attitude, as shown by individuals from one ethnic group who stood as guarantors for someone outside his community, shows a much deeper commitment to the cross-ethnic relationships than is normally the case in a plural society. Further, the breaking down of ethnic barriers occurred to a larger degree in Melaka through a long history of mixed-marriages and cross-cultural sexual liaisons.

In the period under study, Melaka moved towards a higher degree of melding of cultures and interaction between the different ethnic communities. As we have seen, Melaka witnessed the emergence of new cultural forms and practices, as seen in the ways of the Dutch Burghers, the Portuguese-Eurasians, the Baba Chinese and the Jawi-Pekan as well as more comfortable and binding inter-ethnic relationships. Melaka had developed a character that was neither pluralistic nor integrated. It had elements of both.

NOTES

1   T.J. Newbold, *Political and Statistical Account*, p. 110.

2   Ibid., p.138.

3   Ibid., p. 110.

4   See, for example, Portuguese Melaka's encouragement to the Portuguese to marry local women, which resulted in a new ethnic group called Portuguese-Eurasians. For further discussion on this, see Colin Jack-Hinton, 'Malacca and Goa and the Question of Race Relations in the Portuguese Overseas Provinces', pp. 513–557.

5   There were many such marriages. For further reference, see P.A. Christiaans, 'De Europese Bevolking van Malakka Onder Het Laatste Nederlandse Bestuur, 1818–1825', in *Jaarboek Centraal Bureau voor Genealogie*, pp. 257–287.

6   Ibid., pp. 260–277.

7   Ibid.

8   See Appendix 9: List of Registered Slaves in Melaka 1819–1824 and Appendix 10: List of Registered Slave Children in Melaka 1819–1824, in Nordin Hussin, 'Melaka and Penang 1780–1830: A study of two port towns in the Straits of Melaka', Ph.D. thesis, Amsterdam: Vrije Universiteit, 2002, pp. 437–458.

9   T.J. Newbold, *Political and Statistical Account*, p. 138.

10   Ibid., p. 162.

11   See Appendix 6: Property and Ownership in Melaka 1787/88 and 1805/11, in Nordin Hussin, 'Melaka and Penang 1780–1830', pp.432–433.

12   Ibid.

13   'Dutch Protestant Mission Activity: A Survey', p. 87.

14   Ibid.

15   J.J. Sheehan, 'Seventeenth Century Visitors to the Malay Peninsula', p. 92

16   Ibid.

17   Ibid.

18   Ibid.

19   See, for example, P.J. Begbie, *The Malayan Peninsula*, where he notes: 'the ground floors are generally bricked and mats are seldom spread over them, under the idea that the house are cleaner and less dust accumulated. The Dutch houses are the most part neatly furnished', p. 366.

20   T.J. Newbold, *Political and Statistical Account*, pp.110–111.

21   J.J. Sheehan, 'Sevententh Century Visitors to the Malay Peninsula', p. 92.

22   Ibid.

23   See the series of records on auction books 1767–1822: records of auctions of estates held by the Orphan Chamber listing properties sold and the names of purchasers in R/9/13/1; R/9/13/2, and R/9/13/3.

24   Walter Caulfield Lennon,'Journal of a voyage through the Straits of Malacca', p. 59.

25   Sheehan, J.J. 'Seventeenth Century Visitors to the Malay Peninsula', p. 92.

26   Walter Caulfield Lennon, 'Journal of a Voyage through the Straits of Malacca', p. 59.

27   Ibid.

28   Ibid.

29   Walter Caulfield Lennon, 'Journal of a Voyage through the Straits of Malacca', p. 66.

30   T.J. Newbold, *Political and Statistical Account*, p. 139.

31   Charles Lockyer, *An Account of the Trade in India*, p. 75.

32   Ibid., see also T.J. Newbold, *Political and Statistical Account*, p. 139.

33   John T. Thomson, *Glimpses into Life in Malayan Lands*, p. 22.

34   Walter Caulfield Lennon, 'Journal of a Voyage through the Straits of Malacca', p. 66.

35   Muhammad Ibrahim Munsyi, *Kisah Pelayaran Muhammad Ibrahim Munsyi* (Anotasi Mohd Fadzil Othman), Kuala Lumpur: Dewan Bahasa Pustaka, 1980, pp. 11–42. See also Abdullah bin Abdul Kadir, *Kesah Pelayaran Abdullah terkarang oleh Abdullah bin Abdul Kadir Munshi*, Singapore: Malaya Publishing House, 1947.

36   See, for example, Schouten's report of his visit to Malacca, in P.A. Leupe, 'The Siege and Capture of Malacca from the Portuguese in 1640–1641', *JMBRAS*, vol. 14, pt. 1, 1936: 'The city will be well provided with all kinds of fruit, and the fine agriculture will be saved from further decay. For this some 800 to 1,000 Chinese settlers would be very useful', p. 133.

37   See, for example, 'Francis Light, Fort Cornwallis, 25 Jan 1794', in Notices of Pinang, Vol. 5, 1851, pp. 8–11.

38   See, for example, in Penang where this attitude was shown by the Lieutenant-Governor, George Leith, who wrote in his report, *A Short Account of the Settlement*, .that: 'The population of Malay inhabitants is fortunately very small, they are an indolent, vindictive and treacherous people and generally speaking seem fit for little else but cutting down trees at which they are very expert. They are incapable of any labour beyond the cultivation of paddy. But though so rude and uncivilized a race some of them are most excellent goldsmiths and work in Filigree in a very beautiful manner', p. 50.

39   See Schouten's report in P.A. Leupe, 'The Siege and Capture of Malacca from the Portuguese in 1640–1641', where he suggested that the ruined gardens between the river Bukit Cina and the southern suburbs should be lent to the Netherlanders.

40   Kernial Singh Sandhu, 'Chinese Colonization in Melaka', in Kernial Singh Sandhu and Paul Wheatley, (eds) *Melaka*, pp. 93–136. See also John Clammer, 'The Straits Chinese in Melaka', in Kernial Singh Sandhu and Paul Wheatley, (eds) *Melaka*, pp. 156–173.

41   Carl A. Trocki, 'Chinese Pioneering in Eighteenth-Century Southeast Asia', p. 84. See also Victor Purcell, *The Chinese in Southeast Asia*, London: Oxford University Press, 1965, where he divided the history of Chinese migration into three phases prior to 1942. The first stage was between 1300–1800, the second stage between 1800–1920 and the third stage from 1920–1942, pp. xi-xii; for further information, see also W.L. Blythe, *Chinese Secret Societies in Malaya: A Historical Study*, London: Oxford University Press, 1969.

42   See, for example, 'Francis Light, Fort Cornwallis, 25 Jan 1794', in *JIA*, vol. 5, 1851, p. 9.

43   Walter Caulfield Lennon, 'Journal of a Voyage through the Straits of Malacca', p. 66.

44   Charles Lockyer, *An Account of the Trade in India*, London: Samuel Crouch, 1711, p. 75.

45   John T. Thomson, *Glimpses into Life in Malayan Lands*, p. 23.

46   Walter Caulfield Lennon, 'Journal of a Voyage through the Straits of Malacca', p. 66.

47   Ibid.

48   See Letter Farquhar, Lieutenant-governor of Prince of Wales Island, dated 25 May 1805. in G/34/9; see also Extract letter from Governor MacLister to the Chairman and Deputy Chairman, dated 7 November 1808, in SSFR Vol. 9.

49   John Turnbull Thomson, *Glimpses into Life in Malayan Lands*, p. 22.

50   A detailed account of Malik Farizullah's wealth can be found in R/9/12/14, and a detailed account of the number of houses and lands owned by Muthu Manga, in R/9/9/1.

51   See also Letter by W.T. Lewis, dated 30 June 1827, in G.34/172.

52   T.J. Newbold, *Political and Statistical Account*, p. 138.

53   Walter Caulfield Lennon, 'Journal of a Voyage through the Straits of Malacca', p. 59.

54   Ibid.

55   J.J. Sheehan, 'Seventeenth Century Visitor to the Malay Peninsula', p. 91.

56   Ibid.

57   Letter from W.T Lewis Acting Assistant Resident of Malacca, 30 June 1827, G/34/172.

58   Brian Harrison, 'Holding the Fort', p. 48.

59   Obligatie boek 15 Jan 1787–5 Oct 1788, in R/9/8/5, Obligatie boek 1 Jan 1798–24 Apr 1800, in R/9/8/6, Obligatie boek 1 May 1800–10 Jan 1805, in R/9/8/7, Obligatie boek 15 Jan 1805–1 Mar 1811, in R/9/8/8, Obligatie boek 15 Mar 1811–15 Dec 1821, in R/9/8/9.

See also Notitie boek van de debiteuren, 28 Feb 1787, in R/9/9/1, to Notitie boek van de debiteuren Feb 1799, in R/9/9/11.

60   Obligatie boek 15 Jan 1805–1 Mar 1811, in R/9/8/9.

61   Notitie boek van de debiteuren 28 Feb 1791, in R/9/9/5.

62   Muhamad Ibrahim Munsyi, *Kisah Pelayaran Muhamad Ibrahim Munsyi*, pp. 11–44. See also Abdullah bin Abdul Kadir, *Kesah Pelayaran Abdullah*.

63   See notarized wills 7 Apr 1788–22 Sept 1791, in R/9/11/17; Notarized wills 24 Dec 1794–6 Sept 1795, in R/9/11/18; Notarized wills 28 Mar 1797–5 Jan 1801, in R/9/11/19; Notarized wills 18 Feb 1821–8 Nov 1822, in R/9/11/20 and Notarized wills 11 29 Aug 1823, in R/9/11/21.

CHAPTER TEN

Penang: a Port-town of Migrants, 1786–1830

INTRODUCTION

PENANG WAS CREATED AT THE END of the eighteenth century. Before the English opened it as a colonial port-town, the island, almost uninhabited, had only a small settlement of a few hundred Malays whose history and background are not clearly known. Thus, unlike the Dutch in Melaka who took over a thriving entrepot and trading emporium, there was no existing foundation on which the English could build an urban centre. Penang was therefore a creation of the English. However, its physical and societal shape and form were less determined by English traditions than by a combination of factors, of which its geographical location and the purpose for its existence were the most important. Located in the northern part of the Straits of Melaka, the main artery in the long established intra-Asian sea trade, and serving the purpose of assisting the East India Company to gain control of that trade, Penang developed more in the tradition of other colonial port-towns in Southeast Asia but possessed some unique features.

As we have seen, Penang was a port-town of migrants and the population came from several places in Asia and Europe. The population could be divided into three major categories: the Europeans, Asians and mixed-race groups. The European community, mainly English, was very small, as befitted its role as the rulers and elite of society: Company officials and merchants, traders, businessmen and planters. The Asian population was almost the same mix as that found in Melaka with a few exceptions, so that there were the natives (Malays) and the Asian migrants, the Chinese and Indians (Chulias and Hindus), a small number of Arab and Armenian traders and some Siamese and Burmese due to the proximity of Penang to Siam and Burma. Of the mixed-race groups, the most numerous were the Jawi-Pekans. This was due to the fact that there was already a Jawi-Pekan community in Kedah, and when Penang was opened a sizeable number moved there. Their numbers subsequently increased with the presence of the Chulia merchants from India. Similarly, as in Melaka, there were also Eurasians, also of Portuguese and Asian descent, although their numbers were relatively small and most appear to have come from Siam, their migration probably due to the Siamese persecution of Christians in 1779. In the ensuing years, the Eurasian community became more complex, ranging from English-local, English-Portuguese Eurasian, English-Dutch Burgher, English-Siamese and even English-Burmese, although the numbers were very small. Among the Asian population, there also emerged a small group of Baba or Peranakan Chinese.

While Melaka had a settled population when the Dutch took over its administration, Penang's society was entirely made up of migrants who came together and built the town from scratch. Although the English administration did not have a policy of separating the ethnic communities, from the start the tendency was towards self-segregation. The majority of Europeans were found on the northern and western part of the town. The Malays were mostly concentrated in the southern part of Penang, while the Chinese and Indians (Chulias and Hindus) were grouped together in different streets in the town centre. Although there were some Europeans who lived in the Asians areas, their numbers were small.

The majority of the Europeans resided to the west and south of Fort Cornwallis or in the northern part of Penang, in an area towards the fort that was situated close to the administrative centre, at the northern part of Beach Street, north of Penang Street, Light Street, Bishop Street, north of King Street, north of Pitt Street, Penang Road, Farquhar Street and Leith Street. On the other hand, the majority of the Chinese, Jawi Pekans and Chulias resided in the central business district, in the central part of Pitt Street, south of King Street, south of Penang Street, the middle of Beach Street, Chulia Street, Market Street, Queen Street, China Street and Church Street. A small number of Chinese, Chulias, Jawi Pekans and Malays also resided to the west and south of the fort, in predominantly European areas. In addition, a few Malays and Europeans also settled in the central business district. However, most Malays lived in the southern part of the central business district, namely, Aceh Street, Malay Street, the southern part of Pitt and Beach Streets and on Armenian Lane. A small number of Chulias, Jawi Pekans and a few Armenians (probably fewer then 10) also lived in the predominantly Malay areas. The Armenians were merchants who, although few in number, were so distinctive that the small street on which they lived, Armenian Lane, was named after them. However, they were not officially classified as a separate ethnic group.

Due to the fact that all the ethnic communities were new to the environment, the cultural contrasts tended to be stark and were more so because many came with no intention of staying permanently. Thus, they went about their own way, practising their own customs and traditions. This can be clearly seen in the way the European community lived, as we shall see, for while there was some adaptation made to living in the East, both the form and substance in their life style were Western. Similarly, many Chinese and Indians were birds of passage, seeing Penang as a place for making their riches and then returning to their kith and kin in their homeland.

THE EUROPEAN COMMUNITY IN PENANG

As was the case in Melaka, most Europeans in Penang were Company officials and their relatives and European merchants and traders. The official community was small right from the start, as it was in charge of a small population. In fact, the inability of the British to establish Penang as a naval base subsequently led to the reduction of European officers working there. The establishment was reduced from a Governor and three Councillors to a Governor and two Councillors and there were retrenchments in the administrative departments.[1] Besides, there were few Europeans in Penang who did not work for the government, and these were mostly traders, merchants, planters and real estate owners. Thus the European community remained small throughout the period under study. In the first 25 years or so of Penang's opening, Europeans were already overwhelmingly outnumbered by the other communities, making up only 1.5 per cent of the population in 1788, while in 1810 they represented only 0.6 per cent of the total. The small European community was a matter of concern to the administration so that when the English were in Melaka, they also tried, as they did with the Chinese, to entice the European population there to migrate to Penang. In fact those who were willing to leave Melaka were given a cash incentive equivalent to the value of the property they had to leave behind.

Although they were a small minority, the Europeans were the elite of society and some were among the most wealthy on the island due to their business ventures. Table 49 below shows that the Europeans owned more than three-quarters of the wealth in property compared to the other races in 1806, which would have given them an early advantage. They owned some of the choicest land in Penang. The liberal policy of encouraging the merchants and Company servants to own land during Light's administration made many wealthy. Francis Light himself and his friend James Scott and Scott's

Table 49: Value of property according to ethnicity – land, houses and premises in an area around 340 yards from Fort Cornwallis in 1806

Ethnic group	Value of property	Percentage
Europeans	417,550.00	79.26
Chinese	86,500.00	16.42
Europeans and Chinese	4,000.00	0.75
Chulias	2,700.00	0.51
Malays and Jawi Pekans	16,000.00	3.03
Total	526,750.00	100

Source: G/34/19, F/4/262 5848.

close associate, David Brown, owned vast areas of land in the town and hinterland.

In the early years, particularly during the administration of Francis Light, his friendship with European merchants, his background as a country trader and the need for assistance to develop Penang as a port gave the European mercantile community a great deal of say in the running of the new settlement, thus increasing their influence in the government and the community. Following the administration of the third Superintendent of Penang, who saw this direct involvement as interference, there appears to have been some distance between the mercantile community and the government. Nevertheless, this did not affect subsequent relations as cooperation between the two sectors appears to have been maintained, as we have seen. This was largely due to the fact that many European businessmen were former Company servants who probably found that the business opportunities on offer in Penang were more lucrative and could make them wealthy quicker. Indeed, the career path that a company official had to follow was long and the rise to the top was slow. Many started their careers as writers or storekeepers, where they remained for six years before being promoted to the next level, rising up to the positions of Junior and Senior Merchants only from the ninth to the eleventh year of holding their job.

At the social level, the European community interacted as one group. Although European men always outnumbered the women, Penang's European society, even in the early days, was grounded around family life. Phillip Mannington, who succeeded Francis Light as Superintendent in 1794, arrived in Penang with his wife and children one of whom, Elizabeth, was married in Penang in 1803 to a Charles Sealy. Francis Light himself was married and had children although his wife was a Eurasian by the name of Martina

Rozells (in his will Martina was also named as Nonia Abuy),[2] a Portuguese-Eurasian from Siam who had migrated to Kedah and subsequently came to Penang.[3] Evidence shows that many marriages were carried out in Penang. Among the early marriages, besides that of Elizabeth Mannington, was the union between Thomas Burston Pierce, Commander of H.C.S. Taunton Castle, and Anna Maria Fearon in 1801. In the second decade many more marriages were seen in the European community so that by the 1820s there were many children growing up in the European residential areas. Writing in 1837, Martin observed that, 'there must have been more European children in Penang in 1822 than there are today. There were many nice homes with boys and girls growing up together.'[4]

In a new settlement, single European males, usually of a lower social standing, who came to work there were just as likely to form marriage alliances with Asians or other ethnic groups as they were to keep native mistresses, due to the absence of European women of similar standing. Thomas Layton, merchant and owner of a slaughter house and farmland, set up home with a Burmese woman called, Mallo, with whom he had a son, named George.[5] From the will of Mathew Shepherson, a mariner, it appears that he had a mistress in Melaka with whom he had a few children.[6] Another European, Christopher Smith, a botanist and superintendent of the EIC spice plantation, had a child with Rosina, who did not appear to be a European.[7] The case of Smith is interesting because from the information given in the will it would seem that Rosina's sister, Elisabeth, might have been his mistress before he lived with the former.

Among the elite, however, mixed marriages were rare. James Scott, Light's friend and an influential merchant who lived in a typical Malay home, dressed like a Malay and spoke the language, might have been co-habiting with a Malay woman. But 'going native' was probably not well accepted among the community and only a wealthy and prominent member of society, such as Scott, might have been able to challenge the norm with some impunity.[8]

The norm was to preserve the purity of the race, which meant that in time, as in Melaka, familial relations were forged and the Europeans came even closer together through blood and friendship ties. As we have seen, Elizabeth Palmer Mannington, daughter of Phillip Mannington, a wealthy merchant and land owner in the town, was married to Charles Sealy.[9] Phillip Mannington, who died in 1795 and was succeeded by Major Macdonald, had two sons, named Phillip and Robert. Phillip worked as a Second Assistant to the new Superintendent and the Magistrate but died in Penang in 1806. Robert, who also lived on the island, was the godfather to his sister Elizabeth's son.

Besides the Manningtons, the Raffles were also a well connected family which knew many people in the town.[10] A famous member of this family was Sir Stamford Raffles, who later obtained Singapore from the Sultan of Johor. Stamford Raffles had a sister in Penang who married Quinton Dick Thompson. They had a son, christened William O'Bryen Drury, and his godfathers were Rear Admiral William O'Bryen Drury and Thomas Raffles. However, Quinton Dick Thompson died a few months after his son was baptized. Two years later his widow re-married, this time to Captain Flint in Melaka. Leonora, the younger sister of Stamford Raffles, also resided in the town and was married to Billington Loftie, a surgeon.[11]

The Bannerman family had close relationships with various people in the town.[12] One member of that family, J.H. Bannerman, became Governor of the island in November 1817. He had a nephew, named Reverend James Patrick Bannerman, who was a clergyman in the Anglican Church. Both of them had daughters to whom they gave the name Janet. The daughter of Reverend James Patrick Bannerman was married to Henry Burney, a Lieutenant in the Bengal Army, while the daughter of J.H. Bannerman was married to a member of the Phillips family, also one of the senior merchants. The Bannermans were considered an influential family in the town and had nieces and cousins living in Penang.[13]

Two other prominent families were the Carnegys and the Caunters. The Carnegys were related by marriage to various people in the town.[14] In 1817 Margaret Carnegy, the sister of James and Patrick Carnegy, married a Mr Clubley who was the owner of Clubley's Hill on the island and who later became Senior member of the Council of Administration. Another sister, named Mary Alison, was married to John Anderson, a government servant. The town had two Caunter brothers. Their sister, Harriet Georgina, was first married to W. Bennett. After her husband passed away in 1817, however, she married a Mr Ibbetson, who later became Governor of the island. Ibbetson had a sister named Sarah Sparke Caunter who was the wife of either G. or R. Caunter. Later, when her husband died, she married Captain Thomas Larkins.

However, little is known about the lives and family connections of the early pioneers. Although the famous Scott, Light and Brown families possessed wealth in the town, their family connections are only vaguely known. James Scott had two sons, but one died at an early age while the other survived until the ripe old age of 83 years.[15] The long-surviving son, named William, was a philanthropist, well known for his benevolence, hospitality and charitable works. He had the reputation of being a kind person who had many friends and was well liked in the colony. Unlike his father, James Scott, he had a good relationship with the administration and held several appointments in the East India Company. He was educated at Edinburgh High School and later became a member of the Volunteer Cavalry and Royal Archers of the city of Edinburgh.[16] Most of his inheritance came from his wealthy father, which he later left to the Brown family. He also owned a successful plantation that was the envy of many.

The members of the Light family did not stay long in the town after their father's death in 1794. His widow, Martina, remarried and one of his sons, William, pioneered the establishment of Adelaide.[17] All his daughters were married to wealthy gentlemen in Madras and Bengal. As for the Brown family members, their activities were not clearly documented. David Brown went into the plantation business but did not survive to see the results of his hard work on his land.[18] After his death in 1825, his son was the sole survivor of his estate.[19] Little is known about this son except that he inherited a large spice plantation which was pioneered by his father.

Thus it can be seen that many families within Penang were interconnected with one another. This human network went beyond the island, covering the wider community of overseas British nationals in all the colonies set up by the EIC. From this big community the Company drew many of its officials, but it also provided a pool of single men and women that made possible ties of marriage which in turn helped to preserve the integrity of the Europeans as a separate social unit.

This social separateness was reinforced by the distinctive way of life that they pursued. One area in which the European way of life was perpetuated was in the community's link with the Church, as also in Melaka. Although, in sharp contrast to the VOC in Melaka, a strong relationship between the Church and the Company did not exist with the English EIC, and though the Company's charter prohibited any attempt at spreading religion and giving religious education in the colonies, this did not prevent the European community from exercising their religious rights and making their own provisions for the practice of their religion. Their resourcefulness was quite remarkable in view of the obstacles they faced arising from the charter, which took a long time to overcome.

Challenges to the provision of the Company charter regarding religious proselytizing were mounted by the English Evangelicals, who were keen to spread the Anglican faith to the EIC colonies, as early as 1793 when they tried, but failed, to change it in the British Parliament. Following that they tried to publicize widely the matter by drawing public attention, leading finally to the formation of the London Missionary Society in 1795.[20] The Society soon tested the East India Company's policy by proposing to send a group of its missionaries to Bengal, but permission for this was refused. Not until 1813 was the Company's charter amended to permit independent missionary and educational activities in India.[21]

In the meantime, the European society in Penang could not build a church and had to conduct their activities in makeshift premises. There was also no minister or clergyman for the Anglican faith for some time. As a result, evidence of the activities of the Anglican Church in Penang in the early years is scanty. In 1800, when George Leith was appointed the new Lieutenant-Governor of the island, G. Caunter, the First Assistant Secretary, served as Acting Chaplain for the Anglican faith.[22] As a chaplain, Caunter baptized, solemnized marriages and carried out burial ceremonies for members of the Anglican community in the colony. Thus, the community had to make do with the First Assistant Secretary as their religious leader until 1805, when the first Anglican clergyman, Reverend Atwell Lake, arrived on the island. The first Anglican church, St George's Church, was built only in 1818, in contrast to the Roman Catholic Church, which was already standing in Church Street long before the Anglicans had their own permanent place of worship.

As the ruling group, the elite of society and being among the wealthiest people on the island, the Europeans were able to set a high standard in terms of their way of life, just as the Dutch did in Melaka. In Penang, most houses owned by Europeans stood at the northern part of town, mostly facing the sea. Those who lived near the harbour were able to enjoy the beautiful view of the harbour and fort. Most of the houses were large, elegant and spacious. A description of one such house is given by John Turnbull Thomson, an Englishman who worked as a surveyor in Penang from 1838 to 1841. [23] In his book, *Glimpses into Life in Malayan Lands*, he wrote:

> The house belongs to a merchant and planter. It is situated within the precincts of Penang. It is a pillared and verandahed mansion, with ground and upper floor. Green venetians close in the upper rooms, which admit or close out the shifting breezes, at pleasure. A large red-tiled roof of rigidly plain features covers the whole. Various fruit trees are planted in the enclosure or compound, clean gravel roads lead up to the portico, under which the visitor arrives. The front of the house commands a view of the esplanade, the fort, and the harbour.[24]

Penang's European community retained more European characteristics than its counterpart in Melaka. This was probably because the English, who made up the majority of the European population, had not been in the East as long as the Dutch. Perhaps, more importantly, many never envisaged spending the rest of their lives in Penang, so that although far from the mother-land, they regarded it very important to maintain their European way of life.

Thus, although the European community worked and lived in the East, their orientation was towards the West. Nowhere was this more obvious than in the way they kept in touch with what was happening in Europe. When they started the *Prince of Wales Gazette*, the only newspaper available to the community for a long time, almost all of the coverage was about the international scene, particularly news from Europe and other English colonies.[25] The *Gazette*, published in English twice weekly on Wednesday and Saturday, was the European community's window on the world, as it was the only source of news and information for the merchants and the European community. Local news consisted of government notifications, general orders and advertisements and law reports. The auction of revenue farms, which was attended by the Governor and members of his Council, was also reported, with those who succeeded in the bidding meriting a mention. Social events were also reported, such as performances and reviews of them. Another activity reported in the newspaper was the club meetings of the European community. For example, the monthly meetings of the Prince of Wales Island Club, held at Nicholl Tavern, were published. After 1818, when the Anglican Church was officially opened, the newspaper also published news regarding the Mass and the activities of the church. In addition, advertisements made by the general European public, such as information about the sale of property and rentals available and announcements of births, deaths, engagements and marriages were also given space in the paper.[26] The paper showed little interest in other communities.

Another example of the way the European style of life was preserved was seen in their attire and the style with which they conducted their social life. Thomson provides a good picture of the Englishness of a dinner at which he was a guest:

> [T]he party proceeds down stairs and enters the dining hall, where the family silver is spread in its full extent and variety. The visitors now advance solemnly to their respective positions. The ladies seat themselves, and the gentlemen follow. Exquisitely white napkins with fancy bread are laid before each chair. If a clergyman be present, in deference to him, a grace is asked for. Different soups, in silver tureens, occupy the ends and middle of the table, mock turtle and mulligatawny being the favourites. The native servants, in their gaudy liveries, advance and stand with folded arms behind their masters and mistresses. Now the soups are served, and the clattering of spoons commences; the ice is broken, and the joke, laugh, and repartee go round.[27]

The writer went on to describe the after-dinner scene, noting that the ladies retired to the drawing-room (on the upper floor), the gentlemen later joining them, presumably after smoking a cigar or having a few drinks. Then coffee and tea were served, followed by a piano recital by a young lady. Later on, a dance commenced, ending at midnight. The scene, minus the native servants, could just as well have occurred in England and although Thomson was describing a dinner he attended in the 1830s, it would not have been far from the way things were in the earlier period.

British patriotism was also nurtured. When the practice of celebrating important events in the mother country was started is unclear, but even the birthday of the consort of the King of England merited a celebration in Penang. Thus, on 25 January 1817, the Governor entertained the European community to a ball and supper in honour of the 73rd birthday of the Queen of England. The Gazette reported the occasion thus:

> On Monday evening the governor entertained the ladies and gentle-men of the settlement with a ball and supper in honor of the 73rd anniversary of her most gracious majesty's birthday. The spacious suite of room in the mansion of 'Suffolk' was brilliantly illuminated and thrown open at an early hour for the reception of the most numerous assemblage of which our green island has had to boast for many years. An extensive verandah afforded ample space for the accommodation of the dancers while such of the party as gave the preference to cards or chefs, found tables laid for their favorite pursuits in the adjoining rooms. The grateful coolness of the evening tended materially to aug-ment the pleasures of the mazy dance which however was indebted for its unbounded spirit to the unusual number of ladies who graced the party with their preference. Dancing having been kept up to a late hour, after the usual finale of Le Boulanger, the company adjourned to the supper-room where they sat down a table full of elegant supper and at an advanced hour of the night retired equally delighted with the festivities of the evening and the urbanity and unremitting attentions of their honorable host".[28]

At one level, these dinners, receptions and social gatherings were a reminder of home, but at another level their lavishness served to provide the elite with entertainment, as only the rich could afford, and the chance to meet and maintain their status and prestige in the port-town. At such gatherings, the etiquette was European, as we saw above. However, some Eastern tastes and flavours were also appreciated in the food they served and ate. This was due to many of the European settlers arriving not directly from their motherland but from another base in Asia, usually India, where they had worked or set up their businesses in ports on the coast of the Bay of Bengal and where they had first acquired a taste for Eastern cuisine. As described by Thompson, writing in 1830, at these parties the guests were welcomed and entertained according to Western standards although some food was a mix of Western and Eastern dishes.[29] Thus a feast could consist of strange combinations of dishes. One selection could include the best fish from the island, Bengal mutton, Chinese ducks, Kedah chicken and ducks from Ligor, Yorkshire hams, Java potatoes and local tapioca while the last course of another menu could consist of rice, curry, *sambals*, Bombay ducks, Kampar roast, salted turtle's eggs and omelettes.[30] The meal was usually served with wines and complimented by dessert which could consist of maccaroni pudding or custard followed by champagne. According to Thomson, the European merchants and planters who enjoyed lavish dinner parties had grown accustomed to eastern delicacies.[31] The local fruits were a favourite, but they singled out the *durian* and the jack fruit and *cempedak*, which had very strong smells. Thus, from Thomson's account, it would appear that the European community enjoyed an active social life in Penang of which the dinner parties were a favourite. Such parties were designed to tickle the palate as well as provide, for the men, an opportunity to keep up with current affairs and news pertaining to daily life in the East.[32]

The European community also made sure that they did not miss out on their arts and culture. Thus, plays, dramas and comedies and other types of performances were organized from time to time. When a performance was organized by the official community it was attended by the cream of the European society as happened at a performance reported in the 13th December 1817 issue of the Gazette:

> .[O]n Saturday evening the settlement was again assembled at the theatre by a polite invitation from the officers of H.M. ship, Orlando, to witness the representation of Colman's excellent comedy of the Heir at Law and the mockheroic Farce of Bombasters Furioso ... their complete success was fully marked by repeated bursts of applause from the delighted audience who were totally convulsed with inextinguishable laughter. The Governor, Colonel Bannerman, with his family and suite, who honored the theatre with his presence, was received with the usual marks of respect, the guards presenting arms and the band, upon his entrance, playing 'God Save the King'., ... among the crowded company were observed, in addition to the Governor, the Members of Council, Sir George and Lady Cooper, one of the Supreme Court Judges at Madras, Sir Ralph Rice, Colonel Loveday, Captain Clanvell, Paterson and Barnard, R.N.[33]

It seemed that official gatherings such as the performance by the crew of the ship belonging to the British Naval Force and the function in honour of the Queen's birthday, referred to earlier, were only attended by the Europeans in the town. There was no mention in the reports in the paper that the other communities were invited, although it would not have been suitable to invite the non-English speaking communities to an English comedy performance.

Due to the fact that the European community was very small and their social life was restricted to their own group, they probably knew one another. This situation was further assisted by the institution of the club, which was an integral feature of the British colonial scene. The notion of having a club in itself was built around the principle of organizing an association of persons united by a common interest with the object of providing a regular meeting place for conviviality or co-operation. In Penang the European community formed the Prince of Wales Island Club. The club facilitated social interaction and provided a venue away from home where the Europeans could meet or entertain among themselves. Particularly, for the men, it was a place for recreation and relaxation although the Prince of Wales island Club appeared to have been located at the Nicholl Tavern, another European institution serving the needs of the men who liked to retire to a pub for a drink after a hard day's work in the heat.

The social life of the European community living in a colonial town far away from the European social environment was not as bad as some might have anticipated. As Garnier rightly described, 'the social life must have been very pleasant at that time and one finds that many of one's preconceived ideas of life in the East in those days have to be revised and life was not the exile that one sometimes imagined it to have been.'[34] In fact, for some, life was probably even better than they were accustomed to in their homeland. As the elite, they had the best of everything. The hot climate was a drain on their energies, but they developed a hill station called Penang Hill to which they could escape temporarily from the stifling heat. They had servants, and in the early years before slavery was banned, some even had slaves at their beck and call. Moreover, much went on in Penang to keep life interesting. The visit of the HMS Orlanda is a case in point. For many, their world was not only limited to Penang as the opportunity to travel was wide open. The good life to be had in Penang was noted by an author in the following terms: "[T]here was much coming and going. People went to Calcutta, Madras, Malacca, Bencoolen and further afield to the Cape and to China on business or for health – not perhaps for pleasure!"[35]

ASIAN ETHNIC GROUPS IN PENANG

As was with Dutch in Melaka, the English also depended on the Asian communities to develop and turn Penang into an important port-town with permanent settlers. Right from the start, the authorities were convinced that the Chinese were necessary for the task. Francis Light noted that, 'The Chinese constitute the most valuable part of our inhabitants...'[36] His successor Mannington observed, 'From the long experience I have had of the indefatigable industry of the Chinese, they are the only people I am so confident will effectually cultivate this island and be serviceable as mechanics and merchants'.[37] Later, in the first decade of the nineteenth century, the English even tried to force the ethnic Chinese in Melaka to settle in Penang when they, the English, had to abandon Melaka in 1808.[38] At that stage, the Chinese were promised that they would be compensated to the value of one-eighth of their property. However, the scheme was a failure when most Chinese refused to budge from Melaka.[39]

The English also felt that the Chulias should be encouraged to settle permanently in Penang since the majority of them were traders and merchants. This could help trade to flourish between India and Penang and secure the Chulia's trading network, which covered the Bay of Bengal, Southern Thailand, the Straits and north Sumatra. The Chulias were also needed to supply the port-town with cheap labour by bringing men out from India. However, the English had a problem with the attitude of the Chulias, as most of them had no intention of staying permanently but merely saw Penang as a place to make their fortune, after which they would return home.

The Malays in general were perceived as a less important group, being not economically useful in the way that the Chinese and Chulias were. However, an exception was made with the Bugis, who were classified as Malays, for their trading skills were readily acknowledged and they were therefore encouraged to trade and stay in Penang. The English saw these Malays as good traders and honest merchants.[40]

Of the people of mixed descent, the Eurasians were very small in number and had little impact on the population.[41] The majority of them had come from Siam and Kedah. As Penang progressed, their presence was no longer noticed in the annual census of the town and island. On the other hand, the Jawi Pekans were considered a group that 'inherits the boldness of the Malay and the subtlety, acuteness and dissimulation of the Hindu, indefatigable in the pursuit of wealth and most usurious in the employment of it when gained'.[42] The Company perceived the Jawi Pekans as assets because their skills were needed and, as Penang developed, those who were not in the business sector were found to be suited for work in the government departments. A few made good interpreters, some proved useful for policing the town and those who performed the clerical work in the administration were found to be good and trustworthy workers. In the beginning, the Jawi Pekans were mostly shopkeepers who came from Kedah. Some later found work with the Company as interpreters, controlling the immigrants from Kedah, and also as guards for the Company. One of the Jawi Pekans known to have worked with the Company was Nakhuda Kechil, who came from Kedah. Their usefulness lay in the fact that most were able to converse in more than two languages. Although their presence in the town was encouraged, some were regarded as outlaws and a nuisance to society, their bad behaviour being seen as the effect of their mixed parentage, which in their case was Malay and Indian.[43]

THE MALAY COMMUNITY

When Penang began to prosper, many Malays began to arrive from the Malay peninsula and Sumatra to settle in the port-town. Officially, the English classified all natives from the archipelago as Malays, so that the Javanese, Bugis, Minangkabaus and other Sumatrans were all pooled together. The English divided the Malays into two groups, namely, those who resided in the town – mostly merchants and traders – and those who resided in the outskirts and the interior, who were mostly paddy cultivators and wood cutters.[44] Many Malays belonged to that group which resided on the outskirts of the town. In the early period, this group of Malays were especially useful because they felled trees and cleared the jungle on the island for spice cultivation.

The Malay trading community was large enough to form a separate settlement in the southern section of the town. They arrived seasonally to the island from Sumatra, the Malay peninsula and the archipelago. Among these traders were the Bugis, who came from their homeland in South Sulawesi and other Bugis settlements in the archipelago and the Straits. They were a big group, totalling between one to two thousand by 1800.[45] The British viewed them as a proud, warlike, independent people whose vessels were always well equipped with arms, which they used with dexterity and vigour. Although the English regarded them as warlike, it seems that their redeeming feature was that they were easily controlled and were normally obedient. They were also considered as the best merchants among the inhabitants of the Eastern islands.

There were also a few people of Arab descent in Penang, the most prominent being Tuanku Syed Hussain, a member of the royal family of Aceh and a wealthy trader with business connections with Aceh.[46] His family left Aceh in the 1770s for Riau but later settled in Kuala Selangor, where they built a flourishing business. When Penang was established, he moved his trading base to the island and became one of the first settlers there. In 1790 he was appointed leader of the Malay and Muslim communities of Penang. As his business prospered he became associated with several European merchants and was even able to establish ties with John Palmer of Calcutta, an influential figure in official circles and widely known as the 'Prince of Merchants'.[47] Tuanku Syed Hussain was certainly one of the richest men in Penang mostly due to his business ties with Aceh, which were helped by his social standing and connections there. As a result, he was able to acquire a fleet of ships that called regularly at Susu and Singkil.[48] His trade with Aceh consisted mainly of procuring pepper from the Acehnese west coast and betel-nut from the Pedir coast. In return, he brought in opium and piece-goods from India and sold some of these to Aceh. He was granted exemptions from various taxes and trade duties by the ruler, Jauhar al-Alam, until he took the latter to the Penang court over a debt settlement.[49] Through his wealth and philanthropic contributions he emerged as an influential leader of the Malay and Muslim communities in Penang.

Tuanku Syed Hussain was well known in official circles and were even said to have lent money to the administration on several occasions. The British also rented the official residence of the Governor from him. His influence in Penang was immense, leading in May 1815 to his being suggested as a person who could influence the locals into giving assistance to the authorities in defending the island from a possible attack by American privateers. Since the defence of the island was inadequate, the British felt he was the only person who could unite and control the Malays.[50]

Syed Hussain's business connections and influence was such that when he was embroiled in the civil war in Aceh, which ended with his son being made ruler of the kingdom, the Penang commercial community was split into two camps, as discussed earlier. Due to his stature, he was one of the few Asians socially accepted by the Europeans so that his activities were reported by the European press. *The Prince of Wales Gazette* covered the lavish parties he organized to which local European dignitaries and merchants were invited.

As befitting a royal personage and a leader of society, Syed Hussain led an opulent lifestyle, showing off his wealth through huge parties which he gave from time to time. A party he organized was extensively reported in the 7 December 1806 [?] issue of the *Gazette*. It was reported that he had thrown a lavish party to which he invited most of the wealthy European planters, merchants, traders and Company servants, including all the wealthy Malays, Chinese and Indians of the town.[51] The whole residential area of his mansion was illuminated with beautiful lights, including the street and his compound. In order to control a crowd that had gathered near his premises, he asked police and guards to handle the uninvited guests. Such a rich and illustrious event generated much talk among the people. The dinner consisted of all the luxuries and delicacies that generous hospitality could afford. It included the best wines and the best foods in the town. The party was followed later in the night with entertainment in the form of Malay and Indian dances, until late morning.[52] For certain, no other Asian except Syed

Hussain, the richest man on the island, could throw such a lavish party or invite as many guests or bring together prominent members of all the communities under one roof.

Other rich Malays in Penang, along with Syed Hussain, lived in the way to which they were accustomed. As we have seen, when the rules introduced by the government did not suit them, they simply sent petitions, as when they made known that they should be allowed to keep their slaves and practice their way of life without interference. That Syed Hussain built a mosque for the Malay-Muslim community also points to the fact that they looked after their affairs themselves and provided the facilities for their social and cultural needs. The ability to get together a Malay dance troupe on the occasion of Syed Hussain's party also shows that the Malays were not devoid of the finer things in life.

THE ASIAN COMMUNITY

The Chinese were active in trade and spice cultivation and they also monopolized the government revenue farms and dominated the retail business. But they also provided Penang with its skilled, semi-skilled and unskilled workers. The wealthiest Chinese were mostly merchants, revenue farmers, traders and planters who resided in the town centre and owned shops, shophouses, godowns and trading vessels. The majority of the Chinese worked for wages, with some being employed by wealthy Chinese businessmen. According to the English, most Chinese workers received good wages because they were good labourers. Others were carpenters, blacksmiths, tailors, shoemakers, fishermen and gardeners, the last being particularly useful, as they supplied the markets with all sorts of vegetables.[53] Thus, there was no doubt that, as a community, they were to be found in a variety of economic activities and at all levels. It is therefore no wonder that the English found them so useful for the development of Penang.

As a group, the Chinese formed a complex and sometimes divided community because of the existence of sub-ethnic divisions, although in Penang, in the period under study, there were only two main sub-divisions, the Cantonese and Chinchews.[54] The Cantonese came from Macao and the Chinchiews from Fukien. Each spoke its own dialect and showed a strong loyalty only to its own group. Each group also developed certain specialities and monopolised particular trades. Most Cantonese were carpenters, blacksmiths, shoemakers and labourers. Only a small number worked as goldsmiths, tailors and shopkeepers.[55] According to the English, the Chinese who came from Macao or Canton were more robust and hard working than the Chinchews from Fukien.

Due to this division, the early history of the Chinese in Penang was marred by rivalry and infighting. It was a common practice among the Chinese immigrants to form clubs or friendly societies to foster close relationships among their members and to give assistance to newly arrived migrants.[56] Such assistance was much needed, as the Chinese who arrived in Penang were mostly uneducated. In fact, many became the victims of unscrupulous practices among some of the Europeans who took advantage of their ignorance and induced them to sign bonds without their consent or understanding. Many were thus cheated and subsequently lost their property and were forced to move out from their lands and plantations due to their ignorance regarding the signing of papers or bonds.[57]

Membership in a club was restricted to those who came from the same area, spoke the same dialect and shared the same sub-culture; those from other districts or villages were excluded.[58] These clubs only heightened the differences between the sub-groups, often encouraging hostilities and rivalry. At times they ended in physical violence. It should be noted that these clubs were not secret societies but were friendly societies more for socializing and helping the needy and the newly arrived Chinese from China.[59] Nevertheless, the rivalry and animosity engendered were intense and when such attitudes were related to questions of material gain, they were sometimes explosive and long-term.

In Penang much of the problem between the Cantonese and Chinchews arose over competition for lucrative businesses on the island. For example, the revenue farms were a bone of contention, as can be seen in the case of the arak farms. Che Toah, Che Ee, Che Seong and Oosey, all Chinchews, were partners in the opium and *arak* revenue farms. Since 1816, these farms were in the hands of the Chinchews and it became their major and most lucrative monopoly. However, in 1824, the Cantonese group succeeded in breaking the Chinchew monopoly of the opium and *arak* farms through smuggling and illicit trading, and so won control of the *arak* farms from 1824–25. However, in 1827–28 the *arak* farms were back in the hands of the Chinchews and only in 1828–29 did they revert back to the Cantonese.[60]

This rivalry for the monopoly of the revenue may have started in the early nineteenth century. In 1806, Chewan, a Chinchew and also the Chinese Capitan, lodged a complaint about Cantonese smuggling, which he alleged had ruined his monopoly. He also sought assistance from the police magistrate to stop the operations of the Cantonese smugglers. However, the police magistrate was involved in corruption and instead of resolving the issue, he asked for favours from Chewan. Thus the matter became a long-term problem that saw ownership of the farms changing from one group to the other several times.[61]

Rivalry was also seen in the pork farms controlled by the Cantonese. In 1813, the Cantonese pork farmer, Cha Sye, made a complaint to the government that some Chinchews had violated the regulations of the pork farm by killing hogs secretly in their backyards in Beach Street. To substantiate this complaint, the Cantonese farmer claimed that he had not been able to sell even 20 dollars worth of pork to the Chinchew Chinese in Beach Street in two months.[62]

In 1830 the Chinchew Chinese had the monopoly of both *arak* and opium in Penang. Even the regulations and contracts of revenue farms were in the Chinchew dialect, which was not understood by the Cantonese.[63] This showed the stranglehold the Chinchews had over the two farms. More importantly, this state of affairs led the Macao Cantonese to accuse the Chinchews of conspiring to destroy their business. To aggravate the situation, the Chinchew group also encouraged their people to breed hogs and to offer them for sale at high prices. The competition became so intense that finally the Cantonese farmers had to cease their business. Further violence and hostilities broke out the groups. As the monopoly of the opium farms was in the hands of the Chinchews, the Cantonese tried to ruin their revenue from the farms through smuggling, which led to more fighting and clashes.

Thus, there was a tendency among some Chinese to ignore or circumvent the laws and to live according to their own rules and inclinations. Another example of this was in the slave-smuggling activities that they engaged in, even as late as the 1820s. The English also saw them as extravagant in their mode of living, as a large portion of their wages was spent on gambling or smoking opium.[64] Most Chinese were addicted to gaming and opium and were fond of attending Chinese operas or plays, all common leisure pastimes.[65] But they worked hard and helped to develop Penang so that their contribution was apppreciated by the English authorities.

If the Dutch used the terms Moors (Muslim) and Kelings (Hindus) to describe those who came from the Indian subcontinent, the British used the term Chulias (Muslim) and Hindus. Most of the Chulias in Penang came from several ports on the Coromandel Coast although some came from Kedah. The majority of Chulias were shopkeepers, merchants or coolies.[66] By the end of eighteenth century, about one thousand Chulias had settled in the town with their families. Besides this number, there were 1,500 to 2,000 Chulia immigrants from the Coromandel Coast who came to the town annually.[67] However, most were sojourners who, after earning enough money, returned home.[68] Although the Chulias made up the majority of the population in the town, their lifestyle did not make a great impact in proportion to their numbers, perhaps because most of them were 'passing-through' and more inclined to stay for shorter periods than the Chinese.

Thus, most Chulia settlers were men who did not bring their wives and families to the island. They concentrated on their business dealings, led simple lives and cut down on expenses by living in small houses packed with as many people as possible.

Like the Eurasians, the Asian Christians were a small minority and consisted mostly of Siamese and Burmese inhabitants who had converted to Roman Catholicism. In Penang most of them were farmers.[69] The numbers that settled in the town were very small and their impact on the social and economic activities negligible. However, probably because they were Christians, the women seemed to have been seen as suitable partners by some European men.

PENANG AS A MIGRANT COLONIAL PORT-TOWN

As a new settlement, Penang went through a time of adjustment made more problematic by the multi-ethnic nature of its population. An early feature of Penang as a migrant port-town was intermarriages and co-habitation due to the imbalance in the sex ratio. There were intermarriages and co-habitation between the English and the Eurasians and locals, with their offspring being counted as Europeans because the term Eurasians was only used for the descendants of the Portuguese population who had intermarried with the locals. A good example was Francis Light, who married a Portuguese-Eurasian, and James Scott, who adopted Malay culture and way of life and lived with a Malay woman. Since the number of natives was large in the early period, other migrants, namely the Chinese and Chulias, often married or had children with these natives. The Chulias in particular, who came every year and stayed only for a short while, were mostly males.

While the search for companionship encouraged the breaking down of ethnic barriers, the separate existence, which was the norm in Penang's pluralistic society, was more likely than not to cause conflict and tensions. We have seen the intra-ethnic tensions in the Chinese community; other instances of strained relationships existed between the government and the natives and Asian population. While such tensions arose between those on the side of the authorities and the citizens, the ethnic equation could not be discarded. This can be seen when the Police Magistrate, who was in charge of the security of the town, indulged in corrupt practices by receiving illicit payments from the public. In addition, prior to the introduction of the Charter of Justice in Penang, the island was not a peaceful place. Conditions were chaotic and the inhabitants severely harassed by the Indian sepoys and other members of the military. In 1794, there were numerous complaints made against the European Marines and the Indian Sepoys.[70] These complaints involved the fleet of trading vessels that were seized by the military force. They took all the merchandise from the vessels and paid only half of the value of the goods. In addition, the sepoys acted violently in the towns and bazaars and only paid for goods according to their own inclination. The inhabitants of Penang were paralyzed with fear due to the conduct of the military and the sepoys. Consequently, this incident prompted a resolution directing that all goods were to be sold at the marketplace and that every individual was free to dispose of his property.

Intolerance of strange cultural practices was also seen in the early days. A case in point was a complaint made by a Chinese shopkeeper named Gee against Captain Drummond, the Town Mayor of Penang. The complaint involved a brutal action taken by the Town Mayor following an incident. On the eve of the Chinese New Year, Bunee Kha, a police Peon in Penang, arrested a Chinese who was brought to police headquarters. By the orders of Captain Drummond, he was confined to a cell to enable the police to conduct an investigation. However, he was then set free on bail and badly beaten when he appeared the next day before the police magistrate. During the investigation, it was alleged that Gee was badly beaten by Captain Drummond, who was alleged to have been angry at Gee for having thrown firecrackers at the Captain's horses when he was passing in a carriage. After the incident, various rules and regulations were introduced to ensure that the practice of a religious belief should not disrupt another's belief or culture.[71]

It would have been difficult for the Malays to adjust to the rule that, at all times, they had to ride a saddled horse or suffer a dozen strips of the rattan if they disobeyed. The rule was imposed to prevent accidents from occurring, as was the case with the stipulation that the sharp points on the horns of the buffaloes must be cut off and that animals had to be secured by a rope on public roads.[72] These rules and regulations would have been regarded by the Malays as unfair and were tantamount to interfering in their affairs. Thus, ill-feeling could well have arisen. The examples given relate to the English government and its servants, but it is possible that problems also arose between ethnic groups, although such evidence is not available.

Nevertheless, there was much goodwill shown and this could be seen when individuals were prepared to bring together all the different groups, such as was done by Tuanku Syed Hassain and a few European planters. A well documented event was a party organised by a certain European planter who invited leading members of all communities to it. There were also instances when a European planter would throw a feast near his mansion and open it to all his friends and neighbours. Those who came to the party included Malays, Chinese, Indians and also his close European friends.

Since the planter knew that all his guests belonged to different faiths and cultures, in order not to offend them, he ensured that all the food preparation for the feast followed each particular belief or culture. Therefore, the feast included different kinds of cuisine prepared under the strict beliefs and dietary rules of each ethnic group.[73]

After the meal the feast was followed with games and plays, and in the night the host provided guests with special entertainment, which consisted of *Wayang Kulit* (Leather Puppets) from Java, the Merry and Andrew performance (an English play), followed by the Keling Theatre (*Main Kling*) and lastly the fireworks display. The entertainment offered by the European planter thus combined both Eastern and Western features. The Asian guests sat on the ground while the Europeans sat on chairs. Such a congregation was unique, because it involved people of different races, cultures and religions. There was, however, no equality between the guests.

Some planters who had stayed in the country for a few decades were well acquainted with the natives and Asian communities on whom they depended for labour on their estates or plantations.[74] As a result, such men often understood and perhaps even admired aspects of multi-ethnic cultures and beliefs. They were close to their neighbours, who were mostly Malays, Indians and Chinese. However, it was not only in the employer-employee relationship that some understanding and even affection were cultivated. Some Europeans and Asians were close friends who understood each other very well.

The relationship of inequality between the Europeans and Asians, as noted above, in the manner with which the Asian guests at the planter's party were treated, was that of a master to his underlings. This approach was also seen in the way some Europeans treated their Asian wives or mistresses, as is evident from the wills they made. For example, Thomas Layton, who registered his will in September 1806, gave most of his money to his natural son, while his mistress, a Burmese lady, was to inherit her choice of ten of his slaves. The money from the sale of the rest of the slaves was to be divided equally between the mother and the son. Layton also willed his clothes and household furniture to his mistress but wanted his gold watch to go to his nephew. A slaughterhouse was to go to a Joseph Porter, 'for his kind services'. Thus most of the valuable property was not given to the Asian mistress despite her having given him a son.[75]

The European attitude towards Asian mistresses appears to have been one in which they kept some distance. Mathew Shepherdson, in his will, merely referred to 'the mother of my children' when referring to his mistress, and Christopher Smith gave most of his wealth to his European family and close friends, bequeathing only SpD 1,000 to one mistress and SpD 240 per year to the other for the maintenance and education of his child by her.[76]

CONCLUSION

Due to gaps in the sources, it has not been possible to provide a fuller picture of society in Penang. Nevertheless, Penang, whose newness tended to amplify the contrasts between groups, came close to the classic model of a plural society, in the period under study. It was because of these contrasting features that observers, usually the Europeans, were wont to compare and contrast each ethnic group with the other and to draw conclusions about them which were later to become stereotypes. The fact remains, however, that a huge cultural chasm existed between one ethnic group and another, as described earlier. This situation was not helped by the fact that the different ethnic groups lived apart from one another. Further, their economic functions and activities although overlapping in some instances, were more often then not, different so that there was little sharing of common interests across ethnic boundaries. The cultural gap is forcefully put across by a writer who, in describing the atmosphere at a party in which all the ethnic groups were invited, observed:

> Several buffaloes had been killed for the Malays, dozens of pigs for the Chinese, and there was no want of vegetables and curry-stuffs for the Hindoos. Thus the whole area was full of savoury pungent smells, no doubt attractive to the taste of each and all. As the food was ready, so did the people squat down on the ground and devour. The Malays with their tubs of rice, bowls of curried buffalo, and sauces of sambals (condiments). They dug into the contents with their right hands, carefully keeping their left hands from the dishes, for reasons it would offend good taste to mention. The Chinese with their kits of rice, and cups full of stewed pork, shovelled mouthfuls into their wide open jaws, laughing and joking in their uncouth dialects. Then again, the Hindoos eat their simple, quiet, and unsocial meals, hidden in some out-of-the-way corner where nobody could see them – nay, not even their entertainer. Yet the aroma of their meals is agreeable; and they grunt satisfaction at intervals in a manner that is not to be described to ears polite.[77]

The scene above also shows that there was really not much mixing and social interaction despite the fact that the various groups were placed together.

Nevertheless, the society was not devoid of harmonizing features. The understanding shown by the host of the party described above, understood the customs and habits of the various groups and the necessity not to give offence; he and other individuals brought them together at parties, even though such attempts were rare. More importantly, the acceptance by the population of British rule and their preparedness to live next to one another implied, or forced upon them, a tolerance and willingness to work together.

Penang was indeed a migrant port-town built and administered by European powers. The population was composed of various Asians ethnic groups, while the Europeans were in the minority. Although segregation by ethnic groups was not officially practiced in Penang, there was some form of segregation in terms of the social relationships among the ethnic groups. Nevertheless, all groups were united in some ways. Although there were seldom social gatherings between them all, they still met and gathered in the town in order to deal with their business and daily life. The town was considered as a meeting place for all the groups, and it seems that business and trade comprised the main meeting ground. They shared a common knowledge and had common matters to talk about. Beside these meetings, each individual group had their own particular social and religious gatherings.

NOTES

1 See C.D. Cowan, 'Early Penang and the Rise of Singapore', pp.5–6.
2 The will of Francis Light, IOR/L/AG/34/32/1.
3 See List of Roman Catholic inhabitants men, women and children in Prince of Wales Island in December 1788 in appendix to consultation, 10 April 1789, in G/34/3. The majority of them were Portuguese-Eurasians. In this list there are eight persons with the family name Rozells and all of them came from Siam. This indicates that Martina Rozells also came from Siam and she must have been a Catholic too.
4 R. Montgomery Martin, *History of the British Possessions in the Indian and Atlantic Oceans*, p. 10.
5 The will of Thomas Layton registered 28 September 1806, in IOR/L/AG/34/32/1.
6 The will of Mathew Shepherson registered 12 November 1807, a mariner born at Ramsgate in Kent, England, in IOR/L/AG/34/32/1.
7 The will of Christopher Smith, 11 December 1806, in IOR/L/AG/34/32/1.
8 Notices of Penang, in *JIA*, vol. 5, 1851, pp. 93–119 where, for example, it was remarked in a report written by Major Macdonald, the second Superintendent of Penang, that James Scott's adoption of the Malay way of life was an 'unpleasant thing'.
9 Keppel Garnier, 'Early Days in Penang', p. 8.
10 Ibid., pp. 8–9.
11 Ibid., p. 9.
12 Ibid.
13 Ibid., p. 10.
14 Ibid.
15 John Turnbull Thomson, *Glimpses into life*, pp. 231–235. See also the will of James Scott, registered in the Registry of Wills, in IOR/L/AG/34/32/1: 'Be it known that by letter from Edinburgh dated March last, there was then and there alive and in good health, three sons and five daughters, residing with their aunts and my sisters Mary and Barbara, now it is my intent to leave to seven of these children ten thousand Spanish Dollars each and to my oldest son William the residence making him my successor in trust all and several my estates real or personal'.
16 John Turnbull Thomson, *Glimpses into life*, p. 232.
17 A.F. Steuart, *The Founders of Penang and Adelaide*, London: Sampson Low, 1901, pp. 28–38. See also the will of Fancis Light, in IOR/L/Ag/34/32/1.
18 A.F. Steuart, *The Founders of Penang and Adelaide*, pp.28–38. The author writes that: 'The late David Brown stood alone in 1810 as a spice planter on an extensive scale and instead of finding encouragement in the sympathy of those around him, he was

considered by many to be in search of an El Dorado and no one ventured to follow his steps', p. 133. See also the will of John Brown registered on 25 July 1808, in IOR/L/AG/34/32/1.

19 R. Montgomery Martin, *History of the British Possessions in the Indian and Atlantic Oceans*, p. 133.

20 For details on the work of the Anglican Church missionary in India and in the East, see, for example, Brian Harrison, *Waiting for China: The Anglo-Chinese College at Malacca 1818–1843, and Early Nineteenth-Century Missions*, Hong Kong: Hong Kong University Press, 1979; William Milne, *A Rretrospect of the First Ten years of the Protestant mission to China*, Malacca: Anglo-Chinese Press, 1820; Robert Morrison, *Memoirs of the Reverend William Milne*, Malacca: Mission Press 1824. See also Council of World Missionary Archives of the London Missionary Society Ultra Ganges in SOAS Library.

21 Brian Harrison, *Waiting for China*, p. 3.

22 Keppel Garnier, 'Early Days in Penang', p. 8.

23 John Turnbull Thomson (1821–84) was born in north England on 21 August 1821. After completing a course on mathematics at Aberdeen University, he went to Penang in 1838 (at the age of 16) and later became a surveyor. He explored the island extensively and travelled widely in the peninsula. His book, *Glimpses into Life in Malayan Lands*, was a personal account of his travel experiences. For further details, see the introduction to his book: John Turnbull Thomson, *Glimpses into Life in Malayan Lands*, Kuala Lumpur: Oxford University Press, 1984 (first published in 1864), pp. v-viii.

24 John Turnbull Thomson, *Glimpses into Life*, pp. 31–32.

25 *The Prince of Wales Island Gazette* was first published on 1 March 1806. Its last issue came out on 21 August 1827. For further information, see Patricia Lim Pui Huen, *Singapore, Malaysian and Brunei Newspapers an International Union List*, Singapore: Singapore Institute of Southeast Asian Studies, 1992. See also Ibrahim Ismail, 'Early printing in the Straits Settlements by Missionaries of the London Missionary Society', unpublished MA Thesis, University College, London, 1980.

26 For example, the gazette of Saturday 19 July, 1817 published government advertisements, personal and private advertisements, such as a list of real estate for sale, rental and hire, will disputes and claims, articles for sale, proclamations by the government, naval register and brief news regarding shipping. This issue contained four pages; the first page was devoted to local news while the other three pages gave coverage to overseas news, especially England, Europe and other British colonies, particularly Calcutta and Madras. There was also a report on a session of the British Parliament.

27 John Turnbull Thomson, *Glimpses into Life in Malayan Lands*, p. 33.

28 *The Prince of Wales Island Cazette*, 25 January 1817.

29 John Turnbull Thomson, *Glimpses into Life in Malayan Lands*, Here again the author describes that: "All having arrived, the first difficulties of the host commence. The ladies and gentlement are apportioned, and their rights of precedence weighed with the strictest regard to rule, not always giving entire satisfaction to the ladies", p. 33.

30 Ibid. pp.33–34.

31 John Turnbull Thomson, *Glimpses into life in Malayan Lands:* Where he remarks: "Here he is introduced to the hostess sitting in state. Compliments are passed, and mine host asks him if he has brought his white jacket. If so, he retires, and dons the easy, cool, upper dress of India. Other visitors arrived, and the same process is gone through. Such gentlemen as have brought their ladies, hand them over to the obliging care of the hostess and her maid servants or ayahs. Sherry and bitters stand on a side table for the gentlemen to partake of, and whet their tropical appetites", p. 32.

32 Ibid., p. 34.

33 *The Prince of Wales Island Gazette*, Saturday, December 13, 1817.

34 Garnier, 'Early Days in Penang', p. 10.

35 Ibid., p. 10.

36 See, for example, 'Francis Light, Fort Cornwallis 25 Jan. 1794', in *JIA*, Vol. 5, 1851, p. 9.

37 See, for example, Phillip Mannington to Governor General, Fort William, 25 Feb. 1795, in G/34/7.

38   Letter from, Farquhar, Lieutenant-Governor of Prince of Wales Island, dated 25 May 1805, in G/34/9.

39   See Letter written by Farquhar, Lieutenant-Governor of Prince of Wales Island, dated 25 May 1805, in G/34/9; See also Extract letter from Governor Maclister to the Chairman and Deputy Chairman, dated 7 November 1808, in SSFR Vol. 9.

40   George Leith, *A Short Account of the Settlement*, pp. 50–51.

41   A good description of the life of a Eurasian family in Penang can be found in John Turnbull Thomson, *Glimpses into Life*, pp. 250–254.

42   James Low, *A Dissertation on the Soil and Agriculture of British Settlement*, pp.250–251.

43   Ibid..

44   'Francis Light, Fort Cornwallis, 25th Jan. 1794', in Notices of Pinang, Vol. 5, 1851, p. 10.

45   George Leith, *A Short Account of the Settlement*, pp. 50–51.

46   A good account on the life and activities of Tuanku Syed Hussain can be found in Lee Kam Heng, *The Sultanate of Aceh*.

47   Lee Kam Heng, *The Sultanate of Aceh*, p. 219.

48   Ibid., p. 220.

49   Ibid., p. 202.

50   Ibid., p. 220.

51   Sarina Hoyt, *Old Penang*, p. 30. The date as stated in this book could be wrong because there was no issue printed on 7 December 1806.

52   Ibid., pp. 30–31.

53   See 'Notices of Pinang', *JIA*, Vol. V, 1851, pp. 1–14.

54   For further description of the sub-ethnic groups of the Chinese community, see 'Note on the Chinese of Pinang', *JIA*, Vol VIII, 1854, pp. 1–27.

55   'Note on the Chinese of Pinang', *JIA*, Vol VIII, 1854, pp. 1–27.

56   L.F. Comber, *Chinese Secret Societies in Malaya*, p. 32.

57   George Leith, *A Short Account of the Settlement*, p. 48.

58   Ibid., p. 14.

59   'Notes on the Chinese of Pinang', pp. 14–15.

60   Petition of Opium farmers 25 April 1825, in, G/34/100.

61   See proceedings of a special committee of assessors, 25 August 1806, in F/4/ 262 5837.

62   Petition of Pork farmers in 1813, in G/34/38.

63   Petition of Amboon and Ah Keow, pork farmers, 31. May 1830, in G/34/133.

64   'Note on the Chinese of Pinang', *JIA*, Vol VIII, 1854, pp. 1–27.

65   Ibid., p. 25.

66   'Francis Light, Fort Cornwallis, 25th January 1794', in, *JIA*, vol. 5, 1851, p. 9.

67   Ibid.

68   'Notices of Pinang', *JIA*, Vol. 5, 1851, p. 9.

69   Ibid.

70   Phillip Mannington to Captain Robert Hamilton, 20 November 1794, in G/34/7.

71   Minute by Governor, February 1807, in G/34/17.

72   *The Prince of Wales Island Gazette*, Saturday 3 May 1806: 'serious accidents riding horses to the watering place without saddle: no native will be allowed to ride on a horse without its being properly saddled on pain of being punished with one dozen stripes with a rattan any horse loose on the road will be taken by the police and the owner fined five SpD and two *Copang* for subsequent day that the horse was being taken care off'. See also *The Prince of Wales Island Gazette*, Saturday, 21 March 1807: 'Regulation regarding buffaloes on the island: all buffaloes must have the points of their horns cut and holes pierced through the horns through which rattan is to pass by a strong wood roped at all times well secured and no buffaloes shall appear in the public roads without a man walking close to the head and holding the rope in his hand. Any people who did not abide by the regulation would be fined five SpD if a male buffalo and if a female buffalo ten Spanish Dollars and shall pay a *Copang* for each day maintainance of the buffaloes failure to abide the buffaloes would end up in the auction market'. See also *The Prince of Wales*

Island Gazette, Saturday, 21 March 1807: 'several accidents have occured by the very improper conduct of the natives in their present festivals. On Tuesday night two gentlemen returning in a buggy from the country passing some natives with tomtoms etc the horse took fright and ran down Chulia street at full speed at the bottom of the street near the former market meeting with another party the horse turned back continuing speed when unfortunately opposite the Chulia church he knocked down an old fakeer and the buggy passing over his thigh fractured it. The men taken to the police station and later sent to the hospital. Servant of a Chinese running over an old woman, etc'.

73 John Turnbull Thomson, *Glimpses into Life*, p 80.

74 Ibid. The author described that: 'The European proprietor or planter, and especially he whose family has been long resident in the country, generally maintains a good under-standing with his tenants or neighbours. The tenants and neighbours may be Hindoos, Mussulmans, or Buddhists, whithout producing either dislike or prejudice.If his family be of good repute, tradition upholds his favourable influence; his creed may be opponent to theirs, yet they forget the naserani, and see only the European gentleman, liberal in sentiment, superior in understanding, just in dealing, and affable in intercourse. These qualities, when they exist, easily win the affection of an unsophisticated race – simple in mind, credulous, superstitious, sensitive to kindness, and patient under injury', p. 78.

75 The Will of Thomas Layton registered 28 April 1806, in IOR/L/AG/34/32/1.

76 The Will of Mathew Shepherdson registered 12 November 1807, in IOR/AL/AG/34/32/1.

77 John Turnbull Thomson, *Glimpses into Life*, p. 78.

CHAPTER ELEVEN

Conclusion

INTRODUCTION

ALTHOUGH MELAKA AND PENANG SHARED a broadly common location and trade environment in the Straits of Melaka, they differed in specific ways, namely, in the nucleus of their trading environment, in historical depth, and hence social identity, and in the nature of the politico-economic regimes under which they were shaped. In 1780, Melaka, was a stable settled port-town with a small population and the status of a secondary settlement subordinated to Batavia. It was no longer the confident player, unchallenged in its position as a centre of trade in the region. It faced fierce competition from the Bugis in Riau and the English EIC and country traders. Nevertheless, it still retained some of its international entrepot function within the Asian maritime trading system for which it was once renowned. It continued to attract many traders, including the English. Melaka's small but stable population was sustained mainly by its trade and the attachment of permanent settlers that its long history had nurtured. On the other hand, Penang, newly opened in 1786, had the advantage of being owned by the English and a more open trade policy. In the 1780s it was still a very small settlement with the atmosphere of an unruly frontier town, experiencing teething problems and facing an unsympathetic EIC headquarters. Nevertheless, it was able to immediately attract traders from far and near, a small number of new settlers mainly from the surrounding areas and an important core of European traders and merchants who became pioneers in initiating its development.

The years between 1780 and 1830 saw Melaka face several challenges that shaped the nature of its evolution in that period. Foremost among these were the ascendency of the English in the region and their control of the China trade, the opening of Penang with the attendant diversion of part of its trade to the latter, the temporary takeover of Melaka between 1794 and 1818 by the British as caretakers and the rise of Singapore as the new centre of trade in the region. These developments worked to some extent to Melaka's detriment but its social stability and long established local trade function guaranteed its survival. The fact that Melaka's decline as a trading centre occurred in a period of increased trading and commercial activities was significant, for it was able to sustain its activities and take advantage of the newly opened economic ventures in the peninsula. This situation also ensured that it experienced some increase in population. In essence, Melaka lost its international entrepot status but retained its role as the collecting and distributing centre in its immediate vicinity and around it.

By 1830 Melaka was under British rule, its port was silting, its trading reach had contracted and it could no longer harbour any ambition of being an important centre of trade in the region. Despite that, the stability of its population persisted, and in fact the numbers increased moderately. But Melaka was a sleepy hollow, peaceful, quiet and pleasing in appearance, gaining a reputation as an attractive holiday destination and well on its way to being a historical town with a significant past.

Meanwhile, the intervening years saw Penang develop in several significant respects. It managed to attract a sizeable proportion of Melaka's trade and traders. More importantly, its existence was less dependent on its role as a usurper and Melaka's rival, but on its ability to establish itself as a legitimate centre of trade with its own networks up north in the Straits in the regions facing the Bay of Bengal. Its success is evident from the fact that it became an important centre for Indian traders, especially the Chulias, a base for Chinese intra-regional traders and a profitable market for the native peddling trade. In this it owed its success to the fact that the China tea trade was rising in importance and the cloth and piece goods trade with India was mainly handled by the Indians and the English. However, as a new settlement with more promise than guarantees, its population, as we have seen, although growing, was less stable, fluctuating according to the economic fortunes experienced by the island.

By 1830 Penang was a thriving port with a steady trading pattern, an important destination especially for traders from around the Bay of Bengal. It had become part and parcel of the newly formed Straits Settlements colonies, along with Melaka and Singapore. With that came the responsibility of continuing to maintain the thriving trade within the Bay of Bengal not just for its own development but also in conjunction with Singapore in the overall interest of British imperial ambitions in the region.

ADMINISTRATION

In Chapters Eight and Nine the subject of administration was discussed in which it was shown how the political and cultural context affected administrative policies and approaches. In 1780 the Dutch, a small colonial power, had already put into place an administrative framework that exhibited Dutch traditions of urban management and social and moral control. The Melaka situation also indicated Dutch management of limited resources and how such limitations had not stood in the way of their creativity, resourcefulness and a passion for creating a moral, clean and orderly environment. The English in Penang, on the other hand, were starting from scratch and were handicapped by the lack of funds. However, they belonged to a nation on its ascendency, with a liberal attitude and a robust self-confidence in their ability to adopt a piecemeal approach and yet get things right in the end.

Unlike Penang, which was a British colony throughout the period under study, Melaka's administrative history was chequered: taken over temporarily by the British in 1794 following the Dutch defeat in the Napoleonic Wars, then returned to the Dutch in 1818 and finally transferred permanently to the British in 1824 with the determination of separate spheres of influence between the two Western colonial powers in Southeast Asia. The first period of British rule in Melaka, however, did not see fundamental change in administrative procedures or policies largely because the British saw themselves merely as caretakers. Moreover, the Dutch had left an administrative framework that had stood the test of time. When the Dutch returned in 1818, the status quo was maintained. Thus Melaka remained essentially a Dutch colony from 1780 to 1824. The period between 1824 and 1830, when Britain controlled Melaka was, from an administrative perspective, too short to allow grand changes, thus the port-town remained much the same as it was before the transfer. Further, the changing political and economic environment that saw Singapore's rapid rise reinforced Melaka's position and status as a secondary port-town.

Penang, on the other hand, was established as an English settlement amidst continuing grave doubts on the part of the EIC authorities in Calcutta about whether it could become a strategic naval base and trading centre as England pushed to expand trade with China. The EIC approach was to allow Penang to prove itself worthy of Calcutta's attention. In the meantime, the new colony was to fend for itself. Penang essentially grew as a frontier town and was only marginally important in the EIC's scheme of things. The renewed search for a strategic trading base, which culminated in the founding of Singapore in 1819, was testimony to the fact that Penang never became an integral or indispensable part of the India-China trading network. Thus, persistent doubts about its viability and its less strategic position in relation to the intra-Asian trade gave it the character of a frontier settlement for much of the period under study.

In the circumstances, and possessing limited financial resources, Penang's approach to administration in the early years was necessarily ad hoc. This lack of a clear-cut direction affected the day-to-day running of the new port and, in turn, shaped the development of the town in all its dimensions. Administratively, once the Presidency was instituted, the Governor made decisions in a Council made up of government officials. The administration of the township was assisted by committees of assessors that were not permanent bodies, unlike the case of the various councils in Melaka under the Dutch. These committees of assessors, whose members came from the official and unofficial communities, acted as advisory bodies on a variety of matters all concerned with the running of Penang. Their ad hoc character suggests that despite the small establishment that was made available to Penang by the EIC authorities, the administration did not garner the services of the unofficial population to the extent that the Dutch did in Melaka. Even the work of policing and defending the town was given to sepoys brought out from India, which, as we have seen, caused some friction with the population. Labourers, mostly convicts, were also shipped from India. Both these elements of mercenaries and convicts as well as some degree of lawlessness exhibited by the criminal elements in the population, as seen in the conflicts between rival Chinese dialect groups, added to the flavour of Penang as the wild frontier town.

Urban administration evolved haphazardly. A systematic revenue collecting method through taxation was not fully implemented until the 1820s. Taxes on houses and shops were introduced only in 1795 but, in the face of opposition from the inhabitants, were not successfully collected until 1826 when a tax regime was regularized. In order to obtain money the administration, especially in the early years, resorted to selling land and property which it later sought to repurchase when the need for land for its own use occurred. The division of the town into districts or wards was not a well-rounded administrative approach, as it was in the case of Melaka, but an expedient instrument of policing. No credit facilities were available such as the banking system introduced by the Orphan Chamber in Melaka, so that even the Government had to borrow from private individuals, especially in the early years. Further, unlike the situation in Melaka, the welfare of the community was left mostly to the inhabitants. There was no Orphan Chamber or Church Council in Penang.

This was in sharp contrast to life in Melaka. The Dutch had made life there more cultured and refined and their long stay in the port-town had enabled them to adjust many aspects of the Dutch system to local conditions.

Thus, when the English occupied Melaka they introduced few changes and in fact appear to have emulated some elements of the Dutch system of administration by transferring them to Penang. While this also shows that the English were more liberal and laissez-faire in their attitude, it also indicates that the people of Melaka were already strongly rooted in their social existence and lived in harmony within the system that had been introduced by the Dutch. The Penang case was therefore a sharp contrast, for the fluidity of the economic and social scene created a less stable environment and more social tensions.

TRADE

In Chapters Two to Five, we saw that the trade of Melaka and Penang was shaped by factors of geography, the character of the colonial powers and companies involved and the historical age of the port-town. Also, each had its own orbit of trade thus rendering them quite independent of each other in some ways while in others creating interlocking interests.

In 1780, Melaka was the only colonial port in the Straits of Melaka (before the British occupied Penang in 1786) and despite the decline in its overall trade compared to the seventeenty century, it remained a player in the intra-Asian trade of the period. It had won a new lease of life economically after 1784 due to the Dutch defeat of Riau, a serious trade competitor. However, the Dutch soon lost their advantage due to increased competition from the English traders. Although there were regulations requiring the channeling of trade to Batavia, many English and Portuguese ships anchored at Melaka on their way to India or China. However, this trend came close to a halt when the Napoleonic Wars broke out. With the founding of Penang and later Singapore, Melaka became even less attractive as a trading destination.

Nevertheless, on the whole, it could be said that Melaka was able to maintain a useful but diminished role as a trading centre in the Straits of Melaka throughout the period under study. Its long tradition of trade and successful role as an entrepot and its strategic location in terms of proximity to a wide extent of the east coast of Sumatra and the wider Malay archipelago to its south, were factors that worked to its advantage. Melaka's slide downward to the position of an obscure port accelerated after its temporary transfer to British hands in 1794. The almost quarter century under British rule meant that it continued to be seen, in the long term, as Penang's rival. Thus as we have seen, not only did the British, as caretakers, make little effort to improve the situation but attempts were even made, with some degree of success, to divert Melaka's trade to Penang.

However, many of the old trade networks appear to have survived although the volume of trade decreased. Old connections and familiarity with Melaka as well as considerations of accessibility continued to be important factors. Particularly for short-distance traders who came from the southern half of the Malay peninsula, the south and middle sections of eastern Sumatra and the wide expanse of the Malay archipelago south of the Straits, Melaka was a more convenient port of call compared to Penang. In view of these factors and despite trade restrictions imposed by the Dutch and continued under the British, Melaka survived as an entrepot. Only after the acquisition of Singapore and its rapid rise to the unassailable position as the main trading centre in Southeast Asia in the 1820s was Melaka truly relegated to the position of an inferior regional port.

At a time when Melaka was facing the dilemma of declining trade amidst stiff competition from the English, Penang was opened as a free port. English naval supremacy, which was soon affirmed during the Napoleonic Wars, and their efforts to spread trading activities worldwide meant that a free trade policy could only benefit them. This more open trading system gave the initial fillip to growth in Penang and placed the new port at some advantage compared to Melaka, saddled as it was with an outmoded trading policy. Thus, in the early years, Penang was able to attract enough trade to justify its existence. In the first year of its opening in 1786, a total of 85 ships and prahus visited the port. By 1802 the number of ships trading at Penang rose to 3,569. Although figures for incoming ships in subsequent decades are not available, Penang's slow rise as a port can be seen from figures showing the value of its imports and exports, which between 1806 and 1817 had a value within the range of SpD 1.5–2 million. This indicates that while trade did not show a sharp increase, Penang nevertheless was able to maintain its trading activities at a steady level for a decade in the period following its initial growth.

Overall, Penang, having been set up to rival Melaka and to eventually supercede the latter as the main entrepot in the Straits of Melaka, developed only gradually. Hampered, as we have seen, by the reluctance of the EIC officials at the company headquarters in Calcutta to commit themselves to a clear-cut policy towards it, Penang's rise owed much to the determination of its early administrators and the support of its trading and merchant communities. The fact that Melaka had long captured the bulk of the trade in the Straits did not help matters. Nevertheless, as has been shown, Penang was able to hold its own and establish itself as a viable centre of trade, and although its location at the furthermost northwestern corner of the archipelago made it less central in terms of trading networks within the region, it had good links with the areas facing the Bay of Bengal, including Aceh, an important trading centre on the northern tip of Sumatra. Further, its status as a free port was able in some measure to offset its less strategic position.

The English occupation of Melaka had a significant impact on Penang's growth and in the long run more then 3,000 native Southeast Asian traders (Malay, Bugis, Javanese and Minangkabaus) began arriving in Penang. Some, such as the Bugis, even built their own settlements on the southern part of the town. The coming of native traders was greatly encouraged, as they supplied the new port with goods needed for exchange with ships coming from India and China. Although there were downward trends in Penang's trade between 1814 and 1820s, the decline did not affect the demographic pattern in the port-town except for a small reduction in the numbers of ethnic Chinese. Even with the founding of Singapore, when most of the Straits trade was pooled there, Penang was still able to maintain its own trading networks in the Straits. Furthermore, the opening of Singapore also did not greatly effect its population, partly because towards the 1830s active investments and trade developed between Penang and the native states of Perak and Selangor, where the tin industry was beginning to expand. Besides opportunities for investment in tin, many traders in Penang were also involved in trade on the peninsula and in supplying Chinese migrants as labourers to the tin mining industry. In addition, when Penang, Melaka and Singapore were later united as the Straits Settlement Residencies in 1830, Penang fared better then Melaka, not only because it was further away from the smothering effect of Singapore's existence but also because it became an important English colony in the tin industry and acted as a base for financial and investment houses for traders and merchants to invest in tin mining and agricultural industries in the western Malay states.

In viewing the development of trade of Melaka relative to that of Penang, an important factor is that both ports dealt with similar goods and were therefore competing for the same traders and markets. However, the fact that both ports had their strengths as well as weaknesses meant that neither was able to achieve a position of dominance. Penang's free trade policy, opposed to outdated monopolistic trading system of Dutch-Melaka, benefitted many traders. Melaka, mainly by virtue of its strategic location and long tradition of trade, continued along with Batavia, to capture the bulk of the trade with the archipelago. Many local rulers in Sumatra and the Malay peninsula were forced by the Dutch authorities not to sign any trading agreements with the English. Thus most of the important goods from the region such as spices, pepper, forest products, tin and gold, went to Melaka. On the other hand, this period saw the more aggressive English gain ascendency in the intra-Asian trade, giving them virtual control of the cloth and opium trade from India, tin from the Straits and the tea trade from China, thus helping establish Penang's more prominent role. In the circumstances, neither port could gain a clear dominance over the other in the trading activities of the period.

While there were some changes and shifts to the pattern of trade experienced by both ports, such as those brought about by the Bugis-Dutch wars in the 1784, which saw fewer Bugis from Riau coming to trade in Melaka, the Anglo-Dutch war in the 1780s that resulted in fewer English country traders visiting Melaka; the Napoleonic wars which affected the volume of trade in general in both ports and the Aceh dynastic conflicts, which reduced Penang's valuable trade with the northern Sumatran port, these were developments that did not appear to have long term consequences on the general trends discussed above.

The long established and flourishing Asian trade whose attractiveness to the Europeans had increased through the centuries and whose success was, to a considerable extent, tied to the Straits of Melaka as a favoured passageway, could not but benefit both Melaka and Penang as strategic ports of call. During the period under study, both ports played an important (though not pivotal) role in the intra-Asian trading activities. This was true despite the fact that the period under study represented one of stagnation for Melaka and of initial uncertainty followed by only gradual growth for Penang.

The opening of Singapore as a British colony in 1819 freed the British to choose a policy of developing a main centre of trade in Southeast Asia. The choice of Singapore as this centre spelt the end of the claim of Melaka to its former status as the leading entrepot in the Straits and the ambition of Penang to aspire to that position. However, while both Melaka and Penang declined as trading centres of significance, their societies remained vibrant and many among the population turned the two ports into financial and business centres from which new enterprises, particularly in tin mining, were launched in the Malay states beginning from the 1830s. This in turn led to British intervention in the affairs of the western Malay Sultanates of Perak, Selangor, Negeri Sembilan and Pahang. Thus both Melaka and Penang could be said to have been important stepping stones in the forward movement of the British in the Malay peninsula, leading to the so-called period of intervention and the establishment of British rule of the Malay states beginning from 1874.

SOCIETY

In Chapters Six, Seven, Ten and Eleven we discussed the development of the societies in Melaka and Penang and established the fact that trade had been largely responsible in determining population size as well as the multi-ethnic character of the two port towns, and that geographical location influenced to some extent the ethnic combinations involved. However, the complexity of the ethnic amalgam, the social configurations, the cultural diversity and the styles of life were to a large extent shaped by the historical age of the port-towns.

As two port-towns serving the interests of traders, merchants and financiers, Melaka and Penang grew largely through the profit motive. This affected the physical and population growth of both ports at this time, this growth being dependent on the expansion of trade. In view of the fact that Melaka and Penang did not experience rapid growth in trade, their populations also remained small. The dependence on trade and the failure to develop local industries or an agricultural hinterland, the last by design in the case of Melaka, and through failure because of the lack of market demand, in the case of Penang, further worked against the growth of a larger population.

Melaka saw very little trade expansion, as shown by the figures given above, as its trade developed more in the direction of serving as a collection centre for the southern end of the Straits of Melaka within the wider trading network of the Asian trade system. This limited trade role coupled with the lack of development of other sectors of the economy hampered its overall development. With the scope for economic expansion limited, the ability of the port to develop or encourage a bigger population and provide more trade and greater commercial opportunities for its traders and merchants was also curtailed. Melaka reached a maximum of less than 13,000 inhabitants during this period, the numbers fluctuating slightly depending on the ebb and flow of trade. In 1766 Melaka's population stood at 7,216, and in 1829 there were 12,950 inhabitants in the port-town.

However, despite declining trends and fluctuations in its trade, Melaka's population remained stable for much of the nineteenth century up to 1830. This was probably due to the core of permanent settlers, especially the Malays and Portuguese-Eurasians and a smaller number of Dutch Burghers and Peranakan Chinese and to long-term traders and merchants who had found a niche in the commercial activities conducted in and out of Melaka. As we have seen, during the first period of British rule, they were only partially successful in enticing Melaka's trading and commercial population to move to Penang. It is also evident that in the 1820s when the Dutch withdrew from the port-town, many Dutch Burghers chose to stay on in Melaka. Furthermore, the 1820s saw the beginnings of new economic opportunities in the western Malay states, particularly in the tin mining industry, and Melaka's proximity to these states made it an important place for supplying Chinese labour and investment.

By 1780 Melaka had existed as an important trading centre in the Straits for three centuries. It had also been a colonial port town under two European powers, and in the previous three centuries it had seen people from diverse ethnic backgrounds come together to seek their fortunes. Among them were birds of passage, sojourners and settlers, all of whom contributed to the vitality and life of the port-town. The Dutch had no clear policy on migrants in Melaka; only in the early period of Dutch rule did the VOC stress that they needed Chinese migrants to revive Melaka's ecomonic fortunes, which were at a low ebb at the time they took over Melaka from the Portuguese. However, the port-town was already settled by many Asian ethnic groups, including Chinese, a trend that had started since the days of the Malay sultanate. The majority was, of course, the Malays. But the Chinese migrants were encouraged to come to Melaka, as it was felt that they could provide the stimulus to revive, quickly, the town's trade. Furthermore, Chinese migrants could also increase the income of the port-town from the poll tax that the Dutch imposed on the Chinese community in areas under their control. In addition, the Chinese were also a source of increased revenue, which could be obtained from taxes on pig farms and gambling. Nevertheless, in the long term, as Batavia was more important to the Dutch any policy to revive Melaka's position could not jeopardize the former's position as the centre of the VOC administration in the East. Thus company policies and the direction in which Melaka's trade developed militated against the expansion of its population.

Since Penang was a newly created port-town and since it had, originally, only a few hundred Malay inhabitants, the English needed more people to settle permanently. Therefore they encouraged migrants from China, India and the surrounding areas to settle there. The Indian migrants, mostly from the Coromandel Coast, made Penang their trading base, with some settling permanently. Native Southeast Asian traders (Bugis, Malays, Javanese and Minangkabaus) built a small town of their own in Penang. The English had encouraged these traders who mostly came from the Straits, Java and Makassar to settle. A similar policy was also adopted towards the Chinese migrants and traders to the island. While the free trade policy and new opportunities probably provided incentives for traders and migrants alike to come to Penang, its uncertain future and lack of infrastructure worked to its disadvantage. In 1788 Penang had a population of 1,283, and in 1829 the number stood at 12,060. Thus, like Melaka, its population did not exceed 13,000 although, unlike the former, it had a shorter history and had grown from a few hundred to a maximum that matched Melaka. Factors that impeded further growth in Melaka's population also applied in Penang: over-dependency on trade, few agricultural products and absence of industries.

Melaka is unique in the history of Malaysia in that it was the first important breeding ground for new mixed groups in the peninsula, the result of co-habitation of traders and others from outside, mainly males, with native women. Thus, in 1780 Melaka had a population mix of various ethnic groups: Malays, Chinese, Indians (Muslim Chulias and Hindus) and Europeans. It also had a population that was formed from mixed marriages. Historically, the mixed groups in Melaka had emerged before the Dutch period. The Babas or the Peranakans evolved during the Malay Sultanate period as a result of co-habitation between Chinese migrants with the Malay locals, mainly slaves, while the Christian Catholics or the Portuguese-Eurasians were formed during the Portuguese occupation.[1] Another group to emerge during the Malay Sultanate period, the Jawi-Pekans (a mix of Indian and Malay) persisted into the Dutch period. However, due to their small numbers and the Chulias' adherence to the same religion as the Malay women they married, they were more easily absorbed into the dominant, long established and stable Malay population. With the Babas, the pre-dominant position of males in the Chinese value system was an impediment to assimilation. The Portuguese-Eurasians, on the other hand, during the long period of Portuguese rule, were more aligned to the ruling power than to the local Malays, both in culture and religious affiliation. Thus, through the years, both the Babas and Portuguese-Eurasians emerged as new permanent categories and not as groups existing at a certain point along the process towards assimilation. Their permanency was further ensured by their success in maintaining a cohesiveness and self-sufficiency through the presence of mechanisms of social control such as religious and social insti-tutions which were instrumental in creating a sense of belonging. With the Portuguese-Eurasians, the strong influence of Catholicism and their partial descendency from a once powerful conquering power were important factors in the perpetuation of their unique identity. Likewise, the Chinese propensity to form mutual help societies and their strong sense of filial obligations, which made ancestor worship an important part of their lives, meant that the bonds with the Chinese elements in their existence were not easily severed.

Penang provided an interesting contrast to Melaka in terms of the character of its population. Some similarities were seen as could be expected in a port-town in Southeast Asia ruled by a European power and serving similar economic purposes. However, significant differences and contrasting factors and developments also existed. Like Melaka, Penang had its main groups of Malays, Indians, Chinese and Europeans and smaller groups of mixed racial types. It also had the mixed groups of Eurasians and Jawi-Pekans right from the start although not from the local evolution of new types over time as in the case of Melaka. The Eurasians were mostly Portuguese-Eurasians who migrated to the island from Siam following their expulsion by the Siamese authorities. The Jawi-Pekans were migrants from Kedah who sought new opportunities and to expand their business in the new environment, using their already established commercial ties in Kedah to advantage.

The Eurasian community formed the pool from which the earlier European migrants to Penang, mostly males, found their brides. Indeed, many of the early English traders and merchants in Penang intermarried with Portuguese Eurasian ladies who had migrated to the island, thus increasing the numbers of the Eurasian community there. Nevertheless, their numbers remained small and many also intermarried with Asian groups so that their existence as an ethnic category was not even acknowledged in census reports. Unlike the Dutch policy of assimilating the Christian children born of Dutch males with other ethnic groups by accepting them as 'Dutch', the English, in general, did not accept half-castes as 'English' and treated them as an intermediate class, inferior to Europeans but better than Asians. The above factors and the fact that they were new migrants meant that the impact of the Eurasian group in Penang was small compared to their counterparts in Melaka.

However, the impact of the Jawi-Pekans in Penang was greater and had a lasting influence in contrast to Melaka. Although the earlier Jawi-Pekans in Penang were migrants from Kedah, intermarriage between Chulia merchants from the Coromandel Coast and local females helped to increase the population of Jawi-Pekans in the port-town. Due to the fairly large number of Chulias and the already existing core of the Jawi-Pekan community early in the development of Penang, they were, in the long term, able to exist as a separate category without being assimilated into the Malay population as happened in Melaka. Moreover, the Malays in Penang were a group of new migrants still in the process of defining their own social and cultural identity within the context of the new environment. Further, within the context of Penang society, the Jawi Pekans were a more successful community compared to the Malays so that the push to assimilate was not as strong.

Similarly, the impact of the Babas or the Peranakans was also greater and had a lasting identity in Melaka as compared to Penang. The Baba community in Melaka was formed during the Sultanate period when many Chinese migrants cohabited with the locals. Such a practice continued during the Portuguese and Dutch periods because few Chinese women migrated to Melaka. Therefore the Chinese settlers were exclusively males who lived with Javanese and Malay slaves as concubines or married the children of these mixed unions. The effect of this was that the Melaka Chinese had about as much Malay blood in their veins as Chinese. Their offspring were brought up as Chinese and they retained Chinese culture, custom and dress, though they lost their language, speaking a kind of Malay of their own creation.[2]

Another contrasting pattern emerged in the character of the societies of Melaka and Penang: the Asian ethnic mix was not necessarily identical. This was to some extent influenced by the location of the port-towns. While both had attracted Malays, Indians, Chinese and Bugis, Melaka, with its proximity to Java and central Sumatra, had an additional distinct mix of Javanese and Minangkabau, while Penang, close to Aceh, Thailand and Burma, saw more Acehnese and a small number of Thais and Burmese in its population.

While the contrasts between Melaka and Penang were significant, the similarities belied the fact that they had different historical and administrative backgrounds. Such similarities were largely determined by external factors. The multi-ethnic nature of the society, the fact that the Europeans were in the minority and the predominance of the migrant population were all shaped by the circumstances and the direction of the intra-Asian trade. Firstly, the intra-Asian trade had always been conducted by many ethnic groups; secondly, the opening and maintenance of European colonial ports were successfully achieved not from strength of numbers but from the ability and power to dominate, and thirdly, a share in riches to be had from the trade had attracted immigrants to both Melaka and Penang. Thus, in both ports Europeans, Indians, Chinese, Malays and several other ethnic groups made the societies heterogeneous. The status of these ports as trading outposts from the point of view of the European powers, however, meant that Europeans were in the minority, yet at the top of the administrative and social strata by virtue of their position as the controlling power, overseeing the growth of a largely Asian population.

Another similar feature was that both societies suffered from an imbalance in the ratio of men to women – to be expected of ports of call with a seasonal traffic. As this imbalance is in the nature of an outpost, it could not be redressed and led to intermarriages as well as cohabitation, especially of masters with their slaves in a society where slavery remained an important component of the labour force. The mixed groups of Portuguese-Eurasians, the Baba-Chinese and the Jawi-Pekans are among the most enduring contributions made by Melaka and Penang to the social and cultural history of Malaysia.

Although neither of the settlements had an explicit policy of segregation, traditional security considerations reserved the Melaka fort for Europeans. However, self segregation was common. In Penang the European official community withdrew from the rest of the population, settling in an area that became the town center; in Melaka other Europeans tended to live in their own enclaves, but such self-segregation was not necessarily a colonial pheno-menon. Although there was no clear policy to segregate the other com-munities, there was no real encouragement to intermingle. In both Melaka and Penang the different ethnic communities tended to live separately, although there was more intermingling and fewer clear-cut boundaries between the settlements of one ethnic group and another, particularly in Melaka. The Melaka case is to some extent a consequence of its long history, which brought about some measure of integration, thus blurring the sharp lines of division. In Penang, the intermingling was probably determined by the concentration of commercial and mercantile activities in a small area at the start of the settlement. As such activities were not the exclusive preserve of a particular ethnic group, members of different communities found them-selves co-existing alongside one another. Nevertheless, certain areas were easily identifiable as belonging to a particular group as mutual social and cultural needs and practices tended to encourage each group to come together and form itself into a separate cluster.

The physical separation reflected the lack of, as well as discouraged, social interaction. As we have seen, the social and religious tolerance shown by the authorities allowed each community to practice its own way of life and observe its religious beliefs without obstruction. Socially, the Europeans lived a life of considerable comfort, entertained by lavish dinner parties that appear to have been common in both Melaka and Penang and the avail-ability of clubs to socialise in and the occasional play for their amusement, as shown by the evidence for Penang. This situation describes a society where the different communities intermingled mostly in the marketplace. Only a few individuals, such as James Scott and the wealthy Arabs in Penang, were able to cross the social boundary and bridge the cultural gap. Scott, of his own choice, had Asian friends and Syed Hussain, by virtue of his wealth and usefulness to the authorities, was acceptable to the European community. Thus, despite the existence of the mixed groups which indicated some degree of integration, essentially achieved by stealth, there existed alongside this process forces and circumstances that kept the ethnic groups apart.

Another contrast in the history of the two port-towns can be seen in the physical environment of each town and its effect on the perception of observers as well as the population. Melaka, with its long history, had become a place that was home for many migrants from Asia and Europe. Located on the coast of the Straits and blessed with good weather and living conditions, it was hailed as the healthiest port-town in the East. Life was easy and less stressful due to the pleasant environment and good facilities provided by the Dutch. Living in a town with a long legacy and history definitely made a difference to its population compared to living in a newly created town whose infrastructure was still minimal and whose management was poor as was the case in Penang. Due to its long history and rule by Malays and later European powers, this collective experience gave Melaka an edge over Penang in terms of good living conditions and management of a port-town, including sustainable policies pertaining to fire hazards, the construction of buildings, security and judicial matters. As the Dutch were also particular about order and cleanliness, Melaka was also a well kept port-town.

THE CATEGORY OF COLONIAL PORT-TOWNS

Having discussed aspects of the history of Melaka and Penang, it is pertinent to show what the case studies tell us about the category of 'colonial port-town'. At a superficial level and due to the presence of features that have been identified as typifying a colonial port-town, Melaka and Penang, in the period under study, could be said to fit into this category. Among the defining features cited are European imposed urban concepts, the fort or castle as the central focus of the town, separate European and indigenous spheres, a seemingly pluralistic structure, the importance of ethnicity in the scheme of things, a large migrant population, the relative absence of females, a large slave population and an urban centre that was somewhat isolated and poorly integrated with the hinterland.[3] Many of these features were undoubtedly present in both Melaka and Penang. The term 'colonial port-town' also presupposes an externally induced settlement rather than a naturally developing internal phenomenon.

In the introductory chapter the history of the evolution of the concept of the colonial port-town was briefly outlined and it was indicated that the debate regarding its validity is still on. There is, however, a growing consensus that the concept is rather limited in its applicability and that too much emphasis has been put on European elements, such as political control, types and structure of the defence works, administration and ethnic make-up and segregation of population groups. This was the case in Horvath's work and with other scholars of a similar persuasion.[4] In Horvath's case, the over-emphasis might have arisen from the fact that his model was put forward in order to distinguish it from both the industrial city and the pre-industrial city models.[5] Therefore the idea and concept of a colonial port-town needs further scrutiny, as suggested by Nagtegaal, who rightly points out that many of the elements, such as those mentioned in Horvath's work, were not new to many non-colonial Asian port-towns. Much of the problem arose from a presumption. As most Europeans who arrived in Southeast

Asia resided largely in cities and many port-towns were also administered by them, the inclination was to see this as a new phenomenon and therefore distinctive. Moreover, it is hard to ignore the European colonial features of a city altogether as many cities governed by European powers in Asia seemingly shared specific features. Thus the existence of similar features encouraged the idea that 'colonial port-town' is a valid category.

Critics of those who subscribe to the 'colonial port-town' category have also pointed out that case or micro studies of the so-called 'colonial port-towns' have sometimes been undertaken to the exclusion of certain indigenous elements of a town.[6] This is to say that such studies concentrated on highlighting the European or colonial features to the exclusion of other factors. Nagtegaal uses the term 'self affirmative' in describing this tendency, which he regards as flawed.

Nagtegaal also emphasised the need to compare colonial port towns with indigenous cities to ascertain if in fact there are real differences and to examine the circumstances that have led to such differences, if any.[7] From his own research, he has found no big difference between colonial and other port-towns in Southeast Asia. He cites Pontianak as an example of a town that was founded by an Arab and his followers on the west coast of Borneo in 1772. He notes that almost all the inhabitants were migrants from other parts of Southeast Asia. Further, he points out that as with any other early colonial port-town, Pontianak also had a very limited integration with the hinterland areas. Furthermore, when Pontianak was founded the need for labour encouraged the use of slaves, as happened in colonial cities such as Penang.[8] Thus he concludes:

> Therefore, it seems more justified to consider Colonial Cities as examples of *externally induced* settlements in their early stages. This means that the cities had not developed organically within the society itself, but that they were imposed by outside forces who needed a point of entry. In the eighteenth century, it was still possible in Southeast Asia for a leader with a group of followers to start an entirely new settlement at a well-situated location, and to redirect existing trade routes to it. Whether that leader was European, Arab or Buginese was only to a limited extent relevant to the nature of such a city.[9]

The term 'externally induced' as suggested by Nagtegaal is less narrow than the 'colonial port-town' category because not all 'externally induced' towns were colonial. This term can be applied to both Melaka and Penang. For Melaka, even its early opening was 'externally induced' as it was founded by a group of Malays who came to settle there sometime in the fourteenth century. Indeed, externally induced urban centres were common in much of

Southeast Asia and closely linked to physical mobility and trade in the region in the pre-nineteenth century period. However, contrasting 'externally induced' urban centres to 'internal organic' towns is also problematic, as when traders and locals get together to trade and form a settlement it is difficult to prove whether the site was externally induced or locally nurtured.

Given the above shortcomings in the concept of 'colonial port-town', it is hard to accept the validity of a separate colonial urban typology.

The concept 'colonial port-town' is essentially political, referring to the dominant ethnic group, and its usefulness is much more related to a colonial town's place in the wider colonial system. Its usefulness, however, becomes doubtful when we expect it to adequately describe relationships as complex as the economic and social life of a city. Therefore, it is more sensible to look at towns according to their functions (political, economic and social) within specified systems and then divide them into types depending on the different functions that they have within such systems. This means that there can be many different typologies depending on what is being studied and the aim of the analysis. Melaka and Penang, as historical studies, might be better served by looking at them as ports located in the Straits of Melaka, serving a specific trade system in the pre-steamship and pre-high imperialism era. The emphasis on location and function appears more relevant and meaningful than the nature of the political control or the power structure.

Moreover, the acceptance of this 'colonial port-town' label at face value tends to obscure some of the nuances, mechanics and contextual elements of the evolution of the two settlements discussed here. The contrasts that we have seen in the form, structure, content and direction of the development of Melaka and Penang go to show that port-towns did not necessarily share identical or similar characteristics and that with the two settlements under study, other circumstances and historical developments were equally important in defining their respective identities.

Melaka was already an urban centre and a renowned emporium of trade from the fifteenth century. At that stage it was also the seat of a Malay-Muslim kingdom and the centre of an extensive trading system. More than a century of Portuguese occupation beginning from 1511, followed by a longer period of Dutch rule and finally British control in 1824, meant that Melaka evolved from an indigenous trading centre to a port-town under colonial rule. The position established by the Malay sultanate of Melaka as an important trading port in the Straits was later maintained by the three European rulers until late in the eighteenth century. The Melaka trading system did not change drastically and many of the practices during the Portuguese period, such as the pass trade trading system, were later inherited by the Dutch. Although changes were implemented by the three European powers, many of the administrative and trading policies were in fact modified to suit the needs of those who were in power. The length of time that the Malay sultanate and European powers held Melaka greatly shaped the daily life in Melaka. Thus Melaka in the eighteenth century was a unique port town with a blend of many Asian and European elements.

Penang, on the other hand, opened as a colonial port-town right from the start. Melaka's growth and prosperity during the European occupations depended upon its ability to control trade that passed through the Straits and the enforced use of a trading pass system started during the Portuguese period and continued by the Dutch and the English. However, such trading practices could no longer prevail in the light of new challenges which emerged in the Asian trade. Penang, on the other hand, was built from scratch by the English as a colonial trading post, remote in culture and location from the major centers of trade in the Malay-Indonesian archipelago. Its growth and prosperity depended upon its ability to absorb the local Malay traders and other Asian traders, exploit the Chinese tea trade and forge relationships of mutual economic interests with the native kingdoms in the Malay peninsula and in Sumatra. In this way, though Penang was founded to serve a colonial purpose, its success depended on its ability to function as an Asian port. Despite the dissimilarities in historical development and function in the trading policies of the European companies, the same can be said about Melaka, which catered to a regional shipping network.

Therefore, while Melaka and Penang might be labeled 'colonial port-towns' in Southeast Asia, many of the details as well as some of their essential features were not necessarily unique to them. We have seen that the European character of the 'colonial port-towns' was not particularly obvious and that some features said to define the category in fact pre-dated the colonial period and were also commonly seen in indigenous port-towns. Most indigenous port-towns also had a large migrant element by virtue of their participation, either directly or indirectly, in the intra-Asian trade, and ethnic segregation was practised in pre-colonial Melaka. It would appear that the main defining feature of a colonial port-town was European political rule and some morphological and architectural elements.

Thus, the classification 'colonial city' tends to obscure common features and emphasize distinctive elements to the detriment of achieving a more holistic picture. Many port-towns in Southest Asia, irrespective of whether they were ruled by Europeans or not, had a fairly strong Chinese presence, a clear dependence on a migrant population for their economic well-being and exhibited strong elements of cultural diversity. The inclination to look for defining features could lead to the overlooking of small or subtle historical realities, which are nonetheless significant in understanding the dynamics of a society. For example, seeing the Dutch in Melaka as the imposing colonial power denies the level of adaptation to local norms that was seen on the part of the foreign ruling group. The dichotomy of colonial versus natives and external versus organic tends to emphasize stark differences while ignoring significant merging of economic interests, norms and values.

As mentioned above, Melaka and Penang were both Straits trading ports administered and ruled by European powers. Although they were ruled by European powers and many of the characteristics of a colonial port-town were at work, Melaka and Penang cannot be set apart from the other port-cities in Asia. This is because many features of a colonial port-town were also found in other port-towns not ruled by a colonial power. The only significant feature of a colonial port-town that can be seen in Melaka and Penang was the presence of Europeans who held power and controlled the town. Some of the colonial characteristics were more clearly seen in Melaka compared to Penang due to the former's lengthy period under European rule. Many of the European officers during the VOC period were born and grew up in Melaka, which gave the government a decidedly local flavour. This in turn influenced the development and function of the port-town. Both port-towns were controlled and administered by Europeans who were in the minority. Penang was controlled by merchant country traders, and Melaka was run by officers from the VOC. Both port-towns grew more of an Asian character rather than being dominated by any European character-istics, as European quarters were very small compared to the whole town area, which was mostly peopled by Asians.

A TIME OF TRANSITION

The period we have considered, from 1780 to 1830, coincides with the era of transition after the 'Age of commerce' and before the age of high imperialism, which was characterised by two major trends in Southeast Asia, namely, the predominance of the English in the China tea trade and its attendant impact on the region and the increasing role played by the Chinese in its over-all economic development. Our study of Melaka and Penang has shown that the growth and development of trade and society in these two port-towns reflected general trends occurring in that period. Thus, Melaka and Penang were microcosmic representations of the era, as our case study shows the dominant role of the English and the activities of the Chinese within and without the two port-towns.

In examining the first trend, we have seen its co-relation with the in-creasing activities and rivalry of the Europeans in trade in the region, when a pre-industralised Europe was engaged in expanding trading links in the rest of the world. If before the 1760s European traders were content to fit into the long established Asian trading axis, by the 1780s the tide was already turning in their favour, during which they were becoming the principal determinants in the trading system. The achievement of this status had earlier manifested itself in the control of a number of bases in Asia from which they launched their trading offensive. In the Straits of Melåka, the port-towns of Melaka and Penang played out Dutch and British rivalry until the demarcation of spheres of influence agreed upon in the Anglo-Dutch treaty of 1824 gave to the Dutch the Malay archipelago to the south and west of the Straits of Melaka, and to the British, the Malay peninsula. With the transfer of Melaka, the British quest for control of the Straits of Melaka and therefore the main trade route between India and China, which began with the opening of Penang in 1786 followed by their acquisition of Singapore in 1819, was complete.

In many respects the trade of Melaka and Penang charted the rise to an unchallenged position of the Europeans in Asia's trade. Note the European dominance in long-distance trade from the large sizes of the ships and cargoes and the large number of their crews. Between 1780 and 1830, statistics showing the arrival and departure of ships for Melaka consistently show the imposing presence of European traders.[10] Unfortunately, data for Penang are not available, but it could be assumed that the pattern there was similar, besides the fact that Penang being an English port would have been the natural port of call for English traders, the main players in the India-China trade.

Further, the Europeans, especially the English, were able to take control of the main goods in demand, such as opium and cloth from India, tea and porcelain from China and tin, gold and jungle and sea products from Southeast Asia. Thus opium and cloth were conveyed to the ready markets of Southeast Asia, Southeast Asian products to India and China and tea, porcelain, Chinese silk, Indian cloth and Southeast Asian spices to Europe. For example, the total exports of Chinese tea were over 7,000 tons in the 1760s and the English East India Company imported 2,800 tons of tea in 1760 alone. This figure represented 40 per cent of the EIC's total imports to England.[11] Therefore, the English interest in the Southeast Asian trade was increasing tremendously, the main motivation being the need to obtain trade goods to be exported to China in exchange for tea. Lucrative goods, such as opium and tin, thus came under the control of large trading companies. The opium that fed the addiction encouraged in the archipelago was exchanged for tin and other natural products, which found a ready market in China, which in turn provided the tea for the seemingly insatiable European market.

As a result of the European presence and competition, Southeast Asia saw the slow demise of its own peoples in long-distance trading activities. The facts show that during the period under study, Asian long-distance traders remained active but such traders were confined to the Indians and Chinese who were based in their own countries or in Southeast Asia. For example, the majority of the Chinese made Bangkok their major port of call in Southeast Asia, while the Chulias preferred Penang.[12] But even these traders faced challenges to their survival. In the period under study, their arrival in Melaka and Penang became irregular. The survival at least of the Indians appears to have been possible because of the existence of finance houses on the South Asian subcontinent. The Chulia trader who left Penang after the loss of his property following a fire points to the limited resources that Asian traders had, in general, which did not allow them to survive a disaster.

Interestingly, while the period under study saw the rise of Chulia traders in Penang, it witnessed their demise at Melaka. The decrease in numbers of Chulia traders in Melaka could be due to the fact that the free port of Penang provided them the opportunity to trade in Indian cloth, formerly a monopoly of the Dutch VOC at Melaka. Penang was also closer to the Indian subcontinent and within the orbit of the regular trading networks of most Chulia traders, which covered the Bay of Bengal region encompassing the eastern coast of India, southern Burma, southwestern Thailand, northern Sumatra and the northwestern section of the Malay peninsula. Penang was therefore an appropriate choice for a new centre of their network in this region.

While Indian traders managed to some extent to hold their own, and the Chinese expanded into other economic enterprises, the native Southeast Asian long-distance traders had all but disappeared. From the Melaka shipping lists, no native Southeast Asian traded beyond Southeast Asia, their main activities being confined to the conveyance of goods within the region, the main networks being within the Straits of Melaka and between the Straits and the wider Malay archipelago. In fact, a large majority of them were peddlers who sailed along the coast in small boats with limited cargoes. This was in sharp contrast to their position during the height of Asian commerce in Southeast Asia, when Malay and Melakan traders (Melakan-Moors, Melakan-Burghers and Melakan-Kelings) made regular trips to India and China. Rich Melakan traders such as Malik Farizullah, Tso Anko, Mira Mahomat Sia, Malim Moeda and Joost Koek, who owned vassels plying between Melaka–Coromandel–the archipelago–China, were not found in the nineteenth century.

Nevertheless, as has been shown, native Southeast Asian traders continued to play an integral part in the regional trading networks, and although their trading activities were limited in terms of distance and range, many of the goods they brought to collection points such as Melaka and Penang were destined to go beyond the region and as far as Europe. This trend can be seen clearly from the trading activities they conducted with Melaka and Penang. Native Southeast Asian traders not only brought goods, but they also took goods away from the two ports for distribution to native ports in Southeast Asia. In this respect, along with the European, Indian and Chinese long-distance traders, they played a not insignificant role in the overall development of both Melaka and Penang as collecting and distributing centres of goods in the intra-Asian and the inter-regional trade.

But while the Asian share in the India-China wholesale trade was not increasing at a time of increased trading activities, the eighteenth century saw the rise of Chinese business networks and a new wave of Chinese migration into the whole of Southeast Asia after a lull for most of the six-teenth and seventeenth centuries. Not only did this period see the beginnings of Chinese domination in most small- and medium-range business and trade sectors, Chinese labour – skilled and semi-skilled – also came to dominate the service sectors of Southeast Asia economies. Melaka and Penang attracted many of these Chinese migrants and, in the 1820s and for many decades thereafter, both port-towns became centres and important gateways from which most of Chinese migrants left to work in the tin mining industry in the western Malay states. In fact, Penang also became the gateway for Chinese migrants bound for South America. EIC ships were very active in the 1790s carrying Chinese labourers to that continent.

Thus this transition period saw a growing Chinese involvement in short and medium distance trade and commercial activities, and also Chinese migra-tions to Southeast Asia. For many port-towns controlled by Europeans, the arrival of Chinese traders, the exodus of Chinese migrants and the setting up of Chinese settlements were greatly encouraged. The English, for instance, favoured them because they believed that the Chinese were essential for the port-town's prosperity. The coming of Chinese traders was also seen as the primary foundation which enabled many port-towns to grow and expand. The Dutch had also shown an interest in encouraging the Chinese to come to Melaka in order to revive its trade and to invest in agricultural and mining industries in the hinterland. Therefore, an important feature of the 'Chinese century' was the formation of Chinese settlements in many port-towns in Southeast Asia.[13] These settlements were fostered in two forms: the urban merchant settlement and the labourers' settlement. The Chinese urban settlements were varied but the core was the locally domiciled Chinese merchants, and their occupations were largely focused on trade.[14] By the end of the seventeenth century their activities began to expand, focusing on trade but also agricultural production and mining. The latter two enterprises led to Chinese labourer settlements being formed in the interior or hinter-land, thus assisting in the integration of the port-town with the hinterland. More significantly, this development helped to extend the boundaries of colonial influence.

The main points above assert that although Melaka and Penang shared a broadly common context – both were colonial trading ports situated in the Straits of Melaka – they differed in the local context, colonial maritime traditions, urban traditions and historical experience. Melaka was a stable settled town, a secondary settlement under Batavia, and essentially formed by the central Melaka straits local trading environment. As such, by the 1780s it was part of a declining system, but because of its social stability and local economic function it did not suffer much because of this. Penang, on the other hand, was a laissez-faire frontier town, oriented towards the northern Melaka Straits and the Bay of Bengal, run by adventurer merchants, with a floating population and part of the newly emerging trade system. This new system had two orientations: one to the Anglo-Chinese trade axis within which country traders from India and Chinese were dominant, the other the Bay of Bengal system within which Indian merchants, particularly Chulias, played a central role. Although the development of Singapore had further eclipsed Melaka, it only partly effected Penang's future. However, with the advancement in shipping technology and the advent of steam ships where sheltered harbours and monsoon winds were no longer important variables, both port-towns lost their advantage. Furthermore, with the establishment of Singapore, with its great strategic importance and ability to take advantage of nineteenth century technical revolutions, both in terms of shipping trends and the nature of port-towns, both Melaka and Penang were sidelined, leav-ing them as minor players in an accelerating political and economic scene in the region.

NOTES

1   For further discussion on the Babas and Peranakans, see Victor Purcell, 'Chinese Settlements in Melaka', *JMBRAS*, June 1947, pt. 1, vol. xx, pp. 115–125; J.R. Clammer, *Straits Chinese Society*; and J.R. Clammer, 'The Straits Chinese in Melaka'. For further references regarding the Portuguese-Eurasians, see Colin Jack-Hinton, 'Malacca and Goa and the Question of Race Relations in the Portuguese Overseas Provinces'; and Chan Kok Eng 'A Study in the Social Geography of the Malacca Portuguese Eurasians'.
2   Victor Purcell, 'Chinese Settlement in Malacca', p. 125.
3   See Luc Nagtegaal 'The pre-modern city in Indonesia', pp. 45–46.
4   See, for example, A.D. King 'Colonial Cities', pp. 7–10; M.E.P. Bellam, 'The Colonial City', where he says that culturally imports from abroad and were founded by Europeans to satisfy the needs of metropolitan administration, trade and commerce, p. 67; D. Simon, 'Third world colonial cities in context', where he argues that colonial cities should be

defined in terms of external domination and control in a culture-contact situation, p. 502;

5   R.J. Horvath, 'In search of a theory of urbanization: Notes on the Colonial city', p. 72.

6   See Nagtegaal 'The pre-modern city in Indonesia', p. 46.

7   Ibid., p. 45.

8   Ibid., p. 47.

9   Ibid.

10 See Appendix 11: Melaka Shipping Lists, 1780–82 and 1791–93, in Nordin Hussin, 'Melaka and Penang 1780–1830', pp. 459–480.

11 Anthony Reid 'Shipping on Melaka and Singapore as an index of Growth 1760–1840', p. 62.

12 See J. Cushman, *Fields from the Sea: Chinese Junk Trade with Siam During the Late Eighteenth and Early Nineteenth Centuries*, and S. Arasaratnam, 'The Chulia Muslim Merchants in Southeast Asia 1650–1800'.

13 Carl A. Trocki, 'Chinese Pioneering in Eighteenth-Century Southeast Asia', pp. 85–87.

14 Ibid.

Bibliography

ARCHIVAL MATERIAL

Algemeen Rijksarchief, The Hague

Overgekomen Briven en Papieren (VOC):
I. Copie gemene resolutien genomen in rade van Politie der stad en fortresse Malacca
II. Copie secrete resolutien genomen in rade van Politie der stad en fortresse Malacca
III. Copie lijsten van aangekomen en vertrokken vreemde en particuliere vaertuijgen in genoemd tijdperk
IV. Lijste van alle inwoonders tot Malacca

Private Collectie and Collectie Familiearchief:
I. G.J.C. Schneither
II. Couperus
III. Flack
IV. Verhuell
V. Maps Collectie

Oriental and India Office Library, London
I. Straits Settlements Factory Records
II. Board's Collections
III. Dutch Records relating to Malacca
IV. Newspaper: Prince of Wales Island Gazette 12 July 1806–10 Oct 1807; 17 Oct 1807–22 Apr 1815; 20 May 1815–21 July 1827. *Prince of Wales Island, Singapore and Malacca Government Gazette* 25 Oct 1828–3 July 1830.
V. India Office Records Reference Map Collections.
VI. Prints and Drawings: Print Collection in Oriental and India Office.

British Library, London
I. Map Collections in the Map Reading Room

National Archives of Malaysia, Kuala Lumpur

I.   Microfilm of Straits Settlements Factory Records
II. Microfilm on Inventories and accounts of deceased estates
III. Dutch Church Records
IV. Microfilm of VOC records relating to Malacca
V.   Map Collections

School of Oriental and African Studies Library, London

Missionary archives: Council of World Missionary Archive of the London Missionary Society Ultra Ganges

Universiti Kebangsaan Malaysia Library, Bangi

Microfilm copies of Dutch records from India Office Library, London

University of Malaya Library, Kuala Lumpur

Microfilm copies of VOC records relating to Malacca

BOOKS AND ARTICLES

A Catalogue of Manuscript and Printed Reports, Field Books, Memoirs, Maps, etc. of The Indian Surveys, Deposited in the Map Room of the India Office, London: W.H. Allen, 1878.

Abdullah Abdul Kadir, *The Hikayat Abdullah* (An annotated translation by A.H. Hill), Kuala Lumpur: Oxford University Press, 1970.

———, *Kesah Pelayaran Abdullah terkarang oleh Abdullah bin Abdul Kadir Munshi*, Singapore: Malaya Publishing House, 1947.

Abeyasekere, S., 'Slaves in Batavia: Insight From a Slave Register'. In Reid, *Slavery, Bondage and Dependency in Southeast Asia*, pp. 286–313.

———, *Jakarta A History*, Singapore: Oxford University Press, 1987.

Abu-Lughod, Janet, *Before European Hegemony: the World System, A.D. 1250–1350*, New York: Oxford University Press, 1989.

Alston, R.C., *Handlist of Unpublished Finding Aids to the London Collections of the British Library*, London: The British Library, 1991.

An Exposition of the Political and Commercial Relations of the Government of Prince of Wales Island with the States on the East Coast of Sumatra from Diamond Point to Siack, Prince of Wales Island, 1824.

Andaya, Barbara Watson, 'Adapting to Political and Economic Change: Palembang in the Late Eighteenth and Early Nineteenth Centuries'. In Anthony Reid (ed.), *The Last Stand of Asian Autonomies in the Diverse States of Southeast Asia and Korea 1750–1900*, London: Macmillan, 1997.

———, 'The Cloth Trade in Jambi and Palembang Society During the 17th and 18th Centuries', *Indonesia*, vol. 48, 1989, pp. 27–46.

———, 'An Examination of Sources Concerning the Reign of Sultan Mansur Syah of Trengganu 1741–1793, with Reference to the Thufat al-Nafis', *JMBRAS*, 49, 1976, pp. 80–104.

———, 'The Indian "Saudagar Raja" (the King's Merchant) in Traditional Malay Courts', *JMBRAS*, vol. 51, pt. 1, 1978, pp. 13–35.

———, *To Live As Brothers, Southeast Sumatra in the Seventeenth and Eighteenth Centuries*, Honolulu: University of Hawaii Press, 1993.

———, 'Melaka Under the Dutch'. In Sandhu and Wheatley, *Melaka: The Transformation of a Malay Capital*, vol. 1, pp. 195–241.

———, 'Political Development between the Sixteenth and Eighteenth Centuries'. In Tarling, *The Cambridge History of Southeast Asia*, vol. 1, pp. 402–459.

Andaya, Barbara Watson and Leonard Y. Andaya, *The History of Malaysia*, London: Macmillan, 1982.

Andaya, L.Y., 'The Bugis-Makassar Diasporas', *MBRAS*, vol. 68, pt. 1, 1995, pp. 119–138.

———, 'Historical Links Between Aquatic Populations and the Coastal Peoples of the Malay World and Celebes'. In Muhamad Abu Bakar (ed.), *Historia*, Kuala Lumpur: The Malaysian Historical Society, 1984, pp. 34–51.

———, 'Interactions with the Outside World and Adaptation in Southeast Asian Society, 1500–1800'. In Tarling, *The Cambridge History of Southeast Asia*, vol. 1, pp. 345–400.

———, *The Kingdom of Johore 1641–1728: Economic and Political Developments*, Kuala Lumpur: Oxford University Press, 1975.

———, *The World of Maluku: Eastern Indonesia in the Early Modern Period*, Honolulu: University of Hawaii Press, 1993.

Anderson, John, *Acheen and the Ports on the North and East Coasts of Sumatra: with Incidental Notices of the Trade in the Eastern Seas and the Aggressions of the Dutch*, London: W.H. Allen, 1840.

———, *Mission to the East Coast of Sumatra in DCCCXXIII, Under the Direction of the Government of Prince of Wales Island; Including Historical and Descriptive Sketches of the Country an Account of the Commerce, Population and Manners and Customs of the Inhabitants and a Visit to the Batta Cannibal States in the Interior*, London: William Backwood, Edinburgh and T. Cadell, 1826.

———, *Political and Commercial Considerations Relative to the Malayan Peninsula and the British Settlements in the Straits of Malacca*, Prince of Wales Island: William Cox, 1824.

Arasaratnam, Sinnappah, 'Aspects of the Role and Activities of South Indian Merchant Communities 1650–1750'. In Arasaratnam, *Maritime Trade, Society and European Influence*, pp. 582–595.

———, 'Ceylon in the Indian Ocean Trade 1500–1800'. In Das Gupta and Pearson, *India and the Indian Ocean*.

———, 'The Chuliar Muslim Merchants in Southeast Asia 1650–1800'. In Arasaratnam, *Maritime Trade, Society and European Influence*, pp. 126–143.

———, 'Coromandel Shipping and Seafaring in the Indian Ocean 1650–1800', *Journal of East-West Maritime Relations*, vol. 3, 1994, pp. 19–41.

———, 'The Coromandel–Southeast Asia Trade 1650–1740'. In Arasaratnam, *Maritime Trade, Society and European Influence*, pp. 113–135.

———, 'The Dutch Administrative Structure in Sri Lanka', *Modern Sri Lanka Studies*, vol. 2, no. 1 and 2, 1987, pp. 120–132.

———, 'Dutch Commercial Policy and Interests in the Malaya Peninsula, 1750–1795'. In Blair B. Kling and M.N. Pearson (eds), *The Age of Partnership:*

Europeans in Asia before Dominion, Honolulu: University of Hawaii Press, 1979, pp. 159–189.

———, 'The Dutch East India Company and its Coromandel Trade 1700–1740'. In Arasaratnam, *Maritime Trade, Society and European Influence*, pp. 325–346.

———, 'European Port Settlements in the Coromandel Commercial System 1650–1740'. In Broeze, *Brides of the Sea*, pp. 75–96.

———, 'Factors in the Rise, Growth and Decline of Coromandel Ports 1650–1720. In Arasaratnam, *Maritime Trade, Society and European Influence*, pp. 19–30.

———, 'India and the Indian Ocean in the Seventeenth Century'. In Das Gupta and Pearson, *India and the Indian Ocean*, pp. 94–131.

———, 'Indian Commercial Groups and European Traders, 1600–1800: Changing Relationships in Southeastern India'. In Arasaratnam, *Maritime Trade, Society and European Influence*, pp. 42–53.

———, 'Indian Merchants and the Decline of Indian Mercantile Activity: the Coromandel Case'. In Arasaratnam, *Maritime Trade, Society and European Influence*, pp. 27–42.

———, *Islamic Merchant Communities of the Indian Sub-continent in Southeast Asia*, Kuala Lumpur: University Malaya Press, 1989.

———, 'Mare Clausum, the Dutch and Regional Trade in the Indian Ocean 1650–1740'. In Arasaratnam, *Maritime Trade, Society and European Influence*, pp. 73–91.

———, *Maritime Commerce and English Power: Southeast India 1750–1800*, Aldershot: Variorum, 1996.

———, *Maritime Trade, Society and European Influence in Southern Asia, 1600–1800*, Aldershot: Variorum, 1995.

———, 'Merchants and Commerce in Coromandel: Trends and Tendencies in the Eighteenth Century', (unpublished paper).

———, *Merchants, Companies and Commerce on the Coromandel Coast 1650–1740*, New Delhi: Oxford University Press, 1986.

———, 'Merchants of Coromandel in Trade and Entrepreneurship 1650–1700'. In Ptak and Rothermund, *Emporia, Commodities and Entrepreneurs*, pp. 37–51.

———, 'Monopoly and Free Trade in Dutch-Asian Commercial Policy: Debates and Controversy Within the VOC'. In Arasaratnam, *Maritime Trade, Society and European Influence*, pp. 1–15.

———, 'The Politics of Commerce in the Coastal Kingdom of Tamil Nadu 1650–1700'. In Arasaratnam, *Maritime Trade, Society and European Influence*, pp. 1–19.

———, 'Slave Trade in the Indian Ocean in the Seventeenth Century'. In Mathew, *Mariners, Merchants and Oceans*, pp. 195–208.

———, 'Some Notes on the Dutch in Malacca and the Indo-Malayan Trade 1641–1670'. In Arasaratnam, *Maritime Trade, Society and European Influence*, pp. 480–490.

———, 'The Use of Dutch Material for Southeast Asian Historical Writing', *JSEAH*, vol. 3, 1962, pp. 95–105.

———, 'Weavers, Merchants and Company: The Handloom Industry in Southeastern India 1750–1790'. In Arasaratnam, *Maritime Trade, Society and European Influence*, pp. 257–281.

Archer, Mildred and John Bastin, *The Raffles Drawings in the India Office Library, London*, Kuala Lumpur: Oxford University Press, 1978.

'Archives and Fieldwork: The Dutch East India Company Documents As Source Material on Indian History in the Seventeenth and Eighteenth Centuries', *Itinerario*, no. 2, vol. vii, 1983, pp. 38–49.

Banga, Indu (ed.), *Ports and Their Hinterlands in India 1700–1950*, New Delhi: Manohar, 1992.

Barendse, Rene J., 'The East India Companies in the Indian Ocean, XVIth–XVIIIth Century: Some General Problems', *Moyen Orient & Ocean Indien*, 7, 1990, pp. 13–26.

Bassett, D.K., 'The "Amboyna Massacre" of 1623', *JSEAH*, vol. 1, no. 2, 1960, pp.1–19.

———, 'Anglo-Malay Relations, 1786–1795'. In Bassett, *British Trade and Policy*, pp. 72–107.

———, 'British Commercial and Strategic Interest in the Malay Peninsular During the Late Eighteenth Century'. In Bassett, *British Trade and Policy*, pp. 50–71.

———, 'The British Country Trader and Sea Captain in Southeast Asia in the 17th and 18th Centuries', *Journal of the Historical Society*, no. 1, vol. 2, 1961, pp. 9–14.

———, 'The British Missions to Kedah and Acheh in 1772: Some Belated Reflections'. In Bassett, *The British in South-East Asia*, pp. 1–32.

———, *The British in South-East Asia During the Seventeenth and Eighteenth Centuries*, Hull: Occasional Papers, Centre for Southeast Asian Studies, University of Hull, no. 18, 1990.

———, 'British Trade and Policy in Indonesia 1760–1772'. In Bassett, *British Trade and Policy*, pp. 1–29.

———, 'The British Trader and Mariner in Southeast Asia, c.1660–1715'. In Bassett, *The British in South-East Asia*, pp. 1–32.

———, 'Changes in the Pattern of Malay Politics, 1629–1655'. In *JSEAH*, vol. 10, no. 3, 1969, pp. 429–452.

———, 'European Influence in the Malay Peninsula, 1511–1786', *JMBRAS*, vol. 33, pt. 3, 1960, pp. 9–35.

———, 'The Surrender of Dutch Malacca 1795'. In Bassett, *British Trade and Policy*, pp. 108–123.

——— (ed.), *British Trade and Policy in Indonesia and Malaysia in the Late Eighteenth Century*, Hull: University of Hull Monographs, no. 3, 1971, pp. 72–107.

Bastin, Christopher and John, 'Some Old Penang Tombstones', *JMBRAS*, vol. 37, pt. 1, 1964, pp. 126–165.

Bastin, John, *The British in West Sumatra (1685-1825) A selection of documents, mainly from the East India Company records preserved in the India Office Library*, Kuala Lumpur: University Malaya Press, 1965.

———, 'Historical Sketch of Penang in 1794', *JMBRAS*, 32, pt. 1, 1959, pp. 1–32.

———, *The Native Policies of Sir Stamford Raffles in Java and Sumatra: An Economic Interpretation*, Oxford: Clarendon Press, 1957.

Bastin, John and C.A. Gibson-Hill, 'Short notes: Five Early Watercolour Sketches of Penang and Malacca', *JMBRAS*, 31, part 1, 1958, pp. 163–171.

Bastin, John and Pauline Rohatgi, *Prints of Southeast Asia in the India Office Library: The East India Company in Malaysia and Indonesia 1786–1824*, London: India Office Library, 1979.

Basu, Dilip, K. (ed.), *The Rise and Growth of the Colonial Port Cities in Asia*, University of California, Berkeley, Centre for South and Southeast Asia Studies, Monograph Series no. 25, Lanham: University Press of America, 1985.

Baumgarten, F.L., 'Agriculture in Malacca', *JIA*, Series 1, vol. 3, 1849, pp. 707–723.

Baxter, Ian, *A Brief Guide to Biographical Sources: India Office Library and Records*, Second Edition, London: The British Library, 1989.

———, 'Dutch Records from Malacca in the India Office Library', *JMBRAS*, vol. 56, pt. 2, 1983, pp. 105–133.

Begbie, P.J., *The Malayan Peninsula*, Madras: Vepery Mission Press, 1834.

Bellam, M.E.P., 'The Colonial City: Honiara, A Pacific Islands' Case study', *Pacific Viewpoint*, vol. II, number 1, May 1970.

Bernard, Fernand, *A Travers Sumatra de Batavia & Atjeh, etc.,* Paris: Hachette, 1904.

Bhattacharya, Bhaswati, 'The Dutch East India Company and the Trade of the Chulias in the Bay of Bengal in the late Eighteenth Century'. In Mathew, *Mariners, Merchants and Oceans*, pp. 347–361.

Bland, Robert Norman, *Historical Tombstones of Malacca Mostly of Portuguese Origin with the Inscriptions in Detail and illustrated by Numerous Photographs*, London: Elliot Stock, 1905.

Blundell, E.A., 'Notices of the History and Present Condition of Malacca', *JIA*, Series I, vol. 2, 1848, pp. 726–754.

Blusse, Leonard, 'Chinese Century: The Eighteenth Century in the China Sea Region', *Archipel*, 58, 1999, pp. 107–130.

———, 'An Insane Administration and an Unsanitary'. In Ross, *Colonial Cities*, pp. 65–86.

———, *Strange Company: Chinese Settlers, Mestizo Women and the Dutch in Batavia*, Dordrecht: KITLV Press, 1986.

Blusse, Leonard and F. Gaastra (eds), *On the Eighteenth Century as a Category of Asian History: Van Leur in Retrospect,* Aldershot: Ashgate, 1998.

Blythe, Wilfred, *The Impact of Chinese Secret Societies in Malaya, A Historical Study*, London: Oxford University Press, 1969.

Boelen, H.J., 'Iets over Malakka', *Ned. Indie Oud en Nieuw*, vol. 5, 1920/21, pp. 366–78.

———, 'Iets over Malakka', *Ned. Indie Oud en Nieuw*, vol. 6 (1921/22), pp. 63–4.

Bonney, R, 'Francis Light and Penang', *JMBRAS*, xxxviii, I, 1965, pp. 135–158.

———, *Kedah 1771–1821 The Search for Security and Independence,* Kuala Lumpur: Oxford University Press, 1971.

Bort, Balthasar, 'Report of Governor Balthasar Bort on Malacca, 1678', *JMBRAS*, vol. 5, pt. 1, 1927, pp. 1–232.

Bouchon, Genevieve, 'Sixteenth Century Malabar and the Indian Ocean'. In Das Gupta and Pearson, *India and the Indian Ocean*, pp. 162–184.

Boxer, C.R., *The Dutch Seaborne Empire 1600–1800*, London: Hutchinson, 1965.

———, 'The Maritime Twilight of the VOC 1780–95: Some Sources and Problems', *Tijdschrift voor zeegeschiedenis*, no. 1, April 1982, pp. 114–123.

———, *The Portuguese Seaborne Empire 1415–1825*, London: Hutchinson, 1969.

Braddell, T., 'Gambling and Smoking in the Straits of Malacca', *JIA*, Series II, vol. 1, 1856, pp. 66–83.

———, 'Notes on Malacca', *JIA*, Series II, vol. 1, 1856, pp. 43–65.

———, 'Notes on Naning With A Brief Notice of the Naning War', *JIA*, Series II, vol. 1, 1856, pp. 193–232

———, *Statistics of the British Possessions in the Straits of Malacca With Explanatory Notes*, Pinang Gazette Printing Office, 1861.

————, 'Map of Malacca', *JIA*, Series II, vol. 1, 1856, pp. 296–298.

Broeze, Frank (ed.), *Brides of the Sea: Port Cities of Asia from the 16th to 20th Centuries*, Kensington: New South Wales University Press, 1989.

Brohier, Deloraine, 'Who are the Burghers?', *Journal of the Sri Lanka Branch Royal Asiatic Society*, vol. xxx, 1985/86, pp. 101–119.

Brown, C.C (ed.), *Sejarah Melayu (Malay Annals)*, Kuala Lumpur: Oxford University Press, 1970.

———— (ed.), *Sejarah Melayu (Malay Annals)*, *JMBRAS*, vol. 25, pts. 2 and 3, 1952, pp. 1–276.

Brown, Stubbs, M., 'The Failure of Penang as a Naval Base and Shipping Centre', *JMBRAS*, vol. 32, pt. 1, 1959, pp. 1–32.

Bruijn, Jaap R., 'Between Batavia and the Cape: Shipping Patterns of the Dutch East India Company', *JSEAS*, vol. xi, no. 2, September 1980, pp. 251–165.

Bruijn, J.R., F.S. Gaastra and I. Schöffer (eds), *Dutch-Asiatic Shipping in the 17th and 18th Centuries*, Rijks Geschiedkundige Publicatien Grote Serie 165, 166 and 167, The Hague: Martinus Nijhoff, 1979–87.

Bruijn, P.G. de, 'Trade in the Straits of Malacca in 1785: A Memorandum', (translated from the Dutch by B. Harrison), *JMBRAS*, vol. 26, pt. 1, 1953, pp. 56–62.

Bulbeck, D. (ed.), *Southeast Asian Exports Since the 14th Century: Cloves, Pepper, Coffee, and Sugar*, Singapore: Institute of Southeast Asian Studies, 1998.

Burns, Peter, 'The Netherlands East Indies: Colonial Legal Policy and the Definitions of Laws'. In Hooker, *The Laws of Southeast Asia*, vol. II, pp. 147–297.

Butcher, John, 'Revenue Farming and the Changing State in Southeast Asia'. In Butcher and Dick, *The Rise and Fall of Revenue Farming*, pp.19–44.

Butcher, John and Howard Dick (eds), *The Rise and Fall of Revenue Farming: Business Elites and the Emergence of the Modern State in Southeast Asia*, London: Macmillan Press, 1993.

Cabaton, Antoine, *Java, Sumatra and the Other Islands of the Dutch East Indies*, London: Fisher Unwin, 1911.

Cameron, John, *Our Tropical Possessions in Malayan India, Being a Descriptive Account of Singapore, Penang, Province Wellesley, and Malacca, the People, Products, Commerce and Government*, London: Smith & Elder, 1865.

Cardon, R., 'Old Malacca: Tranqueira and Gajah Berang', *JMBRAS*, vol. 21, pt. 1, 1948, pp. 104–16.

Cave, Jonathan, 'Naning in Malacca', *MBRAS*, 1989, Kuala Lumpur.

Chan Kok Eng, 'Population Growth and Ethnic Composition in Melaka Since 1826', *Sarjana*, 1994, pp. 199–216.

————, 'The Distribution of the Portuguese Eurasian Population in Malacca: A study of Spatial Continuity and Change', *Geographica*, vol. 6, 1970, pp. 56–64.

Chaudhuri, K.N., *Asia before Europe: Economy and civilization of the Indian Ocean from the rise of Islam to 1750*, Cambridge: Cambridge University Press, 1990.

————, *The English East India Company, The Study of An Early Joint-Stock Company 1600–1640*, London: Franks Cass, 1965.

————, *Trade and Civilization in the Indian Ocean: An Economic History from the Rise of Islam to 1750*, Cambridge: Cambridge University Press, 1985.

————, *The Trading World of Asia and the East India Company 1660–1740*, Cambridge: Cambridge University Press, 1967.

Chaudhury, S., *From Prosperity to Decline: Eighteenth Century Bengal*, New Delhi: Manohar, 1995.

———, 'Merchants, Companies and Rulers: Bengal in the Eighteenth Century', *Bengal Journal of the Economic and Social History of the Orient*, 31, 1988, pp. 74–110.

———, *Trade and Commercial Organization in Bengal 1650–1720: with Special Reference to the English East India Company*, Calcutta: Firma K.L. Makhopadhyay, 1975.

Che'en Kuo-tung, 'Shipping and Trade of Chinese Junks in Southeast Asia, 1730–1830: A Survey'. In S.P. Ville and D.M. Williams (eds), *Management, Finance and Industrial Relations in Maritime Industries: Essays in International Maritime and Business History*, St. John's: International Maritime Economic History Associations, 1994, pp. 203–214.

Cheong Weng Eang, *The Hong Merchants of Canton: Chinese Merchants in Sino-Western Trade*, NIAS Monographs, 70, London: Curzon Press, 1995.

Chijs, J.A. van der, 'Koepang Omstreeks 1750', *Tijdschrift voor Indische taal-, land-en volkenkunde*, 18, 1872, pp. 209–227.

——— (ed.), *Nederlandsch-Indisch Plakaatboek 1602–1811*, The Hague: Nijhoff, 1885–1900.

Christiaans, P.A., 'De Europese Bevolking van Malakka Onder Het Laatste Nederlandse Bestuur, 1818–1825', *Jaarboek Centraal Bureau voor Genealogie*, Deel 40, 1986, pp. 257–287.

Clammer, John, 'The Straits Chinese in Melaka'. In Sandhu and Wheatley, *Melaka: The Transformation of a Malay Capital*, vol. 2, pp. 156–173.

———, *Straits Chinese Society: Studies in the Sociology of the Baba Communities of Malaysia and Singapore*, Singapore: Singapore University Press, 1980.

Clodd, H.P, *Malaya's First British Pioneer: The Life of Francis Light*, London: Luzac, 1948.

Comber, L.F., *Chinese Secret Societies in Malaya: A Survey of the Triad Society from 1800–1900*, New York: Monograph of the Association for Asian Studies, 1959.

———, *An Introduction to Chinese Secret Societies in Malaya*, Singapore: Donald Moore, 1957.

Coolhaas, W.Ph., *A Critical Survey of Studies on Dutch Colonial History*, The Hague: Martinus Nijhoff, 1980.

———, 'Malacca under Jan Van Riebeek', *JMBRAS*, vol. 38, pt. 2, 1965, pp. 173–182.

Coolhaas, W.Ph. and J. van Goor (eds), *Generale Missiven van Gouverneurs-generaal en Raden aan Heren XVII der Verenigde Oostindische Compagnie*, Rijks Geschiedkundige Publicatien Grote Serie, 104, 112, 125, 134, 150, 159, 164, 193, 205 and 232, The Hague: Nijhoff, 1960–97.

Copland, Ian and Michael R. Godley, 'Revenue Farming in Comparative Perspective: Reflections on Taxation, Social Structure and Development in the Early-modern Period'. In Butcher and Dick, *The Rise and Fall of Revenue Farming*, pp. 45–68.

Cortesao, Armando, *The Suma Oriental of Tome Pires, An Account of the East from the Red Sea to Japan, written in Malacca and India in 1512–1515*, London: Hakluyt, 1944.

Couperus, Abrahamus, 'Berigt aangaande de Gamber, derzelver planting en bewerking op Malacca', *Verhandelingen van het Bataviaasch Genootschap der kunsten en wetenschappen*, Tweede Deel, 1780, pp. 356–382.

Cowan, C.D., 'Early Penang and the Rise of Singapore 1805–1832', *JMBRAS*, 23(2), 1950, pp.1–20.

———, 'Governor Bannerman and the Penang Tin Scheme 1818–1819', *JMBRAS*, vol. 23, part 1, 1950, pp. 52–83.

Crawfurd, John, F.R.S., *Memorandum on the British Settlements in the Straits of Malacca*, London: C.W. Reynell, 1858.

Cushman, Jennifer (ed. by Craig J. Reynolds), *Family and State: the Formation of a Sino-Thai Tin-Mining Dynasty 1797–1932*, Singapore: Oxford University Press, 1991.

———, *Fields from the Sea: Chinese Junk Trade with Siam During the Late Eighteenth and Early Nineteenth Centuries*, Ithaca: Cornell University Press, 1993.

Cushman, Jennifer and A.C. Milner, 'Eighteenth and Nineteenth Century Chinese Accounts of the Malay Peninsula', *JMBRAS*, vol. 52, pt. 1, no. 235, 1979, pp. 1–56.

Dam, P. van, F.W. Stapel and C.W.Th. van Boetzelaer (eds), *Beschrijvinge van de Oostindische Compagnie*, Rijks Geschiedkundige Publicatien Grote serie 63, 68, 74, 76, 83, 87 and 96, The Hague: Nijhoff, 1927–1954.

Dampier, William, *Voyages and Discoveries: With An introduction and Notes by Clennell Wilkinson*, London: The Argonaut Press, 1931.

Das Gupta, A, 'Gujarati Merchants and the Red Sea Trade 1700–1725'. In B. Kling and M.N. Pearson (eds), *The Age of Partnership: Europeans in Asia before Dominion*, Honolulu: University of Hawaii Press, 1979, pp. 123–158.

———, 'Trade and Politics in 18th Century India'. In D.S. Richards (ed.), *Islam and the Trade of Asia: A Colloquium*, The Near Eastern History Group, Oxford, and The Near Eastern Center: University of Pennsylvania, 1970, pp. 181–214.

Das Gupta, A.K., 'Acheh in the Seventeenth Century Asian Trade', *Bengal Past and Present*, January–June 1962.

Das Gupta, Arun, 'The Maritime Trade of Indonesia: 1500–1800'. In Das Gupta and Pearson, *India and the Indian Ocean*, pp. 240–275.

Das Gupta, Ashin, 'India and the Indian Ocean in the Eighteenth Century'. In Das Gupta and Pearson, *India and the Indian Ocean*, pp. 131–161.

———, *Malabar in Asian Trade 1740–1800*, Cambridge: Cambridge University Press, 1967.

Das Gupta, Ashin and M.N. Pearson (eds), *India and the Indian Ocean 1500–1800*, Calcutta: Oxford University Press, 1987.

Davies, Donald, *Old Penang*, Singapore: Donald More, 1956.

De Silva, Gregory. W, *Lupe: An Historical Romance of Portuguese Malacca*, Kuala Lumpur: International Printers, 1939.

Deb, Raja Binaya Krishna, *The Early History and Growth of Calcutta*, Calcutta: Riddhi, 1977 (first published in 1905).

Dick, Howard, 'A Fresh Approach to Southeast Asian History'. In Butcher and Dick, *The Rise and Fall of Revenue Farming*, pp. 3–17.

Dillo, I.G., *De Nadagen van de Verenigde Oostindische Compagnie 1783–1795: Schepen en Zeevarenden*, Amsterdam: De Bataafsche Leeuw, 1992.

Doetichum, Joannes A., *A Series of Prints Illustrative of the Manners and Customs of the People of Malacca, Java, China, the East Indies*, Amsterdam, 1600.

Ellen, R.F., 'The Trade in Spices', *Indonesia Circle*, 12, 1977, pp. 21–25.

Elmore, H.M., *The British Mariner's Directory and Guide to the Trade and Navigation of the Indian and China Seas*, London: T. Bensley, 1802.

Elson, Robert E., 'International Commerce, the State and Society: Economic and Social Change'. In Tarling, *The Cambridge History of Southeast Asia*, vol. 1.

End, T. van den, 'Dutch Protestant Mission Activity: A Survey', *Itinerario*, no. 1, vol. vii, 1983, pp. 85–108.

Evers, Hans-Dieter, 'Traditional Trading Networks of Southeast Asia', *Archipel*, 35, 1988, pp. 89–100.

Eyck van Heslinga, E.S. van, *Van Compagnie naar koopvaardij: De Scheepvaart-verbinding van de Bataafse Republiek met de kolonien in Azie 1795–1806*, Amsterdam: De Bataafsche Leeuw, 1988.

Fieldhouse, D.K., *The Colonial Empires: A Comparative Survey from the Eighteenth Century*, London: MacMillan, 1982.

Fielding, K.J. (ed.), 'The Settlement of Penang by James Scott', *JMBRAS*, xxxviii, I, 1955, pp. 37–51.

Forrest, T., *A Voyage from Calcutta to the Mergui Archipelago*, London: J. Robson, 1792.

Foster, William, *The Founding of Fort St. George, Madras*, London: Eyre and Spottiswoode, 1902.

Fox, J., 'For Good and Sufficient Reasons: An Examination of Early Dutch East India Company Ordinances on Slaves and Slavery'. In Reid, *Slavery, Bondage and Dependency in Southeast Asia*, pp. 246–262.

Fraassen, Ch. F. van, 'Ternate de Molukken en de Indonesische Archipel', Proefschrift Leiden, 1987.

Frank, A.G., *Re-ORIENT: Global Economy in the Asian Age*, Berkeley: University of California Press, 1998.

Furber, Holden, *John Company at Work, A Study of European Expansion in India in the late 18th century*, Cambridge: Harvard University Press, 1951.

———, *Rival Empires of Trade in the Orient 1600–1800*, Minneapolis: University of Minnesota Press, 1976.

Furnivall, J.S., *Colonial Policy and Practice: A Comparative Study of Burma and Netherlands India*, Cambridge: Cambridge University Press, 1948.

Gaastra, F.S., 'The Dutch East India Company's shipping 1602–1795 in a comparative perspective'. In F.S. Gaastra and J.R. Bruijn (eds), *Ships, Sailors and Spices*, Amsterdam: NEHA, 1993, pp. 177–208.

———, *De geschiedenis van de VOC*, Zutphen: Walburg Pers, 1991.

———, 'The Organization of the VOC'. In Meilink-Roelofsz et al, *The Archives of the Dutch East India Company*, pp. 11–29.

———, 'The Textile Trade of the VOC: The Dutch Response to the English Challenge', *South Asia*, 19, 1996, pp. 85–95.

Gall, H.C., 'De Weeskamer in Nederlands-Indie als Negentiende-eeuws Instituut'. In C.J.H. Jansen, E. Poortinga and T.J. Veen (eds), *Twaalf Bijdragen Tot De Studie van de Rechtsgeschiedenis van de Negentiende Eeuw*, Faculteit der Rechts-geleerdheid, Universiteit van Amsterdam, 1996, pp. 29–43.

Garnier, Keppel, 'Early Days in Penang', *JMBRAS*, vol. 1, pt. 1, 1923, pp. 5–12.

Ghosh, Murari, *Calcutta: A Study in Urban Growth Dynamics*, Calcutta: Mukho-padhuay, 1972.

Gibson-Hill, C.A., 'The Fortification of Bukit China Malacca', *JMBRAS*, vol. 29, pt. 3, 1956, pp. 157–181.

Glamann, K., *Dutch-Asiatic Trade 1620–1740*, The Hague: Nijhoff, 1981.

Godley, Michael R., 'Chinese Revenue Farm Networks: The Penang Connection'. In Butcher and Dick, *The Rise and Fall of Revenue Farming*, pp. 89–99.

Goode, S.W., *Municipal Calcutta, its Institutions in their Origin and Growth*, Calcutta: Bibhashgupta, 1986.

Goor, J. van, 'Jan Kompenie as Schoolmaster: Dutch Education in Ceylon 1690–1795', Proefschrift Utrecht, 1978.

——— 'A Madman in the City of Ghosts: Nicolaas Kloek in Pontianak', *Itinerario*, 9/2, 1985, pp. 196–212.

———, *De Nederlandse Kolonien: Geschiednis van de Nederlandse Expansie 1600–1975*, The Hague: SDU Uitgeverijkoninginnegracht, 1993.

———, 'Seapower, Trade and State-formation: Pontianak and the Dutch'. In van Goor, *Trading Companies in Asia*, pp. 83–106.

——— (ed.), *Trading Companies in Asia 1600–1830*, Utrecht: HES Studies in Colonial and non-European History, 1986, pp. 83–106.

Goslings, B.M., 'Een Batik van Jambi'. In *Nederlandsch-Indie Oud en Nieuw*, vol. 12, pp. 279–283.

Graaf, H.J. de, *De Geschiedenis van Ambon en de Zuid-Molukken*, Franeker: Wever, 1977.

Graham, T., 'Historical Sketch of Penang in 1794', *JMBRAS*, 4, 1977, pp. 286–310.

'Grondbezit op Malakka'. In *Tijdschrift voor Nederlandsch Indie*, vol. 19, no. 2, 1857, pp. 65–105.

Groot, H.F.W. Cornets de, 'Slavernij en Het Pandelingschap in de Residentie Lampongsche Districten', *TBG*, xxvii, 1882, pp. 454–487.

Haan, F. de, *Priangan: De Preangen-regentschappen onder het Nederlandsch bestuur tot 1811*, Batavia: Kolff en Co., 1910–12.

———, *Oud Batavia, Gedenkboek Uitgegeven door het Bataviaasch Genootschap van Kunsten en Wetenschappen naar Aanleiding van Driehonderdjarig Bestaan der Stad in 1919*, Batavia: Kolff en Co., 1935.

Hællquist, Karl Reinhold (ed.), *Asian Trade Routes: Continental and Maritime*, NIAS Studies in Asian Topics, 13, London: Curzon Press, 1991.

Hall, D.G.E., *A History of Southeast Asia*, London: MacMillan, 1968.

Hall, Kenneth, R., 'Economic History of Early Southeast Asia'. In Tarling, *The Cambridge History of Southeast Asia*, vol. 1, pp.183–275.

———, *Maritime Trade and State Development in Early Southeast Asia*, Honolulu: University of Hawaii Press, 1985.

Hanna, W.A., *Indonesia Banda: Colonialism and Its Aftermath in the Nutmeg Island*, Philadelphia: Institute for the Study of Human Issues (ISHI), 1978.

Harfield, Alan, *Bencoolen, A History of the Honourable East India Company's Garrison on the West Coast of Sumatra 1685–1825*, Barton-on-Sea: A and J Partnership, 1995.

———, *British and Indian Armies in the East Indies 1685–1935*, Chippenham: Picton, 1984.

———, *Christian Cemeteries of Penang and Perak*, London: British Association for Cemeteries in South Asia, 1987.

Harrison, Brian, 'Holding the Fort', *MBRAS*, 1985.

———, *Waiting for China: The Anglo-Chinese College at Malacca, 1818–1843, and Early Nineteenth-Century Missions*, Hong Kong: Hong Kong University Press, 1979.

———, 'Malacca in the Eighteenth Century: Two Dutch Governors' Reports', *JMBRAS*, vol. 27. pt. 1, 1954, pp. 24–33.

Hayes, Sarina, *Old Penang*, Kuala Lumpur: Oxford University Press, 1991.

Heidhues, M.F. Somers, *Banka Tin and Mentok Pepper: Chinese Settlement on an Indonesian Island*, Singapore: Institute of Southeast Asian Studies, 1992.

———, 'The First Two Sultans of Pontianak', *Archipel*, 56, 1998, pp. 273–294.

Heringa, R., *Een Schitterende Geschiedenis: Weefsels en Batiks van Palembang en Djambi*, the Hague: Museon, 1993.

Hervey, D.F.A., 'Malacca in the Eighteenth Century', *JSBRAS*, no. 12, 1883, pp. 261–267.

Heydt, J.W., *Allerneuester Geographisch und topographischer schau-platz, von Africa und Ost-Indien*, Willhermsdorff: Tetschner, 1744.

Hill, A. H., 'The Demolition of Malacca Fort', *British Malaya*, vol. 2, no. 2, 1953, pp. 99–102.

———, 'Munshi Abdullah's Account of the Malacca Fort', *JMBRAS*, 23(1), 1950, pp. 84–99.

Historical Guide of Malacca, The Malacca Historical Society: Singapore Printers Limited, 1936.

Hoevell, W. R van, *De Emancipatie der Slaven in Neerlands-Indie*, Groningen: Van Bolhuis Hoitsema, 1848.

Hoffman, J.E., 'Early Policies in the Malacca Jurisdiction of the United East India Company: The Malay Peninsula and Netherlands East Indies Attachment', *JSEAS*, vol. 3, no. 1, 1972, pp. 1–38.

———, 'The Siege of Malacca, 1640–1641', M.A. Preliminary course, University of Melbourne, (n.d.).

Hogendrop, W. van, 'Beschryving van het eiland Timor voor zoover het tot nog toe bekend is', *Verhandelingen van het Bataviaasch Genootschap der Kunsten en Wetenschappen*, 1, 1779, pp. 192–214 and 2, 1780, pp. 405–434.

Hohendorff, J.A. van, 'Radicale Beschrijving van Banjermassing, 1757', *Bijdragen tot de taal-, land- en volkenkunde van Nederlandsch-Indie*, 8, 1862, pp. 151–216.

Hooker, M.B., 'English Law in Sumatra, Java, the Straits Settlements, Malay States, Sarawak, North Borneo and Brunei'. In Hooker, *The Laws of Southeast Asia*, vol. II.

——— (ed.), *The Laws of Southeast Asia – Vol. II: European Laws in Southeast Asia*, Singapore: Butterworths, 1988.

Horridge, George Adrian, *The Prahu: Traditional Sailing Boat of Indonesia*, Singapore: Oxford University Press, 1985.

Horvath, Ronald, J., 'In search of a Theory of urbanization: notes on the Colonial city', *East Lakes Geographer*, 5, 1969, pp. 69–82.

Hossain, H., *The Company Weavers of Bengal: The East India Company and the Organization of Textile Production in Bengal 1750–1813*, Oxford: Oxford University Press, 1988.

Hullu, J. De, 'A.E. van Braam Houckgeest's Memorie over Malakka en den Tinhandel Aldaar (1790)', *Bijdragen tot de taal-land- en volkenkunde*, 76, 1920, pp. 284–309.

———, 'De Engelschen op Poeloe Pinang en de Tinhandel der Nederlandsche Oost-Indische Compagnie in 1788', *BTLVNI*, 77, 1921, pp. 605–615.

———, 'De Instelling van de Commissie voor den Handel der Oost-Indische Compagnie op China in 1756', *Bijdragen tot de taal-, land- en volkenkunde van Nederlandsch-Indie*, 79, 1923, pp. 523–545.

―――, 'Over de Chinasche Handel der Oost-Indische Compagnie in de eerste dertig jaar van de 18de eeuw', *Bijdragen tot de taal-, land- en volkenkunde van Nederlandsch-Indie*, 73, 1917, pp. 32–151.

Ibrahim Ismail, 'Early Printing in the Straits Settlements by Missionaries of the London Missionary Society', unpublished M.A. thesis, University College, London, 1980.

―――, 'Missionary Printing in Malacca 1815–1843', *International Library Review*, vol. 32, no. 3, 1982, pp. 177–206.

Inventaris van de Archieven van de Weeskamer te Batavia: Boekhouder-generaal te Batavia: Schepenbank te Batavia, The Hague: ARA, 1980.

Irwin, Graham W., 'The Dutch and the Tin Trade of Malacca in the Seventeenth Century'. In Jerome Chen and N. Tarling (eds), *Studies in the Social History of China and Southeast Asia*, London: Oxford University Press, 1970, pp. 267–287.

―――, 'Governor Couperus and the Surrender of Malacca 1795', *JMBRAS*, vol. 29, pt. 3, 1956, pp. 86–133.

―――, 'Malacca Fort', *JSEAH*, vol. 3, no. 2, pp.19–44.

―――, 'Melaka Fort'. In Sandhu and Wheatley, *Melaka: The Transformation of a Malay Capital*, vol. 1, pp. 782–805.

Ishii, Yoneo, *The Junk Trade from Southeast Asia: Translations from the Tosen Fusetsu-gaki, 1674–1723*, Singapore: Institute of Southeast Asian Studies, 1998.

Israel, Jonathan, *Dutch Primacy in World Trade 1585–1740*, Oxford: Clarendon, 1992.

―――, *The Dutch Republic; Its Rise, Greatness and Fall 1477–1806*, Oxford: Oxford University Press, 1995.

Ito, Takeshi, 'Elephant Trade of Aceh in the 1640s–60s', *Journal of East-West Maritime Relations*, vol. 3, 1994, pp. 1–11.

Jack-Hinton, Colin, 'Malacca and Goa and the Question of Race Relations in the Portuguese Overseas Provinces', *JSEAH*, vol. 10, no. 3, 1969, pp. 513–539.

Jackson, James, *Planters and Speculators: Chinese and European Agricultural Enterprise in Malaya 1786–1921*, Kuala Lumpur: University of Malaya Press, 1968.

Jacobs, Els M., 'Koopman in Azie: De Handel van de VOC tijdens de 18de eeuw', Academisch Proefschrift, Rijkuniversiteit Leiden, May, 1999.

Joerg, C.J.A, *Porcelain and the Dutch China trade*, The Hague: Nijhoff, 1982.

Jong, J.K.J. de, M.L. van Deventer and L.W.G. de Roo (eds), *De opkomst van het Nederlandsch gezag in Oost-Indie: Verzameling van onuitgegeven stukken uit het oud-koloniaal archief*, 17, The Hague: Nijhoff, 1862–1909.

Joseph, K.T., 'The Malacca Land Laws', *Federation Museums Journal*, xv, 1970, pp. 131–179.

Kathirithamby-Wells, J., 'The Age of Transition: The Mid-eighteenth to the Early Nineteenth Centuries'. In Nicholas Tarling (ed.), *The Cambridge History of Southeast Asia*, vol. 1.

―――, 'Banten: A West Indonesian Port and Polity During the 16th and 17th Centuries'. In Kathirithamby-Wells and Villiers, *The Southeast Asian Port and Polity*, pp. 106–125.

―――, *The British West Sumatran Presidency 1760–1785: Problems of Early Colonial Enterprise*, Kuala Lumpur: Penerbit University Malaya, 1977.

―――, 'Early Singapore and the Inception of a British Administrative Tradition in the Straits Settlements (1819–1823)', *JMBRAS*, 62, (ii), pp. 48–73.

——, 'The Islamic City: Melaka to Jogjakarta, c. 1500–1800', *Modern Asian Studies*, 20, 2, 1986, pp. 333–351.

——, 'The Johor-Malay World, 1511–1784: The ideology of Kingship in the Context of Change', *Sejarah*, no. 1, 1988, pp. 35–64.

——, 'Siak and its Changing Strategies for Survival, 1700–1870'. In Anthony Reid (ed.), *The Last Stand of Asian Autonomies*.

Kathirithamby-Wells, J. and John Villiers (eds), *The Southeast Asian Port and Polity: Rise and Demise*, Singapore: Singapore University Press, 1990.

Kattenhorn, Patricia, *British Drawings in the India Office Library: Oriental and India Office Collections*, vols 1, 2, and 3, London: The British Library, 1994.

Kellenbenz, Herman, 'The Herwarts of Augsburg and their Indian Trade During the First Half of the Sixteenth Century'. In Mathew, *Studies in Maritime History*, pp. 69–83.

Kemp, P.H. van der, 'De overtreding van het wettelijk gebod op de afschaffing der slavernij', *De Indische Gids*, I, 1879, 2, pp. 822–833.

Kerlogue, Fiona, *Scattered Flowers, Textiles From Jambi, Sumatra*, Hull: Centre of Southeast Asian Studies, University of Hull, 1997.

Ketelaars, Toine, 'Van Inheemse stapelmarkt tot tweederangs koloniale stad: een geschiedenis van Malakka van 1403 tot omstreeks 1690', Doctoraalscriptie Geschiedenis, Rijksuniversiteit Utrecht, June, 1985.

——, 'Living Apart Together: Ethnic Diversity in Dutch Melaka 1640–1690', (unpublished seminar paper, Asian History and Dutch Sources 17th and 18th centuries).

Khoo Joo Ee, *The Straits Chinese: A Cultural History*, Amsterdam: Pepin Press, 1998.

Kidwai, Atiya Habeeb, 'Conceptual and Methodological Issues: Ports, Port Cities and Port-Hinterlands'. In Banga, *Ports and Their Hinterlands in India*, pp. 7–44.

King, Anthony, D., 'Colonial Cities: Global Pivots of Change'. In Ross, *Colonial Cities*, pp. 7–32.

——, *Urbanism, Colonialism, and the World-Economy, Cultural and Spatial Foundations of the World Urban System*, London: Routledge, 1990.

Klein, P.W., 'The China Seas and the World Economy Between the 16th and 19th Centuries: the Changing Structure of Trade'. In C.A. Davids, W. Fritschy, L.A. van der Valk (eds), *Kapitaal, ondernemerschap en beleid: Studies over economie en politiek in Nederland, Europa en Azië van 1500 tot heden*, Amsterdam: NEHA, 1996, pp. 385–408.

——, 'Schaarste aan bekwame zeelieden luidde ondergang van VOC'. In Dillo, *De nadagen van de Verenigde Oostindische Compagnie*.

Klerk, R. de, *Belangrijk verslag over den staat van Banda en omliggende eilanden aan Zijne Excellentie den gouverneur-generaal van Ned.-Indie Jacob Mossel, met eene korte beschrijving van Banda in het bizonder en de Molukken in het algemeen van 1795 tot 1894 door*, C.A.M. van Vliet (ed.), The Hague, 1894.

Knaap, Gerrit, 'A City of Migrants: Kota Ambon at the End of the Seventeenth Century', *Indonesia*, 1991, no. 51, April, pp. 105–128.

——, 'Coffee for Cash: The Dutch East India Company and the Expansion of Coffee Cultivation in Java, Ambon and Ceylon 1700–1730'. In van Goor, *Trading Companies in Asia*, pp. 39–50.

——, *Kruidnagelen en Christenen: De Verenigde Oost-Indische Compagnie en de bevolking van Ambon 1656–1696*, Dordrecht: Verhandelingen van het KITLV, 1987.

——, *Memories van Overgave van Gouverneurs van Ambon in de Zeventiende en Achttiende Eeuw*, Rijks Geschiedkundige Piblicatien Kleine serie 62, The Hague: Nijhoff, 1987.

——, 'Monopolie en monocultuur: Economische geschiedenis van Ambon van 1656 tot 1863', *Intermediair*, 17/6, 1981, pp. 45–51.

——, *Shallow Waters, Rising Tide*, Leiden: KITLV, 1996.

Knaap, Gerrit and Luc Nagtegaal, 'A Forgotten Trade: Salt in Southeast Asia 1670–1813'. In Ptak and Rothermund, *Emporia, Commodities and Entrepreneurs*.

Kooeing, J., 'Journal of a Voyage from India to Siam and Malacca in 1779', *JMBRAS*, 26, 1894.

Kooiman, Dirk, 'Bombay: From Fishing Village to Colonial Port'. In Ross, *Colonial Cities*, pp. 207–230.

Korte, J.P. de, *De Jaarlijkse Financiele Verantwoording in de VOC*, Leiden: Nijhoff, 1984.

Kraan, A. van der, 'Bali: Slavery and Slave Trade'. In Reid, *Slavery, Bondage and Dependency in Southeast Asia*, pp. 315–340.

Kratoska, Paul, H., 'Land law and Land Tenure in British Melaka'. In Sandhu and Wheatley, *Melaka: The Transformation of a Malay Capital*, vol. 1, pp. 497–534.

Laarhoven, R., 'The Power of Cloth: The Textile Trade of the Dutch East India Company, 1600–1780', Australian National University, Ph.D. thesis, 1994.

Lawson, Phillip, *The East India Company: A History*, London: Longman, 1993.

Lee, F.G., *The Catholic Church in Malaya*, Singapore: Eastern Universities Press, 1963.

Lee Kam Hing, 'Indonesian and Malaysian History from Dutch Sources: Reconstructing the Straits of Malacca's past'. In Abu Hassan Sham (ed.), *Malay Studies from Dutch Sources*, Kuala Lumpur: Penerbit Universiti Malaya, 1998, pp. 45–62.

——, 'The Shipping Lists of Dutch Melaka: A Source for the Study of Coastal Trade and Shipping in the Malay Peninsula During the 17th and 18th Centuries'. In Mohd Yusoff Hashim (ed.), *Ships and Sunken Treasure*, Kuala Lumpur: Persatuan Muzium Malaysia, Universiti Malaya, 1986, pp. 53–76.

——, *The Sultanate of Aceh, Relations with the British 1760–1824*, Kuala Lumpur: Oxford University Press, 1995.

Lee Poh Ping, *Chinese Society in Nineteenth Century Singapore*, Kuala Lumpur: Oxford University Press, 1978.

Leith, G., *A Short Account of the Settlements, Produce and Commerce of Prince of Wales Island in the Straits of Malacca*, London: J. Booth, 1805.

Lennon, Captain Walter Caulfield, 'Journal of a Voyage through the Straits of Malacca on an Expedition to the Molucca Islands Under the Command of Admiral Rainier', *JSBRAS*, June 1881, vol. 7, pp. 51–74.

Leupe, P.A., 'Besognes der Hooge Regering te Batavia gehouden over de commissie van Paravacini naar Timor 1756', *Bijdragen tot de taal-, land- en volkenkunde van Nederlandsch-Indie*, 25, 1877, pp. 412–494.

——, 'The Siege and Capture of Malacca from the Portuguese in 1640–1641', *JMBRAS*, vol. 14, pt. 1, 1936, pp. 1–178.

Leur, J.C., van, *Indonesian Trade and Society*, The Hague: W. van Hoeve, 1967 (first published in 1955 by The Hague-Bandung).

Lewandowski, Susan, 'Changing form and Function in the Ceremonial and the Colonial Port City in India: An historical analysis of Madurai and Madras', *Modern Asian Studies*, II, 2, 1977, pp. 183–212.

———, 'Urban Growth and Municipal Development in the Colonial City of Madras, 1860–1900', *Journal of Asian Studies*, vol. xxxiv, no. 2, February 1975, pp. 341–360.

Lewis, Dianne, 'British Policy in the Straits of Malacca to 1819 and the Collapse of the Traditional Malay State Structure'. In Brook Barrington (ed.), *Empires, Imperialism and Southeast Asia*, Clayton: Monash Asia Institute, 1977, pp. 17–33.

———, 'The East India Company and the Straits of Malacca 1700–1784: Trade and Politics in the Eighteenth Century', Ph.D. thesis, Australian National University, 1970.

———, 'The Growth of the Country Trade to the Straits of Malacca 1760–1777', *JMBRAS*, vol. 43, pt. 1–2, 1970, pp. 114–130.

———, *Jan Compagnie in the Straits of Malacca 1641–1795*, Athens: Ohio University Monographs on Southeast Asia, 1995.

———, 'The Tin Trade in the Malay Peninsula during the Eighteenth Century', *The New Zealand Journal of History*, vol. 3, no. 1, April 1969, pp. 52–69.

Li Zhijyan and Cheng Wen, *Traditional Chinese Arts and Culture: Chinese Pottery and Porcelain*, Beijing: Foreign Language Press, 1984.

Lieberman, Victor, 'Mainland-Archipelagic Parallels and Contrasts c. 1750–1850'. In Reid, *The Last Stand of Asian Autonomies*, pp. 27–53.

Light, F., 'A Letter from Captain Light to Lord Cornwallis Dated 20th June 1788', *JMBRAS*, xvi, I, 1938, pp. 115–22.

Lim Chong Keat, *Penang Views 1770–1860*, Singapore: Summer Times, 1986.

Lim, Patricia Phui Huen, *Singapore, Malaysian and Brunei Newspapers: an International Union List*, Institute of Southeast Asian Studies, Singapore: Institute of Southeast Asian Studies, 1992.

Lim Pui Huen, 'Bibliography of Melaka Studies'. In Sandhu and Wheatley, *Melaka: The Transformation of a Malay Capital*, vol. 1, pp. 632–761.

Lo Man Yuk, 'Chinese names of streets in Penang', *JSBRAS*, 33, 1900, pp. 197–246.

Lockyer, Charles, *An Account of the Trade in India*, London: Samuel Crouch, 1711.

Logan, J.R., *Journal of an Excursion from Singapore to Malacca and Pinang, Miscellaneous Papers Relating to Indo-China and the Indian Archipelago*, second series, vol. 1, London, 1887.

Lombard, D., 'The Indian World as Seen from Acheh in the Seventeenth Century'. In Prakash and Lombard, *Commerce and Culture in the Bay of Bengal*, pp. 183–196.

Lovett, R., *The History of the London Missionary Society, 1795–1895*, London: Oxford University Press, 1899.

Low, J., 'An Account of the Origin and Progress of the British Colonies in the Straits of Malacca', *JIA*, III, 1849, pp. 559–617; *JIA*, iv, 1850, pp. 11–26, 106–118 and 360–79.

———, *A Dissertation on the Soil and Agriculture of the British Settlement of Penang or Prince of Wales Island including Province Wellesley on the Malayan Peninsula*, Singapore: Singapore Free Press, 1836.

Macalister, N, *Historical Memoir Relative to Prince of Wales Island in the Straits of Malacca and Its Importance Political and Commercial*, London: J.H. Hart, 1803.

Manguin, P.Y., 'Late Medieaval Asian Shipping in the Indian Ocean: A Reappraisal', *Moyen Orient & Ocean Indien*, 2, 1985, pp. 1–30.

———, "Manpower and Labour Categories in Early Sixteenth Century Malacca". In Reid, *Slavery, Bondage and Dependency in Southeast Asia*, pp. 209–215.

———, 'Palembang and Sriwijaya: An Early Malay Harbour-City Rediscovered', *JMBRAS*, vol. LXVI, pt. 1, 1993, pp. 23–46.

———, 'The Southeast Asian Ship; An Historical Approach', *JSEAS*, 11, 1980, pp. 266–276.

———, 'The Vanishing *Jong:* Insular Southeast Asian Fleets in Trade and War: Fifteenth to Seventeenth Centuries'. In Reid, *Southeast Asia in the Early Modern Era*.

Manning, Catherine, 'French Interest in Asian Trade 1719–1748', *Moyen Orient & Ocean Indien*, 7, 1990, pp. 145–156.

Marsden, William, F.R.S., *The History of Sumatra Containing An Account of the Government, Laws, Customs and Manners of the Native Inhabitants, with a Description of the Natural Production and a Relation of the Ancient Political State of that Island*, London: Payne, 1783.

Marshall, P.J., *Bengal: The British Bridgehead: Eastern India 1740–1828*, Hyderabad: Orient Longman, 1990.

———, 'Eighteenth-Century Calcutta'. In Ross, *Colonial Cities*, pp. 87–104.

———, 'Private British Trade in the Indian Ocean before 1800'. In Das Gupta and Pearson, *India and the Indian Ocean*, pp. 276–316.

———, 'Reappraisal: the Rise of British Power in Eighteenth Century India', *South Asia*, 19/1, 1996, pp. 71–76.

Martin, Montgomery R., *History of the British possessions in the Indian and Atlantic Oceans*, London: Whittaker, 1837.

Matelief, Cornelis, *Historiale ende ware beschrijvinge vande reyse des admiraels Cornelis Matelief de jonghe, naer de Oost-Indien,* Tot Rotterdam: By Jan Janssz, 1608.

Matheson, V. and M.B. Hooker, "Slavery in the Malay Texts: Categories of Dependency and Compensation". In Reid, *Slavery, Bondage and Dependency in Southeast Asia*, pp. 182–207.

Mathew, K.S., 'Trade in the Indian Ocean during the Sixteenth Century and the Portuguese'. In Mathew, *Studies in Maritime History*, 1990, pp. 13–27.

——— (ed.), *Mariners, Merchants and Oceans: Studies in Maritime History,* New Delhi: Manohar Publications, 1995

———, *Studies in Maritime History*, Pondicherry: Pondicherry University, 1990.

Matos, A.T. de, 'Timor and the Portuguese trade in the Orient During the 18th century'. In A.T. de Matos and L.F.F. Reis Thomaz (eds), *As relacoes entre a India Portuguesa, a Asia do Sueste e o Extremo Oriente*, Macao-Lissabon, 1993, pp. 437–445.

Maxwell, J.R. and R.J Maxwell, *Textiles of Indonesia*, Melbourne: Indonesian Arts Society, 1976.

Maxwell, Peter Benson, *An Introduction on the Duties of Police Magistrates in the Settlements of Prince of Wales Island, Singapore, and Malacca,* Pinang: Pinang Gazette Office, 1866.

Maxwell, R.J., 'Textiles and Tusks: Some Observations on the Social Dimensions of Weaving in East Flores'. In M. Kartomi (ed.), *Five Essays on the Indonesian Arts*, Clayton: Monash University, 1981.

Maxwell, William E., 'Raja Haji', *JSBRAS*, no. 22, 1890, pp. 173–224.

McGee, T.G., *The Southeast Asian City, A Social Geography of the Primate Cities of Southeast Asia*, London: G. Bell and Sons, 1967.

McPherson, Kenneth, 'Anglo-Portuguese Commercial Relations in the Eastern Indian Ocean from the Seventeenth to the Eighteenth Centuries', *South Asia*, vol. xix, 1996, pp. 41–57.

Meilink-Roelofsz, M.A.P., 'Asian Trade and European Influence in the Indonesian Archipelago', *JSEAH*, vol. 5, no. 2, September 1964, pp. 184–197.

———, *Asian Trade and European Influence in the Indonesian Archipelago Between 1500 and about 1630*, The Hague: Martinus Nijhoff, 1962.

———, 'A Comparative Study of the Administration and Trade of the Dutch and English Trading Companies in Asia During the First Half of the Seventeenth Century'. In M.A.P Meilink-Roelofsz (ed.), *Dutch Authors on Asian History: A Selection of Dutch Historiography on the Verenigde Oostindische Compagnie*, Dordrecht: KITLV, 1988, pp. 430–453.

———, "De Europese Expansie in Azie", *Bijdragen tot de taal-, land-en volkenkunde*, vol. 135, 1979, pp. 401–442.

———, 'The Structures of Trade in Asia in the Sixteenth and Seventeenth Centuries', *Mare Luso-Indicum, L'Ocean Indien, Les Pays Riverains et Les Relations Internationales xvi-xviii siecles*, iv, 1980, Paris: Société D'Historie De L'Orient, pp. 1–43.

——— et al. (eds), *The Archives of the Dutch East India Company, 1602–1795*, The Hague: Algemeen Rijksarchief, 1992.

Miller, W. G., 'Robert Farquhar in the Malay world', *JMBRAS*, 51, 2, 1978, pp. 123–138.

Mills, L.A., 'British Malaya 1824–67: Penang 1786–1830', *JMBRAS*, vol. xxxiii, pt. 3, 1960, no. 191, pp. 36–59.

Milne, W., *A Retrospect of the First Ten Years of the Protestant Mission to China*, Malacca: Anglo-Chinese Press, 1820.

Miltone, Pauline Dublin, 'Queen City of the East: the Metamorphosis of a Colonial Capital', Ph.D. thesis, University of California, 1966.

Moor, J.H., *Notices of the Indian Archipelago and Adjacent Countries*, Part One, Singapore: Singapore Free Press, 1837.

Morrah, Patrick, 'The History of the Malayan Police', *JMBRAS*, vol. xxxvi, pt. 2, no. 202.

Morrison, E., *Memoirs of the Life and Labours of Robert Morrison*, (compiled by his widow), London: Longman, 1839.

Morrison, R., *Memoirs of the Reverend William Milne*, Malacca: Mission Press, 1824.

Muhammad Ibrahim Munsyi, *Kisah Pelayaran Muhammad Ibrahim Munsyi*, (Anotasi Mohd Fadzil Othman), Kuala Lumpur: Dewan Bahasa dan Pustaka, 1980.

Muhammad Yusoff Hashim, *Hiikayat Siak, dirawikan oleh Tengku Said*, Kuala Lumpur: Dewan Bahasa dan Pustaka, 1992.

———, *The Malay Sultanate of Malacca: A study of various aspects of Malacca in the 15th and 16th centuries in Malaysian history*, Kuala Lumpur: Dewan Bahasa dan Pustaka, 1992.

Murphey, Rhoads, 'The City in the Swamp: Aspects of the Site and Early Growth of Calcutta', *The Geographical Journal*, vol. 130, 1964, pp. 241–255.

———, 'Traditionalism and Colonialism: Changing Urban Roles in Asia', *Journal of Asian Studies*, vol. xxix, no. 1, November, 1969, pp. 67–84.

Nagtegaal, L., 'The Pre-Modern City in Indonesia and its Fall From Grace With the Gods'. In *Economic and Social History in the Netherlands*, vol. 5, Amsterdam: Het Nederlandsch Economisch-Historisch Archief, 1993, pp. 39–60.

————, *Riding the Dutch Tiger: The Dutch East Indies Company and the Northeast Coast of Java, 1680–1743*, Leiden: KITLV, 1996.

Nair, D. Thankappan (ed.), *British Life in Ancient Calcutta 1750–1850*, Calcutta: Sanskrit Pustak Bhandar, 1983.

Nas, Peter J.M. (ed.), *The Indonesian City: Studies in urban development planning*, Dordrecht: Foris, 1986.

Neild, Susan M., 'Colonial Urbanism: The Development of Madras City in the Eighteenth and Nineteenth Centuries'. In *Modern Asian Studies*, 13, 2, 1979, pp. 217–246.

Netscher, E., 'Twee Belegeringen van Malakka: 1756/57 en 1784', *TBG*, vol. 13, 1864, pp. 285–361.

————, 'Was Malakka Tusschen 1795 en 1818 eene Nederlandsche of eene Britische bezitting?', *TBG*, vol. 17, 1869, pp. 68–9.

————, *De Nederlanders in Djohor en Siak, 1602 tot 1865*, Batavia: Bruining, 1870.

Newbold, T.J., *Political and Statistical Account of the British Settlements in the Straits of Malacca, Pinang, Malacca and Singapore*, London: John Murray, 1839.

Newell, H.A., *Madras the Birth Place of British India*, Madras: Times printing, 1919.

Newitt, M.D.D., 'East Africa and Indian Ocean Trade: 1500–1800'. In Das Gupta and Pearson, *India and the Indian Ocean*, pp. 201–223.

Niemeijer, H.E., 'Calvinisme en Koloniale Stadscultuur Batavia 1619–1725', Vrije Universiteit Academisch Proefschrift, 30 May 1996.

Nish, Ian, 'British Mercantile Cooperation in the India-China Trade from the End of the East India Company's Trading Monopoly', *JSEAH*, vol. 3, no. 2, 1962, pp. 74–91.

Noorlander, J.C., *Bandjarmasin en de Compagnie in de tweede helft der 18de eeuw*, Leiden: Dubbeldeman, 1935.

Nordin Hussin, 'Melaka and Penang 1780–1830: A study of two port towns in the Straits of Melaka', Ph.D. thesis, Amsterdam: Vrije Universiteit, 2002.

—— 'The Social World of Dutch Malacca: 1770s to 1820s'. In Abu Hassan Sham (ed.), *Malay Studies from Dutch Sources*, Kuala Lumpur: Penerbit Universiti Malaya, 1998, pp. 93–115.

'Notices of Pinang', *JIA*, vol. 4, 1850, pp. 97–9; 629–663.

————, *JIA*, vol. 5, 1851, pp. 1–14; 53–65; 155–73; 400–429; 354–366; 189–210; 93–119; 292–305.

————, *JIA*, vol. 6, 1852, pp. 18–32, 83–93, 143–172, 218–238, 521–544, 618–635.

————, *JIA*, vol. 7, 1853, pp. 325–57.

————, *JIA*, vol. 8, 1854, pp. 1–27; 97–111; 329–48; 403–19.

————, *JIA*, vol. 9, 1855, pp. 53–65; 442–82.

————, *JIA*, vol. 2, 1857, pp. 182–203.

O'Connor, Richard A., *A Theory of Indigenous Southeast Asian Urbanism*, Singapore: ISEAS, 1983.

O'Sullivan, R.L., 'A History of the London Missionary Society in the Straits Settlements, 1815–1847', Ph.D thesis, SOAS, London, 1987.

Oosterhoff, J.L. Zeelandia, 'A Dutch Colonial City on Formosa'. In Ross, *Colonial Cities*, pp. 51–64.

Oostindie, Gert (ed.), *Fifty Years Later: Antislavery, Capitalism and Modernity in the Dutch Orbit*, Leiden: KITLV, 1996.

Pearson, M.N., 'India and the Indian Ocean in the Sixteenth Century'. In Das Gupta and Pearson, *India and the Indian Ocean*, pp. 71–93.

'Penang in the Past, compiled by "Bookworm": Reprint of a series of articles from the *Pinang Gazette*', Penang: The Pinang Gazette Press, 1925.

Penang Past and Present 1786–1963, *A Historical Account of the City of Georgetown Since 1786*, Penang: Ganesh printing works, 1966.

Penny, Frank, *Fort St. George Madras: A Short History of Our Possession in India*, London: Swan, 1900.

Phillips, C.H., *The East India Company 1784–1834*, Manchester: University of Manchester Press, 1961.

Pinkerton, John, *A General Collection of the Best and Most Interesting Voyages and Travels in all Parts of the World*, vol. 8, Edinburgh: Blackwood & Murray, 1811, pp. 333–336.

Popham, Home Riggs, *A Description of Prince of Wales Island in the Straits of Malacca with its real and probable advantages and success to recommend it as a marine establishment*, London: J. Stockdale, 1805.

———, *Description of Prince of Wales Island in the Streights of Malacca with its Advantages as a Marine Establishment*, London, 1799.

Prakash, Om, *The Dutch East India Company and the Economy of Bengal 1630–1720*, Princeton: Princeton University Press, 1985.

———, 'The Dutch East India Company in the Trade of the Indian Ocean'''. In Das Gupta and Pearson, *India and the Indian Ocean*, pp. 185–200.

———, *European Commercial Enterprise in Pre-Colonial India*, Cambridge: Cambridge University Press, 1998.

———, 'Europeans, India and the Indian Ocean in the Early Modern Period', *South Asia*, vol. xix, 1996, pp. 15–25.

———, 'Long Distance Maritime Trade in Asia: Decline and revival'. In Mathew, *Studies in Maritime History*, pp. 29–38.

———, 'Opium Monopoly in India and Indonesia in the Eighteenth Century', *Itinerario*, vol. xii, number 1, 1988, pp. 73–90.

Prakash, Om and D. Lombard (eds), *Commerce and Culture in the Bay of Bengal, 1500–1800*, New Delhi: Manohar, 1999.

Proudfoot, I., *Early Malay Printed Books: A provisional account of materials published in the Singapore-Malaysia area up to 1920, noting holdings in major public collections*, Kuala Lumpur: Penerbit University Malaya, 1993.

Ptak, Roderich, *China's Seaborne Trade with South and Southeast Asia, 1200–1750*, Aldershot: Ashgate, 1999.

———, 'From Quanzhou to the Zulu Zone and Beyond: Questions related to the Early 14th Century', *JSEAS*, 1998, vol. 29, pp. 269–294.

——— (ed.), *Portuguese Asia: Aspects in History and Economic History (16th and 17th Centuries)*, Stuttgart: Steiner, 1987.

Ptak, Roderich and Dietmar Rothermund, *Emporia, Commodities and Entrepreneurs in Asian Maritime Trade, c. 1400–1750*, Stuttgart: Franz Steiner Verlag, 1991.

Ptak, Roderich and Karl Anton Sprengard (eds), *Maritime Asia: Profit Maximization, Ethics and Trade Structure, 1300–1800*, Wiesbaden: Harrassowitz, 1994.

Raben, Remco, 'Batavia and Colombo: The Ethnic and Spatial Order of Two Colonial Cities 1600–1800', Proefschrift, Rijkuniversiteit Leiden, 28 March 1996.

————, 'Facing the Crowd: the Urban Ethnic Policy of the Dutch East India Company 1600–1800'. In Mathew, *Mariners, Merchants and Oceans*, pp. 209–235.

Raffles, Sophia, *Memoir of the Life and Public Services of Sir Thomas Stamford Raffles*, London: J. Murray, 1830.

Raja Ali Haji ibn Ahmad, *The Precious Gift: Thufat al-Nafis*, (annot. trans.) Virginia Matheson and Barbara Watson Andaya, Kuala Lumpur: Oxford University Press, 1982.

Reed, Robert R., *Colonial Manila: The Context of Hispanic Urbanism and Process of Morphogenesis*, Berkeley: University of California Press, 1978.

————, 'The Colonial Origins of Manila and Batavia: Desultory notes on nascent metropolitan primacy and urban systems in Southeast Asia', *Asian Studies*, 5, 1967, pp. 543–562.

————, 'The Foundation and Morphology of Hispanic Manila: Colonial Images and Phillippine Realities'. In Basu, *The Rise and Growth of the Colonial Port Cities in Asia*, pp. 187–202.

Reeves, Peter, 'Study in the Asian Port City'. In Broeze, *Brides of the Sea*, pp. 29–52.

Reid, Anthony and Radin Fernando, "Shipping on Melaka and Singapore as an Index of Growth 1760–1840", *South Asia*, vol. xix, 1966, pp. 59–84.

Reid, Anthony, 'An Age of Commerce in Southeast Asian History', *Modern Asian Studies*, 24, 1990, pp. 1–30.

————, *Charting the Shape of Early Modern Southeast Asia*, Singapore: Institute of Southeast Asian Studies, 2000.

————, 'Economic and Social Change, c. 1400–1800'. In Tarling, *The Cambridge History of Southeast Asia*, vol. 1, pp. 460–507.

————, 'From Betel-chewing to Tobacco-Smoking in Indonesia', *Journal of Asian Studies*, vol. xliv, no. 3, May 1985, pp. 529–547.

————,'Introduction: Slavery and Bondage in Southeast Asian History'. In Reid, *Slavery, Bondage and Dependency in Southeast Asia*, pp. 1–43.

————, "A New Phase of Commercial Expansion in Southeast Asia 1760–1850. In Reid, *The Last Stand of Asian Autonomies*, pp. 57–81.

————, 'The Origins of Revenue Farming in Southeast Asia'. In Butcher and Dick, *The Rise and Fall of Revenue Farming*, pp. 69–80.

————, *Southeast Asia in the Age of Commerce 1450–1680 vol. 1: The Lands below the Winds*, New Haven: Yale University Press, 1988.

————, *Southeast Asia in the Age of Commerce 1450–1680, vol. 2: Expansion and Crisis*, New Haven: Yale University Press, 1993.

————, *Southeast Asia in the Early Modern Era*, Ithaca: Cornell University Press, 1993.

————, 'The Structure of Cities in Southeast Asia, Fifteenth to Seventeenth Centuries', *JSEAS*, vol. xi, no. 2, September 1980, pp. 235–250.

————, 'The Unthreatening Alternative: Chinese Shipping in Southeast Asia, 1567–1842'. In *Review of Indonesian and Malaysian Affairs*, 27, 1993, pp. 13–32.

———— (ed.), *The Last Stand of Asian Autonomies: Responses to Modernity in the Diverse States of Southeast Asia and Korea 1750–1900*, London: Macmillan, 1997.

————, *Slavery, Bondage and Dependency in Southeast Asia*, St. Lucia: University of Queensland Press, 1983.

————, *Sojourners and Settlers, Histories of Southeast Asia and the Chinese*, ASSAA, Sydney: Allen & Unwin, 1996.

Remarks Concerning The Protestant Mission at Prince of Wales Island, Malacca: The Mission Press, 1826.

Resandt, W. Wijnaendts van, *De gezaghebbers der Oost-Indische Compagnie op hare buiten-comptorien in Azie*, Amsterdam: Liebaert, 1944.

Roberts, D.E., *History of British India under the Company and the Crown*, Oxford: Clarendon, 1938.

Roche, Patrick A., 'Caste and the British Merchant Government in Madras 1639–1749', *Indian Economic and Social History Review*, vol. 12, no. 4, 1975, pp. 381–407.

Roessingh, M.P.H., "A Pretender on Gowa's Throne: The War of Batara Gowa I: Singkilang in South West Celebes 1776–1790", *Itinerario*, 9/2, 1985, pp. 151–178.

Ross, Robert (ed.), *Colonial Cities: Essays on Urbanism in a Colonial Context*, Dordrecht: Martinus Nijhoff, 1985.

Rost, R. (ed.), 'Formation of the Establishment on Pulo Pinang'. In *Miscellaneous papers relating to Indo-China*, 1st series, vol. 1, 1886.

Rowntree, Joshua, *The Opium Habit in the East*, Westminister: P.S. King and Son, 1895.

Rumbi Mulia, 'The Ancient Kingdom of Panai and the Ruins of Padang Lawas (North Sumatra)', Bulletin of the Research Centre of Archaeology of Indonesia, no. 14, 1980.

Rush, James R., *Opium to Java: Revenue Farming and Chinese Enterprise in Colonial Indonesia 1860–1910*, Ithaca: Cornell University Press, 1990.

Sandhu, Kernial Singh, 'From Capital to Municipality'. In Sandhu and Wheatley, *Melaka: The Transformation of a Malay Capital*, vol. 2, pp. 495–600.

———, 'Tamil and other Indian convicts in the Straits Settlements, A.D. 1790–1873'. In *Proceedings of the First International Conference Seminar of Tamil Studies, Kuala Lumpur, April, 1966*, vol. 1, 1968, pp. 197–208.

Sandhu, Kernial Singh and Paul Wheatley (eds), *Melaka: The Transformation of a Malay Capital 1400–1980*, vols 1 and 2, Kuala Lumpur: Oxford University Press, 1983.

Sar Desai, D.R., 'The Portuguese Administration in Malacca 1511–1641', *JSEAH*, vol. 10, no. 3, 1969, pp. 501–512.

Scammell, G.V., 'European Seafaring in Asia c.1500–1750', *South Asia*, vol. xix, 1996, pp. 27–40.

———, 'The Patterns of European Trade in the Indian Ocean 1500–1700'. In Mathew, *Studies in Maritime History*, pp. 1–12.

Schneider, Jane, 'The Anthropology of Cloth', *Annual Review of Anthropology*, 1987, pp. 409–448.

Schoutens, Wouter, *Oost-indische Voyagie*, Amsterdam: Jacob Meurs, 1676.

Scott, James, 'The Settlement of Penang', *JMBRAS*, 28, pt. 1, 1955, pp. 35–51.

Sen, S.P., 'The Role of Indian Textiles in Southeast Asian Trade in the Seventeenth Century', *JSEAH*, vol. 3, no. 2, September 1962, pp. 92–110.

Shaharil Talib, 'The Port and Polity of Trangganu during the Eighteenth and Nineteenth Centuries'. In Kathirithamby-Wells and Villiers (eds), *The Southeast Asian Port and Polity*.

Sheehnan, J.J., 'Seventeenth Century Visitors to the Malay Peninsula', *JMBRAS*, vol. 12, pt. 2–3, pp. 69–88.

———, 'Seventeenth Century Visitors to the Malay Peninsula: My Voyage to Malacca and Stay There', *JMBRAS*, vol. 12, pt. 2–3, pp. 89–107.

Shellabear, W.G., *Sejarah Melayu*, Kuala Lumpur: Fajar Bakti, 1977.

Simon, David, 'Third World Colonial Cities in Context: Conceptual and Theoretical Approaches with Particular Reference to Africa', *Progress in Human Geography*, vol. 8, no. 4, 1984, pp. 493–514.

Sjoberg, G., *The Pre-industrial City*, New York: Free Press, 1960.

Skertchly, E.F., *A Guide to Penang 1905*, Penang: Criterion Press, (n.d.).

Skinner, A.M., 'Memoir of Captain Francis Light', *SBRAS*, 28, 1–17, August 1895, pp. 1–17.

Smyth, H. Warington, 'Boats and Boat-Building in the Malay Peninsula', *The Indian Antiquary*, April, 1906, pp. 97–115.

Souza, G.B., 'Maritime Trade and Politics in China and the South China Sea'. In Das Gupta and Pearson, *India and the Indian Ocean*, pp. 317–330.

———, *The Survival of Empire: Portuguese Trade and Society in China and the South China Sea, 1630–1754*, Cambridge: Cambridge University Press, 1986.

Steensgaard, N., *The Asian Trade Revolution of the 17th Century: The East India Companies and the Decline of the Caravan Trade*, Chicago: University of Chicago Press, 1974.

———, 'The Growth and Composition of the Long-distance Trade of England and the Dutch Republic before 1750'. In J.D. Tracy (ed.), *The Rise of Merchant Empires: Long-Distance Trade in the Early Modern World 1350–1750*, Cambridge: Cambridge University Press, 1990, pp. 102–152.

Steuart, A.F., *The Founders of Penang and Adelaide*, London: Sampson Low, 1901.

Stevens, F.G., "A Contribution to the Early History of Prince of Wales Island", *JMBRAS*, vol. 7, pt. III, October 1929, pp. 377–414.

Subrahmanyam, S., *The Portuguese Empire in Asia 1500–1700*, London: Longman, 1993.

Sutherland, H., 'Eastern Emporium and Company Town: Trade and Society in Eighteenth-Century Makassar'. In Broeze, *Brides of the Sea*, pp. 97–128.

———, 'Ethnicity, Wealth and Power in Colonial Makassar: A Historiographical Reconsideration'. In Peter J.M. Nas (ed.), *The Indonesian City*, Dordrecht: KITLV, 1986, pp. 37–55.

———, 'Mestizos as Middleman? Ethnicity and Access in Colonial Makassar', Papers of the Dutch Indonesian Historical Conference, Lage Vuursche, Nederland, Leiden, June 1980.

———, 'Slavery and the Slave Trade in South Sulawesi, 1660s–1800s'. In Reid, *Slavery, Bondage and Dependency in Southeast Asia*, pp. 261–285.

———, 'Trade in VOC Indonesia: The Case of Makassar'. In B. Dahm (ed.), *Regional and Regional Developments in the Malay-Indonesia World*, Wiesbaden: Harrassowitz, 1992, pp. 45–62.

———, 'Tripang and Wangkang: The China Trade of Eighteenth Century Makassar, 1720s–1820s', *Royal Institute of Linguistics and Anthropology International Workshop on Indonesia Studies*, no. 2, pp. 1–19.

Tan Soo Chye, 'A Note on Early Legislation in Penang', *JMBRAS*, vol. 23, pt. 2, 1950, pp. 100–107.

Tarling, Nicholas, *Anglo-Dutch Rivalry in the Malay World 1780–1824*, Cambridge: Cambridge University Press, 1962.

———, 'The Establishment of the Colonial Regimes': In Nicholas Tarling (ed.), *The Cambridge History of Southeast Asia*, vol. 2, Cambridge: Cambridge University Press, 1992, vol. 2, pp. 5–78.

——— (ed.), *The Cambridge History of Southeast Asia*, vols 1–3, Cambridge: Cambridge University Press, 1992.

Taylor, Jean Gelman, *The Social World of Batavia: European and Eurasian in Dutch Asia*, Madison: University of Wisconsin Press, 1983.

The Town and Fort of Malacca, a Guide Book Published to Commemorate the Centenary of the British Occupation at Malacca 17th March 1824 – 17th March 1924, Singapore: Methodist Publishing House, 1924.

Thijssen, D. Meyer Timmerman, *Twee Governeurs en een Equipagemeester: in en om Malakka 1778–1823*, Buren: Knuf, 1991.

Thomaz, Luis Filipe F.R., 'The Economic Policy of the Sultanate of Malacca (XVth–XVIth Centuries)', *Moyen Orient & Ocean Indien*, 7, 1990, pp. 1–12.

Thomson, John Turnbull, *Glimpses into Life in Malayan Lands*, Singapore: Oxford University Press, 1984.

Till, Margreet van, 'Social Care in Eighteenth Century Batavia: The Poorhouse, 1725–1750', *Itinerario*, vol. xix, no. 1, 1995, pp. 18–31.

Tregonning, K.G., 'The Early Administration and Agricultural Development of Penang', *JMBRAS*, vol. 39, pt. 2, 1966, pp. 34–49.

———, 'The Early Land Administration and Agricultural Development of Penang', *JMBRAS*, 39, 2, 1966, pp. 34–49.

———, 'Penang and the China Trade'. In *Malaya in History*, v, I, 1959, pp. 8–12.

Trocki, Carl, 'Chinese Pioneering in Eighteenth-Century Southeast Asia'. In Reid, *The Last Stand of Asian Autonomies*, pp. 83–102.

———, *Prince of Pirates: The Temenggongs and the Development of Johore and Singapore, 1784–1885*, Singapore: Oxford University Press, 1979.

Turnbull, C.M., *A History of Singapore 1819–1988*, Singapore: Oxford University Press, 1989.

———, 'Melaka Under British Colonial Rule'. In Sandhu and Wheatley, *Melaka: The Transformation of a Malay Capital*, vol. 1, pp.242–298.

———, *The Straits Settlements 1826–67: Indian Presidency to Crown Colony*, London: Athlone Press, 1972.

Valentijn, F., *Oud en nieuw Oost-Indien*, Dordrecht: Joannes van Braam, 1724–26.

———, 'Valentyn's description of Malacca', *JSBRAS*, no. 13, 1884, pp. 49–61.

Vanvugt, E., *Wettig Opium: 350 Jaar Nederlandse opiumhandel in de Indische archipel*, Haarlem: In de Knipscheer, 1985.

Vaughan, J.D., 'Notes on the Malays of Pinang and Province Wellesley', *JIA*, vol. II, 1857, pp. 116–175.

Verhoeven, F.R.J., 'The Lost Archives of Dutch Malacca 1641–1824', *JMBRAS*, vol. 37, pt. 2, 1964, pp. 11–27.

———, 'Some Notes on the History of the Tamil Community in Dutch Malacca (1641–1825)', *Proceedings of the First International Conference Seminar of Tamil Studies, Kuala Lumpur, April 1966*, vol. 1, 1968, pp. 156–196.

Villiers, Alan, *Monsoon Seas: Story of the Indian Ocean*, New York: McGraw-Hill, 1952.

Villiers, John, 'As Derradeiras Do Mundo: The Sandalwood Trade and the First Portuguese Settlements in the Lesser Sunda Islands'. In Villiers, *East of Malacca*, pp. 59–90.

———, 'Da Verde Noz Tomando Seu Tributo: The Portuguese in the Banda Islands in the Sixteenth Century'. In Villiers, *East of Malacca*, pp. 1–30.

————, *East of Malacca: Three Essays on the Portuguese in the Indonesian Archipelago in the Sixteenth and Early Seventeenth Centuries*, Bangkok: Calouste Gulbenkian Foundation, 1985

————, 'Makassar and the Portuguese Connection'. In Villiers, *East of Malacca*, pp. 31–58.

————, 'Trade and Society in the Banda Islands in the Sixteenth Century', *Modern Asian Studies*, 15, iv, 1981.

————, 'Makassar: The Rise and Fall of an East Indonesian Maritime Trading State, 1512–1669'. In Kathirithamby-Wells and Villiers, *The Southeast Asian Port and Polity*, pp. 143–159.

————, 'The Vanishing Sandalwood of Portuguese Timor', *Itinerario*, 18/2, 1994, pp. 86–96.

Vink, Marcus, 'Passes and Protection Rights: The Dutch East India Company as a Redistributive Enterprise in Malacca, 1641–1662', *Moyen Orient & Ocean Indien*, 7, (1990), pp. 73–101.

Vink, Mark, 'Mare Liberum and Dominium Maris: Legal Arguments and Implications of the Luso-Dutch Struggle for the Control Over Asian Waters 1600–1663'. In Mathew, *Studies in Maritime History*, pp. 38–68.

Vos, Reinout, *Gentle Janus: Merchant Prince, The VOC and the Tightrope of Diplomacy in the Malay World 1740–1800*, Leiden: KITLV, 1993.

Wang Gungwu, *The Nanhai Trade: The Early History of Chinese Trade in the South China Sea*, Singapore: Times Academic, 1998.

————, 'The Nanhai Trade: A Study of the Early History of Chinese Trade in the South China Sea', *JMBRAS*, vol. xxxi, pt. 2, 1958.

Warren, J.F., *The Sulu Zone 1768–1898: The Dynamics of External Trade, Slavery and Ethnicity in the Transformation of a Southeast Asian Maritime State*, Singapore: Singapore University Press, 1981.

Wathen, J., *Journal of a Voyage in 1811 and 1812 to Madras and China*, London: J. Nichols, 1814.

Watson, Bruce, 'Indian Merchants and English Private Interests: 1659–1760'. In Das Gupta and Pearson, *India and the Indian Ocean*, pp. 301–316.

Welch, J.M. (ed.), *The Spice Trade: A Bibliographic Guide to Sources of Historical and Economic Information*, Westport: Greenwood Press, 1994.

Westerhout, J.B., 'Notes on Malacca' *JIA*, Series I, vol. 2, 1848, pp. 171–181.

Winius, George D., 'A Tale of Two Coromandel Towns: Madraspatam (Fort St. George) and Sao Thome de Meliapur', *Itinerario*, vol. xviii, no. 1, 1994, pp. 51–64.

Winstedt, R.O., 'Abdul Jalil, Sultan of Johore (1699–1719), Abdul-Jamal, Temenggong (ca. 1750) and Raffles' Founding of Singapore', *JMBRAS*, x, iii, 1932.

Wolters, O.W., *The Fall of Srivijaya in Malay History*, Ithaca: Cornell University Press, 1970.

Wong Choon San, *A Gallery of Chinese Kapitans*, Singapore: Government Printing Office, 1964.

Wong Lin Ken, 'The Trade of Singapore 1819–69', *JMBRAS*, vol. 33, pt. 4, 1960, pp. 11–215.

————, 'The Revenue Farms of Prince of Wales Islands 1805–1830', *The Journal of South Seas Society*, Singapore, vol. 19, 1964, pp. 56–127.

Yeoh, Brenda, S.A., *Contesting Space Power Relations and the Urban Built Environment in Colonial Singapore*, Kuala Lumpur: Oxford University Press, 1996.

Index